CIVIL WAR ARMS MAKERS

AND THEIR CONTRACTS

A facsimile reprint of the Report by the Commission on Ordnance and Ordnance Stores, 1862.

— edited by —

Stuart C. Mowbray & Jennifer Heroux

ANDREW MOWBRAY PUBLISHERS, P.O. BOX 460, LINCOLN, RI 02865 USA

LIBRARY OF CONGRESS
CATALOG CARD NO: 97-075489
    Stuart C. Mowbray & Jennifer Heroux, editors
        Civil War Arms Makers and Their Contracts
    Lincoln, R.I.: ANDREW MOWBRAY, INC. — PUBLISHERS
        608 pp.

ISBN: 0-917218-77-9

frontmatter ©1998 by Andrew Mowbray, Inc. — Publishers

To order more copies of this book, call 1-800-999-4697.

Printed in the United States of America.

For a free catalog of books about collectible firearms and swords,
write to Andrew Mowbray Publishers, P.O. Box 460, Lincoln, R.I. 02865 or call (401) 726-8011. Toll-free in the United States, 1-800-999-4697. Fax (401) 726-8061.

10 9 8 7 6 5 4 3 2 1

TABLE OF CONTENTS

Editors' Note: For ease of reference, the page numbers listed in the Table of Contents remain true to the original document and do not correlate with the actual pagination of this book. Additionally, since the entries in this report are organized by case number, and not alphabetically, readers searching for specific manufacturers are encouraged to consult the alphabetical list at the back of the book for quick reference.

INTRODUCTION

The report reprinted in this book is — for arms historians — one of the most important documents of the Civil War. It includes the correspondence, testimony and decisions of the Commission on Ordnance and Ordnance Stores, which met in 1862 to review (and in many cases rewrite) all federal contracts for guns, carbines, pistols, ammunition and swords. The case histories for these contracts are remarkably in depth, making this material extremely useful for firearms and military historians. Terms of contracts are outlined, factories are described, machinery is listed and the fairness of prices is argued. This report has long been a mainstay of Civil War researchers. However, it was only available at a select number of federal depository libraries and could not be brought home for detailed study. Now, with this facsimile reprint, the report is available to all students of firearms in a convenient and affordable format.

When the Civil War erupted, the United States Military was faced with an unprecedented expansion of their forces. Recruits were available, but all of these new men needed supplies, uniforms, equipment and weapons before they could effectively fight the South. And though the North had a staggering array of industrial assets to call upon in its need (factories, skilled workmen and inventors), we must remember the exciting, yet confusing, state of the arms industry during those years.

The American Industrial Revolution was at a fever pitch, and firearms manufacturing (along with the textile industry) was leading the way. However, along with all of this growth came uncertainty. Countless inventions vied for the attention of ordnance purchasers, many of whom had severely antiquated or unrealistic ideas about how military firearms were to be used on the modern battlefield. Some of these new inventions would rewrite firearms history, but others were utterly useless.

Amidst all of this debate and confusion was the pressing rush to equip thousands and thousands of men with guns that would work. As a result, a wide range of contracts were given out without planning or proper thought. These agreements were often overly ambitious, calling for delivery dates and production quantities that were impossible to meet. These manufacturers were all competing for the same resources, and they often found themselves unable to acquire the machinery, raw material and skilled labor that they had counted on when determining their original production schedules. Not only did this drive up prices, but defaults became common, as many factories found themselves still setting up at a time when they should have been delivering finished goods. The Ordnance Department discovered, quite early in the war, that it couldn't count on expected deliveries of firearms until the guns had actually been inspected and shipped.

In an effort to impose some order upon this chaotic and inefficient situation, a Commission on Ordnance and Ordnance Stores was established to review all existing federal arms contracts. Most contracts were in a state of technical default because of failure to meet delivery schedules or because initial deliveries had failed inspection. Therefore, the Commission had a unique opportunity to cancel unfavorable contracts and to rewrite others to better meet current military needs. Government lawyers also sited a remote legal argument, which held that many of the contracts were invalid because the government itself had not followed proper procedures in issuing them.

The goals of the Commission were quite simple. They sought to reduce the total number of arms under contract, eliminate pricing abuses, and uncover fraud and political influence in contract appropriation. A reduction in total number of arms under contract was a clear necessity. For example, 1,164,000 Springfield-style muskets had been ordered from private contractors, when the actual number needed for the coming year was only 500,000. Also, bidding procedures and contract oversight had been neglected. Prices varied widely, and sometimes were even higher than retail. Many politicians and government bureaucrats were investors in arms factories, or had factories in districts that they represented. Contracts were often offered to these well-connected companies based upon favors rather than fair and open competition. A few of the "manufacturers" actually turned out to be middle men who purchased the items from subcontractors, or even on the open market, and passed them on to the government at an inflated price. In order to reveal these operators, the Commission demanded that manufacturers prove (through equipment lists, etc.) that they were, indeed, fabricating the items that they were selling.

Naturally, many manufacturers felt threatened by this review process, which could result in the loss or reduction of their contracts. They had purchased machinery and buildings, hired workers and raised capital from investors — all in an effort to tool up for their original contracts. An unfavorable judgement by the commission could easily spell financial ruin. All the elements of a politically charged soap opera were in place.

While some companies were devastated by the eventual decisions, it appears that the Commission made a genuine effort to be fair, and tried to reward good intentions and honest effort. If a factory was working hard to fulfill its contract, the Commission would try to be protective of their interests and investment. From the government's point of view, the Commission was an unqualified success. Aside from imposing order upon what was previously a corrupt and inefficient system, the Commission also saved almost $17 million in the form of canceled/reduced contracts and price adjustments.

Manufacturers and suppliers reviewed in the report range from the famous to the unheard of, and the contracts discussed cover longarms, pistols, carbines, swords, ammunition, equipment, accouterments, and much more. The report is full of minute details and high drama, and we hope that you will find it both entertaining and useful.

About the Commission:
The Commission, originally called the "Commission on Ordnance Claims and Contracts," was established in March of 1862. Edwin M. Stanton, Secretary

of War, appointed two commissioners — Joseph Holt (Judge Advocate General of the U.S. Army) and Robert Dale Owen (politician and respected moralist) — who were sworn in on March 18th. Major Peter V. Hagner of the Ordnance Department was assigned to assist in technical matters and James Wise was appointed as their secretary. The commissioners were given sweeping powers and their decisions were final and beyond appeal.

About the Commission Members

Joseph Holt (1807–1894) was a native of Kentucky. He practiced law during the 1830s and '40s, and became an important political figure in Washington, D.C. during the 1850s, serving as United States Commissioner of Patents and then Postmaster General. In 1861 he was appointed Secretary of War. In 1862, he became Judge Advocate General of the U.S. Army — a post he held until 1875. In his role as Judge Advocate General, Holt was chosen to prosecute John Wilkes Booth's conspirators. He was later accused of withholding evidence and preventing a recommendation of clemency for Mrs. Surratt from reaching President Johnson.

Robert Dale Owen (1801–1877) was the son of Welsh author and socialist Robert Owen. The elder Owen was a partner of Jeremy Bentham and a world-renowned innovator in the treatment of factory employees. Along with his followers, the "Owenites," he founded several unsuccessful cooperative communities in England and the United States, the most famous of which was at New Harmony, Indiana. His son, Robert Dale Owen, followed him to New Harmony, where he taught school and edited newspapers. He was elected to the U.S. House of Representatives in 1843 and served as U.S. Minister to Italy in the late 1850s. A prominent abolitionist, he wrote several books on the topic, including *The Policy of Emancipation* (1863) and *The Wrong Slavery* (1864).

Major Peter Valentine Hagner (1815–1893) is well known to students of Civil War ordnance. His long and distinguished career began with his graduation from the the U.S. Military Academy at West Point in 1836. He served in the war in Florida and then in the Mexican War, where he was wounded once and given brevet promotions for gallantry twice. He was posted to Europe in the late 1840s. Named Inspector of Contract Arms and Ordnance Stores in April of 1861, he served in that role through the end of 1863, when he became commander of the Watervliet Arsenal. He remained at Watervliet through the end of the Civil War.

Acknowledgements:

The editors wish to thank the staffs of the Providence Public Library, the Adams Library at Rhode Island College, the Rhode Island State Library and the U.S. Government Printing Office for their kind assistance with this project.

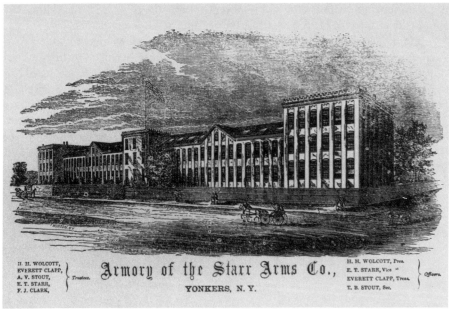

On this page are shown two of the factories that are discussed in this report. The view at top is the Eli Whitney Armory in Whitneyville, Connecticut. At the bottom is an engraved illustration of the Starr Arms Company Armory in Yonkers, New York. This illustration appears on one of the company's Civil War era brochures. *(Stuart C. Mowbray collection)*

LETTER

OF

THE SECRETARY OF WAR,

TRANSMITTING,

In answer to a resolution of the Senate, a copy of the report of the commission on ordnance and ordnance stores made to the War Department.

JULY 17, 1862.—Read, ordered to lie on the table, and be printed.

WAR DEPARTMENT,
Washington City, D. C., July 17, 1862.

SIR: Since the passage of the resolution of the Senate of the 11th instant calling for a copy of the report of the commission on ordnance and ordnance stores, the chairman, Hon. Joseph Holt, has been diligently engaged in preparing the general report, the special decisions on the several cases, and the evidence, for transmission to the Senate.

A copy of the general report is herewith transmitted; the copy of the decisions on the several cases, and of the evidence, cannot be completed for several days.

Very respectfully, your obedient servant,

P. H. WATSON,
Assistant Secretary of War.

Hon. SOLOMON FOOT,
President of the Senate pro tem.

Letter transmitting proceedings.

COMMISSION ON ORDNANCE AND ORDNANCE STORES.
July 5, 1862.

SIR: I have the honor to submit herewith the proceedings of the commission on ordnance claims and contracts.

Very respectfully, sir, your obedient servant,

P. V. HAGNER,
Major of Ordnance, Assistant to Commission.

Hon. E. M. STANTON,
Secretary of War.

PROCEEDINGS OF THE COMMISSION ON ORDNANCE CONTRACTS AND
CLAIMS—1862.

WASHINGTON, *March* 17, 1862.

Messrs. Joseph Holt and Robert Dale Owen, and Major P V. Hagner, of the ordnance department, met this day at No. 472 15th street, in conformity with the following letter of appointment from the honorable E. M. Stanton, Secretary of War.—(See letter in proceedings of the 18th of March.)

It was ordered, That the commission be organized as "Commission on Ordnance Claims and Contracts," and that the hours of session be from 10 a. m. to 4 p. m., daily, except Sundays.

It was ordered, That a secretary be appointed, and that the commissioners take the oath of office to discharge faithfully the duties imposed upon them by their letter of appointment, that the oath be indorsed upon the original letter of the Secretary of War, and be signed by the commissioners before a justice of the peace and be filed with the proceedings, and be recorded on the journal of to-morrow.

The resolution was adopted and the commission adjourned.

MARCH 18, 1862.

Commission met. Present: Honorables Joseph Holt, Robert Dale Owen, and Major Hagner. Messrs. Holt and Owen took, before N. Callan, justice of the peace, an oath of office, faithfully to discharge their duties as commissioners, which oath was indorsed upon the following letter of appointment:

WAR DEPARTMENT,
Washington City, D. C., March 13, 1862.

Ordered, That the honorable Joseph Holt and the honorable Robert Dale Owen be, and they are hereby, appointed a special commission to audit and adjust all contracts, orders, and claims on the War Department in respect to ordnance, arms, and ammunition, their decision to be final and conclusive as respects this department on all questions touching the validity, execution, and sums due or to become due upon such contract, and upon all other questions arising between contractors and the government upon such contracts.

2d. The said commission will proceed forthwith to investigate all claims and contracts in respect to ordnance, arms, and ammunition in the War Department, or pending settlement and final payment, and adjudicate the same. All persons interested in such contracts may appear in person, but not by attorney, before said commissioners and be heard respecting their claims, at such time and place as the commissioners shall appoint. The chief of ordnance and all other officers in the department will furnish such books and papers as the commissioners may require.

Major Hagner, of the ordnance department, is specially assigned to aid and assist the commissioners in their investigations. All claims that they may award in favor of shall be promptly paid. No application will be entertained by the department respecting any claim or contract which they shall adjudge to be invalid.

3d. If, in their investigation, they shall find reason to believe that any agent or employé of the War Department was directly or indirectly interested in any contract for ordnance, arms, or ammunition, or received any consideration for its procurement, they shall give notice thereof to the claimant and proceed to investigate and determine the fact, taking such testimony as they may deem proper; and, if the fact of such interest be established, it shall be good cause for adjudging the claim to be fraudulent.

EDWIN 'M. STANTON,
Secretary of War.

DISTRICT OF COLUMBIA,
    County of Washington:

Joseph Holt and Robert Dale Owen make oath that they will faithfully discharge the duties imposed upon them by the within letter of appointment from the honorable Edwin M. Stanton, Secretary of War, and that they will make him, the said Secretary, a true and faithful report of their action and decisions under said appointment.

J. HOLT.
ROBERT DALE OWEN.

Sworn to and subscribed before me this 18th day of March, 1862.

N. CALLAN, [L. S.]
Justice of the Peace.

James Wise was appointed secretary to the commission, and it was ordered that the following notice to claimants be inserted three times in the *National Intelligencer* and three times in the *National Republican:*

CORCORAN'S BUILDINGS, FIFTHTEENTH STREET.

OFFICE OF COMMISSION ON CONTRACTS AND CLAIMS
FOR ORDNANCE AND ORDNANCE STORES, *March* 17, 1862.

Ordered, That all persons having claims and contracts for investigation and decision under the letter of appointment of the honorable Edwin M. Stanton, Secretary of War, dated 13th of March, 1862, and hereto subjoined, be and are hereby notified to present the same. The commission will continue in session for their reception and examination from day to day, from 10 o'clock a. m. to 4 p. m.

J. WISE, *Secretary.*

By resolution of the commission, a request was made to General Ripley, chief of ordnance, to furnish all the papers connected with the various contracts and claims to be considered by the commission, in compliance with the orders of the Secretary of War.

The following letter, received in reply to the request above communicated, shows the general character of the cases submitted. The list having been published in Executive Document No. 67, House of Representatives, 37th Congress, 2d session, it is not deemed necessary to append it to these proceedings.

ORDNANCE OFFICE, *Washington, March* 7, 1862.

GENTLEMEN : In answer to your resolution of this date, I have to state that each of the contracts and orders for Springfield rifles and other arms has been, furnished in full, with the tabular statements of contracts and purchases called for by resolution of the House of Representatives, and will be printed; thus enabling the commission to ascertain all particulars respecting each case, in much less time and in a more convenient form than if furnished in manuscript. In view of this and of the press of business at the Ordnance office, permit me to suggest that the printed document be used by the commission. If any further information is desired than may be found therein, it will, of course, be promptly furnished.

I respectfully transmit herewith certain papers which were filed in the War Department in compliance with the published order of the Secretary, dated January 29, 1862, which will be found useful to the commission in the prosecution of their labors. Also, certain claims which I think come properly before it, under the War Department orders of the 13th instant. Lists of the papers and claims, so transmitted, accompany this letter.

Respectfully, your obedient servant,

JAS. W. RIPLEY, *Brigadier General.*

Hon. J. HOLT and ROBERT DALE OWEN,
    Commissioners, Washington, D. C.

[Indorsement.]

ORDNANCE OFFICE, *March* 7, 1862.

General J. W. Ripley—transmitting papers in relation to contracts and claims presented in compliance with published order of Secretary of War of 29th January, 1862.

Letters ordered to be appended to the proceedings of the commission.

No. 1.

COMMISSION ON ORDNANCE AND ORDNANCE STORES,
Washington, April 17, 1862.

GENERAL: Many of the orders for pistols, carbines, swords, and sabres, and some foreign arms, which have been referred to the commission, require that deliveries shall have been made in certain quantities prior to the order of the Secretary, stopping deliveries.

As it is expedient for the action of the commission that it shall be known how far parties have complied with the stipulations of their orders, they request that you will inform them of the deliveries actually made under each order, and the date thereof, prior to March 12.

Very respectfully, your obedient servant,

P. V. HAGNER, *Major of Ordnance.*

Gen. J. W. RIPLEY, *Chief of Ordnance.*

No. 2.

ORDNANCE OFFICE,
Washington, April 19, 1862.

SIR: In compliance with the request of the commissioners, contained in Major Hagner's note of the 15th instant, I annex a statement of the arms actually delivered by each of the contractors named, and the dates thereof, prior to March 12, 1862, viz:

Sabres.

J. D. Millard, none.
Mansfield, Lamb & Co.:

1862—Jan. 11		500
17		500
30		500
Feb. 8		500
1862—Feb. 13		500
21		500
March 4		500
8		500
Total		4,000

J. Kepman, none.

Revolver pistols.

Starr Arms Co.:
1862—Feb. 5 .... 1, 000
        24 600
                        ————
            Total........ 1, 600
                        ════
W. C. Freeman, none.
Savage Arms Co.:
Separate report in this case made on
the 17th inst.

Carbines.

J. Hartshorne—Burnside's:
1862—Feb. 18 60
S. B. Smith—Lindner's:
1861—Nov. 26 391
J. C. Palmer—Sharpe's:
1861—Sept. 13 300
      Oct. 2 1,000
           19 1,000
      Nov. 4 500
           25 1,000
      Dec. 7 500
           13 500
           23 500
           31 500
1862—Jan. 20 500
          22 500
          31 500
      Feb. 8 500
           19 500
      March 8 500
                          ————
        Total........... 8,800
                          ════

Carbines.

C. Jackson—Burnside's:
1861—Dec. 30 580
Merrill, Thomas & Co.—Merrill's:
1862—Jan. 27............... 200
      Feb. 10.............. 200
      Mar. 10.............. 200
                          ———
            Total........... 600
                          ════

Enfield rifles.

Howland & Aspinwall:
1861—Sept. 10............. 1, 600
          30............. 2, 400
      Nov. 9............. 1, 000
           13............. 1, 000
           30............. 300
      Dec. 18............. 1, 100
1862—Jan. 6............. 600
                          ————
            Total.......... 8, 000
                          ════

Samuel Colt—Enfields:

	Long.	Short.
1861—Nov. 8......	1, 800	1, 360
18......	400	220
30......	200	60
Dec. 16......	280	300
1862—Jan. 7......	400	....
Total......	3, 080	1, 940

The following named persons have not made any deliveries:
J. Hawthorne, Burnside's rifle muskets; Frank Otard, French St. Etienne sabre bayonets; W. A. Seaver, Enfields; Mickle & Hopkins, muskets; Hewett & Randall, Enfields; Weigart & Otard, French muskets; H. Simon & Son, Enfields.

P. S. Justice has delivered several kinds of arms bearing different names, none of which are recorded in this office as "rifled muskets," under the order for 4,000, although some of them may have been delivered under that order. The fact will be ascertained and communicated to the commissioners.

The dates of delivery above stated are the dates when the accounts were examined and approved in this office. The arms were actually delivered to the United States a few days prior to the dates stated.

Respectfully, your obedient servant,

JAS. W. RIPLEY,
Brigadier General.

Mr. J. Wise, *Secretary, Washington, D. C.*

[Indorsement]

General Ripley.—April 19, 1862. Information concerning deliveries on contracts, &c.

Several contractors named in the enclosed whose papers are not before the commission.

No. 3.

ORDNANCE OFFICE,
Washington, D. C., April 28, 1862.

SIR: I have to acknowledge the receipt of Major P. V. Hagner's communication on the subject of the number of arms which it may be necessary to procure for the service during the next twelve months, either by purchase or contract, in addition to the number on hand, or to be fabricated at national establishments.

It is impossible to furnish exact data on this subject owing to the number of contingencies to be considered, over which the department can have no control; but I present the following figures as being, in my opinion, what we shall require:

500,000 Springfield muskets, Springfield pattern, model 1855.
50,000 Harper's Ferry rifles, with sword bayonets, steel scabbards.
30,000 breech-loading carbines, for cavalry.
30,000 revolver pistols, army size.
10,000 sabres, for cavalry.
5,000 sabres, for light artillery.
10,000 non-commissioned officers' swords.
10,000 musicians' swords.

Respectfully, your obedient servant,

JAS. W. RIPLEY,
Brigadier General.

J. WISE, Esq.,
Secretary Commission on Ordnance Stores.

[Indorsement.]

Letter from General Ripley, April 28, 1862, relative to number of arms needed for the service.

No. 4.

ORDNANCE OFFICE,
Washington, March 15, 1862.

SIR: The undermentioned are regular manufacturers of arms for this department, and I recommend that special authority, under your order of 10th of March, 1862, be given for receiving from them such arms as may be presented *under existing orders to them*, and as may be approved on inspection, for the next three months, unless sooner revoked, viz:

E. K. Root, Colt's Arms Company, Hartford, Connecticut; J. C. Palmer, Sharpe's Arms Company, Hartford, Connecticut; J. T. Ames, Massachusetts Arms Company, Chickopee, Massachusetts; Knap, Rudd & Co., Penn Foundery,

Pittsburg, Pennsylvania; R. P. Parrott, West Point Foundery, Cold Spring, New York; C. Alger & Co., South Boston Foundery, Boston, Massachusetts.

Respectfully, your obedient servant,

JAS. W. RIPLEY,
Brigadier General.

Hon. E. M. STANTON,
Secretary of War.

[Indorsement.]

General Ripley to Hon. E. M. Stanton, giving names of regular manufacturers.

ORDNANCE DEPARTMENT, *March* 15, 1862.

James W. Ripley, brigadier general, submits the names of regular manufacturers of arms for ordnance department, and recommends that special authority be given for receiving such arms as may be presented under existing orders to them for the next three months.

The chief of ordnance is authorized to receive, as within recommended, such arms as may be manufactured by the within named parties, under existing orders approved by the Secretary of War.

By order of the Secretary of War:

P. H. WATSON,
Assistant Secretary of War.

A true copy.

J. G. BENTON,
Captain of Ordnance.

No. 5.

COMMISSION ON ORDNANCE AND ORDNANCE STORES,
Washington, April 26, 1862.

SIR: The commission respectfully submits for your approval the enclosed form of advertisement, with the recommendation that it be published immediately. It has been examined by the chief of ordnance, and is reported by him to be in every way satisfactory, in connexion with your declaration of yesterday that you desired the law to be enforced by the commission in cases where the public interest seemed to require it. It is important to inaugurate at once this legal mode of procedure for obtaining army supplies.

Very respectfully, your obedient servant,

J. HOLT.

Hon. E. M. STANTON,
Secretary of War.

[Indorsement.]

Letter of commission to the Secretary of War submitting form of contracts.

No. 6.

ORDNANCE OFFICE,
Washington, D. C., May 20, 1862.

SIR: I have received the Hon. R. D. Owen's letter of the 16th instant, approved by the Assistant Secretary of War, requesting copies of all the bids made in accordance with the advertisements for proposals for small arms. As these bids are numerous, and the copying of them would involve great labor, I transmit herewith an abstract of all the bids, which will probably afford all the information required. Be pleased to return the copy when no longer wanted.

Respectfully, your obedient servant,

JAS. W. RIPLEY,
Brigadier General.

J. WISE, Esq.,
Secretary Commission on Ordnance Stores.

[Indorsement]

May 21, 1862.—General Ripley; abstracts.

No. 7.

ORDNANCE OFFICE,
Washington, May 21, 1862.

SIR: In compliance with your instructions I have the honor to transmit herewith ninety-five proposals for small arms, offered under the advertisement recently published by this office.

Respectfully, your obedient servant,

JAS. W. RIPLEY,
Brigadier General.

Hon. E. M. STANTON,
Secretary of War.

[Indorsement.]

ORDNANCE OFFICE, *May* 21, 1862.

J. W. Ripley, brigadier general, transmits herewith ninety-five proposals for small arms offered under the advertisement recently published by this office.

Proposals referred herewith to Messrs. Holt and Owen, commissioners, &c., for examination and recommendation.

By order of Secretary of War:

P. H. WATSON,
Assistant Secretary of War.

No. 8.

COMMISSION ON ORDNANCE AND ORDNANCE STORES,
Washington, May 26, 1862.

SIR: The commission have examined in part the proposals for furnishing small arms, and respectfully recommend that they be returned to the chief of ordnance, to be carried out by that department in conformity with the law and the regulations.

The commission have already expressed their recommendation in favor of executing the contract for 40,000 Springfield muskets with Messrs. Remington & Son, of Ilion, New York, at $16 each, and with the same firm for 20,000 revolvers, at $12 each, and have also confirmed to this firm, in accordance with their proposition to the commission, (based upon the award to them of the above-named numbers and arms at the prices named,) the orders previously given for 10,000 Harper's Ferry rifles, at $17 each, and 5,000 army revolvers, at $12 each, being a reduction of $3 upon each rifle and pistol from the price named in the original orders. They hope that these contracts will be at once ordered to be executed by the Secretary of War, as they look upon it as highly important to thus establish the above reasonable prices as a standard for future guidance.

The commission have also recommended the award of 10,000 Springfield muskets, at $17, to J. D. Pitts, of Trenton, New Jersey, as the quantity, time of delivery, and price, combined, make it an advantageous proposal for the government.

They also recommend the award to the Colt's Arms Manufacturing Company of 15,000 army revolvers, at $14 50, (as the chief of ordnance reports the immediate need of revolvers,) promised earlier by these parties than by others, and as the price to be paid shows a reduction of $10 50 upon that heretofore paid this company for like arms. The commission would also add now to their former recommendation to meet the immediate wants of the ordnance department the acceptance of the proposal, made under the recent advertisement, by Eli Whitney & Co., of New Haven, to finish 6,000 navy revolvers, at the price of $10, a reduction upon his proposed price which he now offers to accept.

Although the commission consider that they should not make any further recommendation as to the numbers or kinds of revolvers and small arms to be now contracted for, it is proper that they should state that their investigations have shown satisfactorily that the prices paid heretofore for such arms have been unnecessarily high, as well for securing suitable and effective arms for troops as for a fair remuneration to the manufacturer. No one pattern of patent arms has been proved the best, and, as many of them are, as far as known, equally effective, the simplest and cheapest of such arms are the best for the service. The government can establish the grade of work and price when selecting the pattern, and judge very accurately of the true cost to be incurred and the proper price to be paid for it. Excessive charges for special patents, and the erection of large factories to make *experimental* arms, ought to be discouraged, and the purchase of more than a moderate number, say 1,000 at most, ought not to be made until after satisfactory trial by troops in the field.

The commission respectfully urge, therefore, increased restrictions upon the multiplication of patterns of arms for use in service:

1. That the sample arm shall be tried, by competent officers, *in comparison with the best in use;* that it shall be proved *superior* in essential qualities, or in probable cheapness of manufacture, to such.

2. That after a sample has been approved, as above, 1,000 be ordered for trial by troops, and that no larger numbers be ordered until satisfactory trial has been made by them.

3. That general orders be given requiring all captains of companies to report *quarterly* to the chief of ordnance the kind of arms in use by his company; his opinion of the suitableness of the arm and the general extent of service, and the number requiring repairs since last report. Such reports, if regularly and carefully made, would best check the purchase of unsuitable arms, and soonest show the best and strongest for service.

We are, sir, &c.,

J. HOLT,
Commissioner, &c.

Hon. EDWIN M. STANTON,
Secretary of War.

[Indorsement.]

Report of commissioners in relation to proposals for furnishing small arms.

No. 9.

Indorsements on letter of Major Hagner referring to Emerson & Silver's proposition to furnish cast steel scabbards.

ORDNANCE OFFICE,
Washington, June 6, 1862.

Respectfully returned. These scabbards are only recommended for trial, to ascertain their comparative advantages or otherwise over those now in use. For that purpose I think that 1,000 of them would be sufficient, and that no further order shall be given until the result of the trial shall be known. This is in accordance with the report of the commission of the 26th ultimo, approved and adopted by the War Department, in regard to procuring new kinds of arms for the military service, and is equally applicable to new kinds of accoutrements.

Your obedient servant,

JAMES W. RIPLEY,
Brigadier General.

Referred to the commission on ordnance for examination and report.
Signed by order of the Secretary of War.

P. H. WATSON,
Assistant Secretary.

COMMISSION ON ORDNANCE, *June* 9, 1862.

Respectfully returned to the War Department, with the recommendation that all the new Springfield pattern arms hereafter issued be furnished with sheet steel bayonet scabbards, and that all non-commissioned officers' and musicians' swords to be obtained under future orders be likewise furnished with sheet steel scabbards.

As experience has induced the abandonment of leather scabbards for the sabre bayonet, and our own as well as foreign trials have been favorable to the use of steel sword scabbards, and as the rapid destruction of the leather bayonet scabbard in service proves it unsuitable for the purpose it is applied to, the commission consider that, though the suggestion of the steel scabbard for the ordinary bayonet is novel, it is not of that untried kind that needs slow introduction as a substitute for what is admissibly fragile, costly, and inefficient. The commission therefore recommend that contracts be now made under the recent proposals for procuring a supply of the above articles as above recommended, and that no more leather scabbards be purchased for bayonets or swords.

Very respectfully,

J. HOLT,
ROBERT D. OWEN,
Commissioners.

RESOLUTION OF COMMISSION TO ADJOURN UNTIL FURTHER ORDERS.

JULY 16, 1862.

The final report of the commission, testimony, decision, &c., having been prepared to be transmitted to the War Department, it was

Ordered, That the commission on ordnance and ordnance stores be adjourned, to meet again when called together by the Secretary of War.

J. HOLT, *Commissioner.*

P. V. HAGNER,
Major of Ordnance, Assistant to Commission.

INDEX.

Name.	No. of case.	Name.	No. of case.
Townsend, E	107	Wilstach & Co	27
Treasy, James	58	Wilstach & Co	57
Treadwell, Samuel	105	Ward, Norman	31
Union Arms Co	64	Wheeler, W. A	43
Whitney, Eli	84	Windmuler, L.	46
Wigert & Otard	52	Welch, W. W	80

COMMISSION ON ORDNANCE AND ORDNANCE STORES.

WASHINGTON, *July* 1, 1862.

SIR: The undersigned, commissioned by your authority "to audit and adjust all contracts, orders, and claims on the War Department in respect to ordnance, arms, and ammunition," have the honor to submit the following report:

They met on the 17th day of March, 1862, and, after having appointed a clerk, had publication made that they were in session, and all persons interested in the cases referred to them for examination and decision were invited to appear and offer such suggestions and proofs as they might deem advisable in support of their respective claims. To this notice your letter of appointment was appended, in order that there might be no misapprehension as to your purpose in organizing the commission, or as to the powers with which it was invested. To this appeal the parties, with a single exception, have responded, and, either verbally or in writing, we have been put in possession of their views. Most of them have been examined before us under oath, and their statements, carefully taken down and revised by themselves, accompany this report, and are submitted for your consideration in support of the action which has been taken.

The cases referred to us were one hundred and four in number, and the demands upon the treasury which they involved amounted to about fifty millions of dollars. All of these cases, after patient and careful investigation, have been disposed of, and special reports have been made, showing, either in terms or by reference, the grounds of the decisions rendered. The amount, from the payment of which the government, by the action of this commission, will be relieved, will fall but little short of seventeen millions of dollars. This result has been reached by the rejection of some claims and contracts, by the curtailment or modification of others, and by the reduction of prices when found excessive or extravagant. We are well satisfied that no principle of law has been violated in the conclusions at which we have arrived; that considerations of equity, when these existed, have not been overlooked; and that no undue advantage has been taken of the power of the government in dealing with its citizens. In our desire to protect, as far as practicable, the public interests no private right has been infringed, nor is it believed that any one of the contractors whose engagements have been the subject of our investigations will, if provident and reasonably skilful in the execution of his contract, suffer loss, or fail to realize a fair profit.

A longer time than was anticipated has been occupied in the discharge of our duties. The magnitude of the issues submitted to us forbade that they should be determined either hastily or in the absence of a thorough scrutiny of the merits of each claim separately considered. It has been the endeavor of the commission not only to be just, but, as far as possible, to satisfy the claimants that we had been so. Accordingly, by repeated conferences with frank explanations offered to the parties, both as to the strict legality of the action proposed and as to its absolute necessity from considerations of public policy, we have sought to secure their acquiescence in our decisions. Our efforts in this direction have met with even unlooked for success. It may be safely affirmed that a large majority of the claimants are content with the disposition made of their cases. Many of them, public spirited citizens, have cheerfully expressed their assent; some verbally, others in writing. That amid the variety of character presented by so large a number of shrewd business men, exceptions to this should have presented themselves, will surprise no one who reflects that in every society will be found those who—setting up a distinction between honesty in public and honesty in private affairs—find it difficult to realize that the government has any rights, or the law, which protects its treasury, any obligatory force as against their own personal interests. Such men seem to delude themselves with the belief that however much they may be bound to respect the property of its individual citizens, the country, as a whole, is a fair subject of plunder—a belief of ready growth amid the disorders consequent upon great national convulsions. A few such men we have encountered, and while our action has necessarily left upon them an unpleasant impression, it is altogether probable that their baffled schemes against the public treasury will hereafter become the basis of appeals to Congress.

As the reports made in the particular cases fully exhibit the details of our labors, a very brief resumé of their results and of the considerations suggested in the course of our investigations may here suffice.

It may be stated, generally, that we have found the system, under which have been issued the numerous orders or contracts for ordnance and ordnance stores that have been referred to us, strongly marked with improvidence. The amount of these orders or contracts has been ascertained to be largely in excess of the public wants, and the prices fixed by many of them beyond necessity or reason.

The unexampled demand for arms consequent upon the sudden breaking out of the present gigantic rebellion, and the extraordinary circumstances under which the government arsenals were drained of their best weapons before a blow was struck, afford some explanation of the excess of price referred to; yet, it must be confessed, not by any means a full and satisfactory one. It is to be traced, in a large degree, to a neglect of those common precautions which prudent men of business exercise in the conduct of their private affairs; some of which, too, had been specially provided for and required by acts of Congress.

First, as to foreign arms; it was of course absolutely necessary to resort to these in equipping, within a few months, more than half a million of men, and it was impossible, in all the workshops of Europe, to have had arms manufactured as rapidly as our public necessities required. Under such circumstances prices naturally rose, and inferior (often second-hand) arms had, to some extent, to be purchased.

But these difficulties were greatly aggravated by the lack of system which prevailed. The States and the general government entered the market together as rival purchasers, and thus the members of the same national family bid directly against each other. The folly of this is the more remarkable when it is remembered that these arms bought by the States were, in fact, for the use of the general government, and will, no doubt, in the end, be paid for by it. The general government itself employed, directly or indirectly, numerous agents not acting in unison, and often becoming, therefore, competitors of each other. A few of these made purchases directly for the government; the greater number sprang up in the shape of "middle men," to whom, though not dealers in arms nor skilled in their value, contracts were awarded upon their own terms, only to be sub-let to the actual importers. Under a system so ill considered, extravagance was unavoidable. It was greatly increased by many of these contracts being loosely worded and imperfectly guarded, while some were granted at prices much beyond even the highest rates which could be fairly considered as engendered by the system itself.

Two examples may here be given in illustration: In the first—that of a large contract granted to a "middle man," who had never dealt in arms and knew nothing of their value—the reduction, partly in price and partly in quantity, effected by the action of the commission, amounted to five hundred and eighty thousand dollars. In the second. granted to a *bona fide* importer—being a contract of immense amount, namely, for upwards of one hundred and eighty-eight thousand guns and thirty-eight thousand sabres—the reduction in price alone, as compared with the rates paid under the contract up to the time of our decision, exceeded one million of dollars. In both these examples the reductions w re ordered under proposals finally made by the parties themselves after repeated conferences with them, and accepted by the commission. Other large contracts for foreign arms, of which the owners had incurred forfeiture by failure as to times of delivery, were rescinded by the commission.

Yet, withal, it has been impossible for us to protect the government against lamentable losses in these loose and irregular transactions. In regard to a considerable portion of these foreign arms, government inspection was permitted in Europe before shipment, but so utterly inadequate and so incompetent was the force assigned to this duty, that it became a mere empty form, devoid of all utility or protection. Of this, and other negligences and imprudences. the practical result has been that a large proportion of our troops were armed with guns of a very inferior quality; that tens of thousands of the refuse arms of Europe are at this moment in our arsenals, and thousands more still to arrive, not one of which will outlast a single campaign, while most of them will never be issued at all, being entirely unfit to be placed in the hands of civilized troops. Add to this, that, in many cases, these unserviceable arms were paid for at rates which, under a system of vigilance and obedience to law, would have procured improved rifles of the first class.

As regards orders or contracts for domestic arms, though the abuses in this branch are less glaring than those above referred to, yet the system here also has been essentially faulty, and the loss to the government thence resulting very large, while evils other than excess in prices have resulted from neglect of wholesome precautions and of checks and guards strictly demanded by law.

These contracts are chiefly for the Springfield rifle musket. The quality of this weapon—the best infantry arm in the world—has been carefully and sufficiently guarded.

But, first, the orders were greatly in excess of what the Ordnance office estimates to be the wants of the service. One million one hundred and sixty-four thousand Springfield muskets had been contracted for, while the chief of ordnance reports to this commission that half a million is the number actually needed for a year to come, beyond what the Springfield arsenal can supply.

To relieve the government as far as, with due regard to equitable considerations, lay in our power, from this excess of arms, the commission, governed as to the amount in each case by its peculiar features, have made certain reductions in a large majority of these—the total reductions thus made amounting to four hundred and seventy-three thousand guns. This leaves a margin, over and above the half million estimated to be needed, of one hundred and ninety-one thousand guns for probable or possible failures to make prompt deliveries, in part or in whole, by the contractors.

The legal grounds on which the right to make these deductions rest are fully set forth in the decision in Mason's case, No. 72. While actual investments, made in good faith, have, as far as the public interests would permit, been respected, the maxim has been recognized that the citizen must, in his dealings with the government, as in his general conduct, be held to know the law, and cannot be permitted to profit by its violation. The government of no civilized people has ever been administered on a different principle, nor, indeed, could it be.

Secondly. The price—in every instance twenty dollars per gun, including appendages—is, the commission now believe, higher by several dollars than it need or ought to have been, at least when the contract was for a greater number than twenty-five thousand.

It is true that the vast and unnecessary number of Springfield muskets contracted for, especially at such high rates, has very sensibly increased, to the manufacturer, the cost of the arms, by causing an unexampled demand for materials (particularly of suitable iron for gun barrels, an article of which the present supply is limited) and for skilled labor; and in the early part of our investigations, this consideration, together with the want of accurate and reliable information on the subject, so far weighed with us that we confirmed the first four contracts for fifty thousand guns each, made with experienced manufacturers, at the price of $20, which had been fixed by the Ordnance office. But as we proceeded in our investigations, and as additional evidence came before us, we became satisfied that, for any amount over twenty-five thousand, sixteen dollars per gun would afford a fair profit to the manufacturer. A contract for forty thousand of these muskets, at that rate, has been recently taken by an experienced and responsible firm, Messrs. E. Remington & Sons, of Ilion, New York. And it should be here stated that to Mr. S. Remington, of this firm, we are indebted for the first trustworthy information received touching the actual cost to private manufacturers of this arm. His public spirit, in frankly and voluntarily making this disclosure, is worthy of all commendation, and should it result, as we believe it will, in fixing the price of this gun at not exceeding sixteen dollars, his action will save millions to the public treasury. It should be added that the holder of one of the contracts for 50,000 Springfield muskets confirmed by us, consented, as a part of the conditions of the confirmation, that 25,000 of the guns should be paid for at $16, instead of $20 each. A similar reduction to $16 was made, on the proposal of another contractor, for all the guns embraced in his order over twenty-five thousand.

Thirdly. The neglect to obey the law of the 3d March, 1809, and the stringent regulations founded upon it, which provide that all contracts for army supplies shall, except in cases of emergency, requiring and admitting of "immediate delivery," be preceded by public advertisement inviting proposals, has been prolific in evil results. Indeed, it is to the persistent disregard of this law, which for more than fifty years has been the guardian of the integrity of the contract service, that speculators and "middle men" are indebted for the saturnalia of success they have enjoyed since the commencement of the war. Nor can such disregard of law and duty be excused on the plea that the pressing exigency of the case afforded no opportunity to conform to the provision in question, since, in all the contracts for domestic arms, the deliveries were fixed at distant periods of time.

That better terms might have been obtained for the government is conclusively shown by the fact, that when, a few weeks since, under your direction, proposals for the manufacture of arms were thus invited, responsible bids for the Springfield musket were put in as low as sixteen dollars, while almost all fell below the price of twenty dollars.

In October last, E. Remington & Sons solicited an order for the manufacture of their revolver—acknowledged to be in all respects equal to Colt's army revolver—at $15, but could get a contract for only five thousand. At the same time, an order was given to Colt's Company for an indefinite number of his army revolvers, at $25; and under this there has since been delivered 31,000. That company, under the recent advertisement, proposed to furnish this revolver at $14 50, and a contract at that rate has been executed—thus proving that the charge made and submitted to was $10 50 in excess of the worth of the arm, and showing that in this single item of pistols alone there has been paid to that company, within the time named, at least $325,500 beyond the full value of the arms received. The proposals for sabres indicate a still more marked reduction in price—a responsible offer being made for the best cavalry sabres at $4 12, for which $8 50 has been heretofore paid, and an offer of $5 by the very party who has been, under the private contract system, receiving $8 50.

But an enforcement of the law in regard to advertising would effect more than a mere reduction in price. It would cut up by the roots an abuse which during the present war has threatened, in this branch of the administration, serious injury, alike to the interests of the service and to the public morals. Contracts based on private proposals favor, and indeed necessarily lead to, the creation of a class of "middle men," most of them mere speculators and adventurers, to whom, instead of to the manufacturers themselves, orders for supplying the wants of the government have been often directly or indirectly granted. To this evil we have already, in a report recently printed, accompanying Case No. 72, adverted at length. The class of men referred to are generally rapacious and unscrupulous, and thrust themselves between those whose interest it is to deal, and who ought in every case to deal, directly with each other—the government in need of arms and the manufacturer producing them. Having thus, through unavowed instrumentalities, obtained their contracts, many of them at once put them on the market for sale. A large manufacturer who has failed to get a contract for muskets, assures us that within a few days past such contracts to the amount 200,000 guns have been offered to him by these traders in government patronage. Under a system of open competition invited by public notice, as contemplated by law, no such interposition could take place, and no such class of men could exist. A few illustrations of the practical workings of the system, as it has prevailed in the ordnance department, may be here stated.

A holder of one of these orders or contracts for Springfield muskets appeared before the commission, as did a member of the United States Senate, and from their testimony we learned that the order had been obtained from the Secretary of War by the senator, and that for the service he had charged and is to receive $10,000. It seems to have been in contemplation by the principal party to pay him five per cent. commission, being $50,000; but it was finally settled. so far as his partners were concerned, at the sum named. For this he holds the notes of the parties, who are responsible, and will no doubt make payment at the maturity of the paper in August and September next.

A large manufacturing firm being anxious to secure a contract for their pistols, and being satisfied, from some cause, that their personal application would be unavailing, employed as "middle man" or agent, an individual who represented that he could obtain it for them. His success as one of the partners in a heavy beef contract given out soon after the commencement of the rebellion, seems to have inspired confidence in his representation, and no doubt led to his retainer. He did not overestimate his influence; for, on the 16th October, 1861, an order was issued by the chief of ordnance to the firm, addressed to him, for 5,000 pistols at $20 each, for which the firm paid him $10,000. Subsequently, on the 25th October, 1861, this firm made a written application to the Secretary of War for a contract for 10,000 of the same pistols, which, having been referred to the chief of ordnance, was by him reported against on the 31st of October, upon the ground that the pistol was not, in his opinion, "a desirable one for the service;" and so the application failed.

Some time afterwards a person well known to the country as having neither official position nor capital, but who had probably ascertained the preceding facts, visited the same manufacturers at their establishment, and asked them if they did not want an additional pistol contract, to which they answered that they did. He then inquired what they were willing to give for it? As a little while before they had paid $10,000 for an order for 5,000, it probably occurred to them that the same rate of compensation would be expected in this case, and it was accordingly offered. The "middle man" then—evidently with other reasons, for the purpose of increasing his fee—urged that 22\frac{50}{100}$, instead of $20, should be charged the government for the pistols. This was declined, the manufacturers stating that the pistols were not worth more than $20, and that at this rate they had been previously sold to the government. The price to be paid him for his services was fixed at $2 per pistol, or $10,000 for the 5,000, for which he agreed to secure the order. He returned to Washington, and "in a week or two," the manufacturers received an order bearing date November 28, for the 5,000 pistols, being again the same that a few weeks before had been pronounced "unserviceable," in answer to their own personal application to manufacture them. This order, from some unexplained cause, was not submitted to Congress, and is not found in Ex. Doc. No. 67, H. R. It was, however, referred to us, and was confirmed with a reduction of the price to $18, with the assent of the parties. This change in the price has given rise to a controversy between the broker in government patronage and his employers, as to where the loss thus occasioned should fall, or whether his influence and services shall still be estimated at $10,000, or be reduced to half that sum.

In the first case referred to, the commission was offered to the United States senator, because the manufacturer was assured that it was usual to pay for similar services, and he expressed to us, under oath, the opinion that the assurance was true, and that, in a majority of cases, he believed such compensation to have been made. The public are very sharpsighted in such matters, and when they are found employing, at high rates of compensation, the services of this class of men, there is no hazard in assuming that they have ascertained it is necessary for them to do so. One of the saddest consequences of this course of administration, is the tendency of the public mind to press its imputations of demoralization beyond the mere broker in patronage, who, probably having little to lose in this way, is indifferent to criticism or reproach, so long as he is permitted to put money in his purse. Men are prone to believe that an influence which hawks itself about in the market, rests on foundations which could not be safely laid bare; or, in other words, that what is thus openly sold has been possibly bought. Of course, no such reflections could arise in reference to a member of Congress who should feel himself justified in making pecuniary profit out of his position, in the manner suggested, since the origin and character of his influence over the administration of the executive branch of the government are well understood. Whatever use may be made of it, its source is pure, springing, as it does, from the genius of our institutions, which gives power everywhere to the representatives of the people, in the generous confidence that it will be loyally exercised only for their protection.

For the names, dates, and other details connected with these transactions, reference is had to the written testimony which accompanies this report.

Another deplorable consequence following the substitution of a system of private contracts for that based on advertisement and open competition, is the indiscriminate condemnation which, in public journals and otherwise, such substitution has brought in its train upon all contractors. In many cases this is wholly undeserved, and to none will the advantage be greater than to the *bona fide* contractors themselves, of a change of system which, once in regular operation, will relieve them from imputations of dishonesty or extortion. In no class of persons are the qualities which distinguish the best business men of our country—talent, integrity, enterprise, resource, perseverance—more needed than in them. But if wholesale slurs affecting their character, because of their relations to the government, finally render the very name of a contractor a reproach, what can be the result, except that the honest and the reputable will stand back, and that their places will be filled by men careless of their good name, if only money can be made by the sacrifice?

We beg, therefore, respectfully, to urge the expediency of adhering, in all future contracts for ordnance and ordnance stores, to the principle of advertising, so earnestly impressed by the law and the regulations of your department. This law and these regulations embody the wisdom which long years of experience have taught, and they rest upon a profound knowledge of human character—of the unscrupulous avarice that is to be baffled on the one side, and of the infirmity which is to be guarded against temptation on the other. The absolute necessity of the course suggested is more powerfully illustrated by the facts which we have brought to your notice than it would be by any arguments we could employ. This course on your part would furnish a prompt and complete remedy—and it is the only one—for the evils of extravagance and alleged demoralization, of which so much and such lamentable complaint is heard.

That vast interests and influences will array themselves against a restoration of this branch of the service to the basis of the law, may well be expected. Opposition to this great principle, which has so faithfully guarded the public treasury, has been signally manifested in past years, and the success of that opposition opened then a wide field for rapacity on the one hand and fraudulent collusion on the other. The abuse, in a particular branch of the service, assumed such proportions that Congress, feeling itself called upon to interfere, declared, by solemn enactment on the 31st August, 1852, that "all contracts, of every description, which have been made without public notice having been given, shall be cancelled." While, in dealing with illegal and irregular contracts, we have sought to act in harmony with the spirit of this legislation, we have done so with a tenderness of regard for the interests of *bona fide* contractors which, it is believed, will protect our action from all imputations of harshness or injustice hereafter.

We cannot close this report without bearing testimony to the constant aid and support we have derived from Major Hagner, who has been associated with us as an advisory member of the commission. His labors have been arduous and incessant, and his thorough knowledge, as an accomplished ordnance officer, of the subject-matter of all the contracts submitted for our examination, has enabled him to render us invaluable assistance, alike in our investigations and in the preparation of our decisions.

We are, sir, very respectfully, your obedient servants,

J. HOLT,
ROBERT DALE OWEN,
Commissioners.

Hon. EDWIN M. STANTON, *Secretary of War.*

CASE No. 1.

CYRUS ALGER.

COMMISSION ON CONTRACTS AND CLAIMS
FOR ORDNANCE AND ORDNANCE STORES,
Washington, March 21, 1862.

SIR: The within claim of Cyrus Alger, submitted to the commission through the ordnance department, having been subsequently reduced in amount in accordance with the views of the chief of ordnance, and being now approved by him, is herewith returned with the recommendation that it be paid. Amount approved four thousand eight hundred and sixty-one dollars and forty-three cents, ($4,861 43.)

Very respectfully, your obedident servants,

J. HOLT,
ROBERT DALE OWEN,
Commissioners.

P. V. HAGNER,
Major Ordnance, Assistant to Commission.

Hon. E. M. STANTON, *Secretary of War.*

[Indorsement.]

Case No. 1, no papers. Cyrus Alger. Account in Second Auditor's Office.
Cyrus Alger.

Original amount $5,050 40
Reduced amount.. 4,861 43
Received March 25, 1862. Recommended to be paid.

Directed by Hon. Secretary of War to be referred to the chief of ordnance.

CASE No. 2.

JOHN POUDIR, of Philadelphia.

Contract received from ordnance department for 10,000 *Minie rifles with sabre bayonets, at* $18 50, *July* 26, 1861.

ORDNANCE OFFICE, *Washington, July* 26, 1861.

SIR : I acknowledge your offer to furnish to this department ten thousand rifled arms, calibre 58-inch according to sample left here by you, at $18 50, eighteen dollars and a half each in bond, the first delivery to be made one hundred and five days from this date, and the other deliveries every three weeks thereafter till ten thousand are furnished. The first delivery is to be of not less than one thousand arms, the residue to be delivered from one thousand to two thousand per month. All these arms are to be delivered and inspected at the United States arsenal on Governor's Island, by such officer as may be designated by this office for the purpose. Payments are to be made on certificates of inspection and receipt by the inspecting officer when presented at this office. Please state in writing whether you will agree to furnish the ten thousand arms on the foregoing terms and conditions; and, if so, you may consider your offer accepted.

Respectfully, your obedient servant,

JAMES W. RIPLEY,
Brevet Brigadier General.

Mr. JOHN POUDIR,
221 *Chestnut street, Philadelphia.*

Extension of contract received from ordnance department by John Poudir, *July* 26, 1861.

ORDNANCE OFFICE,
Washington, November 1, 1861.

SIR : I have received your letter of the 30th ultimo, requesting forty to forty-five days longer time on the first delivery of the rifled arms under your order from this office of July 26, 1861. For the reasons stated by you the extension is granted, provided that the delivery of the whole number of arms shall be made within the time allowed by the order.

Respectfully, your obedient servant,

JAS. W. RIPLEY,
Brevet Brigadier General.

Mr. JOHN POUDIR, *Philadelphia.*

Extension of contract received from ordnance department by John Poudir, *July* 26, 1861.

ORDNANCE OFFICE,
Washington, December 18, 1862.

SIR : In answer to your letter of the 17th instant, I have to state that for the reasons stated by you the time of your first delivery of arms under the order of July 26, 1861, for 10,000 rifled arms, calibre 58, is extended, not to exceed thirty days. All the other terms and conditions of the original order remain unchanged.

Respectfully, your obedient servant,

JAS. W. RIPLEY,
Brevet Brigadier General.

Mr. JOHN POUDIR, *Philadelphia.*

WASHINGTON, *February* 3, 1862.

DEAR SIR : My object in writing these lines is to inform you that I find it utterly impossible to deliver the guns under the order which I received July 26, 1861, in exact accordance with the conditions of said order.

Sometimes the deliveries will be, perhaps, a little less than 1,000 ; sometimes more ; but I will deliver the entire order in the specified time. I delivered 200 on the 31st of December to Major Hagner, and have now one hundred and eighty in port, twenty-six cases having been left behind by the steamer. I also have 1,100 at Southampton, which have been stopped in transit, but have taken steps to regain them, and hope to have them here by the end of this month or beginning of next. These are the beautiful Minies, which you will remember are at the low price of $18 50. You are well aware of the difficulties encountered in the transportation, and I respectfully request that you will issue an order that these fine arms of mine shall be received in whatever quantities they arrive, even if not exactly in accordance with the requirements of the order ; that is, up to the time specified for the order to be completed.

Very respectfully,

JOHN POUDIR.

Brevet Brigadier General RIPLEY,
Ordnance Department.

True copy.

CHAS. W. MORRIS, *Chief Clerk.*

[Indorsement.]

ORDNANCE OFFICE, *February* 3, 1862.

Respectfully submitted to the Secretary of War. Mr. Poudir's order was for 10,000 light Minie rifles, with sword bayonets, at $18 50 each, deliverable in New York—first delivery of 1,000 to be in January, 1862. The residue to be delivered from 1,000 to 2,000 monthly, provided that the whole were delivered by the end of August, 1862. He delivered 200 in December, and now has 120 in the port of New York. He applies to have his order so modified as to allow him to deliver the rifles as they arrive from Europe, instead of binding him to specific monthly deliveries, still retaining the condition that the whole 10,000 shall be delivered by the end of August next. These arms are stated, by the inspector, to be of superior quality, and being light, they may be used by mounted troops. I therefore recommend that Mr. Poudir's application be granted.

JAS. W. RIPLEY,
Brevet Brigadier General.

Approved February 4.

EDWIN M. STANTON.

WASHINGTON, *February* 11, 1862.

DEAR SIR : I have the honor of delivering to you herewith copies of the contracts for the delivery of arms made by the ordnance department with me. They are respectively of the following dates, viz :

July 26, 1861.—For 10,000 Minie rifles, with sabre bayonets, at $18 50 each.
November 1, 1861.—The extension of the contract of July 26, 1861.
December 18, 1861.—A second extension of the contract of July 26, 1861.

These extensions were granted for reasons set forth in the letters of application for the same, of the same date as the official extensions.

Under this contract of July 26, and extensions thereof, I have delivered 380 guns, more not having been delivered for reasons set forth in a letter now in your possession, the principal reasons being the difficulties of transportation and 1,100 being withheld from shipment in Southampton. But by a little further modification of the terms of this order I shall be enabled to deliver the full 10,000 by the time of the expiration for the last delivery, being August 30, 1862.

I, in reality, do not ask an extension on the original order, as I will deliver the full amount or number of guns by the time the original expires, but I cannot exactly conform to the terms for each separate delivery.

Yours, very respectfully,

JOHN POUDIR.

Hon. EDWIN M. STANTON, *Secretary of War.*

[Indorsement.]

Papers relating to order to John Poudir, of Philadelphia.
No. 8 of printed list, page 11.—(No. 18, Ordnance office list.)

Statement of deliveries of arms by John Poudir, under contracts of July 26, 1861.

1862.

Feb'y 3.	200	Minie rifles, as per bill.	
19.	168	do	do
20.	492	do	do
27.	908	do	do
March 6.	100	do	do
11.	420	do	do
	2,288		

ORDNANCE OFFICE, *Washington, March* 20, 1862.

Before commission.

Mr. Poudir states that his arms are made at Liege for his order, and that all are now in hand.

COMMISSION ON CONTRACTS FOR ORDNANCE AND ORDNANCE STORES,
Washington, March 21, 1862.

SIR: The commission have the honor to report as follows:

CASE No. 2.—JOHN POUDIR, of Philadelphia.

Order dated July 26, 1861.—(*No.* 8 *of printed list, page* 11.)

To deliver 10,000 light Minie rifles, with sword bayonets, at the New York arsenal. Price, $18 50 per gun. Rate of delivery altered by chief of ordnance, upon application by claimant.

The commission find that Mr. Poudir has delivered about 2,000 arms, which are reported to be of good quality for service, and at a reasonable price, and that he has now in port a number ready for delivery, and that the order can be completed as originally agreed upon.

It is therefore recommended by the commission that Mr. Poudir's future deliveries of the arms above described be accepted according to terms of original order as to quality and price.

The papers received in this case are returned herewith.

We are, very respectfully, your obedient servants,

J. HOLT,
ROBERT DALE OWEN,
Commissioners, &c.

P. V. HAGNER,
Major of Ordnance, Assistant to Commissioners.

Hon. EDWIN M. STANTON, *Secretary of War.*

[Indorsement.]

JOHH POUDIR.—*Case No.* 2,

Recommends that future deliveries of the arms within described be accepted according to terms of original order as to quality and price.

Ordered by the honorable Secretary of War to be referred to the chief of ordnance.

$\frac{8}{32}$. Decision. Received March 25, 1862.

CASE No. 3.

H. G. LEISENRING.—*Order for sabres.*

FRANKFORD ARSENAL, *September* 19, 1861.

SIR : I am authorized by the chief of ordnance to order from you cavalry sabres, to be equal in material and workmanship to the government pattern, and inspected according to the rules prescribed by the Ordnance Manual; to be delivered at the Frankford arsenal packed in suitable boxes for transportation, fifty in each box, at the rate of six hundred (600) per week up to the 10th of October, and 1,000 per week after that date to the 1st of January; the price to be seven dollars ($7) apiece, and if you deliver twenty thousand (20,000) sabres by the 1st January that pass inspection, then a price of seven dollars and fifty cents ($7 50) each to be allowed; the above terms and conditions subject to the approval of the chief of ordnance.

Payment to be made on certificates of inspection, in such funds as the government may allow, and deliveries to be made daily after one week.

Respectfully, your obedient servant,

T. J. TREADWELL,
1st Lieutenant of Ordnance.

Mr. H. G. LEISENRING, *Philadelphia, Pa.*

ORDNANCE OFFICE, *Washington, September,* 1861.

SIR : Take Mr. Leisenring's sabres, at the rate of delivery and on the terms he proposes, until further orders on the subject.

Respectfully, your obedient servant,

JAMES W. RIPLEY,
Brigadier General.

FRANKFORD ARSENAL, *September* 19, 1861.

SIR : I am authorized by the chief of ordnance to order from you cavalry sabres, to be equal in material and workmanship to the government patterns, and inspected according to the rules prescribed by the Ordnance Manual ; to be delivered at the Frankford arsenal packed in suitable boxes for transportation, fifty in each box, at the rate of six hundred (600) per week up to the 1st of October, and one thousand (1,000) per week after that date to the 1st January ; the price to be seven dollars ($7) apiece, and if you deliver twenty thousand (20,000) sabres by the 1st January that pass inspection, then a price of seven dollars and fifty cents ($7 50) each to be allowed ; the above terms and conditions subject to the approval of the chief of ordnance.

Payment to be made on certificates of inspection, in such funds as the government may allow, and deliveries to be made daily after one week.

Respectfully, your obedient servant,

T. J. TREADWELL,
1st Lieutenant of Ordnance.

Mr. H. G. LEISENRING, *Philadelphia.*

FRANKFORD ARSENAL, *September* 19, 1861.

GENERAL : I have the honor to enclose herewith copy of an order given by me to Mr. H. G. Leisenring, of Philadelphia, for cavalry sabres, subject to your approval.

I understand the pistol cartridges ordered to be made for the Washington arsenal to be the round ball cartridge for percussion pistol.

Very respectfully, your obedient servant,

T. J. TREADWELL,
First Lieutenant of Ordnance.

General J. W. RIPLEY,
Chief of Ordnance, Washington, D. C.

[Indorsement.]

Letter of Lieutenant Treadwell, from Frankford arsenal, September 19, 1861, transmits copy of order he has given to Leisenring for sabres, and states what he understands pistol cartridges to be which are wanted at Washington arsenal.

P. V. H.

Received September 21, 1861 ; answered same day.

PHILADELPHIA, *December* 19, 1861.

MY DEAR SIR : The order for cavalry sabres given me by direction of General Ripley, of the ordnance department, I find it will be impossible for me to fill by the time specified, January 1, 1862.

Since your order reached me I have put three large factories to work, and stocked them with machinery suitable for manufacturing cavalry sabres. This took upwards of two months longer time than was calculated upon, in consequence of getting the machinery made requisite for the work, notwithstanding the most positive promises to have it delivered in season to enable me to get the sabres out by the close of this month. This, you will observe, was a serious drawback, and could not be avoided, inasmuch as those with whom I contracted for the machinery were among the most reliable and best machinists in the country. This has all been overcome now, however, and I am enabled to manufacture at least two thousand (2,000) per week from this time forward.

The whole number delivered to the arsenal since September 19, 1861, (the date of your order,) is 6,350, and by the first of January it will be increased to upwards of 10,000.

In view of my difficulties, which have been overcome through much hard labor and the closest attention to the manufacture of the sabres, (as you doubtless are aware,) and the expenditure of large sums of money for machinery, much of which will be comparatively worthless, except for old iron, I respectfully ask an extension of my order until the 1st or 10th of February, 1862, *as well as the condition of payment.*

Hoping, sir, that you will give this matter your earliest attention and communicate with General Ripley upon the subject, giving him such facts relative thereto as you may be familiar with,

I am, with great respect, very truly, your friend,

H. G. LEISENRING.

Lieutenant T. J. TREADWELL.

FRANKFORD ARSENAL, *December* 21, 1861.

GENERAL: I have the honor to enclose herewith a copy of a letter received from Mr. H. G. Leisenring, of Philadelphia. In my opinion Mr. Leisenring has given his time, energy, and means, and used every endeavor to complete his whole order for 20,000 sabres in the time originally agreed upon, and has done so with the expectation of being able to accomplish it. I think the facts are clearly stated in his letter, and therefore respectfully recommend that the extension of time asked for be granted.

Respectfully, your obedient servant,

T. J. TREADWELL,
First Lieutenant of Ordnance.

General J. W. RIPLEY, *Washington.*

ORDNANCE OFFICE, *Washington, December* 23, 1861.

SIR: For the reasons stated in your letter of 21st instant, you are authorized to extend Mr. H. G. Leisenring's time for the delivery of cavalry sabres, as requested in his letter to you of December 19, 1861.

Respectfully, your obedient servant,

J. W. RIPLEY, *Brigadier General.*

Lieutenant T. J. TREADWELL,
Frankford Arsenal.

FRANKFORD ARSENAL, *February* 13, 1862.

SIR: I enclose herewith triplicate certificates of inspection for 988 cavalry sabres, completing your order for 20,000, which were delivered by the time specified in letter dated Ordnance office, December 23, 1861, but the inspection was not finished until to-day.

Respectfully, &c.,

T. J. TREADWELL,
First Lieutenant of Ordnance.

H. G. LEISENRING, *Philadelphia, Pa.*

FRANKFORD ARSENAL, *February* 19, 1862.

GENERAL: I have the honor to enclose herewith a statement of the number of sabres received and inspected at that arsenal on Mr. Leisenring's order for 20,000. These sabres were delivered by the 10th of February, but I was unable to have them all inspected before the 13th. I have given Mr. Leisenring's certificates of inspection for 20,000 sabres in all, but do not feel authorized to receive the large surplus without your instructions to do so. In the original order to Mr. Leisenring to secure the delivery of the whole 20,000 sabres by January 1, 1862, it was agreed to allow fifty cents extra on condition of the completion of the entire order by the time specified.

By your letter of December 23 an extension of time was granted to the 10th of February, and Mr. Leisenring stated *there* his understanding of the conversation had with you at the time the extension was granted was, that the condition of the payment should remain as originally expressed. I have therefore caused a statement of this condition to be added to the last certificate of inspection for your approval.

I am, very respectfully, your obedient servant,

T. J. TREADWELL,
First Lieutenant of Ordnance.

General J. W. RIPLEY,
Chief of Ordnance, Washington, D. C.

[Indorsement.]

(Ord. 45. E B. Feb. 24, 1862. B. M., 32.)

ORDNANCE OFFICE, *February* 22, 1862.

Respectfully submitted to the Secretary of War. Leisenring had an order dated September 19, 1861, when we were in urgent need of such arms, for cavalry sabres, to be delivered at the rate of 600 per week up to the 1st of October, 1861, and 1,000 per week thereafter up to the 1st of January, 1862, at $7 each, and, as an incentive to urge on deliveries, it was agreed to allow him $7 50 per sabre, provided he delivered 20,000 by the 1st of January, 1862. He did not deliver the 20,000 by that time, but finding it impossible to do so, he applied on the 19th of December, 1861, for an extension of the time for delivering that number of sabres to the 10th of February, 1862, "as well as the condition of payment." This application was made to Lieutenant Treadwell, who forwarded it to this office, with the recommendation that the extension of "time asked for be granted." He was authorized to extend Mr. Leisenring's time for the delivery of the sabres as requested in his letter. By the 10th of February, 1862, Mr. Leisenring delivered 21,173 sabres, which passed inspection. He now claims that he is entitled to the additional fifty cents on the 20,000 sabres ordered, and asks that the surplus may be accepted and paid for. He says that he understood when I wrote to Lieutenant Treadwell, authorizing the extension of time, that the condition of payment was also included. I know not what he understood, but I am sure that no such authority was granted by my letter, and it is not probable, when the sole object of granting the extra fifty cents, viz: prompt delivery, was defeated, that that condition should have been continued. I see no objection to taking the surplus 1,173 sabres at $7 each, but I do not think that the additional charge of fifty cents per sabre, amounting to $10,000, is fair under the circumstances, or ought to be allowed.

JAMES W. RIPLEY,
Brigadier General.

Statement of sabres received at Frankford arsenal for account of Mr. H. G. Leisenring, of Philadelphia.

Number examined.. 25, 372
Number rejected... 4, 199

Number passed 21, 173

COMMISSION ON CONTRACTS, &C., FOR
ORDNANCE AND ORDNANCE STORES,
Washington, March 21, 1862.

SIR: The commission have the honor to report:

CASE No. 3.—H. G. LEISENRING, of Philadelphia.

Order September 19, 1861.—(*Number* 10 *of printed list, page* 17.)

To deliver at the Frankford arsenal 20,000 cavalry sabres. Price, $7 per sabre, and deliveries to be completed by January 1, 1862.

" If the stipulated number of accepted sabres is filled at the date of completion above stated, January 1, 1862, $7 50 will be allowed for each sabre."

The commissioners find that on the 19th December the claimant states that he has delivered to that date 6,350 sabres, and that this number will be increased to 10,000 by January 1, 1862, and requests that an extension of the time for filling the original order may be granted until the 1st or 10th of February, " as well as the condition of payment."

In forwarding this request, the commanding officer of Frankford arsenal recommends that the extension of time asked for be granted, and the chief of ordnance replies to this letter, authorizing him to extend the time of delivery as requested by his letter to you of the 19th December.

The final delivery of the 20,000 was made February 10.

The question presented in this case is, whether the additional fifty cents per sabre, stipulated to be paid in the event of the delivery of the whole by the 1st of January, 1862, shall be now allowed.

It is clear that this increment of price was promised as an inducement to secure the delivery of the whole number by the 1st of January. The party, however, failed to make the delivery by the day named, and, of course, with a failure to perform the condition he lost the benefit which, from such performance, would have ensued to him.

It is manifest from the declaration of the chief of ordnance that in extending the time for delivery it was not his purpose to carry with it the increased price. Inasmuch, therefore, as $7 is a full price for the sabre, and as the department has lost the advantages of a delivery on the 1st of January, and the party has been already favored in the extension granted him, we recommend that the additional fifty cents per sabre shall not be allowed.

We are, very respectfully, your obedient servants,
J. HOLT,
ROBERT DALE OWEN,
Commissioners, &c.
P. V. HAGNER,
Major of Ordnance, Assistant to Commission.
Hon. EDWIN M. STANTON, *Secretary of War.*

CASE No. 4.

H. G. LEISENRING.

PHILADELPHIA, *February* 14, 1862.

DEAR SIR: Lieutenant Treadwell advised me yesterday that my contract for 20,000 cavalry sabres had been filled—the whole number delivered on the 10th of February, but not all inspected until the 13th.

He also stated that in the inspection of the whole number delivered on and before the 10th there was an excess of 1,234. This excess occurred by the factories turning out more during the last week than I anticipated or calculated upon.

It will give me great pleasure, sir, to dispose of these 1,234 cavalry sabres to the government, at such price as you or Lieutenant Treadwell may suggest. They are of the same character I have been manufacturing for months past, and have already been inspected by Lieutenant Treadwell. The whole lot are in boxes at the arsenal, awaiting your decision in the matter, which I hope may be favorable.

Please send an order for that number, and greatly oblige,

Very truly yours,

H. G. LEISENRING.

Gen. J. W. RIPLEY, *Chief of Ordnance Bureau.*

MARCH 20, 1862.

GENTLEMEN: The whole number of sabres delivered at the Frankford arsenal, on my order of 20,000 to pass inspection, was 25,433. Out of this number 4,199 were rejected in consequence of not coming up to the requirements of the Ordnance Manual.

There are now at the arsenal *that have been inspected,* 1,173 over and above my contract of 20,000, which I have asked the government to purchase.

Very respectfully, &c.,

H. G. LEISENRING.

Messrs. HOLT and OWEN, *Commissioners, &c.*

COMMISSION ON CONTRACTS, &c., FOR
ORDNANCE AND ORDNANCE STORES,
Washington, March 21, 1862.

SIR: The commission have the honor to report as follows:

CASE NO. 4.—H. G. LEISENRING, of Philadelphia,

Has delivered at the Frankford arsenal 1,234 sabres in excess of his order of September 19th, and requests that orders be given for their purchase. The sabres have already been inspected and passed by the government inspector. These sabres are of American manufacture, and of good quality; $7 is a reasonable price for them, but the department is under no obligation whatever to receive them, they being in excess of the number contracted for. Whether, therefore, they shall be accepted or not, is a question which addresses itself entirely to the discretion of the department and must be decided with reference to the actual or anticipated exigencies of the service, in regard to which we are not informed, and therefore will not express any opinion.

We are, very respectfully, your obedient servants,

J. HOLT,
ROBERT DALE OWEN,
Commissioners, &c.
P. V. HAGNER,
Major of Ordnance, Assistant to Commission.

Hon. EDWIN M. STANTON, *Secretary of War.*

CASE No. 5.

RICHARDSON & OVERMAN.

WASHINGTON, *April* 19, 1862.

GENTLEMEN: The subscribers, manufacturers of the "Gallagher" patent breech-loading carbines, beg leave respectfully to submit for your consideration the following statement in reference to their works: They are now delivering for the use of the United States two hundred breech-loading carbines per week, and will have completed by the close of July the whole number ordered of them, say five thousand. That all the various parts for the whole number are now forged and machined, and that consequently their forges and all the machinery connected with that portion of their works are at present unemployed. That in case the United States should desire to order a further supply of these arms, their early completion and delivery would be very much expedited by an order for the same at an early date, as they would in that case be enabled to commence at once to forge all the various pieces for the different parts of the gun, and thus avoid all the delay which would attend an order at a later date. That their present facilities enable them to finish two hundred carbines per week, which, in case of an addditional order, could be still further increased in capacity.

In the hope that the above statement may be deemed worthy of your consideration, the writer will wait upon you in person.

Very respectfully, your obedient servants,

RICHARDSON & OVERMAN, of Philadelphia.

Hon. JOS. HOLT, ROBERT DALE OWEN, and Maj. HAGNER, *Comm'rs.*

Statement of carbines and cartridges delivered under order of September 17, 1861.

1862.

January 23,	100 carbines;		4,000 cartridges.	
February 3,	100 "		4,000 "	
" 14,	160 "		11,000 "	
" 24,	140 "			
March 4,	100 "			
" 10,	140 "			
" 11,	100 "		11,000 "	
	840		30,000	

March 16, 1862, 200 cartridges ready for delivery.
Deliveries made to Lieutenant Treadwell.

WASHINGTON, *March* 20, 1862.

The subscribers, manufacturers of fire-arms, respectfully represent that, on the seventeenth day of September last, they received from the ordnance department an order for five thousand breech-loading carbines, of the "Gallagher" patent, (which arms they were then engaged in manufacturing;) also an order for two hundred thousand metallic cartridges, being forty rounds for each gun, to be paid for by the United States at the rate of thirty dollars ($30) for each carbine and twenty-five dollars ($25) for the metallic cartridges.

These arms and cartridges are ordered to be delivered at the rate of five hundred carbines per month; deliveries to commence within thirty days from the date of order, (that is on the 17th day of October last,) and to continue until the completion of the order.

That, in consequence of the large amount of additional machinery necessary to be built and put up in their works, in order to manufacture this amount of arms, they were delayed in their deliveries for the first three months, and did not make the first delivery until the 23d of January; since which time they have been making deliveries of carbines and cartridges as fast as the arms were completed, as will be seen by the annexed statement; that their works are now in complete order, and that they are now prepared to furnish from two hundred to two hundred and fifty carbines per week, including the necessary appendage and ammunition, and that they are able to deliver the whole five thousand within the time specified in the order.

That in view of these circumstances, and the fact that the various parts of the whole five thousand carbines are at present in process of manufacture, they would most respectfully ask to be permitted to go on and complete the order as early as possible.

Very respectfully, your obedient servants,

RICHARDSON & OVERMAN,

Manufacturers, Phila.; Factory, corner 12th and Thompson sts.

Hon. JOSEPH HOLT and ROBERT DALE OWEN,

Commissioners, &c.

COMMISSION ON ORDNANCE AND ORDNANCE STORES,
Washington, March 22, 1862.

SIR: The commission have the honor to report as follows:

CASE No. 5.—Messrs. RICHARDSON & OVERMAN, of Philadelphia.

Order dated September 17, 1861.—(No. 6 of printed list, page 15.)

To deliver 5,000 breech-loading carbines, of the Gallagher patent, and 40 metallic cartridges with each gun. Deliveries to be made at the rate of 500 carbines per month from date of order. Price per gun, $30.

Price per M. for cartridges, $25.

Delivery refused under general order.

The commissioners find that the parties made their first delivery January 23, and of 100 guns and 4,000 cartridges only, and that, since that date to March 11, they have delivered 840 carbines and 30,000 cartridges, and they have 200 carbines additional ready for delivery on the 16th March.

The commission find that, in consequence of the non-fulfilment of the order in point of time up to this date, the government is not bound to receive these arms, (by special proviso in the order to that effect;) but as the parties seem now able to proceed more rapidly, having offered over 540, in March, up to the 16th, and promise at least 200 guns per week in future, and as the guns are represented to be of good quality and of a kind needed in service, and as the price is not unreasonable as compared with that paid for like arms by the government, they, therefore, *recommend* that these parties be permitted to continue their work under the terms of their order, and that the number orignally specified be received. The papers in case all returned.

We are, very respectfully, your obedient servants,

J. HOLT,
ROBERT DALE OWEN,
Commissioners.

P. V. HAGNER,
Major of Ordnance, Assistant to Commissioners.

Hon. EDWIN M. STANTON,
Secretary of War.

Approved.

EDWIN M. STANTON, *Secretary of War.*

CASE No. 6.

G. W. RAMSDELL.

WAR DEPARTMENT, *July* 25, 1861.

I refer to you a letter and telegram from Major General Frémont in regard to rifled muskets.

General Frémont pronounces the musket "a good serviceable weapon, and much better than the Enfield's, or any others he has seen in this country."

Upon this recommendation, as the department needs arms, I would say purchase them at the lowest price you can.

Respectfully,

SIMON CAMERON, *Secretary of War.*

General RIPLEY, *Bureau of Ordnance.*

ASTOR HOUSE, *July* 21, 1861.

SIR : Captain Garrison has shown me a rifled musket of French make, (Liege,) rough, but well made, which I think is a good serviceable weapon. I like it much better than the Enfield, or any others I have seen here, and would be glad to have ten thousand of them, for our western force.

With great consideration, I am your obedient servant,

J. C. FRÉMONT.

Hon. Mr. CAMERON, *Secretary of War.*

[Telegram.]

117. Dated London, July 24, 1861, — o'clock, — min. m. To C. K. Garrison:

Are your arms to be sent on immediately ? If so, when ? Answer to Cincinnati.

J. C. FRÉMONT, *Major General.*

ORDNANCE OFFICE, *Washington July* 20, 1861.

SIR : The Secretary of War has referred to me a letter to him from General J. C. Frémont, dated July 21, 1861, in regard to certain rifled muskets of French make (Liege) which you have shown him, and of which he states that he would be glad to have ten thousand for our western force, and also a telegram from the general to you, asking if your arms are to be sent on immediately. In referring these papers the Secretary of War states that upon this recommendation, (of General Frémont,) as the department wants arms, he would say "purchase them at the lowest price I can." As that lowest price is fixed at twenty-seven dollars, ($27,) I have to inform you that this department will take your ten thousand rifled muskets, of the kind shown to, and approved of by, General Frémont, at that price.

Send these arms to General Frémont at such place as he may designate; obtain his acknowledgment of their receipt in a satisfactory condition. Transmit that acknowledgment with your bill for the arms to this office for examination, and the proper reference for settlement.

Respectfully, &c.,

JAMES W. RIPLEY,
Brevet Brigadier General.

Mr. C. K. GARRISON, *New York, N. Y.*

WASHINGTON, D. C., *October* 31, 1861.

SIR : I propose to fill the order of the department in July last to C. K. Garrison for 10,000 rifled muskets, which he has failed to execute, with an arm equal in every respect to the one he agreed to furnish, and at a price $6 per gun less than the price named in his order.

A sample of the gun I propose to supply is in General Ripley's office.

G. W. RAMSDALL.

Hon. SECRETARY OF WAR.

WAR DEPARTMENT, *November* 16, 1861.

Please give letter of authority to George Ramsdall to furnish 10,000 guns in accordance with his proposition.

The Secretary desires this to be done to-day, in order that advices may go abroad to secure the guns.

Very respectfully,

THOMAS A. SCOTT,
Assistant Secretary.

Colonel MAYNADIER.

ORDNANCE OFFICE,
Washington, November 16, 1861.

SIR : Your letter to the Secretary of War of the 31st October, 1861, was referred to this office, indorsed by the Assistant Secretary : " Buy the arms, if they can be furnisned at $6 less than former contract, thus saving $60,000 to the government."

To-day I have received instructions from the War Department to " give letter of authority to George Ramsdall to furnish 10,000 guns in accordance with his proposition." The Secretary desires this done to-day, in order that advices may go abroad to secure the guns.

In compliance with these instructions, I hereby authorize you to furnish the ten thousand (10,000) arms in accordance with your proposition as contained in your letter to the Secretary of War dated October 31, 1861, and filed in this office.

Respectfully, your obedient servant,

WILLIAM MAYNADIER,
Lieutenant Colonel Ordnance.

G. W. RAMSDALL, Esq., *Washington, D. C.*

P. S. The price named in the order to C. K. Garrison for the 10,000 arms was twenty-seven dollars ($27) each.

W. M.

JANUARY 13, 1862.

SIR : I am now ready to deliver the ten thousand guns ordered by the United States government November 16, 1861, and which I agreed to deliver as per order of that date. You will recollect that I deposited a sample in the Ordnance office.

Mr. Samuel B. Smith is my agent in New York, and will deliver for me to such agent as you may direct the above-named guns. His address is, care of Colonel Dodge & Co., Wall street, New York.

The guns are now in warehouse under control of Major P. V. Hagner, in New York.

Please advise Mr. Smith what to do in the premises.

Respectfully, your obedient servant,

G. W. RAMSDALL.

Brigadier General RIPLEY, *United States Army.*

WASHINGTON, D. C., *November* 20, 1861.

Samuel B. Smith, of the State of California, having agreed to furnish me ten thousand (10,000) guns according to sample deposited by me in the United States Ordnance office, I hereby authorize him to deliver to the general government, in my name, the said number of ten thousand guns as per order of the Bureau of Ordnance to me directed, bearing date November 16, 1861, and signed by William Maynadier, lieutenant colonel ordnance. And I give to him, the said Smith, full and complete authority to collect and receive from the United States government the money due or to become due upon the delivery of said guns, and to sign all necessary receipts and vouchers in the premises to the government for me, in my name or otherwise.

GEORGE RAMSDALL.

Witness: JAMES BURNS.

ORDNANCE OFFICE,
Washington, January 17, 1862.

SIR: In answer to your letter of the 13th instant, I have to state that the sample arm to which you refer has been sent to Major Hagner, of which he has been advised from this office.

Respectfully, your obedient servant,

JAS. W. RIPLEY, *Brigadier General.*

Mr. G. W. RAMSDALL,
Care Mr. Samuel B. Smith, New York, N. Y.

ORDNANCE OFFICE,
Washington, January 17, 1862.

SIR: Mr. G. W. Ramsdall informs me that the ten thousand muskets ordered from him, as per letter from this office of the 16th of November, 1861, which he will show you, are ready for delivery.

The sample of these arms which Mr. Ramsdall left in Washington will be sent to you to-day. He informs me that Mr. Samuel B. Smith is his agent in New York, and will attend to the delivery of the arms under the order before mentioned.

Mr. Smith's address is, care of Clark, Dodge & Co., New York, in Wall street.

Respectfully, your obedient servant,

JAS. W. RIPLEY, *Brigadier General.*

Major P. V. HAGNER,
No. 55 White street, New York.

ORDNANCE OFFICE,
No. 55 White street, New York, January 26, 1862.

GENERAL: Your letter of the 17th instant, relative to ten thousand stands of arms ordered from Mr. George Ramsdall, together with a letter from your office of the 16th of November, 1861, alluded to therein, and a copy of the offer of Mr. Ramsdall to the honorable Secretary of War, dated October 31, 1861, to furnish arms to the government on the Garrison contract, have been presented to this office by Mr. S. B. Smith, the agent of Mr. Ramsdall. As the purchase of these arms is a matter of some moment, involving a considerable amount, I have deemed it advisable to communicate with you on the subject, prior to making the necessary arrangements for their inspection and reception. The sample gun, purporting to come from your office, is at hand; and I find it, on examination, to be an Austrian rifle, calibre 715—an altered arm, said to be from the model adopted for the use of gun cotton, and known at this office as the Bulkley arm. This arm is of an inferior grade, and has been purchased in this market at $10 and $10 50 per gun, about fifteen thousand having been purchased at those prices. A letter from Major Hagner dated December 4, 1861, refers to these arms.

Ex. Doc. 72——3

Now as the price stipulated to be paid for the guns to be furnished by Mr. Ramsdall ($21) is so much above the amount for which the same arms (according to sample presented) have been secured in New York, ($10,) I have thought it absolutely necessary, in order to avoid any mistake or misapprehension whatever, to have the identity of the sample arm thoroughly established before completing the transaction, especially as it reaches this office through private hands. Sample No. 2, forwarded to you by express, as per letter of advice from this office dated December 24, is, I am informed, the identical gun. Be pleased to inform me if the Ramsdall arm forwarded from your office accords with sample No. 2, and if this office is to be governed by it in the inspection and reception of the ten thousand stand.

Very respectfully, your obedient servant,

S. CRISPIN, *Captain of Ordnance.*

General J. W. RIPLEY,
Chief of Ordnance, Washington, D. C.

WASHINGTON, *March* 15, 1861.

This letter, written during my illness, was afterwards shown me, with the gun presented as a sample, and application made by Mr. Ramsdall's agent for an order from me to accept the arms he offered like the sample. As the sample gun was only worth from $7 50 to $10, (by my purchases in New York,) I was convinced that some mistake had occurred, and therefore refused to receive the arms offered by Mr. R.   It is evident, from the first order to Garrison, that there *was a mistake,* as G.'s arms were to be French, (Liege make,) and, as General Frémont stated, "much better than the Enfield or any others I have seen."

P. V. HAGNER, *Major of Ordnance.*

ORDNANCE OFFICE,
Washington, January 23, 1862.

SIR : The arm referred to in Mr. Ramsdall's order, and which was forwarded from this office, may be identified with the seal of the Ordnance office upon it.

Respectfully, your obedient servant,

JAS. W. RIPLEY, *Brigadier General.*

Captain S. CRISPIN,
No. 55 White street, New York.

KIRKWOOD HOUSE,
Washington, January 30, 1862.

SIR : Your communication of the 17th instant, informing me that the sample gun under my contract with government had been forwarded to Major Hagner at New York, and that he was advised in reference to the same, was duly received on 18th instant. On the 19th I called at his office, and for the reason (as stated by Captain Crispin) that he was not sufficiently satisfied of the genuineness of sample, and for the further reason that the price named in contract was larger than had been paid by Major Hagner for a similar arm, he informed me he should decline receiving and inspecting the guns—10,000 offered by me to him—until he should be further advised from you. I again called at his office on the 27th instant, at which time he informed me he had read a reply from you, and that the guns would be received as soon as he had seen Major H., and settled the point as to whether the guns could be considered in bond or not.

On yesterday he informed me that the guns could not be received until Major

Hagner was fully advised by the authorities in Washington whether the guns were to be received from me in bond or otherwise, as the order to me was silent on that point, and until it was also settled whether the guns were not already entirely under Major Hagner's control, they having been drawn out of the custom-house by H. Boker & Co. (through whom I shipped the guns) by a permit from Major H., and stored in a warehouse belonging to them, and used by them for storage of arms sold by them to the government. In this connexion I will only state that I ordered these guns from Europe through H. Boker & Co. to fill my contract with the government, and they were shipped for that purpose.

I then called upon Major Hagner, who informed me that he thought there must be a mistake as to the price of guns, and that he would not accept them unless ordered so to do directly, and until he was satisfied that the authorities understood the matter fully.

In conclusion, I have to say the guns are in New York, ready for delivery, and have been since the 13th instant, and I am prepared to deliver them as per contract. I ask that as speedy action be had in the premises as possible. You will recollect it was understood at the time that the guns were deliverable in bond, as has been the case with all guns sold to the government.

Very respectfully,

GEORGE RAMSDALL,
By SAM. B. SMITH, *Agent.*

Brigadier General J. W. RIPLEY.

WASHINGTON, D. C., *February* 10, 1862.

SIR: On the 16th day of November, 1861, I received an order from the Ordnance bureau bearing date that day, signed William Maynadier, lieutenant colonel of ordnance, authorizing me to furnish ten thousand arms in accordance with a proposition made by me October 31, 1861, and as per sample deposited by me in the Ordnance bureau at that date. I immediately ordered that number of guns to be purchased in Europe. On the 13th day of January, 1862, having then received the whole number, I notified General Ripley, chief of the Ordnance bureau, that I was prepared to deliver the guns contracted for, and asking him for instructions as to where they were to be delivered. As you are aware, the government has not yet received the guns, nor have they been inspected, the government officers having failed so to do. The guns are in my possession, and have been paid for. They have been in my possession since the 13th day of January, and I am prepared now, as I was then, to deliver the guns in accordance with the provisions contained in my contract with the government.

I would respectfully ask the immediate attention of the department to this my communication.

Respectfully, your obedient servant,

GEORGE RAMSDALL,
By his agent, SAMUEL B. SMITH.

Hon. E. M. STANTON,
Secretary of War.

WASHINGTON, *February* 21, 1862.

SIR: As directed by you, personally, this day, I have the honor to submit to you the following statement:

On the 16th November, 1861, George Ramsdall was authorized by the United States Ordnance bureau to furnish to the government 10,000 guns in accordance with a sample deposited by him before that date in the Ordnance office, as you will see by reference to copies of his proposition, with reply of Ordnance bureau, accompanying this. On the 20th of same month I having agreed with Ramsdall to furnish for him the guns named in said order, was authorized by him in writing to do so. I immediately ordered the guns from Europe. They have been bought and paid for, and on the 13th of January, 1862, they were in New York city in bond, ready for delivery, and I notified the Ordnance bureau on that day to that effect, signing myself as agent for Ramsdall.

The Ordnance bureau have failed to inspect or receive the guns, and they are now, as they were six weeks since, in bond in New York ready for delivery.

I have made frequent application to General Ripley by letter, and in person, requesting that action be taken in the premises, and the invariable answer has been that the case had been removed from the Ordnance department to the War Department proper, and that nothing could be done until action was had by the Secretary of War. I therefore address you and request that such action be had as will relieve me from my present embarrassing position. The delay which has already occurred has damaged me seriously; a much further delay will prove ruinous.

Yours, respectfully,

SAMUEL B. SMITH,
Agent for GEORGE RAMSDALL.

Hon. E. M. STANTON,
    Secretary of War.

WASHINGTON, February 26, 1862.

SIR: On yesterday I received an advertised letter from the Washington post office, which I found upon examination to be a circular letter from you, with a memorandum calling my attention to the fact that in giving notice to the War Department of its contract with George Ramsdall for arms, I had failed to furnish the department with the original or copy of the contract. On the 13th January, 1862, Mr. Ramsdall was prepared to fill his contract, and I so notified the chief of the Ordnance bureau. The ordnance officers have failed to inspect or receive the arms. On or about the 24th of January I called upon General Ripley personally to ascertain the cause of the delay, when he informed me that all the papers in the case, including a copy of the contract, had been referred to the Secretary of War, and that nothing further would be done until the Secretary had acted upon them.

Knowing thus that a copy of the contract had been filed with the Secretary of War, I did not deem it necessary to furnish another copy at the time I sent in my letter stating what had been done under the contract.

Since then, however, on the 21st of February, I sent to the Secretary of War a copy of the contract. I beg leave to again call your attention to the fact of the extraordinary delay which has occurred in the premises, and to ask of you most earnestly that some action will be taken by the department. If it is necessary for me to make any further showing, or to do anything more in the premises, please inform me by note at the Kirkwood House, Washington city.

Yours, respectfully,

SAMUEL B. SMITH,
Agent for GEORGE RAMSDALL.

Hon. P. H. WATSON,
    Assistant Secretary of War.

WASHINGTON, February 28, 1862.

SIR: On the 21st instant, at a personal interview which I had the honor to have with you, I stated the facts in reference to a contract made in November last between the government and George Ramsdell for 10,000 arms, which arms Mr. Ramsdell has had on hand in New York city, ready for delivery since the 13th of January, 1862, on which day I, as agent for him, notified the chief of the Ordnance bureau to that effect. You will remember that you then intrusted me to make out for you a statement in writing of all the facts, together with a copy of the contract, and furnish the same to you, and that, as soon as I had done this, the case would be referred to the Ordnance bureau, who would act on the matter. On the 22d instant I forwarded to you these papers, and each day since I have called at the Ordnance office in reference to the matter, but have been invariably informed that the papers were still in the War Department, awaiting the action of the Secretary of War. I called this morning, and was so informed. Will you allow me again to call your attention to this matter, and to state that the delay is ruinous? I have been ready now nearly two months to deliver these arms, which have been *purchased and paid for,* and it seems hard that no action has been yet taken toward receiving or inspecting them.

Please excuse me if I seem importunate, but it is very important for me to know what is to be the action of the government toward me in the premises.

Yours, very respectfully,

SAMUEL B. SMITH,
Agent for GEORGE RAMSDELL.

Hon. E. M. STANTON,
Secretary of War.

WASHINGTON, *March* 4, 1862.

SIR: You will please excuse me for again calling your attention to the contract made by government on the 16th November, 1861, with George Ramsdell for 10,000 arms, which contract I have filled for him, having been authorized by him, in writing, so to do. You will remember that nearly two months since I notified you that I had purchased the guns, and that they were at New York city, in bond, ready for delivery, and you will further remember that the government has as yet failed to receive them, or to give me any indication of what they intended to do in the premises.

I cannot understand why I am thus treated. My position is, to say the least, a very critical one. My creditors are daily calling upon me for money advanced by them for me in the purchase of these arms, and I have been compelled to put them off from week to week, until they are tired out, and unless action is taken at once by the government in the premises, I shall be ruined. My case is a very hard one, and I again call your attention to it, with the request that final action be taken by the government in the premises at once.

Yours, respectfully,

SAMUEL B. SMITH,
Agent for GEORGE RAMSDELL.

Brigadier General J. W. RIPLEY,
Chief Ordnance Bureau.

In the matter of the contract made by government with George Ramsdell for arms, November 16, 1861.

KIRKWOOD HOUSE,
Washington City, March 18, 1862.

I am a party in interest in this contract, having furnished the guns.

On the 20th November, 1861, I agreed to furnish the guns, and that I might be certain of receiving the money to become due for said guns, Ramsdell executed to me a power of attorney, directing me to deliver the arms to the government for him in his name, and authorizing me to collect all sums due from government upon said contract, and to receipt for same in his name or otherwise.

I immediately ordered the guns from Europe. On the 13th of January, 1862, I had the guns in bond in New York city, and on that day I, as agent for Ramsdell, notified the Ordnance bureau in writing to that effect. The guns were sold to government by sample deposited with Ordnance bureau. The guns ordered from Europe, and proposed to be delivered, were in accordance with sample deposited, and named in the order of Ordnance department directing the purchase.

The Chief of Ordnance, in response to my letter, wrote me that the sample had been forwarded to Major Hagner, Ordnance office in New York city, and referred me to him. Major Hagner declined to receive or examine the arms, and gave me, personally, as his reason for so doing that the price agreed to be paid for the guns was so large that he thought there must be some mistake, and said he would not act in the matter until further advised. Since then I have had the guns on hand and ready for delivery, but have not been able to get any action taken by government, all contracts for arms having been suspended by order of the Secretary of War. I admit that the price named for the guns was, at date of order, large ; that the government has since bought the same arms for about half the price ; but I assert that the contract was fairly made with the proper department of the United States government, and that I have acted throughout the matter in entire good faith. I will state further, that, at the time the order was made, the government was in great need of arms, and was paying much higher prices than they have since, and that parties furnishing arms from Europe had to take war risks, at that time serious. I rely, however, on the record in the case, believing that the government will not undertake to go beyond her written promise. If any doubts are entertained as to the genuineness of the contract, or as to the means used to obtain it, I am prepared and anxious for the most rigid examination. I only ask that speedy action be taken, as the delay which has already occurred is almost ruinous.

Should you desire my presence, please address me at the Kirkwood House in this city.

Respectfully, your obedient servant,

SAMUEL B. SMITH,

Hon. J. HOLT and ROBERT DALE OWEN,
    Commissioners on Contracts, &c.

ORDNANCE OFFICE,
Washington, March 22, 1862.

SIR : In compliance with your request in your letter of this day's date, I send you this, the sample arm referred to in General Frémont's letter to the Secretary of War of 21st of July, 1861, agreeably to which sample 10,000 arms were ordered from C. K. Garrison on the 26th of July, 1861.

The sample gun referred to in Mr. G. W. Ramsdell's letter to the Secretary of War of October 20, 1861, is not in this office. It was sent to your office at New York, on the 17th of January last, and it is presumed to be there at this time. I enclose copies of two letters from this office on that subject, one to yourself, dated 17th of January, and one to Captain Crispin, dated January 23 last, which is all the evidence that exists in this office in relation to the sample arm.

For the information in relation to this contract, or order, I respectfully refer to Executive Document No 67, current session of Congress, pages 41, 42, 43, 44.

Respectfully, your obedient servant,

JAMES W. RIPLEY, *Brigadier General.*

Major P. V. HAGNER,
    Commissioner on Ordnance and Ordnance Stores.

KIRKWOOD HOUSE,
Washington City, March 24, 1862.

GENTLEMEN : In the matter of the "Ramsdall" contract for arms, a statement in reference to which I had the honor a few days since to submit to you, and in the discussion of which Major Hagner raised the point in your presence, that the gun to be delivered by Ramsdell must be equal to the gun originally proposed to be delivered by Garrison, I beg leave to state what then I neglected to do, that the fact of General Ripley having forwarded to Major Hagner at the city of New York, as a sample to guide him in the inspection, the identical sample gun originally deposited by Ramsdell, and which guided me in my purchase, shows that the government fully understood, in ordering the ten thousand (10,000) guns from Ramsdell, that they were to be controlled by the sample originally deposited, and that when the order was given the government had passed upon the comparative value of the two guns. I beg leave further to state that, in making up my statement, I did not deem it necessary to go back of the papers in the case, as to make explanations of points not necessarily involved. As I said in my statement, however, I am willing and anxious to undergo the most searching examination, if any doubts are entertained by the commissioners as to the validity of the contract, to the means used to obtain it, or as to my having acted in good faith in all that I have done in the premises.

Respectfully, your obedient servant,

SAMUEL B. SMITH.

Hon. J. HOLT and ROBERT DALE OWEN,
Commissioners on Contracts, &c.

JERSEY SHORE, *April* 19, 1862.

DEAR SIR : I received yours of the 16th instant, asking me whether or not I authorized James Duffy to use my name in making proposition to the government to furnish such articles as they might need. In a conversation last spring with Mr. Duffy I did authorize him to use my name to make any such proposition as he should wish to. I understood soon after that he had so used it in proposing to furnish some guns.

Yours, truly,

GEORGE RAMSDELL.

Mr. SMITH.

ORDNANCE OFFICE,
No. 55 *White street, New York, March* 26, 1862.

SIRS: In accordance with your instructions communicated to me through Major P. V. Hagner, I have this day forwarded to his address, per express, the gun deposited at this office by Mr. S. B. Smith, agent for G. W. Ramsdell, as the sample of the 10,000 stand of arms which he was authorized to furnish under his order from the Ordnance office, dated November 16, 1861.

On the presentation of this sample arm, Mr. Smith informed me that the 10,000 to be delivered were in port, imported by the Messrs. H. Boker & Co. I found, from the statement of this firm, that they had made arrangements with the agent of Mr. Ramsdell, and were ready to supply the above number of Garibaldi arms that they had imported at various times in connexion with arms deliverable under their order from the War Department, and I found from the records of this office that about five thousand (5,000) had already been purchased of this firm at the price of $10 per gun.

The price offered to Mr. Garrison, $27, evidently contemplated the securing to the United States first-class arms, and, accordingly, from the tenor of Mr. Ramsdell's letter, I was led to the belief that an arm of good quality was to be submitted for inspection and reception. These facts led me to suppose that there existed some misapprehension relative to this case at the War Department and Ordnance bureau, as the arm presented by Mr. Smith was of such an inferior grade as not to command $10 in the market at the time it was offered me for acceptance. My letter of January 20 was accordingly written.

It may not be improper to state, in this connexion, that this same style of arm has been since offered at low rates at this office, but that I have rigidly refused to purchase, deeming any expenditure for them only justified by the wants of the service; also, the records of this office show that the same arm, purchased by Mr. Sanford, United States minister at Brussels, cost thirty-five (35) francs delivered in Antwerp.

Very truly, your obedient servant,

S. CRISPIN,
Captain of Ordnance.

Hon. JOSEPH HOLT and ROBERT DALE OWEN,
Commission on Ordnance, &c., Washington, D. C.

COMMISSION ON ORDNANCE AND ORDNANCE STORES,
Washington, April 1, 1862.

GENERAL: Mr. S. B. Smith, to whom the order No. 6, of printed list, Executive Document No. 67, pages 33 and 40, has been transferred, has requested of the commission that he may have the benefit of being present before the commission during the examination of *yourself, Captain Benton,* and the *keeper of the ordnance seal,* in relation to the above-named case.

The commission request, therefore, that, if convenient, you will appear tomorrow at 11 a. m., or as soon thereafter as may suit your engagements, and that Captain Benton and the "keeper" may be informed of the desire of Mr. Smith and the request of the commission, so that all may be examined between 11 and 2 o'clock, if possible, during which hours Mr. Smith has been notified to be present.

Very respectfully,

P. V. HAGNER,
Major of Ordnance.

General J. W. RIPLEY, *Chief of Ordnance.*

Before commission, April 5, 1862.

Mr. James Duffy, of Lancaster county, Pennsylvania, being duly sworn, states:

I got in the arms business last July, through Garrison, who asked me if I could sell a gun like the Chasseur de Vincennes. I went to the Secretary of War, and was, by him, referred to General Ripley. I told him the price of the gun was $29, which he said was too high. A week after this Garrison brought me a despatch from General Frémont and a letter. I took the letter and the telegram to the Secretary of War, who sent for and conferred with General Ripley. After the interview the Secretary of War told me to go with General Ripley. He disparaged the gun, and said he would not pay that price; that neither the gun that Garrison had offered as a sample nor the one I proposed to substitute for it was worth anything; and in answer to the question, "Whether there was $6 difference between the guns?" he said, "both together are not worth $6." I reported the substance of this conversation, either immediately or some days thereafter, to Assistant Secretary of War Thomas A. Scott, and told him that General Ripley did not think well of either gun; to which he responded: "If the gun business were left to General Ripley the government would get no guns," and thereupon he gave me the order. I took the order to the Ordnance office, (General Ripley then being absent with the Secretary at Springfield,) and Colonel Maynadier wrote the order, addressing it to G. Ramsdell, at my request. I signed Ramsdell's name by permission. Ramsdell has no interest in or knowledge of the contract. He is my partner in private transactions; believe I had authority to sign his name, from the fact of having signed it, but I do not know that I had specific authority for this particular signature. I had general authority to sign Ramsdell's name if I found an occasion in which it would be of advantage to use it. Ramsdell is a man pretty well off. He has been employed by me; he is an honest, common man. Mr. Scott, and, I think, General Ripley (though I cannot swear to this) knew that the contract was not with Ramsdell, but with me. Ramsdell does not consider himself responsible under the contract. Smith and myself are interested in and own the entire contract. Ramsdell has never received anything from either of us. Ramsdell gave the power of attorney to Mr. Smith without consideration. When I applied to Mr. Scott I do not know whether Ramsdell knew anything of it or not. I did not wish some men to know that I had a contract, because they threatened to have it broken, &c.

I did not know the law on the subject of transfers of contracts. Ramsdell is a lumberman, in the employ of Mehaffy, House & Co., New York, of which firm I am a member.

General Ripley thought my bayonet better than that of the Garrison gun. I thought the gun was better than it is. . I was to have $4 (half profit) on each gun, but now, in consideration of the inferior quality of the gun, I relinquish my claim.

Before commission, May 2, 1862.

General J. W. Ripley, chief of ordnance:

Question. Do you recollect making a comparison in the presence of Mr. Duffy (Colonel Maynadier and Captain Benton, or either of them, being present) between the two guns now shown you?

Answer. I recollect comparing two guns when Mr. Duffy and Colonel Maynadier were present, but I cannot identify the two guns.

Question. Did you ever acknowledge that a gun brought by Mr. Duffy to the Ordnance office, as the sample alluded to in the proposal of Ramsdell, was, in your opinion, a satisfactory substitute for the guns to have been delivered under the order of Garrison?

Answer. I do not recollect having ever expressed any opinion upon the subject. I may have done so, but not as a judgment upon the case, and I did not look upon it as my duty to establish the agreement of the samples. Under the order the receiving or inspecting officer was required to consider as to the sufficiency of the substitute. The Garrison sample was still in the office, and was acknowledged in the proposal, as known to the proposer, by the statement that his gun was "in all respects equal to it." Hence, when the guns were offered under the order given to him, the inspecting officer at New York was directed to examine and see that those offered complied with the terms of the order. He decided that they did not, and I referred the matter to the Secretary of War, with the inspecting officer's opinion.

Before commission, May 3, 1862.

Answers in writing submitted by General J. W. Ripley, chief of ordnance, to questions of Samuel B. Smith relative to Ramsdell contract.

Question. Do you remember a contract made by the government with C. K. Garrison in July last for 10,000 guns? and, if so, please state what was the price agreed to be paid, also whether this contract was filled or annulled.

Answer. This question is fully answered at pages 40 and 41, Executive Document No. 67, 2d session 37th Congress.

Question. Did G. W. Ramsdell propose to fill this contract with another gun, and did the government agree to purchase the gun he proposed to substitute, and if so, at what price?

Answer. This question is also fully answerad at the same pages of the same document as the answer to question 1st.

Question. When, in January last, I notified you (as the agent of Ramsdell) that the 10,000 guns, as per terms of his contract, were ready for delivery in New York, and you forwarded to Major Hagner a sample gun, were you not satisfied that it was the sample gun proposed by Ramsdell to be substituted for the Garrison arm?

Answer. I am satisfied, from the fact of having the official seal upon it, that the sample gun sent to Major Hagner on the 17th of January, 1862, is the identical sample gun substituted by Mr. Ramsdell for the Garrison gun.

Question. When the Ramsdell proposition was made were you not shown his sample, and did you not object to the purchase, and have several conversations with Colonel Thomas A. Scott, Assistant Secretary of War, on the subject; and if so, what passed on the subject?

Answer. I have no recollection of any specific conversation with Colonel Thomas A. Scott, Assistant Secretary of War, in relation to Mr. Ramsdell's proposition; but I have no doubt that if such conversation took place I objected to the whole proposition, both as regarded the quality and kind of arms and the prices to be paid for them.

Five papers relating to an order to G. W. Ramsdall for 10,000 rifled muskets at $21 each.

The history of this case in brief is as follows, viz; The Secretary of War, on the 21st of July, 1861, directed the purchase for General Frémont of 10,000 rifled muskets from C. K. Garrison at the lowest price I could. Mr. James Duffey, acting for Garrison, stated the price to be $29 each. I refused to pay so much. He then, after some time, came down to $27 each, as the very lowest price in which the arms could be sold, (Paper No. 1.) I then gave the order to Garrison to furnish the arms as directed by the Secretary of War, at $27 (Paper No. 2.) That order was not executed, and on the 31st of October, 1861, Mr. G. W. Ramsdall proposed to fill it with an arm equal in every respect at a price $6 less per gun. The War Department, on the 31st of October, sent the proposition to this office with directions to buy the arms, (Paper No. 3,) and reiterated the directions on the 16th of November, 1861, with instructions to have it done to-day, in order that advices may go abroad to secure the guns, (Paper No. 4.) The order was accordingly given to Mr. Ramsdall, who, I am informed, has imported the arms and has them in bond at New York ready for delivery. Similar arms are reported by Captain Crispin, (Paper No. 5,) to have been purchased at New York for about half the price agreed to be paid to Ramsdall.

The contract with Ramsdall was evidently a bad bargain, and I do not and never did consider the arms ordered from him worth the price agreed to be paid. Still, as the contractor has gone on to fulfil his obligations in good faith, and has been at the expense of importing the arms, I do not see how the contract can now be revoked.

JAMES W. RIPLEY,
Brigadier General.

ORDNANCE OFFICE, *January* 24, 1862.

See letter enclosed, No. 95, from Captain Crispin with indorsements.

P. V. H.

Before commission, May 2.

Nathaniel Mulligan, sworn:

Question by commission. Do you affix the seal of the Ordnance office to guns deposited in the sample room?

Answer. I do; I know of no one else who does.

Question. Did you affix the seal on the gun I now show you?

Answer. It looks to me like a seal that I put on, I cannot be positive, although I have some recollection of a seal put on, not of full size, as this is.

Question. When did you affix this seal, and under what circumstances?

Answer. I was ordered to do it by one of the officers; I do not recollect when, but I should suppose it was some five or six months since, if I put it on this gun.

Question. Is this the gun sealed by you in January last?

Answer. I cannot say positively, but I think it is from the peculiarity in the break of the seal. I notice the swell on the stock of this gun, and I recollect that the gun with a deficient seal had such a swell.

Before commission, April 5, 1862.

Mr. S. B. Smith, being duly sworn, states:

I had learned, incidentially, that Mr. Duffy was interested in a contract for 10,000, which he feared he could not comply with. I called on Duffy, who told me I had been correctly informed, and that his contract was held in connexion with C. K. Garrison. I told Duffy I could furnish him 10,000 guns, and I showed him a sample afterwards in my room. This sample I had received from the Messrs. Boker & Co., of New York, and the price fixed at that time, in case I should need the guns, was $13. Mr. Schleischer, of that firm, had the sample gun here in Washington. Mr. Duffy examined the gun, and said it was as good as the Garrison gun, and that he would try and get it substituted. This was some time in October. Some two or three weeks after this, Mr. Duffy informed me that he had made the proposition in the name of Ramsdell, whose name he had been authorized to use, and that he had gotten a contract for the gun at $21. He showed me the order of the ordnance department. Very shortly thereafter I saw Ramsdell, who executed to me the power of attorney, authorizing me to furnish the guns in his name to the government; to receive and receipt for the moneys for them. Immediately after its execution I ordered the guns to be delivered in New York, of the foreign house above mentioned, on the 13th of January. I had all the guns delivered in New York in time, and I saw that the ordnance department was notified that they were there to the number of 10,000. They were the same guns as the sample in the rooms of the commission. Boker & Co. did not tell me the cost of the guns. My purchase of the guns was not conditional, it was absolute. It was made on the 20th of November, through Mr. Schleischer, of Boker & Co., who was then in Washington, and had the sample in his room. I wanted sabres, which he told me he could not furnish, but he said he could furnish guns. I do not recollect that Mr. Boker told Major Hagner what the guns cost when we both visited him at his hotel, in January. Boker told the major that like guns had been purchased by him, (Major Hagner,) at $10. I thought it was a good gun; the lock was strong when I first got it. I got the power of attorney from Ramsdell, here in Washington; he was here a few days after the order was given. The profit on the guns is $8 each. Duffy and I were to have $4 each. Ramsdell has no interest at all in the contract. My interest is $40,000.

Before commission, May 2, 1862.

Captain J. G. Benton:

Question by Mr. Smith. Do you recollect the sample gun in the Ramsdell contract?

Answer. I have a general recollection of the gun; I recognize this (pointing to a sword bayonet, Vincennes rifle) as the original garrison contract sample. I think this other (pointing to Mr. Smith's sample) is the one which I heard was accepted by the War Department, as a substitute for the first-named. I understood it was so accepted.

Question. Do you ordinarily write cards to be attached to sample guns, and do you know the handwriting on this?

Answer. I have never done so myself; this handwriting I do not know.

Question. Do you recollect having been asked to compare the two guns shown you in company with General Ripley and Captain Maynadier?

Answer. I do not recollect any comparison; I did try the Vincennes gun by order of General Ripley, and found the bayonet bent over more than at present. Mr. Duffy was present at this time.

Question. Are you not positive that this is the sample gun handed in by Mr. J. Duffy, at the time he submitted the Ramsdell proposition?

Answer. It is my strong impression that this is the kind of gun.

Question. What do you think was the difference in the market value of the two guns at the time the substitute was proposed?

Answer. If the bayonet was of proper temper, I should say the difference in value was $10. I suppose the sword bayonet to cost $2.

Question. How do the two sword bayonets compare, in your opinion?

Answer. Both the Duffy sample and the other are badly tempered. They are about the same, but the Vincennes is the best model.

Question. How do they compare in quality of lock, stock, rod, and barrel?

Answer. The Vincennes is decidedly the best. The grooves of the Duffy gun are two numerous and fine, the lock plate patched and altered, and I think the barrel has been altered from a flint-lock. The stock is inferior, and the ramrods of the Duffy gun are very defective. The Vincennes gun is a carbine antique.

Question by Mr. Smith. How did you arrive at the impression that the Duffy gun was to be substituted for the Garrison gun?

Answer. I heard a conversation in the Ordnance office about it; I think from some remarks by Colonel Maynadier. General Ripley was present at the time. Colonel Maynadier has the business of writing out the orders of the Secretary of War about small arms. My knowledge is only incidental, and not from official connexion.

J. G. BENTON, *Captain of Ordnance.*

WASHINGTON, *May* 2, 1862.

GENTLEMEN: Representing George Ramsdell in his contract of November 16, 1861, for 10,000 arms, as I have heretofore explained to you, and having full and absolute control over the interests of the parties concerned therein, in order to obtain a settlement with the government, and finally close the matter, I make to you this proposition for a compromise, as per your suggestion of yesterday.

I will deduct six dollars and fifty cents ($6 50) on the price agreed to be paid for each arm, leaving the price per arm, to be paid *in bond* in New York city, fourteen dollars and fifty cents ($14 50.) In this connexion I will state that the sample gun is *iron mounted.* There are, I am informed by the shippers, in my lot of arms some which are *brass mounted.* I wish this understood, and as a part of this proposition I desire that the difference in the mountings be not considered in the inspection. I offer this as a compromise in order to obtain money to meet obligations incurred in this connexion, and respectfully ask a prompt reply.

Yours, respectfully,

SAMUEL B. SMITH.

Messrs. HOLT and OWEN,
Commissioners on Contracts, &c.

WASHINGTON, *May* 7, 1862.

GENTLEMEN: Referring to my letter of May 2, 1862, in reference to the order to George W. Ramsdell, dated November 16, 1861, for 10,000 guns of character and quality indicated by said order, and the proposal on which it was based, I have to state that for the reasons set forth in said letter, and understanding that the commissioners, in view of the inferior quality of the gun, as asserted by them, are unwilling to allow a higher price than eleven dollars ($11) each, I agreed to deliver said 10,000 guns to the government at that price.

Allow me to call your attention to that portion of my letter referring to variations in sample, and to connect that with this my proposition for final settlement.

GEORGE RAMSDELL,
By his attorney in fact, SAMUEL B. SMITH.

My action in presenting the above proposition is both as the fully authorized attorney in fact of George W. Ramsdell and in my own right, I having an interest in the contract, as will appear from testimony heretofore given.

SAMUEL B. SMITH.

Messrs. HOLT and OWEN,
Commissioners on Contracts.

COMMISSION ON ORDNANCE AND ORDNANCE STORES,
Washington, May 9, 1862.

GENERAL: The commission have the honor to report as follows:

CASE No. 6.—G. W. RAMSDELL, transferred from C. K. Garrison, and by power of attorney, to S. B. SMITH.

Original order, by direction of Secretary of War, to C. K. Garrison, dated July 26, 1861.

To furnish 10,000 rifled muskets of French make (Liege) of the kind shown to General Frémont, at $27 each.

Authority by officer in charge of the ordnance department, by direction of the Assistant Secretary of War, Thomas A Scott, esquire, dated November 16, 1861, to G. W. Ramsdell. (See Case 6, Ex. Doc. No. 67, p. 40.)

To furnish 10,000 guns in accordance with his proposition, viz: "I propose to fill the order of the department in July last to C. K. Garrison for ten thousand (10,000) rifled muskets, which he has failed to execute, with an arm equal in every respect to the one he agreed to furnish, and at a price $6 per gun less than the price named in his order. A sample of the gun I propose to supply is in General Ripley's office."

The commission find that the arm proposed to be furnished by C. K. Garrison was one of French pattern, made at Liege, with sword-bayonet, known as the Chasseur de Vincennes model; that Mr. Garrison having failed in his agreement, a Mr. Duffy, in concert with Mr. S. B. Smith, made proposal October 31, 1861, to the Assistant Secretary of War, using the name of G. W. Ramsdell, in the words above stated, "to fill the order of the department to C. K. Garrison;" that this proposal was referred by Mr. Scott to General Ripley at the date named with the indorsement, "buy the arms if they can be furnished at $6 less than former contract;" and that Mr. Duffy at the time took the letter to the Ordnance office, and showed to General Ripley a sample gun known as the Garibaldi arm; that, although some conversation took place at this time as to the value of the sample, no definite action was taken, and no order given; that subsequently, (November 16,) during the absence of General Ripley from the city, Colonel Maynadier was directed by Mr. Thomas A. Scott, Assistant Secretary of War, "to give letter of authority to George Ramsdell to furnish 10,000 guns in accordance with his proposition. The Secretary desires this to be done to-day," &c.

Colonel Maynadier accordingly wrote, narrating the *two* orders received from the Assistant Secretary of War, and without further details or particulars as to the kind of arms to be required, stated that "in compliance with these instructions, I hereby authorize you to furnish the 10,000 arms in accordance with your proposition, as contained in your letter to the Secretary of War, dated October 31, 1861." This letter was addressed, by request of Mr. Duffy, to G. W. Ramsdell. A postscript to it states "the price named in the order to C. K. Garrison for the 10,000 arms was $27 each."

No seal or stamp was placed upon the sample at the time, and no further action appears to have been taken until the 17th January, when a letter of instructions to the ordnance officer in New York (enclosing copies of the above-named proposal by G. W. Ramsdell and of Colonel Maynadier's letter of November 16) was, together with the sample gun, (sealed that day with the seal of the Ordnance office,) delivered to Mr. S. B. Smith, authorized by power of attorney to act as G. W. Ramsdell's agent, to be taken to New York.

Mr. Smith presented his letter and the sample, and informed Major Hagner, the officer in New York, that he had a number of arms like the sample ready for his inspection. As the words of the proposition descriptive of the sample gun required that it should be an arm " equal in all respects" to the one proposed by Mr. Garrison, which was well known to the ordnance officer, while the sample proposed was manifestly a much inferior arm, and of the kind recently purchased and then offered in open market at prices from 50 per cent. to 66 per cent. less than stated in the order to Mr. Ramsdell, Major Hagner declined to receive guns of that kind, under this order, without more specific instruction.

The commission, after a careful examination and consideration of the case, find that the 10,000 arms called for by the order are actually in the country; that Mr. S. B. Smith, who had undertaken the execution of the order under a power of attorney from Mr. Ramsdell, had some reason to consider that the sample gun taken to the Ordnance office by Mr. Duffy would be used as the standard of inspection, and thus was induced to make a contract with Boker & Co. for their importation.

But the commission being fully convinced that these guns are of inferior quality and wholly undesirable in kind, and that the price named is exorbitant, and that the order was not given in compliance with law and regulations, called upon Mr. Smith to make a proposition based upon the allowance of a smaller profit to himself, upon condition that the arms of serviceable quality in the lot offered, not exceeding ten thousand, be accepted by the government.

A proposition has been therefore submitted by Mr. Smith, in his own right, and as the attorney in fact for Mr. Ramsdell; and, in accordance therewith, the commission have agreed that eleven dollars ($11) shall be paid for each arm which, upon inspection, shall be found of as serviceable quality as the best of the class of arms like sample, sound and in good condition, provided that no additional expense whatever shall be incurred by the United States, and also that no rejection shall be made for any difference that may be found in the mountings of the arm offered, if strong and substantial.

We are, sir, very respectfully, your obedient servants,

J. HOLT,
ROBERT DALE OWEN,
Commissioners, &c.
P. V. HAGNER,
Major of Ordnance, Assistant to Commissioners.

Brig. General J. W. RIPLEY,
Chief of Ordnance.

CASE No. 7.

MANHATTAN ARMS COMPANY.

GREENCASTLE, *Indiana, December* 18, 1861.

DEAR SIR: Enclosed I send you a letter from his excellency the governor of Indiana, in relation to a certain box of pistols. In addition to the facts therein stated, I desire to add the following: On the 23d of September I filed in the office of the clerk of the United States district court a libel of information against said box of pistols and other goods which had, prior to that time, been reported to me by the surveyor of the port of New Albany as having been seized at that port by him as contraband of war; and a warrant of arrest issued immediately thereon, and was placed in the hands of the marshal for execution. On the 28th of September this box was turned over to the governor, as appears from the date of his receipt, and this was before the United States marshal had executed the process in his hands; and hence this box was never in the hands of the marshal.

Facts have come to my knowledge which satisfy me beyond all doubt that this box of pistols was never intended for rebel use, the owners being loyal; and this box was a sample which this agent was using in effecting sales to Union men. I therefore unhesitatingly state that the amount realized by the governor ought, in justice to the claimant and owner, to be paid, as the pistols received in exchange are now in the service of the United States.

Yours truly,

JOHN HANNA,
United States District Attorney.

Hon. S. P. CHASE, *Secretary of the Treasury.*

STATE OF INDIANA,
Executive Department, Indianapolis, December 7, 1861.

SIR: In reply to your inquiry as to the disposition made of the box of pistols marked "S. H. Harrington," and turned over to the State of Indiana by the surveyor of the port of New Albany, I beg leave to submit the following statement of facts:

Some time in September last I was informed that a large quantity of pistols had been seized as "counter-band" by the surveyor of the port at New Albany. I sent the following message to Hon. S. P. Chase, Secretary of the Treasury:

"INDIANAPOLIS, *September* 23, 1861.

"Please direct, by telegraph, the surveyor of the port at New Albany to turn over the revolvers in his hands to me. I am in great need of them. It is an absolute necessity. Answer.

"O. P. MORTON, *Governor of Indiana.*

"Hon. S. P. CHASE, *Secretary of the Treasury.*"

To which despatch I received the following reply:

"WASHINGTON, *September* 23, 1861.

"The surveyor of the port at New Albany is hereby authorized to turn over to Governor Morton, taking his receipt, all revolvers in his hands not absolutely needed for effective discharge of office duties.

"S. P. CHASE, *Secretary of the Treasury.*

"Governor O. P. MORTON, *Indianapolis, Indiana.*"

In accordance with the above despatch, the surveyor of the port turned over to me a large lot of pistols, ammunition, &c., for which he now holds my receipt. Among the lot was one box, marked "S. H. Harrington, New Albany," containing 33 Manhattan pistols and 4,600 pistol cartridges, in boxes. Shortly after they were received I exchanged them for navy revolvers, now in the service of the United States.

Respectfully,

O. P. MORTON, *Governor of Indiana..*

By W. R. HOLLONAY,
Governor's Secretary.

Hon. JOHN HANNA,
United States District Attorney for Indiana.

I hereby certify that in pursuance to an order of the Secretary of the Treasury, in regard to a box of pistols and cartridges in the reputed care of a Mr. Harrington, as agent for the Manhattan Fire-arms Company, seized by me as surveyor of New Albany, some time last August, I retained two of the pistols and 400 of the cartridges, and delivered all the rest over to the order of the governor of Indiana. I do not recollect the number of pistols or cartridges so delivered over to the governor. Those in my hands are subject at all times to the order of the United States government.

JACOB ANTHONY,
Surveyor of the Port, New Albany.

STATE OF NEW YORK, *City of New York, County of New York:*

Be it remembered that on this ninth day of January, in the year 1862, personally came before the undersigned, a notary public of and for the State and county above written, Albert Beach, who, being duly sworn according to law, says that he is the secretary of the Manhattan Fire-arms Manufacturing Company, a corporation of said State of New York, engaged in the manufacture and sale of fire-arms; that he superintended the packing and forwarding of a box of pistols and pistol cartridges to the agent of said company, Stephen H. Harrington, to New Albany, in the State of Indiana, on the 9th day of August, 1861; that said box contained 26 blued 7-shot cylinder pistols, at wholesale of the value and price, at that time, of $10 80 each, and 10 plated 7-shot cylinder pistols, at the wholesale price of $11 80 each, and 5,000 cartridges, number one, at wholesale of the value and price of $5 per thousand; and in the aggregate of the value, at wholesale prices, of $423 80; but that the wholesale prices previous to the war excitement were usually, for blued 7-shot cylinder pistols, $9 60 each; also for plated 7-shot cylinder pistols, were $10 40 each, (and for cartridges, $5 per thousand.) So that the aggregate value, at prices current previous to the war excitement. would have been $378 60. Which pistols and cartridges were sent in one box by express to S. H. Harrington, the agent of the company, to New Albany, Indiana, on the 9th day of August, 1861.

ALBERT BEACH.

Subscribed and sworn to before me the day and year above written.

[L. S.]
THOMAS S. RIVETT,
Notary Public, City and County of New York.

DECEMBER 5, A. D. 1861.

UNITED STATES CIRCUIT COURT, *District of Indiana, to wit:*

THE UNITED STATES
vs. } Libel of information.
ONE BOX OF PISTOLS, &c.

Comes now John Hanna, esq., prosecuting the pleas of the United States, and dismisses her libel as to one box of pistols; and thereupon it is ordered that the same be returned to the possession of the Manhattan Fire-arms Manufacturing Company.

UNITED STATES OF AMERICA, *District of Indiana, ss:*

I, John H. Rea, clerk of the district court of the United States for the district of Indiana, do hereby certify the above and foregoing to be a true and correct copy of an order of court made in the above entitled cause on the 5th day of December, A. D. 1861, as now appears of record in my office.

In testimony whereof, I have hereunto set my hand and affixed the [L. S.] seal of said court, at Indianapolis, this 16th day of December, A. D. 1861.

JOHN H. REA, *Clerk.*

INDIANAPOLIS, *Indiana, February* 28, 1862.

SIR: I have the honor to enclose the claim and voucher of the Manhattan Fire-arms Manufacturing Company against the United States for 36 pistols and 5,000 cartridges, amounting to $423 80.

In August, 1861, the box containing this property was seized by the surveyor of the port at New Albany, in this State. Upon the seizure a libel was filed by the district attorney in the United States district court, but before trial 33 of the pistols and 4,600 of the cartridges were delivered to the governor of the State, pursuant to the order of the Secretary of the Treasury of September 23, 1861, and the residue of the property retained by the surveyor, as allowed by said order, except one pistol, which neither the surveyor nor the governor account for. When the cause came up in the district court the judgment of that court was for the claimant, and an order made for the return of the property, but that order could not be executed by the marshal, for the reason that the property had been converted to the public service. This claim now is for the *wholesale* value of the property at the date of the seizure, and its conversion to the public use. It is not supposed that there can arise any question in regard to the payment by the government. The prices charged are below what would have been realized had there been no seizure. In respect to the one pistol, which neither the surveyor nor the governor account for, there can be no question as to the right of the claimant, as the box when seized contained the whole number, and, by some mistake on the part of the government officer, it has become confused with other property in executing the Secretary's order.

Mr. Smith, the president of the company, called upon you in person, and you were kind enough to say that upon presentation of the claim it would receive early attention. May I ask that the claim be allowed, and the warrant sent to my care? The vouchers are as full as the nature of the case allows.

Very respectfully,

THOS. A. HENDRICKS,
Attorney for Claimant.

The ASSISTANT SECRETARY *of the Treasury.*

[Indorsement.]

Referred to ordnance department.

E. M. STANTON.

ORDNANCE OFFICE, *March* 19, 1862.

Respectfully recommended that this claim be referred to the commission ordered March 13, 1862.

JAMES W. RIPLEY,
Brigadier General.

MARCH 19, 1862.

Referred as recommended. By order of the Secretary of War.

P. H. WATSON,
Assistant Secretary of War.

———

COMMISSION ON ORDNANCE AND ORDNANCE STORES,
Washington, March 22, 1862.

SIR: The commission have the honor to report as follows:

CASE No. 7.—MANHATTAN FIRE-ARMS COMPANY, New York.

Referred by special order of War Department. Claim for value of 36 pistols and 5,000 cartridges. Amount, $423 80.

The commission find that 33 pistols were received by the governor of Indiana, upon order of the Secretary of the Treasury, and applied by him to the service of the United States, also 4,600 pistol cartridges. Two pistols and 400 cartridges were received under the same authority by the surveyor of the port of New Albany, who acknowledges that he is still responsible for them to the United States. One pistol lost or mislaid without fault of the claimants, after passing out of their control and into the possession of government officers. They further find that the prices charged are reasonable, and they therefore recommend that this account be paid to the full amount of the claim, $423 80.

We are, sir, very respectfully, your obedient servants,

J. HOLT,
ROBERT DALE OWEN,
Commissioners.
P. V. HAGNER,
Major of Ordnance, Assistant to Commission.

Hon. EDWIN M. STANTON,
Secretary of War.

By direction of the Secretary of War the reports in future are to be addressed to the chief of ordnance for execution, without reference to the War Department.

P. V. HAGNER,
Major of Ordnance.

CASE No. 8.

BEN. MILLS.

COMMISSION ON ORDNANCE AND ORDNANCE STORES,
Washington, March 22, 1862.

GENERAL : The commission have the honor to report as follows :

CASE No. 8.—BEN. MILLS, Louisville, Kentucky.

Referred by special order of the War Department.
Claims pay for work done in inspecting and repairing arms in the hands of the 19th regiment of Kentucky volunteers. Amount of claim, $151 70.

The commission find that the colonel of the regiment (19th Kentucky volunteers) ordered the work to be done while commanding officer in Camp Harrod ; that it was absolutely necessary for the efficiency of his regiment to have the work done at the time ; that it was the only means at hand, and that the account is correct and just.

The commission, therefore, approve the account for the full amount, viz : $151 70.

We are, sir, very respectfully, your obedient servants,

J. HOLT,
ROBERT DALE OWEN,
Commissioners.

P. V. HAGNER,
Major of Ordnance, Assistant to Commission.

General J. W. RIPLEY,
Chief of Ordnance.

CAMP WOOD, KENTUCKY,
February 12, 1862.

GENTLEMEN: Enclosed I return your bill for sighting my guns, approved. Your explanation in regard to the amount of the bill is quite satisfactory, and I presume you will have no difficulty in collecting it. I will say that I had the work done by order of General Sherman, then commanding department of Cumberland.

I remain, very respectfully, your obedient servant,

CHAS. S. COTTER.

Messrs. AINSLEE & COCHRAN, *Louisville, Ky.*

LOUISVILLE, *February* 10, 1862.

DEAR SIR : Enclosed we hand you for your approval bill and duplicate for the work done by your orders on four guns. The bill looks high, $50, but it is not as much as it would come to, at our regular rates, for the time we were engaged on it, which, as you will recollect, was this: The guns were brought to us about half-past 3 o'clock Saturday afternoon, and worked on from that time all of Saturday night and Sunday until 2 o'clock p. m., for which time we had to pay double wages. The number of mechanics and assistants for handling was eight, and the cash actually paid by us for wages was $30. We had to make saddles for placing them on our lathes, and auger drills and taps to suit the screw. So what is left pays but little for the fuel consumed and wear and tear of machinery. We had expected Captain Gilbert to certify to it, as we had a bill under his orders for work done on other guns, which he approved yesterday; but he informs us that they were done under your orders.

We would be pleased to have you approve these as soon as practicable, and return to us by express, as the writer wishes to start to Washington this week with other bills.

Please state, in approving, the reason for having it done.

> Yours, truly,
>   AINSLEE & COCHRAN.

Captain COTTER,
      U. S. Army, Mumfordsville, Ky.

CASE No. 9.

AINSLEE & COCHRAN.

COMMISSION ON ORDNANCE AND ORDNANCE CLAIMS,
              Washington, March 22, 1862.

GENERAL: The commission have the honor to report as follows:

    CASE No. 9.—AINSLEE & COCHRAN, Louisville, Kentucky.

Referred by special order of the War Department   Three accounts for projectiles and sighting cannon. Total amount of claims, $890 52.

The commission find the accounts for sighting gun and *one* for projectiles are duly approved by the general commanding the department, and the articles are acknowledged to have been received by the company officers. Although the last account is not dated, it is made explicit beyond error by the above signatures. The other account for projectiles is only supported by the informal receipt of the lieutenant colonel of the regiment, but is for articles only of use to the government.

The prices charged do not appear unreasonable under the circumstances stated. The claim is therefore approved for the total amount—$890 52.

We are, sir, very respectfully, your obedient servants,
>   J. HOLT,
>   ROBERT DALE OWEN,
>   *Commissioners.*
>   P. V. HAGNER,
>   *Major of Ordnance, Assistant to Commission.*

General J. W. RIPLEY,
      Chief of Ordnance.

CASE No. 10.

HEDDEN & HOEY.

ORDNANCE OFFICE,
      Washington, November 23, 1861.

GENTLEMEN: By direction of the Secretary of War, I offer you an order for fifty thousand (50,000) muskets of Prussian manufacture, corresponding and equal to the sample exhibited to the War Department, with appendages, on the following terms and conditions, viz: These arms are to have the cones altered by you in a good and substantial manner, so as to receive the army caps, and are to be inspected by Major P. V. Hagner, or such other officer as the department may designate for the purpose, and none are to be received or paid for but such as are approved by the United States inspector. Five thousand of the arms and appendages are to be delivered in New York within ten days from this date, and the residue on or before the 15th of January, 1862. In case of any failure to make deliveries to the extent and within the times above specified, the government is to be under no obligation to take any of the arms then deliverable and remaining undelivered at the time of such failure, but may revoke and annul this order as regards these arms and appendages. Payments will be made for each delivery in such funds as the Treasury Department may provide, on certificates of inspection and receipt of the United States inspector, at the rate of seven dollars ($7) for each arm, including appendages, in bond.

Please signify in writing your acceptance or non-acceptance of this order, on the terms and conditions herein stated.

Respectfully, &c.,

JAS. W. RIPLEY,
Brigadier General.

Messrs. JOSIAH HEDDEN and JOHN HOEY,
Washington, D. C.

H. & H.'s proposal dated November 15.
Their acceptance of the order November 26.

OFFICE OF THE ADAMS'S EXPRESS COMPANY,
No. 59 Broadway, New York, January 3, 1862.

SIR: I am advised by my friends in Europe that the steamer of December 24 has on board 16,000 Prussians, to be delivered on the contract of Messrs. Hedden & Hoey. My correspondent found it impossible to make the shipment complete of 40,000, as the room was pre-engaged by our minister to Belgium (Mr. Sandford) for government arms. The balance of our lot will leave Europe by steamer of the 11th January, and reach here about the 28th or 1st of next month, so that all the guns will be in the inspector's hands very shortly after the time given in contract.

Considering all things, I think we have done well, and kept our word with the government. I delivered them, December 6, 6,620, to-day 5,000, and next week will place in the inspector's hands 16,000 more, and before he is through inspection I hope to complete the contract in full.

You have no idea of what my friend in Europe has had to put up with. Freights have advanced 100 per cent., insurance has doubled, and no ship will take arms unless freight is engaged months ahead; besides that, American credit does not stand well at present. I give you all these facts to let you see that, considering the time we have had the work, (since November 26,) we have done well. I think there are not many of the outstanding contracts which have been turned in as quickly as ours. I suppose you will lay all these facts before the Secretary of War, or Major General Ripley, and see that the usual grace is extended to us on the delivery.

Please advise me by return mail, and oblige.

Yours, very respectfully,

JOHN HOEY.

Hon. GEO. ASHMAN.

UNITED STATES MILITARY TELEGRAPH.

Received from New York, February 1, 1862.

Hedden & Hoey have twenty thousand (20,000) Prussian muskets in port to be delivered under order from your office, dated November twenty-third, for fifty thousand. I am requested to relieve them from bond, as time has expired. This office awaits further instructions in this case. Order limited to fifteenth January. Ponder has one hundred and eighty rifles in port. Time also expired.

Please reply.

S. CRISPIN.

General J. W. RIPLEY.

[Indorsement.]

ORDNANCE OFFICE, *February 3, 1862.*

Respectfully submitted to the Secretary of War.

Messrs. Hedden & Hoey's order, dated 23d November, 1861, is for the delivery in New York, by the 15th January, 1862, of 50,000 Prussian muskets, at $7 each. They delivered between the 6th December, 1861, and the 11th January, 1862, 28,352 of those muskets, and have now 20,000 more in port ready for delivery.

Shall they be released from bond and inspected by the United States officer?

JAMES W. RIPLEY,
Brigadier General.

FEBRUARY 4.

The failure to deliver according to the terms of the contract releases the government from the obligation to receive them, but if the arms are required by the necessities of the government, and the contract is fair and reasonable in its terms, the Secretary will be disposed not to stand upon the breach of the condition; he therefore requests the chief of ordnance to report: 1st. Whether the arms yet to be delivered under the within mentioned contract are requisite to the government. 2d. Whether the stipulated price and the terms of the contract are fair and reasonable, and whether it is for the interest of the government to have it completed.

An early report is required.

EDWIN M. STANTON,
Secretary of War.

ORDNANCE OFFICE, *February 20, 1862.*

Respectfully returned with reports from Major Hagner and Captain Crispin, in regard to Messrs. Hedden & Hoey's arms, which are respectfully submitted for your further information in the case. After considering all the evidence I can obtain, I have to report: In answer to the first question, that, in my opinion, the arms yet to be delivered by Messrs. Hedden & Hoey will answer to arm troops effectively, and may and will be required for that purpose, in the event of an insufficient supply of arms of better pattern and higher finish, which I regard as quite probable from the tardiness of contractors in making deliveries. In answer to the second question, the price depends on the quality and finish of the arm. It is represented to be strong, though not manufactured with much regard to smoothness and neatness of finish. Captain Crispin states that the last purchase of Prussian smooth-bore muskets was at $5 50 each, from Messrs. Boker & Co.; and Major Hagner reports that the price of such arms as Messrs. Hedden & Hoye's should not exceed $6 each, if no appendages are furnished. The price fixed by the order is $7 each, *including* appendages, and also the alteration of the cones, at the cost of the contractors, so as to make them receive the army caps. Under all these circumstances, I think the price and terms of the contract fair and reasonable, and that it will be to the interest of the government to have it completed.

JAMES W. RIPLEY,
Brigadier General.

WASHINGTON, *February* 4, 1862.

GENERAL: The Prussian smooth-bore arms in store now are more than sufficient to meet all orders for issue.

They do not prove to be of good service in the hands of troops. The price allowed under this contract is too high, I think, according to the market price of such arms. It should not exceed $6, if no implements are furnished *including* spare cones and screw-drivers.

The deliveries made are said to have been of better quality than the sample gun sent us—that is, not so much worn by service; but the general quality of all these arms is about the same, some having been rather less used than others.

As far as I can judge, I cannot think that the Secretary's questions can be answered affirmatively.

Very respectfully, your obedient servant,

P. V. HAGNER,
Major of Ordnance.

Gen. J. W. RIPLEY, *Chief of Ordnance, Woshington.*

ORDNANCE OFFICE,
No. 55 White street, New York, February 7, 1862.

GENERAL: Your communication of the 5th instant, requesting reports as to the character and quality, serviceability and value, compared with price, of the "Prussian musket" delivered by Messrs. Hedden & Hoey, under their order from the department of November 23, 1861, is received. I have to reply as follows:

The arm is the Prussian smooth-bore musket, of the model previous to 1839, altered from flint lock to percussion, calibre .70, and weight 11 pounds. The plan of alteration from flint to percussion, of both lock and barrel, has, I believe, secured as much strength and durability as can be obtained in an altered arm. The lock appears to be a strong and serviceable one; the barrel is about 41 inches in length, and compares favorably in manufacture with the generality of smooth-bore ones. The stock and mountings appear strong. The arm, however, has not been manufactured with much regard to smoothness and neatness of finish. They are all either old or have been in service.

From the above facts it would seem that the arm, if placed in the hands of troops, would probably withstand the rough usage and handling incident to service; but there are other considerations so important as to render extremely doubtful, in my mind, the propriety of using it in the field, except the emergency of the service require it. The calibre is so large as to render the recoil, even with an allowable diminution in weight of powder and ball, great; which, added to the weight of the gun, and the fact that it is a smooth-bore and an abandoned pattern, makes it objectionable as a weapon, especially to the troops who are to carry and use it.

That it may, in the absence of more approved models, be serviceable to the government, is of course, from its make, apparent; but I conceive, in view of the abovementioned defects, that its purchase and use should be determined by necessity alone.

The last purchase of these arms was at $5 50 apiece, of the Messrs. H. Boker & Co. I would regard the price paid Messrs. Boker & Co. a reasonable one, and probably a fair equivalent for this quality of arm.

Permit me to suggest, in connexion with the above, for the consideration of the department, the propriety of using (in the event of these Prussian arms being extensively issued) the "Nessler" ball as a projectile for them. Its weight is about the same as the round ball, and it is stated on reliable European authorities that by its use the smooth-bore musket has an accurate and effective range of 300 or 400 yards, or at least double that obtained by using the spherical projectile.

I do not deem it improper to state that the majority of arms heretofore delivered by Messrs. Hedden & Hoey have been pronounced by the inspector, Mr. Marston, superior to the sample, and that the rejections were but few.

Very respectfully, your obedient servant,

S. CRISPIN, *Captain of Ordnance.*

Gen. J. W. RIPLEY, *Chief of Ordnance, Washington, D. C.*

WASHINGTON, *March* 13, 1862.

DEAR SIR: In response to your inquiry as to how the Prussian muskets procured of you, through the War department, and sent to Kentucky, were liked by our troops, I have to say that our men liked them as well as any guns sent us, except the Springfield musket, and better than any foreign arm received, although many others were more costly. In addition to the testimony of the troops, Lieutenant Eason, chief of ordnance, spoke very favorably and with gratification of the recent receipt of 16,000 of these guns.

Last summer I had some of them rifled. I am satisfied that it was a useless expense, since the musket is now preferred to the rifle.

I can say of you that at a time when we were sorely pressed for arms, and our State invaded, you rendered us valuable service, and through your instrumentality we procured arms at fair prices and of good quality, for which I desire to thank you.

Your friend, &c.,

J. F. SPEED, of Kentucky.

JOHN HOEY, Esq. ·

WAR DEPARTMENT,
Washington City, D. C., March 20, 1862.

GENTLEMEN: Herewith I submit the claim and contract of Messrs. Hedden & Hoey for arms to be delivered to the United States. While pending and under investigation in this department, it was withdrawn previous to the organization of your commission, and submitted to the President, and appears to have been adjudicated by him, so far as relates the waiver of the time limited for performance, as will be seen by his letter of yesterday's date to the Secretary of War. Designing that in the action of the department all claims and contracts for arms, &c., shall stand on the same ground, this contract is referred to you, with the President's order, to be acted upon according to your judgment and the facts that shall appear in respect to the conformity of the arms, with the terms of the contract.

Very respectfully, your obedient servant,

EDWIN M. STANTON,
Secretary of War.

Hon. JOSEPH HOLT and ROBERT DALE OWEN,
Special Commissioners.

EXECUTIVE MANSION,
Washington, March 19, 1862.

MY DEAR SIR: Messrs. Hedden & Hoey having had a contract with the United States government, closed on the 26th day of November last, to deliver fifty thousand arms to the government by the 15th day of January then next, upon specified terms and conditions, and having actually delivered above twenty-eight thousand within the time. which were accepted and paid for, and having been ready and offered to deliver the remainder, not within, but about ten days after, the contract time, which were refused solely on the question of time, and they having acted in good faith, and the arms being still needed by the government, I think fit to order that the question of time be waived by the government, and that the arms be accepted, if again tendered in conformity to the contract in all other respects.

Yours truly,

A. LINCOLN.

Hon. SECRETARY OF WAR.

COMMISSION ON ORDNANCE AND ORDNANCE STORES,
Washington, March 24, 1862.

GENERAL: The commission have the honor to report as follows:

CASE NO. 10.—HEDDEN & HOEY, New York.

Referred by special order of the War Department.   Contract for 50,000 Prussian muskets, smooth bore, deliverable on or before January 15, 1862.

The commission find that 28,000 only out of 50,000 guns were delivered up to the time specified, leaving 22,000 still to be delivered; that by the terms of the contract, in case of failure to make deliveries to the extent and within the times specified, the government was to be under no obligation to take the arms; that consequently no legal obligation rested on the government to take the 22,000 arms not delivered up to January 15, 1862.

But the commission find, further, that the President of the United States, in a communication to the Secretary of War, dated March 19, 1862, after stating that the contractors, acting in good faith, were ready and offered to deliver the said 22,000 guns within about ten days after the contract term, and that the arms are still needed by the government, orders that the question of time be waived by the government, and that the whole 50,000 arms be accepted.

Therefore, regarding the questions at issue as settled by the above communication of the President, the commission decide that the remaining portion of the 50,000 arms, namely, 22,000, be received in accordance with the terms of the contract and with the President's order in the premises.

We are, sir, very respectfully,

J. HOLT,
ROBERT DALE OWEN,
Commissioners, &c.

Brigadier General RIPLEY,
Chief of Ordnance.

CASE No. 11.

LOUIS MILLER.

ORDNANCE OFFICE,
Washington, February 1, 1862.

These accounts of Louis Miller and John Cross, for horse equipments, are respectfully submitted to the Secretary of War.

The circumstances of the purchases are stated, and payments recommended by General Buell. There is evidence of the delivery of the equipments for the United States service, and the prices are reasonable.

Under the 3d section of the act of February 8, 1815, your approval of the purchases is necessary, which, under the circumstances, I recommend.

JAMES W. RIPLEY,
Brigadier General.

COMMISSION ON ORDNANCE AND ORDNANCE STORES,
Washington, March 24, 1862.

GENERAL: The commission have the honor to report as follows:

CASE No. 11.—LOUIS MILLER, Louisville, Kentucky.

Referred by special order of the War Department.   Bill for 300 sets of horse equipments, at $24 25 each, amounting to $7, 275.

The commission find that the above equipments were furnished by the claimant at the price mentioned, which was reasonable, and that the articles have been received into the United States service. The transaction being in all respects fair, and the payment of the bill having been recommended by General Buell, and also by the chief of ordnance, the commission decide that payment of the full amount shall be made accordingly.

We are, sir, very respectfully, your obedient servants,

J. HOLT,
ROBERT DALE OWEN,
Commissioners, &c.
P. V. HAGNER,
Major of Ordnance, Assistant to Commission.

Brigadier General J. W. RIPLEY,
Chief of Ordnance.

CASE No. 12.

JOHN CROSS.

COMMISSION ON ORDNANCE AND ORDNANCE STORES,
Washington, March 24, 1862.

GENERAL: The commission have the honor to report as follows:

CASE No. 12.—JOHN CROSS, Louisville, Kentucky.

Referred by special order of the War Department   Bill for 350 complete sets of saddles and bridles, halters, cruppers, breast-straps, saddle-bags, surcingles, curry-combs, horse-brushes, and knapsack cloths, at $24 25 each, amounting to $8, 802 50.

The commission find that the above equipments were furnished by the claimant at the price mentioned, which was reasonable, and that the articles have been received into the United States service. The transaction being in all respects fair, and the payment of the bill having been recommended by General Buell, and also by the chief of ordnance, the commission decide that payment of the full amount claimed shall be made accordingly.

We are, sir, very respectfully, your obedient servants,

J. HOLT,
ROBERT DALE OWEN,
Commissioners, &c.
P. V. HAGNER,
Major of Ordnance, Assistant to Commission.

Brigadier General J. W. RIPLEY,
Chief of Ordnance.

CASE No. 13.

COLT'S ARMS COMPANY.

Samuel Colt, Hartford, Connecticut.—25,000 *rifled muskets, model* 1855 *July* 5, 1861.

This agreement, made this fifth day of July, eighteen hundred and sixty-one, between Brevet Brigadier General James W. Ripley, of the United States army, acting by authority of the Secretary of War, and the Colt's Patent Fire-arms Manufacturing Company, by their president, Samuel Colt, witnesseth:

1. The said company binds itself and its assigns to deliver, to such officers of the United States as may be authorized to receive them, twenty-five thousand (25,000) muskets of the exact pattern of the muskets made at the United States armory in Springfield, according to sample to be furnished to the contracting party; all and each of the said twenty-five thousand muskets to interchange in their similar parts with each other, and with the Springfield muskets, and to be subject, before receipt or payment therefor by the United States, to the same kind and degree of inspection, by the United States inspectors appointed for the purpose, as the muskets made at the Springfield armory are subjected to; and any of the aforesaid muskets to be delivered by the said company under this agreement which do not in all respects and particulars of pattern, material, workmanship, and finish, come up to the standard of excellence as established at the United States armory, which is to be determined and decided by the United States inspectors, shall be rejected.

2. The said company does further bind itself and its assigns to manufacture and have ready for inspection and delivery to the United States the aforesaid twenty-five thousand muskets not later than the following periods, namely: one thousand muskets not later than six months from the date of this agreement, and not less than one thousand muskets per month for the next three months, and not less than two thousand muskets for each and every month thereafter until the whole twenty-five thousand muskets shall have been delivered; with the distinct understanding that each or all of these deliveries must be made in as much shorter time as possible; and that on any failure to make deliveries to the extent and within the times above specified, all the obligations of the United States to receive or pay for any muskets then deliverable under this agreement shall be cancelled and become null and void.

3. The said company does further bind itself and its assigns to deliver, with the aforesaid twenty-five thousand muskets, the following appendages, of the regular pattern, subject to the same inspection as the muskets, namely: one

wiper, one screw-driver, one spare cone, and one tompion, to each musket; and one ball-screw, one spring vice, and one tumbler and wire punch to every ten muskets; and also to put up in good boxes, to be provided by the company, of the regular patterns and quality, the aforesaid muskets, twenty in each box, with their due proportion of appendages.

4. It is expressly understood and agreed between the parties to this agreement before named, that payments shall be made to the said company, or its order, on the receipt at the Ordnance office, in Washington, District of Columbia, of certificates of inspection and evidences of delivery, of not less than one thousand muskets, with appendages, at the following rates, namely: twenty dollars for each musket and set of appendages, inclusive, and such price in addition for each packing box as may be certified by the inspector to be just and fair. It is further understood and agreed that no member of Congress shall be admitted to any share or part of this agreement, or to any benefit to arise therefrom.

In witness whereof the parties to this agreement have hereunto set their hands and affixed their seals—the said James W. Ripley, at the city of Washington, the fifth day of July, eighteen hundred and sixty-one, and the said Samuel Colt, at the city of Hartford, Connecticut, the eighth day of the same month and year.

JAMES W. RIPLEY,
Brevet Brigadier General.
SAMUEL COLT,
President.

Witness to signature of General Ripley:
WILLIAM MAYNADIER, *Major of Ordnance.*
Witness to signature of Samuel Colt:
HUGH HORBISON.

WAR DEPARTMENT, *July* 10, 1861.

Approved.

S. CAMERON.

SIR: On the 5th day of July, 1861, the "Colt's Patent Fire-arms Manufacturing Company," of Hartford, Connecticut, entered into a contract with the United States War Department for the manufacture and delivery of *rifled muskets*, to the number of twenty-five thousand, (25,000,) upon the terms and conditions set forth in said *contract*, (reference to which may be had in the files of the department,) and in good faith, and in expectation of fulfilling all its requirements, the company immediately made preparations for the erection of suitable additional buildings, and the manufacture and purchase of adequate machinery, and the purchase abroad of barrels, locks, and such other parts as might be necessary.

The buildings which have been erected for this purpose are, "the main building," 500 feet by 60 feet; "the second building," 500 feet by 40 feet, and the third building 200 feet by 50 feet; all of which are of brick and constructed in the most substantial manner, two of them being each three stories high, and all connected with each other and with the buildings of the old establishment.

The cost of the new buildings up to the *present time* is not less than $100,000, and into two of them machinery has been placed, which is now at work. The cost of the steam-engine and boilers, machinery, and tools, has not been less than $300,000, and the cost of stock and work in progress about $40,000.

But unexpected difficulties have impeded and delayed the progress of the work, so that it has been wholly impossible to make any delivery of muskets up to the present time, according to the terms of the contract.

1st. Soon after the date of the contract, orders were received from the War Department to turn the entire force of our establishment to the production of "holster pistols," of which the government stood in *great immediate* need. These orders were repeated *constant* and *urgent*, and we felt it our imperative duty to conform to the wishes of the government in this respect. This, necessarily, not only diverted our attention to some extent, from the work essential to a prompt fulfilment of the terms of the contract, but made it impossible for us to manufacture in our own establishment the machinery necessary for the new work; we were therefore compelled to contract for it outside, with other parties.

2d. These contracts with other parties have *not* been by them promptly fulfilled, whereby we are embarrassed in our contract with the government.

3d. Since the execution and date of the contract there has been a very large increase in the demand for mechanical labor, which has seriously impeded all similar operations. This has been caused to a great extent by the competition created by the government, in giving out an immense amount of prospective contracts for arms, which though most of them cannot possibly be performed, have stimulated *workmen* into an uneasy and restless demand for *increased wages*.

4th. Colonel Colt, who had always, during his lifetime, the sole active management of the establishment, was so seriously ill during much of the autumn and prior to his death, on the 10th day of January, 1862, as greatly to interfere with the speed of the operations which we had in progress.

It is proper in this connexion to state the condition and capacity of our works to execute the work contemplated in the contract of *July* 5, 1861:

1st. Our capital is *one million of dollars cash* paid in. This has been increased by reserving and appropriating dividends to the erection of the new buildings and the machinery and tools adapted to them.

2d. We have in our employ *fifteen hundred* hands, and work day and night.

3d. We have *now received* most of the machinery needed for the production of at least *one thousand muskets per week*, and the remainder will be delivered in a few days. Our small tools are completed, and we shall be ready to turn out arms as soon as the "stocking machinery" is delivered to us. (This was due two months ago, and has been partly delivered.)

4th. We are in every respect, in power, capacity, and preparation, far in advance of every other private establishment in the country, and have facilities which no other has.

This is all which it seems necessary to say in relation to the contract of July 5, 1861, and what has been done under it. It only remains for the Secretary of War to give his assent to such modification of that contract, as to the time of the early delivery of arms, as the circumstances may justify.

During Colonel Colt's late *illness* the company received from the ordnance department a proposition dated December 26, 1861, for an additional contract for the manufacture of twenty-five thousand (25,000) more arms, upon the terms and conditions set forth in the proposition; the only reply which could be made at that time was, that the condition of Colonel Colt's health rendered it impossible for him then to give his attention to a matter of such importance.

Colonel Colt having died January 10, 1862, the corporation which has been established under a special charter from the State of Connecticut will continue its business under the same organization, and with the same capital as formerly existed, the undersigned having been chosen president in the place of Colonel Colt, deceased.

We are now ready, therefore, to enter into arrangements with the government for the execution of an *additional* contract upon such terms and conditions as can be mutually agreed upon, and we feel entire confidence in our ability to serve the government usefully and to its perfect satisfaction.

Very respectfully, &c.,

E. K. ROOT,
President Colt's Patent Fire-arms Manufacturing Company.
Hon. E. M. STANTON, *Secretary of War.*

ORDNANCE OFFICE, *February* 26, 1862.

Respectfully returned. The Colt's Arms Company had a contract dated July 5, 1861, for 25,000 Springfield muskets, deliverable 1,000 in six months, from date of contract; 1,000 a month for the next three months, and 2,000 a month thereafter, till the whole 25,000 shall be delivered; also an order, dated December 26, 1861, for 25,000 Springfield muskets additional, deliverable 500 in each of the months of July, August, and September, 1862; 1,000 in each of the months of October and November, 1862; 1,500 in December, 1862; and 2,000 a month thereafter, till the whole 25,000 should be delivered. There are 3,000 arms now due under the first contract, and none have as yet been delivered; and the company request an extension of time so as to give them six months more for their first delivery, making it in July next, and delivering 4,000 muskets in that month and continuing monthly deliveries at 2,500 for six months, 3,000 per month thereafter. No deliveries of arms have been yet made under any one of the four contracts entered into at the same time, on the same terms. I believe that the Colt's company are as far, and probably further, advanced in their preparations than any of the other companies, and that we are more likely to get good home manufactured arms from them, and in less time than elsewhere, outside of the national armory. I therefore recommend that the extension of time be granted.

JAMES W. RIPLEY,
Brigadier General.

HARTFORD, CONN., *February* 21, 1862.

SIR: Your valued favor of 17th instant is just at hand. In reply, we beg to submit for your consideration the following proposal for changing the rate of delivery of the 25,000 United States rifled muskets contracted for July 5, 1861:

We will engage to furnish, say, 4,000 of the rifles before the 1st of August, 1862, and 2,500 per month for the next six months succeeding July, after which time we will deliver 3,000 per month for two months, which will complete the delivery of the whole 25,000 muskets. Although we name the 1st of August as the time of first delivery, yet we feel confident that we can commence before that time, but hesitate to fix a date that would not warrant the certainty of fulfilling our engagement.

We beg leave to call your attention to the fact that the modification above proposed in the time and rate of delivery of the arms does not prolong the time at which, by the original agreement, the whole number of muskets would have been delivered. Hoping the preceding proposition will prove acceptable and meet your approbation, we await your acceptance of same.

Remaining respectfully, sir, your obedient servants,

E. K. ROOT,
President Colt's P. F. A. M. Co.

Brigadier General JAMES W. RIPLEY,
Chief of Ordnance Department, Washington, D. C.

ORDNANCE OFFICE,
Washington, March 26, 1862.

SIR: I have to acknowledge your letter of this date, asking for the original of the two contracts or orders to the Colt's Fire-arms Manufacturing Company for 25,000 Springfield muskets each, and, in reply, have to state that the original of the first contract, dated 5th of July, 1861, was transmitted to the Second Comptroller on the 10th of July, 1861, in compliance with section six of the act approved 16th of July, 1798; the second one, dated 26th of December, 1861, was in the shape of a letter offering an additional order for 25,000 Springfield muskets, the original of which is presumed to be in the possession of the said Colt's Fire-arms Manufacturing Company.

Respectfully, your obedient servant,

JAS. W. RIPLEY, *Brigadier General.*

J. WISE, Esq.,
  Sec'y to Commission on Contracts, Washington City.

Before commission, March 26, 1862.

Mr. E. K. Root, president of the Colt's Arms Manufacturing Company, states upon examination:

We have engaged 54,000 skelps of Marshall iron; have on hand 19,000; also have engaged 25,000 barrels of steel, solid, to be bored, and by us; we have also 20,000 barrels made in England, rough bored and first smooth bored. They have turned breech pins fitted. These breech pins may each interchange, although we ordered them by the Springfield pattern for this order. We have also ordered bar steel for 25,000 barrels in case our iron will not answer. Have machinery enough to roll over 1,500 barrels per week, and to finish over 1,000 guns per week, (except in stocking machines, which we are now extending.) Have been much delayed on this work, thinking that the Secretary's order annulled the contracts. Knows of no stocking machine in private hands, and thinks six months at least necessary to get up a full set. Some of our order to Mr. Ames was taken by the Springfield armory, and this has delayed us. Thinks $20 per gun as low a price as the Springfield musket can be made for with any profit, and considers that an order for 50,000 requires that price.

COMMISSION ON ORDNANCE AND ORDNANCE STORES,
Washington, March 26, 1862.

GENERAL: The commission have the honor to report as follows:

CASE No. 13.—COLT'S PATENT FIRE-ARMS MANUFACTURING COMPANY, Hartford, Connecticut.

Referred by special order of War Department. Two contracts, each for 25,000 Springfield rifles, at $20. First dated July 5, 1861; second, December 26, 1861.

It appearing to the commission that the company have made ample preparations for carrying out their contract of date July 5, (being provided with a thorough outfit for the manufacture of Springfield muskets;) and it further appearing that the government is in need of the guns contracted for under both contracts, and that the price is reasonable, it is therefore directed by the commission that the question of forfeiture for failure to deliver up to this date be waived, and that the extension asked for by the company in their written communication addressed to the honorable Edwin M. Stanton, Secretary of War, and received by the Ordnance office on the 10th of February, 1862, be granted, and that the company be allowed in accordance therewith to proceed to the fulfilment of both their contracts.

We are, sir, very respectfully, your obedient servants,

J. HOLT,
ROBERT DALE OWEN
  Commissioners.

P. V. HAGNER,
  Major of Ordnance, Assistant to Commission.

Brigadier General J. W. RIPLEY,
  Chief of Ordnance.

COMMISSION ON ORDNANCE AND ORDNANCE STORES,
Washington, May 16, 1862.

GENERAL: The commission have decided that their confirmation of the contracts and subsequent orders extending the numbers given in the cases of the Colt's Arms Company for 50,000 in all, Jenks & Co. for 50,000 in all, Lamson, Goodnow & Yale for 50,000 in all, Providence Tool Company for 50,000 in all, shall be, as in other cases since decided, upon condition that each of the parties shall, within fifteen days after notice of this decision, execute bond with good and sufficient sureties, in the form and with the stipulations prescribed by law, and the regulations for the performance of the contract as thus modified, resulting from said order and acceptance; and upon his failure or refusal to execute such bond, then the said order shall be declared cancelled and of no effect.

The commission further decide that the deliveries under the contracts to be executed shall be as required in the decisions heretofore made in these cases respectively. You will observe that the formal contract or agreements made in these cases only embraced the number of 25,000 arms each, and also that no sureties were given. It is understood that the bond with sureties now required in each of the above cases shall cover the whole 50,000 muskets to be delivered.

We are, sir, very respectfully, your obedient servants,

J. HOLT,
ROBERT DALE OWEN,
Commissioners.

P. S.—GENERAL: The commission have also decided that the confirmation in the cases of the Union Arms Company for 25,000 rifled muskets and 12,500 Marsh's breech-loading muskets shall be in like manner, upon condition that contracts be entered into by the parties as directed in cases since decided.

J. HOLT.
ROBERT DALE OWEN.

P. V. HAGNER,
Major of Ordnance, Assistant to Commission.

General J. W. RIPLEY.
Chief of Ordnance.

ORDNANCE OFFICE, *Washington, May 15, 1862.*

SIR: My attention having been called to the number of pistols to be delivered under the order to Samuel Colt, dated September 17, 1861, as stated in Ex. Doc. No. 67, I submit the following for the information of the commissioners:

In making up the statement of pistols contracted for, printed on page 19, the number of pistols to be delivered under the order mentioned was estimated at 30,000. The number actually delivered under that order, at the time of preparing the statement, was 19,700; and the average rate of delivery at that period would extend the number to 30,000 in about nine weeks. It was believed that the statement would be made more perfect by inserting an estimated number for that order than by leaving it blank. The estimate has proved to be quite near the truth, for the number since delivered under that order is 11,500; making the whole number delivered 31,200.

Respectfully, I am your obedient servant,

JAS. W. RIPLEY, *Brigadier General.*

Mr. J. WISE, *Secretary to Commissioners.*

CASE No. 14.

ORISON BLUNT.

ORDNANCE OFFICE, *Washington, September* 10, 1861.

SIR: Your proposition of this date to furnish 20,000 Enfield rifle muskets, to be delivered prospectively, and also to furnish twenty thousand (20,000) rifle muskets, as per sample, to be manufactured in this country, at the rate of five hundred in sixty days, or less, and the residue five hundred to a thousand per month, has been submitted to the Secretary of War. I am directed by him to reply that the proposition in regard to the arms to be delivered by importation will not be accepted, but that this department will take as many of the arms of the sample you submit as you can manufacture in this country by the first day of January next, at eighteen dollars per arm, including appendages.

The arms are to be subject to inspection by such officers as this department may designate for the purpose, and none will be accepted or paid for but such as are approved by the United States inspector. Payments will be made on certificates of inspection and receipt in such funds as the Treasury Department may provide. Please signify in writing whether you will agree to deliver the arms on the terms and conditions herein stated.

Respectfully, your obedient servant,

JAMES W. RIPLEY.

Mr. ORISON BLUNT, 118 *Ninth Street, New York.*

WASHINGTON, *January* 15, 1862.

SIR: You gave me an order September 10, 1861, for muskets to be manufactured by me in this country, as per sample deposited with you. The time having expired, January 1, 1862, and I have not as yet been able to turn in any muskets to the department, I have spent the entire time in preparing my factory building, my machinery and tools, and making preparations to make the barrels, which has been very difficult for me to get parties to make barrels without a positive and large order from me. My factory is now all in running order. My men are making 300 barrels per week, and can increase to any reasonable extent if necessary, so that I am now prepared (as I have expended a large amount of money) to furnish the government with from two to five hundred Enfield pattern muskets per month, as per sample, and to increase the number if required, for the sum of eighteen dollars each gun, including implements, consisting of lock-vise to take lock apart, screw-driver, nipple wrench, and ball draw or worm for each gun. I would now ask the department to extend the time until the 1st of May, 1862, or longer if the department will do so.

I herewith present a sample, which is $\frac{58}{100}$ of an inch bore, and 40-inch barrel, and all the guns shall be made in every respect equal to the sample.

By complying with the above you will oblige, yours, respectfully,

ORISON BLUNT,

118 *Ninth street, New York City.*

General RIPLEY, *Chief of Ordnance department.*

ORDNANCE OFFICE, *January* 29, 1862.

Respectfully submitted to the Secretary of War. The order of Mr. Blunt reads, "This department will take as many of the arms of the sample you submit as you can manufacture in this country by the 1st of January next, (1862,) at eighteen dollars per arm, including appendages." The arm referred to is the Enfield rifle musket.

JAMES W. RIPLEY,
Brigadier General.

NEW YORK CITY, *February* 6, 1862.

SIR: I made an application on the 10th day of September to the Secretary of War as follows: To furnish them with 20,000 rifle muskets with triangular bayonets, $\frac{58}{100}$ bore, and 40-inch barrel, of the English Enfield pattern, the same to be imported by me, and delivered to the United States in bond for the sum of eighteen dollars per gun. I also proposed to furnish the United States government with 20,000 the same as the above, and of my own manufacture in this country, for the sum of eighteen dollars each, including appendages, and deposited a sample gun in the ordnance department. My first proposition to import 20,000 guns was rejected, but my second proposition, to manufacture 20,000 guns in this country, was accepted by the ordnance department, and less than four months' time given me to manufacture them. I immediately commenced preparing my factory building, machinery and tools, and have gone to a great expense, knowing that the government would require this arm. I am now all in working order, and can produce from 500 to 1,000 per month like the two I now present, which I have made myself, and are like the pattern gun filed in the ordnance office.

I am a practical manufacturer of guns, and understand it in all its branches, and can make any part of the gun with my own hands. I would respectfully submit that the War Department will extend the time for the manufacture of these guns at least one year, with permission to turn in from 500 to 1,500 per month.

Yours, respectfully,

ORISON BLUNT,
118 *Ninth street, New York.*

Hon. EDWIN M. STANTON.

[Indorsement.]

Referred to chief of ordnance for report.

EDWIN M. STANTON,
FEBRUARY 9, 1862. *Secretary of War.*

ORDNANCE OFFICE,
Washington, February 10, 1862.

Respectfully returned. Mr. O. Blunt received an order dated September 10, 1861, for as many arms of the pattern he submitted then as he could manufacture in this country by the 1st January, 1862, at eighteen dollars per arm, including appendages. He has not yet delivered any of these arms, but says that he has now the means of producing from five hundred to one thousand per month, and asks for an extension of the time of delivery for at least one year, with permission to turn in from five hundred to fifteen hundred per month. The sample arm is a good and effective one, and the price is reasonable as compared with other contracts. It is, therefore, recommended that the time for delivery be extended to the 1st January, 1863—the government to take as many of the arms as Mr. Blunt shall deliver in that time, not exceeding one thousand for any one month, on the same terms and conditions as stated in his order of the 10th September, 1861, herewith enclosed.

JAS. W. RIPLEY,
Brigadier General.

NEW YORK, *March* 3, 1862.

DEAR SIR: I have been informed this morning that you are going to Washington this evening. If so, will you be kind enough to call on General Ripley, and ask him if has made and completed the order to me for one thousand Enfield rifle muskets per month from the 1st of January, 1862, to the 1st of January, 1863—twelve thousand in all. The parts not to interchange, but to be equal as sample I deposited with you.

When I was in Washington a week ago to-day, Mr. Secretary Stanton directed General Ripley to give me the above order on the spot, and he would sanction it. I left Washington on Tuesday. General Ripley did not have it ready for me, but said he would send it in a day or two. If it has been sent, it has been miscarried, as I have not received it. I have made great preparations, and invested a large amount of money in machinery and tools for the manufacturing of this arm. I had no time to build a factory of sufficient capacity. I consequently hired one. My time has expired, and if I do not get this order for muskets at once, I must throw up my factory and stop my barrel works, and throw a great many mechanics out of employment.

You will also be kind enough to say to General Ripley that I have the captured schooner Stephen Hart entirely unloaded, and the cargo is much more valuable than I expected. There are a very large quantity of Enfield rifle muskets on board of her, which will be very useful to our army, together with ammunition and an entire rig-out for a brigade.

By attending to the above you will save me a visit to Washington, as it will be impossible for me to leave until I get this cargo appraised.

Yours, respectfully,

ORISON BLUNT.

S. DRAPER,
  Corner of White and Centre streets.

ORDNANCE OFFICE,
Washington, March 26, 1862.

SIR: In answer to your note respecting the extension of Mr. O. Blunt's order, I deem it proper to make the following statement: Mr. Blunt's application for extension of time on his order of 10th September, 1861, was referred to this office on the 10th February, 1862, and was returned to the War Department with the following indorsement, viz:

"ORDNANCE OFFICE,
" *Washington, February 10, 1862.*

"Respectfully returned. Mr. O. Blunt received an order dated 10th September, 1861, for as many arms of the pattern he submitted then as he could manufacture in this country by the 1st January, 1862, at eighteen dollars per arm, including appendages. He has not yet delivered any of the arms, but says that he has now the means of producing from five hundred to one thousand per month, and asks for an extension of the time of delivery for at least one year, with permission to turn in from five hundred to fifteen hundred per month. This, if granted, will be the same as giving him an order for from six thousand to eighteen thousand muskets, deliverable in monthly instalments, in one year from the date of the order.

"If any new agreement is made with him, (the former one having been forfeited by its terms,) I would respectfully suggest that it be for rifle muskets and appendages of the Springfield pattern, interchangeable with the muskets and appendages made at the national armory.

"JAS. W. RIPLEY,
" *Brigadier General.*"

Subsequently, by verbal direction of the Secretary of War, as understood by me, that indorsement was modified, and the paper sent back to the War Department for the Secretary's action on it under the modified indorsement. The paper has not since been returned to this office, and I understand is now before the commission.

I am, sir, very respectfully, your obedient servant,

JAS. W. RIPLEY,
Brigadier General.

Hon. J. HOLT, *Washington, D. C.*

MARCH 28, 1861.

The paper alluded to within was not among those sent to the commission. As it is properly a part of Mr. Blunt's case, the commission request that this be filed with the papers of that case, and sent yesterday to the chief of ordnance.

P. V. HAGNER,
Major of Ordnance.

COMMISSION ON CONTRACTS.

———

COMMISSION ON ORDNANCE AND ORDNANCE STORES,
Washington, March 26, 1862.

GENERAL : The commission have the honor to report as follows :

CASE No. 14.—ORISON BLUNT, New York.

Referred by special order of War Department.   Contract for as many Enfield rifles as he can make up to January 1, 1862.

The commission find that the contract is forfeited by non-delivery of the arms within the time specified ; that the arm, not being interchangeable, is very much inferior to the Springfield rifle musket, and therefore it is not desirable greatly to increase the number of such in the service.   But they find that Mr. Blunt has proceeded in good faith in the manufacture of these arms, and being now nearly prepared to make certain deliveries of the same, has incurred expenses in this effort to furnish arms to the government which an abrupt suspension would render unreasonably heavy upon him.   They find further that the price is reasonable, and, on inspecting a specimen gun, the workmanship seems fair for a hand-made arm, except as to an accidental omission to temper the ramrod properly.

The commission, therefore, consider that Mr. Blunt's establishment may be relied on to produce arms of this English pattern fully equal to those made abroad, if definite instructions as to details of material and finish, for his guidance and for that of the inspector, be given him by the Ordnance department, and decide upon the acceptance of as many, fully approved as above, as he may be able to make by July 1, 1862, not to exceed 3,000 in all.

Very respectfully, &c.,

J. HOLT,
ROBERT DALE OWEN,
Commissioners, &c.
P. V. HAGNER,
Major of Ordnance, Assistant to Commissioners.

Brig. Gen. J. W. RIPLEY,
Chief of Ordnance.

CASE No. 15.

HERMAN BOKER & Co.

WASHINGTON, *September* 4, 1861.

SIR: Our resident partner in Europe advises us by last steamer of a lot of upwards of one hundred thousand stand of arms—rifled percussion muskets, new, and in good condition—having been placed in his control by making advances thereon.

We desire to offer them to your department, and should it appear to you of sufficient importance to secure the immediate delivery there of so large a quantity of good arms, we would invite your attention thereto.

We offer the arms at a price not exceeding eighteen dollars each, subject to the inspection and approval of an armorer whom you shall select to accompany an authorized agent. If the article is not satisfactory the government will incur no expense, and if approved you will secure an article much needed.

We also control, by advances thereon, over 18,000 cavalry sabres, which we offer as above, at a price not to exceed $7 50 apiece.

Very respectfully, your obedient servants,

HERMAN BOKER & CO.,
50 *Cliff street, New York.*

Also of Liege, Solingen, Remscherd, Birmingham, and Bonn.

Hon. SIMON CAMERON,
Secretary of War.

[Indorsement.]

SEPTEMBER 5, 1861.

I approve the carrying this through carefully, cautiously, and expeditiously. Avoid conflicts and interferences.

A. LINCOLN.

WAR DEPARTMENT,
Washington, September 5, 1861.

GENTLEMEN: Your proposition to furnish one hundred thousand, or upwards, of rifled muskets, with angular or sword bayonets—necessary fixtures as usual with such supplies—properly packed for shipment, price not to exceed eighteen dollars per musket and fixtures, deliverable in New York to an agent of this government; and eighteen thousand cavalry sabres, deliverable as above, price not to exceed seven dollars and fifty cents each, has been submitted to the President, and by him approved.

Your proposition is, therefore, accepted, with the following conditions: All the arms and sabres shall be subject to the inspection and approval of an armorer or officer of this government, to be sent to Europe with your agent; and when duly approved by said armorer or officer payments will be made therefor on presentation of the certificates of inspection and of delivery at New York.

As time is important in this matter, the government will not be deemed responsible for this acceptance unless deliveries for inspection in Europe are commenced within thirty days after the date of the agent sailing for Europe, nor for any deliveries on account thereof, for inspection, that may not be made within sixty days from date of sailing.

Very respectfully,

SIMON CAMERON,
Secretary of War.

Messrs. H. BOKER & Co., *New York.*

[Indorsement.]

WASHINGTON, *September 5*, 1861.

SIR: Your acceptance of our proposition, as within stated, is satisfactory, though it requires delivery at New York instead of at a shipping port in Europe, as proposed by us.

We wish it distinctly understood that the articles are to be delivered to the United States government *in bond* at New York *free of duty.*

Your approval, noted on this acceptance, will much oblige,

Your obedient servant,

HERMAN BOKER,
50 Cliff street, New York.

Hon. SIMON CAMERON, *Secretary of War.*

WAR DEPARTMENT,
Washington City, September 5, 1861.

DEAR SIR: This department has made an arrangement with Messrs. H. Boker & Co., of New York, for muskets and sabres. It is desirable to the government that the arms shall be secured and forwarded at the earliest possible date; please aid the firm, or such agent as they may send, in sending them promptly.

Yours, respectfully,

SECRETARY OF WAR.

Hon. HENRY S. SANFORD,
Resident Minister, Brussels, Belgium.

ORDNANCE OFFICE,
Washington, September 6, 1861.

SIR: For your better information in regard to the inspection and approval of the 100,000, or upwards, of rifled muskets, with angular or sword bayonets, with the necessary appendages, and 18,000 cavalry sabres, properly packed for shipment, deliverable to an agent of this government in New York, I have to give the following instructions: All the fire-arms are to be of one or other of the calibres .58 or .69-inch, or with such slight shades of difference that they will take one ammunition for those calibres. Without exacting all the accuracy and nicety observed in the inspection of our own arms, it will be necessary to see that the arms you are to inspect are of good and suitable material in all respects, and are altogether serviceable, and particularly in regard to the sabre blades, which must be of good steel. It is not necessary to go into minute details of instruction on these points, as your own experience and familiarity with the manufacture of arms and their quality will enable you to see that none but good, serviceable arms are accepted for government use. An express condition of the acceptance of the proposition for the delivery of the arms is, that the government will not be deemed responsible for accepting them unless deliveries for inspection in Europe are commenced within thirty days after the date of agent's sailing for Europe, nor for any deliveries on account thereof, for inspection, that may not be made within sixty days from date of sailing.

During your absence on this inspection service you will be borne on the rolls of the Washington arsenal at your recent rate of compensation, and all the necessary expenses of your voyage to Europe and back, and your stay there, will be paid by the agent whom you are to accompany.

Respectfully, &c.,

JAMES W. RIPLEY,
Brigadier General.

Mr. GEORGE WRIGHT, *Washington, D. C.*

NEW YORK, *October* 19, 1861.

We have just received advices, per Arabia, from our resident partner in Europe, Mr. H. Boker, who writes as follows:

"After a thorough and careful examination of the *guns* in market, I am satisfied that it will be a difficult matter to furnish *rifled* muskets of the calibre exactly .58 and .69, all such arms having to be contracted for in advance. The best arms shown to us are smooth-bore muskets, calibre .70 to .72. I think (and Mr. Wright, the armorer, thinks with me) that a smooth-bore musket, loaded with buckshot and ball, is far more serviceable than any ordinary rifled piece, and is willing to pass good first class arms, if the chief of ordnance will so modify the instructions, instead of being held strictly to rifled muskets of .69 calibre.

" We respectfully ask that the War Department will make this reasonable change, in order that not a moment may be lost in shipping with all possible despatch.

" If this change is made, we can ship all the muskets promptly, and, if desired by the department, can increase the quantity. As we wish to write by earliest steamer, will you please communicate to us *here* the views of the War Department upon the matter referred to in Mr. Boker's letter."

We have the honor to be, with great respect, your obedient servants,

H. BOKER & CO.

Hon. SIMON CAMERON,
Secretary of War.

WAR DEPARTMENT, *October* 22, 1861.

Your favor of 19th was held over until the Secretary arrived, and this morning the enclosed report from chief of ordnance in due form was approved by him. Send this abroad, and Mr. Wright will at once conform to the modifications as ordered by the chief of ordnance. We need the guns as soon as possible, and hope your firm will be able to secure the 100,000 stand of arms as agreed.

Very respectfully,

THOMAS A. SCOTT,
Assistant Secretary.

Messrs. BOKER & Co., *New York.*

ORDNANCE OFFICE, *Washington, October* 22, 1861.

SIR: In answer to Messrs. H. Boker & Co. of the 19th instant, referred to this office, I have to report. Under the circumstances I recommend that the instructions heretofore given be so modified as to allow the reception of good first class arms of smooth bores, the calibre to be .70 in preference to .72; but the latter may be taken, if essential to the procurement of arms, *all* of which should be of one calibre if possible. The cones of the arms should fit our regular army percussion caps, if it be possible to obtain arms with such sized cones. The letter of Messrs. Boker & Co. is returned herewith.

Respectfully, &c.,

JAMES W. RIPLEY,
Brigadier General.

Hon. SIMON CAMERON,
Secretary of War.

Mr. Wright will consider his instructions modified as above.

JAMES W. RIPLEY.

NEW YORK, *November* 23, 1861.

SIR: We have the honor to inform you that in accordance with an order from the ordnance office, dated September 5, 1861, we have purchased in Europe 125,000 stand of arms and 28,000 sabres, which are now being delivered and forwarded by steamers as rapidly as they can be shipped.

In addition to these already purchased we have engaged, deliverable in equal quantities in the months of January, February, March, and April, 50,000 new rifled muskets, calibre .58, with bayonets, at $18, as also 25,000 cavalry swords at $7 50, deliverable in January, February, and March—all in bond—which we offer to the department, in addition to our former order, subject to the inspection of the government agent in Europe.

Soliciting your prompt reply *to-day*, we remain, sir, your obedient servants,

HERMAN BOKER & CO.

Hon. SIMON CAMERON,
    Secretary of War.

In the foregoing letter the expression is used, "in accordance with an order from the ordnance office, dated September 5, 1861, we have purchased," &c. No such order can be found on the books of the ordnance office, and no such order ever emanated from that office. The writer evidently refers to the order of the Secretary of War, dated September 5, 1861, already given.

WAR DEPARTMENT,
Washington, November 25, 1861.

GENTLEMEN: I have received your letter of November 23, and am pleased to learn that you have so promptly secured the arms contracted for by this department. Owing to the numerous failures of other contractors to deliver arms, I deem it advisable to accept your proposition of this date, to deliver 50,000 stand of rifled muskets, new, .58 calibre, in the months of January, February, March, and April next, at $18 for each gun, with angular bayonet and usual fixtures complete; also for 10,000 cavalry sabres, at $7 50 each, deliverable in January and February next. The arms and sabres to be subject to inspection by an armorer of the ordnance department in Europe, and to be delivered in bond in the city of New York without charge to the United States other than the price specified.

Yours, respectfully,

SIMON CAMERON,
    Secretary of War.

Messrs. HERMAN BOKER & CO., *New York.*

WASHINGTON, *November* 8, 1861.

SIR: We are delivering and will deliver to your department by every steamer coming from the continent of Europe the arms we have contracted for in September last. To secure to the department a speedy delivery in New York, and to save to us a good deal of inconvenience as also unnecessary expense, we beg leave to ask of you, through the instrumentality of the Secretary of the Treasury, such instructions to the collector of New York, Hon. Hiram Barney, as to grant to our house a free permit for all arms destined for the government, and upon delivery to the said collector the bills of lading belonging thereto. The latter clause will prevent any trespass on the privileges to be granted.

Our applications for free permits as heretofore, although having been attended to with commendable alacrity, do not return to New York until the goods have gone under general order and are scattered in various bonded warehouses, thereby causing a delay in the delivery for several days, and our advices of shipment generally arrive simultaneously with the goods.

Craving your early attention to this matter, and a prompt reply,

We remain, sir, very respectfully, your obedient servants,

HERMAN BOKER & CO.,

50 Cliff street, New York.

Hon. SIMON CAMERON,
Secretary of War.

NEW YORK, *November* 13, 1861.

GENERAL : Messrs. Boker & Co. have called upon me, showing their contract of the 5th September for the delivery of 100,000 rifled muskets, 18,000 cavalry sabres, required to be inspected and accepted by the United States agent in Europe. They also produce certificates of inspection, signed by "George Wright, inspector," for

1. 400 rifled muskets, calibre .69, Liege—arrived November 7.

2. 1,680 rifled muskets, calibre .69, Liege—960 arrived November 7, balance to arrive.

3. 5,000 rifled muskets, calibre .69, Cologne—4,080 arrived November 7, balance to arrive.

4. 2,500 cavalry sabres, Solingen—arrived November 7.

I have distributed the above arms and sabres, as stated in my letter to you of the 11th instant, and have given receipts to Messrs. Boker & Co. for those which have arrived. As I have had no special instructions upon this subject, I report as above, in order that I may be informed whether the course pursued is satisfactory, and if I shall continue it in future.

The conditions stipulated in the order of the Secretary of War are stated to have been complied with.

Very respectfully, your obedient servant,

P. V. HAGNER,
Major of Ordnance.

General J. W. RIPLEY,
Chief of Ordnance, Washington.

NEW YORK, *November* 20, 1861.

SIR : We have the honor to inform you that we have received, per Saxonia, from Hamburg, arrived this morning, 443 cases rifled muskets—in all about 10,000 ; as also, 73 cases of chasseur sabres—in all 3,650.

We have also, in same steamer, 180 cases of arms ; information about their contents will be received by steamer Asia, due to-morrow.

You will please instruct the government's agent in New York to receive said goods.

Very respectfully, your obedient servant,

HERMAN BOKER & CO.

Hon. SIMON CAMERON,
Secretary of War.

ORDNANCE OFFICE,
No. 55 White street, New York, December 2, 1861.

GENERAL : I have received no instructions relative to Herman Boker's contract. Are the arms to be accepted by me without inspection ?

Of the last delivery, I sent 2,300 Austrian, calibre .69, 1,656 French, calibre .69, to the State of New York, as per statement made to you. To-day, I have had returned to me samples of these arms. The "French" are of two kinds, both old and altered—one original percussion and rifled afterwards, barrels differing two inches in length, *without sights;* the other altered from flint, with patent breech, rifled, *with sights.* As both are roughly made and second hand, since alteration, their value here should not exceed $7 and $8.

The "Austrian" are an inferior arm still; bayonets, locks, and rods very common; three modes of attachments for bayonets; locks old flint, patched in some cases; rods of iron, and some with small ends. Barrels, old flint with small cone-seat brazed on and rivetted, plug in old vent. Mixed with the barrels of usual length are many short barrels, thirty-three inches long. Such guns are of little or no value, and ought not to be imported.

Some of the French arms were issued yesterday to a regiment before departing, but I have requested General Welch to detain the Austrian until I receive your instructions. Wright's certificates of inspection embrace, I believe, all of these arms, but it is evident that no proper inspection was made, as one of the bayonets snapped into three pieces upon very slight pressure in my hands.

Very respectfully, sir, your obedient servant,

P. V. HAGNER,
Major of Ordnance.

General J. W. RIPLEY,
Chief of Ordnance, Washington.

ORDNANCE OFFICE,
No. 55 White street, New York, December 7, 1861.

GENERAL: *   *   *   *   *   *   *   *

What am I to do about Herman Boker's Austrian arms, declined by the State of New York, as stated in my letter of the 2d of December? I have now three large storehouses filled or filling with arms. As soon as I can empty one of them I can probably get along with this one and the one hired to-day to receive Hoey's and the United States arms by the Bavaria. This one I have to keep for sabres and purchased Enfields and small stores. Am I to pay storage in bonded warehouses or the quartermaster, (some cases have been so stored by custom-house officers,) and also the freight upon United States arms purchased in Europe? The quartermaster declines to pay this, I hear.

Very respectfully, your obedient servant,

P. V. HAGNER,
Major of Ordnance.

General J. W. RIPLEY,
Chief of Ordnance, Washington.

ORDNANCE OFFICE,
No. 55 White street, New York, December 19, 1861.

GENERAL: *   *   *   *   *   *   *   *

I have also sent 5,963 sabres to Colonel Ramsay, and I send, to-day, 1,050 more from Boker's contract. * * * Mr. Boker has delivered 1,524 short Austrian muskets, calibre .70, length of barrel *thirty-three inches*, with triangular bayonets, eighteen inches long. There are also some of the same in the lot delivered to the State of New York and declined. What shall I do with them? They are altered from flint-lock by priming and brazing on the cone-seat. * * *

Very respectfully, sir, your obedient servant,

P. V. HAGNER,
Major of Ordnance.

General J. W. RIPLEY,
Chief of Ordnance, Washington.

NEW YORK, *December 7, 1861.*

SIR: We have been informed by Major P. V. Hagner, New York, that he is still without instructions from the Ordnance office to receive goods furnished under our contract, September 5, 1861, and as arms have accumulated very rapidly by recent shipments, we will be much obliged if you will cause the Ordnance department to instruct their agents in New York to receive all goods from us as soon as they arrive with certificates of inspection.

It is very important that the instructions may be given at once, as our warehouses are completely filled and large arrivals (about 30,000 stands) expected every day.

We remain, sir, very respectfully, your obedient servants,

HERMAN BOKER & CO.

Hon. SIMON CAMERON,
    Secretary of War.

COLOGNE, *November* 24, 1861.

SIR: I respectfully beg leave to report that the sixty days within which H. Boker & Co. were required to deliver arms for inspection by me, under their contract of September 5, 1861, expired on the 11th day of November instant.

The arms submitted by them for my inspection were lying at different points in France, Belgium, Prussia, and Austria, and from the number of places, and the great distance apart, I have been unable to inspect and forward only a portion of them up to date.

A lot of chasseurs de Vincennes carbines, stored in the French arsenals at Metz, Grenoble, and Marseilles, have been ready for inspection since October 26, but for the reasons above specified I have not yet had time to examine them, which is much to be regretted, as they are represented as being a superior lot of arms.

Appendages to the arms in the early shipments were not ready in every instance to be sent with them, but the proper number have been forwarded, and hereafter will accompany each case.

The United States minister at Brussels, Mr. Sanford, telegraphed me at Vienna to report to him for the examination of a lot of arms for which he has recently contracted. Although this additional duty will necessarily protract my stay here, I trust it will meet with the approbation of the department.

Respectfully, your obedient servant,

GEORGE WRIGHT.

General J. W. RIPLEY,
    Chief of Ordnance, Washington, D. C.

ORDNANCE OFFICE,
Washington, January 10, 1862.

SIR: As mention is frequently made, in papers coming to this office, of a contract with Messrs. Herman Boker & Co., dated September 5, 1861, requiring a reference to that contract, which is not to be found on the files of this office, I respectfully request to be furnished with a copy of it.

Respectfully, &c.,

JAMES W. RIPLEY,
    Brigadier General.

Hon. SIMON CAMERON,
    Secretary of War.

ORDNANCE OFFICE,
Washington, January 10, 1862.

SIR: As mention is frequently made, in papers coming to this office, of a contract with Messrs. Herman Boker & Co., dated September 5, 1861, requiring a reference to that contract, which is not found on the files of this office, I respectfully request to be furnished with a copy of it.

Respectfully, your obedient servant,

J. W. RIPLEY,
Brigadier General.

Hon. SIMON CAMERON,
Secretary of War.

ORDNANCE OFFICE,
No. 55 White street, New York, February 13, 1862.

GENERAL: In answer to your letter of the 1st instant, requesting a report of the character and number of each kind of arm delivered by the Messrs. Herman Boker & Co. under their contract with the United States, I have to reply as follows: Up to the present, we have received 61,485 rifled muskets, of various calibres, and 26,050 cavalry sabres, from this firm.

I find, on examination, that the aggregate of 61,485 is made up—except 876, of which we have no samples—of eleven different varieties of arms, the distinctive feature being, of course, in the majority of cases, the calibre; but some I have classed as varieties which simply differ from others, not in calibre, but in their finish and some other minor features. The following descriptions are such as my facilities for examination have enabled me to make, viz:

Sample No. 1.—This arm is calibre .70 inch, rifled with four very light grooves, the ——— broader than the grooves. The length of the barrel is 34.5 inches. The stock is of white wood, common to the Austrian manufacture of arms. The lock is inferior in finish, but the material appears to be good. From the indications around the cone-seat, I believe this to be an altered arm from flint lock to percussion. It is finished with the angular bayonet, the provision for securing which is a steel spring or catch rivetted on the barrel; its weight is 9.25 pounds. This gun is the Austrian smooth-bore musket rifled. From its general appearance, inferiority in the manufacture of the lock, and large calibre, besides its being an old model and altered, I should class this as a poor arm, only to be used in the absence of better models. It is furnished with an elevating sight, which turns down on the barrel, and has several notches for different ranges up to 900 paces. The implements accompanying these arms are screw-drivers and cone wrenches, and wipers of the Austrian pattern. No ball-screws, spare cones, or spring vises are furnished. 10,268 of these arms have been received.

Sample No. 2.—This arm is the Austrian rifle musket, new model; calibre about .55. Its description is already in the possession of the department.—(See Major Mordecai's report, Military Commission to Europe, page 151.) Like all Austrian arms, the lock lacks smoothness of finish and snugness in the fitting of the different parts. We have received of these arms, from Messrs. H. Boker & Co., 15,528, 12,384 of them having the simple block rear sight, and the remainder—3,144—being furnished with elevating screws, ranging up to about 800 yards. Of the two samples of this arm which I have examined, I find the bayonet of one an apparently serviceable one, but that of the other is soft, and stays permanently bent when sprung. I should apprehend, from one inspection of these and similar arms, that this defect exists, more or less, in all Austrian arms provided with the new model bayonet, which lacks quantity and quality of metal in the blades to secure a proper degree of stiffness and strength. These guns may be regarded, on the whole, as fair, and will probably prove, as a general rule, serviceable. The implements furnished are the same as accompany No. 1.

Sample No. 3.—This arm is calibre .58 full. In external finish, character of stock, lock, and barrel, bayonets and sights, it is identical with sample No. 2, and I should infer, from the fact that the weight of the barrel of this arm is less than that of No. 2, their exterior dimensions being the same at the muzzle and breech, that this gun is No. 2 bored up to .58 and re-rifled. In quality it is equal about to No. 2. Implements the same as those furnished with No. 1. The quantity received up to date is 984.

Sample No. 4.—This arm is calibre .58-inch. It is finished, in some respects, in imitation of the Enfield rifle; barrel and lock blued, and tompion and snap-cap attached; the bayonet the usual Austrian model. It is the Austrian rifle musket, but of our standard calibre, and identical in other features of length of barrel, weight, &c., to samples Nos. 2 and 3. It appears, however, to be some-what superior, in every respect, to these samples. Implements the same as furnished with No. 1. 7,376 of these arms have been received to date.

Sample No. 5.—This arm is about calibre .72, rifled with five grooves, weight about 10.25 pounds, length of barrel 41 inches; the breech piece contains the cone-seat and a portion of the bore of the gun. From this fact, and from the dimensions of the breech piece and other particulars, I infer that this arm is the Prussian percussion musket, model 1839, rifled. I am more fully convinced of the identification of this arm by the fact that the mountings are brass, and but-plate of iron, also features of the Prussian arm. The Prussian wall-piece, a rifled arm, same calibre, carries a bullet weighing only 488 grains, being lighter than our .58-inch rifled musket ball. Would it not be well to consider the Prussian bullet in preparing ammunition for this arm, and in fact all .71 calibre rifled? The bayonet is angular, and secured by a catch and spring attached to the barrel. The lock is well made and finished. On the whole this arm is solid and substantial, but the calibre is, of course, objectionable. 4,286 of them have been received. Ball screws and worms of the Prussian model are furnished with these arms; spare cones, screw-drivers, cone wrenches, and spring vises will have to be provided.

Sample No. 6.—An Austrian arm; calibre .70, length of barrel 42 inches, weight of gun 10 pounds, rifled with four grooves.

This is the old Austrian smooth-bore rifled and altered to percussion, sufficient evidence of this fact existing in the appearance of the lock-plate and barrel. The lock, like all Austrian arms, is rough and loose in working, lacking snugness and a nice adjustment of the parts. A simple projection on the breech-pin answers for a rear sight. No front sight. The bayonet is fastened by a spring and clasp, and is of the old Austrian model. Implements the same as furnished with No. 1. 3,804 of these arms have been received. Their use in the field should be deter-mined by necessity.

Sample No. 7.—This is also an Austrian gun, and is identical with No. 6 in calibre, length of barrel, weight, and finish. It is rifled with five grooves, and furnished with large range sights, up to a thousand paces, (eight hundred yards.) It is an old model, altered arm, roughly gotten up, and should not be put into the hands of troops in the field except in cases of necessity and in the absence of good weapons. It has been originally adapted for the old model bayonet, but a stud brazed on the barrel has rendered it suitable for the modern class bayonet. Implements the same as furnished with No. 1. 3,767 of these arms have been received.

Sample No. 8.—This arm is of French manufacture, .71 calibre, weight 10.25 pounds, length of barrel 41 inches, rifled with four grooves. The lock is a back-action, and the rear and main spring are in one. This is a solid and substantial arm—well made in lock, stock, and barrel. The bayonet is of the angular form, with clasp; the rammer is not cupped for the accommodation of the elongated ball; and a simple notched projection at the breech-pin constitutes the rear sight. No appendages are furnished with this arm. The large calibre renders, of course, this arm objectionable; but in other respects it is acceptable. We have received 6,940.

Sample No. 9.—This is the same style musket as the French rifled muskets à Liege, being the same calibre, (.71 inch;) about the same weight, (10.5 pounds;) and the same length of barrel, (.41 inches.) It is equal in make and finish to No. 8, and differs but little from it, except in the lock, which is front action. The rammer is cupped to suit the elongated ball. No implements are furnished with them. 1,320 of them have been received.

Sample No. 10.—This arm is calibre .69 full, weight 10.55 pounds. It is the Prussian new percussion musket, rifled with four grooves, and is identical with No. 5, except in not being provided with long-range sight, and the lock being front action. It is a well-made arm, with a strong, substantial lock; its great defect, of course, is its large calibre. The ordinary Prussian ball, screw, and worm are the only implements that accompany this arm. 848 of them have been received.

Sample No. 11.—This is the Austrian rifle, new model, calibre about .54, length of barrel twenty-eight inches, and total weight of gun about ten pounds. A complete description of this arm is found in Major Mordecai's report, "Military Commission to Europe," page 161, except that the arms imported by the Messrs. Boker & Co. have been bored in the stock to receive a steel rammer. No spring for securing the rammers was inserted when this alteration was made. Implements furnished the same as for No. 1. 1,488 of these rifles have been received. These arms are well made, and might answer as personal weapons for artillery, or, deprived of their sword bayonets, might be issued to cavalry regiments in the absence of appropriate weapons.

It would appear from the above that 17,839 inferior arms, principally, if not all, abandoned Austrian models, all inferior in workmanship and finish, of objectionable calibre, and all altered guns, have been received from the Messrs. H. Boker & Co. Also, of the remainder of the 60,609 of which I have examined samples, that 25,376 of them are the present Austrian model, calibre .55 and .58, rifled, fair arms in workmanship and finish, and in weight and calibre according more nearly with our established model than any other arms of continental manufacture. Also, that the rest of the aggregate (17,394) are arms of French and Prussian manufacture, more substantial and solid, better in workmanship, finish, and material than the Austrian models, but open to grave and serious objections as superior military weapons, on account of their large bores, and necessitating the use of ammunition weighty to carry, and giving a recoil inconveniently great. The weights of these arms are also in a majority of cases objectionable, ranging as they do from 10.55 to 11.25 pounds.

I have made an examination of a few of the sabres furnished by the Messrs. H. Boker & Co. Out of the twenty-three examined only ten came up to our standard as first quality; the remainder (thirteen) are either of inferior quality, or, in accordance with our rules of inspection, rejected. I do not regard this inspection as a just criterion of the quality of the sabres furnished, but it shows that we may be apprehensive of finding among them a number of inferior grade.

These arms have been received from the Messrs. H. Boker & Co. by this office on the presentation of the certificates of the United States inspector, Mr. George Wright, in accordance with the instructions of the Assistant Secretary of War, as indorsed on the communication from the above-mentioned firm to the honorable Secretary, dated January 7, 1862, and transmitted in a letter from your office, dated January 11, 1862. The original contract or letter of the Secretary to the Messrs. H. Boker & Co., dated September 5, 1861, is not on the files of, nor has been forwarded to, this office. This paper has not been deemed necessary, as I have interpreted the instructions above referred to as clearly authorizing the reception of these arms on the presentation of the certificates, but I have since thought it proper to advise the department of this action, in order, if there is anything in the letter above referred to which may be necessary for our information and government in the matter, that a copy may be forwarded to this office.

Very respectfully, your obedient servant,

S. CRISPIN,
Captain of Ordnance.

Brigadier General J. W. RIPLEY,
Chief of Ordnance.

NEW YORK, *February* 10, 1862.

SIR: In accordance with your order of January 29, 1862, we herewith enclose copies of all the papers relating to our contracts for arms, and remain,

Very respectfully, your obedient servants,

HERMAN BOKER & CO.

Hon. EDWIN M. STANTON,
Secretary of War.

WASHINGTON, *March* 4, 1862.

SIR: Referring to our communication of February 10, 1862, covering copies of our contracts agreeably to your order of January 29, 1862, we have respectfully to state that we have delivered to the United States government arms to the amount of nearly $1,000,000, for which we have not been paid. The invoices and certificates furnished by us have partly been approved by the Ordnance department and the accounting bureaus of the Treasury Department. Upon application for payment we are given to understand that our accounts had been suspended by your order, of which no official information had reached us. For all the arms so furnished we have paid the money, and it is *indispensably necessary* to the existence of our house that the obligations of the government should be promptly met. The delay already incurred has been seriously detrimental to us, and its further continuance will be *fatal.*

We therefore earnestly request that you will without further delay permit the payment of our accounts by the Treasury Department, and remain, with much respect,

Your obedient servants,

HERMAN BOKER & CO., *New York.*

Hon. EDWIN M. STANTON,
Secretary of War.

Please address your reply to 478 Fourteenth street, Washington.

WASHINGTON, *March* 13, 1862.

SIR: We beg respectfully to state to you that we entered into a large contract for arms with the government at a time when it was of *vital* importance to the country to procure a large quantity of arms in the *shortest possible space* of time. In this business we not only embarked our own fortune but very large amounts commanded by an untarnished credit for thirty years.

We will not disguise from you that we expected to realize a handsome profit on the transaction, and we frankly state to you that we would not have perilled both fortune and credit in one transaction without the expectation of better profits than those usually realized in our current business, which has been chiefly confined to guns and hardware. With equal frankness we state to you that in a business with the government, where we are subjected to the errors of judgment or caprices of inspectors, we are entitled to a larger margin of profits than when dealing with regular and well established firms with whom friendly relations exist arising from a business intercourse of many years standing, and of mutual reciprocity. We trust that you will excuse what will seem to *you* a long preamble, but to *us*, in a business matter of *life and death*, is as short as justice to ourselves will permit. We will now come direct to the point. The accounts rendered by us for arms since December 21, 1861, and the delivery of arms since that date to your ordnance officer in New York, amount to upwards of *one million and a half dollars*. *To save our credit*, which we value beyond profit, we require *this week* $500,000. If you will pay us that amount *this week*, on account of these invoices and deliveries, (which would be less than $7 per arm) it will *save us from utter, ruin* and unless we do receive it *the house cannot stand*. We have not seen the report of your ordnance officer, but are willing to adjust the balance of our accounts upon a price to be fixed at the market value of the arms at the time they were purchased by us for the United States government, that market value to be controlled by the prices paid by the United States officers stationed in New York or elsewhere for purchasing arms at the date of our purchases. It does not seem just and right to us that our arms which have been received by the government, and with which battles have been fought and victories won, should be appraised now at a loss to us of both profit and capital without giving us an opportunity to prove their value. In the dark hour of the government, when her credit was at a discount, and when she was beset by foes at home and abroad, *we risked* our *all, and now in our hour of need* we simply ask to be treated with just consideration. In this appeal to you for your assistance in our extreme need, we do so confidently relying on your high reputation for justice and integrity. In conclusion we beg to state that, by our proposition, we evince our readiness to risk our legitimate profits *to save our credit*, which is dearer to us than anything else in business; but the offer also demonstrates our confidence that you will deal uprightly and fairly with us.

Earnestly praying that you will act promptly in this matter, and relieve us from our perilous position,

We remain, sir, very respectfully, your obedient servants,

HERMAN BOKER & CO.

No. 50 Cliff street, New York.

Hon. E. M. STANTON,
Secretary of War.

WAR DEPARTMENT,
Washington City, D. C., March 14, 1862.

SIR: Under your orders of this date I have the honor to report:

Prior to March 3, 1862, 81,770 rifled muskets had been placed under control of the Ordnance department by Messrs. H. Boker & Co., stated by them to be deliveries under their contract of September 5, 1861, and as such ordered to be received by the purchasing ordnance officer at New York by Assistant Secretary of War, Thomas A. Scott, dated January 9, 1862; also 31,300 cavalry sabres.

Of the above muskets I find—

1. 34,692 are of kinds unsuitable for issue in future, on account of worn condition, fragile parts, or defective construction. 12,524 of the above 34,692 have been issued under pressing "orders for supplies from Ordnance department." 22,168 still remain in store in New York and should not be issued except upon emergency.

The value of the 12,524 already issued should not exceed (upon liberal appraisment)	$71,116
At same rates the 22,168 (of same marks) remaining on hand in New York would be	155,869
Total valuation of 34,692 inferior arms	226,985

2. 41,727 muskets are of kinds suitable for issue, although of various calibres. We have had to purchase like arms and must continue to issue such until our own model is more abundantly supplied. Of this kind 15,106 have been issued, value at fair rates (exceeding no doubt their true value to the government, as, owing to their variety and imperfect construction, repairs will be difficult, although probably very soon necessary)................. $208, 690
At the same rates 26,621 (of same marks) remaining on hand in New York would be....................................... 370, 186

Total valuation, 41,727, *fit for issue*.................... 578, 876

3. 5,351 muskets (including 1,464 returned as worthless by the State of New York, and now at the New York arsenal) are entirely useless for government service, being of inferior quality originally, badly altered in workmanship and plan, of unsuitable calibres, length of barrel, &c. No value stated.
Since March 3 other cargoes of arms have arrived, but remain in store, and should be inspected and appraised before being received.
Sabres.—31,300 sabres have been in like manner placed at the disposal of the Ordnance department by the Messrs. Boker.
24,600 have been issued. Valued in accordance with the like quali-
ties at an average rate, the amount is........................ $87, 330
6,700 on hand, valued as above.............................. 23, 785

Total value of 31,300 sabres....................... 111, 115
Deduct from above value of 3,300, at same, delivered in excess of
order 11, 715

Balance 99, 400

Orders on file authorize *only*—
First order (sabres)... 18, 000
Second order (sabres)....................................... 10, 000

28, 000

Paying Messrs. Boker & Co. for—
1. Inferior arms issued and on hand......................... $226, 985
2. Serviceable arms issued and on hand...................... 578, 876
3. Sabres (authorized) issued and on hand................... 99, 400

Total amount due to March 3, less advances already made.... 905, 261

Advances made (as acknowledged by Messrs. Boker & Co.) by Minister San-
ford in Europe:
November, £29,760, at $5.................................... $148, 800
November, £6,000, at $5.................................... 30, 000
France—November, 200,000 francs, at 20 cents 40, 000
December, 102,600 francs, at 20 cents 20, 520
December, 146,100 francs, at 20 cents 29, 220
January, 421,775 francs, at 20 cents 84, 355
January, 250,000 francs, at 20 cents 50, 000

Carried forward.......... 402, 895

Ex. Doc. 72——6

Brought forward...... $402, 895 00
Amount of voucher paid, as per certificate December 10 .... 249, 922 50
_____
Total paid to Messrs. Boker & Co., as far as appears at present.. 652, 817 50
_____
Balance 252, 443 50
_____

If payment is not made for the 22,168 inferior guns still on hand at New York, deduct appraised value, $155,869, leaving due Messrs Boker & Co. $96,574 50.

Respectfully submitted.

P. V. HAGNER, *Major of Ordnance.*

Hon. E. Stanton, *Secretary of War.*

Washington, *March* 19, 1862.

Papers in the case of Herman Boker & Co. referred to the commission on ordnance claims, &c., by direction of the Secretary of War.

P. H. WATSON,
Assistant Secretary of War.

Commission on Ordnance, &c.,
Washington, March 20, 1862.

Sir : Having taken a cursory view of the purchases of H. Boker & Co., of New York, for foreign arms, we are of opinion that it is highly important that an order should be sent out by the *first steamer* to Mr. Sanford, United States minister to Belgium, not only to make no further purchases, but also to make no further *payments,* out of any money which may remain in his hands for that purpose. Unless this precautionary measure is taken, any decision which this commission may hereafter make in the premises may be comparatively unavailing.

We are, sir, your obedient servants,

J. HOLT,
ROBERT DALE OWEN,
Commissioners.

Hon. Edwin M. Stanton,
Secretary of War.

Before commission, March 24, 1862.

Mr. Schlesscher came before the commission and in the name of Messrs. Boker & Co. made a proposition for the settlement of their account with the United States. It was to the effect that Boker & Co. would ship no more arms if the government would consent to receive all the arms they have now in store, as well as those in transitu, and would pay cost price for their arms, and all expenses, with freight, storage, insurance, &c., allowing Boker & Co. 2½ per cent. commission on their purchases for their services in the premises.

This proposition was acceptable to Boker & Co. on condition that the government would immediately make an advance to their house of $500,000 upon account.

P. V. HAGNER, *Major of Ordnance.*

Before commission, May 5, 1862.

Mr. George Wright, being duly sworn, states :

I received my orders in Washington September 6, and left Washington same day, and New York in steamer of the 11th. My order was to go to Europe and inspect arms to be delivered by Boker & Co. These orders, in words, required all the arms to be new and in good condition, rifled, and of .69 or .58 calibre.

My impressions derived from my knowledge of the wants of the government for arms, and for some I had seen before leaving, and also from the rate of payment prescribed, (not to exceed $18,) convinced me that I should not refuse serviceable arms even if not "new;" and as to calibre, I was ordered to receive those near enough to the calibres of .58 and .69 to use our ammunition. Under subsequent instructions, dated October 22, I considered myself authorized to accept from .69 to .72. I met in Liverpool Mr. Funke, of the firm of Boker & Co. He accompanied me to Liege or Cologne, where I commenced duty.

I found in Cologne samples which were submitted to me of lots of guns ready for inspection. I selected from these samples such as I considered might answer and went to Liege to inspect. I have retained copies of all the certificates I gave.

My course of inspection was to take up a gun from the box, requiring a box here and there to be opened for me, to feel the strength of the mainspring, the spring of the ramrod, the fit and the material of the bayonet. I did not take a lock off, except once. I suppose I have taken off a dozen barrels and taken out the breech pins, to see about the rifling. I went away in such haste I had nothing to inspect a gun with except a taper gauge for calibre. My trade originally was a tinsmith, but I have practiced myself as a machinist. I have had no experience as an armorer, except in repairing our own arms in the shops in the Washington arsenal. When I left the country I professed to be a good judge of an arm.

Question. How many arms would you look at in a box, and how many boxes would you have opened in a hundred, for example?

Answer. It depended upon the locality, number, and time. In Vienna 25,000 .55 calibre, from the government arsenal, were examined but little; I took off no barrels and no locks, as they were in the government arsenal; and I only handled a few of them, feeling satisfied that they had been thoroughly inspected by the Austrian government. These arms were made in 1860–'62. Mr. Schuyler bought a lot of the same arms from the same storehouse before, and Mr. Rhuleman had inspected them, as I heard, and I believe rejected none.

Of the other lots of guns inspected at Vienna I handled at least 30 per cent. I do not know how many I inspected there, and I can form no estimate. I do not intend to say that I took off the locks or took out the barrels or the breech pins of any. I have visited often the shops of manufacturers in Vienna and examined barrels, locks, and stocks.

I looked upon my orders as to the time within which I should inspect and receive as limiting me to the time specified; and when I gave the certificates at the expiration of that time I conceived it to be optional with the government to receive the arms thus inspected and certified to, or not to receive, as they might choose after arrival in New York. I, of course, except from this the new arms of .58 calibre, delivered under the second contract, which I received.

The terms of that contract allow until April to fill it, but I had received all before I left Vienna on the 7th April.

This contract requires the exact calibre, .58, but I did not require it exactly. I think all the arms will receive our .58 ammunition. I considered the same instructions to apply to the second contract as to the first, those dated September 6. I received no other instructions, and no notice of the second contract, except a copy of it shown me by Mr. Funke. I kept no account of the work done and no records, except the triplicate copy of certificates. I took the number they offered, as they told me they had orders, and I supposed it was correct. I do not know how many I received under the first contract. I examined all they offered me, and do not recollect about the number. Mr. Funke told me which lots were offered under the first contract and which under the second, but I made no note of this on the certificates and made no report to the department. The arms of which I stated I examined thirty per cent. in Vienna I should have said were on the second contract. I did not handle thirty per cent. of those I received under the first contract, but only a few here and there. I inspected, under the first contract, in Marseilles, the arms styled "Chasseurs de Vincennes," of which Captain Crispin writes. Of these I only opened a few boxes. They were in the freight depot of the railroad.

May 7.—By direction of the commission Mr. Wright again appeared and produced a statement, showing the dates of certificates given by him, together with the place of inspection, and the number of arms inspected and certified by him under the order to H. Boker & Co. of November 25, 1861.

The commission direct that Mr. Wright shall report, in addition to the above, upon each statement, the marks upon the boxes of arms passed by him and referred to in each certificate; and also that he shall furnish a statement like the above regarding sabres inspected and certified to; and that he also have permission to submit a detailed statement of his official acts abroad, with copies of the orders under which he acted.

Question. Did the Messrs. Boker & Co. offer you arms for inspection, under the first order of September 5, after the expiration of sixty days from the date of your sailing?

Answer. They did.

Question. Did you inspect and give certificates for such arms?

Answer. I did.

Question. Under what authority?

Answer. I thought my letter of instructions justified it, and I was also induced to do it by the declarations of Boker & Co.

Question. Can you tell how many of the arms were offered before November 11, and how many after it?

Answer. I cannot, definitely.

Question. Can you say approximately?

Answer. I can from the papers, and will when I produce them. I can be certain about some of those offered after November 11.

Question. What declarations were made to you by Boker & Co. about the date of the expiration of the sixty days?

Answer. Mr. Funke called my attention to my letter of instructions, stating that I was not limited to sixty days to make my inspections; that they had the arms at different places.

Question. Did you consider that under your instructions you could inspect any arms not delivered, on account of the order of September 5, for inspection after the expiration of the sixty days from the date of your sailing?

Answer. I did not so consider,

Question. Did you inspect any such?

Answer. I cannot say; they told me in a general manner that they had the arms in several places. I took no account at the time, made no record of numbers, and did not visit at once the places.

COMMISSION ON ORDNANCE AND ORDNANCE STORES,
Washington, March 27, 1862.

GENERAL: The commission have the honor to report:

CASE NO. 15.—HERMAN BOKER & Co., New York.

Orders.—First dated September 5, 1861, and second November 23, 1861; specially referred by Secretary of War. No. 24, page 11, and No. 50, page 13, printed list.

For 100,000, and upwards, rifled muskets, new and in good condition, and 18,000 sabres.

Price of muskets not to exceed $18; price of sabres not to exceed $7 50. To be delivered in New York, to be inspected abroad, to be delivered for inspection between the 30th and 60th day from the date of the agent or inspector sailing for Europe. The terms of the second order as follows: to deliver 50,000 .58 calibre rifled muskets and 10,000 cavalry sabres; the muskets at $18 each, and the sabres at $7 50, properly packed for shipment, inspected abroad and delivered prior to May 1st.

The commission find—

That 142,000 arms (about) are offered under the first order, and 28,000 sabres, and about 30,000 arms and 10,000 sabres will be in New York, in fulfilment of the second order, before notice to cease shipments can reach Europe.

The arms delivered by the Messrs. Boker include many of patterns unsuitable for issue to troops, not "new and in good condition," as described in their proposition to the Secretary of War, upon which is based his acceptance.

It appears, however, that the inspector, duly appointed by the government to proceed to Europe and inspect these arms, has given certificates of inspection to the full extent of the 142,000, (about,) describing the boxes, by marks thereupon, as containing certain numbers of arms conforming in all respects, in his judgment, to the requirements of the order given to the Messrs. Boker & Co.

Under such circumstances the arms thus inspected and approved by the inspector, it may be, should be received by the government, but it remains by the terms of the first order for the government to affix a suitable price to each kind and quality, not exceeding $18.

The appraisement, with this purpose, has been ordered by the Secretary of War, and is before the commission.

The Messrs. Boker & Co., represented by their Mr. Schleicher, having appeared before the commission and stated the extreme urgency of an immediate advance to enable their house to meet its business engagements, proposed a plan of adjustment, which the commission has carefully considered, and agree to accept as follows:

WASHINGTON, *March* 25, 1862.

To settle our contracts made with the War Department, dated September 5, 1861, and November 23, 1861, we propose that we will furnish proof, based upon original invoices, fortified, if required, by affidavit, of the bare cost of the goods, including actual expenses, and agree to receive the same, with two and a half per cent. commission, in lieu of personal expenses and time employed, in full of all demands.

In conformity with this, we will now give our obligation, providing the commission is willing now to grant us the advance of money necessary to save our house from bankruptcy. No more arms to be shipped, but the commission agreeing to receive those already in the country or on the voyage hither.

Very respectfully,

HERMAN BOKER & CO.

Hon. JOSEPH HOLT,
Hon. R. D. OWEN,
Commissioners on Contracts.

In accepting the above the commission require that the Messrs. Boker & Co. shall supervise, as heretofore done by them, the delivery to the ordnance officer in New York, or to such other as the ordnance department may appoint to receive,. without charge, for services of self or agent, of—

1st. All arms and sabres now in port in New York, found to be covered by certificate of inspection, withholding such as may be broken or rusted since being packed.

2d. That a number not exceeding 142,000 be presented under the first order, and only those *here actually, now on the voyage hither, or which may leave a European port not later than April* 11, 1862, under the second order.

3d. That the expenses chargeable, under this agreement, be only—

1st. The prime cost of the arms boxed for shipping.

2d. The freight to port of shipment.

3d. The freight on shipboard to New York and insurance.

4th. The actual cost of cartage and storage in New York. The commission understanding that the two and a half per cent. upon "the bare cost, including actual expenses," is in lieu of all other charges whatever, except as above stated.

The commission find that the $500,000 now requested to be advanced by the Messrs. Boker & Co., together with all payments and advances heretofore made to them on this account, in this country and in Europe, as far as known to the government authorities, does not equal the amount to be due them under this agreement; therefore direct that $500,000 be now paid to them.

As a proper protection, however, to the interests of the United States, they require that sufficient bond be given by Messrs. Boker & Co. to reimburse the United States any excess of advances now ordered, and payments and advances heretofore made at home and abroad, should any such excess appear over the sum due to them upon final settlement of this account according to this agreement.

We are, sir, very respectfully, your obedient servants,

J. HOLT,
ROBERT DALE OWEN,
Commissioners, &c.

General J. W. RIPLEY, *Chief of Ordnance.*

WASHINGTON, *May* 8, 1862.

GENTLEMEN: In accordance with your direction of yesterday, I beg leave to submit the following report of my inspection of arms in Europe:

On the evening of the 5th of September, 1861, about ten o'clock, I was sent for by General J. W. Ripley, chief of ordnance, and directed to call on him immediately at Willard's hotel. In compliance with the order I called, and was told by him that I would be required to perform some special duty in Europe, and was directed to call at the Ordnance office on the following morning for instructions. I called accordingly and received some verbal instructions, together with a letter, more fully defining my duties, which will be found on page 78 in House of Representatives Ex. Doc. No. 67, second session 37th Congress.

With the above-mentioned order I left Washington on the 6th September and proceeded to New York, whence I sailed for Europe on the 11th of September, as directed by Messrs. Boker & Co., into whose hands my instructions placed me, and to whom alone I looked for information in reference to the localities of their arms, as well as for my personal expenses whilst abroad.

On or about the 22d September I landed in Liverpool, where I met Mr. Funke, a partner in the firm of H. Boker & Co., and, in company with him, proceeded to the continent to enter upon the discharge of the duties assigned me.

I beg leave here to remark that before leaving Washington I was fully impressed with the urgent demands upon government for small arms, and that these demands must be met speedily, if at all; that scrutinizing inspection into the quality could be far more easily made in this country, where the government had sufficient inspectors at their disposal, than by myself, charged with the inspection of so large a number in so short a space of time.

I knew, also, that the government had an adequate safeguard for its protection in the clause in the contract given to Messrs. H. Boker & Co., that the guns were to cost not more than $18; thus leaving the arms subject to a valuation by the government.

At or about the termination of the sixty days limited in my instructions, Mr. Funke requested me to continue my inspection, using language to the effect that if I had not inspected the arms it was no fault of theirs. This caused me to look more carefully over my letter of instructions, and my construction of it was that I was directed to inspect arms delivered within the sixty days, and not that my inspections were to cease with the sixty days. How many arms Boker & Co. had ready for inspection at various points in Europe within the sixty days specified I am totally unable to say. I do know, however, that I was constantly employed in inspecting arms and sabres during the whole time that I remained in Europe. During my stay in Europe I was constantly and intimately associated with Mr. Funke. This association engendered confidence, and this confidence was strengthened by seeing letters, or extracts therefrom, from the War Department, in corroboration of verbal statements previously made to me by him; in fact, I was led to rely almost entirely on Boker & Co. for directions, as my letters to the department had remained unanswered.

On the 22d February, 1862, however, I received, through Mr. Dayton, our minister at Paris, two official communications from the Ordnance office. The purport of these orders had reached me some time previous to their receipt by or through the ordinary channel of intelligence—the Messrs. Boker & Co.

These orders I regarded as emphatically confirming all which I had previously done in Europe, as a reference thereto will show that my sphere of action in reference to the inspection of arms had been materially enlarged from the dates of said orders.

Copies of these orders you will please find enclosed; also abstract of arms and sabres inspected by me.

Holding myself in readiness to make to the honorable commission any further statements they may require, I subscribe myself, very respectfully, your obedient servant,

GEO. W. WRIGHT.

Hon. JOSEPH HOLT and Hon. ROBERT DALE OWEN,
Commissioners, &c.

Signed by me, and given in as a part of my testimony.

GEO. WRIGHT.

ORDNANCE OFFICE,
Washington, November 27, 1861.

SIR: By direction of the Secretary of War, you will remain in Europe until April, to look after the inspection of arms to be secured by our ministers and others Respectfully, &c.,

J. W. RIPLEY, *Brig. General.*

Mr. GEO. WRIGHT,
Care of United States Minister, Paris, France.

ORDNANCE OFFICE,
Washington, December 7, 1861.

SIR: I am directed by the Secretary of War to instruct you to remain subject to the instructions of Mr. Sanford, United States minister at Belgium, until all the guns ordered by him, Mr. Schuyler, and Mr. Boker are inspected and shipped to this country.

This letter is intended to supersede mine of the 27th ultimo.

Respectfully, your obedient servant,

J. W. RIPLEY, *Brig. General.*

Mr. GEO. WRIGHT,
    Care of United States Minister, Paris, France.

Before commission, May 13, 1862.

Mr. George Wright:

Question. Where did you see the sample of the Marseilles arm first ?
Answer. I do not recollect; I think it was in Paris.
Question. Are you sure it was like these arms now shown you ?
Answer. I think so.
Question. Would you pass such arms as these, under your instruction, as you see them, knowing them to be of large calibre, grooved in the barrel without a twist, and having the Delvigne chamber so long that the ball cannot bear upon the powder when the gun is loaded ?
Answer. I do not know that I should, had I examined them sufficient to know all this.
Question. Did you examine the sample with any more care than the guns generally ?
Answer. No, sir.
Question. It appears from your statement that you examined over 38,000 sabres. State how it happened that you exceeded the number ordered.
Answer. Mr. Funke told me that the order had been increased to 28,000, under the first contract; this, with the 10,000 of the second contract, makes the total, very nearly.
Question. Did you hear of the price paid for any of the Boker arms ?
Answer. I did hear Mr. Funke say that they had agreed to pay $16 for one lot of 10,000, which came out of the arsenal at Vienna. I am not sure whether he meant Prussian thalers or American dollars, as it did not impress itself upon me particularly.

Before commission, June 5, 1862,

Appeared M. H. Boker, jr., of the firm of Herman Boker & Co., and presented the accounts of that firm for arms purchased for the United States, prepared as required by the decision of the commission, dated March 27, 1862.

WASHINGTON, D. C., *June* 7, 1862.

As there seems to be a misunderstanding with your honorable commission as to why the government inspector continued his inspection of arms after the sixty days specified in his instructions had elapsed, and why our firm continued their shipments after that period, we beg leave to submit the following for your consideration:

Before the expiration of the sixty days above mentioned, we were informed by our partners in Europe that the government inspector had written to Washington, stating that it would be impossible for him to inspect all the arms offered in sixty days, and asking further instructions.

Referring to his letter we called on Hon. Thomas A. Scott, Assistant Secretary of War, and asked that instructions might be sent him. The Assistant Secretary of War assured us verbally that such instructions had been forwarded, and this we immediately communicated to our partners in Europe, and at their instance the inspection of arms offered by us was continued. Upon the verbal assurance of our partners, based upon the assurances we had received from Mr. Scott, our inspection was continued, and the inspector acted solely under the direction of our partners in Europe, until he received the letters of the Ordnance department of November 27 and December 7, which confirmed what he had previously done, and directed him to remain subject to the instructions of Mr. Sanford, United States minister at Brussels, until *all the guns ordered by him, Mr. Schuyler, and Mr. Boker are inspected and shipped to this country.*

Respectfully, your obedient servant,

HERMAN BOKER & CO.

Hons. JOSEPH HOLT and ROBERT DALE OWEN,
Commissioners, &c.

ORDNANCE OFFICE,
No. 55 White street, New York, April 28, 1862.

GENERAL : I have on the files of this office a certificate of inspection, signed by George Wright, the United States inspector appointed to examine and approve arms to be delivered to the government under the first contract of the Messrs. H. Boker & Co., of New York, calling for 8,748 rifled muskets, marked R. A. Eight thousand six hundred and eighty-nine have been released from bond, contained in cases, marked as above stated. They have been examined and counted, and now await reception.

These guns, I find, are all old and have evidently seen long and hard service. They are a French model, calibre .708, and in peculiarities of shape of lock, stock and barrel, and dimensions, are about the same as the present French rifle, well known as the French carbine. They are, however, a chambered arm, the old and abandoned plan of M. Delvigne, for destroying windage, using the round ball—relics of the past in the history of rifled arms.

The ramrod is cupped for a round ball, as of course should be expected.

The hausse is a simple standing sight and leaf folding on the barrel with notches for different ranges, a clumsy and inefficient sight as compared with the present model. I should judge the barrel to have belonged to the French smooth-bore musket, and been altered at the time when Delvigne's plan was in vogue. The most peculiar feature of the arms, if they are all like the samples examined, is, however, that they are lightly grooved, straight, or if any twist at all exists, it cannot be detected with the eye.

As they are grooved, but so grooved as to be incapable of giving rotary motion to the ball, I can neither call them a rifled arm nor a smooth-bore musket. From the above it would appear that the arms are old, of an abandoned model, and inferior, if anything, to a smooth-bore musket in consideration of the chamber and straight grooves ; and in consequence, if received, should only be used in cases where the emergency of the service demand their issue.

In the offer of the Messrs. H. Boker & Co. to the Secretary of War, dated September 5, 1861, they propose delivering arms " new and in good condition." The commission on ordnance and ordnance stores, in their decision of this case, state that " under the circumstances it *may be* that the arms thus inspected and approved by a United States inspector should be received by the government;" providing, I infer from this phraseology, for the possibility of the contingency of points arising, in the course of the reception of these arms, which might require a further consideration on their part, or at least render it proper for me to refer to them for instructions.

Under these circumstances, and from the character of the arms, I think it proper and necessary for me not to assume the responsibility of the reception of these arms without a reference to higher authority. I have accordingly to request, if meeting your approval, that you will refer this communication to the commission on ordnance and ordnance stores, in order that I may receive such instruction as they may have to give in the matter. In the meantime I shall await their decision.

I forward two samples of these arms to you by express to-day, in accordance with previous instructions.

Very respectfully, your obedient servant,

S. CRISPIN,
Captain of Ordnance

General J. W. RIPLEY,
  Chief of Ordnance, Washington, D. C.

(Report on above.)

COMMISSION ON ORDNANCE,
Washington, June 10, 1862.

The commission direct that these arms be accepted, as having been shipped upon certificate of inspection given by George Wright; they are embraced in the number to be paid for by the United States.

P. V. HAGNER, *Major of Ordnance,*
Assistant to Commission.

Before commission, June 10, 1862.

Major P. V. Hagner submitted the following statement showing the result of his examination of the various abstracts of deliveries as charged by Boker & Co., compared with the "STATEMENT OF ARMS DELIVERED BY H. BOKER & CO., *in accordance with certificates of inspection signed by George Wright, on file at the ordnance office, No.* 55 *White street, New York,*" furnished to the commission by Captain Silas Crispin, ordnance department.

The prices opposite each variety of arm are made up, in accordance with the decision of the commission, from—

1st. The actual cost price from the manufacturer or holder, as shown by original or certified bills rendered against H. Boker & Co., supported by affidavit and acknowledged before the United States consul.

2d. Freight bills to port of shipment.

3d. Freight on shipboard to New York and insurance.

4th. Bills for storage in New York, (all of these classes supported by original bills duly authenticated.)

5th. Charges for cartage in New York.

6th. Commission of 2½ per cent. on above.

The numbers of each class in the two statements of Captain Crispin and H. Boker & Co. agree.

Sabres.

10,650 at 15 francs each.
23,650 at 18 francs each.
3,850 at 19 francs each.

Total.......... 38,150

Estimating the franc at $22\frac{80}{100}$ cents, giving average price per sabre, $3 $90\frac{15}{100}$.

Fire-arms, (muskets and rifles.)

Class 1.................... 4,440 at $22\frac{50}{100}$ francs.
" 2.................... 600 at 24 "
" 3.................... 1,992 at 25 "
" 4.................... 7,931 at $27\frac{50}{100}$ "
" 5.................... 12,332 at 30 "
" 6.................... 5,488 at 35 "
" 7.................... 4,588 at 38 "
" 8.................... 847 at 45 "
" 9.................... 3,928 at 46 "
" 10.................... 6,940 at 47 "
" 11.................... 4,100 at 50 "
" 12.................... 9,350 at $50\frac{50}{100}$ "
" 13.................... 236 at 55 "
" 14.................... 3,486 at $56\frac{25}{100}$ "
" 15.................... 21,945 at $57\frac{50}{100}$ "
" 16.................... 1,824 at 60 "
" 17.................... 25,247 at $63\frac{75}{100}$ "
" 18.................... 2,272 at 65 "
" 19.................... 51,819 at $68\frac{75}{100}$ "
" 20.................... 18,689 at $16\frac{40}{100}$, (sixteen dollars and forty cts.)

Total............ 188,054 muskets and rifles.

I certify that I have carefully collated the items of these statements, and find that the total number of sabres authorized to be received by the decision of the commission, dated March 27, 1862, amounts to 38,150, (thirty-eight thousand one hundred and fifty,) and that the average price (as authorized to be charged) is $3 $90\frac{15}{100}$, three dollars and ninety cents and fifteen one-hundredths of a cent,) each sabre; and that the total number of fire-arms, authorized as above to be received, amounts to 188,054, (one hundred and eighty-eight thousand and fifty-four,) to be charged as stated opposite each class, of the twenty classes, in francs, and that the rate of $22\frac{80}{100}$ cents per franc is the correct rate of charge, including all and every allowance awarded to be paid by the United States, by the decision of the commission of the above date.

P. V. HAGNER,
Major of Ordnance, Assistant to Commission.
WASHINGTON, *June* 10, 1862.

Condensed statement of H. Boker & Co.'s account.

To 38,150 cavalry sabres, at $3 $90\frac{15}{100}$.................... $148,842 22½
To 188,054 rifles and rifle muskets........................ 2,413,407 04

2,562,249 24

By payments made—
By U.S. minister, H.L. Sanford, Dec. 6, 1861.... $30,000 00
Do. do. do. Dec. 19, 1861.... 40,000 00
Do. do. do. Dec. 11, 1861.... 20,520 00
Do. do. do. Dec. 17, 1861.... 29,220 00
Do. do. do. Dec. 26, 1861.... 84,355 00
Do. do. do. Jan. 2, 1862.... 50,000 00
Do. do. do. Feb. 13, 1862.... 40,000 00
Do. do. do. Nov. 20, 1861.... 148,800 00
By payments made from United States treasury,
Nov. 21, 1861 .... 117,430 00

By payments made from United States treasury,
Dec. 16, 1861 ....$249,922 50
By payments made from United States treasury,
March 31, 1862.......................... 500,000 00
———————— $1,310,247 50

June 10, 1862. Balance due H. Boker & Co................ 1,252,001 74

Balance due to H. Boker & Co., one million two hundred and fifty-two thousand and one dollars and seventy-four cents, ($1,252,001 74.)
 E. E.   P. V. HAGNER,
                 Major of Ordnance.
WASHINGTON, *June* 10, 1862.

          OFFICE OF COMMISSION ON ORDNANCE, &c.,
            Washington, June 10, 1862.

The items of the above accounts have been carefully examined by the commission and are approved, it appearing that the number of arms (and sabres) stated agree with the numbers acknowledged to have been received by the United States ordnance officers at New York, and as reported upon the certificates of inspection signed by G. Wright, United States inspector, in Europe; that the prices charged are in conformity with the decision of this commission, dated March 27, 1862; and that the credits acknowledged agree with the sums stated to have been paid to the Messrs. Boker & Co. on this account.

The commission, therefore, direct that this account, accompanied by the statement of arms, &c., forwarded by Captain S. Crispin, ordnance officer, No. 55 White street, New York, and bearing certificate of Major P. V. Hagner, assistant to commission, be examined and audited, without objection as to the number of arms and sabres or as to the price per gun or sabre as therein stated.
          J. HOLT,
          ROBERT DALE OWEN,
                Commissioners.
          P. V. HAGNER,
      Major of Ordnance, Assistant to Commission.
The CHIEF OF ORDNANCE.

        COMMISSION ON ORDNANCE AND ORDNANCE STORES,
           Washington, June 10, 1862.

GENERAL: By direction of the commission, I enclose herewith the account of H. Boker & Co. for arms furnished by them under the orders given by the Secretary of War dated September 5 and November 25, 1861, duly approved by the commission, and directed to be examined and audited as usual, without objection as to the number of arms or sabres or to the prices charged therein.
   Very respectfully, your obedient servant,
          P. V. HAGNER, *Major of Ordnance.*
Brigadier General J. W. RIPLEY,
     Chief of Ordnance.

        COMMISSION ON ORDNANCE AND ORDNANCE STORES,
           Washington, June 11, 1862.

SIR: The commission directs me to say that the examination made by them has shown that H. Boker & Co.'s account for arms is correct, according to their decision, in the number of arms charged and in the price for each kind. The price as stated includes every expense whatever that is authorized to be charged to this transaction.

This leaves for examination—

1st. The accuracy of the calculations in the main account—that is, whether the number of arms, at the price stated, amounts to the sum stated in each case.

2d. The correctness of the credits at your office, as per previous payments. The commission have examined the statement of receipts from the United States minister, H. L. Sanford, esq., and find these agree, as stated in the account current of the Messrs. Boker, with Mr. Sanford's charge against this firm.

These facts are stated to relieve you from the labor of examination into details, which has already been made by the commission, under the orders from the Secretary of War; and the statement is necessary, as it appears that the papers explanatory of these details have accompanied the main account to your office from the ordnance office. It was supposed by the commission, and is so stated in their decision, that Captain Crispin's "statement of arms received, as per certificates of inspection," need in fact only be sent to your office, as the duty assigned to the commission required of them a settlement of other points. The sole object of this communication is to inform you officially of the facts, so that you may relieve yourself, as far as you may think proper, from labor in auditing the account, and save delay to Mr. Boker in the settlement.

Very respectfully, your obedient servant,

P. V. HAGNER, *Major of Ordnance.*

Mr. E. B. FRENCH,
    Second Auditor.

COMMISSION ON ORDNANCE,
Washington, June 12, 1862.

SIR: In reply to your request, the commission directs me to say that they consent to state to the Secretary of the Treasury that in the adjustment made of H. Boker & Co.'s accounts for arms they expected payment would be made without loss to Messrs. Boker & Co. by delay.

Very respectfully, your obedient servant,

P. V. HAGNER, *Major of Ordnance.*

J. MADISON CUTTS, Esq.,
    Second Comptroller.

CASE No. 16.

W. V. BARKALOW.

ORDNANCE OFFICE,
Washington, November 2, 1861.

By direction of the Secretary of War, I offer you an order for twenty-six thousand (26,000) *long English Enfield rifles*, with angular bayonets and appendages, to be fully up to the government standard in every particular, and to be delivered at the United States arsenal on Governor's island, as follows, viz: three thousand (3,000) in sixty days from this date, three thousand (3,000) more in ninety days from this date, and four thousand (4,000) per month thereafter until the whole 26,000 shall have been delivered. These arms and appendages are to be subject to inspection by such officers as this department may designate for the purpose, and none are to be received or paid for by the government but such as are approved by the United States inspector. In case of any failure to make the deliveries as above specified, the government is authorized to revoke and annul this order immediately.

Payments will be made on each delivery, as before specified, in such funds as the Treasury Department may provide, on certificates of inspection and receipt by the United States inspector, at the rate of twenty dollars ($20) for each rifle, including appendages, in bond. The deliveries of the 26,000 arms and appendages may be made as much sooner than the times specified as you may choose.

Please signify your acceptance or non-acceptance of this order on the terms and conditions herein stated.

Respectfully, your obedient servant,

WM. MAYNADIER,
Lieutenant Colonel of Ordnance.

Mr. W. V. BARKALOW,
  No. 1 Park Place, New York.

ORDNANCE OFFICE,
Washington, January 14, 1862.

SIR: By direction of the Secretary of War, the times for the delivery of the 26,000 *long English Enfield* rifles, with appendages, ordered from you on the 2d November, 1861, are extended as follows, viz: three thousand (3,000) in ninety days from this date, three thousand more in four months from this date, and four thousand per month thereafter until the whole 26,000 shall have been delivered. The deliveries may be made as much sooner than the time specified as you may choose. All the other terms and conditions of the order of the 2d November, 1861, are to remain unchanged.

Your obedient servant,

JAMES W. RIPLEY,
Brigadier General.

Mr. W. V. BARKALOW,
  No. 1 Park Place, New York.

[Per "Africa," *via* Queenstown.]

LIVERPOOL, *January* 18, 1862.

DEAR SIR: The proclamation prohibiting the export of arms was withdrawn last night, and I believe the shipments to the United States are now being resumed. I have therefore informed Mr. Linder that I am ready to take charge of your goods.

You may be aware that arms can be shipped only by the Inman (propeller) line of steamers. We may mutually congratulate one another on the issue of the late difficulty between the two countries.

I am, dear sir, yours truly,

ALFRED THORNEBY.

S. KIRKPATRICK, Esq.,
  No. 1 Park Place, New York.

NEW YORK, *February* 3, 1862.

SIR: In compliance with your order of January 29, permit me to give notice of an order issued to me by the War Department on November 2, 1861, for 26,000 Enfield rifles, as per copy herewith.

Immediately on receipt of the order I despatched an agent to England to purchase and forward the arms, which has been attended with considerable expense to me. He arrived in England about the time that the news of the taking of Mason and Slidell reached there. He had purchased and had 3,000 arms ready for shipment in time to comply with the terms of the order when the proclamation prohibiting the shipment of arms to *America* was put in force, and although he used every means in his power to get them shipped, it was at that time impossible. He left an agent in England to forward the arms to fill the order as soon as an opportunity offered, and returned to lay the matter before the department, and ask for an extension of time to enable me to make the deliveries, feeling confident, from what he saw of the feeling of the people of England, that if Mason and Slidell were given up all would be quiet, and the prohibition would be removed.

I give you those facts to show you that everything has been done on my part to furnish the arms, and the failure to comply with the terms of the order was only owing to a misunderstanding between the two governments, a circumstance over which I could not have any control. I laid a statement of those facts before the department in January, and on the 14th received an extension of time, as per copy herewith.

I enclose a letter from my shipping agent, per Africa, dated Liverpool, January 18, (see copy enclosed,) informing me that the prohibition had been withdrawn, and he was ready to ship the arms.

After getting the renewal on January 14 I wrote my agent in England to go on and make his purchases and contracts for the whole 26,000, and ship the first opportunity, which will cause a heavy loss to me in case the order should now be annulled. As there is now no doubt about my ability to comply with the terms of the renewal, I beg that you will take the circumstances into consideration, and sanction the renewal or issue a new order on the same terms.

Respectfully, &c.,

W. V. BARKALOW.

Hon. E. M. STANTON,
Secretary of War.

ORDNANCE OFFICE, *February* 13, 1862.

Respectfully returned: Mr. Barkalow, by direction of the Secretary of War, received an order dated November 2, 1861, for 26,000 *long English* Enfield rifles to be delivered, 3,000 in 60 days from 2d November, 1861; 3,000 more in 90 days from same date, and 4,000 per month thereafter, till the whole 26,000 were delivered. By direction of the Secretary of War the time was extended, on the 14th of January, 1862, to the delivery of the first 3,000 in 90 days from that date; 3,000 more in four months from said date, and 4,000 per month thereafter, till the whole 26,000 were delivered. He has not delivered any of the arms, but states his ability to comply with the order, as extended, and requests a sanction of that extension, or a new order. The order of Mr. Barkalow is among those revoked and annulled by your published order of the 29th of January last.

JAMES W. RIPLEY, *Brigadier General.*

WASHINGTON, *March* 20, 1862.

GENTS: Enclosed please find copies of order, and renewal of my order for arms, with a statement from memory, being in substance a copy of my letter of February 1 or 3, to Secretary Stanton. On February 3 or 4 I called at the War Department to see the Secretary of War and hand him the papers of which the enclosed are copies. I could not see him but saw the assistant, Mr. Tucker, who read the papers and said, in reply to my letter to Mr. Stanton, that Mr. Stanton had said it was not intended by his order of January 29 to annul any orders made by direction of the former Secretary of War if the party to whom the order was granted complied with the conditions. I told him that the banker through whom we attained our credit in England required to have that explanation in writing or the order indorsed by the present Secretary of War. He said he presumed the Secretary would not object to state in writing what he had said verbally, but as I could not then see the Secretary himself, I requested Mr. Tucker to obtain a written statement from the Secretary confirming his, Mr. Tucker's, verbal assurance that the order of January 29 did not interfere with orders that were being filled in good faith. I returned to New York and made my arrangements to leave for England thence by the steamer of the 12th, as I had missed the steamer of the 5th. I could not, however, make a move further until I received the above letter from the Secretary of War. As it did not arrive, I came again to Washington and called upon Mr. Tucker at the War Department, and found that Secretary Stanton had been ill and nothing had been done. He said that the Secretary was so very much occupied that he could not say when he could reach it, but hoped to reach those matters within a week. I came here again and did not get any more information than on former occasions. I then returned to New York and wrote to the Secretary of War on the 22d of February, begging him to give me the desired information, and that I would call upon him on the 24th of February. I came here on the morning of the 24th and could not see the Secretary; the department was closed (although it was Monday) in consequence of the funeral of the President's son. I remained here two days and then saw Mr. Watson, who said he could not say anything about the matter; he said all such matters were in his hands, but he did not know when they would be reached. I have made in all seven trips from New York since I left the papers with Mr. Tucker, and each time remained from two days to one week in endeavoring to get an answer to my question in my letter of the 1st of February to Secretary Stanton. This portion of the business alone has cost me over $300 and six weeks time. If I could have received an answer to my letter I could have had the first 3,000 arms here now, and could have delivered the whole in less time than the order gives me, but as I have lost that time by the impossibility to obtain that reply, I feel that I am justly entitled to sufficient time, say, grant me the time I have lost, say from February 5 to the date on which you decide this matter, and I will increase the last five deliveries to 5,000 each, thereby reducing the time for the whole delivery one month. With this statement of facts, all of which I am satisfied Mr. Tucker will corroborate, I leave the matter in your hands to be adjusted. As I only want to have justice done me, I feel that I am safe in your hands. As you will see by the dates on which these papers were left with Mr. Tucker, that it was only a few days after the order of January 29, and perhaps the first notice of court under the order, I think you could, without injustice to others, make it one of the first to be decided. Please let me know your decision as early as possible at No. 1 Park Place, New York.

Respectfully, &c.,

W. V. BARKALOW.

Hon. ROBERT DALE OWEN,
Hon. JOSEPH HOLT,
    Commissioners, &c.

No. 1 PARK PLACE, *New York, March* 18, 1862.

SIR: The bearer, Mr. I. Kirkpatrick, is my partner in an order which I have from the government for 26,000 Enfield rifles. He is fully authorized to act in all matters connected with said order in my stead. Mr. Kirkpatrick will hand you a letter from Messrs. Winslow, Lavine & Co. As Mr. Kirkpatrick went to England to purchase the arms, he can explain it all to you more fully than I could myself.

Yours, respectfully,

W. V. BARKALOW.

Hon. ROBERT DALE OWEN, *Washington.*

WASHINGTON, *March* 27, 1862.

GENTS: In reply to your proposition to compromise my order for twenty-six thousand Enfield rifles by granting me a new order for eight thousand instead. I hereby accept the terms you propose, and will deliver the eight thousand Enfield rifles in bond in New York at twenty dollars each as follows, viz: two thousand in sixty days from April 1; three thousand more in ninety days from April 1, and three thousand more in four months from April 1.

Yours, respectfully,

W. V. BARKALOW,
Per KIRKPATRICK.

I should like to have the privilege of delivering all or any of the arms as much sooner than the terms specified as I may choose—all the arms to be subject to inspection by such officers as the government may appoint, and none to be taken or paid for except such as are fully up to the government standard.

Yours, respectfully,

W. V. BARKALOW,
Per KIRKPATRICK.

COMMISSION ON ORDNANCE AND ORDNANCE STORES,
Washington, March 27, 1862.

GENERAL: The commission have the honor to report as follows:

CASE No.16.—W. V. BARKALOW, of New York, represented by J. KIRKPATRICK, of New York, at his request.

Order dated November 2, 1861, No. 39, printed list, page 11. Referred by order of the Secretary of War. — To deliver in New York 26,000 first class long Enfield muskets, $20 each, with implements; time of first delivery, 3,000, February 2, 1862; subsequently extended to 14th of April. Suspended under general order.

The commission find that, upon receipt of this order, Mr. Barkalow immediately entered upon its fulfilment in good faith and with all zeal; that his progress in England was entirely interrupted by the Queen's proclamation; that upon return to this country and withdrawal of the proclamation, they asked and received an extension, but that immediately thereafter the general order in reference to the suspension of contracts made it prudent for him to await more explicit instructions. Mr. Barkalow's agent represents that advances have already been made by Mr. B., and that he is absolutely responsible for the acceptance from the manufacturers of at least 6,000 arms.

The commission, considering that it is not advisable to receive from this source to the full extent of this order of Enfield arms, but that under the circumstances a portion should be accepted, direct that 8,000 arms be received in accordance with the terms of the original order, provided that the quality of the arms be of the *first class*, only, at the high price named ($20;) and that all slightly inferior arms be graded at lower prices according to the judgment of the inspecting officer; and also provided that the first delivery, of not less than 2,000, be made on or before the 1st day of June, and that the whole number be delivered on or before the 1st September, 1862.

Mr. Kirkpatrick, representative and partner of Mr. Barkalow, has notified the commission in writing of his acceptance of the above as perfectly satisfactory.

We are, sir, very respectfully, your obedient servants,

J. HOLT,
ROBERT DALE OWEN,
Commissioners.

P. V. HAGNER,
Major of Ordnance, Assistant to Commission.

Brigadier General J. W. RIPLEY,
Chief of Ordnance.

Ex. Doc. 72——7

CASE No. 17.

HORSTMANN BROTHERS & CO.

PHILADELPHIA, *July* 22, 1861.

The undersigned manufacturers agree to furnish the following articles, delivered at the Frankford arsenal, agreeable to samples furnished by Lieutenant Treadwell:

Dragoon sabres, at $6 87½ per piece, and deliver 50 sabres per day, the first delivery within a fortnight from receipt of order.

Sergeants' swords, at $5 12½ per piece, and deliver 50 swords per day, the first delivery within a fortnight from receipt of order.

Musicians' swords, at $3 62½ per piece, and deliver 50 swords per day, the first delivery within a fortnight from receipt of order.

HORSTMANN BROS. & CO.

Lieutenant T. J. TREADWELL,
U. S. Arsenal, Frankford.

FRANKFORD ARSENAL, *July* 27, 1861.

SIRS: I am authorized by General J. W. Ripley, chief of ordnance, to accept your offer to make cavalry sabres, non-commissioned officers' swords, and musicians' swords, dated July 22.

Please make for this arsenal the following numbers of each, (to be in all respects equal in workmanship and material like patterns furnished, marked U. S.,) viz: 2,000 cavalry sabres, 1,000 non-commissioned officers' swords, and 500 musicians' swords.

I trust you will use your best endeavors to improve on your offer in point of time, as the department is very anxious to have deliveries of each as rapidly as your ability will permit. Any effort on your part to expedite this delivery will be highly appreciated by the department. All the sabres and swords must pass inspection. A copy of the tests required upon the inspection is herewith furnished.

Please notify me in writing of your acceptance of this order.

Fair rates will be allowed you for the packing boxes.

Very respectfully yours, &c.,

T. J. TREADWELL,
First Lieutenant of Ordnance.

Messrs. HORSTMANN BROS. & CO.,
Philadelphia, Pa.

FRANKFORD ARSENAL, *September* 21, 1861.

SIRS: I am authorized by the chief of ordnance to take all cavalry sabres, non-commissioned officers' and musicians' swords you can make and deliver by the 1st of November next, to be subject, of course, to the usual inspection, to be paid for in funds as the government may provide, (at the rates now paid you for these articles,) upon certificate of inspection.

Please acknowledge the receipt and acceptance of this order, and make deliveries as fast as possible.

Respectfully, your obedient servant,

T. J. TREADWELL,
First Lieutenant of Ordnance.

Messrs. HORSTMANN & BROS., *Philadelphia.*

ORDNANCE OFFICE,
Washington, October 26, 1861.

SIR: By direction of the Secretary of War you will extend your order, dated September 21, 1861, to Messrs. Horstmann & Bros., for four months, with the understanding that the sabres and swords are to be of their manufacture, and at the same price.

Respectfulty, your obedient servant,

JAS. W. RIPLEY, *Brig. Gen'l.*

Lieutenant T. J. TREADWELL,
Frankford Arsenal.

FRANKFORD ARSENAL, *October* 28, 1861.

GENTLEMEN: By direction of the Secretary of War I have been instructed to extend your order for swords and sabres, dated September 21, 1861, for four months, with the understanding that all the swords and sabres to be delivered under this extension shall be of your own manufacture, at the same price, and subject to the prescribed inspection.

Respectfully, your obedient servant,

T. J. TREADWELL,
First Lieutenant of Ordnance.

HORSTMANN BROS. & Co., *Philadelphia.*

FRANKFORD ARSENAL, *January* 22, 1862

SIRS: I have been notified by the chief of ordnance that the extension of four months heretofore granted to you under instruction dated Ordnance office, October 26, 1861, has been further extended for six months from the termination of the time mentioned above.

Very respectfully, your obedient servant,

T. J. TREADWELL,
First Lieutenant of Ordnance.

HORSTMANN BROS. & Co., *Philadelphia.*

FRANKFORD ARSENAL, *Pennsylvania, March* 13, 1862.

GENTLEMEN: I have this day received an order from the chief of ordnance, enclosing an order from the Secretary of War, directing that no more arms be received without special authority from the Secretary of War.

I return the sabres sent out by you to-day, as I cannot receive them without the authority above required.

Very respectfully, I am, gentlemen, your obedient servant,

T. T. S. LAIDLEY,
Brevet Major Commanding.

Messrs. HORSTMANN BROS. & Co., *Philadelphia.*

PHILADELPHIA, *March* 15, 1862.

SIRS: On the 13th instant we forwarded to the United States arsenal at Frankford, Peunsylvania, a delivery of sabres as usual on our contract, which were returned to us, with a letter from Major Laidley, of the United States ordnance, stating that he had just received instructions from the ordnance department in Washington, by order of the Secretary of War, to receive no more arms until further orders.

Upon inquiry as to the cause, we are directed to address ourselves to Washington.

The object of this is to state briefly our position, and to ask of your honorable commission an early consideration of our case.

Our house is, to the best of our knowledge, the oldest established manufacturers and dealers in military goods in the United States, and prior to the present war were one of the only two parties engaged in manufacturing swords.

In the early part of July last we were called upon by an officer of the United States ordnance department, who purchased the swords and sabres we had on hand, and were also requested by him to hand in proposals for the manufacture of additional supplies; and on the 27th July we received from the ordnance department at Washington, through Lieutenant Treadwell, in command of the Frankford arsenal, an order for sabres and swords, which was duly executed; and on the 28th of September we received an additional order for all we could make up to 1st November, 1861.

On the 28th October we received, by the directions of the Secretary of War, an extension of this order up to 1st March, 1862; and on the 22d January a further extension was granted up to 1st September, 1862. (Copies of which please find annexed.)

In consequence of the continued demand for these arms, and in order to meet the pressing wants of the department, we were compelled to make extensive outlays for more machinery, &c., to keep up to our contract, and have been in successful operation furnishing articles of the very best make and equal to the requirements of the severe government tests and inspection, and at prices which we believe to be less, and in many instances considerable lower, than paid to other contractors.

To stop the manufacture of said arms, now that we have an accumulation of auxiliary parts ready for mounting, would entail a loss too severe to be borne by a firm who have all their means invested in the manufacture of military goods, in competition to the foreign fabrics, and would most respectfully beg of the honorable commission to forward early instructions to Major Laidley, commanding Frankford arsenal, Pennsylvania, to permit us to continue the delivery and fulfilment of our contract.

Very respectfully, your obedient servants,

HORSTMANN BROS. & CO.

Hons JOSEPH HOLT and ROBERT DALE OWEN, *Commissioners.*

PHILADELPHIA, *March* 20, 1862.

SIRS: As per your request, we forward enclosed the various original letters and contracts appertaining to the statement and copies of vouchers left with you yesterday.

Also please find a copy of the (original on file at the ordnance department) letter of Lieutenant Treadwell, which we omitted in the original list of letters left with you.

Begging your early attention to our case, with special permission to Major Laidley, of the Frankford arsenal, to allow us to resume our deliveries according to contract,

We remain, respectfully, your obedient servants,

HORSTMANN BROTHERS & CO.

Hons JOSEPH HOLT and ROBERT DALE OWEN,
　　　Commissioners on Contracts, Washington D. C

ORDNANCE OFFICE, *Washington, March* 20, 1862.

SIR: I transmit herewith a copy of the letter of 21st September last, ordering sabres from Messrs. Horstmann Brothers & Co., asked for by the commission; and also a copy of letter from this office to Lieutenant Treadwell, dated October 26, 1861, having reference to the same subject.

Respectfully, your obedient servant,

JAMES W. RIPLEY, *Brigadier General.*

J. WISE, Esq., *Secretary of Commission, &c., Washington, D. C.*

Received from Horstmann Brothers & Co. since September 21, 1861.

November 28.—1, 490 cavalry sabres, at........................ $6 87½
788 sergeants' swords, at...................... 5 00
799 musicians' swords, at...................... 3 75
Feb. 4, 1862.—1, 521 cavalry sabres, at....................... 6 87½
400 musicians' swords, at 3 75
446 sergeants' swords, at..................... 5 00
Boxes 75 cents each.

COMMISSION ON ORDNANCE AND ORDNANCE STORES,
Washington, March 21, 1862.

GENERAL: The papers in Horstmann Brothers & Co.'s claim to continue the manufacture of sabres, non-commissioned officers' and musicians' swords, (orders for which were first given by Lieutenant Treadwell, September 20, and subsequently twice extended to September 1, 1862,) refer for the *price* to an offer from them dated July 22. This is not with the papers.

Please furnish, for the use of the commission, a statement of the price to be paid for each kind of sword and sabre, and a statement of deliveries already made under the order, and an estimate of the number likely to be delivered, (the total product of their establishments until September, 1862;) also the number the ordnance department would wish to obtain from this source of supply.

The commissioners also request that you would direct a report to be made for their use by the proper officers, stating the value, in his or their judgment, of the four varieties of arms ordered from H. Holthausen, August 27, *calibre* .69, *for future use in the service.*

Very respectfully, sir, your obedient servant,

P. V. HAGNER, *Major of Ordnance.*

Gen. J. W. RIPLEY, *Chief of Ordnance.*

FRANKFORD ARSENAL, *Pennsylvania, March* 25, 1862.

GENERAL: In answer to your letter of the 22d instant, asking for " an estimate of the number of swords and sabres likely to be delivered by Messrs. Hortsmann Brothers & Co., under their orders from Frankford arsenal," I have to reply that if the estimate be based on the number furnished during the last two weeks prior to the suspension of their order, the probable number that would likely be delivered would amount to 40,000 or 50,000 swords and sabres. But the Messrs. Horstmann Brothers & Co. are not themselves manufacturers of swords, but have these articles made at the manufactories in this vicinity. These establishments have no orders at this time, and can turn their full force on sabres for the Messrs. Horstmann Brothers & Co., and I know of nothing to prevent this firm from delivering from 100,000 to 150,000 swords and sabres under their orders from this arsenal; and as it is evidently to their interest to deliver as many swords as possible within the time of their contract, I think it highly probable that they would deliver as many as 100,000 swords and sabres under their orders.

In reply to that part of your letter asking for the value " of the four varieties of arms ordered from Mr. Holthausen, August 27, 1861," in my judgment or Lieutenant Treadwell's, I have to say that, having examined these arms, I am unable to see any difference in the muskets or in the two varieties of rifles with sword bayonets.

These arms have, in consequence of the delay in their delivery, ceased to be of the same value to the United States that they were at the time they were to be delivered. In my judgment, the muskets are not worth more than ten dollars each, and the rifles with sword bayonets eleven and a half dollars. Lieutenant Treadwell gives, as his opinion, the same figures as above for the value of these arms.

I have the honor to return herewith the letter of Major Hagner.

Very respectfully, I am, general, your obedient servant,

T. T. S. LAIDLEY, *Brevet Major.*

ORDNANCE OFFICE,
Washington, March 22, 1862.

SIR: As requested in your letter of yesterday, I enclose herewith a copy of Messrs. Horstmann Bros. & Co.'s offer to furnish sabres and swords, dated July 22, 1861, and a statement of deliveries made by them since the 21st September, the date of Lieutenant Treadwell's first orders. The estimate of the number likely to be delivered, and of the value, in the judgment of proper officers, of the four varieties of arms ordered from H. Holthausen, August 27, 1861, have to be obtained, and will be sent to the commission, with a statement of the number of Horstmann's sabres and swords desired by this department, as soon as received.

Respectfully, your obedient servant,

JAS. W. RIPLEY, *Brig. General.*

Major P. V. HAGNER, *Office of Commission, &c.*

ORDNANCE OFFICE,
Washington, March 26, 1862.

SIR: In further answer to your letter of the 21st instant, I enclose herewith a copy of a letter from Brevet Major Laidley, of the 25th instant, containing an estimate of the number of swords and sabres which may be delivered by Messrs. Horstmann Bros. & Co., under their order, first given September 21, 1861, and subsequently twice extended up to September 1, 1862; also a report of the value, in the judgment of Major Laidley and Lieutenant Treadwell, of the four varieties of arms ordered from Mr. Holthausen, August 27, 1861.

As regards the number of swords and sabres which the Ordnance department deems it advisable to obtain under the Messrs. Horstmann's order, I have to state that the present supply of sabres renders it inadvisable, in my opinion, to take any more of them; and that 5,000 each of the non-commissioned officers' and musicians' swords will be as many as the wants of the service will require.

Respectfully, your obedient servant,

JAS. W. RIPLEY, *Brig. General.*

Major P. V. HAGNER,
Office of Commission, &c.

WASHINGTON, *April* 7, 1862.

SIRS: We most respectfully represent that, in forming your decision in our case, we believe you have omitted taking into account all our deliveries of sabres.

Thus, from January 31 to March 12 (the date of receiving the order of the department to discontinue deliveries) we have delivered 3,341 sabres, 130 non-commissioned officers' swords, and 50 musicians' swords—besides the lot stated under date of February 4—the vouchers for which are now in the ordnance department, and which we think ought to have been included in your estimate of deliveries by us.

We therefore would ask your honorable commission to allow us to deliver such sabres as are now in process of finishing, which consist of about 5,500 to 6,000.

Very respectfully, your obedient servants,

HORSTMANN BROS. & CO.

Hon. J. HOLT and ROBERT DALE OWEN,
Commissioners on Contracts, &c., Washington, D. C.

CASE OF HORSTMANN & Co., of Philadelphia.

Before commission, April 7.

Mr. Horstmann appeared before the commission and asked that the decision of the commission in their case might be reconsidered; requesting to be allowed to finish up all sabres now under way, and that their deliveries may be continued; states that he means by his own establishment his Philadelphia factory; that he intended in his offer, and understood by the order given him for "sabres of his own manufacture," those manufactured by his men for him. He has no forges, but has his blades and other parts made out, as others do; has had many sabres rejected, and has made but little by them; has opened additional sources of supply since July, but has made no new arrangements since order of September.

PHILADELPHIA, *April* 28, 1862.

SIRS: In our interview with your honorable commission on the 7th instant we respectfully asked your reconsideration of the decision in our case, for reasons then explained.

Not having heard anything in reference to it, we most respectfully ask for a reply.

Your obedient servants,

HORSTMANN BROS. & CO.

Hon. J. HOLT and ROBT. DALE OWEN,
    Commissioners on Contracts, Washington.

Before commission.

Mr. Emerson, of the firm of Emerson & Silver, sabre and sword makers, of Trenton, New Jersey, states that the cost price of a cavalry sabre

blade is	$1 25
Scabbard, of best cast steel	1 25
Hilt, finished in best style	1 25
Fitting and boxing	25
Profit to manufacturer, 33⅓ per cent	1 33
Loss on inspection, 10 per cent	53
Fair cost of a sabre	5 86

Has furnished blades to parties having orders for sabres, but have had no orders direct. Have furnished about 5,000 blades to Horstmann & Co. for the last six months.

COMMISSION ON ORDNANCE, &c.,
    Washington, May 7, 1862.

GENTLEMEN: Your letters asking a reconsideration of your case have been duly received and considered by the commission. In reply, I am directed to inform you that the commission have decided not to reopen the case, as they would not agree, in such event, to increase the number of sabres allowed to be delivered by you.

Very respectfully, your obedient servant,

J. WISE, *Secretary.*

Messrs. HORSTMANN & Co., *Philadelphia.*

COMMISSION ON ORDNANCE AND ORDNANCE STORES,
Washington. March 28, 1862.

GENERAL : The commission have the honor to report as follows:

CASE NO. 17.—HORSTMANN BROS. & CO., Philadelphia, Pa.

Order dated September 21, 1861.—(*No.* 4 *of printed list, page* 17.)

Referred by special order of War Department.   To deliver all sabres, non-commissioned officers' swords, and musicians' swords, that they can make prior to November 1, 1861, subject to prescribed inspections.

October 28.—Extended by order of Secretary of War for four months from November 1, provided that all the swords and sabres to be delivered shall be of their own manufacture.

January 22.—Extended to September 1, 1862, by order of Secretary of War, on same terms.

Deliveries made November 28: 1,490 sabres; 788 non-commissioned officers' swords; 799 musicians' swords.

Deliveries made February 4: 1,521 sabres; 446 non-commissioned officers' swords; 400 musicians' swords.

Further deliveries suspended under general order from War Department.

The commission find that the original order drawn to cover the product of the establishment for one month actually produced nothing for the government, as no delivery was made until November 28, (after the first extension made October 28,) although urged, when receiving this order, to "make deliveries as soon as possible." As it appears that this order was given upon the completion of a previous order, (after an offer to deliver 50 of each kind per day,) it is to be inferred that their establishment was under full headway, and able to produce equal quantities of each kind, at least at the rates proposed in July previous. February 4th a second delivery was made—amounting thus, since their order of the 21st of September, to 5,444 sabres and swords in 136 days, equal to 40 per day. It is fair to presume, therefore, that as their establishment had been up to that time with abundant orders unexecuted, that an estimate of this kind may have induced the prolongation of the order to September 1. Based upon this, we should expect to obtain in the 208 days remaining 8,320 sabres and swords. As the department has been compelled to obtain sabres in large quantities from other sources, owing to the non-fulfilment of promises made by various contractors, (this firm as well as others, as shown above,) it becomes necessary now to limit the deliveries of sabres as much as possible. Both kinds of swords are still desired by the ordnance department.

The commission, therefore, decide that the Messrs. Horstmann Bros. & Co. be required to deliver, prior to September 1, 1862, the following numbers of sabres and swords, to be manufactured at their own establishment, subject to the prescribed inspection, not to exceed—

> 1,500 sabres, at $6 87 ;
> 3,500 non-commissioned officers' swords, at $5 ;
> 3,500 musicians' swords, at $3 75 ;

and that no greater number of either be received under their order of September 21, as extended.

We are, sir, very respectfully, your obedient servants,

J. HOLT,
ROBERT DALE OWEN,
Commissioners.

P. V. HAGNER,
Major of Ordnance, Assistant to Commission.

Brigadier General J. W. RIPLEY,
Chief of Ordnance.

CASE No. 18.

S. Dingee & Co.

NEW YORK, *No. 8 Pine street, February* 5, 1862.

In compliance with your order of the 29th of January, that all parties hold-ing contracts, &c., with the United States government for the supply of arms, &c., that a copy of the same be presented to your department within fifteen days, we herewith hand you a copy of our order of the United States government, together with the directions of the same, by order of the President, under date of January 10, 1862, and a copy of General Ripley's order to Major Hagner, No. 55 White street, New York, dated Washington, January 10, 1862.

Our shipments have thus far been made in compliance with the said order, and the arms are under the direction of the ordnance officer in New York, the inspection of which is going forward.

Yours, very respectfully,

S. DINGEE & CO.

Hon. EDWIN M. STANTON,
Secretary of War.

S. Dingee & Co., in November, 1861, made a contract with the War Depart-ment to deliver to the United States government 53,500 Austrian rifles in ac-cordance with the terms therein specified. This contract was sanctioned by the President, Secretary of War, and General McClellan, and an inspection and delivery began in accordance with the terms of the contract. Proceedings were subsequently suspended by reason of a dispute as to the true meaning and effect of the contract. By consent the whole matter was referred to the Presi-dent of the United States, by whose direction the Secretary of War issued an order, dated January 10, 1862, under which order the ordnance department were directed to carry out and complete the contract as speedily as possible, in accordance with its terms and conditions. That order, together with the neces-sary papers connected therewith, was referred to the proper subordinate officer in New York city, with instructions from General Ripley to have the same carried out.

Under these instructions the government's agents or officers proceeded to in-spect, accept, and grant certificates for the arms; from 42,000 to 45,000 have arrived and were placed in bond, subject to the directions and order of the proper United States officer; the balance are on the way; about 11,000 or 12,000 have been inspected, and certificates given for 8,000 or 9,000, which have been delivered to the government.

On the 12th day of March, 1862, whilst the inspection and delivery of arms, as per contract and order, were proceeding, Captain Crispin, of the ordnance department, detailed at New York to examine and inspect, receive, and certify to the delivery of the arms, notified Messrs. Dingee & Co. that all further pro-ceedings must stop, as, in his judgment, the late order of the Secretary of War, referring all matters of this kind to the commission composed of Messrs. Holt and Owen, applied to this contract, and, until further advised, he should de-cline to proceed to inspect any more arms or to give any certificates for some 3,500 which had passed inspection, and for which certificates had not been granted. These arms were much needed, and were urgently called for by Gen-eral McClellan, and the contractors have, from the start, been ready and willing to carry out to the letter their part of the contract.

Under the circumstances it is deemed but just and right that the inspection and delivery of the arms should proceed and be completed as speedily as possible, saving all further delay, damage, and loss to the contractors and the government, this being an adjudicated and executed contract.

All of which is most respectfully submitted.

Truly, &c.,

S. DINGEE & CO.

ORDNANCE OFFICE,
No. 55 White street, New York, March 12, 1862.

GENTS: In reply to your communication of this date, I have to reply as follows:

The instructions to this office are such as to render it proper, in my judgment, to refer the acceptance of your arms, already inspected, to the decision of the Secretary of War, and that the special authority of the Secretary will be necessary before I can release from bond those now awaiting inspection.

Very respectfully, your obedient servant,

S. CRISPIN, *Capt. of Ordnance.*

Messrs. S. DINGEE & CO.

ORDNANCE OFFICE,
Washington, January 10, 1862.

SIR: I enclose herewith a copy of a letter, of this date, from the Secretary of War, showing the decision which has been made in the case of contracts of Dingee & Co. for arms. You will be governed by this decision in your action in regard to these arms, both as regards their inspection and their valuation. The original contract is in the hands of the contractors.

Respectfully, your obedient servant,

JAS. W. RIPLEY, *Brigadier General.*

Major P. V. HAGNER,
No. 55 White street, New York.

Indorsement of Secretary of War on Captain Crispin's letter of 7th of January, relative to Dingee's contract:

Respectfully forwarded to the President for examination, with request to return, to be placed on file among the records of this department.

SIMON CAMERON.

WAR DEPARTMENT, *January* 10, 1862.

After a careful examination of all the papers of the Dingee & Co. contract by the President, it has been determined that you shall receive the guns offered in accordance with terms of contract, which may be of .58 calibre and pass inspection, on the terms originally agreed upon by ———, nineteen dollars for each gun, with usual implements, including tompion and snap-cap. The guns that may not conform to terms of contract and pass inspection, you will purchase at their value, of which such ordnance officer as you may designate shall be the judge. This adjustment, under all the circumstances, being deemed equitable and just to the parties.

Respectfully, &c.,

SIMON CAMERON, *Secretary of War.*

General RIPLEY, *Chief of Ordnance.*

ORDNANCE OFFICE, *Washington, January* 10, 1862.

SIR: The Dingee & Co. contract, referred to in your letter of this morning, did not accompany it. To enable me to execute the instructions of your letter, it is necessary that the ordnance officer who may inspect the arms should be furnished with the contract, and I respectfully request that it may be sent to this office for that purpose.

Respectfully, &c.,

JAMES W. RIPLEY

Brigadier General.

Hon. SIMON CAMERON, *Secretary of War.*

The sample of these arms is now in General McClellan's headquarters in Washington city.

The said rifles are to be finished to conform to said sample, with the exception that the barrels shall be brown instead of bright, and that the calibre of each arm shall be in accordance with the United States standard, to wit: fifty-eight one hundredths; each arm to be furnished with an angular bayonet, tompion, and snap-cap, and all the usual implements belonging to the army rifle. The said arms shall be finished like the English Enfield rifles.

We agree to furnish to the United States government fifty-three thousand and five hundred arms, in bond, at the price of nineteen dollars per gun, agreeable to above description and the annexed schedule, subject to inspection.

S. DINGEE & CO.

Accepted.

P. V. HAGNER, *Major of Ordnance.*

Schedule of shipments from Europe.

1861—Oct.	26.	From Bremen	3,000
Nov.	2.	From Hamburg	2,000
	16.	From Hamburg	3,000
	23.	From Bremen	2,000
	30.	From Hamburg	2,000
Dec.	1.	From Hamburg	1,500
	14.	From Hamburg	3,000
	15.	From Hamburg	2,000
	21.	From Bremen	3,000
	28.	From Hamburg	3,000
	30.	From Hamburg or Bremen	3,000
1862—Jan.	5.	From Hamburg or Bremen	3,000
	7.	From Hamburg or Bremen	3,000
	14.	From Hamburg or Bremen	4,000
	21.	From Hamburg or Bremen	3,000
	28.	From Hamburg or Bremen	3,000
Feb.	5.	From Hamburg or Bremen	5,000
	16.	From Hamburg or Bremen	5,000

53,500

S. DINGEE & CO.

Attached to paper.

P. V. H.

ORDNANCE OFFICE,

No. 55 White street, New York, December 16, 1861.

SIR: I will give as follows for the arms offered to me by you and inspected by Schmidt, with implements:

198 long sight, calibre .58............................$18 00

200 short sight, calibre .58.......................... 17 00

515 long sight, calibre .57½........................$17 00
685 short sight, calibre .57½........................ 16 50
400 various, of less calibre 16 15

Broken joints and damaged locks to be repaired neatly and satisfactorily. Boxes to be paid for at $1 50 each.

The arms in port to be inspected and assorted under above heads of difference, and to be purchased at the same rates.

I make this offer at your request, as given by Mr. McMaster. You will be pleased to inform me of your acceptance or non-acceptance.

All expenditures incurred thus far upon this lot are to be paid by you.

Very respectfully, your obedient servant,

P. V. HAGNER, *Major of Ordnance.*

Directions given to Captain Crispin on or about January 14, 1862.

The Dingee arms to be received under the decision of the President "as not conforming to the terms of the contract," and which are now offered by Messrs. Dingee & Co., will be charged at the prices stated in my note of December 16, 1861.

P. V. HAGNER, *Major of Ordnance.*

Captain S. CRISPIN.

———

COMMISSION ON ORDNANCE AND ORDNANCE STORES,
Washington, March 28, 1862.

GENERAL: The commission have the honor to report as follows:

CASE No. 18.—S. DINGEE & Co., New York.

Order dated November 5, 1861; No. 41 of printed list, page 11.

To deliver 53,500 Austrian-made Enfield rifles, at $19, commencing about November 15 and ending about March 1. February 16, being date of last shipment from Europe, agreed upon. Deliveries suspended under general order of the War Department.

The commission find that the deliveries of the above arms were being made at the time of suspension under special instructions from the President of the United States, requiring that the arms offered in accordance with terms of contract, and of calibre .58, which pass inspection, with implements, be received at the rate of $19 each, and that all not conforming thereto be appraised by the ordnance officer at New York, and received at such price as he may determine.

This decision being still in force, the commission direct, in conformity therewith, that so many arms as shall have been shipped from Hamburg or Bremen not later than the 16th day of February, 1862, and not exceeding 53,500 in all, be accepted, and that they shall, if they are of .58 calibre, and pass inspection, be paid for at the rate of $19 for each gun, with appendages; but if not, at such rate as the ordnance officer may judge to be the true value.

We are, sir, very respectfully, your obedient servants,

ROBERT DALE OWEN,
J. HOLT,

Commissioners.

P. V. HAGNER,
Major of Ordnance, Assistant to Commission.

Brig. Gen. J. W. RIPLEY, *Chief of Ordnance.*

ORDNANCE OFFICE,
No. 55 White street, New York, April 1, 1862.

GENTLEMEN: In accordance with instructions received from the ordnance department this day, I have to offer you a voucher for that portion of last inspected lot of your arms which have been found according to terms of contract, viz: 1,540 guns, calibre .58, leaf sight, at $19 each. As regards the balance of the lot, I consider it to be clearly my duty, under the instructions of the commission on ordnance, &c., to assess their value before issuing voucher; and as you have expressed yourself unwilling to submit to any other basis of settlement than that heretofore offered you by Major Hagner, I have referred the matter to Washington for decision.

Very respectfully, your obedient servant,

S. CRISPIN, *Captain of Ordnance.*

Messrs. S. DINGEE & Co.,
No. 8 Pine street, New York.

ORDNANCE OFFICE,
No. 55 White street, New York, April 1, 1862.

GENERAL: On the 12th of March I completed the inspection of 3,340 Austrian rifles offered under the contract of Messrs. S. Dingee & Co.

The result of this inspection was as follows, viz:

No. 1.—1,540 guns, calibre .58, leaf sight.
No. 2.—1,040 guns, calibre .58, block sight.
No. 3.—240 guns, calibre .577, leaf sight.
No. 4.—380 guns, calibre .577, block sight.
No. 5.—80 guns, calibre .55, leaf sight.
No. 6.—60 guns, calibre .55, block sight.

The 1,540 (No. 1) comply with the terms of the contract, and are in accordance with my instructions. I have offered payment for them, at the rate of $19 per gun, with the appendages. The remainder, not being in accordance with the original agreement, require to be assessed in value prior to reception and payment. The following prices have been heretofore paid for Nos. 2, 3, 4, 5, and 6, viz: for Nos. 2 and 3, $17; for No. 4, $16 50; and for Nos. 5 and 6, $16 15. These prices were established by Major Hagner in a letter addressed to Messrs. Dingee & Co. dated December 16, 1861, and referred exclusively to that lot of arms which had been inspected and were then awaiting payment, and those that were in port. All lots up to this last have been paid for on this basis or assessment.

Now, as my instructions from the commission on contracts, &c., for ordnance and ordnance stores clearly contemplate the open purchase of all such arms as may not be in accordance with the contract, I conceive it to be my duty to receive each lot just as other purchases are made, viz: at such prices as may be agreed upon, which should be determined altogether, if possible, by the market value of the arms at the time.

For these reasons I do not feel authorized to issue vouchers for the above arms on the old basis. Mr. Dingee refuses to agree to any valuation which will reduce the former rates. Now, as the very acknowledgment that these rates are binding strips the case entirely of its features as an open purchase, and makes it one of contract, or, in other words, renders Major Hagner's letter of the 16th of December, 1861, a contract, binding us in all future purchases, I cannot entertain Mr. Dingee's views, and accordingly see no other course to resort to to obtain a settlement of this case than to refer it to you, with a request that you will be kind enough to forward this communication, through your office, for the consideration of the commission on contracts, &c., for ordnance and ordnance stores.

Please give this matter your early attention, in order that there may be no unnecessary delay in the settlement of this matter.

Very respectfully, your obedient servant,

S. CRISPIN, *Captain of Ordnance.*

General J. W. RIPLEY,
  Chief of Ordnance, Washington, D. C.

Messrs. S. Dingee & Co., early in November, 1861, made a contract with the government to deliver 53,500 Austrian rifles, in accordance with certain terms and conditions therein specified.

Upon the offer to deliver a portion of the arms under said contract, a question arose as to its true meaning and construction. After much difficulty and delay the matter was referred to the President of the United States for examination and settlement, and on the 10th day of January, 1862, an order was issued by the War Department, in conformity with the decision of the President, directing the inspection and delivery of the arms in accordance with the terms of said order. That order, with a letter of instruction from General Ripley, was at once forwarded to Major Hagner, the ordnance officer, at No. 55 White street, New York, and on the 13th of January, in compliance with instructions and at the request of Mr. Dingee, Major Hagner proceeded to fix and settle, with the approbation of Messrs. Dingee & Co., the prices of all the arms that should happen to be out of calibre. These prices ranged from $17 to $16 15, agreeably to a previous offer made by Major Hagner on the 16th of December, 1861. Upon the prices being established, Major Hagner at once wrote Captain Crispin, who was then acting for him, at No. 55 White street, and directed that the arms should be inspected, received, and certified for, in accordance with the prices thus named and determined. The shipment of arms was continued with and under this understanding and agreement, and the inspection and delivery commenced and was carried forward until the order of the Secretary of War, appointing a commission to examine such contracts, when Captain Crispin declined to proceed further without the submission of the contract to the commission, and until further orders. Six invoices had been delivered and inspected, and certificates for five out of the six invoices had been issued, allowing and certifying the prices as established under the President's order and Major Hagner's offer, when Captain Crispin refused to issue a certificate for the sixth invoice until after the commission should render a decision in the case. Upon the ground that the whole matter was fully and finally settled and adjudicated by the President's decision, the instructions of General Ripley, and the establishment of prices by Major Hagner, and the inspections had, and certificates issued in conformity therewith, the counsel of Messrs. Dingee & Co. advised them that it would not be necessary for them to appear before the commission on the merits of the case, satisfied that the decision of the President would be affirmed, and the inspection and delivery of arms be continued as heretofore, and in accordance with the terms and conditions already established. All the papers in the case were placed in the hands of counsel, and I proceeded to consult the commission as to whether the same view would be taken, or whether they would open the question and require the presence of Dingee & Co., or either of them. After deliberation, Mr. Holt informed me the case required no new investigation, and that the President's decision would be confirmed. A decision of the commission was afterwards made to that effect. Captain Crispin now seeks so to construe that decision as to enable him to do what the commissioners declined to do, namely, open the case again on its merits, and virtually nullify and override the decision of the President, and the proceedings had in accordance therewith, by establishing anew and over again the prices already fixed and settled for arms out of calibre, when, in reality, a large proportion of the arms would never have been shipped, except by reason of the decision of the President and the prices named and established in accordance with the terms and understanding thereof, before any delivery and inspection had been had under the same.

I herewith submit certificates and statements and affidavits of Messrs. W. A. Corbier, Solomon Dingee, and James McMaster, showing the establishment of the prices by Major Hagner, conformed and acted on by Captain Crispin, copies of the invoices, with descriptions of the arms as inspected and certified, with the prices affixed.

Messrs. Dingee & Co. claim that under the facts and circumstances, Captain Crispin having referred to General Ripley, as chief of ordnance, for instructions in regard to his further action under the Dingee contract, that it is clearly right and just, and in strict accordance with the true intent and meaning of the decision of the President, and the opinion of the commission confirming the same; that he, Captain Crispin, should be directed to proceed with the inspection of the arms as heretofore, and give certificates for the same, in accordance with the prices as established and agreed upon, and that such inspection should be made and closed as speedily as possible.

Respectfully, your obedient servants,

S. DINGEE & CO.

I, William A. Corbire, of the city of New York, hereby certify that the following are true statements of the Austrian rifles delivered by Messrs. Solomon Dingee & Co. on their contract with the United States government for 53,500 Austrian rifles, and the same have been inspected by the ordnance officer, at No. 55 White street, city of New York.

For all of which the said officer has issued his certificates or vouchers at the prices named and specified in each invoice, with the exception on the sixth invoice the said officer has issued his certificate or voucher for only 1,540 guns, of .58 calibre, long sight. The balance of the said 6th invoice, viz:

52 cases,	1,040 guns,	calibre .58,	block sight	$17	00
12 cases,	240 guns,	calibre .577,	long sight	17	00
19 cases,	380 guns,	calibre .577,	block sight	16	50
4 cases,	80 guns,	calibre .55,	long sight	16	15
3 cases,	60 guns,	calibre .55,	block sight	16	15

These Captain Crispin, the present ordnance officer, refuses to receive at the above prices, which were fixed by Major P. V. Hagner, as per his letter under date of December 16, 1861, as per copy herewith:

First invoice, viz:

220 guns,	calibre	.58,	short sight	$17	00
535 guns,	calibre	.577,	long sight	17	00
665 guns,	calibre	.577,	short sight	16	50
400 guns,	calibre	.55 & .56,	various sight	16	15

1820

91 packing cases	1	50

Second invoice, viz:

26 cases,	520 guns,	calibre .58,	leaf sight	19	00
40 cases,	800 guns,	calibre .58,	block sight	17	00
13 cases,	260 guns,	calibre .577,	leaf sight	17	00
17 cases,	340 guns,	calibre .577,	block sight	16	50

1 case,	20 guns, calibre .55,	leaf sight	$16	15
1 case,	20 guns, calibre .55,	block sight	16	15

98	1,960		

98 packing cases.. 1 50

Third invoice, viz:

15 cases,	300 guns, calibre .58,	leaf sight	19	00
59 cases, 1,180 guns, calibre .58,	block sight	17	00
4 cases,	80 guns, calibre .577	leaf sight	17	00
18 cases,	360 guns, calibre .577	block sight	16	50

96	1,920		

96 packing cases.. 1 50

Fourth invoice, viz:

44 cases,	880 guns, calibre .58	leaf sight	19	00
67 cases, 1,340 guns, calibre .58	block sight	17	00
5 cases,	100 guns, calibre .577	leaf sight	17	00
15 cases,	300 guns, calibre .577	block sight	16	50

131	2,620		

131 packing cases.. 1 50

Fifth invoice, viz:

27 cases,	540 guns, calibre .58,	leaf sight	19	00
26 cases,	520 guns, calibre .58,	block sight	17	00
15 cases,	300 guns, calibre .577	leaf sight	17	00
16 cases,	320 guns, calibre .577	block sight	16	50
33 cases,	660 guns, calibre .55,	leaf sight	16	15
32 cases,	640 guns, calibre .55,	block sight	16	15
1 case,	20 guns, calibre .54,	leaf sight	16	15
1 case,	20 guns, calibre .54,	block sight	16	15
1 case,	20 guns, calibre .59,	leaf sight	16	15
1 case,	20 guns, calibre .59,	block sight	16	15
2 cases,	38 guns, calibre .58,	leaf sight	18	00
2 cases,	40 guns, calibre .58,	block sight	17	00

157	3,138		

157 packing cases.. 1 50

Sixth invoice, viz:

77 cases, 1,540 guns, calibre .58,	leaf sight	19	00
52 cases, 1,040 guns, calibre .58,	block sight	17	00
12 cases,	240 guns, calibre .577	leaf sight	17	00
19 cases,	380 guns, calibre .577	block sight	16	50
4 cases,	80 guns, calibre .55,	leaf sight	16	15
3 cases,	60 guns, calibre .55,	block sight	16	15

167	3,340		

167 packing cases.. 1 50

From all .58 calibre, long sight, and invoiced at $19, a deduction has been on each invoice of 24½ cents, for deficiency in implements, by order of Major Hagner.

WM. A. CORBIERE.

Sworn before me this 5th day of April, 1862.

S. A. PIERCE, *Commissioner of Deeds.*

This is to certify that I, Solomon Dingee, of the firm of Dingee & Co., called on Major P. V. Hagner, United States ordnance officer, office No. 55 White street, New York, immediately after my return from Washington, say about the 13th day of January last, and showed to him the reinstatement of our order for 53,500 Austrian rifles by order of the President of the United States, and Major Ripley, chief of the Ordnance bureau at Washington, after reading the same, he fixed and established prices for all our Austrian rifles that were out of calibre, and I agreed to the same; Major Hagner then wrote out the same in form of instructions to Captain S. Crispin, acting ordnance officer at the time of Major Hagner's indisposition, in which he directed that our arms should be received at said prices. The said instructions he gave to me, and desired me to hand them to Captain Crispin. I delivered the same to Captain S. Crispin. Our rifles have been inspected to the 5th certificate, and Captain Crispin has issued certificates allowing said prices for all the arms that have been inspected, agreeable to annexed copies of inspections.

SOLOMON DINGEE.

Sworn before me this 5th day of April, 1852.

S. A. PIERCE, *Commissioner of Deeds.*

I, James McMaster, of the city of New York, being duly sworn, state that I was present with Major P. V. Hagner and Solomon Dingee at the interview above referred to. I also called on Captain S. Crispin with Mr. Dingee and saw him deliver Major Hagner's instructions to Captain Crispin, also state that the above statement made by Solomon Dingee is true of my own knowledge.

JAMES McMASTER.

Sworn before me this 5th day of April, 1862.

S. A. PIERCE, *Commissioner of Deeds.*

ORDNANCE OFFICE,
Washington, D. C., April 12, 1862.

SIR: I have the honor to enclose herewith, for your action, a statement of O. S. Halsted, esq., counsel for S. Dingee & Co., of New York, in relation to deliveries under their contract for 53,500 arms, dated November 5, 1861. The point is this:

On the 10th of January, 1862, the Secretary of War directed me to receive all guns offered in accordance with the terms of the contract for $19, and that such as did not conform to the contract were to be purchased at a valuation made by such ordnance officer as might be designated by me.—(See paper No. 26, case 41, official statement of arms contracted for.) At that time Major Hagner was the officer whose duty it was to make this valuation; and on the 13th January he put certain prices on certain arms which did not conform to the contract.

In the usual course the case came before the commission on ordnance stores, and their decision was made in accordance with that of the Secretary of War, before quoted.

Captain Crispin is now the officer in charge of the ordnance agency in New York; he does not feel authorized to receive and pay for the arms now presented by Dingee & Co., and which do not conform to the contract, at the prices fixed by Major Hagner, because there is a great difference in the arms offered of this class; and the prices fixed by Major Hagner, in January, are not, in his opinion, such as should be paid for this kind of arms now.

I agree with the views of Captain Crispin, as expressed in his letter to me of April 1, 1862, which is herewith enclosed, and respectfully recommend that, for all arms presented to him by these parties and which do not conform to the contract, he may be directed to fix such prices as are, in his opinion, just, in conformity with the true intent and meaning of the commissioners' decision.

Very respectfully, your obedient servant,

JAMES W. RIPLEY,
Brigadier General.

Hon. E. M. STANTON,
Secretary of War, Washington, D. C.

[Indorsement by the President.]

"APRIL 15, 1862.

"What reason is there that the appraisement made by Major Hagner and adopted and acted upon by Captain Crispin should not stand, so far as it went?"
"A. LINCOLN."

Before commission, April 16, 1862.

Statement by Major Hagner.

My note of December 16, 1861, was written at the request of Mr. Dingee, as an offer for the purchase of the arms which he offered under his contract with me, but which I considered of a quality entirely inferior to the arms contracted for. In my opinion, his contract was null and void at the time, from non-compliance on his part, and I so informed him by letter December 12, 1861, stating, however, that I would agree to purchase such arms as had arrived, or were on the way to him, if suitable for service, at such prices as may be fair and just. Mr. Dingee never replied to my note of December 16, as therein requested, but Mr. McMasters, his agent in this business, informed me that he declined to accept my terms, unless I would acknowledge the contract as still in force. This I could not do, as it was evident that the manufacturers in Europe were not making such arms as were promised, and therefore could not deliver as promised, and I did not wish to increase the number of inferior arms in the country beyond the number necessary to save Mr. Dingee from loss.

It subsequently appeared that Messrs. Dingee & Company were applying at Washington, and about the 13th January they showed me the order of the Secretary of War to consider the contract in force, and to receive such arms as would pass inspection, upon the terms originally agreed upon at $19 each, and such as may not conform to terms of contract and pass inspection to be purchased at their value, "of which I, as ordnance officer then charged with the duty, was to be the judge." As I was ill at the time, I gave directions to Captain Crispin, my assistant, to accept those I had inspected at the prices stated in my note of December 16, and to have the others that might be offered classified, in accordance with that note, as far as he could. This order was not changed while I remained in New York, as it did not seem necessary; none of the guns delivered, by my estimate, were rated as worth $19; but after the President's decision, I believe, some of the best were so rated by Captain Crispin, as it seemed from that decision that a sample gun, shown to General McClellan in Washington, was regarded as a standard of quality and not the Enfield gun, as I had stipulated for. When I was relieved from duty in New

York it became Captain Crispin's duty to judge of the value of the various classes of guns offered by Messrs. Dingee & Co., and as he had to certify to the correctness of the accounts passed by him, he could only allow for arms *purchased* by him such prices as were just and fair at the time the purchase was made. These inferior arms are ordered "*to be purchased at their value,*" and I think the "ordnance officer designated by the chief of ordnance" (Captain Crispin at present) is responsible that the prices paid are not in excess.

COMMISSION ON ORDNANCE AND ORDNANCE STORES,
Washington, April 16, 1862.

SIR : In reply to the inquiry indorsed by yourself upon the papers in S. Dingee & Co.'s claim against the United States, I have the honor to state that it was the purpose of the commission to reaffirm your judgment without qualification, and to this end I believe your own language was employed, as far as practicable.

In adopting the principle of valuation, suggested by yourself, for arms falling short of the requirements of the contract, it was not our intention to ratify the estimate of Major Hagner, made previously to your decision, of the value of a certain number of these guns which had then arrived, for we had no knowledge of the details of this estimate, and considered your order imperative that each arrival was to be appraised "by the ordnance officer in New York," who is bound by the regulation to certify the accounts for payment.

This "appraisement," if left to his judgment, must, we think, depend upon the market value at the time it is made.

The appraisement made by Major Hagner was intended to apply to the arms then before him, (and he thinks it is specifically so stated in his note to Messrs. Dingee & Co.,) and although it is understood some subsequent appraisements were made, under his directions at the same rates, this fact cannot of itself relieve Captain Crispin, the officer who succeeded him, from the obligation to act upon his own judgment in future cases. If such were the case, it would be substituting a new contract for the other by Major Hagner, whereas the decision of the President required the enforcement of the old contract for the arms of a certain class, and an appraisement of the rest upon the principles of an open market purchase.

As the market value of arms is constantly changing, both here and in Europe, we thought it just, alike to the seller and purchaser, that when those not up to the standard of the contract were offered to the government they should be paid for at their value when delivered ; and this we regarded as the true intent and meaning of your language. If, in this interpretation of your words, we have been mistaken, we shall be happy at your suggestion to make the proper correction. If anything more than the reasonable value of the inferior guns is allowed, it will hold out to parties a continual inducement to violate their contracts, and to disappoint the just expectations of the government.

I am, sir, with great respect, your obedient servant,

J. HOLT, *Commissioner, &c.*

His Excellency ABRAHAM LINCOLN,
　　President of the United States

ORDNANCE OFFICE, *Washington, D. C., April* 24, 1862.

SIR : I enclose herewith, for your information and guidance, a copy of a decision made by the President in the case of the contract of S. Dingee & Co. on the point raised by you in your letter of the 1st instant.

Respectfully, your obedient servant,

JAMES W. RIPLEY, *Brigadier General.*

Captain S. CRISPIN,
　　Ordnance Agency, 55 *White street, New York.*

EXECUTIVE MANSION, *Washington, April 23, 1862.*

It is said that in the case of the contract of S. Dingee & Co. in relation to arms a dispute has arisen as to the proper construction of a clause in an order signed by me, which clause is in these words: "and that all not conforming thereto" (the contract) "be appraised by the ordnance officer at New York, and received at such price as he may determine."

This order was prepared with reference to *a definite number* of arms expected to be delivered within a *definite time,* and not in reference to an *indefinite* number to be delivered in an *indefinite time.* I certainly did not expect that under the clause in question a lot of guns would be appraised at one price at one time, and another lot of precisely the same quality appraised at different prices at another time. I expected that when under the clause the price of a particular quality of gun was fixed it would stand throughout the transaction, neither going down or up. I still think this is the just construction.

A. LINCOLN.

[Indorsement.]

A true copy.

S. CRISPIN,
Captain of Ordnance.

A true copy.

J. G. BENTON,
Captain Ordnance and Assistant.

NEW YORK, June 5, 1862.

DEAR SIR: Your favor of yesterday is to hand. We appreciate your suggestion of the substitution of Enfield rifles on our order; and to show you that we are sincere in our offer we will deliver 5,000 English Enfield rifles within ten days, to apply on our order at $19 each, (instead of the Austrian rifles,) and will continue to deliver from time to time sufficient to complete the order within ninety days, provided we can have the privilege or permission of the President.

This is magnanimous on our part, considering that orders are now being filled at $20 and $22. Please act prompt and advise,

Yours, respectfully,

S. DINGEE & CO.

O. S. HALSTED, Esq.

WASHINGTON, June 6, 1862.

DEAR SIR: Herewith find a letter this day received from Messrs. S. Dingee & Co., offering to furnish Enfield rifles as therein stated. This offer arises from a suggestion made by me, that they, having control of a large number of Enfield rifles, should substitute them, under their contract, and save any further difficulty, growing out of a forced construction of the President's decision and the delays and disappointments arising therefrom. Not wishing to trouble the President further about this matter, knowing that Enfield's are now in demand, I trust that Captain Crispin will be at once instructed to receive from Messrs. Dingee & Co. Enfield rifles in place of Austrian rifles, to the number yet due under their contract, at the same price, $19. As that is from *one* to *three dollars* below the market price of Enfields, it will not only be of great advantage to the government, but save any further annoyance and trouble. A speedy decision will much oblige,

Your obedient servant,

O. S. HALSTED, JR.,
Of counsel with S. Dingee & Co., Willard's.

General RIPLEY,
   Chief of Ordnance, &c.

WASHINGTON, *June* 21, 1862.

DEAR SIR: Some days ago I submitted for your consideration a proposition from Dingee & Co. to substitute Enfield rifles for Austrian, under their contract. That offer was made at my suggestion to avoid any further difficulty growing out of certain technical objections to the delivery of a few arms shipped at periods not exactly corresponding with the dates specified in the original contract. The arms referred to were shipped under the contract and the President's decision, and placed in this country long before the government was ready to receive them. Any delay in the shipment and delivery of the arms having been clearly caused by the action of government agents, and not the fault of the contractors, there was no just reason for breaking the contracts or rejecting the arms. The whole matter has been *forced* several times before the President upon mere captious points taken by Major Hagner, or through the ordnance officer at New York. Upon each occasion the President, after a full examination, having expressed his decided disapprobation of the manifest effort to evade or avoid a fair contract on immaterial grounds, with the declaration that he "wanted substantial justice done," uniformly decided in favor of the contractors, waving all such merely technical objections. There are now in the ordnance office at New York 3,060 guns, partly inspected, placed there by *permit* of Captain Crispin. These arms, under a strict construction of the original contract, now again attempted to be insisted on, should have been shipped on the 16th of February; but owing to the temporary suspension of the contract by the War Department, coupled with a delay in the sailing of the steamer, they were shipped a few days later in the month, but reached here long before they were needed for inspection. This is one of that class of futile objections which *I do know* was intended to be forborne and overcome by the President as being, under the circumstances, immaterial and technical, unjust, and at the same time unbecoming a government dealing with its loyal citizens.

Indisposed to trouble the President further, knowing that the chief of ordnance has entire direction and control in such cases, and believing, under the explanations made, the whole matter can be satisfactorily adjusted without further delay, I respectfully suggest that the proposition for the substitution of Enfields be at once considered and adopted, in whole or in part, or that Captain Crispin be directed to continue the inspection of the 3,060 arms now in his charge and above referred to. Should it be deemed necessary to see the President again, I will cheerfully accompany the general, or get the President to make an appointment to see us together at an early day.

Will the general be kind enough to give this early attention, and much oblige,
Very respectfully, your obedient servant,

O. S. HALSTED, JR.,
Of counsel with S. Dingee & Co., Willard's.

General RIPLEY,
Chief of Ordnance, &c.

A true copy.

J. G. BENTON,
Captain Assistant.

List of papers in Dingee case.

1. Decision of the commission made March 28.
2. Captain Crispin's letter of April 1, in relation to the value of arms not conforming to the contract.
3. O. S. Halsted's statement in favor of retaining Major Hagner's appraisement.
4. President's indorsement on Captain Crispin's letter.

5. General Ripley's letter to Secretary of War of April 12, enclosing Captain Crispin's letter and Mr. Halsted's statement.
6. Reply of commission of April 16 to the President's indorsement as above.
7. Opinion of the President on the merits of the points at issue, April 23. (Brought to Ordnance office by Mr. Halsted. Original mislaid, but thought to be in the Second Auditor's office.)
8. General Ripley's letter to Captain Crispin, dated April 24, enclosing copy of President's opinion.
9. Captain Crispin's letters of May 27, (595, 596.) (These letters were sent to the War Department May 29, and have never been returned.)
10. Dingee & Co.'s offer of June 5 (submitted by Mr. Halsted) to give first quality Enfields for allowance due in contract.
11. O. S. Halsted's letter of June 21, calling the attention of General Ripley to offer of June 5.

WAR DEPARTMENT, *June* 24, 1862.

Respectfully referred to the commission on ordnance and ordnance stores, to report whether it would be expedient to accept the offer of the parties owning the Dingee contract to substitute Enfield rifles of first-class quality and of .58 calibre for that class of guns which the contract by its terms calls for.

By order of the Secretary of War.

P. H. WATSON,
Assistant Secretary of War.

———

COMMISSION ON ORDNANCE AND ORDNANCE STORES,
Washington, June 25, 1862.

SIR: The commission have examined the papers in the case of S. Dingee & Co., referred to them by your order of the 24th instant, and respectfully report that they consider it advisable to accept English-made Enfields of the first quality, calibre .58, in place of the Austrian guns, called for by the Dingee contract, at the price stated, $19 each, with appendages, to such extent as the government may still be bound to receive under that contract; but as the current price of first quality Enfields in New York is stated to be $15 at present, no extension of the time stipulated in the Dingee contract should be admitted. The note of S. Dingee & Co., dated June 5, 1862, proposes "to deliver 5,000 English Enfields within ten days, and to continue to deliver from time to time sufficient to complete the order within ninety days." As by the "schedule of shipments from Europe" attached to the contract, and forming part of it, the last shipment from Hamburg or Bremen was to be made February 16, all arms to be examined and received under the President's order, in this case, ought to have been shipped on or about February 16, and to have been in the country within reasonable time thereafter, otherwise they could not, in the language of the President, be "offered in accordance with the terms of the contract."

As there can be no doubt that more than ample time has now elapsed for the arrival of articles that may have been shipped as above, the commission see no ground for recognizing any claim whatever on the part of Dingee & Co. (either under the contract or under the President's orders in their favor) to have arms received not offered in New York prior to this date, and therefore any larger purchase from them at prices exceeding the current market rates would be unjust to the government.

We are, sir, very respectfully, your obedient servants,

J. HOLT,
ROBERT DALE OWEN,
Commissioners, &c.

P. V. HAGNER,
Major of Ordnance, Assistant to Commission.

Hon. EDWIN M. STANTON, *Secretary of War.*

WAR DEPARTMENT, *June* 25, 1862.

Referred to Brigadier General Ripley, chief of ordnance, with instructions to carry into effect the within recommendation of the commissioners, if Dingee & Co. assent.

By order of the Secretary of War.

P. H. WATSON, *Assistant Secretary of War.*

CASE No. 19.

T. POULTNEY.

ORDNANCE OFFICE,
Washington, August 27, 1861.

SIR: By direction of the Secretary of War, I offer you an order for 10,000 Smith's patent breech-loading carbines, on the following terms and conditions: The carbines, with appendages, are to be delivered at the factory of the Massachusetts Arms Company, Chicopee Falls, Massachusetts; the first delivery to commence in the month of September next, and other deliveries to continue at the rate of 1,000 per month thereafter until the whole 10,000 are delivered. The carbines and appendages are to be subject to inspection by such officer as this department may designate for the purpose. In case of a failure to deliver in or within the times before specified, the government is to be under no obligation to take the arms or appendages, but may or may not not do so at its option.

Payments are to be made in such funds as the Treasury Department may provide, on certificates of inspection and receipt by the United States inspecting officer, at the rate of thirty-two and a half dollars ($32 50) for each carbine, including appendages.

Please signify in writing whether you accept the foregoing order on the terms and conditions specified herein.

Respectfully, your obedient servant,

J. W. RIPLEY, *Brigadier General.*

T. POULTNEY, Esq.,
Washington, D. C.

WASHINGTON, *August* 28, 1861.

SIR: Your letter of 27th August, ordering 10,000 Smith's patent breech-loading carbines at $32 50, is received. I accept the offer, and shall proceed at once to execute the order.

Yours, with great respect,

T. POULTNEY.

Brigadier General J. W. RIPLEY,
Chief of Ordnance.

BALTIMORE, *February* 10, 1862.

SIR: In pursuance of an order issued by you January 29, 1862, I have the honor to enclose to you a copy of an order from the chief of ordnance, dated August 27, 1861, for 10,000 Smith's carbines, and my acceptance of the same.

Our factory having been destroyed by fire last year, we had a small delay in procuring new machinery and tools, but having made a large outlay of capital, we are now in full operation, running night and day, and working two sets of hands. I delivered in January 400 carbines, and shall continue now making regular monthly deliveries.

With great respect, your obedient servant,

T. POULTNEY.

Hon. EDWIN M. STANTON, *Secretary of War.*

BALTIMORE, *March* 26, 1861.

In reply to the questions asked of me by Major Hagner yesterday, I would respectfully state that I am a member of the firm of Poultney & Trimble, importers and manufacturers of, and dealers in fire arms, No. 200 Baltimore street, Baltimore; that for five years I have been the principal owner of the patent for Smith's breech-loading gun, and sole manager; and for two years I have had the arms manufactured at the works of the Massachusetts Arms Company, Chicopee Falls, Massachusetts.

In the month of January I delivered 400, and in the month of February 500, under my contract of August, 1861.

I have *now ready for delivery* 600, which have all passed inspection except about 150, which are partly inspected and will require three or four days to finish.

The inspectors have been absent from the factory for some time, and I earnestly beg that their work may be resumed promptly, as it is a matter of serious loss to us if the arms have to be stripped and examined after they have once been put together.

Our factory is now in active operation, working night and day and doing all that our machinery and men can accomplish. We shall certainly deliver 600 per month, and shall in a few months increase the delivery to 800 per month.

The reason why our deliveries were commenced later than stipulated is as follows: in January, 1861, our factory, with all the machinery and tools, was totally destroyed by fire, and after the war commenced the sudden demand for labor and machinery to manufacture arms interfered with our progress to such an extent that we could not work as rapidly as we expected. For five years I have labored constantly and diligently upon this gun, and myself and partners have invested in its manufacture a large sum of money.

I earnestly beg again that we may be permitted to resume our deliveries promptly.

With great respect, your obedient servant,

T. POULTNEY.

Hon. JOSEPH HOLT,
Hon. ROBERT DALE OWEN,
    Commissioners on Contracts.

BALTIMORE, *May* 24, 1862.

SIR: I have sent you a sample of "Smith's patent breech-loading carbine," to which I would most respectfully call your attention; and I also have the honor to present for your consideration a copy of the report of the arms commission on ordnance contracts in reference to my contract of August 27, 1861, for ten thousand of the same.

If the terms of that report are carried out it will ruin me and all others interested in building the arms.

Upon the faith of a contract with the United States government we expended large sums of money in machinery and tools, and have pushed our work diligently and faithfully. We have delivered our arms *as promptly* as any manufacturer, in many cases more promptly, yet we have been cut off from further deliveries and the arms are accumulating in such quantities upon our hands that we are being placed in an embarrassed condition. We would most respectfully call your attention to the report of the commission in the case of Richardson & Overman, whose contract was made at the same time as ours, who, like ourselves, have been behindhand in deliveries, and yet whose contract has been continued.

In the case of the Burnside Rifle Company *no deliveries* have been made, yet the commission *have confirmed their contract* in consideration of a reduction of

$2 50 on each gun, making their price $30 each, and permitting the company to commence deliveries *in June.*

At the suggestion of the commission I reduced the price of Smith's carbine to $30 from $32 50, yet my contract was forfeited, and I have been placed upon the brink of ruin. In *no other case* has such a decision been made, and I feel it due to myself to lay this matter before you, knowing, from your high character for honor, integrity, and justice, you will not permit a contractor who has tried to do his duty to be oppressed in such a manner.

To relieve myself from embarrassment I was compelled to accept $27 from the Ordnance department for 700 carbines, and have also offered an additional 800 at the same price. I would most respectfully ask that you will have me placed upon the *same footing as all the other* carbine contractors, and permit me to furnish the whole number for which I originally contracted at the same price as paid to other contractors, viz: $30. Relying upon your well-known view of fairness and justice,

I remain, with great respect, your obedient servant,

T. POULTNEY.

Hon. EDWIN M. STANTON,
    Secretary of War.

Before commission, June 14.

Letter of T. Poultney to the Secretary of War of May 24, complaining that a more stringent rule has been applied to him in regard to forfeited deliveries than to other contractors.

As the carbine presented is evidently defective as a serviceable arm from having certain important parts made of malleable iron, and as the number ordered will be enough to permit of a fair trial in service, the commission decide to adhere to its decision in the case.

June 28.—It having been shown that all the parts in malleable iron affecting the strength of the gun in use have been, or are to be in future, made of wrought iron, and that the contractors have offered the arm at $27 per carbine in their proposals under the advertisements for small arms, the commission agree to reopen the case of T. Poultney, and to confirm the original order to him for the undelivered number not forfeited under the rule adopted since the order was given to him, viz: "that forfeiture for non-delivery shall extend only to the number due in the month in which the failure occurs," provided the price to be paid does not exceed $27 per carbine, with appendages. Decision therefore recalled, and postscript of June 28 appended thereto.

P. V. HAGNER,
    Major of Ordnance, Assistant to Commission.

WASHINGTON, *April* 23, 1862.

GENERAL: Mr. Poultney left here one of his carbines, and by some accident it seems that the guard has been broken.

The break shows that this guard is of cast iron—called no doubt *malleable*—and also proves that if such a break occurs in service the brass pin is lost, and the gun becomes unserviceable.

As the commission have authorized the reception of some of these arms, Mr. Holt requests me to bring this evidence of bad work to your notice, that steps may be taken to make the manufacturers replace such cast iron parts by wrought iron in all the arms to be received under the decision of the commission.

Very respectfully, your obedient servant,

P. V. HAGNER,
    Major of Ordnance.

General RIPLEY, *Chief of Ordnance.*

COMMISSION ON ORDNANCE AND ORDNANCE STORES,
Washington, March 28, 1862.

GENERAL : The commission have the honor to report as follows :

CASE No. 19.—T. POULTNEY, of Washington.

Order by Secretary of War ; No. 4, page 15, of printed list.　To deliver 10,000 of Smith s breech-loading carbines at the factory of the Massachusetts Arms Company, Chicopee, at $32 50 each, provided the deliveries are made as promptly as stated in his propositions, viz :

First delivery in September, 1861, no number stated, and at the rate of 1,000 per month thereafter, until the whole 10,000 are delivered.

The commission find that the order is forfeited by non-fulfilment as to time, no deliveries having been made until January, 1862, and then only 400 ; that 500 only were delivered in February, and that 600 only are reported to be ready for delivery in March.

As the times of delivery required were exactly those proposed by Mr. Poultney, and as the order was given when the government need for carbines was so great that the hope of securing this number induced the acceptance of Mr. Poultney's proposition, notwithstanding objections on the ground of the high price of the arm, and also that it had not been tried in service, and as the government has lost all the advantage thus expected, and has been obliged to meet its wants by other arrangements, the commission decide that no further deliveries be received under this order of the 27th of August.

As it is reported that 600 of these arms have been already in great part inspected by the government officers, although not received, the commission direct that this number be purchased at the rate of $30 each. Further purchases should depend upon the exigencies of the service, and the price be regulated to conform to that paid for similar arms for mounted troops. Thirty dollars for any cavalry arm is deemed by the commission a higher price than ought to be paid. It has been allowed for the 600 carbines as above only because of the peculiar circumstances under which they are offered.

We are, sir, very respectfully, your obedient servants,

J. HOLT,
ROBERT DALE OWEN,
Commissioners.

Brigadier General J. W. RIPLEY,
Chief of Ordnance.

P. S., *June* 26, 1862.

Since the rendition of the foregoing decision it has been shown to the commission that the contractor, T. Poultney, has, in answer to the public advertisement inviting proposals for arms, dated May 17, 1862, offered Smith's breech-loading carbine at a considerable reduction from the price allowed him by the commission, (which they regarded as a higher price than ought to be paid for any cavalry arm,) namely, at the reduced price of $27 each.

Under these circumstances, although in conformity with the conditions stipulated in this order, the government is not bound to receive the carbines even at such reduced rate. Yet, as in other cases of similar character, where offers of reduction in price had been made, the commission has waived the forfeiture of the entire contract and granted a certain extension of time, and as it has been shown to the commission that the contractor is able to proceed in the delivery of the said carbines forthwith, the commission decide that the forfeiture shall extend to the three first deliveries only, namely, to three thousand carbines, and that the remaining seven thousand be received, deducting therefrom, however, first, the carbines already delivered previously to and under the former decision, namely, 1,500; and deducting, second, 1,500 carbines recently purchased by the Ordnance department, together 3,000, to be deducted from the above seven thousand, thus leaving 4,000 still to be delivered.

These 4,000 carbines the commission decide shall be accepted and paid for at the rate of $27 each, provided they be delivered at the rate of not less than 1,000 per month, commencing in the month of July, 1862; and upon the further condition that Mr. Poultney shall, within fifteen days after notice of this decision, execute bond, with good and sufficient sureties, in the form and with the stipulations prescribed by law and the regulations for the performance of the contract as thus modified, resulting from said order and acceptance, and upon his failure or refusal to execute such bond, then the said order shall be declared cancelled and of no effect.

We are, sir, very respectfully, your obedient servants,

J. HOLT,
ROBERT DALE OWEN,
Commissioners.
P. V. HAGNER,
Major of Ordnance, Assistant to Commission.

CASE No. 20.

H. HOLTHAUSEN.

ORDNANCE OFFICE,
Washington, August 27, 1861.

SIR: By direction of the Secretary of War, I accept your offer of thirty-two thousand arms made in your letter to the Secretary of War of the 30th of August, 1861, on the following terms and conditions: There are to be eight thousand of each of the four kinds of arms of which you exhibited samples, viz: two of rifled muskets, clasp bayonet, and two of carbines, (Minie,) with sabre bayonets, all of calibre .69-inch These arms are to be subject to inspection by such officer as this department may designate for the purpose, and are to be in all respects serviceable, and of as good quality as the samples. The same are to be delivered in Philadelphia in the months of November, December, and January next. In case of a failure to deliver in or within the times specified, the government is to be under no obligation to take the arms, but may or may not do so at its option.

Payments will be made on certificates of inspection and receipt by the United States inspector, in such funds as the Treasury Department may provide, at the following rates, for the arms, including the usual appendages: For No. 2 carbine, sabre bayonets, $19; for No. 5 carbine, sabre bayonets, $18; for No. 2 rifle musket, clasp bayonet, $16; for No. 5 rifle musket, clasp bayonet, $14. The payment to be for the arms in bond.

Please signify in writing your agreement or non-agreement, as the case may be, to deliver the arms on the terms and conditions specified herein.

Respectfully,

JAS. W. RIPLEY, *Brigadier General.*

Mr. H. HOLTHAUSEN,
Philadelphia, Pennsylvania.

ORDNANCE OFFICE,
Washington, November 26, 1861.

SIR: By direction of the Secretary of War, the time for delivery of the 32,000 arms, as per order to you of the 27th of August, 1861, is hereby extended, so as to allow you to commence delivering in the month of December next, and to continue to deliver every forty days up to the end of August, at which time the entire number ordered must be delivered. The arms and appendages are to be all new, and fully up to the samples, and subject to inspection. All the terms and conditions of the order of the 27th of August, 1861, except as regards the times of delivery, are to remain unchanged.

Respectfully, your obedient servant,

JAS W. RIPLEY, *Brigadier General.*

Mr. H. HOLTHAUSEN,
    Philadelphia, Pennsylvania.

WASHINGTON, *February* 4, 1862.

DEAR SIR: I have fifteen cases of guns on the steamer Bavaria to deliver under my order for 32,000 arms. On Saturday last I made application for an order to be issued by the War Department to the Treasury Department to have them delivered free of duty to Lieutenant Treadwell, as per the order. The order was sent to the Treasury; but about an hour after, the War Department sent over to the Treasury withdrawing it, the reason given for which is that the order ran out on January 31. The original order did; but, from and for reasons set forth in an application, I received an extension of the time to deliver these guns, they being new and good arms. I have succeeded beyond my expectations in making the deliveries of them; and my object in writing these lines is to respectfully request you to arrange the matter with the War Department so that the release shall be issued by them for these fifteen cases, and that I may have no further difficulty in delivering the balance as they arrive. The date of the extension is November 27, by which I have the privilege of delivering them up to the end of August next. I am sorry to put you to trouble to arrange this for me, but by so doing you will greatly oblige yours, very truly,

H. HOLTHAUSEN,
Per C. THROCKMORTON.

Brevet Brigadier General RIPLEY,
    Ordnance Department.

[Copy of indorsement on the back of the above.]

ORDNANCE OFFICE,
February 4, 1862.

Respectfully submitted to the Secretary of War.

Mr. Holtshausen, by his order of August 27, 1861, was to deliver 32,000 Minie rifles and carbines in the months of November and December, 1861, and January, 1862. By direction of the Secretary of War, on the 26th November, 1861, the time for delivering these arms was extended so as to allow Mr. Holtshausen to commence the deliveries in December, 1861, and to continue to deliver, every forty days, up to the end of August, 1862. He has delivered, commencing in December, 1861, 3,099 of these arms, and now states that he has 15 cases of them in port ready for delivery, and applies to have them entered free of duty.

Mr. Holtshausen has complied with the terms of his order, as modified, and has till the end of August to complete his deliveries. It is, therefore, recommended that his application be granted.

JAS. W. RIPLEY,
Brigadier General.

Approved.

EDWIN M. STANTON,
Secretary of War.

WASHINGTON, D. C., *February* 7, 1862.

Please to release twenty cases of guns just arrived by the steamer Hausa for Lieutenant Treadwell, of Frankfort arsenal, for contract of H. Holtshausen, of Philadelphia, of thirty-two thousand. The following are the numbers : J. P. 52 *a* 64, 115 *a* 116, 209 *a* 210, 1,099 *a* 1,110. They are consigned to Christ. Fay & Co., of New York.

Yours, respectfully,

H. HOLTSHAUSEN,
Per JOHN PONDIR.

Hon. E. M. STANTON,
Secretary of War.

[Copy of indorsement on the back of the above.]

ORDNANCE OFFICE,
February 7, 1862.

Respectfully returned. My report to the War Department, of February 4, 1862, on Mr. Holtshausen's order for 32,000 arms, is respectfully referred to for full information and for my recommendation in regard to this case. The delivery of the arms herein mentioned is within the terms of his order.

JAS. W. RIPLEY,
Brigadier General.

Secretary of the Treasury requested to give the instructions.

P. H. W.

WASHINGTON, *February* 11, 1862.

DEAR SIR : I have the honor of delivering to you herewith a copy of a contract received by me for 32,000 arms, dated August 27, 1861, and an extension of the same dated November 26, 1861. The reasons for this extension are set forth in a letter of application for the same, dated November 26, 1861.

I have complied with the terms of this extension; in fact, have more than done so. I have delivered in December 3,099, which have been inspected, and found to be first-class arms—fully up to sample—and have now at the arsenal 35 cases being inspected. I shall comply with the terms of this order in every respect.

Yours, very respectfully,

H. HOLTSHAUSEN,
Per JOHN PONDIR.

Hon. EDWIN M. STANTON, *Secretary of War.*

Before commission, March 28, 1862.

Mr. Pondir, a partner in business with Mr. Holtshausen, appeared before the commission, and stated that Mr. Holtshausen was in Europe; that he had the arms embraced in his order actually in process of manufacture, and that he could not now countermand his order for them.

COMMISSION ON ORDNANCE AND ORDNANCE STORES,
Washington, March 29, 1862.

GENERAL : The commission have the honor to report as follows :

CASE NO. 20.—H. HOLTSHAUSEN, of Philadelphia.

Order of August 27, 1861.—No. 20 of printed list, page 11.

To deliver in all 32,000 new arms, calibre .69. equal to samples offered and sealed.

Times of delivery first proposed and accepted, to include January, 1862. Subsequently, upon request made, the terms were modified, November 26, by direction of the Assistant Secretary of War, fixing the month of December for the first delivery, allowing to the end of August, 1862, for the final delivery. Deliveries already made amount to about 4,000, and a still larger number are in port, the delivery of which is suspended under the general orders of the War Department.

The commission find that the terms of the contract, as last extended, have been complied with by the contractor, and as arrangements have been made by them for the whole number, which cannot now be revoked without loss, they direct that the arms be received to the extent and upon the terms of the original order as extended November 26.

We are, sir, very respectfully, your obedient servants,

J. HOLT,
ROBERT DALE OWEN,
Commissioners.

P. V. HAGNER,
Major of Ordnance, Assistant to Commission.

Brigadier General J. W. RIPLEY,
Chief of Ordnance.

CASE No. 21.

ALFRED JENKS & SON, Philadelphia.

On the 13th day of July, 1861, a contract in precisely the same words, and for the same number of rifled muskets as that with Samuel Colt, previously given, was entered into by Brevet Brigadier General J. W. Ripley, acting by the authority of the Secretary of War, with Alfred Jenks & Son, of Philadelphia, Pennsylvania, and was approved of by the Secretary of War.

ALFRED JENKS & SON, Philadelphia, Pennsylvania.—25,000 *rifled muskets, model* 1855, *October* 7, 1861.

WAR DEPARTMENT,
Washington, October 5, 1861.

DEAR SIR: You will increase the orders to Messrs. Lamson, Goodnow & Yale, of New York, and the order to Jenks & Son, of Philadelphia, 25,000 guns in each case, quality and price the same as those previously ordered, the entire contract for 50,000 in each case to be completed within four months after the termination of present contracts for 25,000 each. Notify the parties at once, in order that facilities may be provided to manufacture as promptly as possible.

Yours, respectfully,

SIMON CAMERON,
Secretary of War.

General RIPLEY, *Chief of Ordnance.*

ORDNANCE OFFICE,
Washington, October 7, 1861.

GENTLEMEN: By direction of the Secretary of War, I offer you an order for twenty-five thousand (25,000) muskets, in addition to the 25,000 you contracted to deliver under date of July 13, 1861, on the following terms and conditions, viz: the kind, quality, and price of the arms and appendages now ordered are to be the same as those previously contracted for, and this order is to be an increase of the contract to 50,000 arms, the whole of which are to be delivered within four months after the termination of the contract of July 13, 1861, as therein specified and required.

Please signify in writing your acceptance or non-acceptance of this order, on the terms and conditions herein stated.

Respectfully, &c.,

JAMES W. RIPLEY,
Brigadier General.

Messrs. ALFRED JENKS & SON, *Philadelphia.*

BRIDESBURG MACHINE WORKS,
Philadelphia, October 9, 1861.

SIR: The offer made in your esteemed favor of the 7th instant for 25,000 muskets, in addition to those previously contracted for, is accepted. It will give us pleasure to furnish the same upon the terms and in the time named.

Shall we continue, after the completion of our present contract, to use the present model, or do you design furnishing us with the "last improved model?"

Very respectfully, your obedient servant,

ALFRED JENKS, JR.

General J. W. RIPLEY,
Ordnance Department, Washington.

Before commission, March 28, 1862.

Mr. J. G. Mitchell, of Jenks & Son, appeared before the commission, and states:

We have 14,000 arms passing through our establishment. We have none boxed as yet. We have only one inspector, which is not sufficient. We have been delayed in our work, because a defective model was furnished us from Springfield armory. The octagon, cone seat, and breech-pin were defective. We have now six men at Springfield examining machinery, &c., for us.

Before commission, March 31, 1862.

Mr. Barton H. Jenks, of Jenks & Son, Bridesburg, Pennsylvania, appeared before the commission, and states:

In five months we will furnish all the guns now overdue on our contract. It takes 13,000 guns on hand to turn out 200 per day. Our establishment can make 240 guns per day of ten hours. We have a contract with John Rice to furnish stocks and tips for him. We have finished 20 guns interchangeable in all respects except barrels. We are making all of the gun, except the barrel, sight, and stock, for Sarson & Roberts for 25,000. We have delivered to Sarson & Roberts almost everything under this contract.

COMMISSION ON ORDNANCE AND ORDNANCE STORES,
Washington, April 1, 1862.

GENERAL: The commission have the honor to report as follows:

CASE No. 21.—A. H. JENKS & SON, Philadelphia, Pa.

Orders dated 1st, July 13; 2d, October 7, numbers 3 and 29, printed list. — Orders for 50,000 Springfield rifles, at $20 each, deliverable 1,000 in January, 1862, and monthly, at that rate, to include April, 1862, and then 2,000 per month until 25,000 be delivered, and the remaining 25,000 within four months thereafter.

It appears, to the satisfaction of the commission that Messrs. Jenks & Son have zealously exerted themselves in preparing to carry out their contracts, and that the delay in early deliveries will be soon made good by the increased capacity of their works, the necessary extension of which, now perfected beyond the original expectation of the parties, has been the chief cause of the delay, and will insure a larger and better product to the government; and it further appears that the government is in want of the guns.

It is therefore recommended by the commission that the question of forfeiture for failure to deliver up to time be waived, and that Messrs. Jenks & Son be allowed to proceed to the fulfilment of their contract, provided the whole 50,000 are delivered by the date of their last pledged delivery.

We are, sir, very respectfully, your obedient servants,

J. HOLT,
ROBERT DALE OWEN,
Commissioners, &c.
P. V. HAGNER,
Major of Ordnance, Assistant to Commission.

Brigadier General J. W. RIPLEY,
Chief of Ordnance.

See paper No. 5, case No. 13, for additional condition imposed by the commission.

P. V. HAGNER, *Major of Ordnance.*

CASE No. 22.

COMMISSION ON ORDNANCE AND ORDNANCE STORES,
Washington, April 2, 1862.

GENERAL: The commission have the honor to report as follows:

CASE No. 22.—A. V. DUPONT & CO., Louisville, Ky.

Claim for amount of three bills, $702, October 14, and November 1 and 14. Referred by special order.

Three accounts for powder furnished upon the orders of General W. T. Sherman.

Prices charged—

Cannon powder...... .... 24 cents per pound.
Blasting powder .... 20 cents per pound.

The commission find that the qualities and prices charged are acknowledged by the receiving officer to be correct, and the accounts are fully approved also by General Sherman, commanding the department, who directed the purchase, he says, "at a time when it was of urgent necessity."

The commission therefore direct that payment be made to the full amount of the vouchers, to wit, $702.

We are, sir, very respectfully, your obedient servants,

J. HOLT,
ROBERT DALE OWEN,
Commissioners.
P. V. HAGNER,
Major of Ordnance, Assistant to Commission.

Brigadier General J. W. RIPLEY,
Chief of Ordnance.

CASE No 23.

COMMISSION ON ORDNANCE AND ORDNANCE STORES,
Washington, April 2, 1862.

GENERAL : The commission have the honor to report as follows :

CASE No. 23.—B. F. CRONIN, Frederick, Maryland.

Claim of amount of account for ordnance stores, dated November 22, 1861. Referred by special order.

A voucher for $21 for powder, balls, and material for cartridge bags, ordered by Colonel Link, 12th Rhode Island volunteers, and approved by the commanding officer "as necessary for the public service."

The commission find that the commanding officer of the post directed Colonel Link to prepare certain guns for service, for which no suitable ammunition was at hand ; that, finding the necessary materials in the neighborhood, he purchased and prepared the ammunition ; that he was subsequently called upon by the commanding officer of the department for a statement of the circumstances, and that, after receiving this, General Banks approved the account.

The account is defective in not stating the number of balls purchased, but, under the circumstances, the commission direct that it be paid to the full amount, viz : $21.

We are, sir, very respectfully, your obedient servants,
J. HOLT,
ROBERT DALE OWEN,
Commissioners.
P. V. HAGNER,
Major of Ordnance, Assistant to Commission.
Brigadier General J. W. RIPLEY,
Chief of Ordnance.

[Copy of indorsement on back of the above.]

ORDNANCE OFFICE, *April* 4, 1862.

Under this decision the account will be paid at the Washington arsenal, out of the appropriation for ordnance and ordnance stores.

JAMES W. RIPLEY,
Brigadier General.

CASE No. 24.

ALEXIS GODILLOT.

NEW YORK, *February* 11, 1862.

SIR : I respectfully remit you enclosed—following your general order of the 29th January, 1861—copies of contracts for revolvers and guns given by Major P. V. Hagner, of the ordnance department, United States army.

And remain, respectfully, your obedient servant,
ALEXIS GODILLOT,
By J. B. KING.

Hon. E. M. STANTON,
Secretary of War, Washington, D. C.

ORDNANCE OFFICE,
No. 55 White street, New York, December 19, 1861.

SIR : In compliance with instructions from chief of ordnance, I request that you will deliver to United States ordnance department 1,000 French revolvers, like sample deposited with me, with Ordnance office seal attached.

Ex. Doc. 72——9

The said pistols to be furnished as stipulated in your proposal to the Assistant Secretary of War dated December 16, 1861, and at the price therein stated.

Upon arrival of the arms in New York notice is to be given at this office, and permission will thereupon be furnished to you to receive free of duty from the custom-house the cases which you are to deliver there for inspection at this office.

All not equal to sample in every particular affecting their value or service will be rejected, to be returned by you to the custom-house for payment of duties or for exportation.

Very respectfully, your obedient servant,

P. V. HAGNER,
Major of Ordnance.

Mr. A. GODILLOT, *Paris.*

ORDNANCE OFFICE,
No. 55 White street, New York, December 20, 1861.

SIR: Please furnish United States ordnance department with 1,000 Lefaucheaux revolvers, with fifty cartridges each, at $17, delivered here for inspection free of duty; also 1,500 French model rifle muskets, calibre .69, with 18-inch bayonets, with appendages, delivered here for inspection free of duty, at $15 each.

The whole to be delivered with the least possible delay, not to exceed thirty-five days for the revolvers and a portion of the rifles, the balance as follows, within —— days.

Very respectfully, your obedient servant,

P. V. HAGNER,
Major of Ordnance.

Mr. ALEXIS GODILLOT, *New York.*

COMMISSION ON ORDNANCE AND ORDNANCE STORES,
Washington, April 2, 1862.

GENERAL: The commission have the honor to report as follows:

CASE No. 24.—ALEXIS GODILLOT, of New York.

Orders by Maj. P. V Hagner, Dec. 19, 1861.   To furnish, (by order of Secretary of War,) 1st, 1,000 revolvers, like sample, with 50 cartridges for each, price fixed at fifty dollars each; 2d, 2,000 Lefaucheaux revolvers, with 50 cartridges each, like sample, at $17 each; and 1,500 French model rifled muskets, calibre .69, with 18-inch bayonets, at $18 each.

Deliveries suspended under general orders.

The commission find that, under the first order, 450 have been received, and 100 are in bond ready for delivery. The residue of the order has not been shipped. Under the second order the commission find that of the rifle muskets 336 have been received, 768 are now in port, and besides enough to fill the order, (with some surplus,) 396 of these guns having been previously lost on the passage; also that 6 have been received of the Lefaucheaux revolvers, 1,500 are now in bond, and that 600 of another pattern, valued at $15 90 each, have been sent here to fill the balance of the order, as 500 of the prescribed pattern were lost on the passage, and no similar ones could be obtained by Mr. Godillot in the time to meet the requirements of the orders.

As the arms are needed by the government, and are of good quality, and of reasonable price, the commission direct that all those now in port of the prescribed pattern, which pass the proper inspection, be received, and that the question of purchasing the surplus rifled muskets, and the 600 pistols last mentioned, be referred to the chief of ordnance.

We are, sir, very respectfully, your obedient servants,

J. HOLT,
ROBERT DALE OWEN,
Commissioners.
P. V. HAGNER,
Major of Ordnance, Assistant to Commission.

Brigadier General J. W. RIPLEY,
Chief of Ordnance.

CASE No. 25.

E. REMINGTON & SONS, Ilion, New York.—10,000 *regulation rifles, with sword bayonets, July* 30, 1861.

ORDNANCE OFFICE, *Washington, July* 30, 1861.

GENTLEMEN : You will please make for this department, and deliver with all possible despatch, ten thousand rifles, with sword bayonets, and appendages complete. These rifles are to be of .58 inch calibre, and to have a three-leaf rear sight, and a cupped ramrod, with sword bayonet stud similar to those of the Harper's Ferry rifle model of 1855, in other respects of the pattern of the rifles without bayonets heretofore made by you for this department.

Please send a sample rifle to this office as soon as possible for examination, and to serve as a guide in the inspection of the 10,000 to be delivered by you.

These rifles are to be subject to the regular inspection, and to be paid for on certificates of inspection and receipt, at twenty dollars each, appendages and sword bayonets included. Please signify your acceptance or non-acceptance of this order, and in case of acceptance lose no time in preparing and delivering the arms.

Respectfully, your obedient servant,

JAMES W. RIPLEY,
Brevet Brigadier General.

Messrs. E. REMINGTON & SONS,
Ilion, New York.

ILION, *Herkimer County, N. Y., August* 6, 1861.

SIR : We have the honor to acknowledge the receipt of your communication of 30th ultimo, and to say that we accept the order contained therein for ten thousand rifles, model of 1855, with sword bayonets and appendages complete.

Respectfully, &c.,

E. REMINGTON & SONS.

JAMES W. RIPLEY,
Brevet Brigadier General, Washington, D. C.

E. REMINGTON & SONS, Ilion, Herkimer county, New York.—5,000 *Remington revolvers, army size, July* 29, 1861.

NEW YORK, *July* 18, 1861.

GENERAL : Mr. Remington takes on to you one of his revolvers. I am procuring all of them I can for the western army, and hope to hear I can get all I may need. I have seen no revolver I like as well, and the price is nearer the

cost than with some others.   As Messrs. Remington have done much good work
for the department under my superintendence, I take pleasure in mentioning
them to you.
        Very respectfully, your obedient servant,

                                        P. V. HAGNER, *Brevet Major.*
  GENERAL RIPLEY,
          Chief of Ordnance, Washington.

                                WATERVLIET ARSENAL, *July* 2, 1861.
  SIR : Mr. J. Remington, of the firm of E. Remington & Son, of ——, New
York, has shown me a pistol of their make, which I think deserves the consideration of the ordnance department, and I have therefore advised him to present the pistol in person to you for examination.   Its combination of parts is
very simple.
        I am, sir, respectfully, your obedient servant,
                                        W. A. THORNTON,
                              Brevet Major U. S. Army, Com'g Arsenal.
  Colonel J. W. RIPLEY,
          United States Corps of Ordnance.

                                        ORDNANCE OFFICE,
                                        Washington, July 29, 1861.
  GENTLEMEN : Please make for this department, with the greatest possible
despatch, 5,000 revolver pistols, of the same description as the sample you
showed here, but of the calibre of the army pistol, .44 inch.   Send a sample of
the pistol, calibre .44 inch, such as you are to deliver, for examination at this
office and to serve as a guide in the inspections.   There will be allowed for
these pistols fifteen dollars ($15) each, including appendages ; to be paid, as
usual, on certificates of inspection and receipt.   Please signify your acceptance
or non-acceptance of this order.
        Respectfully, your obedient servant,

                                        JAMES W. RIPLEY,
                                        Brevet Brigadier General:
  Messrs. E. REMINGTON & SONS, *Ilion, N. Y.*

                                WASHINGTON, *July* 29, 1861.
  SIR : We have the honor to inform you that we will accept of your order to
furnish your department with five thousand revolver pistols similar to sample
shown you, but of the army size of calibre, at $15 each.
        Respectfully, &c.,

                                        E. REMINGTON & SONS.
  General JAMES W. RIPLEY,
          Ordnance Department, Washington, D. C.

P. S. JUSTICE, Philadelphia, Pa.—1,000 *Whitney revolvers, August* 21, 1861.

  This contract was made with P. S. Justice by Major P. V. Hagner, and his
authority for making contracts and purchases will be found in the letter from
the Ordnance office to the Secretary of War of August 5, 1861, and which
forms a portion of part 6 of these papers.

                  Before the commission, April 4, 1862.

  Mr. Remington (Ilion Works, New York) came before the commission and
says he has a contract for 1,000 Harper's Ferry rifles, calibre .58, and also

5,000 army revolvers. Has expended $100,000 in preparations; has gone on with diligence twenty hours out of twenty-four, and has left nothing undone. Can now deliver pistols; could have delivered army pistols heretofore, but was delayed on account of the delivery of navy pistols to Major Hagner.

Theirs is an established firm, which has worked for government for fifteen years. Has filled contracts for altering 20,000 smooth-bore muskets to Maynard's primer, and two contracts for guns; has declined, in every instance, to have anything to do with Springfield contracts; has been applied to to take contracts to furnish barrels, make parts, &c., but refused in all cases; uses bored steel barrels; desires to make all things of American manufacture.

April 14.—Mr. Remington stated to commission that he would make 30,000 pistols, additional, at $13, and 10,000 at $14, and 5,000 at $14 50; reducing present order to the above prices, and including the present order.

Before the commission, April 7, 1862.

Mr. Remington, of Ilion, New York, was again before the commission, and says that there should be no difference in price between the government rifle and the musket, except the bayonet. The sword bayonet costs twice as much as the triangular, and the difference between them should be from $1 to $1 50; would be willing to make Springfield guns for $16, if he had assurance of work longer than one year; has all that is requisite to make 100 guns per day, either rifle or musket, as ordered; will deliver the 10,000 already contracted for at $18 each, if the order is allowed to stand. His house had canvassed the question of reducing their prices, but feared their motives might be misconstrued; says $20 is more than the government should pay for his arms, which cost him more than the Springfield gun; will make Springfield guns (with a contract for one year) at $16.

Before the commission, April 24, 1862.

Mr. E. Remington appeared before the commission, and being examined under oath, says: I am engaged in the manufacture of arms, rifles, and revolvers, and am now making rifles with sword bayonets, and revolvers. Our revolvers are made after a patent; those heretofore delivered are upon Beal's patent; those we propose to make in future are in accordance with Elliott's patent. The patented part, in both cases, is the mode of releasing the cylinder from its position and the plan of holding in the base-pin on axle of cylinder.

I have examined the various revolvers now in use—our arm, the Savage, Starr, and Colt's—and as a mechanic, familiar with the mode of doing such work as is required upon these arms, I should say that the Colt's and our own would cost about the same to make, with equal economy in the management; and the same may be said of the Savage and Starr. (The Savage and Starr would cost about the same.)

As to the Colt's arm, we have examined it with care, and have decided that we could make it quite as cheap or cheaper than our own; but we do not think the plan as good as ours. I have not examined either of the others (Savage or Starr) with a view to compare the amount of work, but have handled them frequently, and have formed the opinion expressed upon my general knowledge and experience. I think that the difference of cost between our own and Colt's and the others (Savage's or Starr's) would not be far from one dollar.

In regard to the actual cost of our revolver, I wish to state that we have to pay for two patents. Our profits must therefore be proportionately larger in this, considering the patents, than we should require on rifle or musket work. I will say that should we be dealt with as others have been, receiving a large order for pistols, we would be glad to make them at $12; I mean, by a large order, about 30,000 to 40,000. We can, if the government wish it, turn out 200 to 250 per day of the army size by stopping the manufacture of navy size. Knowing positively that we have a certain large number to make, we can do it at the least cost.

E. REMINGTON.

WASHINGTON, April 5, 1862.

GENTLEMEN : We remarked yesterday, in reply to Judge Holt's inquiry, that United States rifles might be furnished for less than $20, and pay a fair manufacturing profit. Major Hagner has suggested that some explanation of that reply might be desirable, and requested that it be made in writing, together with some proposition to furnish a further supply of arms.

As to the cost of this rifle, or any other arm, several things are to be considered : such as the adaptation of the machinery to the perfect working of the several parts ; systematic division of labor, so that the various pieces shall be manipulated by operatives well skilled in their respective departments ; and then the whole process should be conducted under the personal supervision of a head of sufficient skill and experience to carry forward all the details to the final assembling of a perfect arm. In addition to this, the *quantity* to be furnished and the time for delivery have an important bearing upon the question of cost. These conditions necessarily involve the use of a large amount of capital and the employment of artisans and operatives of skill and training, which cannot well be improvised or suddenly diverted from other callings. This difficulty practical manufacturers have always found serious, and it is now increased by the disturbed condition of the country and the increased demand for such service at the government armories. It will be apparent, from these considerations, that a limited order could not be filled without loss at a rate that would pay a profit when ordered in larger quantities, with more time for delivery.

We are now engaged upon an order given us by the ordnance department for 10,000 United States rifles and 5,000 army revolvers, at $20 each for the rifles and $15 each for the revolvers. This order, it will be observed, is quite limited, as compared with those previously and since given for muskets and revolvers to private establishments. When this order was given we were prepared with machinery and tools for making revolvers, for which there was *then* a brisk mercantile demand. This enabled us to furnish that arm to the government at $15, without particular reference to the *quantity*. At *that time* we could dispose of all we made to the trade, at prices considerably in advance of that paid us by the government ; so that, if the orders from the government were limited, the trade demand would then save us from ruinous sacrifice of capital invested in that branch of our business. But these considerations do not apply to the rifle. The use of that arm is confined almost exclusively to the public service. It requires machinery and tools particularly adapted to its fabrication, involving the investment of capital not applicable to other branches of the trade. If, therefore, the order for this arm was confined to the 10,000, there would be a loss or depreciation of capital thus invested nearly, if not quite, equal to the profit on them at $20. In view of these considerations, and the fact that the rifle with sabre bayonet costs about $1 50 more than the musket, we thought the price of $20 each for that limited quantity was not exorbitant or unreasonable. But intending, as we do, to continue in the business of manufacturing arms permanently, it obviously would be for our interest to furnish them in such quantities as would enable us to reduce the price ; and if the government would engage to take all the rifles we can make in one year after the completion of the present order for 10,000, (or say from 40,000 to 50,000,) we would furnish them, subject to inspection, at $17, and reduce the price on the 10,000 now in hand to $17 each; or, after completing the 10,000 rifles, we would make 50,000 Springfield muskets with the triangular bayonet, subject to inspection of the ordnance department, at $16 each, and in that case we would also reduce the price of the 10,000 in hand from $20 to $17 each.

Our house has been constantly engaged in the fabrication of arms and parts of arms for nearly forty years, and we now possess facilities for completing every part of the rifle and revolver second only to one other private establishment in this country, and we had expected such an increase of orders from the government as would place us on a footing more nearly approaching equality with other private establishments.

Having business correspondence in all the principal cities of the south, we declined all orders for arms when there was the slightest ground to suspect the loyalty of the parties. As early as November, 1860, we commenced returning orders from our southern customers, and we have not furnished any one since who was known to sympathize with the rebellion. Jefferson Davis ordered 5,000 rifles for the State of Mississippi, in November, 1860, which was also peremptorily declined. In this we have only done our duty as loyal citizens. We claim no credit for performing our duty, nor do we wish to disparage others or make uncharitable comparisons; but justice to ourselves requires us to state that we have furnished the government with our army and navy revolvers at $15, while it was compelled to pay $20 and $25 for large quantities of a similar arm confessedly no better than our own; and in all our intercourse we have been governed in all respects by the usages and regulations of the service.

In our dealings with the government, as with the general public, we have desired to secure such legitimate profits as the skill, experience, and capital employed in the business might fairly entitle us to; and we think we may confidently refer to our whole record with the government, and to the facts now brought to the knowledge of the commissioners, to determine whether we have or have not also been mindful of the interest and welfare of the State.

E. REMINGTON & SONS.

Hon. Joseph Holt and others,
Of the Commission for examining Contracts for Arms, &c.

Washington, *April* 11, 1862.

Referring to our communication of the 5th April instant, in which it was proposed to reduce the price named in the order of General Ripley, of the 29th July last, for 10,000 rifles and appendages, we now propose to apply the same principle to the order for revolvers.

The consideration that governed us in that proposal, it will be remembered, was, that arms could be manufactured cheaper and furnished upon more favorable terms in *large* than in *small* quantities. We therefore propose to furnish the government from 40,000 to 50,000 of our army and navy revolvers (or such quantity as our facilities will enable us to make and deliver in one year after completing the order for 5,000) for $13 each, and upon receiving such additional order we will also reduce the price (the 5,000 on hand) from $15 to $13 each. All subject to government inspection.

E. REMINGTON & SONS.

Hon. J. Holt and others,
Of the Commission to examine Contracts for Arms, &c.

Washington City, D. C., *April* 18, 1862.

General: The commission request to be informed whether the ordnance department would desire any additional number of Harper's Ferry rifles, with sword bayonets, such as now ordered from Mr. E. Remington, of Ilion. Mr. Remington has made a proposition to deliver such rifles at $17. If his order were extended to 40,000 or 50,000, including the number now ordered, the price of the 10,000 to be also reduced to $17. He also proposes to furnish 40,000 Springfield muskets at $16 each, if muskets are preferred to the rifles, and in such case also to reduce the price of 10,000 rifles, now ordered, to $17; the commission to have the advantage of your judgment on these propositions. Mr. Remington also proposes to deliver his army or navy revolvers at $13, if he could receive an order occupying his present force about one year. Please inform the commission whether it would be advisable to extend the manufacture of these revolvers, and which kind preferably, and to what extent in numbers, considering the advantage of thus reducing the prevailing high prices of such arms.

Very respectfully, sir, your obedient servant,

P. V. HAGNER,
Major of Ordnance.

General JAS. W. RIPLEY,
Chief of Ordnance.

COMMISSION ON ORDNANCE, *May* 16, 1862.

GENERAL: There are circumstances connected with the proposals of Mr. Remington for furnishing arms, made under your recent advertisement, which render it desirable that they should be communicated to us, and that we should have the privilege of exchanging views with you in regard to them before any action is taken by your department. We trust it will be agreeable to you to favor us with this opportunity.

Very respectfully, your obedient servant,

J. HOLT, *Commissioner.*

General JAS. W. RIPLEY,
Chief of Ordnance.

COMMISSION, &c., *May* 24, 1862.

GENERAL: Mr. Holt, on the part of the commission, Mr. Owen being absent, begs me to state to you that the commission had considered the circumstance that if their recommendation to award the number of 40,000 Springfield muskets to Messrs. Remington was adopted, that the delivery of all could not be made within a year from the date of the advertisement, and in so much would not be in exact accordance with the words of the invitation for proposals. But they consider that it would be perfectly competent for the department to fix its own terms in so small a matter, as the object of the law and compliance with it had been effected without injury to any individual and with benefit to the government interests by the acceptance with such slight departure.

The commission consider it highly important to execute a contract with such a reliable company as that above named at the price of $16, and they trust that you will agree with them that it should be done with as little delay as possible, in order that it may be known as the standard price. Supposing that it would be at once executed, being, as they think, in every way favorable to the government, they have decided upon Mr. Remington's orders of last year, connecting them with the acceptance of this proposal.

Very respectfully, sir, your obedient servant,

P. V. HAGNER,
Major of Ordnance.

General JAS. W. RIPLEY,
Chief of Ordnance.

COMMISSION ON ORDNANCE,
Washington, May 21, 1862.

SIR: In reply to the recent advertisement made by the chief of ordnance for arms, &c., ninety-one proposals have been submitted. Abstracts of these proposals have been examined by us, and the result has satisfied us that this step taken by the ordnance department, if followed up, cannot fail, while guarding the morality of the service, to save many millions to the treasury. Among the proposals is that of E. Remington & Son for forty thousand Springfield guns at $16 each, which is the best offer made. We earnestly recommend, as a means of fixing the price of this arm at a fair rate, that the proposal of Remington & Son shall be at once accepted and a contract closed with them. Mr. Remington is one of the oldest manufacturers of arms in the United States, is a man of high character and undoubted responsibility, and has in his conferences with us displayed public spirit that cannot be too strongly commended. His example, if properly encouraged, will prove invaluable to the government.

Very respectfully, &c.,

J. HOLT, Commissioner.

Hon. EDWIN M. STANTON,
Secretary of War.

P. S.—It would also be important, as answering all objections to the action of the commission in reducing to 20,000 many of the orders for larger numbers, while allowing the price of $20 for each gun, to accept the offer made by John D. Pitts, of Trenton, New Jersey, to furnish 10,000 Springfield muskets at $17, and the commission is therefore anxious that this offer be also accepted.

J. HOLT, Commissioner.

COMMISSION ON ORDNANCE AND ORDNANCE STORES,
Washington, May 23, 1862.

GENERAL: The commission have the honor to report as follows:

CASE No. 25.—E. REMINGTON & SONS, Ilion, N. Y.

Two orders from chief of ordnance.—See pp. 48 and 195, Ex. Doc. No 67 Referred by direction of the Secretary of War.

1st, to deliver 10,000 rifles, with sword bayonets, with all possible despatch; order given July 30. Price, $20 per gun. 2d, to deliver 5,000 revolver pistols, calibre .44, with the greatest possible despatch; price, $15. Order given July 30.

The commission find that the Messrs. Remington have been for a number of years manufacturers of arms for the government; that they have a large and well-supplied factory for gun work; that, upon receipt of the above orders, they enlarged the capability of their establishment by the expenditure of about $100,000; that they are working zealously and at extra hours to expedite their work, and have now parts of all the 5,000 pistols in hand.

The work on the rifles is also fully under way, and parts of a large number are in hand.

Mr. Remington has appeared before the commission, and stated that they desired to devote the full capabilities of their establishment to the use of the government; that they found they could manufacture pistols and rifles with fair profit to themselves at much less prices, provided the government would secure to them work for a reasonable time by giving orders for arms to the extent given to other first class manufacturers; that if permitted to contract with the government for the manufacture of 40,000 rifles additional, or 40,000 Springfield muskets, they would agree to furnish the rifles with sabre bayonets at $17 each, or the Springfield muskets at $16 each, and would then charge the above 10,000 rifles, if confirmed to them, at the rate of $17 only; and, further, that in case their proposal, made in accordance with the advertisement of the ordnance department, to furnish army revolvers was accepted, they would likewise agree to include the number in the above order of July 30 as forming part of any number ordered, and at the rates stated in their proposal. The commission, accepting the above offer of Mr. Remington, postponed action on the above cases, and recommended the execution of contracts for 40,000 Springfield muskets at $16, and for 20,000 army and navy revolvers at $12. As the said contracts have now been executed accordingly on the part of the government, they hereby confirm the above orders of July 30 for 10,000 Harper's Ferry rifles and of July 30 for 5,000 army revolvers, according to all their terms and conditions, provided that the price to be paid for each rifle shall be $17, including appendages, and for each revolver $12 dollars, including appendages; and provided, further, that they shall, within fifteen days after notice of this decision, execute bond, with good and sufficient sureties, in the form and with the stipulations prescribed by law, and the regulations for the performance of the contract, as thus modified, and, upon their failure or refusal to execute such bond, then the said orders shall be declared cancelled and of no effect.

We are, sir, very respectfully, your obedient servants,

J. HOLT,
ROBERT DALE OWEN,
Commissioners.

P. V. HAGNER,
Major of Ordnance, Assistant to Commission.

General J. W. RIPLEY,
Chief of Ordnance.

WASHINGTON, *June* 20, 1862.

DEAR SIR: In the report which we will make to the Secretary of War in a few days we shall take occasion to mention the reduced price at which Springfield muskets have been contracted to be manufactured, and think it would be only justice for us to state that the information on which our action, in insisting on this reduction as reasonable, has been based *came from yourself.* Have you any objections to our referring to you in this connexion by name? If you have, of course we will not do it. Please answer by return mail, and oblige,

Very respectfully,

J. HOLT, *Commissioner.*

Mr. S. REMINGTON, *Ilion, New York.*

OFFICE OF REMINGTON'S ARMORY,
Ilion, New York, June 25, 1862.

SIR: We have your favor of the 20th instant, addressed to one Mr. S. Remington, and, in reply, have to say that we have no objection to your using our name, as suggested, in your report to the Secretary of War in connexion with the manufacturing of the Springfield muskets, &c.

We are, very respectfully, your obedient servants,

E. REMINGTON & SONS.

Hon. JOSEPH HOLT, *Washington, D. C.*

CASE No. 26.

H. J. IBBOTSON.

7 BROADWAY, *New York, February* 10, 1862.

SIR: A contract for the delivery of twenty thousand Enfield rifles was issued to Mr. Henry J. Ibbotson, of Sheffield, then in this city, under date October 23, 1861, and accepted by him.

Mr. Ibbotson at once proceeded to England to procure and ship the same, but, owing to the prohibition placed on the exportation of arms from England within a week after his arrival there, has been unable to deliver according to the terms of the contract.

Mr. Ibbotson took with him funds to the amount of eighty-five thousand dollars, and is now in England with the funds lying idle, waiting an opportunity to ship the guns he has engaged and purchased.

I beg leave, on behalf of Mr. Ibbotson, to append a copy of the contract issued to him, and to request that whatever guns he may have purchased under the same may be received as soon as the prohibition is sufficiently relaxed to enable him to ship them. A different course would subject him to very severe and, in his case, unmerited losses.

Trusting this may receive your favorable consideration,

I am, sir, your obedient servant,

GEO. MACKENZIE,
For HENRY J. IBBOTSON.

Hon. EDWIN M. STANTON,
  Secretary of War, Washington, D. C.

ORDNANCE OFFICE, *Washington, October* 23, 1861.

SIR: By direction of the Secretary of War I offer you an order for twenty thousand (20,000) Enfield rifle muskets, with the usual appendages, on the following terms and conditions, viz:

The arms are to be subject to inspection by such officer as this department may designate for the purpose, and are to be delivered at New York as follows, viz: 2,500 in sixty days from this date; 2,500 in seventy-five days from this date; 2,500 in ninety days from this date; and not less than 5,000 per month thereafter, until the whole 20,000 shall be delivered.

In case of failure to make the delivery in or within the time specified, the government will have authority to revoke and annul this order.

Payments will be made, on certificates of inspection and receipt of the United States inspector, in such funds as the Treasury Department may provide for the purpose, at the rate of twenty dollars ($20) for each arm, including appendages, in bond or free from duty.

Please signify in writing your acceptance or non-acceptance of this order on the terms and conditions stated.

Respectfully, your obedient servant,

J. W. RIPLEY, *Brigadier General.*

HENRY J. IBBOTSON, *New York, N. Y.*

NEW YORK, *March* 20, 1862.

SIR: We are in receipt of one hundred and eight cases, containing twenty-one hundred and forty Enfield rifles, with implements, shipped from Liverpool per steamship "Jura," *via* Portland, by Mr. Henry J. Ibbotson, under a contract made with him by the United States government, dated October 23, 1861.

As Mr. Ibbotson's agents here, we would respectfully ask for an order that the above may be received under the above contract, they having been shipped immediately that shipments became possible after the removal of the prohibition in England, and before the copy of the order "rescinding all foreign contracts," of January 29, was able to reach Mr. Ibbotson.

We remain, sir, your obedient servants,

LARSON & ROBERTS, *Agents,*
For HENRY J. IBBOTSON.

Hon. EDWIN M. STANTON,
  Secretary of War, Washington.

ORDNANCE OFFICE, *March* 24, 1862.

Mr. Ibbotson, by direction of the Secretary of War, received an order dated 23d October, 1861, for 20,000 Enfield rifle muskets, at $20 each, deliverable in New York; 2,500 in sixty days, 2,500 in seventy-five days, and 2,500 in ninety days from date of order, and not less than 5,000 per month thereafter. One of the conditions of the order was, that in case of failure to make the delivery in or within the times specified, the government will have authority to revoke and annul the order. If these are really Enfield rifles, of good quality, we want them, and I recommend that Captain Crispin, in New York, be authorized to receive them by purchase (and not under the order) at their fair market value, if he find on inspection that they are of such kind and quality as are suitable and desirable to obtain for the military service.

JAS. W. RIPLEY, *Brigadier General.*

Referred to ordnance commission.

EDWIN M. STANTON.

NEW YORK, *April* 3, 1862.

SIR: Under a contract, issued October 23, to Mr. Henry J. Ibbotson, for the supplying of twenty thousand Enfield rifle muskets to the United States government, Mr. Ibbotson made his business arrangements here, and taking with him a credit on London for eighteen thousand pounds, started for England, where he arrived early in November, and at once proceeded to purchase and to have manufactured the number of arms called for in the order. By the time he had secured about twenty-two hundred, (within about a week after his arrival,) a prohibition was issued by the English government forbidding the exportation of arms, and, in consequence, Mr. Ibbotson was unable to ship them in time to fulfil the terms of the order, by no fault of his own, but by a cause he was entirely unable to control. Immediately upon the removal of the prohibition, Mr. Ibbotson shipped them, and they were on their way to this country per steamer "Jura" to Portland, within a week after that time. Twenty-one hundred and forty are now in the bonded warehouse in New York, ready for delivery, and we would respectfully ask for an order that they may be received under the contract—their non-arrival here, according to the terms of the contract, being caused solely by the action of the English government in prohibiting their leaving the country.

The delay in realizing the proceeds of this shipment is now causing Mr. Ibbotson very serious embarrassments, and we would respectfully request your early and favorable consideration of this subject.

We are, very respectfully, your obedient servants,

LARSON & ROBERTS, *Agents,*
For HENRY J. IBBOTSON.

Hon. EDWIN M. STANTON,
   Secretary of War, &c., Washington.

Before commission, April 7, 1862.

Messrs. Larson & Roberts, agents for Mr. Ibbotson, of New York, appeared before commission, and state: Has an order for 20,000 Enfield rifles, to be delivered, first, 2,500 within sixty days; the time elapsed before the arms were here; 2,140 have arrived, and are now in New York. Mr. Ibbotson is in Birmingham. Messrs. Larson & Roberts, in his behalf, request that the number in the country be received and the balance be surrendered. These guns were delayed on account of the Queen's proclamation, in part. They cost, some fifty-nine shillings, some sixty-eight, and the cheapest fifty-five shillings. Average cost in bond not less than eighteen dollars.

WASHINGTON, *April* 8, 1862.

SIRS: Referring to the matter of Mr. Henry J. Ibbotson's shipment of Enfield rifles, in regard to which we had the pleasure of speaking to you yesterday, we should esteem it an especial favor, having heavy drafts to meet this week on Mr. Ibbotson's account, if you would kindly cause the matter to be acted upon as quickly as possible, in order to assist us in doing so.

We remain your obedient servants,

LARSON & ROBERTS.

Hon. JOSEPH HOLT and ROBERT DALE OWEN, *Washington.*

COMMISSION ON ORDNANCE AND ORDNANCE STORES,
Washington, April 8, 1862.

GENERAL: The commission have the honor to report as follows:

CASE NO. 26.—H. J. IBBOTSON, New York.

Order dated Oct. 23, 1861. No. 34 of printed list. To deliver 20,000 Enfield rifled muskets in bond in New York, at $20 each, with implements. First delivery, 2,500 in sixty days; second delivery, 2,500 in seventy-five days; third delivery, 2,500 in ninety days; and not less than 5,000 per month thereafter.

The commission find that Mr. Ibbotson proceeded to England upon receipt of his order, arriving early in November; that upon the publication of the Queen's proclamation forbidding the exportation of arms he had to suspend operations, having secured about 2,200; that upon the removal of the prohibition he shipped 2,140, which are now in New York; but he has made no further adequate provision, either by purchase or arrangement for manufacture, for fulfilling this contract, so that up to the present date 17,500 guns are due from him to the government, and he is in a condition to and offers to deliver but the said 2,140.

In consequence of which default on his part, said contract, according to its terms, has become liable to forfeiture, and is hereby declared to be annulled and held for naught.

Mr. Ibbotson having, however, purchased and shipped said 2,140 arms, which are now in this country, the commission direct that these be received as a purchase from him, provided they are found to be of the kind and quality stipulated for, and that payment be made for them at $18 50 each, which sum, in the judgment of the commission, will give him two and a half per cent. on his outlay, and will also reimburse him his actual expenses.

Very respectfully, &c.,

J. HOLT,
ROBERT DALE OWEN,
Commissioners, &c.
P. V. HAGNER,
Major of Ordnance, Assistant to Commission.

Brigadier General J. W. RIPLEY,
Chief of Ordnance.

CASE No. 27.

WILSTACH & Co.

PHILADELPHIA, *April* 3, 1862.

GENTLEMEN: We take the liberty of handing you, with this, a copy of an order for cavalry sabres and non-commissioned officers' swords, given to us by Major R. H. K. Whiteley, commanding the New York arsenal; as also copies of the correspondence that has passed between Lieutenant T. J. Treadwell and Major R. H. K. Whiteley in relation to its state of forwardness and quality of the goods. We were not aware until a short time since that this would be embraced within the requirements of the Secretary of War's order for copies of all unexecuted orders for arms, or we should have taken pleasure in advising you of this within the required time. The balance of the order for cavalry sabres were ready for inspection on the day that Major Laidley received his instructions in regard to the further receipt of arms, and, in consequence, he has declined to accept or inspect these until otherwise ordered by the department. On receipt of Major Whiteley's letter addressed to Lieutenant Treadwell, dated January 16, and a copy of which is annexed, Major Laidley directed us to make the non-commissioned officers' swords, and we now have them in process of finishing, and the larger portion ready for delivery.

In relation to the apparent delay in the execution of this order we have to say that the parties whom we had originally to work upon it were induced by higher prices to quit us and go to work for others, thereby causing us to enter into new arrangements and get up extra sets of tools. The higher rates paid by the government subsequent to this contract admitted of the contracting parties paying higher wages; but we have now succeeded in furnishing an article superior to any, and can deliver the entire order within a very short time.

We would earnestly commend this matter to your attention, and trust that you will authorize us to complete the delivery at an early date. The hands who have been engaged in their manufacture are now idle—an additional reason why we would earnestly solicit an early and favorable reply.

Copies of this correspondence were addressed to the honorable the Secretary of War on the 27th ultimo.

Yours, very respectfully,

W. P. WILSTACH & CO.,
Per EDWIN M. SELLERS.

Hon. JOSEPH HOLT and ROBERT DALE OWEN,
    Commissioners, Washington, D. C.

NEW YORK ARSENAL, *August* 7, 1861.

GENTLEMEN: A few days ago I contracted with Mr. Scott, of your firm, for one thousand light cavalry sabres and one thousand non-commissioned officers' swords, United States pattern. Please send them over in lots of five hundred each, thirty sabres in one box and fifty swords in one box. I loaned Mr. Scott a pattern sabre; please have it returned the first opportunity. I agreed to pay six dollars for the sabre and five for the sword.

I am, gentlemen, very respectfully, your obedient servant,
R. H. K. WHITELEY,
Captain of Ordnance.

Messrs. W. P. WILSTACH & Co.,
    No. 38 *North Third street, Philadelphia.*

FRANKFORD ARSENAL, *January* 13, 1862.

MAJOR: I have received 630 sabres from Wilstach & Co., on your order to them, and have rejected 15; 90 still to inspect. I think them the best lot of sabres we have received thus far, as the percentage of rejected sabres is generally much greater than this. Mr. Scott, who is going to New York, desires to take you a report of them, and desires me to say that if you agree, he will send me the bill for the 1,000 sabres you ordered, and I can give him a certificate of inspection. If you conclude to this arrangement please send me a copy of the order. The price named by Mr. Scott is $6 apiece.

Very respectfully, your obedient servant,

T. J. TREADWELL,
First Lieutenant of Ordnance.

Major R. H. K. WHITELEY,
Commanding New York Arsenal, New York.

NEW YORK ARSENAL, *January* 16, 1862.

DEAR SIR: I received your letter of the 13th instant, by the hand of Mr. Scott. I am much pleased to learn the sabres turn out so well.

I herewith enclose you a copy of my order to Messrs. Wilstach & Co. for one thousand sabres, and the same number of non-commissioned officers' swords. I would much prefer he would turn them all in to the Frankford arsenal, and send his bills to you. If you desire to receive sabres instead of non-commissioned officers' swords, I can see no objection to the change. Still it would be well to consult our chief on the subject.

I am, sir, yours, respectfully,

R. H. K. WHITELEY,
Major of Ordnance.

Lieutenant T. J. TREADWELL,
Commanding Frankford Arsenal, Philadelphia.

Before commission, April 8, 1862.

Mr. Scott, before the commission relative to the claim of Mr. Wilstach, states: We have a contract for sabres, &c. Deliveries have been refused under the general order of the Secretary of War. We commenced the manufacture of swords in November; we did nothing between August 7 and January 16. We have the 1,000 non-commissioned officers' swords made.

COMMISSION ON ORDNANCE AND ORDNANCE STORES,
Washington, April 8, 1862.

GENERAL: The commission have the honor to report as follows:

CASE No. 27.—WILSTACH & Co., Philadelphia, Pa.

Order from Major Whiteley, commanding United States arsenal, dated August 7, 1861.

To deliver at the Frankford arsenal 1,000 cavalry sabres, at $6; 1,000 non-commissioned officers' swords, at $5.

Deliveries stopped under the general order from the Secretary of War.

The commission find that no times of delivery were specified in the written order of Major Whiteley, although it is admitted both parties expected an earlier completion.

The Messrs. Wilstach seem to have exerted themselves in starting this work, and have proceeded in good faith in carrying it on, particularly after a verbal intimation to them, in January last, that swords were still required by the ordnance department. The prices are not unreasonable, and the commission therefore direct that the sabres and swords be received to the extent and according to the terms of the original order.

We are, sir, very respectfully, your obedient servants,

J. HOLT,
ROBERT DALE OWEN,
Commissioners, &c.
P. V. HAGNER,
Major of Ordnance, Assistant to Commission.

Brigadier General J. W. RIPLEY,
Chief of Ordnance.

CASE No. 28.

STROBELL & CO.

WASHINGTON, *March* 24, 1862.

SIR: The prompt attention given by the War Department, under your administration, to all matters of business pertaining to that department of the government induces us to bring to your notice the following statement of facts, and to ask for your favorable attention thereon, to wit: On the 24th day of October, 1861, the firm of Strobell & Co. made application to the Hon. Simon Cameron, then Secretary of War, to furnish the department 10,000 of Gibbs's patent breech-loading carbines, at the price of twenty-eight (28) dollars each. On the 25th of October, 1861, the Secretary of War referred our application to General Ripley, chief of the Ordnance bureau, for a report thereon. General Ripley made a report upon the same day, and on that report the Secretary of War, under date of November 21, 1861, requested General Ripley to contract with Strobell & Co. for five thousand (5,000) of said arms. This contract was not perfected, for the reason that the papers, viz: the order to contract, by reason of omission or otherwise, were not returned to the ordnance department until the twenty-ninth (29th) day of January, 1862. In the meantime, and on the 13th day of December, 1861, one of the parties interested in the patent procured, upon the strength of General Ripley's report made upon our application, an order from the Secretary of War for 10,000 of the same carbines. General Ripley now declines to contract for or to receive from us the 5,000 carbines which he was requested by the Secretary to contract for, upon the ground that the 10,000 above referred to, to be delivered under the contract dated December 13, 1861, annulled or superseded the order to Strobell & Co.

We now very respectfully ask that General Ripley be requested to execute and deliver to us a contract under the order of November 21, 1861, or that the 5,000 mentioned in said order be declared to form a part of the 10,000 to be delivered under the order of December, 1861. Either course will be satisfactory to Strobell & Co., although we believe the interest of the government will be subserved by allowing Strobell & Co. to furnish the 5,000 under the order of November 21, the delivery to commence within sixty days from this date. Any communication of the subject of the above matter may be addressed to Strobell & Co., care of Thomas C. Fields, National Hotel, Washington city, D. C.

All of which is respectfully submitted.

STROBELL & CO.

Hon. EDWIN M. STANTON,
Secretary of War.

COMMISSION ON ORDNANCE AND ORDNANCE STORES,
Washington, April 8, 1862.

GENERAL : The commission have the honor to report as follows :

CASE NO. 28.—STROBELL & Co., Washington, D. C.

Alleged order, November 21, 1861; not on printed list.

To manufacture 5,000 of Gibbs's patent breech-loading carbines, at $28 each.

The commission find that the only document in this case is a memorial dated March 24, 1862, addressed to the Secretary of War, and by him referred to the commission, in which it is alleged that an application made by them to furnish 10,000 of Gibbs's breech-loading carbines was referred to Brigadier General Ripley, chief of ordnance; that a report was made thereon; that the Secretary of War thereupon requested the chief of ordnance to contract with Strobell & Co. for 5,000 of said arms, but that, in point of fact, no such contract was then made. Subsequently another contract for 10,000 of the same arm was made with another party.

Strobell & Co. ask either that the first contract be made, as asked for, or else that it be considered as part of the second.

No evidence whatever is furnished even of the allegations made, and it is admitted that no contract with Strobell & Co. was made or exists. It further appears to the commission that the government is not in want of these additional arms.

The commission decide that no obligation whatever exists on the part of the government to take these arms; that there is no reason why a contract *not* made with one person should be considered part of a contract actually made with another, and that the request of Strobell & Co. be not granted.

Very respectfully, &c.,

J. HOLT,
ROBERT DALE OWEN,
Commissioners.
P. V. HAGNER,
Major of Ordnance, Assistant to Commission.

Brig. Gen. J. W. RIPLEY,
Chief of Ordnance.

CASE NO. 29.

Captain S. H. MOER.—Colorado claims.

DENVER CITY, *Colorado Territory, April* 14, 1862.

MAJOR : In the discharge of my duty at this point, I have had occasion to examine claims against the government for arms and ammunition furnished by citizens of this Territory at a time of threatened insurrection. These claims are based upon the call of the governor of the Territory, and as far as my knowledge of the circumstances leads me to form an opinion I consider all of them that have come under my observation as correct and just, and to effect a settlement of which I have made out accounts in triplicate, and advised the persons interested to cause them to be presented to the commission appointed March 13. The prices I have put in as were promised by the purchasing official. In the accounts that I have examined I have complied with the requirements of the

Ordnance department, by setting forth that the property is in my possession, and is to be accounted for, and return to be rendered for the quarter ending June 30, 1862.

Very respectfully, your obedient servant,

JOHN W. ALLEY.

Captain Third Infantry, A. A. Q. M.

Major PETER V. HAGNER,
Ordnance Department, U. S. A., Washington, D. C.

WASHINGTON, D. C., *April* 8, 1862.

SIRS: This will be handed to you by Mr. J. S. Fillmore, appointed a special paymaster of the United States for Colorado Territory.

He represents the creditors of the United States of that Territory, in other matters; and from his intimate knowledge of the entire transactions, may well do it in regard to the purchase of arms by Governor Gilpin.

By reason of the great distance to that locality, and the consequent inconvenience for the various creditors to appear before you in person, I trust you will permit Mr. Fillmore to appear for the creditors, and make all needed explanations to aid you in reaching just conclusions upon these claims of the citizens of my Territory.

Very respectfully,

H. P. BENNET,

Delegate Colorado Territory.

Hons. JOSEPH HOLT and ROBERT DALE OWEN.

ORDNANCE OFFICE, *Washington, D. C., May* 2, 1862.

SIR: I have the honor to transmit herewith for your approval the accounts of Messrs. Laplin, Smith & Co. for powder, and those of C. W. Durant, for arms delivered to Captain J. W. Alley, United States infantry, by the parties, under the authority of the governor of Colorado Territory.

In the case of Captain Moer's accounts for ordnance stores ordered by governor Gilpin, and receipted for by Captain M., the order of the governor does not appear on the face of the vouchers, being only sworn to by Captain Moer. The commission on ordnance stores, under date of April 10, passed the accounts however, and they have been paid. In both these cases Governor Gilpin's order appears on the face of the vouchers, the property has been regularly receipted for by a United States officer, and all that is further required is your approval.

Respectfully, your obedient servant,

JAMES W. RIPLEY,

Brigadier General.

Hon. E. M. STANTON,
Secretary of War.

MAY 5, 1862.

The within accounts are specially referred to the ordnance commission, with the request that they be investigated.

EDWIN M. STANTON,

Secretary of War.

COMMISSION ON ORDNANCE AND ORDNANCE STORES,
Washington, April 10, 1862.

GENERAL : The commission have the honor to report as follows :

CASE No. 29.—Accounts of Captain S. H. MOER, assistant quartermaster United States army in Colorado Territory.

Quarterly cash accounts, with vouchers and property return, for third quarter, 1861. Referred to commission by special direction of the Secretary of War.

Purchase of ordnance stores made by order of Governor Gilpin, late governor, to meet the exigencies of the public service in that Territory, without proper legal authority. The accounts are also defective in form, not always stating clearly the number and price of items, and in not having the authority for the purchase upon the voucher.

Acting Paymaster J. S. Fillmore is recommended to the commission by Hon. H. Bennett, delegate in Congress from Colorado, as one known to him to be authorized by the many claimants concerned in these accounts to act for them as their agent.

The commission have examined the accounts so far as to find that the articles purchased as per abstract have been taken up upon the quarterly account of Captain S. H. Moer, assistant quartermaster United States army, and that he acknowledges, in his account under date of September 30, 1861, to be accountable for such of the articles purchased as have not been issued and accounted for by him.

The commission further find that although the prices of most of the articles are high, yet that they do not seem to be unreasonable, considering the place and circumstances under which the purchases were made ; and they have the statement of Mr. Fillmore, delivered under oath, that, in his judgment, the prices are fair and just. Mr. Fillmore also swears that he is personally cognizant of the fact that Governor Gilpin actually authorized and approved each purchase, and also of the issues made ; and, further, that the accounts are known to him to be correctly made in number and price of articles and in the names of the claimants.

The commission, therefore, direct that the accounts be examined and audited as usual, without suspension on account of lack of due authority to order the purchases or of informality in stating the accounts.

We are, sir, very respectfully, your obedient servants,

J. HOLT,
ROBERT DALE OWEN,
Commissioners.

P. V. HAGNER,
Major of Ordnance, Assistant to Commission.

Brigadier General J. W. RIPLEY,
Chief of Ordnance.

Approved.

EDWIN M. STANTON,
Secretary of War.

MAY 23, 1862.

SIR: The enclosed despatch has just been received, and the commission direct it to be forwarded to you, as all the Colorado claims have or will be sent to be audited, as usual.

P. V. HAGNER.

SECOND AUDITOR *of the Treasury.*

[Copy of telegram.]

Received May 22, 1862; from Denver 19th.

All Colorado ordnance accounts, except Lafling's, are paid by me. and must be returned here, being same as allowed by your board before.

                                        J. S. FILLMORE, *Paymaster.*

Messrs. HOLT and OWEN,
   Ordnance Commissioners.

CASE No. 30.

S. & A. M. SAWYER, of Massachusetts.

WASHINGTON, *April* 9, 1862.

SIR: There having been some objections made to our bill for ordnance and ordnance stores, which we furnished to Major General B. F. Butler between December 7, 1861, and February 19, 1862, as per order of Major Strong, ordnance officer and acting adjutant general on General Butler's staff, we deem it due to ourselves to make some explanations in relation to some of the items objected to, or, in other words, with which comparison has been made by the Ordnance bureau, which are as follows:

1. *Cast-steel guns.*—In relation to this item, we are compelled to say that there has not been any cast-steel guns made by the Ordnance department; hence, strictly speaking, there could be no comparison made. But there has been some semi-steel guns made, at a cost of 57½ cents per pound, finished weight, which have been brought into comparison by the Ordnance bureau with our guns, which are made of pure homogeneous cast steel, and for which we have charged 70 cents per pound, or some 12½ cents more per pound than has been paid for semi-steel, which in reality is nothing more than a coarse quality of wrought iron.

The forgings for the semi-steel guns (I am informed) costs about 17 cents per pound, and allowing for shrinkage caused by the process of boring, turning, and rifling, which would be about one-half of the original weight, it would make the finished cost of the stock 34 cents per pound, exclusive of the labor, which must be much less than that of finishing cast steel. Now, on the other hand, our cast-steel forgings cost, delivered at the shop, (inclusive of duties and freights, &c.,) 21½ cents per pound, and allowing the shrinkage in finishing to be one-half of the original weight, as in the case of the semi-steel, it would bring the finished cost of the steel to 43 cents per pound, leaving only a margin of 3½ cents for the extra work and tools necessary in finishing cast steel. And, aside from this, the semi-steel guns were only bored three inches in diameter, while our guns were bored 3.67 inch, which would require a day or two more labor to accomplish and leave quite an amount more metal in the semi-steel guns, to be charged for at 57½ cents per pound, than there is in the guns made of cast steel.

Now, in view of these facts, we think that it must be perfectly obvious that we are receiving much less profit on our cast-steel guns than was realized by the manufacturers of the guns made from the (so-called) semi-steel.

2. *Rammers and Staves.*—This is the next item in order in which there is a difference in price, and needs, we think, only a few words of explanation, *i. e.*: These rammers are double-headed—one head being made of wood, for ramming the cartridge, and the other of bronze, for driving home the projectile; and as it is absolutely necessary to have this head fit the conical part of the shot or shell, it will be readily seen that if it was made of wood it would soon become split,

and hence rendered useless. We will here add that these rammers are furnished at the manufacturers' prices, and without any profit to ourselves whatever.

3. *Tompions.*—These tompions were provided with a rubber belt or collar, to prevent the water from getting into and rusting the gun, and also to prevent them from looseing out when on the march. The ordinary tompions are not so provided, which will account for the difference in price.

4. *Solid shot.*—These shot were ordered for proof shot, it being required that there should be double the weight of shot and powder fired for proof charges; and it being deemed unsafe to fire two conical shot or shell in the guns at a time, we were directed to fill our ordinary shell with lead (which would give about the desired weight) for that purpose; and the prices charged for these shot is only the price of the shells that has been previously paid by the Ordnance bureau, and the cost of the lead that was put into them to make up the required weight.

5. *Case shot*—The same may be said (in a measure) of the case shot as of the solid shot, *i. e.*, we have only charged the price for the shells that we have been heretofore paid, and for the actual amount of bullets put into the shells at cost prices. There is another fact which we would mention in this connexion, and that is the capacity of our shell for holding destructive material, whether filled with bullets, powder, or other substances. It has nearly double the capacity of any other similar projectile, and hence we put in nearly double the number of bullets which is put in the case shot referred to in the list of comparative prices which has been submitted to you by the Ordnance bureau.

6. *Shells.*—The shells referred to in this item are the same as we have been furnishing to the government for a year or two past, and at the same prices, without, to our knowledge, there having been any fault found with the price whatever; and, indeed, we have filled one order from the ordnance officer at Fortress Monroe since we received and had nearly completed this order of General Butler, and have received our pay for the same.

Having said thus much, we will now proceed to point out some of the chief differences in the cost and advantages of our shell as compared with other shells of a similar character, which we have not as yet discussed; and will commence by stating that our projectile was patented November 13, 1855, and in our patent then issued we claim, among other things, combining with the butt or rear of the shell lead, or a softer metal than that of which the body of the shell is composed, for a specific object, as described in our specification; and we also claim making the rear part of the shell tapering or conical, and combining therewith a ring or anulus of lead, *or its equivalent,* so that when it is submitted to the action of the powder it shall be forced or crowded up the conical or tapering portion, joining the cylindrical body of the shell so as to cause it to fit closely to the bore of the gun, or, in other words, to ·press it firmly against the bore of the piece. Now we do not claim any particular advantages over others using the same thing, either in cheapness or other ways, except that of having a patent covering those principles, and that of uniting the soft metal upon the butt or rear end of the shell with a similar coating upon the cylindrical portion of the same. Now, if this anti-friction metal is not indispensable, it is quite essential in protecting the nicely finished bore and grooves of the gun from the abrasion which would be caused by coming in contact with the rough and sand-pitted cast iron of the shell; and also in preventing the shell from becoming rusty or corroded by exposure.

Hence, if it is found essential to thus protect the gun and shell, we must admit the necessity of incurring the expense to do so; and furthermore, our detonating cap or fuse is attached to the shell by the means of this alloy, which extends up and around the conical point of the shell. This method of igniting the shell has been recommended by high military authority for its superiority over all others, and for its certainty to burst the shell at the desired point of penetration; but fuses arranged in this way, as well as coating the cylinder of the shell, necessarily involve some expense, as the alloy costs about four times as much as the cast iron.

There is another seeming difference in the comparative cost of our shells, as made by the Ordnance bureau, which, on investigation, does not exist to the extent that is apparently represented, and that is in relation to fuses, boxing, truckage, &c. In our case, we have furnished the fuses, boxing, truckage, &c., and include the expense in the cost per shell, while others have simply furnished the shells, and charged extra for fuses, boxing, &c.

We will now only add, in relation to this item, that the government are paying sixty cents each for the fuses that they are using, and that the boxing must average to cost at least twelve cents per shell.

7. *Canister.* This canister shot was patented November 19, 1861. The can or case is made of *malleable iron*, and is of sufficient strength so as to prevent it from being forced into the grooves, and thereby prevent its usefulness in a rifle gun. The castings for these cans costs about twelve cents per pound, beside the bullets, boxing, covers, and the labor of finishing the cans and charging them, hence the extra price.

8. *Powder.*—This powder was purchased of Mr. Pratt, of Boston, and is the same as that he is furnishing to the government; but we, inadvertently or otherways, have charged four cents less than the government price, hence we can probably get over this objection easily.

9. *Boxing.*—In relation to this item we can only say that the boxing was done as cheaply as we could do it in the manner that it was done, but we could have done it cheaper and consequently coarser, if we had supposed it desirable.

Very respectfully, your obedient servants,

S. & A. M. SAWYER.

Hon. EDWIN M. STANTON,
 Secretary of War.

WAR DEPARTMENT, *September* 10, 1861.

Major General B. F. Butler is hereby authorized to raise, organize, arm, uniform, and equip a volunteer force for the war in the New England States, not exceeding six (6) regiments, of the maximum standard of such arms, and in such proportions and in such manner as he may judge expedient; and for this purpose his orders and requisitions on the quartermaster, ordnance, and other staff departments of the army, are to be obeyed and answered, provided the cost of such recruitment, armament, and equipment does not exceed, in the aggregate, that of like troops now or hereafter raised for the service of the United States.

SIMON CAMERON,
 Secretary of War.

MARCH, 11, 1862.

True copy.

JOHN POTTS,
 Chief Clerk War Department.

WAR DEPARTMENT, *September* 12, 1861.

Major General Butler is authorized to fit out and prepare such troops in New England as he may judge fit for the purpose to make an expedition along the eastern shore of Virginia, *via* the railroad from Wilmington, Delaware, to Salisbury; and thence through a portion of Maryland, Accomac, and Northampton counties, of Virginia, to Cape Charles.

Transportation agents, quartermasters, and commissaries of subsistence will answer General Butler's requisitions for this purpose.

SIMON CAMERON, *Secretary of War.*

MARCH 11, 1862.

True copy.

JOHN POTTS,
Chief Clerk War Department.

———

COMMISSION ON ORDNANCE AND ORDNANCE STORES,
Washington, April 10, 1862.

GENERAL : The commission have the honor to report as follows :

CASE No. 30.—S. & A. M. SAWYER.

Claim for payment of vouchers, suspended by Ordnance department.   Account for ordnance and ordnance stores furnished upon order of Major General Butler, between December 7 and February 19, 1862. Articles received and account approved by General Butler.

The commission find that General Butler received authority from the Secretary of War, dated September 10, 1861, " to raise, organize, arm, uniform, and equip a volunteer force, not exeeding six regiments," "in such manner as he may judge expedient," " and for this purpose" (it was further ordered) " his orders and requisitions on the quartermaster, ordnance, and other staff departments of the army are to be obeyed and answered, provided the cost of such recruitment, armament, and equipment does not exceed, in the aggregate, that of like troops now or hereafter raised for the service of the United States."

The payment of this account has been suspended by the Ordnance department, as some of the items are changed at higher prices than heretofore paid for articles of like use, while the proviso seems to limit the price to such usual amount.

The Messrs. Sawyer have appeared before the commission and stated the circumstances under which the articles were made, being of special pattern, and made in small quantities, and at a cost to them not over ten per cent. less than charged by them ; and that they have had to devote a great deal of their personal attention to the manufacture and the putting in service of these articles, for which they have received no remuneration ; that they proceeded to carry out the orders of General Butler, who was the accredited agent of the department in securing the supplies required in perfect good faith on their part, knowing nothing of any limitation as to prices being placed upon his action. The commission consider that it is difficult to give any practical force to the proviso in this case, as its terms are of such a character that they cannot be applied solely to any one kind of supplies or to any particular period, and, as like prices have been paid for many of the articles by the Ordnance department, when purchased of the Messrs. Sawyer heretofore, the commission direct the payment of the account for nineteen thousand and nine dollars and sixty-nine cents, ($19,009 69,) and also signify their approval of the other account for stores supplied to General Butler under the above authority, amounting to fourteen thousand, nine hundred and fifty-six dollars, ($14,956.)

We are, sir, very respectfully, your obedient servants,

J. HOLT,
ROBERT DALE OWEN,
Commissioners, &c.

P. V. HAGNER,
Major of Ordnance, Assistant to Commission.

Brigadier General J. W. RIPLEY,
Chief of Ordnance.

CASE No. 31.

NORMAN WIARD.

NEW YORK, *February* 20, 1862.

SIR: I enclose duplicate accounts for one (1) six-gun battery, being the "Third Ohio Steel-gun Battery," with carriages and implements complete, purchased for the State of Ohio, upon the authority of Governor William Dennison, by Colonel C. P. Wolcott, and delivered as per receipt attached.

For considerations satisfactory to me, I hereby assign the said account or claim to Mr. John Stephenson, of this city, (No. 47 East Twenty-seventh street,) and request that the amount ($11,500) be paid to him.

I sign receipts to avoid delay.

Yours, very respectfully,

NORMAN WIARD.

$11,500.

General JAMES W. RIPLEY,
    Chief of Ordnance, Washington City.

SIR: The enclosed account is assigned to me by Norman Wiard in payment for the carriages constructed by us for said batteries.

For considerations satisfactory to me, I hereby assign the said account or claim to Shepherd Knapp, esq., president of Mechanics' Bank of this city, and request that the amount ($11,500) be paid to him.

To avoid delay receipts have been signed by Mr. Norman Wiard.

Respectfully, yours,

JOHN STEPHENSON.

General J. W. RIPLEY,
    Chief of Ordnance, Washington City.

NEW YORK, *March* 24, 1862.

SIR: I enclose duplicate accounts for one (1) six-gun battery, being the "Fourth Ohio Steel-gun Battery," with carriages and implements complete, purchased for the State of Ohio, upon the authority of Governor William Dennison, by Colonel C. P. Wolcott, and delivered as per receipt attached.

For considerations satisfactory to me, I hereby assign the said account or claim to Mr. John Stephenson, of this city, (No. 47 East Twenty-seventh street,) and request that the amount ($11,500) be paid to him.

I sign receipts to avoid delay.

Very respectfully, yours,

NORMAN WIARD.

$11,500.

General J. W. RIPLEY,
    Chief of Ordnance, Washington City.

NEW YORK, *March* 24, 1862.

SIR: The enclosed account is assigned to me by Norman Wiard in payment for carriages constructed by us for him.

For considerations satisfactory to me, I hereby assign the said account or claim to Shepherd Knapp, esq., president of Mechanics' Bank of this city, and request that the amount ($11,500) be paid to him.

To avoid delay the receipts have been signed by Mr. Norman Wiard.

Respectfully, yours,

JOHN STEPHENSON.

General J. W. RIPLEY,
    Chief of Ordnance, Washington City.

NEW YORK, *April* 1, 1862.

SIRS: Under date of 28th March the Ordnance department has returned to us two accounts, each for $11,500, not paid because " the time for delivery having expired without the fulfilment of the conditions of the contract."

I am a carriage-builder, and have, within a few months, constructed over 700 carriages for the United States, mostly for the ordnance department, and with entire satisfaction, as we think P. V. Hagner, major of ordnance, will bear witness.

The two invoices now referred to are the first of such occurrence, and from no fault of ours. Mr. Norman Wiard contracts with the State of Ohio for four batteries of steel guns complete. Mr. Wiard applied to us to construct the carriages. After conferring with Major Hagner I consented. We performed our work in time; and, because the guns were not ready, we were obliged to hire storage for the carriages.

The amount ($23,000) has been assigned to us by Mr. Wiard to pay for the carriages, and also about $7,000 of work done by us for the Burnside expedition. All of these carriages are now in the service of the United States, and performing to entire satisfaction. Major Hagner is aware of all these transactions, and we gladly refer to him for testimony. Please instruct us what we shall do with the accounts now here.

Respectfully,

JOHN STEPHENSON.

Hon. Messrs. HOLT and OWEN,
Commissioners for the settlement of Accounts, &c.

ORDNANCE OFFICE,
Washington, September 19, 1861.

SIR: In answer to your letter of the 18th instant, in relation to procuring arms, accoutrements, and equipments for Ohio troops, I have to state that such supplies, so far as they are necessary for troops, which have been or may be authorized by the government, to be raised in your State for the service of the United States, may be procured or contracted for by you, or such person as you may designate for that purpose, at rates not exceeding those paid at the time by the government for similar articles, and will be paid for on proper vouchers in such funds as the Treasury Department may provide for the purpose.

Respectfully,

JAS. W. RIPLEY,
Brigadier General.

Gov. WILLIAM DENNISON,
Columbus, Ohio.

True copy.

CHAS. W. MORRIS, *C. C.*

Before commission.

Certificate attached to Norman Wiard's voucher No. 1, of date January 21, 1862. Amount, $11,500:

" Purchased under authority of Brigadier General Ripley's letter to governor of Ohio, dated September 19, 1861, and part delivery under arrangement reported to Ordnance office by my letter of 22d November, 1861. And I certify that the said battery, with all its implements and appendages complete, has been inspected and received by me, and sent to the governor of Ohio for use of troops of that State, actually mustered into the service of the United States.

" C. P. WOLCOTT,
"Agent of State of Ohio.

"I certify that the above account is correct and just, amounting to eleven thousand five hundred dollars and no cents.

"C. P. WOLCOTT, *Agent of Ohio.*

"FEBRUARY 20, 1862."

True copy.

P. V. HAGNER, *Major of Ordnance.*

Before commission.

Certificate attached to Norman Wiard's voucher No. 2, of date February 26, 1862. Amount $11,500:

I do hereby certify that the above-named battery was purchased under the authority of Brigadier General Ripley's letter to the governor of Ohio, dated 19th September, 1861, and is the last of the batteries covered by the arrangement reported to the Ordnance office by my letter of November 22, 1861. And I further certify that the said battery, with all the implements and appendages named, has been inspected and received by me and delivered to the governor of Ohio for use of the troops of that State, actually mustered into the service of the United States.

C. P. WOLCOTT,
Agent of the State of Ohio.

I certify that the above account, amounting to eleven thousand five hundred dollars, is correct and just.

C. P. WOLCOTT, *Agent of Ohio.*

True copy.

P. V. HAGNER,
Major of Ordnance.

COMMISSION ON ORDNANCE AND ORDNANCE STORES,
Washington, April 11, 1862.

GENERAL: The commission have the honor to report as follows:

CASE No. 31.—NORMAN WIARD, New York.

Vouchers for batteries furnished for troops of the State of Ohio. Referred by special order.
Orders given by Mr. Wolcott, agent of the State of Ohio, under authority from chief of ordnance, dated September 19, 1861. Batteries, by agreement thus sanctioned, to be all delivered within sixty days from November 20, 1861.

Payment of the voucher suspended by the Ordnance department, as the "time for delivery expired without the fulfilment of that condition of the contract."

The commission find that there was delay in delivering to the agent of Ohio in the case presented to us of one month; but as it appears that the battery was satisfactory to the agent, and was received by him and issued for service, they direct that this default as to time be waived, and that the accounts for the four batteries be examined and audited as usual, without objection on account of time.

We are, sir, very respectfully, your obedient servants,

J. HOLT,
ROBERT DALE OWEN,
Commissioners, &c.

P. V. HAGNER,
Major of Ordnance, Assistant to Commission.

Brigadier General J. W. RIPLEY,
Chief of Ordnance.

CASE No. 32.

CHARLES ALBRIGHT.

MAUCH CHUNK, *Pennsylvania, January* 31, 1862.

DEAR SIR: In answer to your published orders in regard to contracts, &c., I herewith send you a copy of an order from the Ordnance department for 13-inch shell.

I am actively and busily at work, and expect to have the order completed the early part of the month.

You will greatly oblige me by acknowledging receipt of this, so I may know that it has reached its destination.

Very truly, your obedient servant,

CHARLES ALBRIGHT.

Hon. E. M. STANTON,
    Secretary of War.

ORDNANCE OFFICE, *Washington. January* 3, 1862.

SIR : In answer to your application I have the honor to offer you a contract to furnish this department with three thousand (3,000) 13-inch mortar shells for the price of 2¾ cents per pound, delivered on Governor's Island, New York harbor.

These shells will weigh not far from 220 pounds each. A drawing of one showing the form and dimensions is herewith enclosed for your information.

If you accept the terms proposed, I desire that you will prosecute the work as rapidly as possible, for the shells are required for immediate service.

An officer will be sent to inspect them as soon as you report them completed. The requirements of the proof and inspection are fully given in the Ordnance Manual, a copy of which I send you by this day's mail.

The price of 2¾ cents per pound, deliverable at the pleasure of this department, is the same as that proposed by a responsible party residing in the western part of Pennsylvania.

Respectfully, your obedient servant,

JAMES W. RIPLEY,
    Brigadier General.

Mr. CHARLES ALBRIGHT,
    Mauch Chunk, Pennsylvania.

———

COMMISSION ON ORDNANCE AND ORDNANCE STORES,
    Washington, April 11, 1862.

GENERAL : The commission have the honor to report as follows :

CASE No. 32.—CHARLES ALBRIGHT, of Mauch Chunk, Pennsylvania.

Order from Ordnance department for 13-inch shell.   Order for 3,000 13-inch mortar shells, at 2¾ cents per pound.

Deliveries suspended under general order.

The commission find that the price per pound of the shells is reasonable, and that they are needed for the service, and therefore direct that further deliveries be accepted to the extent and under the terms of the original order.

We are, sir, very respectfully, your obedient servants,

J. HOLT,
ROBERT DALE OWEN,
Commissioners, &c.
P. V. HAGNER,
Major of Ordnance, Assistant to Commission.

Brigadier General J. W. RIPLEY,
Chief of Ordnance.

CASE No. 33.

Messrs. ATKINS & BROTHERS.

POTTSVILLE, *February* 8, 1862.

DEAR SIR: Agreeably to directions, as per your published order, we hand you enclosed copy of an order for 6,000 10-inch columbiads received by us.

Very respectfully,

ATKINS & BROTHERS.

Hon. E. M. STANTON,
Secretary of War.

ORDNANCE DEPARTMENT,
Washington, D. C., January 11, 1862.

GENTLEMEN: By directions of the Secretary of War I offer you an order for six thousand (6,000) ten-inch columbiad shells on the following terms and conditions to wit: These shells are to be delivered by you at the United States arsenal, Governor's Island, New York, and are to undergo there the regular prescribed inspection and proof by United States inspectors. They are to be delivered by you in or within four months from this date, and none are to be accepted or paid for but such as pass inspection, and are approved by United States inspectors. Payments are to be made in such funds as the Treasury Department may provide for the purpose for as many of the 6,000 shells as may be delivered in the time before stated, at the rate of 2¾ cents (say two and three-quarter cents) per pound, delivered at the arsenal.

Please signify your acceptance or non-acceptance of this order.

Respectfully,

J. W. RIPLEY, *Brigadier General.*

Messrs. ATKINS & BROTHERS,
Pottsville, Pennsylvania.

PIONEER FURNACES,
Pottsville, Pennsylvania, February 18, 1862.

DEAR SIR: Your favor covering order No. 11 in respect to contracts is received, stating that our notice to you covering copy of order from Brigadier General Ripley for 6,000 ten-inch columbiads was defective, inasmuch as we did not state what had been done on account of it. We have spent several hundred dollars to get the necessary flasks, patterns, &c., ready, but have delayed somewhat until we could get assurance from General Ripley that we could get them inspected here instead of at Governor's Island, where they are to be delivered as expressed in the order. We have now this assurance from the general by the same mail that brought yours, and if the order is all right, of which we wait your assurance, will proceed to make the shell as rapidly as possible.

Please let us hear at your earliest convenience, and oblige, truly and respectfully, yours,

ATKINS & BROTHERS.

Hon. EDWIN M. STANTON,
Secretary of War.

COMMISSION ON ORDNANCE AND ORDNANCE STORES,
Washington, April 11, 1862.

GENERAL : The commission have the honor to report as follows :

CASE No. 33.—Messrs. ATKINS & BRO., Pottsville, Pa.

Order given by chief of ordnance, January 11, 1862. To deliver 6,000 ten-inch columbiad shells, subject to inspection, at the rate of 2¾ cents per pound, at Governor's Island, New York. Deliveries suspended under general order from Secretary of War.

The commission find that the parties are prepared to go on with the order; that the shells are needed by the government, and the price reasonable; and therefore direct that they be received under the terms and to the extent of the original order, modified as to the place of inspection, if so directed by the chief of ordnance.

We are, sir, very respectfully, your obedient servants,

J. HOLT,
ROBERT DALE OWEN,
Commissioners, &c.
P. V. HAGNER,
Major of Ordnance, Assistant to Commission.

General J. W. RIPLEY, *Chief of Ordnance.*

CASE No. 34.

J. E. BICKFORD.

DOVER, N. H., *February* 1, 1862.

SIR : In accordance with an order from your department I saw published under date of January 30, I herewith send you a statement of orders for gunpowder, received from General Ripley, chief of Bureau of Ordnance, with our doings thereon.

First order, May 1, 1861, for............................ 800 barrels.
Second order, August 24, 1861, for...................... 1,000 "
Third order, September 25, 1861, for.................... 500 "

In all....................................... 2,300 "

We have made and sent forward, according to directions, as follows, viz:

September 10, 1861, to Watertown arsenal................ 550 barrels.
January 24, 1862, to Watertown arsenal................. 805 "

1,355 "

This leaves a balance of nine hundred and forty-five barrels to be manufactured and delivered. As reason for the small quantity manufactured and delivered, we have at the same time been at work for the navy; but chiefly on account of an explosion destroying three of our mills, causing a stoppage of work for four months.

Very respectfully, your obedient servant,

JOHN E. BICKFORD,
Agent Union Powder Works.

Hon. EDWIN M. STANTON, *Secretary of War.*

ORDNANCE OFFICE, *Washington, May* 1, 1861.

SIR: Please make for this department, in accordance with the requirements of the circular from this office of the 20th April, five hundred (500) barrels cannon and three hundred (300) barrels musket powder.

The powder is to be of the quality requisite to pass the regular United States inspection, and to be packed in 100-pound barrels. The whole of the powder is to be delivered at the New York arsenal, Governor's Island, New York. It is essential that the manufacture and delivery of the powder shall be pressed with the utmost despatch. Please report when you have enough ready for an inspection—say one-half of the order. The price to be paid will be the same as that given to the other manufacturers, viz: eighteen dollars ($18) per barrel, including the barrel.

Respectfully, your obedient servant,

JAS. W. RIPLEY,
Lieut. Colonel of Ordnance.

JOHN E. BICKFORD, Esq., *Dover, N. H.*

ORDNANCE OFFICE, *Washington, August* 24, 1861.

SIR: Please to furnish this department with seven hundred (700) barrels of cannon powder, and three hundred (300) barrels of musket powder. The cannon powder should be of the kind known as No. 5 grain, samples of which will be sent to you as soon as they can be prepared. The density should be at least 1.75; and the price will be 18 cents per pound, delivered at Watertown, Massachusetts arsenal, unless otherwise directed.

It should be packed in white-oak barrels, covered with hickory or cedar hoops, divested of the bark. Each barrel should contain 100 pounds. It will be inspected, as far as practicable, according to the rules laid down in the Ordnance Manual.

Respectfully, your obedient servant,

JAS. W. RIPLEY,
Brevet Brigadier General.

JOHN E. BICKFORD, Esq., *Dover, N. H.*

ORDNANCE OFFICE, *Washington, September* 25, 1861.

SIR: Be pleased to supply this department with five hundred (500) barrels of ordinary cannon powder. Samples of this powder will be furnished to you from West Point or the Watertown arsenal.

The price of the above-named powder will be 18 cents per pound, delivered at the Watertown arsenal.

Respectfully, your obedient servant,

JAS. W. RIPLEY,
Brigadier General.

Mr. JOHN E. BICKFORD,
Union Powder Co., Dover, N. H.

COMMISSION ON ORDNANCE AND ORDNANCE STORES,
Washington, April 11, 1862.

GENERAL: The commission have the honor to report as follows:

CASE No. 34.—JOHN E. BICKFORD, Agent Union Powder Works, Dover, New Hampshire.

Orders from chief of ordnance, dated May 1, 1861; August 24, 1861; September 25, 1861. To deliver in all 2,300 barrels of cannon powder at the Watertown arsenal, unless otherwise directed, at the rate of 18 cents per pound. Deliveries to January 14, 1862, amount to 1,355 barrels. Further delivery suspended under the general order from the War Department.

The commission find that some delay has occurred in the completion of the order, stated to be due to an explosion at the mills, but the company are now going on with their work; that the powder is required, and the price reasonable, and therefore direct that the amount ordered be received according to the terms of the orders.

We are, sir, respectfully, your obedient servants,
J. HOLT,
ROBERT DALE OWEN,
Commissioners, &c.

P. V. HAGNER,
Major of Ordnance, Assistant to Commission.

General J. W. RIPLEY,
Chief of Ordnance.

CASE No. 35.

CULLEN BROWN.

COMMISSION ON ORDNANCE AND ORDNANCE STORES,
Washington, April 11, 1862.

GENERAL: The commission have the honor to report as follows:

CASE No. 35.—CULLEN BROWN, Detroit, Michigan.

Claim for payment of voucher dated December 28, 1861. Account for 108 sets of cavalry equipments, complete, $32 each, including spurs and straps, currycombs, horse brush, picket-pin, lariat rope, nose-bag, hitching straps, and saddle blanket, also 18 packing boxes, at $1 50.

It appears that the above were furnished in excess of order given to Mr. Brown, but as they were accepted by the United States officer, and subsequently deposited at the United States arsenal by order of the chief of ordnance, and are represented to be of good quality, and at reasonable price, and needed by the government, the commission direct that the account be paid to the full amount of $3,483.

We are, sir, very respectfully, your obedient servants,
J. HOLT,
ROBERT DALE OWEN,
Commissioners, &c.
P. V. HAGNER,
Major of Ordnance, Assistant to Commission.

General J. W. RIPLEY,
Chief of Ordnance.

WASHINGTON, *February* 10, 1862.

This is to certify that Mr. Cullen Brown, of the city of Detroit, received authority to contract with Captain N. K. Mizner, acting in behalf of the United States government, for (1,104) eleven hundred and four sets of cavalry equipments, complete, for the use of the 2d regiment of Michigan cavalry, Colonel F. W. Kellogg commanding. Through miscalculation Mr. Brown purchased trimmings sufficient to manufacture (1,212) twelve hundred and twelve sets, and made that number, hoping that he could dispose of the surplus, 108 sets, to the United States government, for the use of the 3d regiment of Michigan cavalry, which at that time required them, but in the interview Colonel Kellogg obtained authority to contract for his regiment, which he did, with Messrs. Duncan & Bro., of Detroit, thereby leaving 108 sets on Mr. Brown's hands, which were received by me, acting as quartermaster at Detroit, I not knowing at the time that they were not included in the number contracted for. I had never read the contract which was made with Captain Mizner. Finding that I had a number of equipments on my hands which I could not turn over to any regiment, I asked for instructions from General Ripley as regards their disposal, and was directed to turn them over to Major H. Bell, at Dearbornville, which command I complied with. They are now in the possession of the United States government, at Dearbornville, subject to their order.

E. G. OWEN,
Captain and Assistant Quartermaster U. S. Army.

CASE NO. 36.

LAMSON, GOODNOW & YALE.

WINDSOR, *Vermont, February* 8, 1862.

DEAR SIR: Pursuant to the requirement of your recently issued order relative to existing contracts for fire-arms, &c., we submit the following report:

1st. In the month of July last we entered into a contract dated the 11th day of July, 1861, with General James W. Ripley, chief of the Ordnance department, for the manufacture of *twenty-five* thousand rifled muskets and their appendages, to be made after the new model musket then just completed, which was shown to us in the department, and the changes from the model then being made at Springfield armory pointed out to us.

2d. In the month of October following we received a further order, dated October 7, from the said General Ripley, for 25,000 muskets, in addition to our contract of July 11, of the same description as those contracted for in July, the same to be delivered within four months after the completion of our first contract of July 11, 1861.

Now as to progress. We will say first that we were somewhat delayed in not receiving the *new model* musket, as we expected, as nearly sixty days elapsed after signing our contract before we received it.

Immediately after closing the first contract we contracted for our musket stocks, ten thousand of which are now on hand, and the balance are to be delivered monthly, so that within twelve months we shall have about fifty thousand stocks delivered.

We also made arrangements for using the establishment known as the Bay State Works, at Northampton, Massachusetts, for the manufacture of our barrels, bayonets, and ramrods. The machinery is now nearly all in, and a part in operation, calculated to make 200 barrels, &c., per day. About seventy men are employed by these works in finishing the barrels, &c., and the number will be increased, now as we have just commenced receiving a good quality of welded barrels from N. Washburn, of Worcester, Massachusetts, who has contracted to furnish the fifty (50) thousand barrels.

At our cutlery works, Shelburn Falls, Massachusetts, an establishment where we have formerly employed some four hundred men, we are now forging the locks, mountings, and appendages of the muskets, and now have more than 25,000 of some parts and quite a quantity of nearly every part of the mountings already made.

We are also making at this establishment, for the Springfield armory, ten drops with dies, &c., for forging the parts of the same new model musket we are now making; six (6) of the drops have been delivered and are now in operation in armory. We have about seventy men employed at Shelburn Falls on the forgings, and are increasing our force.

At Windsor, Vermont, we own a large armory, known formerly as the Robbins & Lawrence armory, somewhat celebrated for making some thirty-five thousand muskets for the United States government of the model of 1842; also for making a large amount of machinery for the English Enfield armory, and also several thousand Enfield rifles.

We have here about (100) one hundred men making gun machinery; and now taking the amount we had on hand when we signed our contract with what we have since made, we have nearly enough to finish the locks and mountings, and to stock (200) two hundred guns per day. We have about 100 men finishing the parts, and are daily increasing. We shall soon be ready for the government inspectors to examine and inspect our work.

We will here say that we have now invested, for the prosecution and fulfilment of our contracts with your department, from one hundred to one hundred and fifty thousand dollars, and now see no reason why we cannot within eight weeks commence delivering the muskets.

We have been somewhat delayed for the want of iron equal in quality to the imported Marshall iron, and are not now without our fears; yet we feel quite confident that the iron we are now receiving will prove satisfactory.

We are making every effort to deliver the guns at the earliest moment, and now if, for any reason, the government will not receive the fifty thousand, we desire to be informed immediately.

We will further state that in consequence of the delay in receiving the new model gun Mr. Cameron, then Secretary of War, granted us an extension of sixty days for the fulfilment of our contract.

We are, very respectfully, your obedient servants,

LAMSON, GOODNOW & YALE.

EDWIN M. STANTON,
Secretary of War, Washington.

This agreement, made this eleventh day of July, eighteen hundred and sixty-one, between Brevet Brigadier General James W. Ripley, of the United States army, acting by authority of the Secretary of War, and Lamson, Goodnow & Yale, of Windsor, Vermont, witnesseth:

1. The said Lamson, Goodnow & Yale hereby bind themselves, their heirs, executors, administrators, and assigns, to deliver, to such officers of the United States as may be authorized to receive them, twenty-five thousand muskets of the exact pattern of the muskets made at the United States armory in Springfield, Massachusetts, according to sample to be furnished to the contracting party; all and each of the said twenty-five thousand muskets to interchange in their similar parts with each other and with the Springfield muskets, and to be subject, before receip for payment therefor by the United States, to

the same kind and degree of inspection by United States inspectors, appointed for the purpose, as the muskets made at the Springfield armory are subjected to; and any of the aforesaid muskets to be delivered by the said Lamson, Goodnow & Yale under this agreement which do not, in all respects and particulars of pattern, material, workmanship, and finish, come up to the standard of excellence established at the United States armory, which is to be determined and decided by the United States inspectors, shall be rejected.

2. The said Lamson, Goodnow & Yale do further bind themselves, their heirs, executors, administrators, and assigns, to manufacture and have ready for inspection and delivery to the United States the aforesaid twenty-five thousand muskets not later than the following periods, namely: one thousand muskets not later than six months from the date of this agreement, and not less than one thousand muskets per month for the next three months, and not less than two thousand muskets per month for each and every month thereafter, until the whole twenty-five thousand muskets shall have been delivered, with the distinct understanding that each or all of these deliveries must be made in as much shorter time as possible; and that on any failures to make deliveries to the extent and within the times above specified, all the obligations of the United States to receive or pay for any muskets then deliverable under this agreement shall be cancelled and become null and void.

3. The said Lamson, Goodnow & Yale do further bind themselves, their heirs, executors, administrators, and assigns, to deliver with the aforesaid twenty-five thousand muskets the following appendages, of the regular patterns, subject to the same inspection as the muskets, namely : one wiper, one screwdriver, one spare cone, and one tompion to each and every musket, and one ballscrew, one spring vise. and one tumbler and wire punch to every ten muskets ; and also to put up in good boxes, to be provided by them of the regular pattern and quality, the aforesaid muskets, twenty in each box, with their due proportion of appendages.

4. It is expressly understood and agreed between the parties to this agreement, before named, that payments shall be made to the said Lamson, Goodnow & Yale, or their order, on receipt at the Ordnance office, in Washington, D. C., of certificates of inspection and evidences of delivery of not less than one thousand muskets, with appendages, at the following rates, namely: twenty dollars for each musket and set of appendages, inclusive, and such price, in addition, for each packing box as may be certified by the inspector to be just and fair

5. It is further understood and agreed that no member of Congress shall be admitted to any share or part of this agreement, or to any benefits to arise therefrom.

In witness whereof, the parties to this agreement have hereunto set their hands and affixed their seals, at the city of Washington, District of Columbia, the eleventh day of July, 1861.

JAMES W. RIPLEY,   [L. S.]
Brigadier General.

LAWSON, GOODMAN & YALE.   [L. S.]

Signed and sealed in presence of—
     W. MAYNADIER.

Approved.   SIMON CAMERON,
                                       Secretary of War.

WAR DEPARTMENT, *July* 11, 1861.

ORDNANCE OFFICE, *Washington, October* 7, 1861.

GENTLEMEN: By direction of the Secretary of War, I offer you an order for twenty-five thousand (25,000) muskets (in addition to the twenty-five thousand you contracted to deliver under date of 11th July, 1861,) on the following terms and conditions, viz: the kind, quality, and price of the arms and appendages now ordered are to be the same as those previously contracted for, and this order is to be an increase of the contract to fifty thousand arms, the whole of which are to be delivered within four months after the termination of the contract of 11th July, 1861, as therein specified and required.

Please signify, in writing, your acceptance or non-acceptance of this order on the terms and conditions herein stated.

Respectfully, your obedient servant,
JAS. W. RIPLEY, *Brigadier General.*

Messrs. LAMSON, GOODNOW & YALE,
New York, N. Y.

NEW YORK, *October* 22, 1862.

DEAR SIR: We were duly in receipt of yours, under date of 7th October, 1861, transmitting an order from the Secretary of War for the furnishing an additional quantity of twenty-five thousand arms, and now inform you of an acceptance of said order upon the terms and conditions therein stated.

While we remain, most truly yours,
LAMSOM, GOODNOW & YALE.

Brigadier General JAMES W. RIPLEY,
Ordnance Department, Washington, D. C.

Memorandum.—In consideration of the fact that Lamson, Goodnow & Yale did not receive a model from which to construct the muskets they contracted for for sixty days after the date of their contracts, thus retarding their operations for that length of time, if it be absolutely necessary in completing their second contract, they may be allowed that sixty days additional, but this shall not apply to their first contract.

SIMON CAMERON, *Secretary of War.*

OCTOBER 25, 1861.

ORDNANCE OFFICE, *Washington, November* 29, 1861.

In answer to your letter of the 27th instant, I have to state that no further papers are necessary to complete the order to you of the 7th October, 1861, from this office, which was accepted by you, as per your letter of the 22d of the same month.

Respectfully, your obedient servant,
JAS. W. RIPLEY, *Brigadier General.*

Messrs. LAMSON, GOODNOW & YALE,
New York, N. Y.

Before commission, April 9, 1862.

Mr. Goodnow, of Lamson, Goodnow & Yale, came before the commission, and states:

"We have a contract for 50,000 Springfield guns. The progress of our work was reported in our letter to the Secretary of War. The work will all be done in our own shop at Windsor. We have a full suit of stocking machines now up. The barrel bedding machines are now belted and being adjusted. We have already finished a stock, except the ramrod groove. We do not know if gauges have been applied. The product of our machines will be from one to two hundred guns per day. We have two establishments making barrels, and barrel machinery will be running in three weeks. We have 15,000 stocks on hand in the rough, 8,000 of them are dry, the remainder are in our dry-house at Windsor. We are now belting and adjusting our stocking machines, to commence work. The product of our machines will be from 100 to 200 per day, and we propose to fix it definitely at 200 per day. This amount will be ample for our orders, and we do not propose to make for others. All our stocking machines will be at Windsor, where we will assemble the guns. We have made a contract with Washburn for 50,000 barrels. He has already delivered to us 2,000, but we have learned that fifty per cent. of these do not turn out well. Our last letters do not confirm this; and it may be that the defect was in the size of the bore; we are not certain. If Mr. Washburn's iron does not prove good, he is bound to get iron that will. His machinery for rolling, &c, is as perfect as any, and he must change his iron until he can secure a good product. He has abundant means and ability, and he will carry out whatever he undertakes. When we took the first order we purposed starting a rolling mill for our barrels, but Mr. Washburn and Messrs. Cooper & Hewitt proposed to start mills for this purpose, and we thought it safer to rely on them. We have at Northampton a shop now at work finishing barrels. The product of this will be 200 per day. We shall have in three weeks like machinery at Windsor sufficient to finish from 100 to 200 barrels per day. We started this second shop as an additional precaution, and if we can produce more than we need, we may make for others; but as yet we have not made any promises, and we must first see our own way clear. Bayonets and ramrods are also being made at Northampton; bayonets now being finished. Locks, mountings, sights, and appendages will all be made at Windsor; machinery for them now running. Locks are being put together in detail. We are forging all the mountings, sights, parts of locks and appendages at Shelburn Falls, twenty miles from Northampton. This work is in advance, and mostly to the extent of 20,000. We have abundant drops and dies to furnish any desired number of those parts. We have many applications for those forged parts, but as yet we have furnished nothing. Colt and ourselves are to make the last pattern of Springfield arms. They have open bands and no swell to ramrods, thinner lock plate, and Enfield hammer. The butt plate and stock also differ. We are ahead of the armory in this pattern, and we are to get up gauges for the armory while finishing our own. We shall turn out the new gun before they do at Springfield. We have been making machines for many parties. We have made stocking machines for the Amoskeag Manufacturing Company, and also a number of machines for finishing barrels. We have made and we are making stocking machines for the Providence Tool Company. We are also making some other machinery. It will be about two months before we are required to deliver to the Providence Tool Company. We have to make our first delivery of guns under our orders from the government very soon. As soon as we can get barrels, we will be ready probably to assemble one hundred per day."

APRIL 10, 1862.

Mr. Goodnow again before the commission :

"We have received 2,000 rolled barrels, all bored by us; 1,200 are turned and ready to grind, and 500 will be ready for proof next week. Expect to certainly turn out 50 finished barrels per day on the 15th May, and we will, in from four to six weeks afterwards, complete 75 to 150 per day. This is to be done at Northampton, and by working night and day we can nearly double this. In two or three days we can rely upon the new shop at Windsor for at least 100 per day. This product may also be increased by working at night. We have 4,000 bayonets forged, and 1,600 partly forged. Ramrods and breech pins are also being forged, and we will soon turn out 200 per day. The machines for finishing and tapping are both at Northampton and Windsor.

"We look upon the price as low enough, leaving only a fair manufacturing profit, such as we always expect to make in ordering work. The forged pieces already made at Shelburn Falls are guard-bows, swivels, bands, stock-tips, sights, lock plates, hammers, tumblers, bridles, sears, main-springs, sear-springs, triggers, cones and screws."

COMMISSION ON ORDNANCE AND ORDNANCE STORES,
Washington, April 12, 1862.

GENERAL: The commission have the honor to report as follows:

CASE NO. 36.—LAMSON, GOODNOW & YALE.

Orders dated, first, July 11; second, October 7; Nos. 2 and 3 of printed list. Orders, first, for 25,000 Springfield rifle muskets; and second, for 25,000 additional ditto, at $20 each, deliverable as follows: 1,000 in January 1862, and monthly at that rate, to include April 1862; and then 2,000 per month until 25,000 are delivered, and the remaining 25,000 within four months thereafter.

The commission find that upon receipt of their order the Messrs. Lamson, Goodnow & Yale commenced work in good faith, preparing to manufacture themselves all parts of the arm except the rolled barrels; that now they are nearly ready to finish each part, and have actually turned out certain parts by their own machines, and if not delayed for barrels, they have given good assurance that they may produce the finished arm during the month of May; that the arm required of them is of the latest pattern, not yet in hand at Springfield, and consequently that they have had to originate some of the gauges and tools, as none such have yet been made at Springfield. The arms they are to make, therefore, will doubtless be of the best kind for the government to secure, and the commission see no reason to doubt that diligent efforts will be made by these gentlemen to speedily meet their engagements with the government. Since the commission acted in the cases of Jenks & Son and the Colt's Arms Company, it has been shown satisfactorily to them that the price stipulated for the Springfield pattern arm is unreasonably high where quantities over fifteen or twenty thousand are to be made by one establishment, and it is manifestly proper that the government should receive all fair advantage due to the large orders it may give to manufacturers; the commission consider that where the order exceeds 25,000 in amount there should have been a reduction in price, and especially as where the work is performed by experienced gun-makers. As the best justification offered for the present price is that the work required had to be done within a specified time, the commission have therefore decided that where any portion of the order has not been delivered as stipulated they will in future decline to receive such portion at the contract price. Considering that arms of the pattern making by the Messrs. Lamson, Goodnow and Yale will be required, and cannot be obtained at so early a period from any other source, the commission direct that the question of entire forfeiture for failure to deliver prior to May first be waived, and that the Messrs. Lamson, Goodnow & Yale be allowed to proceed with their work under the terms of the contract to the extent mentioned therein, deducting such numbers as may not have been or may not in future be delivered within the stipulated period.

We are, sir, very respectfully, your obedient servants,

J. HOLT,
ROBERT DALE OWEN,
Commissioners.

P. V. HAGNER,
Major of Ordnance, Assistant to Commission.

Brigadier General J. W. RIPLEY, *Chief of Ordnance.*

(See No. 5, case No. 13, for further condition of this decision.)

CASE No. 37.

PROVIDENCE TOOL COMPANY.

OFFICE OF THE PROVIDENCE TOOL COMPANY,
Providence, January 31, 1862.

DEAR SIR: We notice to-day your request that all contractors with your department should give written notice to you of their contracts, and we beg promptly to respond to your order.

On the 13th of July last the chief of the ordnance department, by direction of the Secretary of War, issued to this company a contract for 25,000 rifled muskets of the Springfield pattern, at $20 each. On the 3d of August following we received the model.

We engaged at once in the work of getting the necessary machinery and tools for their manufacture, and no moment has been lost in order to make deliveries as early as possible. A large establishment has been devoted to this use, and a large sum of money already expended. We are making the several parts, and have more than two hundred men at work under this contract. We have put in operation, we believe, the first set of barrel rolling machinery ever made in this country.

A further order for 25,000 was issued to us on the 26th of November, at the same price, and we have largely increased our contracts for machinery and stock, that we might deliver the whole as speedily as possible.

About the middle of November General Ripley gave the writer a verbal order for what "light cavalry sabres" we could make by the 1st of January, instant, price same as paid for the best article, $8 50 each. On the 1st instant the writer called upon General Ripley and reported that about 1,000 were ready, and the general proposed to send an inspector to our works. He gave us an additional and verbal order for 5,000, and then to continue the manufacture until further orders. A written order to this effect we expected by mail, which is not yet to hand.

We have stock for all these sabres, and more; have a large number in process of manufacture; have about 2,000 completed, and some seventy men engaged in this branch. The quality of the article was highly spoken of by General Ripley, (a sample having been inspected by him,) and his letter of the 24th instant advises that an inspector had been ordered here.

These are the extent of our contracts, upon which we have entered with honest purposes; and as to our capacity and responsibility, we beg respectfully to refer you to the honorable senators and representatives in Congress from this State.

If this letter is not all that is desired of us, we will respond to any further call.

Respectfully, your obedient servant,

JOHN B. ANTHONY,
Treasurer.

Hon. E. M. STANTON,
Secretary of War, Washington.

PROVIDENCE TOOL COMPANY,
Providence, Rhode Island, February 19, 1862.

DEAR SIR: In addressing you on the 31st ultimo I had before me only a telegraphic synopsis of your order in "respect to contracts." Your order is now at hand, and I beg to reply to your further interrogatories.

The purport of the contracts is shown by copies of the same, which I herewith enclose. Our musket contracts call for 50,000, under which we have already made an investment of more than $160,000, and our engagements for machinery not yet in will amount to fully $50,000 more.

We have made contracts for barrel iron and for stocks sufficient for the full number of muskets. Of steel, for the various parts, we have here and on the voyage of importation enough for 35,000. Much of the labor we have contracted for for the full number of parts. We are rolling, boring, and turning barrels, are forging all the parts, and have our tools nearly ready for milling and finishing. We are exerting ourselves to the utmost to make as early deliveries as possible. Two hundred and fifty men are at work under this contract.

Our contract for sabres is for 6,000, which, however, we have never received in writing. We have stock for the whole number, and nearly all are in process of manufacture, about 2,500 being already finished. An inspector is here and now examining the work. About seventy men are employed in this department.

Very respectfully, yours,

JOHN B. ANTHONY,
Treasurer.

Hon. EDWIN M. STANTON,
Secretary of War, Washington.

My letter of December 3 (copy of which is herewith) speaks of the written order for sabres not having been received.

Copy of contract.

This agreement, made this thirteenth day of July, eighteen hundred and sixty-one, between Brevet Brigadier General James W. Ripley, of the United States army, acting by authority of the Secretary of War, and Providence Tool Company, of Providence, Rhode Island, by John B. Anthony, treasurer thereof, witnesseth:

1. That the said company binds itself and its assigns to deliver, to such officer of the United States as may be authorized to receive them, twenty-five thousand (25,000) muskets, of the exact pattern of the muskets made at the United States armory in Springfield, according to sample to be furnished to the contracting party; all and each of the said twenty-five thousand muskets to interchange in their similar parts with each other and with the Springfield muskets, and to be subject, before receipt or payment therefor by the United States, to the same degree of inspection, by United States inspectors appointed for the purpose, as the muskets made at the Springfield armory are subjected to; and any of the aforesaid muskets to be delivered by the said company under this agreement which do not, in all respects and particulars of pattern, material, workmanship, and finish, come up to the standard of excellence as established at the United States armory, which is to be determined and decided by the United States inspectors, shall be rejected.

2. The said company does further bind itself and its assigns to manufacture and have ready for inspection and delivery to the United States the aforesaid twenty-five thousand muskets not later than the following periods, namely: one thousand muskets not later than six months from the date of this agreement, and not less than one thousand muskets per month for the next three months, and not less than two thousand muskets per month for each and every month thereafter, until the whole twenty-five thousand muskets shall have been delivered, with the distinct understanding that each or all of these deliveries must be made in as much shorter time as possible; and that on any failure to make deliveries to the extent and within the times above specified, all the obligations of the United States to receive or pay for any muskets then deliverable under this agreement shall be cancelled and become null and void.

3. The said company does further bind itself and its assigns to deliver with the aforesaid twenty-five thousand muskets the following appendages of the regular pattern, subject to the same inspection as the muskets, namely: one wiper, one screw-driver, one spare cone, and one tompion to each musket, and one ball-screw, one spring vise, and one tumbler and wire punch to every ten muskets: and also to put in good boxes, to be provided by the company, of the regular patterns and quality, the aforesaid muskets, twenty in each box, with their due proportion of appendages.

4. It is expressly understood and agreed between the parties to this agreement, before named, that payments shall be made to the said company, or its order, on the receipt, at the Ordnance office, in Washington, D. C., of certificates of inspection and evidences of delivery of not less than one thousand muskets, with appendages, at the following rates, namely: Twenty dollars for each musket and set of appendages, inclusive, and such price, in addition, for each packing box as may be certified by the inspector to be just and fair.

5. It is further understood and agreed that no member of Congress shall be admitted to any share or part of this agreement, or to any benefit to arise therefrom.

In witness whereof, the parties to this agreement have hereunto set their hands and affixed their seals—the said James W. Ripley at the city of Washington, the 13th day of July, 1861, and the said J. B. Anthony at the city of Providence, the twenty-fourth day of the same month and year.

JAS. W. RIPLEY,   [SEAL.]
Brevet Brigadier General.

PROVIDENCE TOOL CO.,   [SEAL.]
By J. B. ANTHONY, *Treasurer.*

Signed and sealed in presence of—
    W. MAYNADIER,
        Major of ordnance, witness to General Ripley's signature.
    FRED. W. HOWE,
        Witness to signature of J. B. Anthony, treasurer.

ORDNANCE OFFICE, *Washington, November* 26, 1861.

SIR: By direction of the Secretary of War, I offer you an order for twenty-five thousand (25,000) muskets, (in addition to the 25,000 you contracted to deliver under date of July 13, 1861,) on the following terms and conditions, viz: the kind, quality, and price of the arms and appendages now ordered are to be the same as those previously contracted for, and this order is to an increase of the contract to fifty thousand arms; the whole of which are to be delivered within four months after the termination of the contract of July 13, 1861, as therein specified and required.

Please signify, in writing, your acceptance or non-acceptance of this order on the terms and conditions herein stated.

Respectfully, your obedient servant,
JAS. W. RIPLEY, *Brigadier General.*

J. B. ANTHONY, Esq.,
   Treasurer of the Providence Tool Company, Providence, R. I.

PROVIDENCE, *December* 3, 1861.

DEAR SIR: I duly received your letter of the 26th ultimo. We accept the order for 25,000 muskets contained therein, and attach to this order our original contract of July 13, making it a part of the same.

We are getting on well with the sabres for which you gave us a verbal order; presume you do not desire a delivery until we have several hundred ready. Shall

have as many as we named, and in the time specified. We have not received
your written order for these.

Respectfully, your obedient servant,

JOHN B. ANTHONY,
Treasurer Providence Tool Company.

Brig. Gen. JAS. W. RIPLEY,
Ordnance Department, Washington, D. C.

Before commission, April 12, 1862.

Mr. John B. Anthony, president of Providence Tool Company, states:

We have a contract for 50,000 Springfield guns. None are yet delivered.
We are preparing to make the whole arm, except the sights, in our own shop at
Providence. We have a set of rolls in operation for barrels. We have had
about 4,000 or 5,000, chiefly of Washburn's iron. We found Washburn's iron
bad; nearly every barrel being imperfect. We have suspended its use until we
can succeed in improving his iron, as we have secured 200 tons of Marshall iron.
Our turning and boring machines are all ready. Rifling and milling machines
not quite ready. Tapping for cone-seat ready. We are to have a full suit of
stocking machines, and we should have been ready before this, but others have
disappointed us. Our machines are being made in Pawtucket, in Windsor, and in
our own shops. We have made engagements with Redfield, of New York, to
furnish us with 3,000 to 5,000 stocks. I have been to his shop (some two
months since) in New York, and there saw stocks in the third and fourth stage.
Our own machines should produce finished stocks by the 1st of June; if we
get none from Redfield, we will be obliged to wait for our own.

We have on hand, either complete or nearly so, full sets of milling machines
and tools for every part. We have also machines for appendages. Our sights
are made by contract at Freetown, Massachusetts. Some are already finished,
and 11,000 are forged. This shop is under our control, and cannot make
for others without our permission. Every part of our locks is being forged.
Some of the parts are ready in large numbers. Our milling tools for plates are
running, and our cones are forged. The bayonets and ramrods are made in our
second shop in Providence. Forgings are going on, but neither milling nor
grinding has yet been commenced. The gauges are being made by our men at
Springfield. We have hired a shop there, and verify the work by the armory
gauges. Our delay in delivering has been due mainly to our inexperience, not
well understanding at first what such a job required. We have to teach our
workmen, as but few experienced men can be had. The pattern guns given out
at Springfield are not model guns suitable for making the gauges by, and therefore we have had to start a shop at Springfield, and get opportunities to verify
our work by the true models as we could. Our foreman is an old hand at government work, and knows how to inspect. We understand that our first contract declares forfeiture of monthly deliveries if not made in the stipulated time,
not impairing our right to make deliveries subsequently due.

Our business heretofore was making bevel tools—ship chandlery hardware.
We have taken a separate shop for this work, and we have spent for building,
engine, and shafting, $73,000, and for tools, machines, and materials, we have
disbursed $165,000. We have contracts beyond this for materials and machines
to the extent of $180,000, and for iron to the extent of $48,000.

We have an order for 6,000 sabres, which are in process of manufacture. No
time for delivery of them fixed.

COMMISSION ON ORDNANCE AND ORDNANCE STORES,
Washington, April 12, 1862.

GENERAL: The commission have the honor to report as follows:

CASE No. 37.—PROVIDENCE TOOL COMPANY, Providence, Rhode Island.

Order dated July 11, 1861; No. 4 of printed list.   Order for 25,000 Springfield rifle muskets, at $20 each. Deliverable 1,000 not later than six months, and not less than 1,000 per month for the next three months, and not less than 2,000 muskets for each and every month thereafter, until the whole 25,000 shall have been delivered.

The commission find that this company—previously engaged in manufacturing tools, &c.—upon receipt of the order, invested a large capital in shops, power, machines, and material; that they prepared themselves to manufacture the whole arm, including the barrel rolling, (except the sights,) every portion in an advanced stage, and with machines, foreman and workmen likely to secure work of a good quality, and will probably commence deliveries in July next.

Under the decision made in the case of Lamson, Goodnow & Yale, the commission decide that the Providence Tool Company be allowed to proceed with their work under the terms of the contract and to the extent mentioned, deducting such numbers as may not have been or may not in future be delivered within the stipulated period.

We are, sir, very respectfully, your obedient servants,

J. HOLT,
ROBERT DALE OWEN,
Commissioners, &c.
P. V. HAGNER,
Major of Ordnance, Assistant to Commission.

Brigadier General J. W. RIPLEY,
Chief of Ordnance.

(See paper No. 5, case No. 13, and also No. 5, case No. 36.)

[Additional.]

COMMISSION ON ORDNANCE AND ORDNANCE STORES,
Washington, May 6, 1862.

GENERAL: The commission have the honor to report as follows:

CASE No. 37.—PROVIDENCE TOOL COMPANY.—25,000 *additional order.*

Increase of number ordered July 13, 1861, by order of Secretary of War, dated November 26, 1861.   Order for 25,000 muskets, in addition to the 25,000 already ordered, on the following terms and conditions, viz: The kind, quality, and price of the arms and appendages to be the same. This order to be an increase of the contract to 50,000 arms, whole of which are to be delivered within four months after the termination of the contract of July 13, 1861, as therein specified and required.

The above additional order should have been noted on the record of case No. 37.

The commission decide that the finding in that case be fully applied to the additional number.

We are, sir, very respectfully, your obedient servants,

J. HOLT,
ROBERT DALE OWEN,
Commissioners, &c.
P. V. HAGNER,
Major of Ordnance, Assistant to Commission.

Brigadier General J. W. RIPLEY,
Chief of Ordnance.

PROVIDENCE TOOL COMPANY ARMORY,
Providence, April 23, 1862.

GENTLEMEN : We have received from the chief of ordnance a letter, under date of the 19th instant, enclosing a copy of your instructions to him in relation to our contract for 25,000 muskets, dated July 13, 1861.

It was well understood by the contracting officers that this work could not be done in the time specified in the contract, though we believed that by great energy and perseverance we could accomplish it.

So many other parties starting in the work at about the same time, and the Springfield armory multiplying so largely their production, (we studiously avoiding any interference whatever in their work,) the competition for labor and for tools became so great that men had to be bought for almost every operation. We have undertaken to build a thorough and most complete armory. We are certain our work, so far, will compare favorably with any other. The competition in this work has made the cost of preparing for it much greater than we anticipated. We entered upon the labor, believing the government as well as ourselves would be benefited by it. When we began we were assured that the letter of the contract in regard to deliveries would not be insisted upon by the government if we worked faithfully ; not so assured, it is true, by the contracting officers, but by those in government places whose judgment we respected and whom we believed knew well what course would be pursued. Under your decision, the best we can do our number will be greatly reduced. While this is all our contract gives us, yet, in view of all the circumstances—the fact that we are doing all the work ourselves and in a most thorough manner, have experienced superintendent and foremen, have stock secured of unexceptionable character—and in view of the great difficulties attending the work, we ask that we may be allowed to continue the manufacture to the full number specified in the contracts, especially as we understand some of the contracts to be for much larger numbers than ours. When this contract is finished, if the government desire, we will place one complete armory at their disposal upon the most favorable terms.

You refer to the " decision made in the case of Lamson, Goodnow & Yale." We are not advised what this decision is ; but beg to suggest, without meaning any disparagement to them, that they had a large establishment and all the tools that had heretofore been used in the manufacture of Enfield rifles, and even then contracted for a large share of their work outside of their own shops. When we found we should be late in our deliveries we increased our tools, hoping that the aggregate delivery might be within the time named ; and we now ask that, if consistent with your duties and high position, you will so revise your decision as to make this all that is required of us.

I am, gentlemen, with great respect, your obedient servant,

JOHN B. ANTHONY, *Treasurer.*

Hon. JOSEPH HOLT and ROBERT DALE OWEN,
Commissioners, &c.

COMMISSION ON ORDNANCE,
Washington, May 6, 1862.

SIR: I am directed by the commission (in answer to yours of April 23) to enclose a copy of that portion of their decision in the case of Lamson, Goodnow & Yale, to which reference is made in the finding in your case.

You will perceive that the action is in accordance with a rule adopted, to be applied to all future cases, and is considered necessary and proper by the commissioners.

To show the matter complete it should have been noted in the record in your case that an addition of 25,000 arms was made to your original order on the 26th of November. Although no charge is made in the terms of the second order, (deliveries under which are to be concluded within four months after the completion of the first order,) you will please note that the record will be so changed as to include the second order.

Very respectfully, sir, your obedient servant,

P. V. HAGNER, *Major of Ordnance.*

J. B. ANTHONY, Esq.,
   Treasurer of Providence Tool Company.

CASE No. 38.

DURRIE & RUSHER.

It is supposed that the order of November 23 was given to Durrie & Rusher, on verbal instructions by the Secretary of War, referred to in the above indorsement as "authorized yesterday." No acceptance of the order appears to have been received from these parties.

ORDNANCE OFFICE,
Washington, November 23, 1861.

GENTLEMEN: By direction of the Secretary of War, I offer you an order for twenty-five thousand (25,000) English long Enfield rifles, with appendages, on the following terms and conditions, viz: These arms are to be subject to inspection by Major P. V. Hagner, or such officer as this department may designate for the purpose, and none are to be received and paid for but such as are approved by the United States inspectors. They are to be delivered in New York, N. Y., as follows, viz: Two thousand (2,000) in sixty days from this date; three thousand (3,000) more in ninety days from this date; four thousand (4,000) more in four months from this date; five thousand (5,000) more in five months from this date; five thousand (5,000) more in six months from this date; and six thousand (6,000) more in seven months from this date. In case of any failure to make deliveries to the extent and within the times above specified, the government is to be under no obligation to take the arms deliverable under this order and remaining undelivered at the time of such failures, but may revoke and annul this order so far as regards these arms and appendages. Payments will be made for each delivery, as before specified, in such funds as the Treasury Department may provide, on certificates of inspection and receipt by the United States inspectors, at the rate of twenty dollars ($20) for each arm, including appendages, in bond.

Please signify, in writing, your acceptance or non-acceptance of this order on the terms and conditions herein stated.

Respectfully, your obedient servant,

JAMES W. RIPLEY,
Brigadier General.

Messrs. DURRIE & RUSHER,
   No. 78 *Beekman street, New York.*

DURRIE & RUSHER, 78 Beekman street.

NEW YORK, *April* 10, 1862.

GENTLEMEN : Since the writer presented the facts in the case of the contract given us for 25,000 long Enfield rifles, we have had additional information from the maker of the arms, Mr. Francis Preston, of Manchester, England, whose manufacture we represent, and from whom we have had advices by almost every steamer of his increased ability to produce, and were so governed in seeking the contract.

We have learned more fully of the preparation he made on receiving the contract, and of the engagements and contracts he made to further his ability so as to be able to deliver promptly, according to the terms of the contract. These engagements he made when materials were much higher than at present, and to such an extent that if we are now refused an extension we will suffer very great loss, as we also shall in the putting in jeopardy the advances we have made to him.

In consideration of these facts, we would respectfully propose that if you cannot extend the contract given us, that you substitute in its place another calling for the same deliveries, up to twelve or fifteen thousand of the rifles.

Yours, respectfully,

DURRIE & RUSHER,
Per H. DURRIE.

Extracts from letter of Mr. Francis Preston, received February 6, 1862, *and dated Manchester, England, January* 21, 1862.

" On the 18th I wrote you, saying we expected the proclamation would be withdrawn this week; and I am now glad to say it is so. I have now 1,000 rifles ready for your contract, and, by way of giving you a good position, I will ship this week 600, which you will sell for me to the best of your judgment, and remit me the proceeds on England as soon as possible. They were made up at the high prices, and if I do not get from 68s. to 70s. I shall be loser. How will your finance troubles affect the payment and remittances for transportation? People here are all very much afraid, and advise me not to send without the cash beforehand. Of course, I could not afford to continue to do so ; but being desirous of establishing both your position and mine as A 1 agents and maker, I will spare this shipment without the cash beforehand, although I can ill spare them, as there are now two buyers here already again for the worth, who are paying cash.

"I can now only add that I am yet in a position to deliver 1,000 per week, if the finance arrangements can be carried out. I see the exchange is now 115, which will be against you, and besides that, I suppose it will be another expense to convert your paper money into sterling; so that all the profits will have to be run finer."

In another letter, dated Manchester, January 23, 1862, and just received, he says :

" I find the 600 arms I intended to send yesterday could not be taken, as the steamer was full; therefore, on the 29th, by British steamer, I intend to send you a thousand rifles, which now lay in Liverpool ready for shipping. The proceeds you will remit me at the earliest opportunity. The exchange, I see, is yet 115, and a premium on gold 9.47; so that I fear they will not leave me the market price. I hope, on Monday, to hear something definite from you touching the contract. My next lot of guns will be very superior; in fact, I do not think there will be many sent equal to mine, as all my guns I have viewed twice, besides having the materials viewed separately. If you and an inspector come over, and the payment is all right, I can do a thousand per week, steadily.

"Messrs. DURRIE & RUSHER, *New York.*"

Before commission, April 3, 1862.

Messrs. Durrie & Rusher state: We have received Enfield rifles from England, but none delivered on our contract. Our arms are received from Mr. Preston. The price of Enfields now is sixty shillings. Mr. Preston feared to send more arms because of the order of the Secretary of War revoking contracts; previously he was restricted in England by the Queen's proclamation. All the arms received by us have been sold in open market at $20 each. Captain Crispin refused to take them on our contract.

COMMISSION ON ORDNANCE AND ORDNANCE STORES,
Washington, April 12, 1862.

GENERAL: The commission have the honor to report as follows:

CASE No. 38.—DURRIE & RUSHER, New York.

Order given by direction of the Secretary of War, Nov. 2, 1861. To deliver, in New York, in bond, 25,000 English long Enfield rifles, viz: 2,000 in 60 days, January 23; 3,000 in 90 days, February 23; 4,000 in 120 days, March 23; 5,000 in 150 days, April 23; 5,000 in 180 days, May 23; 6,000 in 210 days, June 23.

In case of any failure to make deliveries to the extent and within the times above specified, the government is to be under no obligation to take the arms deliverable under the order and remaining undelivered at the time of such failure, but may revoke and annul this order so far as regards those arms and appendages. No arms have been delivered under the above order.

Messrs. Durrie & Rusher have appeared before the commission, and represent that they have received some lots of these arms from England, but have sold them to the government agent in New York in open market, at $20 each; that the agent refused to take them upon the contract, as they did not arrive within the time stipulated.

They further represent that the Queen's proclamation and other causes produced the delay in their deliveries.

The commission consider that the order was given at the high prices then ruling in order that the government might receive all the advantage due to the speedy deliveries promised; that as, from causes not under the control of the government, these advantages have been lost, and the government has been obliged to supply its wants from other sources, there remains no obligation, as specially stipulated in the order, to receive these arms. They therefore direct that the order be revoked and annulled, and that no arms be received under it.

We are, sir, &c.,

J. HOLT,
ROBERT DALE OWEN,
Commissioners, &c.
P. V. HAGNER,
Major of Ordnance, Assistant to Commission.

Brig. General J. W. RIPLEY,
Chief of Ordnance.

CASE No. 39.

J. P. FITCH, New York.

NEW YORK CITY, *February* 12, 1862.

SIR: In compliance with your order requiring those holding contracts or orders from the Department of War for supplies, ordnance, &c., to file, in the office of the Secretary of War, notice of the same, with statements of what had been done thereunder, I beg respectfully to represent that, in July last, I submitted to the Secretary of War a proposal to furnish and deliver to the government fifty thousand (50,000) English Enfield rifled muskets, at twenty dollars ($20) each, and that subsequently I submitted another proposal to furnish an additional twenty-five thousand (25,000) of the same kind of guns at the same price; both of which were accepted by the chief of ordnance. A certain number were to be delivered on or before the expiration of a time limited, and then a certain number per month until all should be delivered, as by reference to the original papers on file in the ordnance department will appear.

Immediately upon the acceptance of these proposals I made a contract with New York agents of English gun manufacturers to supply the guns to meet the terms of my engagement with the government. But subsequently these agents, finding that the government was paying a higher price than $20 for these guns, sold directly to the government at $23, having refused to carry out their engagement with me. I could not, of course, obtain guns to fill my contract at $20 while the government and its agents were paying from $23 to $28, as was done. These prices the government continued to pay until the exportation of guns from England to this country was interdicted, after which I could, of course, obtain none at any price.

The time for the delivery of a considerable portion of these guns has now expired; but that I have failed to meet the terms of my engagement I do not regard as my fault, the government having rendered it impossible for me to carry out my agreement by buying in the market the same guns at a much higher price than that fixed in my contract.

Permit me further to say that I still hold the said contracts, not having parted with the same or offered to sell or dispose of them, and that I am still ready to supply either the whole of said 75,000 guns or the portion of them which by the terms of my proposals are yet to be delivered, as soon as exportation of the same from England shall be permitted, and the non-appearance of the government in the market as a purchaser at a higher rate than the price agreed to be paid to me shall render it possible for me to do so; or I will produce and deliver, within a reasonable time, an equal number of American guns of the Springfield pattern at the same price.

To this last proposal I beg to call the special attention of the honorable Secretary of War, and respectfully to request a reply to the same, when I will, if desired, make the proposal more definite, and give satisfactory assurances of having command of the necessary facilities for producing the guns.

I beg also to be informed whether, under the circumstances, the honorable Secretary of War will deem it his duty to correct my said contracts.

Very respectfully, your obedient servant,

J. P. FITCH.

Hon. E. M. STANTON, *Secretary of War.*

NEW YORK, *February* 28, 1862.

SIR: In consequence of having been for some time absent from the city, I have only just now received the printed copy of your order of January 29, 1862, indicating to me that copies of all orders for furnishing arms, &c., must be filed with the Secretary of War. I had intended to comply fully with that order, and supposed I had done so, and failed only because I mistook the import of the words, "and file a copy thereof with the Secretary of War," in the last line of the third division of that order. Supposing the word "thereof" referred to "the statements in writing" mentioned in the next previous line, and not to the "contract, bargain, &c.," mentioned in the first line of the said third division.

I now herewith enclose copies of the orders for guns issued to me by the chief of ordnance referred to in my "*statement*" already transmitted to you, and would respectfully request that said statement may be completed by having the said copies placed on file in the office of the Secretary of War.

Respectfully, your obedient servant,

J. P. FITCH.

Hon. E. M. STANTON,
 Secretary of War.

ORDNANCE OFFICE, *Washington, August* 14, 1861.

SIR: Your letter to the Secretary of War, of the 3d instant, proposing to furnish and deliver to the government fifty thousand Enfield rifles, has been referred to this office, and I am directed to accept your proposition on the following terms and conditions: You are to deliver these arms at New York city as follows, viz: 2,500 in 30 days, 2,500 in 60 days, 6,000 in 90 days, 6,000 in 4 months, 6,000 in 5 months, 7,000 in 6 months, 10,000 in 7 months, and 10,000 in 8 months.

These arms are to be of the best quality and highest grade (No. 1) of English guns. They are to be delivered for inspection at the arsenal on Governor's island, New York, and are to be subject to inspection and approval by Captain R. H. K. Whiteley, or such other officer as may be designated for the purpose. On any failure to deliver the arms according to the quantities, and in or within the time before stated, the government will be under no obligation to receive them, but may or may not do so at its pleasure. Payments in such funds as the Treasury Department may provide will be made for each delivery of arms on certificates of inspection and receipt by a United States officer, and at the rate of twenty dollars ($20) each, including appendages, in bond.

Please inform me, in writing, whether you will agree to deliver the fifty thousand arms on the terms and conditions herein stated.

Respectfully, your obedient servant,

JAMES W. RIPLEY,
Brevet Brigadier General.

Mr. J. P. FITCH, *New York, N. Y.*

[To the above Mr. Fitch returned reply that he accepted terms stated, and in accordance therewith would furnish the arms named.]

ORDNANCE OFFICE, *Washington, September* 9, 1861.

SIR: Referring to my letter to you of the 14th August, 1861, I have now to inform you that, by direction of the War Department, the time of delivery of the fifty thousand Enfield rifles is to date from August 30, 1861. All the other terms and conditions respecting the quality, inspection, delivery, payment, and all else, to remain as specified in my letter to you dated August 14, 1861.

Respectfully, your obedient servant,

JAS. W. RIPLEY, *Brigadier General.*

Mr. J. P. FITCH, *Washington, D. C.*

ORDNANCE OFFICE, *Washington, September* 9, 1861.

SIR: Your proposition to deliver twenty-five thousand English Enfield rifles, (No. 1,) in addition to the fifty thousand you have agreed to deliver on the order from this office of August 14, 1861, as modified in regard to dates of delivery by the letter from me of this date, has been referred to this office. Your proposition is accepted on the following terms and conditions, viz: You are to deliver the 25,000 Enfield rifles, with appendages, for the same, at the following times, dating from August 30, 1861: 2,000 in 45 days, 3,000 more in 75 days, and 4,000 additional in every 30 days thereafter, until the whole 25,000 shall have been delivered. These arms are to be of the first quality, and highest grade (No. 1) of English guns. They are to be delivered for inspection at the arsenal on Governor's island, New York, and are to be subject to inspection and approval by Captain R. H. K. Whiteley, or such other officer as may be designated by this department for the purpose. On any failure to deliver the arms and appendages according to the quality and quantities, and in or within the times before stated, the government will be under no obligation to receive them, but may or may not do so at its option. Payments in such funds as the Treasury Department may provide for the purpose will be made for each delivery of arms with appendages on certificates of inspection and receipt by a United States officer, and at the rate of twenty dollars ($20) each, including appendages, in bond.

Please inform me, in writing, whether you will agree to deliver the twenty-five thousand arms on the terms and conditions herein stated.

Respectfully, your obedient servant,

JAS. W. RIPLEY, *Brigadier General.*

Mr. J. P. FITCH, *Washington, D. C.*

[To the above Mr. Fitch replied that he accepted the terms therein stated, and would supply the 25,000 Enfield rifles.]

COMMISSION ON ORDNANCE AND ORDNANCE STORES,
Washington, April 14, 1862.

GENERAL: The commission have the honor to report as follows:

CASE No. 39.—J. P. FITCH, of New York.

First, order of August 14, 1861, No. 14, printed list, page 11.

1st. To deliver 50,000 Enfield rifles of best quality and highest grade (No. 1) English guns in New York city, at $20 each, in bond; 2,500 in 30 days; 2,500 in 60 days; 6,000 in 90 days; 6,000 in 4 months; 6,000 in 5 months; 7,000 in 6 months; 10,000 in 7 months; 10,000 in 8 months.

Second, order of August 30, 1861, No. 22 of printed list, page 11.

2d. Altering first order to date from 30th August, increasing the number to 75,000, and requiring deliveries as follows: 2,500 in 30 days; 2,000 in 45 days; 2,500 in 60 days; 4,000 in 75 days; 6,000 in 90 days; 10,000 in 4 months; 10,000 in 5 months; 11,000 in six months; 14,000 in 7 months; 13,000 in 8 months. Total, 75,000 in 8 months (prior to May 1, 1862.) No deliveries made. Mr. Fitch stating, under date of February 12, 1862, that he was unable to carry out his agreement owing to the high price of arms and the Queen's proclamation.

The commission find that Mr. Fitch has failed to make the deliveries as promised; and as the government reserved to itself the right, in such "case of failure to deliver in or within the times specified," to take the arms or not at its option, and has already supplied itself from other sources, and no longer needs these arms, they direct that the orders given be revoked and annulled, and that no arms be received under them.

We are, sir, very respectfully, your obedient servants,

J. HOLT,
ROBERT DALE OWEN,
Commissioners, &c.
P. V. HAGNER,
Major of Ordnance, Assistant to Commission.

Brig. Gen. J. W. RIPLEY,
Chief of Ordnance.

CASE No. 40.

JAMES T. AMES.

COMMISSION ON ORDNANCE AND ORDNANCE STORES,
Washington, April 11, 1862.

GENERAL : The commission request that you will send them a copy of your order to Mr. J. T. Ames, of Chicopee, under which he states he delivered 5,000 foreign sabres prior to January, 1862. Also the order, issued October 19, for a second lot of 5,000 foreign sabres, part of which have been delivered.

The commission likewise request to know the prices allowed for the different swords and sabres ordered June 11, as per document No. 67, page 212.

Very respectfully, your obedient servant,
J. WISE, *Secretary to Commission.*

General J. W. RIPLEY,
Chief of Ordnance.

ORDNANCE OFFICE, *April 11, 1862.*

In answer to the request of the commission, communicated in your note of this date, I enclose copies of orders to James T. Ames, dated July 25 and October 19, 1861. The prices allowed for the different swords and sabres ordered June 11, 1861, are all stated on page 20 of Executive Document No. 67.

Respectfully, your obedient servant,
JAMES W. RIPLEY.

Mr. J. WISE, *Secretary to Commission.*

Extract from a letter dated Ordnance office, Washington, July 25, 1861.

" As regards cavalry sabres, I will take the 1,000 you will have by next week, and the 500 to 600 per week, deliverable after eight weeks, to the extent of 5,000 additional, provided they prove on inspection to be of good quality, and to satisfy the inspector that they are as good for service as the inspected sabres."

"JAMES T. AMES, Esq.,
" *Chicopee, Massachusetts.*"

Extract from a letter dated Ordnance office, Washington, October 19, 1861.

" Your two letters of the 16th instant are received. Deliver the remaining sabres due, and 5,000 more at the weekly rates you mention, or as much faster as possible."

"JAMES T. AMES, Esq.,
 "*Chicopee, Massachusetts.*"

CHICOPEE, *October* 16, 1861.

SIR : The steamer Bremen yesterday brought 400 more sabres, which makes 2,500 of the 5,000 ordered that have arrived, and I expect the balance will come within the next three weeks. I can, if you desire, get them out now steadily at the rate of 600 to 800 per week ; and, after a few weeks, at 1,000 per week, (unless a steamer is lost,) if I know at once that you wish them; but the present order will be out by the time I can get a letter over. I have a good inspector looking after them, and Major Whiteley reports that those received are of good quality. It was my intention to call on you to-day, but at New York found it was necessary to return, and now shall not be ready to leave for several days ; meantime, if you can, let me know your wishes about sabres. I will do all in my power to urge them forward, and you will be sure of a good quality.

Very respectfully, your obedient servant,

JAMES T. AMES.

General JAMES W. RIPLEY.

Enclosed is Major Whiteley's letter, which gives his opinion of the quality of sabres:

NEW YORK ARSENAL, *September* 27, 1861.

DEAR SIR: I have received and inspected the six boxes of foreign cavalry sabres. They are all alike, and seem to be very good sabres. Your invoice is 300—I have received 299 ; please send me the other sabre, or invoice for the smaller number. Do one or the other before the end of the month, for I wish to issue them immediately, and they must be included in the transactions of this quarter.

Yours, respectfully,

R. H. K. WHITELEY,
Major of Ordnance.

Mr. J. T. AMES.

WASHINGTON, *February* 5, 1862.

SIR : Enclosed are bills and receipts for 1,300 sabres.

There are 2,000 more of these sabres in New York, and the balance of the order of October 19 are all on the way. The entire order for 5,000 would have been delivered in January, only upon the disturbance caused in England by the Trent affair; they were all returned to Germany, and have now been sent by German steamers, and will be laid down in New York in a few days. I have been at the great expense of having an agent go out with gauges and barrels to have these made with great care, and trust they will all be received, as they conform in quality and model to those made by us here.

Very respectfully, your obedient servant,

JAMES T. AMES.

General JAMES W. RIPLEY,
Chief of Ordnance.

June 11.—10,000 cavalry sabres, 7,030 shipped; 5,000 artillery sabres, 700 shipped; 1,000 artillery swords; 5,000 non-commissioned officers' swords, 1,032 shipped; 3,000 musicians' swords, 700 shipped; 300 staff swords, 27 shipped; 1,500 mounted officers' swords, 80 shipped; 3,000 foot officers' swords, 487 shipped.

The balance of this order is in process of manufacture.

WASHINGTON, *February* 5, 1862.

SIR : Enclosed is a list of such orders for sabres and swords as we had on the 30th of January; since which time about 700 have been completed of the different kinds. I make this list in accordance with what I suppose to be the requirements of the late order from the Secretary of War.

Very respectfully, your obedient servant,

JAMES T. AMES.

General J. W. RIPLEY,
   Chief of Ordnance.

I may add that all the above list are in progress, and materials in hands of workmen.

J. T. A.

ORDNANCE OFFICE, *February* 8, 1862.

Respectfully submitted to the Secretary of War.

The orders to Mr. Ames, of June 11 and October 19, 1861, were for the sabres and swords herein stated, to be of the regular patterns, subject to United States inspection, at the usual prices for such articles. Those under the order of 11th of June, to be delivered as soon as possible, and those under the order of 19th of October, by the 19th of January, 1862. Mr. Ames, having been for many years a manufacturer of such articles for the government, understood perfectly the kind and quality of the articles ordered, and the usual prices. He has gone on to fill the orders to the extent mentioned in his letters, and states that the materials for the residue to be made by him have been provided, and that the work on them is in progress. Also, that 1,000 of the sabres to be imported have been delivered, 2,000 more are in New York, and the residue on board steamer to arrive in a few days. The swords and sabres, heretofore manufactured and delivered by Mr. Ames, are of the best kind and quality. It is recommended that he go on to complete his present orders.

JAMES W. RIPLEY,
   Brigadier General.

Before commission, April 2, 1862.

Statement by Major Hagner.

Mr. Ames has received a higher price for foreign sabres than any one else in New York. He has charged $8 50 each—the same as paid to him for sabres of his new make. It is believed that this was not the intention of the department in assenting to his suggestion to deliver foreign sabres. Nothing was said in giving assent about the price to be paid; but in the original order it was stipulated that the swords and sabres should be paid for at the "usual" prices. Mr. Ames has not charged the usual prices for the foreign sabres delivered by him. He has been paid as if all charged were home-made, no doubt inadvertently. The order given to him is still unfilled, and the accounts under that order open.

COMMISSION ON ORDNANCE AND ORDNANCE STORES,
Washington, April 5, 1862.

MAJOR : The commission as above request that you will state to them in writing—

1st. The number of foreign sabres received by you from James T. Ames under his contracts with the ordnance department, with dates of receipt.

2d. What proportion of the whole, or what particular deliveries you have been enabled to have inspected in this country, and the proportion of loss in such inspections.

3d. The relative value of the foreign deliveries compared with those made at the factory of Mr. Ames.

4th. The relative value of the foreign deliveries by Ames compared with those made by other contractors or sellers.

5th. The prices paid Ames and others as far as known to you.

6th. Whether the foreign-made Ames's sabres are for any reason worth more to the government than those known to you, and referred to by you in your answer to the fourth inquiry above.

Very respectfully, your obedient servant,

P. V. HAGNER,
Major of Ordnance.

Major R. H. K. WHITELEY,
Commanding New York Arsenal, Governor's Island, N. Y.

NEW YORK ARSENAL, *April* 9, 1862.

MAJOR : I have received your letter dated the 5th instant, and answer your questions as follows, viz :

1st. Bar sabres delivered by J. T. Ames, esq., and dates of receipt:

300	September 24, 1861.
800	September 30, 1861.
1,000	October 17, 1861.
400	October 22, 1861.
800	November 2, 1861.
600	November 5, 1861.
50	November 8, 1861.
800	November 25, 1861.
300	December 31, 1861.
1,000	January 27, 1862.
2,116	March 19, 1862.

8,166   Total number receipted for.

2d. The last delivery about one-fourth of the whole number receipted for; 80 boxes, of 50 each, were in the last delivery—4,000 ; 7 boxes were received at once in haste—350. A few boxes arrived wet, were opened for preservation, and the discovery made that the sabres had not been inspected in Europe, though Mr. Ames sent on an inspector there to perform this duty. The balance (3,650) were inspected at this arsenal; 1,766 received, and 1,884 rejected—nearly fifty-two per cent. of the number examined. I do not think any one blade or scabbard would meet fully the requirements of the inspector's regulations.

3d. The relative value of foreign bar sabres and those made by Mr. Ames I would set down at $5 and $8 50.

4th. Equal.

5th. James T. Ames, out of bond, $8 50.

Ph. & L. Lehipplin, (con. by Maj. W.,) in ditto, $3.
Do.   do.   (con. by Maj. H.,) in ditto, $3 50.
Schuyler, Hartly & Graham, (pur. by Maj. H.,) $6.
L. Windmuller,   do. $7.
Jas. A. Lacche,   do. $7 and $6.
Tomes, Son & Melvain,   do. $7.
J. Meyer,   do. $3.
  6th. No.
  I am, sir, very respectfully, your obedient servant,
                                R. H. K. WHITELEY,
                                      Major of Ordnance.

P. V. HAGNER,
    Major of Ordnance, Washington City.

    Questions to which the foregoing answers apply.

  1st. Report the number of foreign sabres received from Ames, and date of receipt.
  2d. What proportion of these have been subjected to inspection at your arsenal, and with what result?
  3d. Relative value of Ames's home and foreign made sabres?
  4th. Relative value of Ames's and other foreign made sabres?
  5th. Prices paid, as far as known, to you for foreign made to different individuals?
  6th. Is there any reason known to you why Ames should have received more for his foreign than others have done?

                                ORDNANCE OFFICE,
                          Washington, D. C., April 14, 1862.

  SIR: I enclose herewith, for the information of the commission, an extract from a letter received from Major R. H. K. Whiteley, commanding New York arsenal, as to the number of foreign sabres received on Mr. J. T. Ames's order.
      Respectfully, your obedient servant,
                                JAS. W. RIPLEY, *Brigadier General.*

J. WISE, Esq.,
    Sec'y to Com'n on Ord. Stores, Washington, D. C.

                                NEW YORK ARSENAL, *April 12, 1862.*

  GENERAL: I have had the honor to receive your letter dated the 9th instant. The whole number of foreign sabres received at this arsenal on account of J. T. Ames, esq., is 8,116. I consider them second class, and worth three dollars and a half in, and about five dollars out of, bond. In my statement to Major Hagner, of the 9th instant, the number appears 8,166 foreign sabres—that is correct; but fifty of them are officers' sabres, and should not have been numbered with the others. Therefore the true number received from Mr. Ames is 8,116.
  I am, sir, very respectfully, your obedient servant,
                                R. H. K. WHITELEY,
                                      Major of Ordnance.

True extract.
                                J. G. BENTON,
                                      Asst. Chief of Ordnance.

Brigadier General J. W. RIPLEY,
    Chief of the Ordnance Department, Washington City.

CHICOPEE, *May* 1, 1862.

SIR: The enclosed I intended to send by same mail as the statement of sabres and swords manufactured by us here, but was not able to get it ready. This relates entirely to the foreign sabres, by which it appears there are 1,884 sabres to be delivered to make the 10,000, the price for which the commission fix at $5 for each sabre. I have not taken any account of the sabres since the deliveries of the last lot in March, and therefore do not know what are on hand only by Major Whiteley's receipts, but think enough are in port to finish the two orders. I will go on at the price fixed by the commission, with what I have in port, at the low price fixed, $5, (which is much less than cost.) This I cannot object to, because the last order for 5,000 sabres being in hand while there was great competition in Germany, I cannot say that they were as fairly inspected in Europe as the first 5,000 were under the arrangement I had made for the purpose. I must infer from the result of the inspection at New York arsenal that the sabres were not of the same quality as the first lot, and if I had known they were inferior, I would not have offered them as of the same character. The first order of 5,000 sabres was shipped under an inspection I had arranged in Europe, and I examined the first delivery of that order and found the sabres to stand the test of our own inspection, and to be of as good quality for service, though perhaps not quite as highly finished as the home-made. For want of time I did not examine them after the first delivery, before they were sent to the New York arsenal, but receiving regular receipts from Major Whiteley, I supposed they were satisfactory—the only objection to quality being confined to the last 5,000. Under the circumstances, I do not think the commission, in going back to the first 5,000 after they had been issued, and cutting them down to the price named, (which is much less than cost,) have treated me fairly. I expected to have had an opportunity to leave before such a decision, and I consider its action in this case entirely in view of the facts I have stated—entirely different from what they would have given if they had known fully the circumstances; and I request that this letter may be sent to them with a view of reconsideration of their decision.

Very respectfully, your obedient servant,

JAS. T. AMES.

General J. W. RIPLEY,
Chief of Ordnance.

COMMISSION ON ORDNANCE AND ORDNANCE STORES,
Washington, May 20, 1862.

SIR: The commission request that you will furnish them with such evidences as you may have of any superiority in value of the first lot of your sabres of 5,000 over the second lot of 5,000.

Should it appear that a marked difference existed, the commission will reconsider their order as respects the first lot.

Very respectfully, your obedient servant,

P. V. HAGNER,
Major of Ordnance.

J. T. AMES, Esq., *Chicopee, Massachusetts.*

WASHINGTON, *June* 13, 1862.

GENTLEMEN: I left two sabres with Major Hagner to-day, and explained to him that one sabre was a sample of those that I supplied to the government in my order for 5,000, or that I believed it to be, but I only opened one lot, and of course cannot say as to the others more than that I honestly believe it to represent the whole. I find they were issued as soon as received, and are all gone into service. I left another sabre which represents what have been sold to the government, and I could have filled my order at a very early day if I had been willing to offer them. I shall be a large loser if I do not get at least $7 each for the first 5,000 sabres, and I think you will see the justice of saving me from a great loss on that order when you see the superiority of the arm.

Very respectfully, your obedient servant,

JAMES T. AMES.

COMMISSION ON ORDNANCE AND ORDNANCE STORES.

Before commission, June 26, 1862.

Statement of sabres delivered, as per receipts of Major Whiteley, by James T. Ames, under his orders from the ordnance department dated July 25 and October 19, 1861.

1861—October	2,100	sabres.
November	1,200	do.
November	1,400	do.
December	300	do.
1862—January	1,000	do.
March	2,116	do.
	8,116	do.

Major Hagner states that the above statement of deliveries is reported as correct.

He has examined the sample of sabres submitted by Mr. Ames, and considers that those delivered before January 1, 1862, (as per sample,) are worth $6 50 and of bond; the others not to exceed $5 out of bond at times of delivery. Thinks that it would be fair to allow at these rates.

The commission agree to modify their decision dated April 15, 1862, accordingly.

COMMISSION ON ORDNANCE AND ORDNANCE STORES,
Washington, April 15, 1862.

GENERAL: The commission have the honor to report as follows:

CASE No. 40.—JAMES T. AMES, Chicopee, Massachusetts.

Two orders by chief of ordnance, dated July 25; case No. 12, page 20, Ex. Doc. 67. "To deliver 10,000 foreign sabres, provided they prove, on inspection, to be of good quality, and to satisfy the inspector that they are as good for service as the inspected sabres." Deliveries under the first order to be "at the rate of 500 to 600 per week, deliverable after eight weeks to the extent of 5,000," and under the second order "from 600 to 800 per week at first, and after a few weeks at the rate of 1,000 per week." By report of the chief of ordnance the whole of the last order was to be delivered by January 19, 1862, and the price to be the usual price for such articles.

The commission find that under the above order 8,116 foreign cavalry sabres have been delivered, 5,000 prior to December 31, 1861, 1,000 January 27, and 2,116 March 19, at the New York arsenal; that on several occasions issues of these sabres have been made under such urgent circumstances that the prescribed rules of inspection were not followed prior to the issue, promise having been made that this should be done in Europe. A more formal inspection was made of the last delivery, amounting to over 25 per cent. of the whole number delivered, when it was discovered that these sabres had not been inspected in Europe; that of 3,050 examined, 1,766 only were received, nearly 52 per cent. of the number examined being rejected, the inspecting officer reporting that, in his opinion, "no one blade or scabbard met fully the requirements of the inspection regulations."

The commission find that the maximum value of the sabres delivered prior to December 31 by Mr. Ames under the above order does not exceed $6 50 each, duties paid, and of those delivered since that date the maximum value does not exceed $5, duties paid.

It appears that bills for a portion of the sabres delivered under the orders have been already presented by Mr. Ames, and paid at the treasury, as is now evident, at prices greatly exceeding their true value, and also exceeding the usual value of foreign sabres purchased from every source except this.

The commission therefore decide that this transaction be considered as still in progress, and that the sabres paid for be considered as "upon account," and that a price of $6 50, duties paid, be allowed upon the 5,000 delivered prior to December 31, 1861, and $5, duty paid, on those since delivered and remaining to be delivered under the orders given to Mr. Ames. The commission further direct that none of those offered in future under these orders be received (at the rate of $5, duties paid) unless proved upon inspection equal to the best quality of foreign sabres now received by the government at like cost. As Mr. Ames has been for a long time most extensively employed by the government in many ways, and particularly in the manufacture of sabres, is perfectly acquainted with the requirements of the government inspection of sabres, and promised that these should be fully equal to such requirements, there is manifest propriety in demanding of him an article of the full value of the price paid.

In addition to the above order for foreign sabres, an order was given by the chief of ordnance June 11, 1861, for 10,000 cavalry sabres, 5,000 artillery sabres, 1,000 artillery swords, 3,000 non-commissioned officers' swords, 1,500 mounted officers' swords, 3,000 foot officers' swords, under injunctions of speedy delivery, stating that they were wanted as soon as possible, particularly the non-commissioned officers' and "musicians' swords." In accepting this Mr. Ames promised "to use all efforts to meet your wants."

The commission find, on reference to this order, that on the 5th February, 1862, Mr. Ames reports that he has shipped only 7,630 cavalry sabres, 700 artillery, 1,032 non-commissioned officers' swords, 700 musicians' swords, 27 staff swords, 80 mounted officers' swords, 487 foot officers' swords.

Major Whiteley reports that 50 mounted officers' sabres, *foreign*, were received by him from Mr. Ames November 8, (possibly under this order,) and included in the 80 reported as shipped.

The commission consider that it is evident, from the small proportions of the order filled, as above shown, the efforts promised by Mr. Ames to meet the wants of the government have not been made; that more than a reasonable time has already been allowed for the completion of the order; that the well known wants of the government required far greater despatch in this work; and as owing to this non-receipt the government has been compelled to supply itself with these articles from other sources, they direct that instructions be given to close at once the above order.

The commission further direct that if any foreign-made swords or sabres have been delivered under the last quoted order, the price allowed for them be only such as were paid by the purchasing officer in New York for like articles at the same period. In the settlement of Mr. Ames's accounts deductions are to be made if foreign sabres have been included in accounts already paid at the treasury.

We are, sir, very respectfully, your obedient servants,

J. HOLT,
ROBERT DALE OWEN,
Commissioners, &c.

Brigadier General J. W. RIPLEY, *Chief of Ordnance.*

CASE No. 41.

F. STEFFENS.

ORDNANCE OFFICE, *Washington, April* 15, 1862.

James W. Ripley, brigadier general, recommends that the five enclosed accounts be referred to the commission on contracts, &c., for ordnance and ordnance stores.

Approved and referred by order of the Secretary of War.

P. H. WATSON,
Assistant Secretary of War.

ORDNANCE OFFICE, *Washington, April* 15, 1862.

SIR: I respectfully submit herewith five accounts which have reached this office, viz:

1. Daniel B. Pond, $1,500, for two Ellsworth guns and ammunition, purchased by General Butler.
2. Putnam Machine Company, by M. Fairbanks, $364 70, for one rifling machine, purchased by the same officer.
3. George M. Maclean, $53.60, for saddler's tools and materials for 11th Illinois cavalry, Colonel Ingersoll.
4. F. Steffens, $206, for twelve pendulum hausses and labor, by order of General F. Sigel.
5. M. G. Anders, $1,681 75, for seventy-five sets horse equipments, purchased by order of General R. Anderson.

As the articles charged for were not procured in accordance with law, but have been received for the service of the United States, I recommend that they be referred to the commission on contracts, &c., for ordnance and ordnance stores, in the same manner as previous similar accounts.

Very respectfully, your obedient servant,

JAS. W. RIPLEY,
Brigadier General.

Hon. EDWIN M. STANTON,
Secretary of War.

ST. LOUIS, *March* 25, 1862.

SIR: I have the honor to transmit a duplicate of an account approved by F. Sigel, acting major general commanding third division, in favor of F. Steffens for twelve pendulum hausses, amounting to $108, and twenty-four and a half days' labor, $98, amounting in all to $206. The work was done on the road from Rolla to Springfield, Missouri, by Mr. Steffens, while the army was moving in that direction last fall. This account has been presented to Captain F. D. Callender, ordnance department, United States army, at St. Louis arsenal, who states that he is not authorized to pay the same, and desires that the same be transmitted to you. Mr. Steffens has placed the account in my hands for collection, he not being a resident of this city.

I have the honor to remain, sir, very respectfully,

G. A. FINKELNBURG.

Brigadier General J. W. RIPLEY,
Chief of Ordnance, Washington.

Address G. A. Finkelnburg, attorney at law, St. Louis, Missouri, box 3,802.

COMMISSION ON ORDNANCE AND ORDNANCE STORES,
Washington, April 17, 1862.

GENERAL : The commission have the honor to report as follows :

CASE No. 41.—F. STEFFENS, St. Louis.

Claim for account of voucher, dated October 30, 1861. Referred by special order of Secretary of War.

For pendulum hausses and labor in attaching them to the guns of Major Backhoff's artillery, Missouri volunteers. Amount of claim, $206. Voucher suspended, the purchase of ordnance stores not having been made in accordance with law.

The commission find that the account is approved by General Sigel, commanding the division, and the articles receipted for by the assistant quartermaster of the division; that the battery was under orders for service, and the articles, such as would be needed, and the work done while on the march, and hence required more time and higher daily wages. Under these circumstances the commission direct that the account be examined and audited as usual, without objection on account of informality in the purchase or of the rates charged.

We are, sir, very respectfully, your obedient servants,

J. HOLT,
ROBERT DALE OWEN,
Commissioners, &c.
P. V. HAGNER,
Major of Ordnance, Assistant to Commission.

Brigadier General J. W. RIPLEY,
Chief of Ordnance.

CASE No. 42.

PUTNAM MACHINE COMPANY.

Before commission.

Bill of Putnam Machine Company for one rifling machine, and indorsed as follows :

This bill was contracted by my orders, has not been paid, and if the price is just, of which I know nothing, should be paid.

B. F. BUTLER,
Major General Commanding.

Amount of bill, $364 70.

FORT MONROE ARSENAL,
March 5, 1862.

The rifling machine ordered by General Butler was received here in August, 1861, and has been used for the public service nearly ever since.

T. G. BAYLOR,
First Lieutenant Ordnance, Commanding.

True copy.

P. V. HAGNER,
Major Ordnance.

COMMISSION ON ORDNANCE AND ORDNANCE STORES,
Washington, April 17, 1862.

GENERAL : The commission have the honor to report as follows:

CASE NO. 42.—PUTNAM MACHINE COMPANY, Fitchburg, Mass.

Claim for account of voucher, dated July 1861.   A rifling machine delivered at the Fort Monroe arsenal, ordered by General Butler, then commanding, and receipted for by Lieutenant Baylor, commanding arsenal. Amount of claim, $364 70. Voucher suspended, the purchase of the ordnance stores not having been made in accordance with law.

The commission find that the machine has been in constant use at the arsenal since its arrival; but as no evidence is presented, upon which its proper price can be predicated, the commission direct that the account be submitted to Lieutenant Baylor, or commanding officer at Fort Monroe arsenal; and if the price be considered reasonable by him, that the account be examined and audited without objection on account of informality of purchase.

We are, sir, very respectfully, your obedient servants,

J. HOLT,
ROBERT DALE OWEN,
Commissioners.
P. V. HAGNER,
Major of Ordnance, Assistant to Commission.

Brigadier General JAS. W. RIPLEY,
Chief of Ordnance.

FORT MONROE ARSENAL,
Virginia, April 23, 1862.

SIR : I enclose the papers relating to the rifling machine finished by the Putnam Machine Company on the order of General Butler. I thought the price of this machine very high, and wrote to the Putnam Machine Company to that effect; but I was informed that they were ordered to make this machine with all despatch, and worked on it day and night until finished. Such being the case, I do not thing the price too large.

Very respectfully, your obedient servant,

T. G. BAYLOR,
First Lieutenant of Ordnance.

Brigadier General JAS. W. RIPLEY,
Chief of Ordnance, Washington, D. C.

CASE No. 43.

W. A. WHEELER.

Before commission, April 16, 1862.

Mr. W. A. Wheeler, of New York, appeared, and stated that he claimed to have a contract to deliver 50,000 Springfield muskets, under the order addressed to him and published, pages 157 and 158, Ex. Doc. No. 67. He explained that, for some reason unknown to him, the original letter from General Ripley had never come to hand, and therefore he has written no acceptance, as stated in the printed document; but that he had since obtained an official copy of this letter, and had sent in his acceptance of the order, and was going on with the work under it. Mr. Wheeler was informed that the original order was never sent to him, but was retained in the War Department, and was now in the hands of the commission, and that, having been thus withheld by the department, it could not be regarded as giving him any right to make arms under it. That it was supposed that he had no thought of doing so, and therefore no written decision had been made in the case, but one would now be made as soon as Mr. Owen (who was then absent) returned to the city. Mr. Wheeler contended that the order was good against the government, only his delay in accepting it; being satisfactorily accounted for, as above, he lost no right in consequence of the delay, and therefore he intended to act under it, as if received and accepted in proper time.

W. A. WHEELER.—*Claim to furnish arms.*—50,000 *United States rifled muskets, model* 1855.—*December* 24, 1861.

WASHINGTON, D. C., *November* 18, 1861.

SIR : I have obtained, in connexion with a number of capitalists in New York, the control of one of the largest manufacturing establishments in the country, which can readily be converted into a manufactory for arms, which enables me to make the following proposition, viz :

I will furnish 100,000 stand of the most approved muskets, with interchangeable parts, equal in every respect to the best Springfield pattern, without the Maynard primer attached to lock, which I learn has been abandoned by the government—delivery as follows : within six months from the date of the contract, 5,000 in thirty days ; thereafter, 6,000 ; and within each succeeding thirty days, 8,000, until the entire number is delivered. The arms to be delivered at Governor's island, or such other arsenal in or near New York as the government may direct, and be subject to usual inspection by an officer of the United States army. Price of each gun and usual fixtures, $20 ; payments to be made on the delivery of each lot of 500 or more guns.

I also propose, if desired, at the last-mentioned rate per month, to further increase the number of muskets for six months longer, making the whole number 150,000.

Believing that the government will at once increase the supply of muskets to at least one million stand, and that our own mechanics and capital should be employed for that purpose, I desire, respectfully, to call your attention to the subject.

The outlay for property, machinery, &c., to start the work, will not fall short of $200,000 before guns can be delivered. By proper encouragement now on the part of the government, a sufficient amount of gun machinery can be started in this country to prevent the necessity, in future, of sending abroad to procure guns to crush out rebellion, or to defend our country from foreign troubles, thus enabling us to use our own resources and weapons, and rendering us independent of foreign nations in any emergency.

I respectfully ask for a definite reply within the next ten days, in order that arrangements may be perfected to start the work.

I have the honor to be, very respectfully, your obedient servant,

WM. A. WHEELER.

Hon. SIMON CAMERON, *Secretary of War.*

(For the order of the Secretary of War, directing contract to be made with William A. Wheeler, of New York, see Assistant Secretary of War Scott's memorandum of December 24, 1861, attached to C. B. Hoard's proposal, No. 59.)

An order from the Ordnance office, dated December 24, 1861, was given, in compliance with the above instructions, to William A. Wheeler, of New York, for 50,000 United States rifle muskets in precisely the same words, and imposing the same conditions as that given to C. B. Hoard on the same date, for which see No. 59.

The records of the Ordnance office afford no evidence that Messrs. Wheeler & Co. accepted the order of December 24, 1861, for 50,000 muskets.

Original letter addressed by the chief of ordnance to W. A. Wheeler, New York, received by me with various other papers in a package marked "Papers found in Mr. Thomas A. Scott's drawer," referred to commission on ordnance claims, &c.

Respectfully, &c.,

P. H. WATSON,
Assistant Secretary of War.
P. V. HAGNER,
Major of Ordnance.

ORDNANCE OFFICE,
Washington, December 24, 1861.

SIR: By direction of the Secretary of War I offer you an order for fifty thousand (50,000) muskets, with appendages, of the Springfield pattern, on the following terms and conditions, viz: These arms are to be furnished with the regular appendages, and are to be in all respects identical with the standard rifle musket made at the United States armory at Springfield, Massachusetts, and are to interchange with it and with each other in all their parts; they are to be subject to inspection by United States inspectors, in the same manner that the Springfield arms are inspected, and none are to be received or paid for but such as pass inspection and are approved by United States inspectors. These fifty thousand (50,000) arms and appendages are to be delivered at your armory as follows, viz: not less than one thousand (1,000) in each of the months of July, August, and September, 1862; not less than two thousand (2,000) in each of the months of October and November, 1862; not less than three thousand (3,000) in December, 1862; and not less than four thousand per month thereafter, until the entire fifty thousand shall have been delivered; and you are to have the right to deliver more rapidly than according to the number of arms before specified, if you can do so. In the case of any failure to make deliveries to the extent and within the times before specified, you are to forfeit the right to deliver whatever number may be deficient in the specified number for the month in which the failure occurs. All these arms and appendages are to be delivered by you, and this order, if transferred to another party, is to be thereby forfeited. Payments are to be made, in such funds as the Treasury Department may provide, for each delivery, on certificates of inspection and receipt by the United States inspectors, at the rate of twenty dollars ($20) for each arm, including appendages. All these arms and appendages are to be packed by you in boxes of the regular pattern, with twenty (20) muskets and appendages in each box, for which a fair price, to be determined by the United States inspector, will be allowed.

Please signify, in writing, your acceptance or non-acceptance of this order on the terms and conditions before stated herein.

Respectfully, your obedient servant,

JAMES W. RIPLEY,
Brigadier General.

W. A. WHEELER, *New York, N. Y.*

COMMISSION ON ORDNANCE AND ORDNANCE STORES,
Washington, April 16, 1862.

GENERAL : The commission have the honor to report as follows :

CASE No. 43.—WILLIAM A. WHEELER, New York.

Order from chief of ordnance, by direction of the Secretary of War, dated December 24, 1861.

To deliver 50,000 rifled muskets, Springfield pattern, at $20 each. Deliveries to commence in July, 1862.

The original order, signed by chief of ordnance December 24, 1861, was never delivered to or received by Mr. Wheeler, but has been sent to the commission from the War Department, having been found there, with other papers, in the drawer of Hon. Thomas A. Scott, Assistant Secretary of War, by whom the order was originally given.

A few days since, on the 29th March, Mr. Wheeler applied for and received a copy of this order at the Ordnance office, and wrote an acceptance of it on the same day, the proposed contract being then inchoate and unclosed, so far as the government was concerned.

The commission consider that, as the original order was never issued from the War Office, but seems from some consideration to have been and is still withheld, it must be regarded as having in fact not been given, and decide that it be treated as null and of no effect.

The acceptance of Mr. Wheeler written upon a copy of the order, which he obtained from the ordnance department, could impose no obligation upon the government, since the original of this order, which was the expression of the government's assent to Mr. Wheeler's proposal, remained at that moment undelivered and inoperative, and still remains so.

We are, sir, very respectfully, &c.,

J. HOLT,
ROBERT DALE OWEN,
Commissioners.
P. V. HAGNER,
Major of Ordnance, Assistant to Commission.

Brigadier General J. W. RIPLEY,
Chief of Ordnance.

NEW YORK, *April* 23, 1862.

GENTS: My contract for Springfield rifle muskets being in process of execution, and desiring not to be delayed, I again respectfully request, if you have any doubts of its legality, that you will refer it to the Secretary of War for a decision.

Your early reply will very much oblige your obedient servant,

WILLIAM A. WHEELER.

Hon. JOSEPH HOLT and R. D. OWEN, *Commissioners.*

COMMISSION ON ORDNANCE AND ORDNANCE STORES,
Washington, April 28, 1862.

SIR: In reply to yours of the 23d instant, I have to state that, so far as this commission knows or believes, you have no "contract" with the government for Springfield rifle muskets. Your attempt to conclude such a contract failed, as we have decided, because the assent of the War Department thereto was not expressed and delivered to you, but was withheld. If the guns are in process of manufacture, as you allege, the work must have been commenced within a few days, and without any sanction from the government. In your interview with the commission on the 16th instant, which your present letter strangely ignores, you did not pretend to have taken any steps towards the fulfilment of what you now very inaccurately call a contract. On the contrary, you then admitted that you had received no notice of the assent of the War Department to your proposal, although you had succeeded in obtaining, as late as March 29, 1862, from the ordnance department a copy of such assent, the original of which you were assured by me was in our possession, and had never been delivered.

Your attempt to treat this transaction as one importing any obligation upon the government is wholly without legal sanction.

Very respectfully, your obedient servant,

J. HOLT, *Commissioner, &c.*

Mr. W. A. WHEELER, *New York.*

NEW YORK, *April* 30, 1862.

SIR: I have received *your* decision in the case of my contract for "Springfield rifled muskets." As I have not asked for any decision at your hands other than to refer the matter to the Secretary of War, I consider it entirely superfluous for you to render a decision in the case. The fact that an original order from the War Department did not reach me, and that upon the representation of the fact to the ordnance department, the proper officer and head of that bureau, whose duty it was to issue such orders, knowing that I was entitled to it, gave me a copy in lieu of the original, and that this order was accepted by me, forms, not only in my own mind, but the minds of the best legal talent of this city, a clear contract, and as such I shall treat it and proceed accordingly, believing that our government, which asks only justice at the hands of others, will concede the same justice when itself is concerned as the party appealed to.

The argument adduced by you would ruin any business man's character, and cannot be tolerated in a great government like ours, which desires to have the reputation of doing right. I am also in receipt of yours of the 28th instant, which I cannot allow to remain unanswered, as it contains statements entirely at variance with the facts as they occurred in our conversation. You say my "attempt to conclude a contract for muskets failed because the assent of the War Department thereto was not expressed and delivered to me, but was withheld." This is entirely an assumption on your part, and destitute of proof, as, even if the original order was mislaid, it forms no argument against me, as the ordnance department promptly supplied the deficiency when notified of the fact, which they had the undoubted right to do, having the written authority of the Secretary of War to do so. You also say, in my interview with you on the 16th, I did not pretend that I had taken any steps towards the fulfilment of what I now very inaccurately call a contract, and that on the contrary I admitted I had received no notice of the assent of the War Department to my proposal, &c. Now, my dear sir, if you can recollect any of the conversation, you must surely know I distinctly stated to you that I had taken the necessary steps towards fulfilling this contract, but that you assumed as I did not get the order till the 29th March, therefore I had done nothing, being, as you said, "very evident," though how you knew this I am at a loss to comprehend.

I make no attempt to treat this as a contract, because it is so in fact, and the very best legal opinions I can get pronounce it so, and those that stand at least as high for legal attainments as yourself. I shall therefore still consider it as a legal contract and carry it out.

Truly yours,

WM. A. WHEELER.

JOSEPH HOLT, Esq.

Before commission, May 3, 1862.

Mr. Keller, clerk in Ordnance office, being sworn, deposes as follows:

Question by the commission. Examine the paper purporting to be a copy of a letter dated Ordnance office, Washington, March 29, 1862, addressed to Mr. W. A. Wheeler, of New York, and in the following words, to wit:

"ORDNANCE OFFICE,
"*Washington, March* 29, 1862.

"SIR: Herewith I enclose a copy of a letter addressed to you from this office on the 24th of December, 1861, tendering to you, by instructions from the War Department, an order for the manufacture of 20,000 Springfield rifle muskets, at $20 each.

"Respectfully, your obedient servant,
"JAS. W. RIPLEY, *Brigadier General.*

"Mr. W. A. WHEELER, *of New York—Present.*

"MAY 10, 1862.

"NOTE.—The twenty thousand above should be *fifty thousand;* and the error was made by myself in writing the letter in a hurry, as the person for whom it was intended was waiting for it. The same error occurs in the original letter to Mr. Wheeler, of which this is an exact copy.

"J. P. KELLER, *Clerk Ordnance Office.*"

and state the circumstances under which the original was written and issued from the Ordnance office.

Answer. Mr. Wheeler, or a gentleman whom I took to be Mr. Wheeler, called at the office on the day of the date of this letter, and asked to be furnished with a copy of a letter which had been addressed him some time previous. In obedience to the standing instructions "to issue to individuals copies of papers in which they are personally interested," Mr. Wheeler, or the gentleman who I suppose was he, was shown the press-book by Mr. Morris, one of the clerks; and the clerk being very busy, he, Mr. Wheeler, made a copy from it; and, as an evidence that it was an official copy, he asked that it might be enclosed to him, which was done in the words of the letter quoted. Captain Benton, or one of the officers in the office, brought Mr. Wheeler to my desk and told me to do what was usual in the premises. I therefore wrote the letter and took it to the general to sign, who did so at once; and I handed it to Mr. Wheeler, who thereupon wrote a letter in the Ordnance office, acknowledging the receipt of the order and accepting it. In writing the letter, I intended only to state the character of the paper enclosed, describing it as it is known to us, viz: as an order issued by instructions of the War Department. The words "by instructions of the War Department" refer to the original order, not to enclosing them a copy of the order. I had no special instructions to furnish this paper as authority upon which action was to be taken by Mr. Wheeler, but the copy was given solely under the general instructions, as a matter of interest to him. Mr. Wheeler stated that the original had never reached his hands, and that he wished to have a copy—did not state his purpose, and I had no knowledge whatever that the original paper was still held by the War Department, but supposed it had merely miscarried by mail, as we know that no acceptance from Mr. Wheeler and no acknowledgment of the order had been received at the office.

JONAS P. KELLER.

Questions propounded to General James W. Ripley, chief of Ordnance department.

1st question by the commissioner. Look upon the paper now shown you, dated "Ordnance office, Washington, December 24, 1861," and signed by yourself, and professing to be an order to W. A. Wheeler, New York, N. Y., for fifty thousand muskets, with appendages, of the Springfield pattern, at the price of $20 each, and which paper is endorsed "$\frac{829}{32}$ W. D.," and state whether or not said paper is the *original* order issued by you, and which is referred to on pages 155, 157, and 158, of "Executive Document No. 67, House of Representatives," 37th Congress, 2d session.

2d. In a letter addressed by said W. A. Wheeler to Joseph Holt, one of the commissioners, dated "New York, April 30, 1862," and now shown to you, occurs the following passage: "The fact that an original order from the War Department did not reach me, that upon representation of the fact to the Ordnance department, the proper officer and head of that bureau, whose duty it was to issue such orders, knowing that I was entitled to it, gave me a copy in lieu of the original, and that this order was accepted by me, forms, not only in my mind, but in the minds of the best legal talent of this city, a clear contract, and as such I shall treat it," &c. Please state whether this sentence, so far as it professes to set forth your action in the premises, is true or false, and detail fully your connexion with the transaction referred to, and the significance which should attach to a delivery of the copy to Mr. Wheeler under the circumstances.

Answer to question 1. I recognize the letter signed by myself, dated December 24, 1861, and addressed to W. A. Wheeler, New York, tendering to him, by direction of the Secretary of War, an order for the delivery of 50,000 Springfield muskets, at $20 each, now exhibited to me, as the original letter which I signed on the day of its date.

Answer to question 2. The copy of the letter referred to in answer to the first question, and which was furnished to Mr. Wheeler on the 29th day of March last, was furnished in pursuance of the regulation, published by Secretary Cameron on the 18th day of that month, in relation to furnishing copies of papers from the War Department. This copy was not given in lieu of an original order. Even if I had been clothed with authority to that effect, I would not have renewed an order involving $1,000,000 without submitting the matter to the Secretary of War. In this case the Secretary, by whose order I had prepared the original order to Wheeler, had resigned after it had been given, and had been succeeded by another, who had, on the 10th day of March, only nineteen days before this copy was furnished, issued a very stringent order prohibiting the purchase or reception of arms after that date, except in pursuance of special directions from himself, and this order I had published to all ordnance officers who had previously been authorized to purchase arms. When the copy was given to Mr. Wheeler it was not contemplated or expected by me that he would make it the basis of the acceptance of the proposal. I had then no knowledge that the original order, now before me, had been withheld by the War Department, and it was furnished as any other copy of a paper would have been furnished by myself or assistants to any person applying for such copy, upon showing that his interest therein was such as was contemplated by the regulation of March 18, before referred to.

JAS. W. RIPLEY, Brigadier General.

ORDNANCE OFFICE, *May* 8, 1862.

Sworn to and subscribed before me this 9th day of May, A. D. 1862.

N. CALLAN, J. P. [L. S.]

ORDNANCE OFFICE, *Washington, March* 29, 1862.

SIR: Herewith I enclose a copy of a letter addressed to you from this office on the 24th December, 1861, tendering to you, by instructions from the War Department, an order for the manufacture of 20,000 Springfield rifle muskets, at $20 each.

Respectfully, your obedient servant,

JAMES W. RIPLEY,
Brigadier General.

Mr. W. A. WHEELER,
    of New York—Present.

MAY 10, 1862.

The "20,000" above should be 50,000, and the error was made by myself in writing the letter in a hurry, as the person for whom it was intended was waiting for it. The same error occurs in the original letter to Mr. Wheeler, of which this is an exact copy.

J. P. KELLER, *Clerk Ordnance Office.*

WAR DEPARTMENT,
Washington City, D. C., May 3, 1862.

SIR: Your proposal, bearing date 18th November, 1861, offering to furnish 100,000 stand of most approved muskets, of the best Springfield pattern, at $20 each, was not accepted by this department.

On the 24th of December, 1861, Thomas A. Scott, Assistant Secretary of War, directed the chief of ordnance to make out an order in your name for 50,000 Springfield muskets at the price named; and such an order was made out and signed by the chief of ordnance on that day. The said order, however, was not delivered or forwarded to you, but was withheld by this department, and is still in its possession. The purpose of the department, being thus inchoate and unconsummated, was not communicated to you.

Some months after the date of this transaction notice of what had occurred seems, through some channel or other, to have reached you; and on the 29th of March, 1862, you obtained from the ordnance department a copy of the order of 24th December, and wrote your acceptance of it. This was without the authority of this department, and was an assent by you to a proposal which, in point of fact, had not been made, the intention to make it having been abandoned.

Having learned that you are endeavoring to treat this action on your part as constituting a contract, and that you profess a determination to proceed in its execution, I deem it proper to inform you that this department recognizes no contract as existing between it and yourself, and that if you take any measures for supplying the arms referred to, you will do so on your own account and at your own risk, and without any obligation on the part of the government to receive them.

I am, sir, very respectfully, your obedient servant,

EDWIN M. STANTON,
Secretary of War.

Mr. W. A. WHEELER, *New York.*

CASE No. 44.

W. F. BROOKS.

NEW YORK, *February* 6.

Report of W. F. Brooks on order for carbines and muskets.

Submits copy of order to furnish 10,000 Gibbs's patent breech-loading carbines, and 10,000 muskets, Springfield pattern.

NEW YORK, *February* 6, 1862.

DEAR SIR: In compliance with "Order No. 11, in respect to army contracts," I hereby respectfully give notice that I have a contract with the War Department to supply ten thousand Gibbs's patent breech-loading carbines, and ten thousand muskets, Springfield pattern.

Appended hereto are respectfully submitted copies of the order and acceptance which constitute the contract. And I also report that the various parts of these respective arms are now being rapidly made; that they will be put together and delivered to the government within the terms provided for delivery in and by said contract.

I would also beg leave to add that I am prepared to receive and execute additional orders should the government require more of these arms.

I am, with respect, your obedient servant,

WM. F. BROOKS.

Hon. EDWIN M. STANTON,
    Secretary of War.

ORDNANCE OFFICE,
Washington, December 13, 1861.

SIR: By direction of the Secretary of War, I offer you an order for ten thousand (10,000) Gibbs's patent breech-loading carbines, with appendages, and ten thousand rifle muskets, Springfield pattern, with appendages, on the following terms and conditions, viz: all these arms are to be subject to inspection and proof in such manner and by such inspectors as this department may designate, and none are to be received and paid for but such as pass inspection, and are approved by the United States inspectors. The carbines are to be equal in all respects to a sample carbine to be furnished by you and approved by this office. The rifle muskets are to be, in all respects, identical with the standard rifle muskets manufactured at the Springfield armory; are to interchange with it and with each other in all their parts, and are to be inspected in the same manner that the Springfield muskets are inspected. These twenty thousand arms are to be delivered in the city of New York as follows, viz: one thousand of either or both kinds on or before the twelfth (12th) day of April, 1862, and not less than one thousand per month thereafter, until the whole twenty thousand shall have been delivered. In case of any failure to make the deliveries to the extent and in or within the times specified, the government is to have authority to revoke and annul this order so far as regards the arms and appendages remaining undelivered at the time of such failure. Payments are to be made for each delivery in such funds as the Treasury Department may provide, on certificates of inspection and receipt by United States inspectors, at the rate of twenty-eight (28) dollars for each carbine, including appendages, and twenty (20) dollars for each rifle musket, including appendages. All these arms and appendages are to be packed by you in boxes of the regular pattern, with twenty arms and appendages in each box, for which a fair price, to be determined by the United States inspector, will be allowed.

Please signify, in writing, your acceptance or non-acceptance of this order on the terms and conditions herein stated.

Respectfully, your obedient servant,

JAMES W. RIPLEY, *Brigadier General.*

WM. F. BROOKS, Esq, *Washington, D. C.*

WASHINGTON, *December* 13, 1861.

SIR: I have had the honor to receive your letter of this date assigning me a contract for ten thousand Gibbs's breech-loading carbines, and ten thousand muskets, Springfield pattern, and requiring me to accept or reject the same in writing.

In conformity therewith, I hereby accept the said contract, its conditions and terms of payment.

I have the honor to be your obedient servant,

W. F. BROOKS.

Brigadier General JAMES W. RIPLEY,
Chief of Ordnance Department.

NEW YORK, *April* 10, 1862.

At the request of Mr. Wm. Marston, (who I have been acquainted with the last four years,) we visited his fire-arms manufactory, in this city, for the purpose of examining the tools and machinery used in making Gibbs's breech-loading carbine. We find he has a large amount of milling, turning, shaping, drilling, edging, rifling, stocking, and other machinery entirely new, and now at work on the different parts of the above arms. Mr. Marston informs us he has been very much delayed by parties who he contracted with to make machinery, and, in consequence of the delay, he is obliged to ask an extension of time on the contract for arms granted to Wm. F. Brooks, who is associated with himself in manufacturing the same. We know Mr. Marston to be a practical gun-maker and machinist, and are certain he can speak knowingly, and will now deliver arms in the time he engages to do so.

R. HOE & CO.

ORDNANCE OFFICE,
No. 55 White street, New York, April 11, 1862.

SIR: Agreeably to your request, I have made an examination of your establishment in which you contemplate to manufacture the carbines which you inform me have been contracted for by the United States with you and Mr. W. F. Brooks. Your facilities for accomplishing that portion of the work which you design fabricating at your factory, viz: the stocks and finishing of locks and other component metallic parts, appear to me to be good, and, if properly applied, will secure a completion of your order in a reasonable time. The party who is to supply you with the principal forged parts required, Mr. J. Stephenson, has good facilities also for fulfilling his engagements, and has always satisfactorily complied with his orders from this office.

The forged barrels and the small parts of locks which you design having made elsewhere can, I should judge from my knowledge of this kind of work, be readily obtained.

Respectfully, your obedient servant,

S. CRISPIN, *Captain of Ordnance.*

Mr. W. M. MARSTON, *New York.*

Before commission, April 15, 1862.

W. F. Brooks, of New York, states: I am a brass and flue manufacturer, in Manchester county. Had no special experience for arms. Mr. Marston, who has been associated with me, is a practical armorer.

Mr. Marston called, and states: We expect to make all the carbine work, except the barrel, in the rough. We are to get the barrels from Dinslow & Chase, Windsor Locks. They are to be of steel, and some of them are already delivered. They are to be bored there, where they have machines for turning, rifling, and milling. We have a suit of stocking machines in my shops, and we can turn out fifty in ten hours. All our machines are ready, except those for letting in locks, which will be ready this week. Mr. Stephenson, who has drops and dies, is forging all my mountings and small parts, and I am finishing them in my shops. We have fifteen new milling machines, five shaping machines, and twenty lathes, all on this work. I think we can deliver in from sixty to ninety days; but Mr. Brooks thinks we cannot in less than four months. I think we have machinery enough to complete 1,000 per month. Our arm is about as costly to make as Sharpe's. None have been made heretofore, except twenty made by hand, one of which has been tried by a military board at West Point.

Nothing has been done on the work for Springfield arms. I think we can use our stocking machinery and our rifling machinery for this work after we finish the carbines. We have been disappointed by machine makers, but we have been preparing for our work from before January.

WASHINGTON, *April 15, 1862.*

GENTLEMEN: On the 13th day of December last I contracted with the Ordnance bureau of the War Department, United States, to manufacture and deliver to said department ten thousand Gibbs's patent breech-loading carbines and ten thousand Springfield muskets; the carbines at the price of $28 each, and the muskets at $20 each. Under said agreement one thousand were to have been delivered on the 12th instant, and one thousand monthly thereafter. Immediately upon the execution of the contract I entered upon the preparation for manufacturing the arms, with the full belief that I should be able to make the first delivery on the day mentioned in the contract. To that end I associated with me Mr. W. W. Marston, an experienced manufacturer of arms, and expended large sums of money for machinery, tools, &c., and have used the utmost exertions to make the delivery; but, from circumstances which were beyond my control, I now find that I shall not be able to make a delivery for some time to come—say four months. This extension I only ask to refer to the first delivery. I still believe that I shall be able to complete the delivery of the whole number within the time stipulated in the contract. In making this request, I beg to say that I rely with confidence upon the favorable consideration of the commission, as the gentlemen of the commission must be aware the great demand of the government for arms at the time and since the date of my contract called into requisition nearly all the mechanics and machinery of the country.

With much respect, I am your obedient servant,

WM. F. BROOKS.

Hon. JOSEPH HOLT and R. D. OWEN, *Commissioners.*

WASHINGTON, *April 22, 1862.*

SIR: Since my appearance before the commissioners on contracts, I am informed there has been no report made on my case by the commission to the ordnance department. My contract with that bureau was dated December 12, 1861, for ten thousand Springfield muskets and ten thousand Gibbs's breech-loading carbines, the first delivery to be made on the 12th instant, which I failed to comply with; the cause of the failure was stated by me to the commission, at which interview I understood that that part of the contract relating to muskets would be stricken out, and that the carbines would be confirmed. The object of the present is to ask, if compatible with the views of the commisson and regular proceedings, that they cancel my contract for the two descriptions of arms, and give me a new contract for carbines only, which would simplify and facilitate the prompt execution of it.

I am, sir, very respectfully, your obedient servant,

W. F. BROOKS.

Hon. Joseph Holt.

Ordnance Office, *Washington, March* 29, 1862.

Sir: In reply to your letter of this date, I have to say that the sample carbine referred to in Mr. W. F. Brooks's contract, made on the 13th of December, 1861, has never been submitted to this office.

I enclose, agreeably to your request, a report of the board convened at West Point, New York, in 1858, for the trial of breech-loading carbines, in which a mention is made of the trial of Gibbs's carbine.

This arm has never been tested that I am aware of in actual service.

Your obedient servant,

JAS. W. RIPLEY,
Brigadier General.

Major P. V. Hagner,
Ordnance Department, Washington, D. C.

Commission on Ordnance and Ordnance Stores,
Washington, April 18, 1862.

General: The commission have the honor to report as follows:

Case No. 44.—W. F. Brooks, New York.

Order from the Secretary of War, through the chief of ordnance, dated December 13, 1861. To deliver 10,000 Gibbs's carbines, with appendages, at $23, and 10,000 Springfield rifle muskets, with appendages, at $20—1,000 of either or both kinds on or before April 12, 1862, and 1,000 per month thereafter.

It is stipulated that, "in case of any failure to make deliveries to the extent or within the times specified, the government is to have authority to revoke and annul this order, so far as regards the arms and appendages remaining undelivered at the time of such failure."

The commission find that Mr. Brooks has associated with him as the manufacturer of these arms a gunsmith of New York, who has commenced to provide suitable machinery for the carbine work, and sufficient, as he thinks, to enable him to complete 1,000 guns per month after three and a half to four months from this date; that he proposes to get his barrels forged and bored by a firm at Windsor Locks, and his other forgings from other parties; but has actually ordered and in part received the machines for finishing all iron work and for stocking.

Nothing has been done towards commencing work upon the muskets, but it is stated that such of the machines as admitted of it have been planned with a view to their use in the musket work as soon as the carbines shall have been completed.

The terms of the order given to Mr. Brooks make it optional with the government to annul and revoke the whole order for carbines and muskets upon failure to meet the first or any other stipulated delivery; and from the evidence it seems probable that the government will lose all the advantages anticipated from the delivery, at the promised time, of at least 4,000 carbines.

The high price agreed to be paid for them was, no doubt, mainly due to the hope of securing, when most needed, these arms.

The order to Mr. Brooks also required that a sample carbine should be furnished by him and approved by the ordnance department. This has been done.

The commission find that the manufacture of these carbines is going on in good faith, and that the price is lower than some others, but that the prosecution of the work is at much voluntarily assumed risk on the part of Mr. Brooks, since he has not yet furnished the sample carbine, which, under the order, is to be inspected and approved by the Ordnance office.

They therefore decide that the said sample carbine be at once furnished, and that upon its approval by the ordnance department Mr. Brooks be permitted to deliver the 10,000 carbines according to the terms of the order, provided that the first delivery of 1,000 be made not later than the 1st of August, and subsequent deliveries of not less than 1,000 monthly, and that the order for 10,000 muskets be withdrawn and annulled.

We are, sir, very respectfully, &c.,

J. HOLT,
ROBERT DALE OWEN,
Commissioners.

P. V. HAGNER,
Major of Ordnance, Assistant to Commission.

Brigadier General J. W. RIPLEY,
Chief of Ordnance.

CASE No. 45.

S. B. SMITH.

WASHINGTON, D. C., *February*, 10, 1862.

SIR: In response to your order requiring the parties holding contracts with the United States War Department for furnishing arms to communicate the nature and contents of such contracts, together with whatever may have been done under such contracts by the holders of the same within the period of fifteen days from the date of order, (January 29, 1862,) I have to state that early in the month of December, 1861, I addressed a communication to the War Department, proposing to furnish the government with forty thousand rifles, a sample of which accompanied my communication, and was left by me with the chief of the Ordnance bureau. On the 11th day of December, 1861, in reply to my proposition, I received a communication bearing that date from Brigadier General J. W. Ripley, chief of Ordnance bureau, a copy of which you will find enclosed. Immediately on receipt of this communication I addressed and delivered to General Ripley a letter accepting the propositions of the government and agreeing to all its provisions. In this connexion, I have to state that on the 13th of the same month (December) I ordered the said lot of guns (40,000,) with the appendages, as per contract, through a responsible foreign house in the city of New York, and that since that time I have been advised by them that the entire number of guns has been purchased in Europe, and a large portion of them have been already shipped to fill my order; and the entire number of guns will be ready for delivery in much shorter time than that fixed by the contract. Should you desire any further or more particular information from me in the premises, please address me at the Kirkwood House, in this city, care of A. J. F. Phelan.

Respectfully, your obedient servant,

SAM. B. SMITH.

Hon. E. M. STANTON, *Secretary of War.*

ORDNANCE OFFICE, *Washington, December* 11, 1861.

SIR: By authority of the Secretary of War, I offer you an order for forty thousand (40,000) rifles, with the usual appendages, on the following terms and conditions, viz: These arms are to be of the same pattern and quality with the sample rifle deposited in the Ordnance office. They are to be subject to inspection by such officer as this department may designate for the purpose, and none are to be received or paid for but such as are approved by the United States inspector. The appendages are to consist of one screw-driver and cone-wrench and one wiper for each arm, and one spring vise and one ball-screw for every ten arms. The whole forty thousand arms, with appendages, are to be delivered in the city of New York before the first day of June, 1862. In case of failure to deliver as specified, this department is to have authority to revoke and annul this order, so far as regards the arms and appendages remaining undelivered at the time of such failure. Payment will be made in such funds as the Treasury Department may provide for the purpose, on certificates of inspection and delivery by the United States inspector, at the rate of twenty dollars for each arm, including appendages, in bond. Please signify, in writing, your acceptance or non-acceptance of this order on the terms and conditions herein stated.

Respectfully, your obedient servant,

JAS. W. RIPLEY,
Brigadier General.

SAM. B. SMITH, Esq., *Washington, D. C.*

WASHINGTON, *March* 18, 1862.

GENTLEMEN: I have the honor to state that on the 11th December, 1861, I was authorized to furnish to the government forty thousand arms, with appendages, of the same pattern and quality with a sample rifle before that date deposited by me in the Ordnance office, I having until June 1, 1862, in which to deliver said arms. A copy of the order I some time since forwarded to the Secretary of War, and I suppose it is now among your papers. Immediately upon receipt of this order I contracted with a European house for the delivery of the arm as per contract. The entire number has been purchased in Europe, and will soon be in my possession in New York city, to fill the order. On the 13th instant I notified the chief of ordnance that I was prepared to deliver four thousand nine hundred and ninety-two (4,992) rifles (under this order,) and asking him for instructions as to what to do with them. I have received no reply, except that nothing could be done until the contract had been passed upon by your commission. I most earnestly request your speedy attention to this contract; the amount involved is large, and a protracted delay will prove ruinous.

If in your investigation you should require my presence, I will be glad to be notified. My address is Kirkwood House, Washington.

Respectfully, your obedient servant,

SAM. B. SMITH.

Hon. J. HOLT,
Hon. ROBERT DALE OWEN,
Commissioners on Contracts for Arms, &c.

KIRKWOOD HOUSE,
Washington City, March 27, 1862.

GENTLEMEN : I have the honor to inform you that, in addition to the four thousand nine hundred and ninety-two (4,992) rifled arms which two weeks ago I notified the chief of ordnance I was ready to deliver under my contract of December 11, 1861, I am now prepared to deliver eleven hundred and thirty-two (1,132) more under the same contract, making a total of six thousand one hundred and twenty-four, (6,124.) Will you allow me to call your attention to the importance to me of your speedy action on this contract? I will very soon have a much larger number in my possession, purchased and shipped, to fill the order of the government, and it behooves me to know at the earliest moment possible whether my contract is to be approved or not.

I have this day notified the chief of ordnance that I am prepared to deliver the number of guns specified. I would call upon you in person, but I am confined to my room by sickness.

Very respectfully, your most obedient servant,

SAM. B. SMITH.

Hon. JOSEPH HOLT and ROBERT DALE OWEN,
Commission on Contracts, &c.

S. B. SMITH.—*Argument relative to* 40,000 *contract.*

In the matter of the contract made by government with S. B. Smith for 40,000 arms.

WASHINGTON CITY, *April* 20, 1862.

GENTLEMEN : In the above matter I have shown to you a written contract made with me by the chief of the Ordnance bureau, " by order," as he states, of the Secretary of War, by which I was bound to deliver to the government 40,000 arms of a pattern agreed upon, at a price agreed upon, and within a time specified. The contract was " bona fide," I being a party capable of contracting, and, at the time the contract was made, able to fulfil its requirements. The government agreed to pay to me a specified price per arm for each one delivered under the contract. I have on two occasions notified the government of my readiness to make delivery of a very considerable number of arms under it, and I have on several occasions informed the War Department proper, and have stated to you, that I should be able to fill the entire order within the time fixed by the contract. As you are aware, no action has been taken by the government towards inspecting or receiving the arms I proposed to deliver. I have shown to you that I purchased the arms to fill the contract at a price less than the government agreed to pay to me. The difference between the price I agreed to pay and that which the government agreed to pay me is my profit, my property, which I can only be deprived of by an arbitrary disregard of law and a positive repudiation of the plighted faith of the government, plighted in the manner prescribed by law.

I stand upon my rights under the contract. My contract with parties to furnish me these arms was unconditional; whether government take them from me or not, I am legally bound to take them, and pay for them the price agreed upon. Should suit be brought against me in the event of my failing to pay for them, the defence that government had not kept its agreement with me would not save me from the judgment of a court of law.

The contract was not a one-sided one. The government needed the arms. I agreed to furnish them, taking the risk of hostile cruisers and a war with England, which would have brought upon us a blockade of all our principal ports.

It may be said that individually I incurred no risk, because I had purchased the arms from other parties, and that I could not by any possibility lose anything. I *did* incur a very serious risk, and I incurred it for the profit. I agreed to pay in *legal tender*, which at the date of contract was *gold* and *silver* coin; and if Congress had not recently passed an act making its late issues legal tender, the depreciation in the value of government securities might have been, and probably would have been, ere this, so great as to have not only swept away my profits, but have subjected me to a very considerable loss by my being compelled to pay the premium on gold and silver. Here is a risk which I took knowingly, and have been liable to from the first. The passage of the act at the date of my contract was highly improbable, and as you are well aware became a law by a bare majority.

What would have been the probable answer to me if I had delivered the entire number of arms, and when I received my pay and found that government securities were only worth 50 cents upon the dollar, I had petitioned for government relief? The reply would have been, "You, for the sake of the profit, incurred this very risk, and you must take the consequences." This being the probable action of government, had such a state of case occurred, places me in position to say, I ask the profit on a contract from which you would not have relieved me had the circumstances been different.

In this connexion, I would respectfully call your attention to the following words used by government in the order to me: "Payments will be made in such funds as the Treasury Department may prepare for the purpose." Thus showing that government contemplated a depreciation in the value of its issues, and would not agree to pay in gold and silver.

Besides this, it seems I took another risk, not then contemplated, viz: the possibility of government refusing to fulfil its agreement, and subjecting me to vexations and interminable delay, almost equivalent to repudiation. If it be said that this is no such risk as would entitle me to profits, it can only be on the ground that the government always fulfils its every legal agreement. The delay which has occurred, and the doubts thereby engendered, as to what would be the ultimate action of the government in the premises, has embarrassed me greatly, in ways not necessary for me now to state. I have been kept in suspense since the 29th of January last, the date of the published order of the Secretary of War, suspending all contracts for arms. I have begged him, time and time again, to pass upon my contract, and, as I have done on several occasions before, I again most earnestly ask of you to decide upon its merits. I want to know where I stand. I am worn out by being kept so long in the dark; nothing can be worse than this long suspense.

Relying upon the justice of my cause, and believing, gentlemen, that it is impossible for you to knowingly do me a wrong, (in accordance with the order of the War Department,) I submit this case to you, as the tribunal created by the Secretary of War to decide upon it and other like cases.

Yours, respectfully,

SAM. B. SMITH.

COMMISSION ON CONTRACTS, &c.

A.

WASHINGTON, *December* 12, 1861.

DEAR SIR: In reply to your favor of yesterday, we beg leave to state that we will agree to furnish you with the quantity of rifled muskets designated in contract of Ordnance office, Wasington, December 11, 1861, and subject to sample deposited by you with the ordnance department, deliverable from January,

1862, to June, 1862, at fifteen dollars ($15) apiece, deliverable in bond in New York, and payable to us in legal tender.

Very respectfully, your obedient servants,

HERMAN BOKER & CO.

SAMUEL B. SMITH, Esq.

A true copy handed by me to commission.

SAMUEL B. SMITH.

B.

In the matter of the contract with Samuel B. Smith for 40,000 arms.

WASHINGTON CITY, *April* 9, 1862.

GENTLEMEN : I propose to deliver to the government 20,000 guns under the above contract, and release the government from the other 20,000, upon the following terms : The government to take at once all guns I am now prepared to deliver, as well as all others under the contract, as I may be prepared to deliver them, up to 20,000 arms, they making no distinction as to block or leaf sights on the guns to be delivered to a greater amount than 50 cents per gun, the government to pay me $2 50 per gun on the 20,000 arms they are released from taking. If this proposition is agreed to, I will at once cause all further shipments to be stopped.

Yours, respectfully,

SAMUEL B. SMITH.

The COMMISSIONERS *on Contracts for Ordnance and Ordnance Stores.*

Before commission, April 9, 1862.

Mr. S. B. Smith, in reference to his contract for 40,000 rifles, at $20, had been previously sworn, and states :

I have made a contract with Boker & Co. to furnish the guns to be delivered by me on my contract, like sample, at $15. All loss for inspected guns failing to equal sample fall on Boker & Co. The only time specified for their delivery is that specified in my proposal and order, on or before June 1, 1862. As the commission was notified in my letter of March 27, I have now ready in New York 6,124 arms and appendages ready for the inspection, and have reason to expect an additional number by the next steamer, to-day or to-morrow.

Question by commission. Who is responsible for storage in New York prior to inspection ?

Answer. I have not thought about this. I made a positive contract to take the arms, subject to the terms of inspection. I have a written contract to this effect, and will show it to the commission if they desire to see it.

Question by commission. Can you stop the order at any time for such as may not have been shipped ?

Answer. I have no right to do this, but I have proposed it to Boker & Co., who have substantially assented to my making a proposition offering to stop arms not yet shipped. That proposition I now hand in in writing.

Question by commission. Do you expect to pay Boker & Co. anything until you receive your money from the United States ?

Answer. No.

(Papers marked A and B signed by Mr. Smith, and handed in by him to commission.)

Before commission, April 10, 1862.

Mr. S. B. Smith appeared and asked to say that the phrase " payable to us in legal tender," in Boker & Co.'s acceptance of his order, would have required him to pay in gold had not Congress made treasury notes a legal tender, and would thus have obliged him to purchase gold had he been paid in notes by the government. This would have absorbed part of his profits. Also, he considers that if Boker & Co. can prove that they supply to him the same gun as the sample, he will be bound to pay for them, whether they pass inspection or not, or are received by the government or not. I made no sort of understanding or qualification to the contrary.

WASHINGTON, *May* 7, 1862.

GENTLEMEN : On May 2, 1862, I addressed and delivered to you a letter, of which the following is a copy :

" WASHINGTON, *May* 2, 1862.

" GENTLEMEN : In accordance with your suggestion of yesterday, that I should propose a compromise in the matter of my contract for 40,000 arms, dated December 11, 1861, and in order to obtain a final recognition of my contract and a settlement with the government, I make the following proposition :

" If the government will receive and pay for all the arms which I now have in New York, and which may arrive there under my contract, the whole number not to exceed 20,000, I will reduce the contract price from $20 per gun to $16 50 (sixteen dollars and fifty cents) per arm, releasing the government from the balance. In connexion with this proposition, and as a part thereof, I will state that while my sample gun has upon it *leaf sights*, I am informed by the shippers that some of my lot of arms has upon them a sight known as the *block sight*, and I desire that they be received and paid for at same price. I offer this as a compromise, in order to obtain the means to meet obligations incurred in carrying out my contract of the date above named, and I most respectfully ask a prompt reply.

" Yours, respectfully,

" SAMUEL B. SMITH.

" Messrs. HOLT and OWEN,
 "*Commissioners on Contracts, &c.*"

Referring to the above letter, and learning from the commissioners that they are *only* willing to settle at $16 (sixteen dollars) per arm, I hereby agree to accept that price, as per terms of letter, and execute such releases as may be necessary.

Yours, respectfully,

SAMUEL B. SMITH.

Messrs. HOLT and OWEN,
 Commissioners on Contracts, &c.

COMMISSION ON ORDNANCE AND ORDNANCE STORES,
Washington, April 9, 1862.

GENERAL : The commission have the honor to report as follows :

CASE NO. 45.—SAMUEL B. SMITH, of New York,

Order from chief of ordnance, by direction of the Secretary of War, dated December 11, 1861.

To deliver 40,000 rifles, of same pattern and quality with sample deposited in Ordnance office, with appendages, in the city of New York, before 1st June, 1862, at the rate of $20 each, in bond, subject to inspection.

Specially referred by the Secretary of War.

The commission find that Mr. Smith had reported, April 9, that he had ready to offer, in New York, 6,124 rifles, under this order, and was expecting more by the next steamer.

The case, as presented to the commission by the evidence submitted, is as follows :

A gun, of the pattern known as .54 calibre Austrian rifle, imported by Boker & Co., was brought to Washington by Mr. S. B. Smith, and shown to the Secretary of War, Mr. Cameron, on the 11th December, 1861, with a proposition to furnish 40,000 of same quality and pattern at $20 each, in bond, in New York. This proposition was referred to the chief of ordnance, with the indorsement signed by Mr. Cameron : "If this proposition meets the approbation of the chief of ordnance, it will be concurred in by me."

On the same day, December 11, an order, in the usual terms, was given to Mr. S. B. Smith for 40,000 rifles, with appendages, to be of the same pattern and quality with sample gun deposited in the Ordnance office, to be subject to inspection, and none to be paid for but such as are approved by the United States inspector, the whole to be delivered on or before the 1st of June, 1862; and in case of failure to deliver, as specified, the ordnance department to have authority to revoke and annul the order, so far as regards any remaining undelivered at the time.

The commission find that the arm thus accepted as a sample is one which, as compared with the interchangeable Springfield arm, is manifestly inferior, while the price to be paid is the same ($20) as was allowed for the Springfield gun, in the order given at the same date, and 20 per cent. higher than that at which responsible manufacturers now propose to make this (Springfield) arm, under orders of equal extent.

Mr. Smith, who received this order, was not in the gun business, but made his bargain immediately with the same firm in New York which was then delivering—under large orders to the government—the same kind of arm, among others, at a less price, while the agent of the ordnance department in New York was also purchasing them at a less price in open market there.

Mr. Smith testifies that he made his bargain with Messrs. Boker & Co. to deliver to him, subject to all the conditions of the order as issued by the ordnance department, the arms at $15 each, he agreeing to pay for such only as were received, and only after their inspection.

As a virtual agent, therefore, bearing the order from Washington to New York, Mr. Smith's services in the matter terminated at this point, not to be again required until called upon to receive the payments.

This order being for guns not desirable for the service, at an unreasonable price, and given in a manner not in accordance with law and regulations, the commission felt it to be incumbent upon them to reduce the numbers as well as the price of these arms, and had many interviews with Mr. Smith with this object. After a full explanation and consideration, Mr. Smith consented to propose the following modification of his orders, and the commission have decided to confirm it so modified, subject to all other terms and conditions as therein stated :

Twenty thousand arms only are to be offered instead of forty thousand, and payment is to be made at the rate of sixteen dollars in bond per gun, accepted and received with appendages, instead of twenty dollars, without any additional charge whatever. As it is represented that some of the guns have block sights instead of the leaf sights as on the sample guns, the commission agree that such may be received without deduction therefor, provided, in all other respects, the arm is equal to the sample.

We are, sir, very respectfully, your obedient servants,

J. HOLT,
ROBERT DALE OWEN,
Commissioners, &c.
P. V. HAGNER,
Major of Ordnance, Assistant to Commission.
Gen. J. W. RIPLEY, *Chief of Ordnance.*

CASE No. 46.

L. WINDMULLER.

COMMISSION ON ORDNANCE AND ORDNANCE STORES,
Washington, April 22, 1862.

GENERAL : The commission have the honor to report as follows :

CASE No. 46.—LEWIS WINDMULLER, of New York,

Letter to Major Hagner, dated 15th March, 1862, and referred to chief of ordnance, and approved by him.

Asks to deliver sabres rejected at inspection on account of defects and since repaired or corrected.

Deliveries of these sabres suspended under general orders. The commission find that Mr. Windmuller was permitted to take away, after inspection and condemnation, certain of his sabres, with the promise on his part to have new blades inserted and to return them. Before they were returned the receipt of all arms was suspended by general order.

As the privilege of repairing these sabres had been granted by the inspecting office, and the expense of making the repair actually incurred by the claimant, the commission direct that these be now inspected and received, not to exceed the number heretofore offered and rejected, provided that none be paid for but such as are of first quality of foreign sabres, according to the standard established at New York.

We are sir, very respectfully, your obedient servants,

J. HOLT,
ROBERT DALE OWEN,
Commissioners, &c.
P. V. HAGNER,
Major of Ordnance, Assistant to Commission.

Brig. Gen. J. W. RIPLEY,
Chief of Ordnance.

CASE No. 47.

JOHN HOFF, Washington, D. C.

20,000 foreign Minie rifles, November 4, 1861.

WASHINGTON, *October* 21, 1861.

SIR: I propose to deliver to the government 20,000 Minie rifles, .58 bore, with cap chain and muzzle stopper, barrel colored as Enfield rifles, and to deliver them as follows : November 30, 1,000 ; December 16, 2,000 ; January 5, 3,000 ; January 16, 2,000 ; February 5, 2,000 ; March 1, 4,000 ; March 16, 2,000 ; April 1, 4,000 ; but, if required, will deliver the whole of them in February for $20 each gun. All to bear government inspection.

Very respectfully,

JOHN HOFF.

Hon. THOMAS A. SCOTT,
Assistant Secretary of War.

[Indorsement on above.]

The Secretary directs that this proposition be accepted, provided the guns are all delivered before the close of February, or earlier, with usual implements, and subject to inspection.

THOMAS A. SCOTT, *Acting Secretary of War.*

ORDNANCE OFFICE, *Washington, November* 4, 1861.

SIR: By direction of the Secretary of War, I offer you an order for twenty thousand (20,000) Minie rifles, .58 inch bore, barrels colored as Enfield rifles, with cap chain and muzzle stopper, and the usual implements, on the following terms and conditions, viz: These arms and implements are to be delivered at the United States arsenal in this city as rapidly as possible, so that the whole twenty thousand shall be delivered before the close of February, 1862, or earlier. They are to be subject to inspection by such officers as this department may designate for the purpose, and none are to be received or paid for by the government but such as are approved by the inspectors.

In case of failure to deliver the arms at the time before specified, the government is to have authority to revoke and annul this order.

Payments are to be made in such funds as the Treasury Department may provide, on certificates of inspection and receipt by the United States inspector, at the rate of twenty dollars ($20) for each gun, including the implements.

Please signify, in writing, your acceptance or non-acceptance of this order, on the terms and conditions herein stated.

Respectfully, your obedient servant,

WILLIAM MAYNADIER,
Lieutenant Colonel Ordnance.

Mr. JOHN HOFF, *Washington, D. C.*

WASHINGTON, *November* 6, 1861.

SIR: Your order for twenty thousand Minie rifles has been received. They will be delivered according to order.

Very respectfully,

JOHN HOFF.

WILLIAM MAYNADIER,
Lieutenant Colonel Ordnance Department.

(Received November 8, 1861.)

[Indorsement on Mr. John Hoff's letter as returned to Ordnance office]

WAR DEPARTMENT, *Washington, November* 26, 1861.

The Secretary directs that deliveries on this contract be made as follows:

January	2,000
February	3,000
March	5,000
April	5,000
May	5,000
Total	20,000

Yours, respectfully,

THOMAS A. SCOTT,
Assistant Secretary.

ORDNANCE OFFICE,
55 *White street, New York, February* 11, 1862.

GENERAL: I forward to you, per express, a sample gun from a lot of arms, 3,140 in all, presented at this office for inspection and reception by the Messrs. M. Guiterman & Co., attorney and general agent for Mr. John Hoff, in part fulfilment of his order for the delivery of twenty thousand .58-inch calibre Minie rifles, dated November 4, 1861, and modified November 26, 1861.

These arms are Austrian rifle muskets, calibre .58-inch, and of the same style of manufacture and finish, with a few minor differences in finish, as the standard Austrian rifle musket, calibre .55. They are identical, judging from sample, with the arms being delivered under the Dingee contract, imported by the same party importing these latter arms, and included in the same bill of lading with a portion of them; also, the importing firm, Messrs. Guiterman & Bro., or one of its individual members, are attorneys for both parties in relation to their contracts or orders with the United States.

It would appear from this that Mr. Hoff's order is to be filled with rifles known at this office as the Dingee arms.

On an examination of Hoff's order, I find that it reads as follows: "By direction of the Secretary of War, I offer you an order for twenty thousand Minie rifles, .58-inch bore, barrels colored as Enfield rifles, with cap-chain and muzzle-stopper, and the usual appendages," &c.

Be pleased to inform me if the arm forwarded is considered by the department as complying with the above terms, in order that, if so decided, I can have the necessary inspection made and receive the guns.

Respectfully, &c.,

S. CRISPIN,
Captain of Ordnance.

General J. W. RIPLEY,
Chief of Ordnance, Washington, D. C.

[Extract.]

ORDNANCE OFFICE,
Washington, February 14, 1862.

SIR: I return the sample gun sent by you to this office. You will perceive by it that the bayonet and ramrod are too soft. In your inspection of small arms you will be particular to receive none in which the ramrod and bayonet do not possess the prescribed hardness and elasticity. * * *

J. W. RIPLEY,
Brigadier General.

Captain S. CRISPIN,
No. 55 White street, New York.

NEW YORK, *February* 11, 1862.

SIR: In accordance with an order issued from your department on the 29th of January, I beg leave respectfully to submit that on the 4th day of November I obtained from the department over which you preside an order for supplying the government with twenty thousand rifles, at $20 each, to be delivered as follows, to wit: 2,000 in January, 3,000 in February, and 5,000 each month thereafter. In the month of January I delivered 3,060, 1,060 more than I was required to do, and of a quality that I do not fear to have compared with any in the service, and will have ready for delivery 3,000 more next week. I can say, moreover, that in point of time for delivery of the rest the contract will be more than complied with.

I have the honor to remain your obedient servant,

JOHN HOFF.

Hon. E. M. STANTON,
Secretary of War.

Ex. Doc. 72——14

WASHINGTON, (328 *H street,*) *March* 21, 1862.

GENTLEMEN : I have come to this city to attend to some business growing out of an order of the War Department to John Hoff for furnishing the government with twenty thousand (20,000) rifles, and am referred by the Ordnance bureau to your commission. I am compelled to communicate with you in writing because of a violent attack of rheumatism, with which I have been laid up for several days.

I am the partner of John Hoff, interested and identified with him in this contract, and have attended to all the business in relation thereto, and therefore request that honorable commissioners will adjudicate the question at once, as the delay already created has been quite disastrous. The transaction is a perfectly clean one, not tainted with corruption, fraud, or anything of the kind. The proposal was made and accepted at a price which the government was willing to pay for guns of their character, and, especially, as the short time within which they were to be made was a matter of great moment. Our first delivery was considerably greater than we were obliged to furnish, and the whole would have been tendered long before the expiration of the time allowed had they been received in accordance with our order. You, of course, are well aware of the peril that contractors may be subjected to by the failure of the government to perform its part, and particularly where the capital involved (as in the present instance) is a matter of some magnitude. I therefore *beg* your honors to give this case your earliest attention. I will state, further, that if you have any questions to propound I will cheerfully answer them, on oath or otherwise, as you may direct.

With great respect, I am your obedient servant,
GEORGE M. LOUMAN.

Hon. JOSEPH HOLT and ROBERT DALE OWEN,
Commissioners, &c.

WASHINGTON, *March* 31, 1862.

GENTLEMEN : At the request of Mr. George M. Louman, I beg to call your attention to an order given to John Hoff for *twenty thousand* Minie rifles. Mr. Louman is a partner of Mr. Hoff, as is shown by the writing of Hoff in your possession. Mr. Louman came here more than two weeks ago to attend to this business, and for the last fifteen days has been confined to his bed by severe indisposition. As a friend of Mr. Louman I address you this letter, asking an early disposition of the case. To me it appears one of extreme hardship. The parties have been delayed since January last, when 3,060 guns were offered to be delivered on the order. If it be in fact, as it seems to me to be, a plain, clear case of contract without fraud, the parties should not be exposed to serious loss—it may be ruin—by uncertainties and delays thrown around them by the action of government agents. A clear contract should be promptly complied with by the government, without vexatious and ruinous delays.

The parties say that no better guns have been imported ; that they are made by the manufacturer of arms for the Austrian government, and are of the same kind and quality uniformly used by that government ; that they are made under the supervision of an army officer, and that no lock is allowed to be used except that purchased of the Austrian government arsenal. The parties now have the permission of the Austrian government to export these arms, which may at any time be revoked.

The guns are claimed to be in strict conformity with the order. Allow me, respectfully, on behalf of Mr. Louman, to ask that you will inform him of the grounds on which the government agents refuse to accept the guns and carry out the contract.

Mr. Louman is at No. 328 H street, where he may be addressed. When informed of the grounds on which the government refuses to carry out the contract he will endeavor to meet every objection and difficulty.

He is ready to answer, upon oath, any inquiries submitted to him touching the integrity and *bona fide* character of the contract.

Very respectfully, your obedient servant,

D. WILMOT.

Hon. Joseph Holt and Robert Dale Owen.

READING, *March* 23, 1862.

GENTLEMEN: Mr. George M. Louman is fully interested with me in the order for 20,000 rifles, and has attended to the details. He can give all the information in reference to the matter, and is authorized so to do.

JOHN HOFF.

Hon. Joseph Holt and Robert Dale Owen,
Commissioners to settle Ordnance Claims, &c.

WASHINGTON, (328 *H street*,) *April* 1, 1862.

GENTLEMEN: In the matter of John Hoff for furnishing arms to the government, you would do him and myself (his associate) a great favor by disposing of our case to-morrow. You will pardon us for pressing this matter so urgently, which we would not do but for the demands made upon us from abroad, which we cannot take care of in the present condition of our contract, it being virtually suspended. We are not afraid of an investigation of the case, and respectfully ask early action.

Very respectfully, your obedient servant,

GEORGE M. LOUMAN.

WASHINGTON, (328 *H street*,) *March* 27, 1862.

GENTLEMEN: Being very ill and unable to leave my bed, I trust you will pardon me for calling your attention to the order of John Hoff, and if there is anything further wanted of me I will endeavor to comply. In accordance with your requirement, I procured Mr. Hoff's acknowledgment of my interest and sent it to you on Tuesday, but I fear it has not come to your notice.

With great respect, your obedient servant,

GEORGE M. LOUMAN.

Hon. Joseph Holt and Robert Dale Owen.

CASE OF JOHN HOFF.

Before commission, April 17, 1862.

Mr. A. Guiterman, of New York, being duly sworn, states that he is the importer of the guns to be furnished the government under Mr. Hoff's order, and also of the guns being delivered by Dingee & Co.; considers that Mr. Hoff's guns are better than those of Dingee & Co., if there be any difference between them. The manufacturer was instructed to be more careful in the manufacture of guns for Mr. Hoff, and we actually paid more for a part of them. We paid, in Vienna, for the arms, packed, 34 florins; which, valuing the florin at 46.19 cents, makes it cost $15 70. Our last invoice, we notice, charges the arms at 33.50 florins; the cost of getting the arm to New York is, for freight, $1 to $1 25 each. In August, or about that time, our house offered samples of these arms to the Secretary of War, in Washington, to be delivered in New York, at $16, at the rate of 8,000 to 10,000 per month. Our offer was not received. We then made an agreement with Mr. Hoff. We did not fix upon a price, but agreed that we should share equally the profits, after deducting all the expenses. The first offer of arms, under the order, was about 3,000, in January. We have 3,000 additional in New York, and we have advices that 13,000, in all, have left Vienna, and the next steamer will probably bring news of a few thousand more. We feel certain that all the 20,000 will be here by the end of May, as stipulated, unless some accident occurs. Think that I could stop about 5,000 guns in Europe, if desirable, and I am not sure that this stoppage would cost us anything, as possibly we could make arrangements for turning them over to other parties—that is, if they are not actually on their way here. I must telegraph to my partner before I can answer definitely; I will do so, and report to-morrow.

April 19.—Mr. Guiterman appeared, and reported to the commission that he had received an answer to the telegram sent to his partner, which was in the following words: "Exercise your own discretion, and be sure to be safe." Under the authority thus given me, I will endeavor to stop all that can be stopped without loss to us, and will use the earliest means of communication.

Mr. Hoff is a citizen of Philadelphia, not known to me personally, but to my partner, Mr. Louman.

COMMISSION ON ORDNANCE AND ORDNANCE STORES,
Washington, April 23, 1862.

GENERAL: The commission have the honor to report as follows:

CASE No. 47.—JOHN HOFF, Philadelphia.

Order from chief of ordnance, by direction of Assistant Secretary of War. Referred by special direction of the Secretary of War.

To deliver in New York, "prior to the close of February, 1862, or earlier, 20,000 Minie rifles, .58-inch bore, barrels colored as Enfield rifles, with cap-chain and muzzle-stopper, and the usual implements. Price, $20 in bond. The arms to be subject to inspection, and none to be received or paid for by the government but such as are approved by the United States inspector."

November 26, 1861, by direction of the Assistant Secretary of War, Thomas A. Scott, the time of delivery was extended, requiring only 5,000 prior to the close of February, and 5,000 monthly thereafter, until all are delivered.

The commission find that in the proposal made by Mr. Hoff no sample gun was referred to, and that no explicit description of the arm to be furnished to the government was given either by the Assistant Secretary of War, in his directions to the ordnance department, by the department in giving the order, or by Mr. Hoff in accepting it. The only positive requirements are: 1st. That the calibre be .58-inch. 2d. That the barrels be colored like the Enfield. 3d. That the price to be paid for such as meet the approval of the inspector shall be $20 in bond.

The term "Minie rifles" can only be considered as requiring the arms to be rifled, as all such can be used to fire the "Minie" ball; and all rifled arms are sometimes called "Minie rifles;" but the words have no reference to the workmanship, quality, or pattern of the arms.

As it is essential, in order to inspect for approval or rejection, that some definite standard of quality, finish, and pattern should be first established, unless this can be fairly done under the terms of the order, there would be no other course than to consider the order incomplete, and consequently nugatory.

The only stipulation of the order bearing upon these qualities in arms is *the price.* This is the usual criterion of quality among dealers, and the only distinctive feature left in this case between the worst and the best "Minie rifles" of like calibre and color of barrel. The commission therefore consider that they must look to it—the price—as a means of establishing the proper sample or grade of arm to be required by the inspection; and, as these have been changed in price, consequently the value prevailing about the date of this order should be the guide.

The order is dated November 4, with the express condition that all arms should be delivered "prior to the close of February, or earlier," and it was so accepted November 5 by Mr. Hoff. On the 26th November, however, the final terms of delivery were modified by the Assistant Secretary by waiving the condition and extending the time, so as to require only one-fourth of the whole number to be delivered prior to the last of February. It is under favor of this alteration that the parties proceeded to carry out their obligation, as only 3,140 guns had been offered up to February 11 to the ordnance office in New York, and, as stated by Mr. Guiterman to the commission, only 13,000 in all had left Vienna at the date of his examination on the 18th of April.

The commission find that a telegram was sent November 16, 1861, by Secretary Cameron to Major Hagner, purchasing officer in New York, directing him "to purchase no more first class Enfields at prices exceeding twenty dollars, including the usual appendages," and stating "this price is liberal, and the government will pay no more."

As this maximum is pronounced by the Secretary liberal for even small quantities in port, there cannot be a doubt that, in the estimation of that officer, it was even more liberal for large quantities to be delivered prospectively, and hence it may be safely affirmed that the price allowed Mr. Hoff, $20, was expected to secure an arm equal in quality at least to the "first class Enfields" alluded to by the Secretary. At the date of this order, and now also, the "first class Enfield" was and is confessedly the highest grade of foreign arms sent to this country, and, although some others are of equal value for service, no foreign rifle muskets can be regarded of a higher grade or higher market value. The commission therefore direct that no arm not reasonably worth $20 in open market in New York in November last be received under the terms of Mr. Hoff's order at the price therein stated.

Should it be necessary, to meet the necessities of the government, to purchase any of these arms offered by Mr. Hoff, found upon inspection to be of inferior grade to that required by the terms of the order, as above explained, the commission direct that they be purchased as in open market, and at rates to established by the inspecting officer in New York, as in his judgment may be fair and just compared with the price paid for like arms so purchased, to an extent not to exceed, with those of first quality, the number mentioned in the original order.

Although this order, being neither an open purchase nor based upon proposals made under previous advertisement, is without legal sanction and therefore not obligatory on the government, yet, as the party has proceeded in good faith to make his purchases to fill it, we have deemed it but just to him to respect its provisions as above expounded.

We are, sir, very respectfully, your obedient servants,

J. HOLT,
ROBERT DALE OWEN,
Commissioners; &c.
P. V. HAGNER,
Major of Ordnance, Assistant to Commission

Brigadier General J. W. RIPLEY,
Chief of Ordnance.

CASE No. 48.

SAVAGE ARMS COMPANY.

MIDDLETOWN, CONNECTICUT, *February* 4, 1862.

SIR: Referring to your order, No. 11, in respect to army contracts, dated Washington, January 29, 1862, we have the honor to report that this company are at present working under an order received from the chief of ordnance dated October 16, 1861, and also under a subsequent order dated November 28, 1861, of which the following are copies, viz:

Copy of first order.

ORDNANCE OFFICE,
Washington, October 16, 1861.

SIR: The proposition of the Savage Revolving Fire-arms Company to deliver their pistols is accepted on the following terms and conditions, viz: The whole number of these pistols, with the usual appendages for each, to be taken by the government is to be five thousand, including the one thousand heretofore verbally ordered. The pistols are to be, in all respects, equal to the sample left by you at this office, and are to be subject to inspection and proof by such officers as this department may designate for the purpose. None of these arms or appendages are to be taken but such as pass inspection and are approved by the United States inspectors. The pistols and appendages are to be delivered as follows, at the armory at Middletown, Connecticut, viz: not less than five hundred in the month of October, 1861; not less than seven hundred in the month of November, 1861; not less than one thousand in the month of December, 1861; and not less than fifteen hundred per month thereafter until the whole five thousand are delivered. In case of failure of any one of the deliveries in the times before specified, the government is authorized to revoke and annul this order immediately.

Payments are to be made, in such funds as the Treasury Department may provide, on certificates of inspection and receipt by United States inspectors, at the rate of twenty dollars per pistol, including appendages.

Please signify, in writing, your acceptance or non-acceptance of this order on the terms and conditions herein stated.

Respectfully, your obedient servant,

JAMES W. RIPLEY,
Brigadier General.

THOMAS DYER, Esq., *Washington, D. C.*

The following is a copy of the second order, viz:

ORDNANCE OFFICE, *Washington, November* 28, 1861.

SIR: By direction of the Secretary of War, I offer you an order for five thousand (5,000) of the Savage Revolving Fire-arms Company pistols, on the following terms and conditions, viz: These pistols are to be subject to inspection and proof by such officers as this department may designate for the purpose, and none are to be received or paid for but such as pass inspection and are approved by the United States inspectors. The arms, with the usual appendages, are to be delivered at the United States arsenal, New York, as follows, viz: 1,666 in March, 1,667 in April, 1,667 in May next, or earlier, if possible. In case of failure to make any one of the deliveries, as before specified, the government is to have authority to revoke and annul this order, so far as regards the arms and appendages remaining undelivered at the time of such failure. Payments will be made for each delivery, in such funds as the Treasury Department may provide, on certificates of inspection and receipt by the United States inspectors, at the rate of twenty dollars per pistol, including appendages.

Please signify, in writing, your acceptance or non-acceptance of this order on the terms and conditions herein stated.

Respectfully, your obedient servant,

JAS. W. RIPLEY, *Brigadier General.*

JAMES A. WHEELOCK, Esq.,
Secretary Savage Revolving Fire-arms Company, Middletown, Conn.

In reference to the first order herein, dated October 16, 1861, we beg to report that its conditions have been fully complied with on our part, inasmuch as the pistols have all been ready for the inspectors.

The following deliveries have been made, viz: In the month of October, five hundred; in the month of December, fifteen hundred; in the month of January, one thousand, and on the first of February we had ready for inspection from seven to nine hundred; the balance of this order, being two thousand, will be ready for delivery during the present month.

In reference to the second order herein, dated November 28, 1861, we beg to report that the whole number are in the works and many of the parts entirely finished, and the balance progressing rapiply. We shall be prepared to turn them all in agreeably to the conditions of the order.

Very respectfully, your obedient servant,

JAMES A. WHEELOCK,
Secretary of Savage Revolving Fire-arms Comp'y.

Hon. EDWIN M. STANTON,
Secretary of War, Washington, D. C.

WASHINGTON, *March* 24, 1862.

SIR: We have an order from the Ordnance department for 5,000 pistols, to be delivered as follows: 1,667 in March, 1,667 in April, 1,666 in May. The pistols were being inspected when orders came discontinuing the inspections. As the pistols are all ready to be delivered under the order, may I ask you to have orders given to resume the inspection.

I am your obedient servant,

JAMES A. WHEELOCK,
Secretary of Savage Revolving Fire-arms Comp'y.

Hon. E. M. STANTON,
Secretary of War, &c.

WASHINGTON, *March* 24, 1862.

SIR: The application of "The Savage Revolving Fire-arms Company," of Middletown, Connecticut, to the chief of the Ordnance bureau, for an order for 10,000 pistols, having been referred to you for decision, we beg leave to state that we are practical gunsmiths of long standing—for three-quarters of a century. Gun and pistol making has been the leading business of our town. We have complied with our contracts with the government, and are now nearly out of work, and heavy outlays to enable us to meet our former government contracts will endanger our permanency unless this application meets your favorable consideration.

We beg to refer you to the representative from our district, Hon. James E. English.

I have the honor to be your obedient servant,

JAMES A. WHEELOCK,
Secretary of Savage Revolving Fire-arms Comp'y.

Hon. E. M. STANTON, *Secretary of War.*

COMMISSION ON ORDNANCE AND ORDNANCE STORES,
Washington, April 16, 1862.

GENERAL: The commission request to be informed in reference to the order for 5,000 revolvers, given November 28 to the Savage Arms Company, no reference to which is made in document No. 67:

1st. Whether any deliveries have been made under the order?
2d. Whether the stipulations have been complied with?
3d. Whether these revolvers are needed by the department?
Also, whether all deliveries under previous orders have been made?

Respectfully, your obedient servant,

P. V. HAGNER,
Major of Ordnance.

General J. W. RIPLEY,
Chief of Ordnance.

ORDNANCE OFFICE, *Washington, D. C., April* 17, 1862.

SIR: I have to acknowledge the receipt of Major P. V. Hagner's communication of the 16th instant, and to enclose herewith, in reply thereto, copies of all the correspondence in this office pertinent to the subject of the Savage Revolving Fire-arms Company's last order, numbered one to nine, inclusive, with the following remarks:

A portion of the papers in this case are printed on page 203, Ex. Doc., (House,) No. 67, being the first effort of the company to obtain a second order, with the indorsement of the Assistant Secretary of War, and the further indorsement of the chief of ordnance, dated October 31, advising that the offer be not accepted. By an oversight in making up the record for document No. 67 the remainder of this case was omitted. Two deliveries have been made under the order of November 28 The first on the 11th of March of 500 pistols, the second on the 21st of March of 500. Regarding the manner in which the stipulations have been complied with, and whether all deliveries under previous orders have been made, I would refer to Captain Balch's letter to this office, dated March 1, No. 7.

One thousand of these arms are now required to fill present orders.

Respectfully, your obedient servant,

JAS. W. RIPLEY,
Brigadier General.

J. WISE, Esq.,
Secretary to Commission on Ordnance Stores.

WASHINGTON, *November* 19, 1861.

SIR: The undersigned respectfully offer to furnish the United States government, delivered at New York, 10,000 six-barrelled self-cocking army pistols, manufactured by the "Savage Revolving Fire-arms Company," which shall be fully equal, in every respect, to the sample submitted with this proposition, at twenty dollars ($20) per pistol, with all fixtures included, and to be furnished at the rate of fifteen hundred (1,500) per month, at the lowest, till the order is complete. The delivery of the above to begin at the close of our present contract with the United States government, say March 1.

Very respectfully,

JAS. A. WHEELOCK,
Secretary Savage Fire-arms Company.

Hon. SIMON CAMERON,
Secretary of War.

[Indorsement on the above letter.]

WAR DEPARTMENT, *November* 21, 1861.

Respectfully referred to the chief of ordnance for such action as may be necessary in the premises.

THOMAS A. SCOTT,
Assistant Secretary.

ORDNANCE OFFICE,
Washington, November 28, 1861.

SIR : By direction of the Secretary of War I offer you an order for five thousand (5,000) of the Savage Revolving Fire-arms Company pistols on the following terms and conditions, viz :

These pistols are to be subject to inspection and proof by such officers as this department may designate for the purpose, and none are to be received or paid for but such as pass inspection, and are approved by the United States inspectors. The arms, with the usual appendages, are to be delivered at the United States arsenal, New York, as follows, viz : 1,666 in March, 1,667 in April, and 1,667 in May next, or earlier if possible. In case of failure to make any one of the deliveries as before specified, the government is to have authority to revoke and annul this order, so far as regards the arms and appendages remaining undelivered at the time of said failure. Payments will be made for each delivery, in such funds as the Treasury Department may provide, on certificates of inspection and receipt of the United States inspectors, at the rate of twenty dollars per pistol, including appendages.

Please signify, in writing, your acceptance or non-acceptance of this order, on the terms and conditions herein stated.

Respectfully,

JAS. W. RIPLEY,
Brigadier General.

JAS. A. WHEELOCK, Esq.,
Secretary of Savage Fire-arms Co., Middletown, Conn.

MIDDLETOWN, CONN., *December* 4, 1861.

SIR : The order received from you for five thousand North's patent pistols, manufactured by the Savage Revolving Fire-arms Company, dated November 28, is accepted upon the terms therein mentioned.

I would state, however, that heretofore all our pistols have been delivered at our factory upon the inspection certificates. Could you not alter that clause in conformity therewith, instead of being delivered at the New York arsenal?

We have had 500 pistols ready for delivery for some days, but as yet have received nothing from Captain Balch. We shall probably have 500 more ready for delivery next week. I trust there will be no delay in getting the pistols off.

I am your obedient servant,

JAS. A. WHEELOCK,
Secretary of the Savage Revolving Fire-arms Co.

General J. W. RIPLEY,
Chief of Ordnance, Washington, D. C.

MIDDLETOWN, *February* 6, 1862.

SIR : Your telegraph, asking how many pistols your department can depend upon receiving from us weekly, was received, and immediately answered that you could depend on 400, and possibly 500.

We have three inspectors now, who should inspect 400 weekly. We have now ready for inspection 1,000, and shall send off 500 on Saturday next.

The inspectors are exceedingly particular, of which, however, I make no objection. My only apprehension is that they will not get them out as fast we can deliver them.

I am yours, very truly,

JAS. A. WHEELOCK,
Secretary of the Savage Revolving Fire-arms Company.

General J. W. RIPLEY,
U. S. A., Chief of Ordnance, Washington.

MIDDLETOWN, *February* 22, 1862.

SIR: The inspectors will complete their inspection of 5,000 pistols in the course of two weeks. May I ask, therefore, to have them continued on to the next lot of 5,000 pistols, which will be ready upon the completion of the present order?

I am your obedient servant,

JAS. A. WHEELOCK,
Secretary of the Savage Revolving Fire-arms Company.

General J. W. RIPLEY,
U. S. A., Chief of Ordnance, Washington.

ORDNANCE OFFICE,
Washington, February 26, 1862.

SIR: I enclose a copy of a letter from the Savage Revolving Fire-arms Company in relation to the inspection of their pistols. Please have the matter attended to. The company had two orders—one of October 16, 1861, for 5,000 pistols, deliverable 500 in October, 700 in November, 1,000 in December, and 1,500 a month thereafter; the other, dated November 28, 1861, for 5,000 pistols, deliverable 1,666 in March, 1,667 in April, and 1,667 in May, 1862. Price, $20.

Respectfully, your obedient servant,

JAS. W. RIPLEY, *Brigadier General.*

Captain G. T. BALCH,
Springfield, Massachusetts.

SPRINGFIELD, MASSACHUSETTS, *March* 1, 1862.

SIR: I have the honor to acknowledge the receipt of your letter of the 26th February, giving times of delivery, and number to be delivered, of Savage's pistols.

I desire to call your attention to the following statement of *promised* and *actual* deliveries, under *order of October* 11, 1861:

To be delivered in October	500	Delivered October 28	500
To be delivered in November....	700	Do. November ....None.
To be delivered in December....	1,000 {	Do. December 6.....	500
		Do. December 16.....	500
		Do. January 2	500
To be delivered in January	1,500 {	Do. January 16	500
		Do. January 28	500
		Do. February 11	500
To be delivered in February	1,300 {	Do. February 19	500
		Do. February 28	500
Total to be delivered to Feb.28..	5,000	Delivered up to Feb. 28.....	4,500

Leaving 500 pistols not deliverred on the expiration of the order of October 11, 1861.

As indicated in your letter of the 26th, the following are to be the deliveries on the order or November 28, 1861:

To be delivered in March.. 1,666
To be delivered in April 1,667
To be delivered in May... 1,667

Total... 5,000

The capability of production of this company, as its force is at present arranged, is not beyond 1,666 per month, and it is doubtful whether they can come up to time on the above order.

As regards the 500 yet undelivered on the previous order, I do not think they should be accepted; but that the general principle that contracts for time deliveries should be *strictly enforced* should be carried out; especially as these pistols, in the opinion of the department, are not such as are best for the service, and repeated reports have been made against them.

I respectfully submit to you the question whether we are to take the 500 yet due or not; and, until I hear from you on the subject, my instructions to the sub-inspectors are not to accept them, but make every pistol better count on the monthly deliveries as given above for the order of November 25, 1861.

Very respectfully, your obedient servant,

GEO. T. BALCH,
Captain Ordnance Corps.

General J. W. RIPLEY,
Chief of Ordnance, Washington, D. C.

SPRINGFIELD, MASSACHUSETTS, *March* 13, 1862.

SIR: I have the honor to acknowledge the receipt of your letter of the 11th instant, covering the order of the Secretary of War, in relation to the purchase of arms.

Am I to understand that this relates at all to the carbines and pistols I am daily receiving from the various parties who have orders on contracts, the inspection of which is in my charge?

Very respectfully, your obedient servant,

GEO. T. BALCH,
Captain of Ordnance.

General J. W. RIPLEY,
Chief of Ordnance, Washington, D. C.

ORDNANCE OFFICE,
Washington, March 17, 1862.

SIR: In answer to your letter of the 13th instant I have to say that the order of the Secretary of War prohibits the receipt by this department of any arms whatever, without his special permission to be obtained in every case.

Respectfully, your obedient servant,

JAMES W. RIPLEY,
Brigadier General

Captain G. T. BALCH,
Ordnance Department, Springfield, Mass.

WASHINGTON, *May* 2, 1862.

GENTLEMEN: The Savage Revolving Fire-arms Company will deliver the pistols now made and making for the government under contract, at the rate of nineteen dollars each, to wit, 4,500 pistols.

I am, gentlemen, your obedient servant,

JAS. A. WHEELOCK,
Secretary of the Savage Revolving Fire-arms Company.

Hon. JOSEPH HOLT and ROBERT DALE OWEN,
Commissioners, &c.

ORDNANCE OFFICE, *Washington, May* 2, 1862.

SIR: In reply to your inquiry of this day, I have to state that no pistols have been received from the Savage Arms Company since the date of my report of 17th ultimo, nor for some time previous.

On the 1st ultimo I recommended to the Secretary of War that a number of them reported ready for delivery be accepted, provided they were delivered by the 1st of May, but no action was had on that letter that I am aware of.

Respectfully, your obedient servant,

JAMES W. RIPLEY,
Brigadier General.

Major P. V. HAGNER, *Commission on Contracts.*

COMMISSION ON ORDNANCE AND ORDNANCE STORES,
Washington, April 23, 1862.

GENERAL: The commission have the honor to report as follows:

CASE NO. 48.—SAVAGE REVOLVING FIRE-ARMS COMPANY.

1. Order from Secretary of War, through chief of ordnance, dated October 16, 1861.

1st. To deliver 5,000 Savage Revolving Fire-arms Company pistols, at $20 each, prior to May 1, 1862.

2d. To deliver 5,000 additional, at $20, prior to June 1, 1862.

2. Also, order dated November 28, 1861.

Deliveries have been made of $4,500 under the first order in due season.

By special directions of the Secretary of War 1,000 have been inspected and received under the second order.

The commission find that the failure to deliver 500 within the stipulated time has released the government from receiving that number, as is expressly provided under the first order. The second order for 5,000, given on the 28th of November, requires the delivery of 1,666 in each of the months of March, April, and May, and the company, in their report to the Secretary of War, state that they will be prepared to fill punctually this condition.

As the chief of ordnance has reported to the commission that his department is in present need of pistols to the full extent of the number not yet delivered, the commission have decided to authorize the acceptance, under the terms of the order, of 4,500, at the price of $19 each, proposed by the secretary of the company as acceptable to them. The commission are convinced, however, that this arm should be made in future free from malleable iron, and at a lower price than $19.

We are, sir, very respectfully, your obedient servants,

J. HOLT,
ROBERT DALE OWEN,
Commissioners.

P. V. HAGNER,
Major of Ordnance, Assistant to Commission.

General J. W. RIPLEY, *Chief of Ordnance.*

MIDDLETOWN, *June* 16, 1862.

GENTLEMEN : Upon my return home on Saturday last I made application to Messrs. Parker, Inow, Brooks & Co., of Meriden, Connecticut, (who made proposals, under the advertisement of the chief of ordnance for small arms, for 50,000 Springfield muskets,) to transfer their proposal to us, to which they readily assented. It appears to me, therefore, that the great difficulty in the way is thus obviated, as I am enabled to come in under the advertisement. Your idea was that the government would want 500,000 Springfield muskets, and you had confirmed the old contracts to the amount of 600,000. I stated to you that one-half that quantity could not possibly be turned in, provided the government adhered to the agreements and did not grant any extensions. To convince you that you will receive but a small proportion of the number confirmed, I will state that on Friday last, in New York, I found quite a number of these contracts in the hands of brokers, who were making it a regular business to sell them upon the best terms. I certainly had not less than 200,000 offered me on that day, and these cannot be all that are in the market. None of these contracts can be executed, as I believe we are the only establishment of any capacity in the country at present idle. So far I have rejected all their propositions, although the price offered is much more liberal than that I offered to the government; in fact, we can get $19 per musket from the speculators, yet I consider a contract made direct with the government under my proposition more desirable. Under the confirmed contracts I do not see how it is possible to deliver 200,000, as the time is limited to sixteen months from July. Certainly none of these contracts now in the market and offered to the lowest bidder can be executed.

If these facts prove to you that you will receive but a small proportion of the contracts, do you consider our company entitled to the consideration of the department, and our proposition favorably received? If you can give me the slightest encouragement, I would willingly make one more effort. I think it would be only necessary for you to give it your approbation. I cannot yet reconcile the idea of being quite overlooked by the government and obliged to take a contract from these speculators, inasmuch as we are the oldest and one of the largest establishments in the country.

Upon a careful reconsideration of this matter, taking in view the fact that Messrs. Parker, Inow, Brooks & Co. will transfer their proposal under the advertisement to us, I feel confident you will favor our application.

I must apologize for thus intruding upon your notice again, but necessity compels me to use every honorable means to obtain a contract. You will oblige me by giving an early answer to this communication.

I am, gentlemen, your obedient servant,
JAMES A. WHEELOCK,
Secretary of the Savage Revolving Fire-arms Company.
Hon. JOSEPH HOLT and ROBERT DALE OWEN, *Commissioners, &c.*

Before commission, June 8, 1862.

Indorsement on proposition of Mr. James A. Wheelock, of Savage Arms Company, to make 50,000 Springfield arms at $16, if an order could be obtained for that number. Referred to commission by the Secretary of War:

"The commission respectfully report that, in their opinion, the price proposed ($16) for 50,000 arms is reasonable and fair; but as the date of first delivery is distant, and the number already engaged, and to be previously delivered, is sufficiently large in all probability to meet the wants of the government, they do not consider it advisable to accept a private proposal at this time and under existing circumstances; nor would it be in accordance with the law to do so, the present proposal not being submitted in response to any previous advertisement upon the subject."

J. HOLT.
ROBERT DALE OWEN.
P. V. HAGNER,
Major of Ordnance, Assistant to Commission.

Before commission, June 11, 1862.

Mr. W. A. Wheelock, treasurer of Savage Revolving Arms Company, appeared before commission in reference to their application to make United States Springfield muskets, asking that an order may be recommended in their behalf at $16 per gun, or that one of the existing contracts confirmed by the commission may be formally transferred to them. Commission informed him that a report had been made on this subject.

Mr. Wheelock stated, in explanation of the present price of their pistols, as complained of in the decision of the commission, that they had to pay $2 per pistol to obtain the orders for those heretofore delivered, and that this tax increased the cost of the arm to the government. The commission summoned Mr. Wheelock to give testimony upon this subject, requiring him to appear at 11 a. m. to-morrow.

P. V. HAGNER, *Major of Ordnance.*

COMMISSION ON ORDNANCE AND ORDNANCE STORES,
Washington, June 12, 1862.

Mr. James A. Wheelock, of Savage Revolving Arms Company, having appeared at the instance of the commission, deposed as follows:

Questions by the commission.

First. State your relation to the Savage Revolving Fire-arms Company.

Answer. I am, and have been for several years, secretary and treasurer of said company.

Second. State what knowledge you have of any money having been paid by said company for obtaining orders or contracts from the War Department for the manufacture of pistols. Set forth fully the date of said orders thus obtained, and their amount; the sum of money thus paid out, and to whom; and all the circumstances of said transaction as known to you.

Answer. On the 10th of September last, Mr. Savage, one of the directors in our company, obtained an order from General Ripley for 5,000 pistols, deliverable in monthly instalments of 1,000. The delivery of the first month failed, in consequence of which, on the 11th of October, the order was revoked by the chief of ordnance. This order was in the name of Mr. Savage, and was never transferred to our company. No action was taken by him for its fulfilment. At the date of this order Mr. Thomas Dyer, known as one of the partners in the first large beef contract given out after the commencement of the rebellion, was retained by our company as an agent to obtain a pistol contract for it. All our personal efforts to procure such a contract from the War Department had failed, and we employed Mr. Dyer, because he said to us that he could obtain it. Accordingly, on the 16th of October, another order was obtained for 5,000 of the same pistols by Mr. Dyer, to whom we agreed to pay $10,000, being two dollars per pistol for his services. On the 25th of October, 1861, I, as the secretary, and on behalf of the Savage Revolving Fire-arms Company, made application to the Secretary of War for an order for 10,000 six-barrelled self-cocking pistols at $20; which application was referred to the chief of ordnance, and by him returned to the Secretary of War, advising that it should be refused, on the ground that, in his opinion, "the Savage arm was not a desirable arm for the service." The application was not granted. Some time after this, Henry Wykoff came to me at our manufactory, at Middletown, Connecticut, and asked me if our company did not want a contract for pistols. I told him we did. He then inquired what we were willing to pay for the order. I told him for an order of not less than 5,000 pistols we would pay him $2 per pistol; and that we would furnish the pistols at $20. He then suggested that we should charge $22 50, but I refused, stating that the pistol was not worth more than $20, and that at that rate we had sold them to the government. He stated that he had an application pending before the department for a pistol contract, in which he proposed to charge $22 50, and, therefore, he wished the same price should be fixed by us, as he desired to transfer the contract, if he obtained it, to us. I told him any order or contract for us must appear in our own name, and not as assigned to us. He then went to Washington, and in a week or two we received an order from the War Department for 5,000 Savage pistols at $20, which order bore date the 28th November. These were the same pistols which I offered to the department, as already stated, on the 25th of October, but which were not accepted. The money has not yet been paid to Mr. Wykoff, it being an unsettled question between him and the company, whether he shall abate any part of his fee or douceur of $2 per pistol, in consequence of this commission, in confirming the contract, having reduced the price from $20 to $19.

JAMES A. WHEELOCK,
Secretary of the Savage Revolving Fire-arms Company.

Sworn to and subscribed before me this twelfth day of June, A. D. 1862.

N. CALLAN, J. P. [SEAL.]

CASE No. 49.

D. B. POND.

COMMISSION ON ORDNANCE AND ORDNANCE STORES,
Washington, April 17, 1862.

SIR: Your communication to the Secretary of War, enclosing voucher for two Ellsworth guns, &c., purchased of you by order of General Butler, February 15, 1862, has been referred to this commission. The commission will sanction the purchase as soon as evidence is furnished that some United States officer actually received the articles and is accountable for them, and also some evidence showing the reasonableness of the price, as the gun is not known by the name given it.

Upon the just requirements it is supposed that satisfactory evidence can be obtained by you in Boston, without the delay of sending to Ship island, and as to the second you can furnish some description of the gun, with a detailed account of the "fixtures" going to make up the price, and the opinion of Captain Rodman, or other officer of Watertown arsenal, or of some expert known to the commission, Mr. Alger, for instance, in case Captain Rodman may not be at his station.

Yours, very respectfully,

P. V. HAGNER, Major of Ordnance.

Mr. D. B. POND, Boston.

P. S.—The voucher is enclosed to be returned to Messrs. Holt and Owen, commissioners, &c., Corcoran's Building, Washington.

CITY, COUNTY, AND STATE OF NEW YORK, *ss:*

I, Daniel B. Pond, of said city, county, and State, hereby certify that on the 9th day of January, A. D. 1862, at the city of Boston, county of Suffolk and Commonwealth of Massachusetts, Major General Benjamin F. Butler, ordered of me two Ellsworth guns and two thousand rounds of ammunition suitable for the same, at a price then agreed upon, to wit: three hundred and fifty dollars apiece for the guns and forty cents per round for the ammunition.

I further certify that Sabin P. Pond, of Brooklyn, county of Kings and State of New York, aforesaid, had the general supervision of the manufacture and delivery of said guns and ammunition, and that said Pond made and delivered to said Butler, or his agent, the two guns and two thousand rounds of ammunition, aforesaid, as will appear by said Pond's affidavit, which is hereto annexed, to which the commissioners are respectfully referred.

I also further certify that on or at about the 25th of November, A. D. 1861, I sold and delivered to the President, Abraham Lincoln, *twenty Ellsworth* guns and four thousand rounds of ammunition suitable for the same, at the prices then agreed upon, as follows, to wit, three hundred and fifty dollars per gun, and forty cents per round for the ammunition; that before said guns and ammunition were accepted, the President required, as per agreement, the certificate of Colonel C. F. Kingsbury; that said Kingsbury fired said guns and examined said ammunition, and gave his certificate of approval and acceptance of the same; which said certificate, contract, &c., is now on file in its proper place, and to which this commission is respectfully referred.

I also further certify that I made considerable improvements upon said guns and ammunition, and caused said improvements to be added to said guns and ammunition at a considerable outlay, and at my own expense. And I further certify that the guns and ammunition sold and delivered to Major General B. F. Butler, as aforesaid, had all of said improvements added and attached to them before their said delivery, and at no extra charge.

I also certify that the balls sold and delivered to Major General B. F. Butler, were turned in a lathe, and covered with *linen twine,* instead of being made of chilled iron and covered with cotton twine, as I had previously made them, and that no extra charge was made for said ammunition, although the expense for making the same was largely increased.

I also certify that the price of three hundred and fifty dollars per gun also included gun-carriages, ammunition boxes, ramrod, priming wire, &c., and that the price of forty cents per round, included tin cartridge case, powder and ball, &c.

DANIEL B. POND.

Sworn to before me this 22d of April, 1862.

FRANK W. BALLARD,
Notary Public in said city.

I, Sabin P. Pond, of the city of Brooklyn, county of Kings and State of New York, hereby certify that I had the management and supervision of the manufacture of two Ellsworth guns and two thousand rounds of ammunition ordered of Daniel B. Pond by Major General B. F. Butler, and that said guns and ammunition were made in a superior and workmanlike manner in all respects, and that on the 15th day of February, A. D. 1862, I delivered said guns and ammunition to Major General B. F. Butler, at his headquarters, in Court square in the city of Boston and State of Massachusetts, and that said guns and ammunition were then and there inspected by Captain Joseph H. Kensel, by the order of Major

General B. F. Butler, and the bill and duplicate as forwarded to the War Department were then and there examined and approved by Major General B. F. Butler; and further, I do certify that, at the order of Major George C. Strong, I was then and there repaid the amount of money I had paid to the Norfolk County Railroad Company for freight of said guns from Blackstone, Massachusetts, to the city of Boston, and that I receipted for the same, which said receipt I presume can be found on file in the city of Washington; and furthermore, I did then and there request Major George C. Strong to forward to Daniel B. Pond. No. 7 Wall street, New York, the aforesaid approved bills, with all the necessary receipts, voucher, and other papers, to insure a speedy auditory of said accounts at the War Department, in the city of Washington, which the said Major George C. Strong then and there agreed to do.

SABIN P. POND.

Sworn to before me this 22d of April, 1862.

FRANK W. BALLARD,
Notary Public in said city.

COMMISSION ON ORDNANCE AND ORDNANCE STORES,
Washington, April 24, 1862.

GENERAL: The commission have the honor to report as follows:

CASE No. 49.—DANIEL B. POND, Boston, Massachusetts.

Claim for amount of vouchers, dated February 15, 1862. Amount of claim, $1,500.

Account for two Ellsworth guns and fixtures; 2,000 rounds of ammunition for ditto. Furnished upon the order of Major General Butler.

Referred to the commission by special direction of the Secretary of War, the ordnance stores not having been purchased in accordance with law.

The commission find that the account is informal, in not showing to what officer of the army the articles were delivered, and in not explaining, as required by regulation, the items embraced in it, so that the reasonableness of the charges may be judged of. They have therefore required an affidavit from Mr. Pond, by which it appears that the same prices have been heretofore paid for the like articles by order of the President of the United States, and also that the articles were delivered at General Butler's headquarters, and the freight upon them paid by Major Strong, the ordnance officer of General Butler's command. It has been shown to the commission that General Butler was specially authorized by the Secretary of War to make purchases of ordnance stores for the command he was organizing at this period, upon certain conditions; and the commission consider the authority applicable in this case. They therefore direct that the account be examined and audited as usual, without objection on account of informality.

We are, sir, very respectfully, your obedient servants,

J. HOLT,
ROBERT DALE OWEN,
Commissioners, &c.
P. V. HAGNER,
Major of Ordnance, Assistant to Commission.

General J. W. RIPLEY,
Chief of Ordnance.

Ex. Doc. 72——15

CASE No. 50.

G. W. MACLEAN.

COMMISSION ON ORDNANCE AND ORDNANCE STORES,
Washington, April, 1862.

GENERAL : The commission have the honor to report as follows:

CASE No. 50.—G. W. MACLEAN.

Claim for amount   Account for saddlers' tools and stores for 11th Illinois
of voucher, dated   cavalry, under command of Colonel R. G. Ingersoll.
October 18, 1861.   Referred by special direction of the Secretary of War, the
purchase of the ordnance stores not having been duly authorized as required by
law.

The commission find that the 11th Illinois cavalry was mustered into service
December 20, 1861, and that Robert G. Ingersoll was mustered as colonel and
William Cunie as quartermaster on the same day.

The articles purchased are regarded as essential for the cavalry service, the
prices not unreasonable, and Quartermaster Cunie acknowledges his accounta-
bility for them in his quarterly accounts for December, 1861.

The commission therefore direct that this account be examined and audited
as usual, without objection on account of informality.

We are, sir, very respectfully, your obedient servants,
J. HOLT,
ROBERT DALE OWEN,
Commissioners.
P. V. HAGNER,
Major of Ordnance, Assistant to Commission.

Brigadier General J. W. RIPLEY,
Chief of Ordnance.

Before commission.

Copy of certificate upon account of M. G. Anders, amounting to $1,631 25.
October 10, 1861.

I certify, on honor, that this account is correct and just; that the articles
named were necessary for the public service, and were bought by order of
Brigadier General Robert Anderson—the order being written, and a copy of it
furnished Colonel Thomas Swords, assistant quartermaster general, in the matter
of the claim of D. Ricketts against the United States for horses furnished the
2d Kentucky cavalry. The said saddles were received, and are now in use by
the said cavalry.
LOVELL H. ROUSSEAU,
Brigadier General 4th Brigade.

True copy.

P. V. HAGNER,
Major of Ordnance.

CASE No. 51.

M. G. ANDERS.

COMMISSION ON ORDNANCE AND ORDNANCE STORES,
Washington, April, 1862.

GENERAL : The commission have the honor to report as follows :

CASE No. 51.—M. G. ANDERS.

Claim for amount of voucher, dated October 11, 1861 ; amount of claim, $1,631 75.

Bill for 75 cavalry saddles, with all equipments complete ; purchased under order of General Robert Anderson, commanding the department.

Referred by special directions of the Secretary of War, the purchase of the ordnance stores not having been made as required by law.

The commission find that, as appears by certificate of Brigadier General Rousseau, these equipments were bought, by order of General Robert Anderson, for the 2d Kentucky cavalry; that they were received and were in use by that regiment ; and Elias Thomasson, quartermaster of the regiment, signs the receipt for the whole amount charged on the account. The items of the account are not stated with sufficient explicitness, but that "all the equipments were complete." The price charged is, therefore, not unreasonable.

The commission direct that the account be examined and audited, without objection on account of informality.

We are, sir, very respectfully, your obedient servants,
J. HOLT,
ROBERT DALE OWEN,
Commissioners, &c.
P. V. HAGNER,
Major of Ordnance, Assistant to Commission.

Brig. Gen. J. W. RIPLEY,
Chief of Ordnance.

WAR DEPARTMENT, *October* 29, 1861.

SIR : I beg leave to call your attention to the following extract from a letter received from George L. Schuyler, esq., our agent at Paris, under date of October 10, 1861:

"The contract made with Mr. Wigert (September 5) to deliver 10,000 Chasseurs de Vincennes rifles in 55 days he cannot, of course, fulfil. Such arms do not exist in the markets at any price. The price he is to obtain ($23 50) may induce speculators to send out guns called 'Chasseurs de Vincennes rifles,' but of very inferior quality. If purchases are made in New York I respectfully suggest a rigid inspection."

General Ripley will please call the attention of his officers in the eastern cities to the matters referred to in the foregoing extract.

Respectfully,
THOMAS A. SCOTT, *Assistant Secretary.*

General RIPLEY, *Chief of Ordnance.*

Indorsed as follows :

ORDNANCE OFFICE, *October* 31, 1861.

Respectfully returned as directed; attention has been called to the matters referred to in the extract. I deem it proper to state, in regard to the contract for the 10,000 Chasseurs de Vincennes rifles, that it was made by direction of the Secretary of War for the delivery of these arms in 55 days—that is, by the 4th of November, 1861. On the 23d of October a letter, directed to this office, was received here, stating that the arms could not be delivered at the time agreed upon, and asking an extension of eight months. That letter was promptly answered (24th October) that the extension of time could not be granted. On the 26th of October a letter to the War Department, from the same party, proposing to deliver the same 10,000 arms, at $23 50 each, in bond, was sent to this office, indorsed "The Secretary desires the guns referred to shall be secured, and directs me to send this to you."

Yours, respectfully,

THOMAS A. SCOTT, *Assistant Secretary.*

In obedience to that order, the 10,000 arms, deliverable in eight months, were contracted for on the same day, and that contract now stands.

JAS. W. RIPLEY, *Brigadier General.*

CASE No. 52.

WIGERT & OTARD.

COMMISSION ON ORDNANCE AND ORDNANCE STORES,
Washington, April 24, 1862.

GENERAL : The commission have the honor to report as follows :

CASE No. 52.—WIGERT & OTARD, New York.

Order, by direction of the Secretary of War, dated September 10, '61. No. 26, page 11, of printed list.

To deliver 10,000 French St. Etienne rifles, with sabre bayonets, calibre .69, price $23 50 per gun, to be delivered, in bond, in the city of New York, in 55 days from date.

In case of failure to deliver, as stipulated, the government may or may not, at its option, take the arms.

Referred to the commission by direction of the Secretary of War.

The commission find that no deliveries have been made under the above order ; and that according to its terms, because of the failure of the parties to comply with their engagements, the government is under no obligation to take the arms. They, therefore, decide that said order be, and is hereby, withdrawn and annulled, and that no arms shall be received under the same.

We are, sir, very respectfully, your obedient servants,

J. HOLT,
ROBERT DALE OWEN,
Commissioners, &c.

P. V. HAGNER,
Major of Ordnance, Assistant to Commission.

General J. W. RIPLEY, *Chief of Ordnance.*

CASE No. 53.

FRANK OTARD.

COMMISSION ON ORDNANCE AND ORDNANCE STORES,
Washington, April 24, 1862.

GENERAL: The commission have the honor to report as follows:

CASE No. 53.—FRANK OTARD, New York.

Order by Secretary of War, dated October 26, 1861. No. 35, printed list.   To deliver 10,000 French sabre bayonet rifles, of the improved pattern, St. Etienne make, calibre .69-inch, at $23 50, with appendages, in bond, at the New York arsenal, Governor's island, at the rate of 750 per month for four months from date of order, and 1,750 per month thereafter. In case of failure, may be revoked and annulled.

Referred to commission by direction of the Secretary of War.

The commission find that no deliveries have been made under the above order; and, as the periods of five deliveries have passed, in pursuance of the authority given by the terms of the order to revoke and annul it for failure to comply with its stipulations, the commission direct that said order be, and is hereby, revoked and annulled, and that no arms be received under it.

We are, sir, very respectfully, your obedient servants,

J. HOLT,
ROBERT DALE OWEN,
Commissioners, &c.
P. V. HAGNER,
Major of Ordnance, Assistant to Commission.

Brigadier General J. W. RIPLEY,
Chief of Ordnance.

CASE No. 54.

MICKLES & HOPKINS, Syracuse, New York.—60,000 *foreign muskets,* October 23, 1861.

No official notice of this order was ever received at the Ordnance office, and there was no knowledge of its existence in that bureau until the parties filed a copy of their offer with the Secretary of War.

The following papers contain all the information which can be obtained from the records of the War Department concerning it.

The date of the contract is uncertain, as no copy of the acceptance of the offer can be found on the files of the War Department, although it is alluded to in the subjoined letter of the Secretary of War to the Hon. H. S. Sanford, United States minister to Belgium, dated December 13, 1861.

WASHINGTON, *October* 23, 1861.

Philo D. Mickles, of the city of Syracuse, and Charles Hopkins, of the city of New York, propose to sell to the United States government 60,000 muskets and bayonets, upon the following conditions, viz:

The muskets and bayonets are new, never having been used, and are now ready for use. The length of the barrel 42½ inches; iron furniture; beech-wood stocks; calibre $17\frac{5}{10}$ millimetres, near the calibre of United States muskets; made according to plan or drawing hereunto attached. To be delivered in the city of New York in lots or parcels of not less than 5,000 at a time, and the whole 60,000 to be delivered in the course of four months, the government not charging the contractors any duties.

The muskets to be inspected by the agent of the United States government, and at their expense, in the city of Antwerp, and to be by him approved as perfect in all respects. The government to pay for said muskets the sum of $7 65 for each musket and bayonet, upon the delivery of each parcel of not less than 5,000 in the city of New York.

(No signatures were attached to the copy forwarded to the Secretary of War.)

WAR DEPARTMENT,
Washington, October 26, 1861.

DEAR SIR : Enclosed you will find a proposition from Philo D. Mickles and Charles Hopkins, of New York, to furnish 60,000 muskets, ready for use, deliverable within four months from the 23d October to the government, at the city of New York, properly packed, with all the usual appendages furnished with guns for army purposes, price seven dollars and sixty-five cents each. Please have the guns examined, and, if adapted to our purposes, make the purchase.

Mr. Hopkins will call upon you with a letter of introduction, and will confer fully in relation to the whole subject. Payment to be made in New York.

Very respectfully, (by direction of the Secretary of War,)
THOMAS A. SCOTT,
Assistant Secretary of War.

GEORGE L. SCHUYLER, Esq.,
United States Government Agent, Paris.

WAR DEPARTMENT,
Washington, October 26, 1861.

SIR : Permit me to introduce to your favorable notice Charles Hopkins, esq., of New York, who visits Europe to confer with you in regard to arms, the proposition for which was sent you by mail, in care of Hon. W. L. Dayton, United States minister at Paris.

Very respectfully,
THOMAS A. SCOTT,
Assistant Secretary of War.

GEORGE L. SCHUYLER, Esq.,
United States Agent, Paris.

Extract of a letter from Thomas A. Scott, esq., Assistant Secretary of War, to Hon. H. L. Sanford, United States minister, Belgium, under date of December 13, 1861.

"A contract was, some time since, made with Philo D. Mickles and John F. Hopkins to deliver in New York sixty thousand new guns, at $7 65 each, if they are found suitable for our purpose. That contract has been recently changed, by transfer, to H. Hall, of New York, whose agent, Gustavus Smith, esq., will visit Europe to complete the negotiation.

"These guns you are requested to receive, after inspection by Inspector Wright, and you will pay for them, after their delivery on board the vessels to bring them to the United States, and after the bills of lading, policies of insurance, and freight bills paid are in your possession.

"The balance of credits there available you are requested to use in payment for guns, to be furnished by Boker & Co. on their contract, and have them delivered as speedily as possible. On the completion of their several contracts for arms, enough will have been received to meet the present wants of the service, and no more foreign guns will be taken, as our own manufactories, we believe, will be able to furnish an ample supply of first class arms.

"THOMAS A. SCOTT,
"Assistant Secretary of War."

WAR DEPARTMENT, *Washington, January 9, 1862.*

DEAR SIR : The parties to the contract of Messrs. Mickles & Hopkins now inform the department that the guns they proposed to furnish the government, with iron mountings, cannot be secured, but an article with brass mountings, similar in every other respect, can be secured and delivered by them within a reasonable period, say sixty days after the time fixed in their contract. If this can be done, you will please receive them under the terms of agreement.

Very respectfully,

THOMAS A. SCOTT,
Assistant Secretary of War.

Hon. HENRY S. SANFORD,
United States Minister, Brussels.

NEW YORK, *February* 8, 1862.

SIR : I herewith enclose copy of proposition made to and accepted by the War Department in October, 1861, and time extended on 9th January, 1862. My agent is now in Europe attending to the same.

Respectfully, yours,

PHILO D. MICKLES.

Hon. EDWIN M. STANTON,
Secretary of War, Washington, D. C.

WAR DEPARTMENT, *Washington, December* 13, 1861.

DEAR SIR : This will be handed to you by Augustine Smith, esq., of New York, the gentleman authorized by Mr. Hall, of New York, to represent him in delivery of guns under contract with this department, as stated in official papers delivered to Mr. Hall, which I presume will be forwarded by Mr. Smith for delivery to you.

Very respectfully, yours,

THOMAS A. SCOTT,
Assistant Secretary of War.

Hon. H. S. SANFORD,
United States Minister, Brussels.

COMMISSION ON ORDNANCE AND ORDNANCE STORES,
Washington, April 26, 1862.

SIR : Your claim to furnish 60,000 foreign muskets under the proposition made by Mickles & Hopkins, dated October 23, 1861, with the copies of papers transmitted by you to the Secretary of War February 8, 1862, has been referred to the above commission. As it is stated in your note that your agent is in Europe, the commission direct me to inform you that they have advised that our minister in Belgium should be notified not to receive any arms for the United States on your account, as the arrangement stated to have been made is regarded as without legal sanction, improvident for the government, and that arms of the kind described are not needed by the army.

So far as appears by the papers before the commission, the stipulations of the proposal on your part have not been fulfilled, and hence may have been already forfeited.   In order, however, to prevent the risk of loss to you, it is deemed proper to inform you at once of the views of the commission before seeing Mr. Sanford's reports.

Very respectfully, your obedient servant,

P. V. HAGNER,
Major of Ordnance.

PHILO D. MICKLES, Esq., *New York.*

COMMISSION ON ORDNANCE AND ORDNANCE STORES,
Washington, April 25, 1862.

SIR: In case No. 36, page 108, Executive Document No. 67, it appears that Mr. Sanford, minister in Belgium, still remains responsible for carrying out the procurement of the arms therein alluded to.

This case is decidedly an illegal binding of the government, and the arms not such as can be of use, and at a high price.

The commission respectfully suggest, therefore, that no time should be lost in notifying Mr. Sanford not to act (further than he may have already done) under the instructions given him on the 9th of January, 1862, and that he be informed that, if possible, no gun should be received under these instructions.

The order to Mickles & Hopkins was given without notification to the ordnance department for valueless arms, at a high price, and without any sufficient stipulation to protect the government interest.

Very respectfully, your obedient servant,

P. V. HAGNER,
Major of Ordnance.

P. H. WATSON, Esq.,
Assistant Secretary of War.

———

COMMISSION ON ORDNANCE AND ORDNANCE STORES,
Washington, April 28, 1862.

GENERAL: The commission have the honor to report as follows :

CASE No. 54.—MICKLES & HOPKINS, Syracuse, N. Y.   (Transferred to H. Hall, Gustavus Smith, agent.)

Proposals accepted by Secretary of War, as stated in letter dated November 25, 1861, addressed to Hon. H. S. Sanford, United States minister to Belgium. No. 36, printed list, page 11.

To deliver 60,000 muskets, iron mountings, new, never having been used, near the calibre of the United States muskets, according to plan or drawing thereunto annexed, in lots of 5,000, and the whole number in the course of four months.   To be inspected in the city of Antwerp, and paid for upon delivery in New York, at $7 65 each.

Referred to commission by direction of the Secretary of War.

The commission find that this order thus acknowledged to have been given, was not so given through the ordnance department, and no notice of it there recorded. The proposition of Messrs. Mickles & Hopkins seems to have been forwarded by Assistant Secretary of War T. A. Scott, October 26, 1861, to George L. Schuyler, government agent in Paris, with directions to have the guns inspected, and if adapted to our purposes, to make the purchase.

Reported copies of this proposition are before the commission, but no signatures are attached to them, although one was forwarded to the Secretary of War by Mr. Mickles, and the other from the ordnance department to the commission, with the statement that no signed copy is on file there. On the 9th January Mr. T. A. Scott, in a letter to H. S. Sanford, United States minister to Belgium, states that Messrs. Mickles & Hopkins now inform the department that the guns they propose to furnish the government, with iron mountings, cannot be secured, but an article with brass mountings, similar in every other respect, can be secured and delivered by them within a reasonable period, say sixty days after the time fixed in their contract.

If this can be done you will please receive them under the terms of their agreement.

No arms appear to have been offered under the order either to Mr. Schuyler or to Mr. Sanford, and none have arrived in the United States, as far as shown to the commission.

An arrangement so informal as this for such a large number of arms, from which the government has derived no advantage, and which, from the character of the arms, cannot, if fulfilled, ultimately prove of benefit, ought not to be allowed to remain without decisive action.

If the terms of Mr. Scott's letter of the 9th of January be considered as establishing a fixed period for the first delivery, it should have been made on the 23d of December, and the whole lot delivered by the 23d of April.

As far as known neither of these conditions have been complied with. Arms of the description stated are probably Prussian smooth bore, not suiting our ammunition; no longer used either in Europe or in our country, except upon great emergency, and no doubt such as have been purchased in New York, at the time of our greatest need, at a price lower than is named for these. That they are positively "new, never having been used," is hardly to be expected; as the whole responsibility of deciding whether they were adapted to our purpose was thrown by Mr. Scott upon our minister to Belgium, in his letter of the 9th of January, it may be that he has already received some of them at Antwerp, but possibly, with the experience he has obtained in his extra official duty, he may not have done so.

The commission suggest that instructions be sent to him not to receive them after such notice. There cannot be a doubt of the illegality of such a mode of giving orders, or making contracts, in the opinion of the commission, as stated in other cases, and therefore the commission unhesitatingly decide that there is no obligation upon the government to accept any not already delivered to the minister, nor any so delivered, except to relieve the minister from any responsibility, should he have complied exactly with the instructions given him.

We are, sir, very respectfully, your obedient servants,

J. HOLT,
ROBERT DALE OWEN,
Commissioners, &c.
P. V. HAGNER,
Major of Ordnance, Assistant to Commission
Brigadier General J. W. RIPLEY,
Chief of Ordnance.

CASE No. 55.

W. A. SEAVER.

COMMISSION ON ORDNANCE AND ORDNANCE STORES,
Washington, April 28, 1862.

GENERAL: The commission have the honor to report as follows:

CASE No. 55.—W. A. SEAVER, New York.

Order from chief of ordnance, under directions of Secretary of War, dated August 14, 1861. No. 15 printed list. Referred by Secretary of War.

To deliver 50,000 Enfield rifle muskets, at $20 each, including appendages, at Governor's island, New York, subject to inspection, as follows: 10,000 in September, 1861, and from 10,000 to 20,000 monthly thereafter, until all are delivered. To be equal to sample with tower mark, deposited in Ordnance office by Messrs. Mitchell and Jones. In case of failure to deliver, the government may refuse at its option.

The commission find that no deliveries have been made as stipulated; and as the government has been compelled to supply its wants from other sources in consequence of this failure, they direct that the order given be revoked and annulled, as provided for by its terms, and that no arms be received under it.

We are, sir, very respectfully, your obedient servants,

J. HOLT,
ROBERT DALE OWEN,
Commissioners, &c.
P. V. HAGNER,
Major of Ordnance, Assistant to Commission.

Brigadier General J. W. RIPLEY, *Chief of Ordnance.*

CASE No. 56.

H. SIMON & SON.

COMMISSION ON ORDNANCE AND ORDNANCE STORES,
Washington, April 28, 1862.

GENERAL: The commission have the honor to report as follows:

CASE No. 56.—H. SIMON & SON, Washington, D. C.

Order by direction of the Secretary of War, dated October 28, 1861. No. 37 of the printed list, page 11. Referred by direction of Secretary of War.

To deliver at the United States arsenal Governor's island, New York, 5,000 long Enfield rifles, equal in all respects to sample exhibited, and subject to inspection, at $19 for each rifle, including appendages, in bonds. Deliveries to be made as follows: 1,500 in eight weeks from the 28th of October; 1,500 in twelve weeks from the 28th of October; 2,000 in sixteen weeks from the 28th of October. In case of failure to deliver, the government may annul this order.

The commission find that no deliveries have been made under this order, and therefore direct, in accordance with its provisions in such case of failure, that it be revoked and annulled, and that no arms be received under it.

We are, sir, very respectfully, your obedient servants,

J. HOLT,
ROBERT DALE OWEN,
Commissioners.
P. V. HAGNER,
Major of Ordnance, Assistant to Commission.

Brigadier General J. W. RIPLEY, *Chief of Ordnance.*

CASE No. 57.

WILSTACH & CO.

PHILADELPHIA, *April* 18, 1862.

SIR : We enclose a copy of a contract from the ordnance department, received through Major Hagner, dated July 1, 1861, for 3,000 sets United States cavalry mountings. By referring to the postscript you will find we were directed to give preference in deliveries to such other orders as the department was about to give out to saddlers for the complete equipment. We did receive a very large proportion of such orders, and were kept busy until late in November, when we continued to make and finish the contract for these 3,000 sets. In the month of December, when prepared to begin to deliver these mountings, we then learned for the first time that Major Hagner thought that the government ought not to take these mountings. No intimation, verbal or written, had been expressed before ; had there been, we would not have caused so large a proportion of the order to be manufactured, all of which has been useless to us for the past five months.

We called General Ripley's attention to this order. He preferred not taking action, and thought it ought to be settled by the ordnance commission ; and our object in addressing you is for permission to place this subject before them for adjudication.

Respectfully,

W. P. WILSTACH.

Hon. EDWIN M. STANTON, *Secretary of War.*

WAR DEPARTMENT, *April* 25, 1862.

Referred to the special commission on ordnance and ordnance stores. By order of the Secretary of War.

P. H. WATSON,
Assistant Secretary of War.

PHILADELPHIA, *July* 1, 1861.

GENTLEMEN : I am authorized by the chief of ordnance to procure for the ordnance department 3,000 sets saddlery hardware for United States pattern horse equipments, to be of established quality and kind, subject to the usual inspections, and consisting, each set, of the articles stated in your proposals made to me June 27, 1861, except 5 per 70 No. 1 riding bits to be furnished instead of 10 per 70, and 45 per 70 No. 3 instead of 40 per 70 ; the No. 1 mouth-piece ring to be 4 inches in diameter.

It is understood that the inspections will be made at the Frankford arsenal, and the articles are to be delivered there for this purpose, at your expense, as often as is now required, and in such quantities as may be convenient, and in suitable bundles and boxes, as usual for such articles.

I accept the offer as to price per 100 sets complete, as stated in your before-mentioned proposals, and agree to pay you at the rate last named therein, viz : seven dollars ($7) per set, upon the production of the prescribed certificates of inspection from the commanding officer of the Frankford arsenal.

If the above is satisfactory to you, you will please notify me by letter addressed to me, care of commanding officer, Frankford arsenal.

Very respectfully, your obedient servant,

P. V. HAGNER, *Brevet Major.*

Messrs. WILSTACH & Co. *Philadelphia.*

P. S.—Three thousand sets of equipments will be ordered to-day from various saddlers, and you will probably be called upon to supply to them the necessary hardware. I request that the execution of the above order may not interfere with such supply ; beyond this, you will please use all practicable despatch.

P. V. H.

COMMISSION ON ORDNANCE AND ORDNANCE STORES,
Washington, April 26, 1862.

GENERAL : Please furnish for use of commission, as above—

1. The offer of Wilstach & Co. to Major Hagner to sell cavalry mountings, as stated in letter to chief of ordnance from Major Hagner, December, 1861, recommending purchase at the prices stated.

2. A statement of purchases made by the ordnance department of cavalry mountings, prior to December, 1861, from Wilstach & Co., by Lieutenant Treadwell, at the Frankford arsenal, or received there under orders given by the ordnance department.

The object of this last is to learn whether deliveries were not made by Wilstach & Co. to the Frankford arsenal since the parts ordered by Major Hagner were fairly due under the order given by him.

Very respectfully, your obedient servant,

P. V. HAGNER, Major of Ordnance.

General J. W. RIPLEY, <i>Chief of Ordnance.</i>

ORDNANCE OFFICE,
Washington, April 26, 1862.

SIR : I have to acknowledge your letter of this date, and transmit the original letter from yourself, recommending purchase of parts for horse equipments from Wilstach & Co.; also a copy of his proposal. Please return these papers to the files of this office.

Upon examination, it appears that Lieutenant Treadwell received from that firm 7,500 sets of horse equipment hardware during November and December, 1861, viz :

By certificate of November 9, 1861, 3,300 sets, at $6 14.......... $20,262
By certificate of December 11, 1861, 7,200 sets, at $6 14.......... 44,208

Respectfully, your obedient servant,

JAS. W. RIPLEY, Brig. General.

Major P. V. HAGNER,
Commission on Contracts, Washington City.

ORDNANCE OFFICE,
No. 55 White street, New York, December 19, 1861.

SIR : I am offered by Messrs. Wilstach & Co., of Philadelphia, 3,000 cavalry regulation bits, of steel ; 3,000 sets of malleable iron parts ; 3,000 lengths for girth webbing, 3½-inch ; 3,000 lengths for swingles, 4½-inch.

Extra parts necessary for repairs of cavalry equipments at prices very favorable for purchase by the government.

Bits at $1 50 ; original price, $2 85. Malleable parts at 65 cents ; original price, 85 cents. Webbing, 3½-inch, at 25 cents ; original price, 30 cents. Webbing, 4½-inch, at 36 cents ; original price, 40 cents.

All to be delivered at the Washington, Watervliet, New York, or Allegheny arsenal, subject to inspection.

The above articles remain in hand with Messrs. Wilstach, after supplying orders, owing to their determined efforts to have an abundant supply to meet all demands that came so suddenly upon them some weeks since. I have no doubt that they are all of the best quality, and recommend that the purchase be made, unless a large supply of spare parts has already been secured.

Very respectfully, sir, your obedient servant,

P. V. HAGNER, *Major of Ordnance.*

General J. W. RIPLEY,
Chief of Ordnance, Washington City.

P. S.—They have also 3,000 watering bits, at 31 cents, and 3,000 curb chains, at 76 cents.

P. V. HAGNER, *Major of Ordnance.*

ORDNANCE OFFICE, *March* 5, 1862.

Captain Balch will please examine the proposition of Messrs. Wilstach & Co., and report if, in his opinion, it be desirable to purchase the articles offered for sale. He will also report the stock of parts for cavalry equipments he has on hand and contracted for.

JAS. W. RIPLEY, *Brig. General.*

ORDNANCE OFFICE, *March* 19, 1862.

Mr. Wilstach, or his agent, states that the 8,000 sets of cavalry equipment trimmings are those ordered by you in your letter of July 1, and that they should be received under that order. Be pleased to read over the enclosed papers, and report the facts to this office.

Respectfully submitted to Major Hagner, ordnance department.

JAS. W. RIPLEY, *Brig. General.*

WASHINGTON, *March* 20, 1862.

Messrs. Wilstach & Co. have no claim whatever to furnish these upon my order. If not needed, (as stated in my letter,) the purchase should not be made.

Very respectfully,

P. V. HAGNER, *Major of Ordnance.*

ORDNANCE OFFICE, *April* 24, 1862.

The letter of Major Hagner, of July 17, explicitly orders 3,000 sets trimmings, and the postscript thus modifies it: "Three thousand sets of equipments will be ordered to-day from various saddlers, and as you will probably be called upon to supply them the necessary hardware, I request that the execution of this order may not interfere with such supply; beyond this you will please use all practicable despatch." The meaning of which clearly is, that Messrs. Wilstach & Co. must furnish but 3,000 sets trimmings to saddlers, and *only three thousand*—a point which is carefully avoided in this letter of the 18th of April, herewith enclosed.

The sales-book of the Messrs. Wilstach will show at what time they had delivered to the saddlers, who had orders from Major Hagner, these 3,000 sets. All deliveries subsequent to these should have been to the government on this order. If, however, deliveries were made to other parties, it appears to me that such deliveries annulled the order, and I respectfully request that, with this view, the matter may be submitted to the commission on ordnance stores for their decision thereon.

JAMES W. RIPLEY, *Brig. General.*

COMMISSION ON ORDNANCE AND ORDNANCE STORES,
Washington, April 29, 1862.

GENERAL: The commission have the honor to report as follows:

CASE No. 57.—WILSTACH & Co., Philadelphia, Pennsylvania.

Claim to deliver *now* three thousand sets of cavalry mountings, upon order given by Major Hagner, under instructions from chief of ordnance, July 1, 1862.

Order to deliver at the Frankford arsenal three thousand sets of cavalry mountings, at the rate of seven dollars per set, to be delivered, subject to inspection, with all possible despatch after supplying the saddlers, to whom orders to the extent of three thousand sets of equipments had been given that day, July 1, 1861. Referred by special direction of the Secretary of War.

The commission find that Major Hagner, under instructions from the chief of ordnance, gave out orders, July 1, 1861, to various saddlers to manufacture for the government three thousand sets of equipments with all despatch; that the mountings required by these saddlers had to be supplied by themselves; that the claimants, who are dealers in saddlery hardware, were informed of this fact, in order that no time should be lost in getting a stock on hand; that at the same time Major Hagner ordered of the claimants three thousand additional sets of mountings, for future use, to be made, and delivered at the Frankford arsenal; and to prevent this last order from interfering with the first, he stipulated that the reserve supply for the arsenal need not be furnished until after these saddlers engaged upon the three thousand sets of equipments (who might call upon these parties for mountings) had been provided; but "beyond this," directed them "to use all possible despatch."

No report was made to Major Hagner, who was on duty in New York, and in frequent communications, personally and by letter, with the claimants as to the non-fulfilment of his order of July 1, until about the 19th December, 1861, when one of the firm called at his office in New York, and after stating that they had three thousand sets of mountings on hand, offered them at nearly fifty per cent. reduction, to be delivered at either Washington, Watervliet, New York, or Allegheny arsenals. It was then stated to Major Hagner that no deliveries had been made under his order of July 1, although a very large number, exceeding twenty thousand sets of the same articles, had been, in the meantime, supplied to saddlers and to the ordnance department at Frankford arsenal under other orders from ordnance officers, so that not only were all saddlers supplied to the full extent of their orders, but the department had in store a large reserve supply.

No claim was then made to deliver these under the original order, and the voluntary offer to deliver at any of the places named, and at the lower rates stated, showed conclusively that the parties themselves did not then consider they had any such claim.

Major Hagner, however, wrote to the chief of ordnance, December 19, and recommended the purchase of this lot, "unless a large supply of spare parts has already been secured," in consideration of the low price.

Major Hagner's recommendation was not approved by the ordnance department, as, upon inquiry, it was found that a very large reserve supply had already been procured, and among the rest 10,500 sets from the Messrs. Wilstach & Co. themselves, during the months of November and December, and delivered by them at the Frankford arsenal.

As it is thus evident that the intention of the government in first ordering the three thousand reserve supply had been filled, even to a greater extent than first intended, with the knowledge of and by purchase from the Messrs. Wilstach & Co., it must be considered that the government regarded the original orders to Messrs. Wilstach & Co. either as substantially complied with by them, or forfeited for non-compliance, and for this reason gave its subsequent orders to the full extent of its wants.

The commission, therefore, decide that the Messrs. Wilstach & Co. have no claim whatever under order of July 1, 1861, forfeited by their own neglect to use the despatch required, and therefore direct that no delivery be accepted under that order.

We are, sir, &c.,

J. HOLT,
ROBERT DALE OWEN,
Commissioners, &c.
P. V. HAGNER,
Major of Ordnance, Assistant to Commission.

General J. W. RIPLEY,
Chief of Ordnance.

CASE No. 58.

J. TREASY.

ORDNANCE OFFICE,
Washington, April 26, 1862.

I have the honor to enclose herewith the following accounts, viz:

One of James Treasy, assigned to Joshua F. Speed, Louisville, for $1,087 50.

Three of Albert Jewett, of Kansas City, viz: One for $103 47; one for $2 10, and one for $2 95—total $108 52.

All the articles included in the above accounts were obtained without the knowledge of this office, but appear to have been received for the service of the United States, and the prices charged reasonable. I respectfully recommend that the accounts be submitted to the commission on contracts, &c., for their action thereon.

Respectfully, your obedient servant,
JAS. W. RIPLEY, *Brigadier General.*

Hon. E. M. STANTON,
Secretary of War.

Before commission, April 29, 1862.

Copy of certificate indorsed upon the account of James Treasy for $1,087 50, dated October 21:

I certify, on honor, that this account is correct and just; that the articles named were necessary for the public service, and were bought by order of Brigadier General Robert Anderson, the order being written, and a copy of which was furnished Colonel Thomas Swords, assistant quartermaster general, in the matter of the claim of D. Ricketts against the United States for horses furnished the second Kentucky cavalry. The said saddles were received, and are now in use by said cavalry.

LOVELL H. ROUSSEAU,
Brigadier General 4th Brigade.

COMMISSION ON ORDNANCE AND ORDNANCE STORES,
Washington, April 29, 1862.

GENERAL: The commission have the honor to report as follows:

CASE No. 58.—JAMES TREASY, Louisville, Kentucky.

Claim for amount of vouchers, dated October 21, 1861.   Bill for fifty cavalry saddles, equipments complete, purchased under order of General Robert Anderson, commanding the department.

Referred to the commission by special directions of the Secretary of War, the purchase of the ordnance stores not having been made as required by law.

The commission find that, as appears by certificate of Brigadier General Rousseau, these equipments were bought by order of General Robert Anderson for the second Kentucky cavalry; that they were received, and were in use by that regiment, and Elias Thomasson, acting assistant quartermaster of the regiment, signs the receipt for the whole number charged on the account.

The items of the account are not stated with sufficient explicitness, but that "all the equipments were complete." The price charged is therefore not unreasonable.

The commission direct that the account be examined and audited as usual, without objection on account of informality.

We are, sir, very respectfully, your obedient servants,
J. HOLT,
ROBERT DALE OWEN,
Commissioners, &c.

Brigadier General J. W. RIPLEY,
Chief of Ordnance.

CASE No. 59.

HEWETT & RANDALL.

COMMISSION ON ORDNANCE AND ORDNANCE STORES,
Washington, April 29, 1862.

GENERAL: The commission have the honor to report as follows:

CASE No. 59.—HEWETT & RANDALL, New York.

Order by direction of Assistant Secretary of War, dated September 26, 1861; No. 28 of printed list. Referred by general directions of Secretary of War.   To deliver at the United States arsenal, Governor's island, New York, within four months from date, 10,000 long Enfield rifles; the first 5,000 to be delivered October 26, and 500 or upwards per week thereafter. Price to be $20, including appendages.

Three dollars are to be forfeited on each rifle short of the number herein contracted for in the time named for delivery.

Accepted, on the terms and conditions and under the penalties named, September 25, 1861.

The commission find that no deliveries have been made under this order, and no explanation of the failure has been made to the commission. The prescribed forfeiture of three dollars per rifle short of the promised number is thus applicable to the whole order.

As the commission have decided that orders of the above character are not such as do bind the government, they consider them equally impotent as affects the other party, and therefore decide that the order be revoked and annulled, and that no arms be received under it, and that the amount of forfeiture be remitted.

Respectfully, your obedient servants,

J. HOLT,
ROBERT DALE OWEN,
Commissioners, &c.
P. V. HAGNER,
Major of Ordnance.

Brigadier General J. W. RIPLEY,
Chief of Ordnance.

CASE No. 60.

A. JEWETT.

COMMISSION ON ORDNANCE AND ORDNANCE STORES,
Washington, April 29, 1862.

GENERAL: The commission have the honor to report as follows:

CASE No. 60.—ALBERT JEWETT, of Kansas City.

Claim for payment of three accounts for ordnance stores: 1st. September 1, 1861, $103 47; 2d. January 21, 1862, $2 10; 3d. January 22, 1862, $2 95.

No. 1 certified to by A. A. Q. M. Thomas S. Case.

Nos. 2 and 3 approved by Captain Jno. J. Boyd, 4th regiment Kansas volunteers, commanding post.

Referred by special directions of the Secretary of War.

The commission find that these accounts are not in proper form; that the ordnance stores were purchased without the approval prescribed by law and regulations, and no evidence is furnished that they were received and are accounted for as government property.

It appears, however, that the articles purchased were such as were necessary for every military post or command for current use; that they are in reasonable quantities and charged at suitable prices, and (as far as appears) were ordered or approved by the post commandant or quartermaster.

The commission direct that they be examined and audited, without objection on account of informality.

We are, sir, very respectfully, your obedient servants,

J. HOLT,
ROBERT DALE OWEN,
Commissioners, &c.
P. V. HAGNER,
Major of Ordnance, Assistant to Commission.

General J. W. RIPLEY,
Chief of Ordnance.

CASE No. 61.

HOWLAND & ASPINWALL.

NEW YORK, *February* 4, 1862.

SIR: In compliance with your order, No. 11, we beg to state that in July last we effected a sale to the ordnance department of 17,000 Enfield rifles, then

Ex. Doc. 72——16

under the control of our friends, at $19 per gun, with bayonet, &c., complete, in bond, deliverable at the rate of 2,000 per month, conditioned only upon their safe arrival and non-interference by the British government.

We hand you herewith copies of our letters of July 16, (marked A,) of July 20, (marked B,) of August 29, (marked C,) and of General Ripley's letter, of August 31, (marked D,) relative to the same.

We beg further to inform you that under this sale we had delivered 8,000 rifles, when further deliveries were stopped by the Queen's proclamation prohibiting the export of munitions of war. After which we inquired, under date of January 13, 1862, (copy of letter enclosed, marked E,) whether the department preferred to consider the deliveries as at an end, or to receive the arms when they could be delivered. On receipt of the reply that the department desired to receive them as soon as possible, we at once communicated the same to our friends in England; and as we are now informed that the prohibition has been removed, we are in hopes to receive the arms without much further delay.

We are, sir, respectfully your obedient servants.

HOWLAND & ASPINWALL.

Hon. E. M. STANTON,
  Secretary of War, Washington.

Eight thousand were delivered when the Queen's proclamation stopped further shipments. The prohibition has been removed, and they expect the arms without much further delay.

No copy of this letter was communicated to the commission prior to July 1, 1862.

P. V. HAGNER,
  Major of Ordnance.

WASHINGTON, July 16, 1861.

SIR: Referring to the verbal agreement made with our Mr. Aspinwall this morning, we now desire to state the same in writing, which, if in conformity with your understanding, please confirm.

Having the control, through parties in England, of 17,000 stand of Enfield rifles, of the best English manufacture, and all having the stamp of English inspection, we offer the same to you, deliverable in New York city, in bond, at the rate of not less than 2,000 per month, and at a price of $19 per gun, in bond, with the usual allowance for the cases. These guns are subject to your inspection upon arrival, and are to be equal to the best English rifle of this manufacture, and are all to be provided with proper barrel stoppers and cap covers, and are sold for cash.

It is further understood that as the parties controlling the contract for delivery in England, from our late advices, have been trying to dispose of the same in England, in the event of their having done so upon receipt of advices of our conditional sale to you, we in that case are held harmless from being called upon to make the deliveries, inasmuch as the sale to you is made with the distinct reservation of the contract not having been sold when the advices of said sale by us reach England. Our advices of conditional sale to you go forward by the "Persia," to sail to-morrow, and we will at once communicate to you the response we may receive.

Believing the above to be in accordance with the verbal agreement,

  We remain your obedient servants,

HOWLAND & ASPINWALL.

Brigadier General J. W. RIPLEY,
  Chief of Ordnance Department, Washington, D. C.

NEW YORK, *July* 20, 1861.

SIR: Referring to the agreement entered into with you by our Mr. Aspinwall when in Washington, we beg now to confirm the sale to the United States government of a contract for 17,000 Enfield rifles, under the conditions as named in our respects of 15th instant; and as we are acting for other parties, we enclose, for your perusal, extracts of our letters of instructions per "Persia," 16th instant, and per "Arago," of this date, with reference to the shipment of these arms. We have had the pleasure of a visit from Captain Whiteley, who has received your instructions to inspect these guns, and have arranged with him to keep him advised of their arrival.

We remain, sir, your obedient servants,

HOWLAND & ASPINWALL.

General RIPLEY,
Chief of Ordnance Department, &c., Washington, D. C.

NEW YORK, *August* 29, 1861.

SIR: Referring to our respects of the 20th ultimo, we have now the pleasure to inform you that our letters per Persia and Arago arrived in England while a negotiation was pending there for a sale of the rifle contract, but our orders, being positive, were in time to prevent it; and letters received to-day inform us that the rifles will come forward without delay. We shall therefore be able to deliver the 17,000 as fast as received, and nothing but interference on the part of the British government or disaster at sea will, in our opinion, interfere with the delivery of 2,000 a month. To avoid the risk of privateers we have recommended a preference be given in shipping to English vessels and to steamers to insure despatch and regularity, although the rate of freight is higher. We can begin on Monday the delivery of 1,000 rifles now on hand, unless you should prefer to wait until the 2,000 for September can be delivered in one parcel.

We have 1,200 rifles on board the steamer "Etna," which has put back disabled.

We shall be glad to hear from you at your early convenience, and to receive authority to withdraw from public warehouse the lots now on hand.

We remain, your obedient servants,

HOWLAND & ASPINWALL.

Brigadier General RIPLEY,
Chief of Ordnance Department, &c., Washington, D. C.

ORDNANCE OFFICE,
Washington, August 31, 1861.

GENTLEMEN: Your letter of the 29th instant is received. Please deliver the Enfield rifles to Major R. H. K. Whiteley, at the arsenal on Governor's island, New York, as fast as possible.

Major P. V. Hagner has general authority to give certificates for the admission, free of duty and charges, of all arms imported or purchased by him in bond, for government use exclusively. I have written to Major Hagner respecting the 17,000 Enfield rifles purchased of you. Please see him at Fifth Avenue Hotel in relation to certificates of admission of the same, duty free.

Respectfully, your obedient servant,

J. W. RIPLEY,
Brigadier General.

Messrs. HOWLAND & ASPINWALL, *New York, N. Y.*

NEW YORK, *January* 13, 1862.

DEAR SIR: We are requested by the parties for whom we have been delivering to the United States government the Enfield rifles sold to you at $19, as detailed in our letters of 20th July and 29th August, to ascertain what are your wishes as to the 9,000 which they have been prevented shipping by the Queen's proclamation.

The original number was 17,000, of which we have received and delivered with entire regularity 8,000 guns, notwithstanding the competition and advance in prices, until one of the contingencies alluded to in our letter of 29th August has prevented their continuing to export the arms; and they now desire us to ascertain whether you prefer to cancel the contract, or whether you desire to receive the remaining 9,000 as soon as the prohibition of export from England is removed and the monthly delivery can be resumed, or possibly the whole 9,000 can be delivered at once if this delay extend beyond two or three months.

If you can conveniently reply to-morrow, you will enable us to write by the steamer Asia leaving this port on Wednesday.

We remain, dear sir, your obedient servants,

HOWLAND & ASPINWALL.

Brigadier General J W. RIPLEY,
Chief of Ordnance Department, Washington, D. C.

No copy of this letter was communicated to the commission prior to July 1, 1862.

P. V. HAGNER,
Major of Ordnance.

ORDNANCE OFFICE,
Washington, January 27, 1862.

GENTLEMEN: In answer to your inquiry concerning the delivery of the remainder of the Enfield rifles you were to furnish, I have to state that they should be delivered as soon as possible to the extent of the residue not yet delivered, and on the same terms with those already supplied on your orders for the seventeen thousand.

Respectfully, &c.,

JAS. W. RIPLEY,
Brigadier General.

Messrs. HOWLAND & ASPINWALL, *New York.*

No copy of this letter was communicated to the commission prior to July 1, 1862.

P. V. HAGNER,
Major of Ordnance.

NEW YORK, *March* 26, 1862.

DEAR SIR: We beg leave to refer to our respects of the 13th January and to your reply of the 27th of the same month, referring to the Enfield rifles which yet remained to be delivered of the 17,000 sold you, as detailed in our letter of 29th August last.

We have now the pleasure to inform you of the arrival, last night, of the steamship Edinburg at this port, having on board the remainder of the arms, and we feel great satisfaction in having been able to furnish the entire quantity within the time originally contemplated, notwithstanding the temporary interference through the Queen's proclamation.

Instead of 9,000 Enfields, the shipment per Edinburg consists of 9,200 Enfields. You will please inform us whether you prefer to receive the extra 200 Enfields on the same terms as the others.

As on former occasions, we gave due notice to Major Hagner and Major Whiteley.

Remaining, dear sir, yours, very respectfully,

HOWLAND & ASPINWALL.

Brigadier General JAS. W. RIPLEY,
Chief of Ordnance, Washington, D. C.

P. S.—We find Major Hagner is absent in Washington, and have telegraphed you for instructions.
H. & A.

Refer to their letter of 13th January, report arrival of remainder of Enfield rifles and 200 over, and ask instructions on the subject.

ORDNANCE OFFICE, *March* 27, 1862.

Respectfully submitted to the Secretary of War, with the recommendation that the 9,000 Enfield rifles due under the order to Messrs. Howland & Aspinwall, and also the 200 over, be received.

JAS. W. RIPLEY,
Brigadier General.

MARCH 27, 1862.

Approved.

EDWIN M. STANTON,
Secretary of War.

No. 54 FOURTH STREET, *March* 26, 1862.

SIR: The steamer Edinburg arrived last evening, brings the remainder of the Enfield rifles to be delivered under our sale to the United States government. We will be obliged if you will request the collector to deliver us the permit, that we may hand it over to the quartermaster.

Respectfully, your obedient servants,

HOWLAND & ASPINWALL.

Major P. V. HAGNER.

Memorandum per steamer Edinburg.

(A) 1—460.—Four hundred and sixty cases Enfield rifles. Howland & Aspinwall.

Wish order on collector for free permit for 460 cases Enfields, balance of their sale to United States government.

ORDNANCE OFFICE, *New York, March* 26, 1862.

Respectfully referred to the chief of ordnance. I do not feel authorized to request the permit desired unless the special authority of the Secretary of War is obtained for the reception of these arms. Deliveries under the Messrs. Howland & Aspinwall's order have heretofore been made to Major R. H. K. Whiteley.

S. CRISPEN,
Captain of Ordnance.

This letter was not communicated to the commission prior to July 1, 1862.

P. V. HAGNER,
Major of Ordnance.

CASE No. 61.

COMMISSION ON ORDNANCE AND ORDNANCE STORES,
Washington, April 22, 1862.

GENERAL : The commission have the honor to report as follows :

CASE No. 61.—HOWLAND & ASPINWALL, New York.

Accepted propo-
sal by the chief of
ordnance, dated
July 16, 1861. No
5, printed list. Pro-
posal conditional
upon the non sale
of the guns in Eng-
land before receipt
of news of accept-
ance.

To deliver in New York, in bond, 17,000 Enfield rifles of the best English manufacture, at the rate of not less than 2,000 per month, and at a price of $19 per gun, with the usual allowance for the cases.

The proposal states that it is made with the distinct reservation that in the event of the sale of the lot of guns offered in England, before the receipt there of the news of this conditional sale, the parties are to be held harmless from being called upon to make deliveries.

The commission find that the parties commenced delivering September 15, 1861, and up to January 6 had delivered 8,000. These deliveries are all that show that the conditional sale was acknowledged as far as made, they have been paid for by the government at the rate stated in the proposal.

Supposing the proposal binding upon the parties, the deliveries, as promised, should have amounted to 12,000 arms prior to January 16, and the whole number of 17,000 should now be in New York.

As the value of the arms to the government depended chiefly upon the exact fulfilment of the promised early deliveries, and as these have not been made as stipulated, but the wants of the government have been supplied from other sources, the commission decide that the receipt of arms in future from these parties, as from others, should depend solely upon the wants of the service, and that only so many of them as may be needed be purchased as in open market, at such prices as may be just and proper, compared with those paid for like arms in New York at the time of purchase.

We are, sir, very respectfully, &c.,

J. HOLT,
ROBERT DALE OWEN,
Commissioners, &c.
P. V. HAGNER,
Major of Ordnance, Assistant to Commission.

Brig. General J. W. RIPLEY,
Chief of Ordnance.

———

COMMISSION ON ORDNANCE AND ORDNANCE STORES,
Washington, July 8, 1862.

GENERAL : Subsequent information having rendered it necessary for the commission to modify their report in Case No. 61—Howland & Aspinwall—it has been amended by the addition of the following postscript.

Very respectfully, your obedient servant,

J. HOLT, *Commissioner.*

Brig. General J. W. RIPLEY,
Chief of Ordnance.

P. S.—Case 61—Howland & Aspinwall, New York, July 1, 1862. The commission withdraw and cancel their decision in the above case, dated April 22, 1862, as it appears that several of the papers explaining it, among them the letter of the chief of ordnance, dated January 27, 1862, were not transmitted to the commission, and are now known to them for the first time.

By said letter of the chief of ordnance, the arms then due were ordered to be furnished as soon as possible, on the same terms as those already supplied, thus virtually renewing the order; and by recommendation of the chief of ordnance, approved by the Secretary of War, March 27, 1862, these arms were ordered to be received without the knowledge of the commission. No action in the case was therefore required of the commission at the date of their decision.

CASE No. 62.

JOHN RICE.

PHILADELPHIA, *November* 27, 1861.

SIR: Your letter of the 21st instant is received.

I hereby accept the order to furnish the United States government 36,000 muskets, on the terms and conditions named therein.

Please send the order at your earliest convenience, and oblige

Your obedient servant,

JOHN RICE.

Brigadier General J. W. RIPLEY,
Washington, D. C.

ORDNANCE OFFICE,
Washington, November 21, 1861.

SIR: By direction of the Secretary of War, I offer you an order for thirty-six thousand (36,000) muskets, of the Springfield pattern, on the following terms and conditions, viz: These arms are to be furnished with the regular appendages, and are to be, in all respects, identical with the standard rifle-musket now made at the United States armory at Springfield, Massachusetts, and are to interchange with it, and with each other in all their parts; they are to be subject to inspection, by United States inspectors, in the same manner that the Springfield arms are inspected; and none are to be received and paid for but such as pass inspection and are approved by the United States inspectors. These thirty-six thousand (36,000) arms and appendages are to be delivered as follows, viz: Three thousand (3,000) in February, 1862, and three thousand in each and every month thereafter, until the whole 36,000 are delivered. In case of any failure to make the deliveries to the extent and within the terms before specified, all the obligations of the United States to receive or pay for any muskets, then deliverable under this order, shall be cancelled and become null and void. Payments are to be made, in such funds as the Treasury Department may provide, on certificates of inspection and receipt by the United States inspectors, at the rate of twenty dollars ($20) for each arm, including appendages. All these arms and appendages are to be packed by you in boxes of the regular pattern, with twenty muskets and appendages in each box, for which a fair price, to be determined by the United States inspectors, will be allowed.

Please signify, in writing, your acceptance or non-acceptance of this order on the terms and conditions herein stated.

Respectfully, your obedient servant,

JAS. W. RIPLEY,
Brigadier General.

Mr. JOHN RICE,
Philadelphia, Pennsylvania.

The Secretary directs that the time for delivery may be extended for the first lot to May 1, 1862, and the balance of deliveries extended in same manner.

THOMAS A. SCOTT,
Assistant Secretary.

Gen. RIPLEY, *Chief of Ordnance.*

ORDNANCE OFFICE,
Washington, November 28, 1861.

SIR: In answer to your letter of the 27th instant, I have to state that my letter to you, dated November 21, 1861, the receipt of which you acknowledge, is an order for 36,000 muskets to be delivered by you on the terms and conditions therein stated and accepted by you.

Respectfully, your obedient servant,

JAS. W. RIPLEY, *Brigadier General.*

JOHN RICE, Esq., *southwest corner of 9th and Sansom streets,*
Philadelphia, Pennsylvania.

ORDNANCE OFFICE,
Washington, December 14, 1861.

SIR: By direction of the Secretary of War, indorsed on the letter to you from this office of the 21st November, 1861, I have to inform you that the times for the delivery of the 36,000 muskets and appendages therein ordered are extended as follows, viz: Three thousand are to be delivered on or before the 1st of May, 1862, and three thousand in each and every month thereafter until the whole 36,000 are delivered. All the other terms and conditions of the order dated November 21, 1861, remain unchanged.

Respectfully, your obedient servant,

JAS. W. RIPLEY, *Brigadier General.*

Mr. JOHN RICE,
Philadelphia, Pennsylvania.

PHILADELPHIA, *January 30, 1862.*

SIR: On the 21st of November, 1861, I received an order from your department for the manufacturing of thirty-six thousand (36,000) muskets; and on the 14th of December, 1861, owing to the disappointment and difficulty in getting machinery, I had the time for the delivery extended to the 1st of May, 1862.

I have made contracts for the different parts of the musket with the best mechanics in the country, and have advanced a large amount of money for the purchase of stocks and machinery, and look forward with confidence to the faithful fulfilment of the order.

It would facilitate my operations if I had permission to deliver the whole or a part of the muskets at the United States armory in Springfield, Massachusetts, and respectfully ask permission for the same, if consistent with the regulations of the department.

I remain your obedient servant,

JOHN RICE.

Hon. EDWIN M. STANTON,
Secretary of War, Washington, D. C.

WAR DEPARTMENT,
Washington, D. C., February 20, 1862.

SIR: Your letter of the 30th ultimo has been received.

I am directed by the Secretary of War to inquire whether you are a manufacturer of fire-arms? Where your workshop is? How many guns you have completed? What materials for the manufacture of arms you have on hand; and where and in whose possession they are? How many men you have employed in manufacturing arms; and how long you have had them so employed: and where? A reply to these inquiries is necessary, preliminary to answering your inquiries in regard to inspection, &c.

Very respectfully, your obedient servant,

P. H. WATSON,
Assistant Secretary of War.

JOHN RICE, Esq.,
Philadelphia, Pennsylvania.

PHILADELPHIA, *March* 1, 1862.

SIR: Your favor of the 20th ultimo has been received, and but for my absence from home would have been sooner answered.

In reply to the questions in your letter, I will state that, until I obtained the order from the ordnance department, I had never been engaged in the manufacturing of fire-arms.

I have, for the last twenty-five years, been very extensively engaged in mechanical pursuits, and felt confident, when I obtained the order, of being able to fulfil it.

I have organized in this city an extensive establishment for the manufacturing of the locks, and have advanced large sums for the purchase of machinery, material, and the payment of workmen wages for the same. It is now in successful operation, having a large number of the different parts of the lock in progress, and will be ready to make deliveries in a very few days.

I have also contracted with the well-known and responsible firm of Alfred Jenks & Son, also of this city, for the stockings and stock lips of the muskets, and have advanced the necessary funds for the purchase of the rough stocks, which are now in the kiln room seasoning.

They are turning out finished stocks daily, and will deliver mine whenever I am ready to receive them.

I have also contracted with the following persons for the remaining parts of the arms: W. Mason, of Taunton, Massachusetts, one of the most extensive machinists in the country, for the barrels, who reports he will be ready in time for the delivery; H. B. Bigelow, of New Haven, for but plates and trigger guard; Humphreyville Manufacturing Company, of Seymour, Connecticut, for bayonets; Coleman & Bro., of Philadelphia, Pennsylvania, for ramrods; Nicholson & Co., of Providence, Rhode Island, for sights and bands; Cole & Brother, of Springfield, for cones; S. Stow, Manufacturing Company, of Connecticut, for band springs; C. B. North, of Springfield, for washers; Dwight & Co., of Bridgeport, Connecticut, for appendages.

The above are responsible parties, and I have every assurance they will deliver according to their contracts.

I have also propositions for assembling, and am only waiting to know where the muskets are to be delivered, so as to decide.

If you need any further information upon the subject, let me know, and it will be cheerfully furnished by your obedient servant,

JOHN RICE.

Hon. P. H. WATSON,
Assistant Secretary of War, Washington, D. C.

PHILADELPHIA, *April* 3, 1862.

SIRS: This will be handed to you by Mr. W. Mason, of Taunton, Massachusetts, the party with whom I have contracted for gun barrels, under my order for furnishing arms to the United States government. He will, no doubt, give you all the information intended to be furnished by myself in relation to the delivery of said gun barrels.

I will also state, for your further information, that I have sent several locks, of which you have a sample, left with you a few days since, to the Springfield armory, and found them perfect in every particular, interchanging in every part; a certificate to that effect will be furnished to you as soon as received.

The ramrods also have been compared in the same manner, and require but very slight alteration in the gauges to make them perfect.

I intend sending the different parts as soon as they are ready, and have them all compared in the same manner, and hope, by so doing, to have no difficulty in the inspection when ready for delivery.

Believing you will give a full consideration as to the difficulties attending the manufacturing of these arms, the delay and disappointment in getting machinery, also the heavy outlay made by the parties with whom I have contracted, I respectfully solicit any further inquiry or investigation as to the manner the order was obtained, holding myself ready at any time to answer cheerfully and promptly any question in relation to the subject.

My sole object in taking this order was, first, that the government required them; that, in the manufacturing of them, it would furnish employment to machinery and labor that would have been otherwise idle, which would be much preferable to the importation of foreign arms of an inferior character.

I am still of the opinion that the government need them, and, from my experience in mechanical pursuits, have no doubt, with your kind consideration for the delay occasioned by circumstances beyond any human foresight or control, that I will fill the order to your entire satisfaction.

I expect to come to Washington early next week, and will then see you again upon the subject.

Hoping to receive a favorable consideration of my case,

I remain your obedient servant,

JOHN RICE.

The COMMISSIONERS ON CONTRACTS FOR ARMS, &c.

PHILADELPHIA, *March* 1, 1862.

SIR: Your favor of the 20th ultimo has been received, and but for my absence from home would have been sooner answered.

In reply to the questions in your letter, I will state that, until I obtained the order from the ordnance department, I have never been engaged in the manufacturing of fire-arms. I have for the last twenty-five years been very extensively engaged in mechanical pursuits, and felt confident, when I obtained the order, of being able to fulfil it.

I have organized in this city an extensive establishment for the manufacturing of the locks, and have advanced large sums for the purchase of machinery, material, and the payment of workmen wages for the same. It is now in successful operation, having a large number of the different parts of the locks in progress, and will be ready to make deliveries in a very few days.

I have also contracted with the well known and responsible firm of Alfred Jenks & Son, also of this city, for the stocking and stock lips of the muskets, and have advanced the necessary funds for the purchase of the rough stocks, which are now in the kiln room seasoning. They are turning out finished stocks daily, and will deliver mine whenever I am ready to receive them.

I have also contracted with the following persons for the remaining parts of the arm:

Mr. Mason, of Taunton, Massachusetts, one of the most extensive machinists in the country, for the barrels, who reports that he will be ready in time for the delivery, and with H. W. Bigelow, of New Haven, Connecticut, for butt plates and trigger guards.

Humphreyville Manufacturing Company, Seymour, for bayonets.

Coleman & Brother, of Philadelphia, for ramrods.

Nicholson & Co., of Providence, Rhode Island, for rear sights and bands.

Cole & Brother, of Springfield, Massachusetts, for cones.

S. Stow, Manufacturing Company, Connecticut, for band springs.

C. B. North, of Springfield, Massachusetts, for washers.

Dwight & Co., of Bridgeport, Connecticut, for appendages.

The above are responsible parties, and I have every assurance they will deliver according to their contracts.

I have also propositions for assembling, and am only waiting to know where the muskets are to be delivered so as to decide.

If you need any further information on the subject let me know, and it will be cheerfully furnished by your obedient servant,

JOHN RICE.

Hon. P. H. WATSON,
 Assistant Secretary of War, Washington, D. C.

PHILADELPHIA, *April* 8, 1862.

GENTLEMEN : On my return from Washington I found a despatch from Mr. Washburn, stating that he had succeeded in getting iron of the proper quality for the gun barrels, and that all anxiety on that point was now removed.

I will visit his and all the places of parties with whom I have contracted. Before doing so, it will be necessary to have the contracts with these parties with me.

The contracts were all left at your office. Will you please send them to me, and on my return I will bring them with me, and also a full and reliable report upon the whole subject.

Very truly, your obedient servant,

JOHN RICE.

Hon. JOSEPH HOLT and ROBERT DALE OWEN.

Before commission, April 1, 1862.

Extracts from letters of sub-contractors to John Rice, informing him of the condition of the parts of his gun :

1. Samuel Norris, Springfield: "The appendages will be promptly delivered according to contract."

2. S. Stow, Manufacturing Company: "We hope to make our first delivery in April 12 to 15, (of gun springs.) Hoping they will be in time."

3. Cole & Brother, Pawtucket, (cones :) "Will be able to furnish 6,000 by the first of April."

4. C. H. Williams & Co. furnish a sample lock to Mr. Rice, "and trust it will convince him of their ability to fill his contract."

5. Humphreyville Manufacturing Company : "We can make 600 bayonets per day. In April, and after, there will be no failure to deliver your bayonets as called for in our contract."

6. W. F. Nicholson & Co., Providence, who furnish Mr. Rice with sights, bands, and swivels : "We see nothing to hinder prompt deliveries."

7. E. P. Coleman, Philadelphia: "Now ready to deliver ramrods."

8. H. B. Bigelow, New Haven, (guard plates, bows, triggers, butt plates, &c.:) "Will be delivered as per agreement."

P. V. HAGNER,
Major of Ordnance, Assistant to Commission.

Before commission, April 7, 1862.

Mr. John Rice states :

Knowing the difficulties I will meet in complying with my contract, I was about to ask for some compromise or adjustment by which I could be made whole. I do not think Mr. Washburn can get his iron. If I could get the government to take the prices I have contracted for, I would be glad to be relieved. I can ascertain my liabilities in ten days. I can get my stocks. I have 1,500 already finished from Jenks. Esler & Brother, of Philadelphia, make my locks, and I can get them as fast as I want them. I have not yet fixed on a place for assembling my guns. I wanted permission to deliver my guns at Springfield, and if it is obtained, I will so deliver them.

CASE No. 62.

COMMISSION ON ORDNANCE AND ORDNANCE STORES,
Washington, May 2, 1862.

GENERAL : The commission have the honor to report as follows :

CASE No. 62.—JOHN RICE, Philadelphia.

Order for 36,000 rifled muskets, Springfield pattern, by direction of the Assistant Secretary of War, dated November 21, 1861. Time extended December 14, 1861. No. 46, printed list, page 13. Referred by special directions of Secretary of War.

To furnish 36,000 muskets, of Springfield pattern, with the regular appendages, to be identical in all respects with the standard rifle musket, to interchange with it and with each other in all the parts. Price $20 for each arm which passes inspection and is approved.

Delivery at first prescribed to be made at the rate of 3,000 per month, commencing in February, 1862. As altered December 14, 3,000 are to be delivered on or before the 1st May, and 3,000 monthly thereafter. In case of any failure to make the deliveries to the extent and within the times specified, all the obligations of the United States to receive or pay for any muskets then deliverable under this order shall be cancelled and become null and void.

The commission find that the stipulation as to the first delivery has not been fulfilled, and that Mr. Rice is now convinced that a first delivery cannot be made before July. Under the express provision, therefore, of the order it is forfeited, and there remains no obligation on the part of the government to receive any arms under it.

Mr. Rice has appeared before the commission, and states that he undertook the order in good faith, and with the known intention to engage various manufacturers to supply the several parts of the arm, not to manufacture himself; that he expected only to devote his efforts to hurry forward and systematically arrange the work; that he commenced at the earliest moment after receiving his order, and has zealously applied himself to his task, securing reliable establishments for doing the work in different parts of the country; that on account of the small quantity of proper machinery in existence, the urgent, immediate demand for such machinery and for competent workmen created by the many orders for like arms, unforeseen difficulties accumulated against him, and, although he has already advanced large sums and has in hand much of the work required for the first delivery, the barrel work is so much behind that he cannot promise it before July; that unless he is permitted to furnish some portion of the number ordered, the pecuniary loss to him will be excessive.

The commission find that the terms of the proposal made by Mr. Rice, (at the time a contractor for stone-work at the Capitol and a carpenter by trade,) requiring early monthly deliveries of large quantities of interchangeable arms—a work of extreme difficulty even to the most experienced armorers—precluded any other mode of fulfilment than that adopted by him; that, having undertaken the duty, Mr. Rice has displayed energy and industry in his endeavors to carry it out, and that his failure to do so is chiefly due to the difficulties of the task and to his inexperience in such work; that the present delay is owing to the non-success of the barrel maker in making barrels of a suitable quality by the methods he has been pursuing; this, it is said, has been corrected, and a lot of good barrels has been recently sent to the finisher.

Under the above circumstances the commission consider that, as the interests of the government require the earliest possible deliveries of this class of arms; as by the terms of the order a quality of gun equal to the Springfield, and none of inferior quality, is to be received; as the mode of manufacture pursued will increase the cost of the accepted arm to the contractor, so that he cannot be expected to furnish to the government at as low a price as a *bona fide* manufacturer; and as expenses have been incurred by him up to this time from which the government will derive benefit by earlier deliveries than can be promised by manufacturers now starting, it is fair to Mr. Rice to confirm in part the order given him at the price stated therein, although assured that it is higher than the arms of this pattern can now be made for. They therefore direct that a number not exceeding in all 25,000 muskets, with the proper appendages, be accepted under the terms and conditions of the order dated November 20, 1861, provided that a first delivery of at least 2,000 be ready prior to July 1, 1862, and that monthly thereafter at least 2,000 per month be delivered until the number ordered is completed.

We are, sir, very respectfully, your obedient servants,

J. HOLT,
ROBERT DALE OWEN,
Commissioners, &c.

P. V. HAGNER,
Major of Ordnance, Assistant to Commission.

Brigadier General J. W. RIPLEY,
Chief of Ordnance.

For additional condition required in this case, see paper No. 5, case 13.

CASE No. 63.

MANSFIELD, LAMB & Co., Smithfield, Rhode Island.

10,000 *cavalry sabres, August* 28, 1861.

WASHINGTON, *August* 27, 1861.

The manufacturing company of Mansfield, Lamb & Co., of Smithfield, Rhode Island, are desirous of contracting with the government of the United States for twenty thousand cavalry sabres, at the regular contract price paid by the government.

For the company,

ANSEL HOLMAN.

I am well acquainted with the firm making the above application, and know them to be responsible, loyal, and reliable.

J. F. SIMMONS.

The sabres offered can be delivered as follows: 1,000 in the month of October next, 2,000 in the month of November, and 3,000 per month thereafter, until the same are completed.

ANSEL HOLMAN.

[Indorsements.]

(A.)

WAR DEPARTMENT, August 27, 1861.

Respectfully referred to General Ripley, chief of ordnance.

THOMAS A. SCOTT,
Assistant Secretary.

(B.)

Received, Ordnance office, August 27, 1862, War Department, 1159, book 31.

(C.)

WAR DEPARTMENT, August 28, 1861.

The Secretary of War desires you to contract with the parties for ten thousand sabres, (10,000.)

THOMAS A. SCOTT,
Assistant Secretary.

General J. W. RIPLEY,

    Chief of Ordnance.

ORDNANCE OFFICE,
Washington, August 28, 1861.

SIR: By direction of the Secretary of War, I offer to the manufacturing company of Mansfield, Lamb & Co., of Smithfield, Rhode Island, an order for ten thousand light cavalry sabres, on the following terms and conditions:

These sabres are to be of the regular United States pattern, and are to be subject to inspection and proof by such as this department may designate for the purpose. They are to be delivered at the company's works at Smithfield, Rhode Island, as follows, viz: 1,000 in the month of October next, 2,000 in the month of November next, and 3,000 per month thereafter, until the whole 10,000 are delivered. In case of failure to deliver in or within the times before specified, the government is to be under no obligation to take the sabres, but may or may not do so, at its option. Payments will be made in such funds as the Treasury Department may provide, on certificate of inspection and receipt of the United States inspector, at the rate of eight dollars and a half ($8 50) per sabre.

Respectfully, &c.,.

JAMES W. RIPLEY,
Brigadier General.

Mr. ANSEL HOLMAN, <i>Washington, D. C.</i>

WASHINGTON, D. C., *August* 28, 1861.

DEAR SIR: I herewith acknowledge the receipt of your letter of the 28th instant ordering ten thousand sabres, and accept the conditions and terms therein contained.

Respectfully, your obedient servant,

ANSEL HOLMAN.

General RIPLEY, *Ordnance Department.*

COMMISSION ON ORDNANCE AND ORDNANCE STORES,
Washington, May 3, 1862.

GENERAL: The commission have the honor to report as follows:

CASE NO. 63.—MANSFIELD, LAMB & CO.

Order by direction of the Secretary of War, dated August 28, 1861. No. 7 of printed list, page 211, Ex. Doc. No. 67. To deliver at the company's works, Smithfield, Rhode Island, 10,000 light cavalry sabres of regular United States pattern, and subject to inspection, at $8 50 per sabre. "In case of failure to deliver in or within the times specified, the government is to be under no obligation to take the sabres, but may or may not do so, at its option." Times specified—"1,000 in October, 2,000 in November, and 3,000 per month thereafter."

The commission find that the company failed to deliver any sabres until January, and then only 1,500, in February only 1,500, and in March 1,000, prior to the 8th of that month, making in all 4,000 delivered, instead of the whole number which was due before that date. Under the terms of the order, therefore, as provided in case of such failure, there remains no obligation upon the government to receive more of these sabres.

Mr. Mansfield has appeared before the commission, and stated that 2,000 sabres made under this order have passed inspection by the United States inspector since the report made by the ordnance department to the commission, and are now boxed ready for delivery; that these are made after the sample furnished him, with malleable iron bands, mouth-pieces and tips, and cannot therefore be offered under the recent advertisement of the ordnance department, which excludes in future all malleable iron, and that he will offer them at seven dollars each.

The commission decide that these two thousand sabres be accepted at the price of seven dollars each, allowing, in addition for the boxes, at the rate of $1 50 for each thirty sabres, if of prescribed quality.

Respectfully, &c.,

J. HOLT,
ROBERT DALE OWEN,
Commissioners.
P. V. HAGNER,
Major of Ordnance, Assistant to Commission.

Brig. Gen. J. W. RIPLEY,
Chief of Ordnance.

CASE No. 64.

UNION ARMS COMPANY.

R. H. Gallaher submits copies of contracts to furnish—
  25,000 B. L. rifles.
  20,000 Springfield guns.
  20,000   "
  20,000   "

OFFICE OF THE UNION FIRE-ARMS COMPANY,
New York, February 4, 1862.

SIR: In obedience to your official order of the 29th of January, 1862, to contractors for arms, &c., I transmit copies of four several orders for the manufacture of Springfield rifle muskets and Marsh's breech and muzzle-loading rifles. The first issued to me individually, the second to John S. Gallaher & Co., the third to S. W. Marsh, patentee, and the fourth to me as agent of the Union Fire-arms Company, of Newark, New Jersey; which several contracts were, on the 3d day of January, by request of those concerned, and by direction of your predecessor, transferred to the "Union Fire-arms Company of New York," of which company I am a member and agent. The said copies are accompanied by a copy of the transfer, or order of transfer, the original being on file in the Ordnance office.

I may be allowed to remark that the first order to myself was sought at the instance, and with a view to their employment, of many of the experienced workmen of the Harper's Ferry armory, who were banished and thrown out of their business and homes by the rebels. Of these workmen (represented for many years by my father in both branches of the Virginia legislature) I have engaged the experts, and many who were trained from boyhood in the manufacture of arms of the best quality. In this connexion, and with a view of showing what guarantee I have for the proper manufacture of the arms I have agreed to furnish the government, I beg leave to call your attention to the accompanying letter from Mr. Dan'l J. Young, who had for many years charge of the government rifle factory at Harper's Ferry, and who is also to have the principal charge of the armory of the Union Fire-arms Company.

To show my identification with the manufacture of fire-arms, I will state that as early as May, 1861, I had become possessed, for the period of ten years, of the patent for S. W. Marsh's breech-loading rifle, and after much time, labor, and expense, demonstrated its value to the satisfaction of experts in arms and of the most skilful officers of the government, all of whom pronounced it a most valuable arm and worthy of adoption in the army. The President of the United States himself examined the rifle, and was so well satisfied of its merits, after a careful scrutiny, that he gave an order to the Ordnance bureau to have it thoroughly tested, which was done by a skilful officer, who gave a most satisfactory report, and upon which report the War Department gave the contract to the inventor, Mr. Marsh, at my instance, for the manufacture of 25,000.

The government found it necessary (because of the insufficiency of the supply of that valuable arm) to give the orders referred to herein for a large number of the Springfield rifle muskets. To render certain a fulfilment of the several orders, I have enlisted the aid of large capitalists in the city of New York and elsewhere, and completed the organization of my Fire-arms Company for a period of ten years, and have been incessantly occupied in the preliminary measures for the establishment of a permanent armory. I have abandoned every other pursuit, incurred very heavy responsibilities myself, and induced many others to make heavy outlays on my account, and an annulment of these contracts would result in my utter ruin, whilst it would also inflict a loss upon others upon whom I had impressed repeated assurances that the government would not disturb my progress in fulfilling the orders it had given me. I, myself, have incurred liabilities to the extent of more than a *hundred thousand dollars*, which I could not have incurred but for my strong reliance upon the good faith of the government, and of my own conscientious conviction of being able to carry out successfully what I had undertaken.

Feeling assured that the government absolutely needed not only all the guns it had ordered from me, but from other contractors, I have never allowed myself to suppose, for a moment, that any of my contracts were to be disturbed. The most casual observer could not but have been impressed with the belief that the efficiency of our army has been greatly retarded for the want of good arms to take the place of the large number of inferior foreign guns the War Department has had to resort to in order to arm the soldiers at all. Reports from the arsenals where repairs are going on will show that thousands of arms are monthly returned for renovation, many of which are entirely worthless, which, of course, render new supplies of good weapons constantly necessary.

The determination of my company to make deliveries of arms within the times specified in the last order of transfer has induced us to call in the aid of extensive manufacturing establishments, one of which furnishes the Springfield armory with a most important limb of the gun. If, therefore, our deliveries be not made within the times specified, it will be because capital, energy, and skill are not competent to the task.

It is but justice to your predecessor to state that, before making the orders above recited, he required the strongest evidence that each and all of them could be faithfully carried out.

I have the honor to be your obedient servant,

R. H. GALLAHER.

Hon. E. M. STANTON, *Secretary of War.*

Copy of contract to H. R. Gallaher for 20,000 *Springfield guns—transferred by consent of War Department to Union Fire-arms Company of New York.*

ORDNANCE OFFICE, *Washington, August* 31, 1861.

SIR: By direction of the Secretary of War I offer you an order for twenty thousand, No. 1, Springfield guns, with appendages and angular bayonets, complete, on the following terms and conditions, viz: These guns are to be, in all respects, identical with the standard rifle musket now made at the United States armory at Springfield, Massachusetts, and are to interchange with it and with each other in all their parts; they are to be subject to inspection by United States inspectors in the same manner that the Springfield arms are inspected, and none are to be received and paid for but such as pass inspection and are approved by the United States inspectors. These 20,000 muskets and appendages are to be delivered as follows: Two thousand (2,000) in sixty days (60 days;) four thousand (4,000) in ninety days (90 days;) five thousand (5,000) in four months (4 months;) four thousand (4,000) in six month (6 months;) each delivery from this date. In case of a failure to deliver in or within the time before specified the government is to be under no obligation to take the arms, but may or may not do so at its option. Payments are to be made, in such funds as the Treasury Department may provide, on certificates of inspection and receipt by the United States inspector, at the rate of twenty dollars ($20) for each arm, including appendages. All these arms and appendages are to be packed by you in boxes of the regular pattern, with twenty muskets and appendages in each box, for which a fair price, to be determined by the United States inspector, will be allowed. Please signify, in writing, your acceptance or non-acceptance of this offer on the terms and conditions herein stated. In case of acceptance an order will be given, on your application, to furnish you with a pattern musket and appendages from the Springfield armory.

Respectfully, your obedient servant,

J. W. RIPLEY, *Brigadier General.*

R. H. GALLAHER, Esq., *New York.*

The times within which the guns ordered in this contract were to be delivered being entirely too short, the Ordnance office, under date of November 26, 1861, extended said times of deliveries, and the contract was subsequently, by the consent of the War Department, as will be seen by accompanying papers, assigned to the Union Fire-arms Company of New York, of which the original contractor is president.

Copy of contract to Jno. S. Gallaher & Co., for 20,000 Springfield guns—transferred by consent of War Department, January 3, 1862, to the Union Fire-arms Company of New York.

ORDNANCE OFFICE, *Washington, October* 11, 1862.

GENTLEMEN: By direction of the Secretary of War, I offer you an order for twenty thousand rifle muskets and appendages, on the following terms and conditions, viz: These arms are to be, in all respects, identical with the standard rifle musket now made at the United States armory at Springfield, Massachusetts, and are to interchange with it and with each other in all their parts. They are to be subject to inspection by United States inspectors, in the same manner that the Springfield arms are inspected, and none are to be received and paid for but such as pass inspection and are approved by the United States inspectors. These 20,000 muskets and appendages are to be delivered as follows, viz: One thousand in five months from the date of this order, and not less than three thousand eight hundred (3,800) per month thereafter, so that the whole 20,000 shall be delivered in or within ten months from this date. In case of failure to make any one of the deliveries, in or within the times before specified, the government is to have authority to revoke and annul this order immediately. Payments are to be made, in such funds as the Treasury Department may provide, on the certificate of inspection and receipt by the United States inspectors, at the rate of twenty dollars ($20) for each arm, including appendages. All of these arms and appendages are to be packed by you in boxes of the regular pattern, with twenty muskets and appendages in each box, for which a price, to be determined by the United States inspectors, will be allowed. Please signify your acceptance or non-acceptance of this offer on the terms and conditions herein specified.

Respectfully, your obedient servant,

JAMES W. RIPLEY, *Brigadier General.*

Messrs. JNO. S. GALLAHER & Co., *Washington, D. C.*

The foregoing contract was transferred and assigned, by the consent of the War Department, January 3, 1862, to "The Union Fire-arms Company," of New York city. See copy of official consent to said transfer accompanying this—original being on file in Ordnance bureau.

Copy of contracts to S. W. Marsh for 25,000 of his breech and muzzle loading rifle—transferred to the Union Fire-arms Company of New York, by consent of the War Department, January 3, 1862.

ORDNANCE OFFICE, *Washington, October* 14, 1862.

SIR: In obedience to the order of the Secretary of War, received to-day, I offer you an order for twenty-five thousand Springfield rifle muskets, with bayonets and appendages complete, and with your breech-loading arrangement attached, on the following terms and conditions, viz : These arms are to be in all respects, except the breech-loading attachment, identical with the standard rifle musket made at the United States armory at Springfield, Massachusetts, and are to interchange with it in all their parts, except those pertaining to the breech-loading attachments, and with each other in all their parts. They are to be subject to inspection, by United States inspectors, in the same manner that the Springfield arms are inspected, and none are to be received and paid for but such as pass inspection and are approved of by the United States inspectors. These 25,000 muskets, with bayonets and appendages complete, are to be delivered as follows, viz : Three thousand to be delivered in four months from this date, and not less than four thousand per month to be delivered monthly thereafter, until the whole 25,000 are delivered. In case of failure to make any one of the deliveries in, or within the times before specified, the government is to have authority to revoke and annul this order immediately.

Payments are to be made, from time to time, as the arms and appendages are delivered, in such funds as the Treasury Department may provide, on certificates of inspection and receipt by the United States inspectors, at the rate of twenty-nine dollars and seventy-five cents ($29 75) for each arm, including the bayonets and appendages complete. All these arms, bayonets, and appendages are to be packed by you in boxes of the regular pattern, with twenty muskets, bayonets and appendages in each box, for which a fair price, to be determined by the United States inspectors, will be allowed.

Please signify, in writing, your acceptance or non-acceptance of this offer on the terms and conditions herein specified.

Respectfully, your obedient servant,

JAS. W. RIPLEY, *Brigadier General.*

S. WILMER MARSH, Esq., *Washington, D. C.*

ORDNANCE OFFICE,
Washington, November 12, 1861.

SIR: By direction of the Secretary of War, the order to you for 25,000 rifle muskets, dated Ordnance office, Washington, October 14, 1861, is modified as follows, viz: Strike out in the order of the 14th of October, 1861, the words: "In case of failure to make any one of the deliveries in or within the times before specified, the government is to have authority to revoke and annul this order immediately," and insert in their stead the following provision, viz: "On any failure to make deliveries to the extent and within the time above specified, all the obligations of the United States to receive and pay for any muskets then deliverable under this order shall be cancelled and become null and void." All the other terms and conditions of your order of the 14th of October, 8161, are to remain in force as therein stated.

Respectfully, your obedient servant,

WM. MAYNADIER,
Lieutenant Colonel of Ordnance.

S. WILMER MARSH, Esq.,
Washington, D. C.

Copy of contract to Union Fire-arms Company for 25,000 Springfield muskets.

ORDNANCE OFFICE,
Washington, November 14, 1861.

SIR: Your letter to the Secretary of War, dated the 13th instant, offering to furnish, as agent for the Union Arms Company of Newark, New Jersey, twenty-five thousand Springfield muskets, has been referred to this office, with instructions from him to authorize the parties to manufacture the guns and fixtures as stated. In obedience to those instructions from the Secretary of War, I authorize the Union Arms Company of Newark, New Jersey, to manufacture and deliver the twenty-five thousand arms and appendages, on the following terms and conditions, viz: These arms are to be, in all respects, identical with the standard rifle musket now made at the United States armory, Springfield, Massachusetts, and are to interchange with it and with each other in all their parts. They are to be subject to inspection by the United States inspectors, in the same manner that the Springfield arms are inspected, and none are to be received and paid for but such as pass inspection and are approved by the United States inspectors. These 25,000 arms and appendages are to be delivered as follows, viz: Not less than two thousand (2,000) per month after five months (5 months) from this date, until the whole 25,000 are delivered. In case of a failure to make deliveries to the extent and within the times above specified, all the obligations of the United States to receive or pay for any muskets then deliverable under this order shall be cancelled and become null and void. Payments are to be made, in such funds as the Treasury Department may provide, on certificates of inspection and receipt by the United States inspectors, at the rate of twenty dollars ($20) each, including appendages. All these arms and appendages are to be packed by you in boxes of the regular pattern, with twenty muskets and appendages in each box, for which a fair price, to be determined by the United States inspectors, will be allowed.

Please signify, in writing, your acceptance or non-acceptance of this order, on the terms and conditions herein specified.

Respectfully, your obedient servant,

WM. MAYNADIER,
Lieutenant Colonel of Ordnance.

R. H. GALLAHER, Esq.,
Agent Union Fire-arms Company, Washington, D. C.

This contract was, by consent of the War Department, January 3, 1862, transferred to the Union Fire-arms Company of New York, as will be seen by accompanying paper, original of which is on file at Ordnance office.

Assent of War Department to the assignment to the Union Fire-arms Company of four contracts; also, an extension of the times of delivery on said contracts.

WAR DEPARTMENT,
Washington, January 3, 1862.

It having been satisfactorily shown that the Union Fire-arms Company of New York, consisting of Edward Robinson, James McKay, Linus Scudder, Enoch Chamberlain, John Hays, Robert H. Gallaher, and others, have the necessary capital and facilities for manufacturing guns for the government, it is agreed by the War Department that a transfer or assignment of the following orders may be made to said company, subject to the conditions and stipulations imposed by the chief of ordnance upon contractors whose deliveries commence in July, 1862, except as to date of first deliveries:

First. An order to Robert H. Gallaher, dated August 31, 1861, for twenty thousand Springfield rifle muskets.

Second. An order to John S. Gallaher & Co., dated 11th October, 1861, for twenty thousand Springfield rifle muskets.

Third. An order to S. Wilmer Marsh, dated 14th October, 1861, for twenty-five thousand patent breech and muzzle loading rifles.

Fourth. An order to R. H. Gallaher, agent of the Union Arms Company of Newark, New Jersey, dated November 14, 1861, for twenty-five thousand Springfield rifle muskets.

It is further agreed and directed that the time for the first delivery of arms under each of the foregoing orders shall be during the month of May, 1862, and the subsequent deliveries to be made monthly thereafter in the proportions stated in said orders, with the privilege of earlier deliveries, if prepared to do so.

SIMON CAMERON,
Secretary of War.

Copy furnished to Ro. H. Gallaher.

JAS. W. RIPLEY,
Brigadier General.

ORDNANCE OFFICE, *January 3, 1862.*

WASHINGTON, D. C., *March 31, 1862.*

GENTLEMEN : The undersigned, for himself and his associates of " The Union Fire-arms Company of New York," is present in conformity with an order of the Secretary of War of the 13th instant, under which your commission has been convened.

By the records of the Ordnance bureau it will be found that under an order of the Secretary of War of January 3, 1862, four certain contracts or orders for Springfield rifled muskets and Marsh breech and muzzle loading rifles were consolidated into one order for ninety thousand guns to the Union Fire-arms Company. A copy of said order of January 3 will be found herewith, marked "A," and will also be found in congressional document published by order of the House of Representatives in relation to contracts for arms, &c.

Prior to the consolidation of the contracts as aforesaid, I, as the original contractor for supplying the guns named in the several contracts transferred to Union Arms Company, had made extensive preparations for the manufacture of the arms, by ordering large amounts of gun machinery, engaging workmen, and securing suitable buildings for the regular establishment of an armory. I had also induced numbers of persons who possessed partial facilities for manufacturing different limbs of the Springfield musket to enlarge those facilities, by a heavy expenditure of money, in order that I might be aided in the prompt and faithful deliveries of my guns to government. In my desire to carry out in good faith all I had undertaken to perform, and relying implicitly upon the government to do nothing to retard my efforts, I involved myself and others to a very large amount, by assuming obligations I could not have assumed but for the faith I had in my own ability to fulfil what I had stipulated to do. After becoming involved myself, and involving others, I found it necessary to enlist a large amount of *cash* working capital beyond what was necessarily to be employed by the parties engaged to make different limbs of the guns, and in order to secure this capital I resolved to organize the Union Fire-arms Company, under the laws of the State of New York, and sell stock in said company to the amount of *two hundred and forty thousand dollars.* This amount of stock I had *actually sold,* and so informed the War Department, when I appeared before it on the 2d and 3d of January asking that all my contracts might be consolidated into one, with authority to transfer to the Union Fire-arms Company. The department, being satisfied with the facilities I possessed for the manufacture of guns so much needed by our army, readily consented, granted me the authority asked for, and accordingly issued the order of January 3, 1862, under which I and my associates, under the name of the Union Fire-arms Company, are now faithfully endeavoring to deliver guns to the government.

Shortly after my return to New York from Washington, with my authority to transfer contracts to my company, and after we were progressing in a most satisfactory manner with all our arrangements for pushing the manufacture of our arms vigorously, my capitalists to whom I had sold the *two hundred and forty thousand dollars* cash stock, became alarmed at rumors that all gun contracts given out by the War Department were likely to be annulled, and they required me to again visit Washington and get a confirmation of said contracts by the present Secretary of War, who had just been called into power. This I declined to do, because I deemed it uncalled for, and I accordingly gave the subscribers to the stock notice that unless they paid up their subscriptions I should at once proceed to make other arrangements for the money they had agreed to furnish, as I had no more time to lose in waiting upon them. Upon the very heels of the alarm which had been created on the minds of my original subscribers, and just when I was about satisfactorily consummating new arrangements for other capitalists to take the place of those who had become unnecessarily alarmed, the present Secretary of War issued his order, addressed to contractors for arms, of January 29, 1862, requiring all contractors to send in, within fifteen days, copies of their contracts, accompanied by statement of progress in the execution of said contracts. I hailed that order with pleasure and responded to it as promptly as possible, by coming on to Washington in person and presenting my statement, to which I beg leave to refer your commission, as said statement is doubtless within your control.

Knowing how *sensitive* capital always is, but finding it particularly so in regard to contracts with government, since the many embarrassments which were continually springing up about contracts during this war, I felt that the order of the 29th January would put at rest all fears as to my contracts, and that after complying with said order, by handing my statement, I should have no further "drawbacks." After handing in copies of contracts, with my statement, I had the most positive assurance, *more than once*, from the department, that my contracts were not to be disturbed, but these assurances, whilst they were satisfactory to me individually were not satisfactory to my capitalists and the many other parties who had agreed to aid in the prosecution of my work, and I thereupon informed the Assistant Secretary of War, Hon. J. Tucker, of the difficulty I labored under and of the ruinous delay I was being subjected to unless I could get the assurances referred to *in writing;* whereupon he informed me that my wishes should be complied with and the written assurances forwarded as soon as the health of the Hon. Secretary of War could himself give his attention to the matter. Thus have matters rested, and my progress in the manufacture of guns been greatly retarded for the want of the promised *written assurance,* and I have now presented myself as the representative of the Union Fire-arms Company for a prompt decision on our case, as the whole subject matter relating to ordnance contracts has been referred to you.

I beg leave to accompany this statement with letters and other testimony as to the ability of the Union Fire-arms Company to carry out faithfully all it has undertaken, and in confirmation of my assertion that we are prepared to make guns equal to any other concern, I would respectfully invite any ordnance officers now in New York, or who might be selected by you for the purpose, to visit the premises and examine into the facilities we claim to control for the prosecution of our work.

In conclusion and in justification of myself, I solemnly aver that no officer of the War Department, or any other department, has had any interest in my procuring the contracts to which this statement refers, nor have I promised, in *any form,* to compensate a government official, directly or indirectly, for any service connected with the fulfilment or procurement of said contracts.

All of which is respectfully submitted.

R. H. GALLAHER.
President Union Fire-arms Company.

Hon. JOSEPH HOLT and ROBERT DALE OWEN,
Commissioners.

WASHINGTON, D. C., *April* 2, 1862.

GENTLEMEN: The subjoined statement was prepared about the middle of January last, upon the appearance of the first report that the honorable Secretary of War intended to *annul* the orders for fire arms given by his predecessor. It was withheld under the impression that the faith of the government could not be broken, as all the usages of the departments were against the idea that one Secretary would review and revoke the acts of his predecessor, unless upon a clear case of fraud on the part of the person or persons with whom the contract was made.

Upon the appearance of the order of the 29th January, requiring contractors to report progress, the undersigned made a statement on behalf of himself and associates, within the time prescribed, and had a verbal assurance, *with the promise of a written one*, from one of the Assistant Secretaries (the Hon. Secretary himself being sick) that a prompt response, to the effect that my contracts were not to be disturbed, would be furnished me, in order that my capitalists, who had become alarmed, should not desert me.

It is now nearly two months since the report was made, and although the time lost has been a serious impediment, the undersigned has continued, under very great disadvantage, his preparations, believing implicitly in the faith of the government. He felt that the order of January 3 removed all existing difficulties, and that it would be held sacred, as Secretary Cameron, before authorizing the *consolidation* of the contracts, had satisfied himself of the competency of " The Union Fire-arms Company," as attested by an honorable gentleman who had given his attention to the subject during two weeks sojourn in the city of New York.

The statement is now submitted as a part of my argument, already addressed to your commission, showing why the contracts to " The Union Fire-arms Company " should not be disturbed.

Very respectfully, your obedient servant,

R. H. GALLAHER.

Hon. JOSEPH HOLT and ROBERT D. OWEN,
Commissioners.

P. S.—Since the preparation of accompanying argument the fact has come to my knowledge that the English government has on hand in its arsenals at this time *one million* stand of small arms, (Enfield rifles,) besides those in private armories, and have made arrangements for the manufacture of a *million* more. Why should the United States have less ?

Ro. H. G.

Argument of R. H. Gallaher, showing why the contracts of Union Fire-arms Company should not be disturbed.

NEW YORK, *January* 16, 1862.

SIR: By referring to the files of the Ordnance bureau you will see that there are now existing contracts with the " Union Arms Company" for the manufacture of 65,000 Springfield muskets and 25,000 additional ones, with the attachment of Marsh's breech-loader. Before these were made I had obtained, by assignment from Mr. Marsh, the exclusive right to manufacture his breech-loader for ten years, and was engaged in the organization of the aforesaid company, so as to provide for the extensive manufacture of arms.

Having subsequently completed the organization, these contracts were, on the 3d instant, by direction of your predecessor, united in said company—having been originally made with individuals, myself included—as they now stand.

In the various steps taken between the date of the original contract, the 31st of August last, and the present time, money and labor have been employed in the faithful execution of the contracts.

Arms for the government must, necessarily, be manufactured in private establishments, to some extent, upon borrowed capital. The formation of the "Union Arms Company" was designed to avoid this as much as possible, by combining in the association a large amount of individual wealth.

Nevertheless, as the government advances nothing for guns until they are delivered, companies are sometimes under the necessity of making loans. This, under ordinary circumstances, there is no difficulty in doing, but for the fact that a recent debate in the House of Representatives has created an impression that these and other similar contracts are to be annulled, has had the effect to create uneasiness. All these contracts were entered into in perfectly good faith, and, notwithstanding what has been said, the undersigned can claim for himself and all others concerned in said "Union Arms Company" that their motives in making them have not been exclusively sordid.

At the commencement of the rebellion the *government was almost entirely without arms.* The armory at Harper's Ferry had been destroyed, and it owned but a single establishment—that at Springfield—which could not manufacture a sufficient number for the public service. Soldiers enlisted all over the country with far greater rapidity than they could be furnished with arms, and many instances occurred where *whole regiments were drilled without a single gun.* The country was clamorous for guns, and your predecessor was abused with as much fierceness *for not having them* as he is now for having merely provided for what is *assumed* to be too large a number. It is altogether probable that this clamor against him would have been greater than it is if he failed to make the amplest possible provision for a future supply. Patriotism, therefore, no less than a sense of duty, demanded of him that he should make as many contracts as possible for guns to be supplied as soon as they could be manufactured. And this duty became the more urgent as the difficulty of procuring them from Europe was increasing in consequence of the policy of the British government towards this country. And the undersigned has the right to claim, on behalf of himself and other private contractors, that they, too, were influenced by motives of patriotism as well as interest when they, at great expense, not only erected new establishments, but provided new machinery for old ones, when it was perfectly evident that this was the only *possible* way to furnish the government with the guns necessary to put down the rebellion, and place itself in a proper state of defence for the future. A moment's reflection will satisfy any unprejudiced mind that private individuals could not, in justice to themselves, make these changes in their business unless they had *contracts beforehand,* upon which they could rely for indemnity—and of this your predecessor, as a business man, must have been fully conscious. Hence, as the government had an insufficient supply, and did not possess the means to furnish enough, and could not procure them in Europe, contracts with individuals or companies became absolutely necessary.

Your predecessor would have been derelict in duty if he had failed to invite, by a liberal course of policy, the investment of private capital in the manufacture of guns. How else could they be procured? No private owners of a manufacturing establishment will engage in making *Springfield* muskets unless they can have a reliable assurance, *before doing so,* that they will be taken *by the government,* for everybody knows that there is no *private* sale for guns of this description. So it may be asserted as true that your predecessor, in making these contracts, adopted the only possible mode of providing for the existing necessity of the country and of answering the public expectation.

But it is *now* said that the number of guns contracted for is too great, because the *rebellion will be put down before they are delivered.* There may now be more convincing evidence that this desirable result is nearer at hand than existed when these contracts were made; but if there is, it cannot justly be made to *relate back* to the time of making the orders, so as to *authorize their cancellation*. Your predecessor, in making them, acted upon the state of things before his mind at the time, not as it might be subsequently; and I need not say to you that *subsequent events cannot vitiate a contract*. But suppose the rebellion is not put down in the time supposed—what then? Is it not manifest that if it is not, and these contracts are cancelled, and private manufactories are closed to the government, and the government has to rely solely upon its Springfield armory, that in a few months it may be unable to supply with guns an army of sufficient magnitude to defend itself? Suppose such a state of things should by possibility occur, would not those who had caused these contracts to be destroyed, be held in the same estimation as a late Secretary of War is held, who took another mode of depriving the country of guns, by putting them in the hands of the rebels? Those who say the country will not need these arms assume to look into the future and to know just what our relations with the rebel States and with Europe will be, three, six, nine, or twelve months hence. Have we any assurance that Great Britain may not, during the next spring, recognize the independence of the southern confederacy, and make the attempt to break our blockade of southern ports; or that the state of public feeling, both in that country and our own, may not drive the two countries into a war upon some other question; or that Great Britain, France, and Spain, or Spain alone, may not attempt to replant European authority in Mexico and Central America, and combine to drive our commerce from the Gulf? In other words, is the future so certain and secure that a great nation like ours can safely rely for its supply of arms and munitions of war *upon a single establishment of its own*, its hopes of erecting one or more others, when local jealousies shall be so accommodated that it can be decided where to put them? Now, in view of all these considerations, may it not be at least feared, that if these contracts are annulled, and it is thereby rendered impossible that private enterprise shall be employed in the future manufacture of arms, Great Britain and possibly other European governments, may take advantage of that very fact to begin war upon us? There could be no better time, so far as they are concerned, for doing so—for they would have no difficulty in seeing that, although we might justly boast of *our twenty millions of population*, we would be compelled to flee before their armies for the *want of arms* to defend ourselves. Suppose fifty thousand troops were to march now from Canada to the interior of New England or New York; how could they be resisted without guns? And are we to continue in this unprepared condition for the future is the question to be decided. How was it with Tennessee and Kentucky? Your honorable predecessor, in view not only of the necessity of being prepared for any possible state of things growing out of the rebellion, but looking both to our *existing and future relations with Europe*, adopted a far-reaching and necessary policy, when he recommended the reorganization, arming, and disciplining the militia of the States. The making of these contracts was, doubtless, a part of that policy, whether so designed by him or not, and if they shall be annulled the most effective means of its adoption will be destroyed.

The undersigned has deemed himself justified in respectfully presenting to your consideration these views in regard to the *public aspects* of the proposition to annul these contracts. He has but a few words to say as it regards the private interests of himself and his associates.

We have expended both time and money in executing our contracts. We have put our company in such a condition that we entertain no doubt of our ability to deliver all the guns we have contracted for, within the time specified; and if we should fail to do so, it may be observed that the government pays nothing.

If there had been any fraud in the contracts represented by the undersigned, he would concede that they should fall. Fraud does and ought to vitiate everything it touches. He avers that there is no ground for a suspicion, either on his own or the part of any officer of the government, so far as he knows or believes. The government *needed guns.* The whole country understood it. There was no other means of getting them than by private contract; and these contracts were applied for. They were awarded and entered into without the slightest suspicion that any objection could arise to them in any quarter.

Hence the undersigned respectfully asks that you will be pleased to give official notice of the fact that the contracts with the "Union Arms Company" shall not be annulled by you, unless you should be directed by Congress to do so. You will perceive the necessity of this from the fact that the credit of their company has been materially injured by the clamors already referred to. It will enable them to proceed without further delay or apprehension in the manufacture of the guns ordered.

I have the honor to be, very respectfully, your obedient servant,

RO. H. GALLAHER,
Agent of Union Arms Company.

Hon. E. M. STANTON,
   Secretary of War, Washington, D. C.

John S. Gallaher & Co., transfer of contract to the Union Fire-arms Company.

WASHINGTON, *April* 17, 1862.

It having been agreed by the War Department, under order of January 3, 1862, that an order to the undersigned from said department, dated October 11, 1861, for twenty thousand Springfield rifle muskets, may be transferred to and carried out by the "Union Fire-arms Company of New York," of which Ro. H. Gallaher is president, we hereby transfer to said company all our right and title to said order for the purposes specified in said order of 3d January, 1862.

JOHN S. GALLAHER & CO.

Witness : GEO. W. PALMER.

S. W. Marsh's transfer of contract to Union Fire-arms Company.

WASHINGTON, D. C., *April* 17, 1862.,

It having been agreed by the War Department, under order of January 3, 1862, that a contract to me from said department, dated October 14, 1861, for twenty-five thousand of my breech and muzzle loading rifle musket, may be transferred to and carried out by the Union Fire-arms Company of New York, of which Ro. H. Gallaher is president, I hereby transfer to said Union Fire-arms Company all my right and title to said contract for the purposes specified in said order of department of January, 1862.

S. WILMER MARSH.

Witness: W. A. SHANNON.

R. H. Gallaher, assignment of contract to Union Fire-arms Company.

WASHINGTON, D. C., *April* 17, 1862.

It having been agreed by the War Department, under order of January 3, 1862, that a contract to me from said department, dated August 31, 1861, for twenty thousand Springfield rifle muskets, and also a contract to me, as agent of the Union Arms Company of Newark, New Jersey, for twenty-five thousand Springfield rifle muskets, bearing date November 14, 1861, may be transferred to and carried out by the Union Arms Company of New York city, to which I am president, I hereby, in my individual capacity, and as agent, transfer all my rights and titles in and to the foregoing contracts to said Union Fire-arms Company of New York city for the purposes specified in the order of War Department of January 3, 1862.

RO. H. GALLAHER.

Witness: J. WISE.

WASHINGTON, D. C., *April* 18, 1862.

GENTLEMEN: As it seems to be the settled policy of your board to curtail the number of guns ordered by the late Secretary of War, and as the Union Fire-arms Company of New York is willing, under existing circumstances, to bear its portion of the reduction deemed advisable, the said company hereby relinquishes to the United States all claim to manufacture forty thousand of the sixty-five thousand Springfield rifle muskets under contracts, which were, on the 17th of April, 1862, transferred, by consent of the War Department, under order of January 3, 1862, to the said Union Fire-arms Company of New York, of which I am president.

In thus relinquishing the right to manufacture and deliver to the government the forty thousand guns aforesaid, it is with the distinct understanding that all the rights and privileges pertaining to the manufacture of the remaining twenty-five thousand Springfield rifle muskets, and the twenty-five thousand breech and muzzle loading rifle muskets, (Marsh's patent,) are to be undisturbed.

As considerable time has been lost by the action of the government, (as will appear from my statement on file.) it is but just that the said company should have a *reasonable* extension of time on its first deliveries of guns. I therefore ask that it may be allowed the whole month of July for its first deliveries, thus putting it upon a footing with other contractors, such as Messrs. Whitney, Sarson, and Roberts & Co.

Further delay in the prosecution of these contracts being fatal to the interests of the company, it is earnestly but respectfully urged that your commission act at once on this case.

I have the honor to be, very respectfully, your obedient servant,

RO. H. GALLAHER,
President Union Fire-arms Company of New York.

Hon. JOS. HOLT and ROBERT DALE OWEN,
Commissioners.

Authorized proposal of R. H. Gallaher, president of Union Arms Company; accepted by commission after modification by George Mattingly, authorized agent of R. H. Gallaher.

COMMISSION ON ORDNANCE AND ORDNANCE STORES,
Washington, D. C., April 23, 1862.

The "Union Fire-arms Company of New York" having relinquished a portion of the contract awarded it by an order of War Department of date January 3, 1862, and the commission being satisfied with the terms of said relinquishment, it is agreed and recommended that the order be confirmed for the delivery of twenty-five thousand Springfield rifle muskets, and twelve thousand five hundred of the breech and muzzle loading rifle muskets, (Marsh's patent,) upon the terms and stipulations therein contained, with the following modifications as to deliveries and price, viz: That said company deliver one thousand of said arms during the month of July, 1862; one thousand during the month of August, 1862; and six thousand monthly thereafter, till the whole fifty thousand guns shall have been delivered, with the privilege of more rapid deliveries if prepared to make them. In consideration of the extension of time herein granted upon all of the deliveries aforesaid, the price of the breech and muzzle loading muskets is to be twenty-seven dollars and seventy-five cents each, instead of twenty-nine dollars and seventy-five cents, as in original contract. The interlineation of the words twelve thousand five hundred, and erasure of the words twenty-five thousand in the within, is made by me as the authorized agent of R. H. Gallaher.

GEO. MATTINGLY.

WASHINGTON, D. C., *April* 23. 1862.

The foregoing arrangement is, under all the circumstances, hereby accepted by the Union Fire-arms Company of New York.

R. H. GALLAHER,
President Union Fire-arms Co. of New York.

Witness : GEO. MATTINGLY.

WASHINGTON, D. C., *April* 19, 1862.

The Union Fire-arms Company of New York having relinquished a portion of its contracts, and the commission being satisfied with the terms of said relinquishment, it is hereby agreed that the said Union Fire-arms Company may have the whole of the month of July, 1862, to make its first deliveries of guns, upon the terms and conditions of a similar contract to Eli Whitney, issued by the Ordnance office December 24, 1862, that is to say : That said Union Fire-arms Company is hereby required to deliver, during the month of July, 1862, one thousand guns; during the month of August, 1862, one thousand guns; and four thousand guns monthly thereafter till all the guns under the contract shall have been delivered, to the number of fifty thousand arms.

The privilege of earlier deliveries, and to a greater extent per month, is also hereby given to the said Union Fire-arms Company, but not to exceed fifty thousand arms in all.

WASHINGTON, D. C., *April* 19, 1862.

GENTLEMEN : I take the liberty of filing the foregoing outline of such an agreement *as to extension of time for first deliveries, &c.,* as would meet my wishes, in view of the relinquishment of certain part of the contracts of Union Fire-arms Company.

Very respectfully,

R. H. GALLAHER,
President of Union Fire-arms Company.

Hon. JOSEPH HOLT and ROBT. D. OWEN,
Commissioners.

R. A. Douglas's letter to R. H. Gallaher, about the 500 *tons of iron contracted for by R. H. Gallaher.*

NEW YORK, *February* 21, 1862.

DEAR SIR : I have now made the necessary alterations in my rolling-mill for turning out the different sizes of iron required for your work, and shall be ready, at short notice, to commence work for you, as per contract of 500 tons, which I hope you will soon be ready to commence ordering.

Your most obedient, &c.,

R. A. DOUGLAS.

R. H. GALLAHER, Esq.,
Union Fire-arms Company.

Letter from Trenton Iron Works to R. H. Gallaher, agreeing to roll all his gun-barrels.

OFFICE TRENTON IRON COMPANY,
Trenton, March 22, 1862.

DEAR SIR : Yours of the 21st instant, asking the price at which we would sell you barrels, you furnishing the stock, is received. If you will let me know the shape in which you would furnish the iron, I will then be able to fix on a price, but not otherwise, as I have no idea of the work necessary to be done to get the iron you mention into proper shape.

Very respectfully,

CHAS. HEWITT.

R. H. GALLAHER, Esq.,
No. 37 Nassau street, New York.

Letter from Collins & Co., the great tool and sword manufacturers, showing their readiness to supply R. H. Gallaher with all the bayonets for his contracts.

NEW YORK, *March 24, 1862.*

DEAR SIR : In reply to your inquiry, we would advise you that we are now forging the triangular bayonet, having some 3,000 to 5,000 ready for finishing up.

Our facilities will probably equal a delivery of about two hundred daily. We have a contract for two or three thousand, but as yet no large contract that would interfere with our supplying you with any quantity equal to your wants. In the rough state we could deliver larger quantities, our facilities for forging being greater than for finishing up.

Respectfully, yours,

COLLINS & CO.

R. H. GALLAHER, Esq.

Important letter from Daniel J. Young, who had charge of the United States rifle factory, Harper's Ferry.

[Mr. Young expresses the conviction that R. H. Gallaher will be better prepared to manufacture guns than any other contractor.]

WASHINGTON CITY, *December 1, 1861.*

DEAR SIR : Your letter of November 28 was received yesterday at noon. It afforded me great pleasure to learn that your arrangements for organizing and commencing operations at Newark, New Jersey, were progressing to your satisfaction. I think you have been very fortunate, indeed, in finding so large a stock of machinery, tools, and fixtures adapted to the manufacture of arms ; and, in my opinion, with competent men at the head of the various departments, success will be the inevitable result.

You desire me to send you a list of names who are suitable persons to be employed on the various branches of work. This I hope you will please excuse me from doing at present, not knowing what connexion I will hold to the establishment, or in what capacity the company or yourself may intend me to act, and for what compensation, &c. I can get, at the shortest notice, a sufficient number of the best armorers to go to work on the various parts of the gun, as well as tools, &c., but think I would not be justifiable in doing so until there is an understanding between you and myself.

If you can get the necessary amount of capital invested, and the management of the work placed in good hands, you will certainly succeed far better than any other man that ever received a contract from the government. This may seem extravagant; but my reason for believing so is based upon the fact that the men will have nothing to learn, and understand precisely what the government inspection will require.

If you should see proper to confer the honor of getting up the tools, machines, &c., upon me, I will require the assistance of Mr. Alexander Grillet, who is competent and willing to come with you. After the work gets in full operation, I would suggest that Mr. Butt act as principal inspector, and see that the work comes up to the model in all respects.

Very respectfully, your obedient servant,

DANIEL J. YOUNG.

R. H. GALLAHER, Esq.

List of machinery ready to be turned over by the Manhattan Arms Company to the Union Fire-arms Company.

6 milling machines.
3 four-spindle drill-presses, finished.
1 rifling machine.
2 edging machines, finished.
4 screw and cone machines, ready April 1, 1862.
6 plain engine lathes, ready April 20, 1862.
4 drilling lathes, ready April 20, 1862.
4 small drill presses, ready April 15, 1862.
3 edging machines, ready April 20, 1862.
3 screw and cone machines, ready May 1, 1862.
1 quadruple drop, (4 drops,) ready May 1, 1862.
1 polishing machine, (6 spindles,) finished.
1 machine for tapping lock-plate, finished.
1 tumbler milling machine, finished.
4 cone lathes for drilling cones, ready April 20, 1862.
30 milling machines, ready May 1, 1862.

NEW YORK, *March* 24, 1862.

List of machinery in the pistol factory of the Manhattan Arms Company ready for use by the Union Fire-arms Company.

20 milling machines.
2 slabbing machines.
1 index milling machine.
2 edging machines.
1 4-gear drill-press.
9 plain drill-presses.
2 cone and screw machines.
13 engine lathes.
30 drilling lathes, large and small.
11 planing machines.
1 shaping machine.

2 power presses.
1 quadruple press, (4 drop.)
7 forges.
10 engine lathes.
6 drills, (machine.)
1 trip hammer, with forge.
Inside polishing machine patterns.
Outside polishing machine patterns.
Rifling machine.
All small tools and a large amount of vacant room.

NEW YORK, *March* 24, 1862.

*Letter from W. C. Hicks, agreeing to turn all the machinery and workmen of
Boston Arms Company on Robert H. Gallaher's gun work.*

NEW YORK, *March* 26, 1862.

DEAR SIR: If your contracts for arms are confirmed by the board of commissioners, consisting of Hon. Joseph Holt and Robert Dale Owen, I shall be prepared, as heretofore, to take hold, to manufacture them in your shops, and can bring all our present machinery and sixty of the best gun workmen in the United States with me. I am confident that we can turn out guns in as short time as any one, if not quicker, as our machinery is now made and can be immediately set at work.

Please inform me as soon as possible, that I may make no other engagement.

Yours, truly,

WILLIAM C. HICKS,
Superintendent Boston Arms Company.

R. H. GALLAHER, Esq.

*Copy of C. K. Garrison's letter agreeing to furnish Robert H. Gallaher with
capital to complete contracts.*

NEW YORK, *March* 20, 1862.

SIR: I hereby agree to furnish you the money you need to aid in completing your gun contracts with the United States, when said contracts shall be confirmed by the board of commissioners, consisting of Hon. Joseph Holt and Robert Dale Owen.

The money to be furnished by me on the terms agreed upon between you and myself.

Yours, respectfully,

C. K. GARRISON.

ROBERT H. GALLAHER, Esq.,
President Union Fire-arms Company.

[Duplicate]

Report of Lieutenant S. V. Benét, United States ordnance, on breech loader.

WEST POINT, U. S., *August* 24, 1861.

SIR: Yesterday I superintended the trial of Marsh's breech and muzzle loading rifle, and have the honor to make the following report:

The arm consists of a United States rifle, calibre .58, fitted with a breech attachment. The latter is connected to the upper edge of the breech of the barrel by a hinge, and consists of a breech plug or bolt, with a gas check at the end next the barrel. The gas check is made of a double ring of steel, breaking joints, that is expanded by means of a steel cone that passes through it, thus closing all escape of gas. The plug or bolt is thrown up by pressing the trigger forward and exposing the opened barrel to receive the cartridge; it is brought back to its place after loading by a blow of the hand, and is held in position by a steel pin that enters the bolt at its rear extremity.

The ammunition used was of two kinds: a common paper cylinder tied to the United States expanding bullet, and the "seamless skin cartridge" used with the Enfield rifle. The same cartridge serves for both breech and muzzle loading, and no material enlargement as a chamber is therefore made.

Forty-four shots were fired with the common cartridge, loading at the breech. At the seventh round the cartridge could not be inserted, the cartridge paper having been driven into the interior orifice of the vent. This was readily removed with a wire, and the firing was continued. At the twenty-eighth round thereafter the bolt moved with difficulty, caused by the escape of gas and consequent fouling. At the forty-first round paper again stuck in the vent; at the forty-fourth fouled and worked with difficulty. The gas check and breech were cleaned, when necessary, by merely rubbing them with a rag or the moistened finger, a very simple, easy, and quick operation, that did not materially interrupt the course of the trial.

The breech attachment being thus cleaned, the rifle was fired seventy-seven rounds with Enfield skin cartridge, loading at the breech. At the twenty-eighth round the breech fouled, and was cleaned with a rag in a moment. At the forty-fifth round it again fouled, and was cleaned. At the fiftieth (or ninety-fourth of the entire firing) the rifle was loaded at the muzzle; the barrel was so foul that the bullet was sent home with difficulty. The firing was then continued, loading at the breech, with ease, and so continued to the seventy-seventh, (or one hundred and twenty-first of the entire firing.) The last round was loaded at the muzzle with great difficulty, because of the excessive fouling of the barrel. The barrel was not cleaned during the trial.

The gun was fired ten rounds in one minute and fifty seconds.

Conclusions.—The mechanism is very simple and strong, and not easily put out of order. The rifle with which the firing was made is evidently an old one, has been much used, and the bolt that closes the breech not at all firm and solid in its place, the steel pin that enters its rear end working loose. This may account in part for the fouling. The fouling was not very great, and the invention has the great merit of permitting the clogged parts being easily cleaned by the finger moistened with saliva, where a moist rag is not convenient. By this simple expedient the rifle was fired one hundred and twenty-one rounds with no difficulty or detention, although the bore had meanwhile become so foul that loading at the muzzle became a tedious and troublesome operation.

The common cartridge was inserted *entire*, without tearing, the cap exploding the charge through the paper without fail. The sticking of the paper in the vent might be easily remedied.

Should, from any cause, the breech attachment fail to work, a few turns of a screw fixes it in its place, and the rifle becomes a muzzle loader, using the same ammunition.

The invention has undoubtedly great merit, and I believe that a new rifle, with the parts more skilfully fitted, would give more satisfactory results.

Very respectfully, your obedient servant,

S. V. BENÉT,
1st Lieutenant United States Ordnance.

Brevet Brigadier General J. W. RIPLEY,
   Chief of Ordnance, Washington, D. C.

COMMISSION ON ORDNANCE AND ORDNANCE STORES,
Washington, May 1, 1862.

SIR: I am instructed by the commission on ordnance and ordnance stores to state to you that your proposal of April 23, 1862, as modified by your agent, Mr. George Mattingly, viz: to reduce the number of guns to be manufactured by you to 25,000 Springfield rifle muskets and 12,500 breech and muzzle loading rifles, has been accepted; that your contract, in that modified form, will be confirmed, so that you may proceed with confidence in carrying it out.

I am, sir, very respectfully, your obedient servant,

J. WISE, *Secretary to Com'n.*

Mr. R. H. GALLAHER, *New York, N. Y.*

COMMISSION ON ORDNANCE AND ORDNANCE STORES,
Washington, May 5, 1862.

GENERAL: The commission have the honor to report as follows:

CASE No. 64.—UNION ARMS COMPANY, New York.

Orders for 65,000 muskets, Springfield pattern, and 25,000 breech-loading muskets, Marsh's patent.

Orders by direction of the Secretary of War: 1st. R. H. Gallaher; 2d. J. S. Gallaher; 3d. S. W. Marsh; 4th. Union Arms Company; dated, respectively, August 31, October 11, October 14, and November 15. All transferred and assigned to the Union Arms Company under order from the Secretary of War, dated January 3, 1862. Case No. 43, Ex. Doc. 67.

To deliver, 1st, 20,000 Springfield rifled muskets, at $20; 2d, 20,000 Springfield rifled muskets, at $20; 3d, 25,000 breech-loading muskets, Marsh's patent, at $29 75; 4th, 25,000 Springfield rifled muskets, at $20, including in each case appendages.

Time of delivery, as finally directed January 3, to commence in May, 1862, and to be monthly thereafter as follows:

In May, 1862, 3,000 Marsh, 5,000 Springfield.
In June, 1862, 4,000 Marsh, 9,800 Springfield.
In July, 1862, 4,000 Marsh, 10,800 Springfield.
In August, 1862, 4,000 Marsh, 10,800 Springfield.
In September, 1862, 4,000 Marsh, 9,800 Springfield.
In October, 1862, 4,000 Marsh, 5,800 Springfield.
In November, 1862, 2,000 Marsh, 2,000 Springfield.
And 2,000 Springfield, monthly, to June, 1863.

By the terms of the order, dated January 3, 1862, "in case of failure to deliver to the extent and within the times specified, the parties are to forfeit the right to deliver whatever number may be deficient in the specified number for the month in which failure occurs."

The commission find that the Union Arms Company was formed and incorporated solely with the view of executing the above orders; that it is not in fact a manufacturing company, but purposes to raise and invest sufficient capital in the work to secure the supply of the various parts of the arm from the several manufacturers, and to assemble the parts thus supplied under direction of Mr. Gallaher, the president of the company.

Mr. Gallaher has appeared before the commission and shown that he has personally devoted much time to the preliminary correspondence and inquiries necessary to start the work, but has not yet actually commenced work in execution of the orders.

According to the terms of the order of January 3, the first delivery of both the Springfield and Marsh patterns should be made in May; but Mr. Gallaher admits that the company cannot be expected to commence deliveries earlier than July, and has proposed to the commission, in behalf of the Union Arms Company, and with the written concurrence of all the original holders of the orders, to surrender at once all claim under these orders to a greater extent than twenty-five thousand of the Springfield pattern, and twelve thousand five hundred of the Marsh pattern, provided the order to the Union Arms Company be confirmed to this amount at the prices of twenty dollars, ($20,) including appendages, for each musket of Springfield pattern, and of twenty-seven dollars and seventy-five cents, ($27 75,) including appendages, for each musket of the Marsh pattern, that may be accepted as fully equal to the requirements of the original orders, respectively, for these arms, and that the stipulated rate and dates of delivery shall be as follows, viz: First delivery of 1,000 in July, second delivery of 1,000 in August, and not less than 4,000 monthly thereafter, so that all will be delivered prior to June 1, 1863.

In consequence of all the circumstances of the case, and especially of Mr.

Gallaher's repeated assurance that he has fully acquainted himself with all the government inspection requires, and can secure the most reliable means to carry out such requirements upon confirmation by the commission; that he has devoted much time to the subject, and incurred responsibilities which will prove extremely oppressive to him should the proposition now made not be accepted. The commission has decided to accept the mode of adjustment proposed by Mr. Gallaher, and to confirm the order as to numbers, prices, and times of delivery, as above, requiring the full execution of the terms and conditions of the original orders in all other respects.

The commission require of Mr. Gallaher that he shall proceed at once to prepare, and shall submit to the chief of ordnance prior to June 15, a satisfactory sample of the proposed breech-loader of Marsh's pattern, to be accepted as a guide in the inspection of those arms, and that the deliveries promised shall include at least one-third of the breech-loaders, in each month after the first delivery, and that the forfeiture for non-compliance as to time shall be strictly enforced, so as to curtail the numbers of each kind to the extent of each monthly delivery that may not be punctually made.

We are, sir, very respectfully, your obedient servants,

J. HOLT,
ROBERT DALE OWEN,
Commissioners, &c.
P. V. HAGNER,
Major of Ordnance, Assistant to Commission.

Brigadier General J. W. RIPLEY,
Chief of Ordnance.

CASE No. 65

C. W. DURANT.

Before commission.

Copy of certificates appended to the account of C. W. Durant, dated September 1 to 30, 1861, amounting to $3,732 12.

"This bill of ordnance was purchased by my order as governor of Colorado at a time of public insurrection, and was necessary for arming the first regiment of Colorado volunteers in the absence of government arms.

"WILLIAM GILPIN,
"*Governor of Colorado Territory.*"

True copy.

P. V. HAGNER, *Major of Ordnance.*

Also as follows:

"I certify that the above articles of ordnance have been received by me, and have been accounted for on a return of ordnance and ordnance stores to be rendered for the quarter ending June 30, 1862.

"JOHN W. ALLEY,
" *Capt. 3d Infantry, Acting Assistant Quartermaster.*"

True copy.

P. V. HAGNER, *Major of Ordnance.*

COMMISSION ON ORDNANCE AND ORDNANCE STORES,
Washington, May 5, 1862.

GENERAL : The commission have the honor to report as follows :

CASE No. 65.—C. W. DURANT, Colorado Territory.

Claim for $3,733 50, for sporting rifles and muskets. Referred by order of Secretary of War.

Purchases of arms made by order of Governor Gilpin, late governor of Colorado Territory, to meet the exigencies of the public service in that Territory, without proper legal authority.

The commission find that the purchases were made by authority of Governor Gilpin; that the arms, as per abstract, have been taken upon the quarterly account of Captain J. W. Alley, acting assistant quartermaster, who acknowledges their receipt, and states that they have been accounted for on a return of ordnance and ordnance stores to be rendered for the quarter ending June 30, 1862.

The commission further find that although the prices for the articles are high, yet they do not seem unreasonable, considering the place and circumstances under which the purchases were made.

The commission, therefore, direct that the account be examined and audited, as usual, without suspension on account of lack of due authority to order the purchases or of informality in stating the account.

We are, sir, very respectfully, your obedient servants,

J. HOLT,
ROBERT DALE OWEN,
Commissioners.

P. V. HAGNER,
Major of Ordnance, Assistant to Commission.

Brigadier General J. W. RIPLEY,
Chief of Ordnance.

CASE No. 66.

LAFLINS, SMITH & CO.

Before commission.

Copy of certificates attached to the account of Laflins, Smith & Co., dated September 27, 1861, *and November* 29, 1861, *amounting to* $10,632.

This bill of ordnance stores was purchased by my order, as governor of Colorado Territory, at a time of public insurrection, and was necessary for arming the first regiment of Colorado volunteers in the absence of government arms and ammunition.

WILLIAM GILPIN,
Governor of Colorado Territory.

True copy.

P. V. HAGNER,
Major of Ordnance.

Also :

" I certify that the above articles of ordnance stores have been received by me, and have been accounted for on a return of ordnance and ordnance stores to be rendered for the quarter ending June 30, 1862.

"J. W. ALLEY,
"Captain 3d Infantry, Acting Assistant Quartermaster."

True copy.

P. V. HAGNER.
Major of Ordnance.

COMMISSION ON ORDNANCE AND ORDNANCE STORES.
Washington, May 5, 1862.

GENERAL : The commission have the honor to report as follows :

CASE NO. 66.—LAFLINS, SMITH & CO., Colorado Territory.

Claim for $10,632 for rifle and cannon powder. Referred by order of Secretary of War.   Purchase of powder made by order of Governor Gilpin, late governor of Colorado Territory, to meet the exigencies of the service in that Territory, without proper legal authority.

The commission find that the purchases were made by authority of Governor Gilpin; that the powder, as per abstract, has been taken upon the quarterly account of Captain J. W. Alley, acting assistant quartermaster, who acknowledges its receipt, and states that it has been accounted for on a return of ordnance and ordnance stores, to be rendered for the quarter ending June 30, 1862.

The commission further find that although the prices are high, yet they do not seem unreasonable, considering the place and the circumstances under which the purchases were made, and that the ordinary roads were closed up so that the ordnance stores had to be conveyed by land by a circuitous route, greatly adding to the expense of transportation.

The commission, therefore, direct that the account be examined and audited, as usual, without suspension on account of lack of due authority to order the purchase or of informality in stating the account.

We are, sir, very respectfully, your obedient servants,

J. HOLT,
ROBERT DALE OWEN,
Commissioners. &c.
P. V. HAGNER,
Major of Ordnance, Assistant to Commission.

Brigadier General J. W. RIPLEY,
Chief of Ordnance.

CASE NO. 67.

D. J. MILLARD.

HOUSE OF REPRESENTATIVES,
December 12, 1861.

SIR: Mr. David J. Millard, of Clayville, Oneida county, New York, is proprietor of a large water power and manufactory, known as the Paris Furnace Company. He is very extensively engaged in the manufacture of scythes, and is entirely prepared to furnish promptly a large number of sabres. He is desirous of entering into a contract for that purpose, and is prepared, at a fair and just price, to furnish any number of these weapons he undertakes to deliver. We commend Mr. Millard to your favorable consideration.

Your obedient servants,

J. P. Chamberlain, M. C., 26th district.   Theo. M. Pomeroy, M.C., 25th district.
S. N. Sherman, M. C., 17th district.   W. E. Lansing, M. C., 22d district.
C. B. Sedgwick, M. C., 24th district.   Roscoe Conkling, M. C.
A. W. Clark, M. C., 23d district.   A. B. Olin, M. C.
R. H. Duell, M. C., 21st district.   R. Franchot, M. C.
Elijah Ward, M. C.   W. A. Wheeler, M. C.
F. A. Conkling, M. C., 6th district.   A. Frank, M. C., 3d district.
John B. Steele.   B. Van Horn, M. C., 31st district.
Ed. Haight, M. C., 9th district.   Wm. Hall, M. C., 5th district.
Steph. Baker, M. C., 12th district.   A. S. Diven, M. C., 27th district.

Hon. SIMON CAMERON,
    Secretary of War.

D. J. Millard, Clayville, Oneida county, New York, submits copy of an order to furnish 10,000 sabres, (issued December 31, 1861,) at $8 50 each:

ORDNANCE OFFICE,
Washington, December 13, 1861.

SIR: By direction of the Secretary of War, I offer you an order for (10,000) ten thousand cavalry sabres, on the following terms and conditions: These sabres are to be of first quality, and are to be subject to the regular inspection of such inspectors as this department may designate for the purpose, and are to be of the regular United States pattern. None are to be received and paid for but such as pass inspection and are approved by United States inspectors. They are to be delivered at Clayville, New York, as follows, viz: Five hundred in ninety days from this date, and two thousand per month thereafter, until the whole ten thousand are delivered. In case of any failure to deliver to the extent and in or within the times specified, this department is to have authority to revoke and annul this order so far as regards the sabres remaining and delivered at the time of such failure. Payments are to be made, in such funds as the Treasury Department may provide, for each delivery, on certificates of inspection and receipt by United States inspectors, at the rate of ($8 50) eight and a half dollars for each sabre complete.

Please signify, in writing, your acceptance or non-acceptance of this order, on the terms and conditions herein stated.

Respectfully, your obedient servant.

(Signed by Brigadier General Ripley, of the ordnance department, and a copy retained in the office.)

Mr. D. J. MILLARD,
    Clayville, Oneida county, New York.

CLAYVILLE, ONEIDA COUNTY, NEW YORK,
December 16, 1861.

DEAR SIR: Referring to your order on me, in behalf of the United States, for ten thousand cavalry sabres, said order dated December 13, 1861, I reply that

I accept of said order on the terms and conditions therein stated, and will try to please the government.

Please accept my thanks for your prompt action in this matter.

Very respectfully, your obedient servant,

D. J. MILLARD.

Brigadier General RIPLEY,
    Ordnance Office, Washington.

Mr. Conkling filed this acceptance.

CLAYVILLE, N. Y., *February* 19, 1862.

The purport of the contract entered into by David J. Millard with the War Department for ten thousand sabres was understood, in the wording of said contract, a copy of which was forwarded to the department, and we conclude the marking of red ink under the words "*and its purport*" in the circular sent in *was not intended.* For the fulfilment of said contract we have made arrangements as follows:

First. We have contracted for all the stock for manufacturing said sabres. We have most of our help engaged, and are actively at work at manufacturing the same. We have increased the capacity of our work for facilitating the manufacture of the sabres by building a culvert 530 feet long, 11 feet span, and 17 feet under ground, now nearly finished. We have added a new wheel, purchased at the Novelty Works at an expense of about $1,500, and have incurred expenses and entered into engagements to the amount of thirty thousand dollars or over, all of which liabilities we have made ourselves responsible for the purpose of carrying out the conditions of the said contract.

Your obedient servant,

DAVID J. MILLARD.

Hon. EDWIN M. STANTON,
    Secretary of War, Washington, D. C.

HOUSE OF REPRESENTATIVES, *February* 22, 1862.

SIR: I have the honor to hand you herewith a response of David J. Millard, of Clayville, New York, which, it is hoped, is in full compliance with the order of supplemental circular, heretofore issued on the subject of giving notice to you of contracts made with your department. "The purport" of the contract fully and particularly appears from the copy of it, heretofore handed you for Mr. Millard by me.

I have the honor to be your obedient servant,

R. CONKLING.

Hon. EDWIN M. STANTON,
    Secretary, &c.

———

COMMISSION ON ORDNANCE AND ORDNANCE STORES,
Washington, May 6, 1862.

GENERAL: The commission have the honor to report as follows:

CASE No. 67.—D. J. MILLARD, of Clayville, New York, 10,000 *cavalry sabres.*

Order by direction of Secretary of War, dated December 13, 1861, Ex. Doc. No. 67, page 225.

To deliver, subject to inspection, at his factory, 10,000 cavalry sabres—500 in 90 days, and 2,000 per month thereafter—at the rate of $8 50 for each sabre complete. Referred by direction of the Secretary of War.

The commission find that the first delivery of 500 should have been made March 13, 1862, but, as Mr. Millard's own factory was not then in complete operation, he purchased sabres from another manufacturer, thinking himself at liberty to supply his deficiency in this way. Upon report to the Ordnance office, he was informed that the department did not permit orders to manufacturers to be filled by purchase.

Mr. Millard has appeared before the commission, and states that he has met with more difficulties in commencing the manufacture of blades and scabbards than he had anticipated; that he now has a lot of blades ready for the inspector, but will be obliged to procure scabbards for these from other establishments; that he has invested a large portion of his means in preparations for the work, and is now in a condition to advance, he hopes, satisfactorily.

By the terms of the order, as given to Mr. Millard, his failure to make the first delivery as stipulated has released the government from all obligation to receive the 10,000 sabres, and the commission find that the price allowed by this order is beyond the usual and reasonable one for such home manufactured work, and much beyond the prices paid for foreign sabres.

As a full equivalent for the work, seven dollars ($7) per sabre, is considered by the commission as much as should be allowed, many manufacturers have made, and are offering to make, at a less price; but as the extraordinary expenses of undertaking a new business must be considered in a first order, and as Mr. Millard has shown to the commission that he entered upon it in good faith, and with the expectation of only fair profit, and has been zealously at work to fulfil his undertaking, the commission decide that he be permitted to fill the original order upon the terms and conditions stipulated, except that the sabres accepted after inspection be paid for at the rate of $7 each.

The commission further agree that Mr. Millard may deliver, in fulfilment of his order, the sabres and scabbards, of American manufacture, which he has already purchased for this purpose, provided they be found acceptable upon inspection; and that the whole number so offered shall not exceed 600 sabres complete, and 1,100 scabbards.

We are, sir, very respectfully, your obedient servants,

J. HOLT,
ROBERT DALE OWEN,
Commissioners, &c.
P. V. HAGNER,
Major of Ordnance, Assistant to Commission.

Brigadier General J. W. RIPLEY,
Chief of Ordnance.

CASE No. 68.

GORDON, CASTLEN & GORDON.

Before commission.

Copy of certificates attached to account of Gordon, Castlen & Gordon, of Louisville, Kentucky, amounting to $1,425, dated October 26, 1861.

" The above arms were purchased to arm the regiment of Colonel Jackson, commissioned by the President of the United States. I approve the contract of purchase, and say it was necessary for the public service.

"W. T. SHERMAN,
" *Brigadier General Commanding.*

" HEADQUARTERS DEPARTMENT OF CUMBERLAND,
" *Louisville, November 5, 1861.*"

Also :

"I certify that the above account is correct and just, amounting to fourteen hundred and twenty-five dollars and no cents, and that I have received the articles enumerated therein.

"J. H. SMYSON,
"*First Lieutenant 5th Artillery, Acting Ordnance Officer.*
"LOUISVILLE, Ky., *October* 26, 1861."

True copy.

P. V. HAGNER,
Major of Ordnance.

COMMISSION ON ORDNANCE AND ORDNANCE STORES,
Washington, May 6, 1862.

GENERAL : The commission have the honor to report as follows :

CASE No. 68.—GORDON, CASTLEN & GORDON, Louisville, Kentucky.

Voucher of Oct. 26, 1861, for navy pistols and musket caps. Amount of voucher, $1.425.   Arms purchased to arm the regiment of Colonel Jackson, commissioned by the President of the United States, approved by Brigadier General W. T. Sherman, commanding department.

The commission find that the account is approved by General Sherman, commanding department, as is shown by his statement upon the voucher ; that the prices are not unreasonable, and that the articles were received, and are receipted for by the acting ordnance officer of Louisville, Kentucky.

The commission, therefore, direct that the account be examined and audited, as usual, without objection on account of informality

We are, sir, very respectfully, your obedient servants,

J. HOLT,
ROBERT DALE OWEN,
Commissioners, &c.
P. V. HAGNER,
Major of Ordnance, Assistant to Commission.

Brig. Gen. J. W. RIPLEY,
Chief of Ordnance.

CASE No. 69.

STARR ARMS COMPANY.

NEW YORK, *February* 7, 1862.

DEAR SIR : A short time since there was published in a newspaper an order from you that copies of all contracts with the War Department should be sent to you to be placed on file, together with a statement of what had been done under said contracts.

As our contracts were made directly with the War Department, we suppose they are already on file ; but, in compliance with your order, we herewith enclose copies of our contracts, with a report of progress under same.

We have received from the War Department the following orders :

September 23, 1861, for 12,000 Starr army revolvers.
January 11, 1862, for 8,000 Starr army revolvers.

November 27, 1861, for 10,000 breech-loading carbines, Starr's patent.

December 24, 1861, for 50,000 Springfield muskets.

Of which we herewith enclose copies, together with copies of our acceptance of same.

In reference to progress, we respectfully report as follows :

We have delivered to government 2,500 pistols, and now have 225 men in our factory at Binghamton, where we are working day and night. We are now turning out there fifty army revolvers per day, and the number is constantly increasing. We have within the last ninety days expended over $150,000 in buildings and machinery at Yonkers, New York, to carry out these contracts. The main building is 400 feet long by 40 feet wide. The blacksmith shop 150 by 30 feet wide. The blacksmith shop and one-half of the main building are entirely finished, and the machinery is going in. We commence work in same next week. This part will be devoted entirely to manufacturing of carbines, the tools for which are now being removed from Binghamton to Yonkers. The other half of main building will be finished in a short time, in which we shall manufacture army revolvers. These extensive and expensive preparations and outlays, in connexion with our Binghamton factory, will enable us to fill our contracts within the specified time.

In regard to Springfield muskets, we have just received from General Ripley an order on the Springfield armory for models, and are preparing ourselves as rapidly as possible for their manufacture.

Respectfully, yours,

For STARR ARMS COMPANY,
EVERETT CLAPP,
Treasurer.

Hon. E. M. STANTON,
Secretary of War, Washington, D. C.

Copy of order for 12,000 *Starr army revolvers.*

ORDNANCE OFFICE, *Washington, September* 23, 1861.

SIR : By order of the Assistant Secretary of War, I offer you an order for twelve thousand of the Starr Company army pistols, on the following terms and conditions, as proposed in your letter of August 31, 1861, viz : The pistols, with appendages therefor, consisting of a bullet mould, a screw-driver, and a cone wrench for each pistol, are to be subject to inspection, by such officer as this department may appoint for the purpose, and are to be delivered at your factory for inspection, as follows : not less than five hundred (500) in October, 1861; not less than five hundred in November, 1861 ; not less than five hundred in December, 1861 ; not less than one thousand (1,000) per month for each month thereafter, till and including June, 1862, and not less than two thousand (2,000) per month thereafter, until the whole twelve thousand pistols, with appendages, are delivered ; which must be prior to the first of September, 1862. In case of any failure to deliver in or within the time before specified, the government is to be under no obligation to take the pistols and appendages then remaining undelivered, but may or may not do so, at its option. Payments will be made, on certificates of inspection and receipt by the United States inspector, in such funds as the Treasury Department may provide, at the rate of twenty-five dollars per each pistol (including appendages) which may be accepted by the inspector as equal in all respects to the sample pistol deposited in the Ordnance office.

Please signify, in writing, your acceptance or non-acceptance of this order, on the terms and conditions herein stated.

Respectfully, your obedient servant,

JAMES W. RIPLEY,
Brigadier General.

EVERETT CLAPP, Esq.,
Treasurer Starr Arms Company, New York, N. Y.

Copy of acceptance of foregoing.

SIR: In consideration of your order, under date of September 23, 1861, for twelve thousand Starr Arms Company army pistols, and appendages, (of which order foregoing is a copy,) the Starr Arms Company hereby accepts the same, and agrees to execute the contract contained in said order upon the terms and conditions therein specified.

For STARR ARMS COMPANY,
EVERETT CLAPP,

Treasurer.

Brigadier General JAMES W. RIPLEY,
Chief of Ordnance, War Department, Washington, D. C.

Copy of order for 10,000 *Starr breech-loading carbines.*

ORDNANCE OFFICE, *Washington, November* 27, 1861.

SIR: By order of the Secretary of War, I offer you an order for ten thousand (10, 000) breech-loading carbines, of Starr's patent, on the following terms and conditions, viz: These arms are to be equal in all respects to the sample submitted to the War Department, and are to have the following appendages, viz: One bullet mould, one screw-driver and cone wrench, and one wiper and thong for each carbine.

The arms and appendages to be subject to inspection and proof by such officers as the department may appoint for the purpose, and none are to be received or paid for but such as pass inspection and proof, and are approved by the United States inspector.

They are to be delivered at the factory of the company, ready for inspection, as follows: Five hundred (500) in February, 1862; five hundred (500) in March, 1862; and one thousand per month thereafter, until the whole 10,000 are delivered, which must be on or before December 31, 1862. In case of any failure to make these deliveries in or within the times before specified, the government is to have authority to cancel and annul this order so far as regards the arms and appendages remaining undelivered at the time of such failure.

Payments will be made for each delivery in such funds as the Treasury Department may provide, on certificates of inspection and receipt by a United States inspector, at the rate of twenty-nine dollars ($29) for each arm, including appendages.

Please signify, in writing, your acceptance or non-acceptance of this order, on the terms and conditions herein stated.

Respectfully, your obedient servant,

JAS. W. RIPLEY,
Brigadier General.

EVERETT CLAPP, Esq.,
Treasurer, Starr Arms Company, Binghamton, N. Y.

Copy of acceptance of foregoing,

DEAR SIR : In consideration of your order, under date of November 27, 1861, for ten thousand breech-loading carbines and appendages (of which order foregoing is a copy) the Starr Arms Company hereby accepts the same, and agrees to execute the contract contained in said order, upon the terms and conditions therein stated.

Respectfully, yours,

For STARR ARMS COMPANY,
EVERETT CLAPP,
Treasurer.

Brigadier General JAMES W. RIPLEY.
Chief of Ordnance, War Department, Washington, D. C.

Proposal of the Starr Arms Company of New York to manufacture 50,000 rifled muskets of Springfield pattern.

NEW YORK, December 14, 1861.

SIR : In perfecting our arrangements for the manufacture of pistols and carbines, we find we can so extend our armories as to include the manufacture of muskets. We therefore propose to furnish to the government fifty thousand (50,000) rifled muskets of the Springfield pattern, conforming in every respect to a sample to be furnished by the government from the armory at that place, upon the same terms as the contracts made with Mr. Colt, of Hartford, and Mr. Jenks, of Philadelphia, as follows, viz : 1,000 in July, 1862; 2,000 in August, 1862; 2,000 in September, 1862; 3,000 in October, 1862; 3,000 in November, 1862; 3,000 in December, 1862; and 4,000 per month thereafter until the whole 50,000 are delivered, with the usual appendages, at twenty dollars ($20) apiece.

We should be glad to hear from you as early as possible, in order that we may commence our preparations promptly.

Respectfully, yours,

For STARR ARMS COMPANY,
EVERETT CLAPP,
Treasurer.

Hon. SIMON CAMERON, *Secretary of War.*

Copy of an order for 50,000 Springfield muskets.

ORDNANCE OFFICE,
Washington, December 24, 1861.

GENTLEMEN : By direction of the Secretary of War, I offer you an order for fifty thousand (50,000) muskets, with appendages, of the Springfield pattern, on the following terms and conditions, viz : These arms are to be furnished with the regular appendages, and are to be in all respects identical with the standard rifled musket made at the United States armory at Springfield, Massachusetts, and are to interchange with it, and with each other, in all their parts; they are to be subject to inspection by United States inspectors in the same manner that the Springfield arms are to be inspected, and none are to be received or paid for but such as pass inspection and are approved by the United States inspectors. These fifty thousand (50,000) arms and appendages are to be delivered at your armory as follows, viz : not less than one thousand (1,000) in each of the months of July, August, and September, 1862; not less than two thousand in each of the months of October and November, 1862; not less than three thousand (3,000) in December, 1862, and not less than four thousand per month thereafter, until the entire fifty thousand shall have been delivered; and you are to have the right to deliver more rapidly than according to the number of arms before specified, if you can do so. In the case of any failure to make deliveries to the extent and within the times before specified, you are to forfeit the right to deliver whatever number may be deficient, in the specified number for the month in which the failure occurs. All these arms and appendages are to be delivered by you, and this order, if transferred to another party, is to be thereby forfeited.

Payments are to be made in such funds as the Treasury Department may provide, for each delivery, on certificates of inspection and receipt by the United States inspectors, at the rate of twenty dollars ($20) for each arm, including appendages. All these arms and appendages are to be packed by you in boxes of the regular pattern, with twenty (20) muskets and appendages in each box, for which a fair price, to be determined by the United States inspector, will be allowed.

Please signify, in writing, your acceptance or non-acceptance of this order, on the terms and conditions before stated herein.

Respectfully, your obedient servant,

JAS. W. RIPLEY,
Brigadier General.

STARR ARMS COMPANY, *Binghamton, N. Y.*

NEW YORK, *January* 2, 1862.

DEAR SIR: The Starr Arms Company hereby accept the contract from the ordnance department, under date of December 24, 1862, for 50,000 Springfield muskets, upon terms and conditions therein stated.

For STARR ARMS COMPANY,
EVERETT CLAPP,
Treasurer.

Brig. General J. W. RIPLEY,
Chief of Ordnance, War Department, Washington, D. C.

Copy of order for 8,000 *Starr army revolvers.*

ORDNANCE OFFICE,
Washington, January 11, 1862.

SIR: By direction of the Secretary of War, the order of September 23, 1861, to the Starr Arms Company, for 12,000 pistols, is hereby extended to 20,000 pistols, provided that the 8,000 additional pistols, with the usual appendages, are delivered in equal monthly quantities, commencing with the month of March, 1862, and ending with the month of September, 1862; the price, $25 dollars per pistol, including appendages, and the other terms and conditions—except as herein modified in regard to delivery—to be the same as in the order of September 23, 1861.

Please signify, in writing, your acceptance or non-acceptance of this extension of your order.

Respectfully, your obedient servant,

JAS. W. RIPLEY, *Brig. General.*

E. CLAPP, Esq.,
Treasurer of Starr Arms Company, New York, N. Y.

Copy of acceptance of the foregoing.

DEAR SIR: The Starr Arms Company hereby accepts the contract from the ordnance department of January 11, 1862, (of which foregoing is a copy,) for an increase from 12,000 to 20,000 of Starr army pistols, upon conditions and terms therein stated.

Respectfully, yours,

For STARR ARMS COMPANY,
EVERETT CLAPP,
Treasurer.

Brig. General JAS. W. RIPLEY,
Chief of Ordnance, War Department, Washington, D. C.

Statement of facts connected with the existing relations between the government. as principal, and the Starr Arms Company, as contractors.

Previous to August last the Starr Arms Company had been for two years employed in the necessary preparations for the manufacture of arms. On the 31st of that month it accepted a contract for 12,000 pistols, upon the faith of which additions and extensions were made to its manufacturing capacity, which enabled it, in November last, to accept an offer of a contract for 8,000 in addition. In that month, and a few days thereafter, it was offered, and it accepted, a contract for 10,000 breech-loading carbines. Immediately upon the acceptance of this contract the necessary preparations were immediately commenced, and they have been continued unabated, and are now almost wholly completed. Very soon after, to wit, on the 14th of December last, a contract for muskets was offered to the company, and on the 24th of that month it was accepted; the additional necessary preparations for its execution were added to those required for the carbine contract.

The unusual demand for gun-makers and gun machinery caused much delay in obtaining the requisite machinery, and a large appreciation in its price.

The erection of the necessary buildings was commenced immediately, and their completion accomplished through storm and frost, at any cost, at any hazard, and in a period almost unprecedentedly short; meantime, an uninterrupted intercourse was kept up with the machine shops throughout New England which had been employed to build gun machinery. These machine shops were kept at work day and night, and every effort was made and inducement offered to effect the prompt completion of the machines. When, at your request, the treasurer first, and afterwards the president, of the Starr Arms Company appeared before your commission, they responded willingly and frankly to your inquiries. From them you have the then existing facts in detail relating to the extent, cost, and classification of the preparations made. As the necessary increase to the facilities for making pistols had been made before the carbine or musket contracts were taken, the energy of the company was directed to the important work of preparing for making carbines and the additional buildings and machinery for making muskets. These preparations consist of an immense building filled with new and suitable machinery, giving employment to many hundred men, who, at great expense, have been collected to operate it; of a very large stock of materials in hand and large orders for steel from England; of many thousand carbines and muskets in various stages of completion, and several thousand carbines almost completed.

The armory at Binghamton is employed exclusively in the manufacture of pistols; that at Yonkers in carbines and muskets. The extent of the latter is only exceeded by the Colt establishment, at Hartford.

The extraordinary exertions that have been made, the increased cost of the machinery and manufacture by reason of the unexampled demand for gun machines and gun-makers, were based upon the conditions of the contracts under which and upon the faith of which the whole enterprise has been prosecuted, and it would not have been attempted or justified under less favorable conditions. Both wages and machinery are almost, and in some cases quite, double the current rates of a year ago. The deliveries of pistols have been quite up to the letter of the existing agreement; the spirit of the carbine contract has not been violated, although the right to deliver, as far as deliveries are due, has been technically forfeited. The first delivery under the musket contract will be due in July, and the guns will be ready.

You can but imperfectly judge of the surprise, embarrassment, and distrust occasioned by the action of the government in declining to receive the pistols—inspected, boxed, and ready to be shipped, in response to requisitions in the hands of the inspecting officer, Major Whiteley—amounting in value to about $40,000.

The Starr Arms Company has built, equipped, and put into operation one of the largest armories in this country, *upon an abiding faith.* The company is up to the spirit, if not to the letter, in all its undertakings—time, quality, and quantity.

At my last interview with your commission it was suggested to me that the contracts accepted by the Starr Arms Company were without the form and authority of law. Certainly it cannot be your wish or the intention of the government to destroy at a blow the just expectations of those parties who have invested their whole property in the business. Should that company suffer by reason of any irregularity on the part of the government, and be ruined by a technicality? If the government has acted without the authority of law, should it, can it, equitably avail itself of such unlawful act?

The conclusions to which the company has arrived are, that the government cannot equitably, and will not wrongfully, destroy or abridge its rights and just expectations. The company therefore asks that the existing hindrances to the delivery of its arms be removed, and that the spirit of their contracts be recognized by the government now, as it was recognized when and at the time of the acceptance of them by the company.

OFFICE OF THE STARR ARMS COMPANY,
New York, April 17, 1862.

GENTLEMEN : It now occurs to me that, in consequence of being interrupted when before you the other day, a statement was not given of all the machinery purchased for the special purpose of manufacturing the Springfield rifle, under our contract for 50,000 guns.

In addition to the machinery then enumerated, we have actually purchased twelve edging machines, fourteen drill presses, and four screw machines—one-half of which are intended for the Springfield rifle—and also six trip-hammers and five forging drops; all of which are now in the factory, and half of them for Springfield gun work.

There are also thirty lathes now in the factory, one-half of which are for the above work.

We have now running a steam-engine large enough to do all the carbine and pistol work, but not the rifle work; and we have under contract, which we are obliged to take, a steam-engine and boilers of 200 horse power, with pulleys and shafting, costing altogether $12,000. The shafting and part of the pulleys are now in the factory.

The above comprises all the large purchases of machinery made for rifle contract; but there are many small things, amounting in the aggregate to a considerable sum, which should be added.

Very respectfully,

H. H. WOLCOTT,
President of Starr Arms Company.

COMMISSIONERS ON ORDNANCE,
Washington, D. C.

OFFICE OF THE STARR ARMS COMPANY,
New York, April 17, 1862.

GENTLEMEN : When before you the other day, Mr. Holt suggested that we should make some proposition to modify our contracts. I have submitted the matter to our company, and am now prepared to make the following proposition :

We will release the government from the contract for fifty thousand Springfield rifles on condition that the time for delivering the twenty thousand revolvers be extended through one year from August next, and that the contract for carbines be increased to twenty thousand, to be delivered in same time as the revolvers, the price of the last ten thousand carbines to be twenty-five dollars each.

In making this proposition, we do not expect to make up any loss of profits that might have accrued on the rifle contract, but simply to employ the machinery purchased and factory built to carry out that contract. Our business is the making of fire-arms, and nothing else, and we intend to continue it permanently.

We have expended large sums of money, in good faith, to place ourselves in a position to carry out these contracts, and we know no reason why we should not be allowed to do so; but as there seems to be a wish to reduce the expenditures, the above proposition will save an outlay of seven hundred and fifty thousand dollars to the government.

We would like an early decision on this matter, as we are constantly increasing our expenditures for carrying out the rifle contract.

Very respectfully,

H. H. WALCOTT,
President of the Starr Arms Company.
COMMISSIONERS ON ORDNANCE, &c., *Washington, D. C.*

Before commission, April 10, 1862.

Mr. E. Clapp, treasurer of the Starr Fire-arms Company, came before the commission, and states: We have a contract for 50,000 Springfield muskets. Cannot answer as to the details of the work, but we propose making the whole arm except the rough barrel. A full set of stocking machines has been ordered by us. Do not know when due to us, or where deliverable. We have an order, dated September 23, 1861, for 12,000 revolvers, deliverable not less than 500 in October, November, and December, each, and not less than 1,000 monthly thereafter, until June, 1862. This order was increased, January 11, by 8,000, deliverable in equal monthly instalments from March to September, 1862. We were not ready to deliver in October, but we sold to Major Hagner, in New York, 500, navy size, at $20, in that month. We also sold, in like manner, 250, navy size, in November, and in the same month we sold 250, navy size, to the agent of Ohio. We have delivered and received certificates for 1,000, army size, in January ; 600, army size, in February; 1,400, army size, in March,. and we notified the department that we had 1,000 ready for inspection March 28 or 29. The department immediately sent inspectors, who are now at work. We think our pistols cost, to make, double as much as Colt's. Our company has paid Mr. Starr $200,000 for his patents for carbines and pistols, and $90,000 additional for perfecting the pistol. I think Mr. Wolcott, the president of the company, told me that the cost of making our pistol was between $14 and $15. We had only made one thousand for the government in 1858, and five hundred for the trade prior to the receipt of our contract, and we have spent $100,000 since in pistol machinery and on our factory. We think our clear profit on each pistol does not exceed $5. When we proposed to make 20,000, at $23, we required eight months longer to deliver; with this time for deliveries, we would have no extras to pay for working at night. We made no proposition to reduce the price of our pistols to $20, nor was it asked of us. We are now turning out regularly two thousand per month. We make our pistols at Binghamton—working all night. This we have done since October, 1861. We expect to fill our whole order in August, and we will start as soon as we can an additional force at Yonkers on the work.

We have also an order for ten thousand breech-loading carbines, deliveries to be made—500 in February, 500 in March, and 1,000 per month thereafter; price, $29 each. No deliveries yet made; 1,500 due at the end of this month. An extension of our time for delivery of our carbines has been asked for, but not yet granted. We asked an extension of Mr. Cameron, and we have a letter from him acknowledging the receipt of our request, and stating that he told me that it was not worth while to change our contract, as, if proceeded with in good faith, the time of delivery would be extended. This letter is here offered. We have now in hand six hundred, which we expect to deliver in May. The barrels we have made out. We have spent $140,000 on factory stock and machinery for this work alone. We have nearly all the stock for the work on hand, and the remainder is all ordered. We are perfectly willing to reduce the numbers by the amount of monthly failures; but having gone on in good faith upon Mr. Cameron's promise, made immediately after Mr. Starr signed the proposal in my name, the loss of the whole contract would be unjust and unreasonably oppressive to us.

Before commission, April 15, 1862.

Mr. Wolcott, president of the Starr Arms Company, states: We propose to make the whole Springfield gun, including barrel. We will make barrels from steel rods. We have our building at Yonkers, and we are getting our machinery for this work. We have one full set of barrel machines, which we are using on the carbines ordered of us. We have ordered another full set from Hewes & Phillips, of Newark, New Jersey. We expect them to be done within four months. We have stipulated to take this one set. They have also agreed to furnish us as many more sets as we need.

We have agreed with Lysander Wright, of Newark, for a full set of stocking machines. He has made some machines—not a full set, I think—which we had the option to take, but did not, as we were not ready for them, and he promised to get ours up in time for us. We have no written contract with him, and his making them is dependent upon our future order to him. Wright is just finishing a set of stocking machines for carbines for us which we are obliged to take. This set, I think, includes four machines, not more, and turns out the work so that it requires more hand work than the Springfield musket machines ought to do.

Nothing done in preparation for our mountings, bayonets, or ramrods. We have contracted for 130 milling machines; seventy of these are for the musket, and we shall use sixty for the carbines. Twenty of this 130 are already delivered, and forty more are to be delivered before the 1st of May, and the remainder during the first two weeks of May. We are getting forty of these from Parker, Snow, Brooks & Co., twenty from the Fishkill Landing Company, and fifty from Putnam Machine Company. The twenty now in shop are part of those by Parker, Snow, Brooks & Co. We have only a few cases of steel suitable for muskets, but we expect to get shapes from England. We have made no bargain for these. We can get a supply in sixty days from date of order in New York. We have done nothing for stocks; we can get some in New York for starting. I think that the Springfield arm, when inspected, will have cost us at least $17, including interest on investment, wear and tear, &c. I judge this from my *own* experience, and I think it holds good if 50,000 are made. Should the order for carbines be filled, we could turn all our stock, machinery, &c., to work upon the muskets without important loss. We are arms makers, have all our capital so engaged, and expect to continue in the business, having been at it now for three years. We therefore must seek this kind of work, even if the government do not employ us.

We have feared that we could not make all our own work in time for the early deliveries, and we have therefore been in correspondence with others to give us about or under 5,000 sets of parts, to enable us to carry out the stipulations as to the deliveries. R. S. Stenton, 229 Pearl street, New York, states that he can furnish the musket complete (1,000 per month) ready to assemble July 1. Mr. Redfield, 177 Broadway, has offered to furnish any number of stocks; says he has a full suit of machinery, and is now turning out stocks. I know nothing myself of either party, but I have talked with Mr. Sackett, and his agent, the partner of Mr. Stenton, and, from his representations, I suppose they must be prepared to do as promised. Their work is said to be done at Rahway and Newark. We have had many propositions from other contractors to furnish guns or parts, but we have uniformly rejected them. We find that up to this time our pistols have cost us to make—say 5,000 in all—about $30 each, including a fair interest on investment and the wear and tear of machinery.

LOCHIEL, *April* 8, 1862.

SIR: The letter accompanying this is respectfully referred to you. The statement of the writer in relation to the extension of the contract is correct. The department had employed this company at their Binghamton works, and being entirely satisfied with the progress they had made in producing arms when we most needed them, I was anxious to retain their services to the government, and when Mr. Clapp objected to closing the contract without an extension, I assured him that if his company should go on in good faith, and endeavor to fulfil their contract, the time of delivery should be extended.

I feel confident that the War Department, under its present head, has no desire to interfere with any contract made in good faith, and have so said to all who have called on me in relation to arms; and this is certainly one of that character.

Very truly,

SIMON CAMERON.

Hon. E. M. STANTON,
    Secretary of War.

[Enclosed.]

NEW YORK, *March* 27, 1862.

DEAR SIR: You will doubtless remember, when I asked the extension of time for delivery of carbines—awarded to the Starr Arms Company under date of November 27, 1861—by the War Department, on the ground that so long a time had elapsed between the time of bid for and award of contract, that you said it was not worth while to change the contract, but gave me the positive assurance that if the Starr Arms Company went on in good faith manufacturing for government, the times of delivery should be liberally extended.

The best evidence of our good faith is to assure you that we have kept our Binghamton factory working day and night with a large force, since last September, expressly for government, and for none else—part of the time at a serious loss, and have expended on our Yonkers works—on the faith of your assurance, and expressly to carry out this carbine contract—over ($140,000) one hundred and forty thousand dollars.

The War Department having no evidence on record of this promise of extension of time, makes it necessary that I should trouble you to confirm this statement, that the department may know the character of our claim for an extension.

Will you, therefore, please oblige me with a letter to the Hon. E. M. Stanton, Secretary of War, who, with such evidence before him, will, I am sure, do us full justice.

Very respectfully, yours,

EVERETT CLAPP,
Treasurer Starr Arms Company.

Hon. SIMON CAMERON.

GENTLEMEN : In response to the request of Major Hagner, we make the following proposition as an arrangement of our contracts for fire-arms :

The Ordnance department has ordered the receipt of 2,000 pistols, now inspected and being inspected, which will, when they are taken, leave 15,000 due on the contract. These we propose to deliver at the rate of 1,200 per month, beginning with the month of June next, at the rate of $20 each, pistol and appendages, we only being held liable to forfeit the amount undelivered in each month, and having the right to deliver as much faster as we can get them out.

The carbines we propose to deliver at the rate of 1,000 per month, beginning with July next, at $29 each, with the same conditions as above in regard to forfeitures and deliveries.

On these conditions we shall be willing to release the musket contract.

We ask for the extension of time in order to enable us to cheapen the cost of the arms to us, that we may meet the great reduction in price which we have proposed, for if compelled to work nights, as we are now doing, we cannot afford the reduction.

Most of the outlay for pistols has already been incurred, so far as materials, machinery, tools, &c., are concerned, and a very large proportion for the carbine. We have also expended $50,000 towards making muskets, which, in case the contract is given up, adds so much to the cost of the pistols and carbines to us.

We have expended large sums to carry out these contracts, and have our whole fortune embarked in the enterprise.

What we have proposed above will barely reimburse us for our outlay, and leave us, when the contracts are completed, with all our means tied up in factories and machinery, for which we shall have little work.

If you would examine our large and costly establishment, you could realize the loss and disappointment to us in surrendering the musket contract.

Commending this matter to your early and favorable attention, I remain your obedient servant,

H. H. WOLCOTT,
President Starr Arms Company.

The COMMISSIONERS ON ORDNANCE, &c.

Before commission, May 5, 1862.

The number of pistols due under the orders are as follows :

First order to be completed prior to September, 1862:
Prior to May 1, 1862.............................. 5,500
Second order to be completed, same date as first order, by equal instalments after March 1 :
Prior to May 1, 1862............................. 2,666

Total due May 1, 1862 8,166
Remaining to be delivered.......................... 11,834

Total ordered................................. 20,000

The commission agree to the reception of not exceeding 15,000 at $20 each—regarding this price as still too high for such arms.

The Starr Arms Company is not among the number whose arms were recommended to be received by the chief of ordnance, in his letter to the Secretary of War, dated March 15, 1862.

P. V. HAGNER, Major of Ordnance.

Decision—Starr Arms Company.

COMMISSION ON ORDNANCE AND ORDNANCE STORES,
Washington, May 6, 1862.

GENERAL : The commission have the honor to report as follows :

CASE No. 69.

STARR ARMS COMPANY, New York.

First order Sept. 23,1861; page 200, Ex. Doc., No. 67.
To deliver 12,000 revolvers, of the Starr Company army pattern, at $25 each ; 500 in October, November, and December each, and 1,000 monthly thereafter.

Second order Nov. 27, 1861; p 186 Ex. Doc., No. 67.
To deliver 10,000 breech-loading carbines, of the Starr Company pattern, at $29 ; 500 in February, 500 in March, and 1,000 monthly thereafter—completing the order before December 31, 1862.

Third order Dec. 24, 1861; page 159, Ex. Doc., No. 67.
To deliver 50,000 rifle muskets, Springfield pattern, at $20 each, as follows : 1,000 monthly in July, August, and September, 1862 ; 2,000 monthly in October and November, 1862 ; 3,000 in December, 1862 ; and 4,000 monthly thereafter.

Fourth order January 11, 1862.
To extend order of September 23 for 12,000 revolvers to 20,000, upon the same terms and conditions, provided that the whole number be delivered within the time stipulated—September 23, 1861.

The terms of the orders for pistols and carbines declare *total* forfeiture for failure in any stipulated delivery ; the forfeiture is limited to the monthly delivery due in the order for muskets.

The commission find that no deliveries of carbines have been yet made, and none can be made prior to July; and that, although 5,000 of the pistols have been inspected and received, the early deliveries were not made as stipulated ; hence, under the provisions above stated, the obligations upon the government to receive 12,000 pistols, 10,000 carbines, and probably several thousands of the muskets would be cancelled.

As the parties are regular manufacturers of arms, have invested a very large capital in the business, and erected extensive buildings and machinery, and as their failures in time cannot be ascribed to a lack of zeal, or to intentional neglect, the commission deem it proper not to enforce measures likely to injure their manufacturing ability ; but, as the price of the revolvers is unreasonably high, compared with the arms furnished by other manufacturers, and as the retention of so large an order as that for muskets must increase the delay and uncertainty in complying with the terms of the others, the commission considered it incumbent upon the company to make a proposition corrective of these objections. Mr. Wolcott, the president of the company, has appeared before the commission, and has offered to relinquish entirely the order for the 50,000 muskets, and to reduce the price upon the remaining 15,000 pistols to $20 each, provided the orders for pistols and that for carbines be confirmed by the commission; and they also request that increased time be allowed for the deliveries; and that forfeiture for failure to deliver extend only to the monthly delivery due—promising to complete the work as soon as possible.

As the rates of delivery originally promised made work by night necessary, and thus increased the cost of production; and as the condition of total forfeiture for failure in amount or in time of a monthly delivery must also add to the manufacturer's risk and expenses, the commission consider that, in the case of so well established a company as this and the present extent of our supplies, the promise to deliver "as rapidly as possible" will probably secure the full product of their factory without more rigorous stipulation. It is therefore directed that the order of December 24 to furnish 50,000 muskets be considered revoked and annulled; that a number not exceeding 15,000 revolvers and 10,000 carbines be received under the terms and conditions of the orders given November 27, 1861, and January 16, 1862, at the rate of $20 for each revolver, with appendages, and $29 for each carbine, with appendages, that may be accepted upon inspection; provided that not less than 1,200 revolvers be furnished monthly, commencing in June next, and 1,000 carbines be furnished monthly, commencing in July.

The commission have considered it proper, under the circumstances, to authorize the prices as above for each of those arms as may be delivered as stipulated, although they regard them as unreasonably high for service arms.

Should the company fail to deliver the above numbers of either arm in any month, the total number remaining to be delivered of that kind must be reduced to the full extent of the number due for that month.

It is further directed that a sample carbine, satisfactory to the Ordnance department, shall be furnished prior to June 1, 1862.

We are, sir, very respectfully, your obedient servants,

J. HOLT,
ROBERT DALE OWEN,
Commissioners.
P. V. HAGNER,
Major of Ordnance, Assistant to Commission.

Brigadier General J. W. RIPLEY,
Chief of Ordnance.

COMMISSION ON ORDNANCE AND ORDNANCE STORES,
Washington, June 30, 1862.

SIR: In reference to the account of the Starr Arms Company for 2,000 revolvers, for which certificates of inspection were given May 20, 1862, and which are charged at $25, the facts of the case are as follows, so far as known to the commission:

All deliveries upon the orders held by the company were stopped by your orders, and this case, with others, referred to the commission to decide as to future deliveries. The commission found that the orders were forfeited by the terms on account of failure to deliver as stipulated, but agreed to receive not exceeding 15,000 revolvers and 10,000 carbines upon certain conditions, one of these conditions being that the price of the pistols should be at the rate of $20 for each revolver and appendages.

This plan of adjustment was accepted by the parties and formed the basis of the commission's decision. As no revolvers could be received after the date of the Secretary's order, except under the decision of the commission, none received since that day should be paid for at a higher price than $20. The charge of $25, therefore, in this account should not be allowed. The fact that the revolvers in question were inspected prior to the date of the decision does not alter the case, as they were not accepted by the government, and were regarded by the commission, as well as by the parties, to come in under the decision.

Very respectfully, your obedient servant,

J. HOLT, *Commissioner, &c.*

Hon. EDWIN M. STANTON,
Secretary of War.

CASE No. 70.

SCHUYLER, HARTLEY & GRAHAM.

ORDNANCE OFFICE,
Washington, September 19, 1861.

SIR: In answer to your letter of the 18th instant in relation to procuring arms and accoutrements and equipments for Ohio troops, I have to state that such supplies, so far as they are necessary for troops which have been or may be authorized by the government to be raised in your State for the service of the United States, may be procured or contracted for by you, or such person as you may designate for that purpose, at rates not exceeding those paid at the time by the government for similar articles, and will be paid for on proper vouchers, in such funds as the Treasury Department may provide for the purpose.

Respectfully, your obedient servant,

JAMES W. RIPLEY,
Brigadier General.

Governor W. DENNISON, *Columbus, Ohio.*

September 20, 1861.

I do hereby designate and appoint Christopher P. Wolcott, judge advocate general of the State of Ohio, to purchase and contract for the within mentioned arms, equipments, and accoutrements.

W. DENNISON,
Governor of Ohio.

Contract made November 18, 1861, between Christopher P. Wolcott, judge advocate general of the State of Ohio, acting for the United States, under the authority of the Ordnance office, in purchasing arms for Ohio troops raised and authorized to be raised for the service of the United States, of the first part, and Schuyler, Hartly & Graham, of New York, of the second part, witnesseth: The party of the second part agrees to deliver to the party of the first part in bond in the city of New York, ten thousand long (39-inch barrel) Enfield rifles of the first quality, with angular bayonets, muzzle-stoppers, and snap-caps, a spare nipple for each gun, and a nipple wrench for every four guns; to be delivered in New York in lots in the months of December, January, and February next, all by the first of March, 1862. The said arms to be subject to the usual inspection for Enfield guns, the barrels all to bear the English proof mark, and the whole to be in complete order; no extra charge except for boxes, and these to be charged at two dollars and fifty cents each. The said party of the first part agrees to pay for the same, cash, on satisfactory inspection and delivery of each lot, at the rate of nineteen ($19) dollars a gun in bond as aforesaid.

C. P. WOLCOTT,
Judge Advocate General of the State of Ohio.

SCHUYLER, HARTLEY & GRAHAM.

New York, *December* 3, 1861.

In consideration of Brown, Brothers & Co. granting to us a letter of credit, No. 269, for £20,000, say twenty thousand pounds sterling, for the purchase of the Enfield rifles referred to in the annexed contract, we hereby assign all our right, title, and interest in the said contract to the said Brown, Brothers & Co.

SCHUYLER, HARTLEY & GRAHAM.

Witness: JAMES S. GILLEN, 59 *Wall street.*

New York, *April* 21, 1861.

GENTLEMEN: Enclosed you have contracts made between C. P. Wolcott, agent for the State of Ohio, assumed by the United States, and ourselves, for 10,000 Enfield rifled muskets, dated November 18, 1861, at $19 each in bond, deliverable in the months of December, January, and February. The embargo laid upon arms by the English government just as we were commencing to deliver (December 4) prevented us from delivering as agreed. As soon as the restriction was removed, we telegraphed to Mr. Wolcott—then in Ohio—asking for an extension of time, and he replied, by telegraph: "Can't answer about extending of contract without consulting governor and War Department. Will advise you next week." We never received any other answer. In the meantime we disposed of them as they arrived to Captain Crispin, ordnance officer in this city, up to March 10, when the order from the War Department was issued stopping the purchase of arms. Thinking that the department would resume purchasing, we took no steps for the disposal of those arriving weekly, until we had accumulated some 3,500. On the 31st of March we offered them to the department, through Captain Crispin, for $17. We have as yet received no answer to our offer. We had entered into contracts with manufacturers on the other side, and our Mr. Tomes had instructions to forward the arms the moment the embargo was raised, intending to carry out our agreement to the best of our ability. If on the other side we had omitted to make arrangements for the forwarding of the arms as above, Mr. Wolcott might have held us liable for damages. Therefore we think, under the circumstances, the government should take the arms. We have some 3,500 in bond *here*, about 2,000 on the way, and about 1,500 more that will arrive between now and the 15th of June. You will observe that our contract price is $19; but we have offered all on hand and to arrive at $17.

These arms are all first class—such as we have been furnishing to the States of Indiana and New York and the United States.

We may have erred in delaying this matter so long, but submitted our case to Captain Crispin here, and he thought the department would buy the arms; but not hearing from them, and as we are accumulating the arms, we submit our case to your consideration.

Awaiting an early answer, we remain yours, respectfully,

SCHUYLER, HARTLEY & GRAHAM.

Hon. JOSEPH HOLT and ROBERT DALE OWEN,
Commissioners on Contracts.

OHIO STATE AGENCY,
No. 25 William Street, New York, April 28, 1862.

GENTLEMEN: I have read your letter addressed to Messrs. Joseph Holt and Robert Dale Owen, under date of the 21st instant, and beg leave to say that the statements there made are substantially correct.

Beyond this general approval of your statement, it seems proper to add that during the last summer I had, on behalf of the State of Ohio, made contracts with you for the then future delivery to that State of a large number of Enfield rifles, which had been executed by you with promptness and fidelity, and that this fact, together with my knowledge of your facilities and of the means taken by you for the fulfilment of the contract mentioned in your letter, leaves me no room to doubt that it too would have been faithfully performed but for the untimely interdict of the British government against the exportation of arms. Of course, this interdict does not give you any right now to deliver the arms contemplated by the contract, but under all the circumstances I think you may justly ask the War Department now to purchase from you, at a reasonable price, any arms which you have been obliged to receive under arrangements made by you prior to the "embargo," for the purpose of enabling you to fulfil the contract in question.

Very respectfully yours,

C. P. WOLCOTT.

Messrs. SCHUYLER, HARTLEY & GRAHAM, *New York city.*

P. S.—The fact that such a contract had been made with you was communicated by me in a letter to the Ordnance office, dated 26th November, 1862, and was sanctioned by it in a reply dated 27th of the same month.

C. P. W.

WASHINGTON, *May* 2, 1862.

GENTLEMEN: Referring to our letter of the 21st April, we will modify our proposition to read as follows:

3,500 Enfields, with angular bayonet, now in port, $16 25.

2,000 Enfields, to arrive, $16 25.

1,500 Enfields, making, on or before the 15th June, in all seven thousand, at sixteen dollars and twenty-five cents.

Yours, respectfully,

SCHUYLER, HARTLEY & GRAHAM.

Hon. JOSEPH HOLT and ROBT. DALE OWEN.

CASE No. 70.

COMMISSION ON ORDNANCE AND ORDNANCE STORES,
Washington, May 8, 1862.

GENERAL: The commission have the honor to report as follows:

CASE No. 70.—SCHUYLER, HARTLEY & GRAHAM, New York.

Contract made by agent of State of Ohio under authority of the governor and accepted by chief of ordnance, dated November 18, 1861. Referred by special direction of the Secretary of War.

To deliver in bond in New York 10,000 long Enfield rifles of the first quality, with angular bayonets, muzzle-stoppers, and snap-caps, and a spare cone for each gun, and a nipple wrench and screwdriver for every four guns. The arms to be subject to inspection, the barrels to bear the English proof mark, and the whole to be delivered in complete order (without extra charges except for boxes, and these to be charged at $2 50 each) in the months of December, January, and February.

The commission find that the contract was made in due form by C. P. Wolcott, esq., agent of Ohio in New York; that he was duly authorized by the governor of Ohio, who, under the direction of the Secretary of War, was authorized by the chief of ordnance, September 19, 1861, "to procure such supplies as were necessary for troops authorized by the government to be raised in Ohio;" that the embargo upon the exportation of arms from England prevented for a time and delayed the performance of their part of the contract by Messrs. Schuyler, Hartley & Graham, but that as soon as the restriction was removed they asked for an extension of time, having previously obtained credits and made arrangements with manufacturers abroad to the full extent of the original contract; that upon arrival of 500 of the arms, in December, 1861, they were delivered to the agent of Ohio and received by him under the contract; that the next arrivals were in March, and as the agent of Ohio had no authority to receive under the contract, 1,200 of the arms were sold to the United States ordnance officer in New York at $20 each, the market rate at that time; that at present 3,500 are in bond in New York, and 2,000 more on the way there, and that 1,500 engaged to be made at Suhl, in Germany, will be there prior to June 15, 1862.

Mr. Hartley has appeared before the commission, and representing the oppressive liabilities incurred in preparing to carry out their contracts, from which they cannot free themselves, has proposed to deliver the 7,000 arms now in port and to arrive prior to June 15, at the rate of $16 25 per gun, including appendages, and subject to all the requirements of the contract as to quality.

Considering that the guns are required to be of the first class, that such a number may be needed, and that the price is reasonable, the commission decide that Messrs. Schuyler, Hartley & Graham be permitted to deliver at the price of sixteen dollars twenty-five cents ($16 25) per gun in bond, conformably to the terms of the contract, not exceeding 7,000 arms (including the 1,500 made at Suhl, if of equally good quality and similar in calibre and finish) provided the whole number be delivered to the inspecting officer in New York, prior to June 15, 1862.

We are, sir, very respectfully, your obedient servants,

J. HOLT,
ROBERT DALE OWEN,
Commissioners, &c:
P. V. HAGNER,
Major of Ordnance, Assistant to Commission.

Brigadier General J. W. RIPLEY,
Chief of Ordnance.

CASE NO. 71.

S. R. PHILLIPS.

PHILADELPHIA, *February* 11, 1862.

RESPECTED SIR: In compliance with your published instructions, I beg very respectfully to inform you that I have the following orders, to wit: an order for twenty-five hundred (2,500) sets of horse equipments from Major General John C. Frémont. This order was given at the time he was in command at St. Louis, the same being subject to the inspection of a government inspector, and at the government regulation price. These equipments are now nearly completed, having all of the stock on hand, and the entire lot being nearly ready to pack up and send away. The order is on file in the Ordnance department, Washington city. All that is required is the order of the Ordnance department as to where they wish them sent.

I have also an order from the Ordnance department direct for 605 sets of horse equipments, which are ready for inspection.

Your obedient servant,

SAMUEL R. PHILLIPS.

Hon. EDWIN M. STANTON,
Secretary of War, Washington, D. C.

PHILADELPHIA, *September* 19, 1861.

RESPECTED SIR: I write to inform you that I have placed in hands 2,500 sets of cavalry horse equipments of the McClellan pattern, according to the order you gave me for General J. C. Frémont. I will finish them as soon as possible, and hope soon to begin to ship said goods.

Will you please be so kind as to have an *official order* sent me by the proper department, it being customary, as you know, to have all orders for the government in writing, to prevent any misunderstanding. I write in haste, and will write you again in a few days. With many thanks for your kindness,

I am your obedient servant,

SAMUEL R. PHILLIPS.

EDWARD M. DAVIS, Esq.,
Quartermaster's Dep't of Gen. John C. Frémont, St. Louis, Mo.

HEADQUARTERS WESTERN DEPARTMENT,
St. Louis, October 5, 1861.

Your letter of the 19th is at hand. The order for the 2,500 cavalry equipments were by order of General Frémont, who is now in the field. The assistant adjutant general, Captain McKeever, has been empowered to sign for the general commanding. His signature will confirm the order.

Respectfully,

E. M. DAVIS,
Assistant Quartermaster.

SAMUEL R. PHILLIPS,
South 7th street, Philadelphia.

WAR DEPARTMENT, *December* 19, 1861.

Order approved. By order of Maj. Gen. Frémont.
CHAUNCY MCKEEVER,
Ass't Adj't Gen.

This contract having been made in good faith, if the articles are delivered subject to usual rates and inspection, I think they should be received.

THOMAS A. SCOTT,
Assistant Secretary.

General RIPLEY, *Chief of Ordnance.*

PHILADELPHIA, *March* 1, 1862.

RESPECTED SIR: Your answer to our letter in which we named the contracts we had from the government was duly received, but owing to the absence of our Mr. Phillips from the city we have delayed answering it until the present time.

Mr. Phillips hopes to be able to call in person at your office (War Department) on Monday next, when he will endeavor to give his answer much more satisfactorily to the Secretary of War than he could by letter. Hoping that you will excuse us for not answering sooner, and that if successful in having an audience with the Secretary, everything may be explained to his entire satisfaction,

I beg to remain your obedient servant,

SAMUEL R. PHILLIPS,
Per W. T. SULLIVAN.

Hon. P. H. WATSON,
Assistant Secretary of War, Washington, D. C.

PHILADELPHIA, *March* 13, 1862.

RESPECTED SIR : Knowing full well the value of your time, I would not trespass upon your attention did not necessity actually compel me to do so. Having received an order from Major General J. C. Frémont for 2,500 sets of cavalry equipments, and having no doubts on the subject as to its binding the government to receive the goods, I ordered all of the stock to complete the order, and commenced working on it.   To confirm this I enclose you my letter to the western department, in which you will see that I requested an official order, which order was received, and is herewith enclosed to you. After hearing that General Frémont had been removed, I ceased for a time on the work, imagining then, for the first time, there would be some trouble.   I made it my business to visit Washington to inquire into the matter. After a great deal of trouble, I had an interview with the Assistant Secretary of War, Hon. T. A. Scott, at the War Department, and represented my case to him.   He said he would consider the matter, and let me know through the Ordnance department what would be done.   You will see that he indorses the order, and therefore that I was (as I thought when I first received the order and commenced working on it) right in filling it.   I beg most earnestly to solicit your kind and immediate attention to my case, as I am inconvenienced very much by my creditors continually coming for their money for the stock which I have bought from them to fill this order. I am compelled to show them the goods on my hands, and tell them that I am unable to do anything until the government receives the work.   *I do, dear sir, beseech you to assist me in this matter,* as I can ill afford to stand so *great a loss* as to have this stock left on my *hands.*   I called upon you at the office in person on Monday, March 10, but was unable to see you, but saw the Assistant Secretary, Mr. Watson, to whom I handed a copy of the order and a few lines to you personally, to which I expected an answer, and not hearing from you, I have thus addressed you. Thinking all that would be necessary to get your sanction and order that the goods are to be received, and that you would have *justice* done me, was to give you a full explanation of the whole transaction, I thought it could be done as well by letter as in person, and therefore have written you a plain statement of facts, and in conclusion would say that I sincerely hope you will favor me with an answer at your earliest convenience.   I herewith enclose you a copy of the order as on file in the Ordnance department, indorsed, as you will see, by Thomas A. Scott, Assistant Secretary.

Your obedient servant,

SAMUEL R. PHILLIPS.

Hon. EDWIN M. STANTON,
    Secretary of War, Washington, D. C.

PHILADELPHIA, *March* 14, 1862.

Samuel R. Phillips—relative to an order received from Major General John C. Frémont to furnish 2,500 sets of cavalry equipments. Encloses copy of his letter to the western department; also copy of the order, with the approval of Thomas A. Scott, Assistant Secretary of War.   Asks that the order be sanctioned and the goods ordered, as he is greatly embarrassed.

Referred to the chief of ordnance for report.

By order of the Secretary of War.

T. H. WATSON,
    Assistant Secretary of War.

ORDNANCE OFFICE, *April* 4, 1862.

Respectfully returned.   The indorsement of Thomas A. Scott, Assistant Secretary of War, of December 19, 1861, is simply an expression of opinion, and not a recognition by the War Department of the order for the purchase of these equipments.   Under the third section of the act of February 8, 1815, this department has not authority to approve an account for their purchase by General Frémont's order, unless sanctioned by the Secretary of War.   The equipments are not now wanted for the public service.

JAMES W. RIPLEY,
Brigadier General.

COMMISSION ON ORDNANCE AND ORDNANCE STORES,
Washington, April 11, 1862.

GENERAL: In the enclosed letter from S. R. Phillips it is stated that Mr. Phillips received a promise from Mr. Scott to consider his claim and "let him know through the Ordnance department what would be done," and he encloses in his letter an indorsement addressed to you and signed by Mr. Scott, giving an opinion favorable to the claim of S. R. Phillips.

Will you please inform the commission whether S. R. Phillips was notified through your department of this indorsement of Mr. Scott; and if so, at what date ?

The commission think it important also to obtain some exact information as to the number of finished sets and quantity of material he may have on hand, and would inquire if such information can be obtained for them through some officer of your department in Philadelphia.

Respectfully, your obedient servant,

J. WISE,
Secretary to Commission.

Brigadier General J. W. RIPLEY,
Chief of Ordnance.

ORDNANCE OFFICE,
Washington, April 11, 1862.

SIR : I have to acknowledge your letter of this date, enclosing a letter from S. R. Phillips, in relation to 2,500 sets of horse equipments ordered of him by General Frémont in October last, which letter has been referred to the commission by the Secretary of War.

In reply to your inquiry, I have to state that for the reason stated in the indorsement made at this office on Mr. Phillips's letter, the indorsement made by Assistant Secretary Scott on General Frémont's order of October fifth last was not communicated by this office to Mr. Phillips.   The copy enclosed by him is a correct one, the original being on file and having been compared with it.

Major Laidley, the commanding officer of Frankford, will be directed to make the inquiry suggested in the last paragraph of your letter, as to how far Mr. Phillips may have progressed in fulfilling the order, the result of which will be communicated to you with the least delay practicable.

Mr. Phillips's letter and enclosure is herewith returned.

I am, sir, respectfully your obedient servant,

JAMES W. RIPLEY,
Brigadier General.

J. WISE, Esq.,
Secretary to the Commission, &c., on Contracts, &c., Washington, D. C.

Relative to order of horse equipments by General Frémont, from S. R. Phillips.

FRANKFORD ARSENAL, *April* 21, 1862.

GENERAL: In compliance with your instructions of the 11th instant, I called, immediately on the receipt of your letter, on Mr. S. R. Phillips, to learn from him where I could find the portions of horse equipments he had prepared, under his order from General Frémont of October last. He stated to me that no one but himself, not one of his clerks, could impart the required information, and that he had an engagement which would prevent his attending to my inquiries at that time, but he would meet me the next day and be prepared to answer any questions I might desire to ask him. This he failed to do, and it was not till *three* days after that he gave me the names of the parties at whose shops I could see the progress of the work made under the order above referred to. In the meantime he had communicated with several of the parties, as I have found out, and sent a special messenger to Newark, New Jersey, where a portion of the work was said to be ordered. He also tried to buy, conditionally, some parts of the equipments, with the understanding that they were to be taken at once to his storehouse, and, if not required, to be returned in a few days, at his expense.

Mr. Phillips has not be able to show me a single order that he has given for material of any kind for these equipments, nor have I been able to find on the memorandum books of any of the parties from whom the different articles are said to be purchased a single order from Mr. Phillips for these sets of equipments.

I am told by business men in the city that this is not the usual way of transacting business on so large a scale.

I have called on several of the parties in the city who are said to have orders to furnish parts of the equipments. One party stated to me that he had *no order* from Mr. Phillips for anything.

Another party said that Mr. Phillips had the *refusal* of 3,000 bits, partly made; but when he found I did not wish to buy, but was making inquiries into the facts of Mr. Phillips's order for 2,500 sets of equipments, I was told that I could not have any of these bits, as they belonged to Mr. Phillips. This party was at first particularly inquisitive who I might be. I learned that Mr. Phillips had been there two days before on private business, which was to be kept secret.

Another party said that they had watering bits, some partly finished, others finished, made for Mr. Phillips; but the same party told other persons, a short time since, that they had no bits.

Mr. McNaulty told me that he had 500 sides of bridle leather which was made for Mr. Phillips, but there was no evidence that it was for these 2,500 sets of horse equipments. I found at Mr. Phillips's store less than fifty saddle-trees, and a hundred or more pairs of stirrups. Mr. Phillips says that much of the material intended for these equipments is ordered from persons in Newark, and some in Harrisburg, Pennsylvania. Of these I have, of course, made no inquiries.

From the facts of the case, as I have been able to discover them by my imperfect investigation, I am impressed with the belief that a further examination of the witnesses would be useless, unless it could be made under oath, and that it would require more time than my other duties will permit to get at the amount of work done by Mr. Phillips under this order.

I have the honor to be your obedient servant,

T. T. S. LAIDLEY, *Brevet Major.*

Brigadier General J. W. RIPLEY,
  Chief of Ordnance, Washington, D. C.

Major Laidley's letter, enclosed by General Ripley, relative to claim of S. R. Phillips. (Major Laidley's letter filed with papers in case.)

ORDNANCE OFFICE,
Washington, D. C., April 22, 1862.

SIR : I enclose herewith, for the information of the commission, Major T. T. S. Laidley's letter of the 21st instant, received this day, in relation to the order of S. R. Phillips from General Frémont, dated October 5, 1861. This and my letter of the 11th instant complete my reply to your letter of the 11th instant on this subject.

Respectfully, your obedient servant,

JAMES W. RIPLEY,
Brigadier General.

J. WISE, Esq.,
Secretary Commission on Ordnance Stores, Washington, D. C.

COMMISSION ON ORDNANCE,
Washington, May 7, 1862.

MAJOR : The commission request that you will report the dates of orders for cavalry equipments given to S. R. Phillips since July 1, 1861, the amount of each order, and the number to be delivered at specified dates thereafter, and the dates of actual delivery.

It is supposed that all orders given him, except the Frémont orders, required delivery at your arsenal. Should this not be the case, please so state.

Very respectfully, your obedient servant,

P. V. HAGNER,
Major of Ordnance.

Major T. T. S. LAIDLEY,
Commandant of Frankford Arsenal.

COMMISSION ON ORDNANCE, &c.,
Washington, April 24, 1862.

SIR : The commission, as above, desire your appearance before them at your earliest convenience, in order that you may be examined, under oath, relative to your claim to furnish cavalry equipments, under order stated to have been given by Assistant Quartermaster Davis, and by authority of General Frémont.

Very respectfully, your obedient servant,

J. WISE, *Secretary.*

Mr. S. R. PHILLIPS, *Philadelphia.*

PHILADELPHIA, *April 26, 1862.*

GENTLEMEN : Your letter of the 24th instant has been received. In answer I beg to inform you that I will with pleasure obey your summons to appear before you in reference to my order for cavalry equipments. I will, if agreeable to you, be in Washington on Thursday, so that I may appear before you on that day. I trust I will not be detained long in your city, my business requiring me to be back in Philadelphia on Saturday morning. May I beg to ask you if you will be through with me on Thursday ? for if that day should not suit your convenience, I will come at any time that may please you.

I am, gentlemen, your obedient servant,

SAMUEL R. PHILLIPS.

Messrs. ROBERT DALE OWEN and JOSEPH HOLT,
Commissioners, Washington, D. C.

FRANKFORD ARSENAL,
Bridesburg, Pa., May 10, 1862.

MAJOR: I enclose herewith the report asked for by your letter of the 7th instant.

Very respectfully, I am your obedient servant,

T. T. S. LAIDLEY,
Brevet Major.

Major P. V. HAGNER,
Washington, D. C.

Statement of orders given to S. R. Phillips, of Philadelphia, for horse equipments; also report of deliveries made.

Order given.	By whom given.	Quantity ordered.	When to be completed.	Actual deliveries.	
				Date.	Quantity.
		Sets.			*Sets.*
1861. July 1	Major P. V. Hagner	500	....	1861. July 29	25
				30	25
				31	25
				Aug. 1	25
				6	50
				7	50
				16	50
				17	25
				19	25
				20	25
				24	75
				28	25
				29	25
				Sept. 2	50
					500
August 30	Lieut. T. J. Treadwell, (by authority from the Ordnance office dated Aug. 24, 1861.)	5,000	5 months	Sept. 4	25
				10	100
				12	50
				13	25
				14	25
				17	75
				18	25
				19	50
				20	50
				21	25
				24	25
				25	75
				30	125
				Oct. 1	50
				3	25
				4	100
				5	50
				11	25
				12	100
				14	100
				15	100
				22	50

Statement of orders given to S. R. Phillips, &c.—Continued.

Order given.	By whom given.	Quantity ordered.	When to be completed.	Actual deliveries.	
				Date.	Quantity.
1861. August 30	Lieut. T. J. Treadwell, &c.—Continued.	*Sets.*		1861. Oct. 31	*Sets.* 270
				Nov. 1	360
				2	60
				4	210
				5	60
				6	30
				7	30
				12	60
				13	210
				14	120
				15	90
				16	90
				18	90
				19	60
				20	30
				21	60
				22	60
				23	30
				25	60
				26	90
				27	90
				28	30
				29	120
				30	120
				Dec. 2	30
				3	120
				4	90
				5	60
				6	90
				7	120
				9	30
				10	120
				12	90
				19	180
				20	240
				21	125
					5,000
June.........	Colonel Young, for Kentucky regiment; transferred to the Ordnance department by consent of General J. W. Ripley.—(See letter from Ordnance office to S. R. Phillips, dated July 24, 1862.)	1,200	....	Dec. 21	25
				23	60
				24	180
				26	60
				27	90
				30	120
				31	90
				1862. Jan. 1	60
				2	30
				3	30
				4	60
				7	60
				8	30
				9	90

Statement of orders given to S. R. Phillips, &c.—Continued.

Order given.	By whom given.	Quantity ordered.	When to be completed.	Actual deliveries.	
				Date.	Quantity.
1861. June.........	Col. Young, &c.—Cont'd .	*Sets.*	....	1861. Jan. 10 11 13	*Sets.* 120 90 5
					1,200
	Inspected and received by authority dated Ordnance office, February 12, 1862.	600	....	Feb. 26 27 28 March 1 3 5 6	30 150 180 120 30 60 30
					600

FRANKFORD ARSENAL, *May*, 1862.

Before the commission, April 30, 1862.

S. R. Phillips came before the commission, and having been sworn, says:

I think the original order given me by Captain Davis was either by messenger or by telegram. I knew Captain Davis in Philadelphia; he is a native and was a resident of Philadelphia. He was at my store before he left for St. Louis, and I made a set of equipments for his personal use. I think, if I received a message from Captain Davis, it was either by his son or his brother, who is a member of Congress.

Question. In your letter to Captain Davis you asked for the written order of September 19; had you any orders from the Ordnance department at that time?

Answer. Yes; I think I had orders at the time that were unfilled. I have been working on orders from the Ordnance department pretty much all the time; there might have been intervals when I had not orders. I think my last delivery under orders from the Ordnance department was made since the first of the year; it may have been in February or March. I do not charge my mind with the dates. I received a draft from the Treasury Department for cavalry equipments delivered at the Frankford arsenal as late as one week since. This draft, I think, is for equipments delivered before the first of January, and there is still due me payments for 600 sets of equipments delivered since the first of the year. I do not recollect at all the dates of delivery, or of last delivery.

Question. What preparation did you make to fill the order of General Frémont?

Answer. When I got this order I told different persons of it, and told them to prepare me the stock. From Mr. Goff, mountings, buckles, and curb chains for 2,500 sets; from Mr. Woastkoop, of Newark, the bits (curb;) from Mr. Shields, of West Philadelphia, watering bits; from Messrs. McNaulty & Sons, of Philadelphia, leather; from Mr. Guenawault, of Harrisburg, leather; from Mr. Elkton, of Philadelphia, leather; from Mr. McBeath, leather. I ordered the stirrups from Mr. Rich, of Philadelphia. I wish to say that when I received orders for equipments, (the manufacturers generally coming into my store every day or two,) I would tell them of my orders, and bid them go on to prepare stock for the amount of the order. I rarely gave my orders in writing. They did not require written orders, as the parties knew me.

Question. Did you regard the orders given as an absolute order?

Answer. I did. I wish to add, I think the parties would not have gone on to prepare the stock which they now have on hand had they not supposed that I would take it.

Question. You have mentioned four names of leather dealers who were to supply the leather; in what proportion did you or they divide the 2,500 sets for each?

Answer. I can't say; there were no written numbers and none agreed upon, as far as I remember.

Question. State whether you consider that the parties named by you do hold you responsible for any particular amount of, or number of articles, on account of the order in question.

Answer. I have not asked the question of any of the parties, but my impression is that from my large dealings with them they would not.

Question. Have you not spoken to any of the parties named by you upon this subject recently?

Answer. After Major Laidley spoke to me, I did speak to all the parties I have named to inquire what they had done.

Question. What answers did you receive?

Answer. Mr. Goff said he had the mountings, web, and curb chains ready for the 2,500 sets, but he did not say that he expected me to take them, as I did not ask him. Mr. Hoarstkoop said he had 600 bits done, and others partly done for this order. I sent to Newark to inquire, I did not see him myself. Mr. Shields said he had 500 to 700; (the number I am not quite certain of.) I saw him myself; he did not say he expected me to take them, and I did not ask him. Mr. McNaulty I saw myself. He had 500 sides, I think, of leather prepared for the order; he did not say he expected me to take them, and I did not ask him. Mr. Guenawault, of Harrisburg, I saw in Philadelphia, and asked him if he had any of the leather done which I had ordered of him for this order. He said he had a lot, I don't think he mentioned any quantity; he did not say he expected me to take this lot, and I did not ask him. Mr. Elkton I saw myself, and he answered about the same, specifying no number; he did not say that he expected me to take what he had, and I did not ask him. Mr. McBeath I saw myself. He answered about the same as Mr. Guenawault, specifying no number; he did not say that he expected me to take what he had, and I did not ask him.

Question. Have you any of the stock in your store?

Answer. I have all or nearly all the stirrups in my store, and all of the brass screws and some rivets.

Question. When did you receive the stirrups?

Answer. Part of them I have had some time; part I received recently.

Question. What proportion recently?

Answer. I do not remember; cannot say the proportion.

Question. How recently was the last lot you speak of received?

Answer. I cannot say; I do not remember.

Question. Was it before or since Major Laidley called upon you upon the subject?

Answer. Since.

Question. How many sets of equipments have you made since July last for the Ordnance department?

Ex. Doc. 72——20

Answer. I think somewhere near 6,000 or 7,000, all assembled in our shop, but parts made outside by journeymen. Upon receipt of orders subsequent to the order for the 2,500, I applied in the same way to the parties I have named to prepare the stock, and they all furnished to me.

Question. Did you tell them at any time to delay the preparations for the 2,500 sets?

Answer. I did.

Question. Did you at any time tell them to resume preparations for the 2,500 sets?

Answer. No, sir; not after I told them to stop them; not to go any further than they had.

Question. About what time?

Answer. I can't remember. It was in consequence of what I saw in the papers about the government going to remove General Frémont. I don't know whether it was before or after General Frémont's removal; but it was in consequence of what I saw in the papers that I suspended my orders.

Question. Have you ordered from the parties above named by you for your subsequent orders?

Answer. These parties have been furnishing me since, as I wanted articles in their line.

Question. When you gave orders to the parties subsequently to giving orders for the 2,500 sets was any reference made by them or you to the prior order of 2,500?

Answer. Not that I remember.

Question. Did you give your orders for material at any time in writing?

Answer. I may have done so, but generally not; my foreman sometimes gives orders, or gets things from stores for use as well as myself.

Question. Have any of the sets been finished?

Answer. No, sir.

Question. You have stated that you suspended your orders upon seeing statements about General Frémont's removal. What did you mean, then, by this sentence in your letter to Mr. Secretary Stanton: "I am inconvenienced very much by my creditors constantly coming for their money for the stock which I have bought from them to fill this order?"

Answer. I meant that they were annoying me to have the goods taken—continually calling and inquiring when I would take them.

Question. What do you mean by "I am compelled to show them the goods on my hands and tell them I am unable to do anything until the government receives the work?"

Answer. The bookkeeper wrote this letter, and I had not read it over. I have no recollection of it. It is not written nor signed by me. I ordered him to write a letter. He writes most of my letters, and has misunderstood me about this.

Question. What is his name?

Answer. William T. Sullivan, He is still my bookkeeper. He writes most of my business letters and signs sometimes for me and sometimes my own name, as if written by me; of the three letters shown me, one is signed in the first-named way; the other two in the second way, neither, however, was actually signed by me.

S. R. PHILLIPS.

COMMISSION ON ORDNANCE AND ORDNANCE STORES,
Washington, May 12, 1862.

GENERAL : The commission have the honor to report as follows :

CASE NO. 71.—SAMUEL R. PHILLIPS, of Philadelphia.

Claim to fill an order for 2.500 sets of cavalry equipments, given originally by Captain E. M. Davis, acting quartermaster, prior to September 19. Order approved by the assistant adjutant general, western department, by order of General Frémont, October 5, 1861. Application to confirm the order made by claimant to the Secretary of War, December 19, and repeated February 11 and March 13.

A verbal order for ordnance stores, by an assistant quartermaster, without special authority through the chief of ordnance. No price nor time of delivery, nor inspection stipulated. The order approved by the assistant adjutant general during General Frémont's absence in the field. Application of December 19 referred to chief of ordnance by the Assistant Secretary of War, Thomas A. Scott, and not approved by him. Referred by special directions of the Secretary of War.

The commission find that the original order for these ordnance stores was not given in accordance with law and regulation. That Mr. Phillips, being himself aware of this, applied to Captain Davis, September 19, to send him an "official" order, that this application was answered by a letter from Captain Davis, dated October 5, 1861, stating that "the order for the 2,500 cavalry equipments were by order of General Frémont, who is now in the field. The assistant adjutant general has been empowered to sign for the general commanding. His signature will confirm the order." This letter, signed by Captain E. M. Davis, acting quartermaster, is followed by the words on the same page, "order approved."

By order of Major General Frémont.

CHAUNCEY McKEEVER.

About December 19 this letter appears to have been presented at the War Department, with an application to confirm the order, and was there indorsed on that day as follows :

WAR DEPARTMENT, *December* 19, 1861.

This contract having been made in good faith, if the articles are delivered subject to usual rates and inspection, I think they should be received.

THOMAS A. SCOTT,
Assistant Secretary.

General RIPLEY,
Chief of Ordnance.

General Ripley, chief of ordnance, states that he regarded this as a mere expression of opinion by Mr. Thomas A. Scott, Assistant Secretary of War, not a recognition of the order by the War Department; that, under the third section of the act of February 8, 1805, this department has not authority to approve an account for their purchase unless sanctioned by the Secretary of War. The equipments are not now wanted for the public service.

February 11, 1862, in compliance with the circular of the Secretary of War, Mr. Phillips's clerk, signing his (Mr. Phillips's) name as if written by himself, reported this order as an "unfilled order;" and again, under date of March 13, the same writer narrates circumstances, in a letter signed in the same way, both of which letters are addressed to the Hon. E. M. Stanton, Secretary of War. In both of these, statements are made relative to the work done under the order which Mr. Phillips, in his testimony before the commission, acknowledges not correct, and testifies that they were not examined by him, but written by the clerk under general directions from him, and either not read by himself or not with sufficient care. Mr. Phillips further stated in his testimony that the preparations actually made by him at the time were merely to mention to the dealers in mountings, leather, &c., from whom he was accustomed to purchase, that he had received such an order and would need stock for it; further, that "he stated no quantities to them and could not say how much was ordered from each dealer;" that he has been receiving from the same parties since for other orders; that he had not called upon them since definitely to furnish the stock for this particular order, and that they had not called upon him to receive such stock under the order he had been given. It further appears that since this commission has been making examinations concerning the case he has called upon or communicated with many dealers, and that they have told him that they had certain quantities ready, but that no one of them said that he expected Mr. Phillips to take what he had, nor did he ask any one of them whether he would so expect him. Mr. Phillips has also testified that he has not actually finished any sets under this order; that he suspended all orders about it upon seeing statements in the newspapers about General Frémont's removal, and that though the same parties have been subsequently furnishing articles in their line of business, as he wanted them to fill other orders, he has not directly ordered any one to resume the orders suspended as above. When asked by the commission whether he considered that the parties would hold him responsible for any amount of the stock, he frankly answered that he does not think they will, as he has dealt largely with them.

The commission find that Mr. Phillips received an order for cavalry equipments from the Ordnance department in July, through Major Hagner, for 500 sets; that before the delivery of these he obtained a second order, through Lieutenant Treadwell, for 5,000 sets; and upon completion of this another for 1,200, and then a fourth order for 600 sets as late as February 12, the last delivery under which was not made until March 6. These many orders, it is admitted by Mr. Phillips, kept his establishment fully occupied upon work for the Ordnance department of the very kind claimed to have been ordered by General Frémont; they fully informed him, too, of the proper and usual course through which such ordnance stores should be ordered, and, as it appears, made him so doubtful of the validity of the order now claimed that he took no timely steps to make deliveries under it, (although he promised in September soon to begin to ship said goods,) and did not notify the Ordnance department until December 19 that 1,200 sets of equipments were expected from them for the use of the western department, at which date General Ripley reports that arrangements have already been made to meet the future wants of all sections of the country.

Considering that this order was originally issued without proper authority, that the claimant was soon fully aware of this and could have at once taken steps to have it made strictly formal; that he has been employed since by the Ordnance department to a very large extent the commission decide, as in a previous case of like circumstances, that it should be considered that Mr. Phillips has either forfeited his order by non-fulfilment as to time, or that the department had deemed it complied with, as far as required, by the deliveries made under later orders. Had Mr. Phillips used proper punctuality in filling the order, or had he given earlier notice to the Ordnance department, arrangements, including the number now in question, would doubtless have been made, by reducing receipts from other sources.

The commission therefore direct that this order be considered annulled and of no effect, and that no equipments be received under it.

We are, sir, very respectfully, your obedient servants,

J. HOLT,
ROBERT DALE OWEN,
Commissioners, &c.

P. V. HAGNER,
Major of Ordnance, Assistant to Commission.

Brigadier General JAMES W. RIPLEY,
Chief of Ordnance.

CASE No. 72.

WILLIAM MASON.

ORDNANCE OFFICE,
Washington, January 7, 1862.

SIR: By direction of the Secretary of War I offer you an order for fifty thousand (50,000) muskets, with appendages, of the Springfield pattern, on the following terms and conditions, viz: These arms are to be furnished with the regular appendages, and are to be in all respects identical with the standard rifle musket made at the United States armory at Springfield, Massachusetts, and are to interchange with it and with each other in all their parts; they are to be subject to inspection by United States inspectors in the same manner that the Springfield arms are inspected, and none are to be received or paid for but such as pass inspection and are approved by the United States inspectors. These fifty thousand (50,000) arms and appendages are to be delivered at your armory as follows, viz: Not less than one thousand (1,000) in *each* of the months of July, August, and September, 1862; not less than two thousand (2,000) in *each* of the months of October and November, 1862; not less than three thousand (3,000) in December, 1862; and not less than four thousand per month thereafter, until the entire fifty thousand (50,000) shall have been delivered, and you are to have the right to deliver more rapidly than according to the number of arms before specified if you can do so.

In case of any failure to make deliveries to the extent and within the times before specified, you are to forfeit the right to deliver whatever number may be deficient in the specified number for the month in which the failure occurs.

All these arms and appendages are to be delivered by you, and this order, if transferred to another party, is to be thereby forfeited.

Payments are to be made, in such funds as the Treasury Department may provide, for each delivery, on certificates of inspection and receipt by the United States inspectors, at the rate of twenty dollars ($20) for each arm, including appendages. All these arms and appendages are to be packed by you in boxes of the regular pattern, with twenty (20) muskets and appendages in each box, for which a fair price, to be determined by the United States inspector, will be allowed.

Please signify, in writing, your acceptance or non-acceptance of this order on the terms and conditions before stated herein.

Respectfully, your obedient servant,

JAMES W. RIPLEY,
Brigadier General.

P. S.—It is further directed by the War Department that double the number of arms and appendages, viz, one hundred thousand, will be received if manufactured at your own establishment in Taunton, Massachusetts, and delivered within the time before specified for the delivery of the fifty thousand arms and appendages. All the other terms and conditions of this order remaining unchanged for the additional fifty thousand.

                                        JAMES W. RIPLEY,
                                              Brigadier General.

WILLIAM MASON, Esq., *Taunton, Massachusetts.*

                              TAUNTON, *Massachusetts, February* 7, 1862.

SIR : In compliance with your orders I have the honor to transmit herewith a copy of an order issued to me from the War Department, through the Ordnance office, for Springfield muskets.

I accepted this order, and am proceeding to manufacture the muskets to the best of my abilities.

I have purchased material and a part of the machinery, and have the remainder in such a forward state of completion that I anticipate being able to deliver muskets as early as many of the parties whose contracts are dated five or six months anterior to mine.

I am, sir, respectfully, your obedient servant,

                                        WILLIAM MASON.

Hon. EDWIN M. STANTON,
      Secretary of War, Washington, D. C.

                                    EXECUTIVE DEPARTMENT,
            State of Rhode Island, &c., Providence, February 10, 1862.

MY DEAR SIR : Allow me to recommend to your favorable consideration Mr. William Mason, of Taunton, Massachusetts. Mr. Mason is one of the largest and most reliable manufacturers in New England, and in the country. He has a contract with the government made by your predecessor. He has performed large contracts with the concern of A. W. Sprague, and always to their entire satisfaction. I also place him among those of my most valued personal friends, and can without hesitation pledge to you that any contract you may make with him will be faithfully carried out.

With high respect, I am your obedient servant,

                                        WILLIAM SPRAGUE.

Hon. E. M. STANTON, *Secretary of War.*

                                    TAUNTON, MASS., *June* 5, 1862.

SIR : I find, on my arrival here, a package from the Ordnance office, containing, for execution, quadruplicate copies of bonds and contract for the manufacture of 30,000 muskets. I presume, from the date of the accompanying letter, that they were sent without your knowledge, and mailed before my last interview with you, last Staturday, when you proposed to have my case reconsidered as soon as Mr. Owen could be present. This is a mater of great importance to me, though it may be a trifling affair to the government, and I hope you will present my case to the commission in its true aspect. I have been investigating my gun business since I returned, and have decided that if my contract is not reduced below 50,000 I can get out of the difficulty without much loss, provided the government pay promptly.

I will be in Washington again in a few days, and will see you.

      Yours, respectfully,

                                        WM. MASON.

Major P. V. HAGNER,
      Office of the Commission on Ordnance, &c., Washington, D. C.

Before the commission, April 4, 1862.

Wm. Mason appeared before the commission, and says that he has barrel machinery being made, chiefly in his own shops; he expects barrels in rough from Mr. Washburne. His machinery for barrels is nearly finished. Stocking tools are to be made by Wood, Slight & Co., Worcester, and George Crompton. A party wants to make my bayonets, but I have effected no arrangement with him yet. Ramrods, buts, and tips I am preparing for myself. First delivery to be made in July. Will be able to deliver in time if stocking machinery is furnished. (Mr. Almy, Eagle Manufacturing Company, has no machinery other than such as may be used for bayonet work; he wants to make for me. I have taken a fortnight since the stock machinery which was under way for Almy.) Is getting a full suit—about twenty machines—some to be duplicated; contract is for 100,000. Is a manufacturer of machinery for cotton mills. I could not finish a musket stock until July. A man in Providence has fitted up to make me 50,000 locks; Colman & Co. work only for Mason. Locks are to be complete; they are now at work; they are now swedjing and milling ports. Bands and guards are arranged for; balance to make myself. Bands made by a man in Fall River. Mason furnishes him a superintendent, and has control over his manufactory. *Hames* makes guards upon like terms. Neither has had experience in gun work, but both are machinists.

The appendages he makes himself. Has not commenced on them. Will finish barrels in May. He depends on Washburne for barrels, who promises them as fast as Mason wants them. If Washburne's iron fails, he will have to get it elsewhere. Everything except bayonets is arranged for. A man who fits up to make guns cannot make fair profit with 50,000. If the government leaves contracts as at present, there cannot be deliveries in time, except in a few cases. As yet no one has furnished suitable barrels, to my knowledge. I learn that several state they depend on me for barrels. I have only promised to Rice & Bodine. Bodine wrote and asked to be released, as he thought he should give it up. Mr. Washburne is trying to make his own iron answer. He has good tools, and can do all the work well, if he uses good materials. Messrs. Tyler, at Springfield, are making my barrel gauges. Each party that undertakes a special piece has to make his own gauges. These I will see compared with the standard gauges at Springfield. I have a sample gun and sample of parts. Never heard of H. E. Robbins, of Hartford, and know of no stocking machines there except Colt's. It is possible I may not be up to time in the first delivery, but I will certainly be with the second. A party in Milbury, Massachusetts, Mr. Waters and Osgood, in Ilion, New York, are now making complete bayonets, and I can get from them if not from Almy; also Dagget, sabre maker at Attleboro', offers to make bayonets.

COMMISSION ON ORDNANCE AND ORDNANCE STORES,
Washington, May 15, 1862.

GENERAL: The commission have the honor to report as follows:

CASE No. 72.—WM. MASON, Taunton, Massachusetts.

Order by direction of the Secretary of War, Jan. 7, 1862 —(See pp. 171–2, Ex. Doc. H. R. No. 67.)

To furnish, at his armory in Taunton, Massachusetts, 50,000 Springfield rifle muskets, at the rate of 1,000 monthly for July, August, and September, 1862; 2,000 monthly for October and November, 1862; 3,000 in December, and 4,000 monthly thereafter.

Permission to double the number, if manufactured by him

at his own establishment at Taunton, and delivered within the times above specified.

In case of failure to deliver to the extent or within the times stipulated, the right to deliver the number deficient for the month in which the failure occurs to be forfeited.

In the letter of the Assistant Secretary of War, of January 6, 1862, written by order of the Secretary of War, granting permission to increase the original order from 50,000 to 100,000, provided the entire 100,000 guns be manufactured at Mr. Mason's own establishment, the inducement for granting such permission to increase the order is declared to be "thus to secure an efficient armory to furnish arms for the government."

The order itself is for 50,000; but, in a postcript, (page 172,) the chief of ordnance adds that 100,000 guns will be received under the above conditions.

Mr. Mason has appeared before the commission. and his statement to them is to the effect that he has relinquished what seems to have been his original proposition, as stated by Mr. Secretary Scott, for manufacturing all the parts of these arms at his own establishment at Taunton, and has contracted for different portions of the same, to be made at various and far distant points; as barrels at Worcester, bands at Fall River, locks at Providence, &c. By the adoption of this policy, violating the condition on which the order was to be enlarged from 50,000 to 100,000, namely, that the entire 100,000 should be made "at his own establishment at Taunton;" and by thus failing "to secure an efficient armory to furnish arms to the government"—the suggestion of which appears from the language of Mr. Assistant Secretary Scott, (page 171,) to have been the chief inducement to doubling the order—Mr. Mason forfeits all claim to the enlargement.

By statement at page 16, Ex. Doc. 67, it appears that the existing contracts and orders for Springfield muskets amount to one million one hundred and sixty-four thousand, while, in the opinion of the Ordnance department, (as has been officially reported to the commission,) there will be required for a year to come, to meet the probable wants of the country, not exceeding half a million of guns of this model. This excess of orders beyond the need of the government may, in part, be due to the expectation of the department that a large portion of the arms contracted for would not be promptly delivered. Some of these contracts have already fallen through from non-compliance; and, from the present aspect of things, it seems likely that others will be added, in part or in whole, to the list of failures. Nevertheless, in view of the vast expenditures to which the present war has given rise, the commission deem it expedient and important to bring down the total number of Springfield muskets, which the government shall be bound to accept, to some six hundred thousand, or as near as may be to that amount, provided the reduction can be made with due regard to law and a reasonable measure of protection to all who have proceeded with energy and in good faith to supply government wants; even in cases in which the contracts or orders, under which they have so proceeded, shall be found to lack some of the sanctions of legality.

In the attainment of this object the commission find it desirable, in the large majority of cases in which Springfield guns have been ordered or contracted for, to confirm such contract or order as to a portion only of the arms proposed to be delivered—having reference in determining the exact number to the particular character and claims of each case.

In four cases only, so far, the commission have confirmed such contracts without reduction. These four cases are the only ones out of thirty-six, in all, in which it was found that a formal contract had been signed and sealed by the contracting parties, and the only ones containing the provision, imperatively demanded by law, that no member of Congress should be admitted to any share therein or to any benefit therefrom. These contracts, also, were made nearly two months in advance of all others, and five months in advance of one-half of all the other contracts for such guns; they were made at a time when the government was at its utmost need, pressed beyond all precedent for arms, and keenly alive to the necessity of securing them with the least possible delay from every reliable source.

In addition to this, in two out of these four cases, the contracts were made with the owners of armories already established—men experienced in the business—the others being practical machinists and working large factories.

In all other cases—except where the number specified to be delivered is so small that further to reduce it would work serious injury to the contractor—the commission either have reduced, or have the intention of reducing, the original number. In Mr. Mason's case, they propose to confirm, under conditions hereafter to be explained, the order for 30,000 guns only.

In so doing, it becomes proper to consider—

1st. The legal right of the commission to make, on behalf of the government, the reduction in question.

2d. If that right should be established, then the equitable claim of the individuals concerned (in this case Mr. Mason) to be allowed to deliver a smaller number, so as to protect from loss those who may have assumed liabilities or made expenditures in good faith.

And, first, as to the legal right to make the reduction.

That right clearly exists, if the contract or order is not obligatory on the government, because essentially defective in its terms or conditions, or in any important notice required to precede it, or in any omission therein of provisions strictly prescribed by law for the protection of the public interests and the prevention of fraud.

Is the contract or order in question, in common with all other similar orders issued by the War Department in the autumn and winter of 1861–'62, thus essentially defective?

The 5th section of the act of 1809, March 3, provides, "That all purchases and contracts for supplies or services which are or may according to law be made by or under the direction of the Secretary of the Treasury, the Secretary of War, or the Secretary of the Navy, shall be made by open purchase, or by previously advertising for proposals respecting the same."

This statute is still in force, and is the basis on which the contract system of the service rests.

The regulations founded upon this law are as follows:

"1044. All purchases and contracts for supplies or services in the army, except personal services, *when the public exigencies do not require immediate delivery of the article* or the performance of the service, shall be made by advertising a sufficient time previously for proposals respecting the same."

"1046. Contracts shall be made with the lowest responsible bidder, and purchases from the lowest bidder who produces the proper article. But when such lowest bids are unreasonable, they will be rejected, and bids again invited by public notice, and all bids and advertisements shall be sent to the bureau."

"1048. When *immediate delivery* or performance *is required by the public exigency*, the article or service required may be procured by open purchase or contract, at the places and in the mode in which such articles are usually bought and sold or such services engaged between individuals."

These regulations are not an enlargement or modification of the act of 3d March, 1809, but are simply an official exposition of its true intent and meaning. They were approved by the President of the United States, and published for the government of the military service, and by an order, dated 10th August, 1861, the Secretary of War declares that "they shall be strictly observed as the sole and standing authority upon the matter therein contained."

The course of legislation upon this subject indicates the object which Congress has desired to secure, and the evil it has sought to avoid. The object evidently was to obtain army and other supplies at the lowest possible rates; the evil to be avoided was exorbitant prices, which might result from refraining to give formal notice as to the wants of the service, or from fraudulent collusion between government officers and sellers. The law, then, as construed by the regulations, is eminently laudable in its intent, and well calculated to effect its object in practice. It ought to be upheld.

Has it been departed from in the present case?

The order for the manufacture of these guns was given on the 7th of January, 1862, six months after the first contracts for Springfield arms were concluded and more than three months after the chief of ordnance had officially expressed his opinion (Ex. Doc. H. R. No. 67, page 137) that orders for the prospective delivery of muskets to a sufficient extent had already been given. Whatever may be alleged as to the earliest contracts made, there is no ground for maintaining that as late as January of the present year a state of things existed requiring instant orders for the manufacture of Springfield arms.

The act of 1809 evidently contemplates two modes of procuring army supplies: first, through contracts providing for future deliveries; second, through open purchases. The regulations and the act—of which these regulations are but a correct and official interpretation—require that in the first class of cases, the contracts shall be made on proposals invited by previous advertisement, and that in the second class, the purchases without advertisement shall be made only where "the public exigency" makes "an immediate delivery" necessary. In such cases, the advertisement is dispensed with, simply because there is not time within which to make it. But however urgent the "exigency" of the service, if the party dealt with has no ability at once to supply it, the duty to advertise remains, because the reason for omitting it—the want of time between the offer to buy and the required delivery—does not exist. In the case now under consideration "the public exigency" may have called for an "immediate delivery" of Springfield muskets, but Mr. Mason was not in a condition to make such delivery. The order given to him, instead of contemplating the immediate delivery, which would have excused the department from advertising, provided, on the contrary, that the deliveries should not begin for six months, and should be continued through a period of one year and three months thereafter. There is therefore no pretence for treating this order or contract as an "open purchase" made in conformity to the law and regulations as quoted. The order and its acceptance constitute a contract manifestly falling with the first classification—that is, being an engagement for the delivery of army supplies, not only in the future, but at remote periods of time. In reference to all such contracts, the requirement is imperative that they "shall be made by advertising a sufficient time previously for proposals respecting the same." This requirement was not complied with in the order to Mr. Mason. It was issued to him without notice to others, and without the chance of competition on the part of those dealing in or manufacturing arms. The law from which the Secretary of War derives his authority to make contracts for army supplies, being thus not obeyed, but violated, the contract itself can impose no binding obligations on the government. There was ample time to advertise: the law and the highest interests of the service required it; and if the principle cannot be enforced in such a case as this, then all the wise and stringent legislation of Congress on the subject will be in vain. Executive innovation will have virtually repealed a statute, the value of whose guardianship over the public treasury and over the morality of the service cannot be overestimated.

The view here insisted upon is not at all called in question by the 3d section of the act of 8th February, 1815, which declares that "it shall be the duty of the colonel or senior officer of the Ordnance department to furnish estimates, and, under the direction of the Secretary of the Department of War, to make contracts and purchases for procuring the necessary supplies of arms, equipments, ordnance, and ordnance stores." This enactment is in no respect in conflict with the act of 1809. It is simply cumulative upon it, by requiring that the directions of the Secretary of War for contracts and purchases of supplies of arms, equipments, &c., shall be given to and executed by the chief of ordnance; but the *mode* of making such contracts and purchases, as prescribed by the act of 1809, is not changed, or even alluded to, by that of 1815. The two statutes are in *pari materia*, and in perfect harmony with each other. The incompatibility between them would have to be marked and wholly irreconcilable to justify a repeal, or even a modification, by implication, of a law so vitally important as that of 1809.

The habitual disregard of this law by the War Department in its contracts for arms has been attended by the evil of exorbitant prices, which the statute intended to prevent. The first contract for Springfield muskets was made on the 8th July, 1861, with Colt's Patent Fire-arms Manufacturing Company, of which Samuel Colt was president. It was entered into on the private proposal of the company, fixing the price of the arm at $20. The prices demanded of the government for arms, by this company, have been generally not only high, but oppressive. Since we have been in session it has come to our knowledge that for years past they have furnished to the Ordnance department, at $22 each, revolvers of the navy size, which, during the Crimean war, they sold to the English government at $12 50. A similar revolver, in all respects equal, and in some perhaps superior to this, was, during the past year, supplied, and is still supplied, to the government by one of the first American manufacturers of arms, at $15. The actual cost of the manufacture of this arm does not, it is believed, exceed $9. For a revolver of the army size, Colt's company has constantly charged the government $25, and on the 14th day of September, 1861, a running order for these pistols, indefinite as to numbers, was given to the company at this rate. An arm fully the equal of this, and so pronounced by the chief of ordnance, is now offered to the government by the American manufacturer referred to, at $15 in small and $13 in large numbers. The same manufacturer, as we have learned since the first cases were decided by us, is willing to contract to supply the Springfield muskets, in large numbers, at $16. This allusion to the spirit in which Colt's company has dealt with the government is made with a view of showing how unsafe it was to permit it, through a private proposal, to determine the price which the government should pay for Springfield muskets. No attempt, however, appears to have been made by advertisements to lower this rate, at which all the subsequent orders for these muskets—that of Mr. Mason included—have been issued. This, with the vast pecuniary losses it has entailed, is the legitimate result of the abandonment of the principle of advertising, so earnestly impressed by the statute and regulations. One of the consequences of the high prices thus improvidently paid by the government was the creation of an unhealthy competition among those seeking the mechanical skill and labor or the materials necessary in the manufacture of arms. Under this undue stimulus, wages and materials rose, and those holding these orders for arms were thus led to enter into contracts, and to proceed in their engagements with the government, on a basis which precludes us from directing such a reduction of the prices as, under other circumstances, we would have felt warranted in making.

The disastrous effect of giving out contracts of such magnitude, without soliciting competition by advertisement has been, probably, even more glaring in the orders for arms to be purchased abroad than in those issued for their manufacture in our own country. One of the worst results has been to call into existence a class of speculators known as "middle men," all of whose profits are unwarrantable abstractions from the public treasury. Merchants engaged in large and successful commerce or extensive manufactures, usually busy at home are best reached by public notice. Failing this, "middle men," who have neither establishments to manufacture, nor business relations enabling them to furnish, in the course of their legitimate operations, the necessary supplies, thrust themselves between the government and the manufacturers and merchants, whose interest it is to deal directly with each other, and thus often realize, as mere factors neither needed nor desired, profits almost fabulous in amount, at the expense of the government. Investigations have shown that this system has extended far beyond the Ordnance department, and that, while involving the loss of many millions, it has been the means of introducing and fostering a deplorable demoralization. At no time and under no circumstances could such a course of administration reasonably expect to escape condemnation, but it especially deserves it at the present moment, when the public debt is being increased at from two to three millions of dollars daily, and when the honest laborious industry of the country is on the point of being taxed to its utmost capacity to bear the burdens thus imposed.

A single case, recently decided by the commission, may here be noticed, in illustration. One of these "middle men," who had never dealt in arms, and had no experience as to their quality or value, obtained an order for 50,000 foreign guns. For these he at once sub-contracted with Boker & Co., of New York, dealers in arms, at such rates and on such conditions that, without the advance of a dollar, and for the labor of a few days at most, his profits, by the terms of the contract, amounted to two hundred and eighty thousand dollars. After repeated conferences with him, so convinced did the individual in question ultimately become of the flagrant injustice to the public of a remuneration so utterly out of proportion to the service rendered, that he, himself, at the suggestion of the commission, proposed to surrender two-fifths of his order, and on the remaining three-fifths to strike from the price of one lot of these guns four dollars each, and from another lot of inferior quality, ten dollars each; and the matter was finally settled with the assent of the claimant, on a basis which reduces his expected profits to about one-tenth their original amount, thus saving to the government a quarter of a million of dollars, and relieving it, in addition, from the payment of $400,000 for 20,000 undesirable guns.

Such a case never could have arisen under a system of obedience to the law.

But the neglect to advertise is not, in the case which we are now considering, the only omission to conform to the requirements of the law.

An act approved April 8, 1808, provides, under a heavy penalty, that "no member of Congress shall, directly or indirectly, himself, or by any other person in trust for him, or for his use or benefit, or on his account, undertake, execute, hold, or enjoy, in the whole or in part, any contract or agreement hereafter to be made or entered into with any officer of the United States in their behalf, or with any person authorized to make contracts on the part of the United States," and a violation of this provision is declared to be a high misdemeanor, rendering null and void the contract, and subjecting the party to a fine of three thousand dollars. The 3d section requires that "in every such contract or agreement to be made or entered into, or accepted as aforesaid, there shall be inserted an express condition that no member of Congress shall be admitted to any share or part of such contract or agreement, or to any benefit to arise thereupon."

There must have been reasons of the gravest character for the passage of this extraordinarily stringent law, which is still in full force.

The subsequent experience of the government, so far from suggesting a relaxation of the rigor of the statute, led to the adoption of the act of 26th February, 1853, the 3d section of which provides that—

"Any senator or representative in Congress who, after the passage of this act, shall, for compensation paid or to be paid, certain or contingent, act as agent or ttor ney for prosecuting any claim or claims against the United States, or shall in any manner or by any means, for such compensation, aid or assist in the prosecution or support of any such claim or claims, or shall receive any gratuity or any share of or interest in any claim from any claimant against the United States, with intent to aid or assist, or in consideration of having aided or assisted in the prosecution of such a claim, shall be liable to indictment, as for a misdemeanor, in any court of the United States having jurisdiction thereof, and, on conviction, shall pay a fine not exceeding five thousand dollars, or suffer imprisonment in the penitentiary not exceeding one year, or both, as the court in its discretion shall adjudge."

This clause is a remarkable enlargement of the act of 1808, and denounces any interested connexion of a member of Congress with a claim against the government, even in the character of agent or attorney, as a misdemeanor, punishable by fine and imprisonment in the penitentiary. It was the obvious purpose of these laws to guard the purity of the national legislature, by making its members the representatives of the nation, and not of their own personal interests, or of those of government contractors. We do not deem it competent for an officer in the executive department, by his action, to disregard and virtually destroy this safeguard, which Congress, in its wisdom and patriotism, has so carefully thrown around itself.

Imperative as are these enactments, in the case of the order to Mr. Mason they have been wholly disregarded. No provision excluding members of Congress from a share in the contract, or from any benefit to arise therefrom, appears in that paper, nor, except in the four first contracts already referred to, has the commission found this provision incorporated in a single contract or order for arms issued since the commencement of the present rebellion. And thus, in a proposed expenditure of more than thirty millions of dollars, the government has been left without that protection to its interests and its honor which a compliance with the law would have afforded.

While, for these reasons, this order and its acceptance cannot be regarded as a contract binding upon the government, still there are equitable considerations in favor of the party, arising out of the transaction as it has progressed, which cannot be overlooked. Mr. Mason, in virtue of the order, which he may have regarded as conformable to law, has made considerable outlays and incurred large obligations, and it is but just that he should, as far as practicable, be protected from loss. Such protection the commissioners feel assured they will afford him in confirming his order to the extent of thirty thousand guns at the contract price. This price, even for a much smaller order, is a liberal one, and is such as to secure Mr. Mason not only indemnity against all loss, but, under reasonably good management, a satisfactory profit on his investment and a fair return for his labor and his risks. This confirmation, however, must be given on condition. Parties to contracts to be executed in future, whether for supplies or services, are required by law and the usages of the government to give bond, with responsible sureties, for the performance of their engagements. The regulations of the War Department upon the subject are as follows :

"1050. The contractor shall give bond with good and sufficient security for the true and faithful performance of his contract, and each surety shall state his place of residence.

"1051. An express condition shall be inserted in contracts that no member of Congress shall be admitted to any share or part therein, or any benefit to arise therefrom."

This case, like all others of the numerous class to which it belongs, is wholly without these ordinary and essential characteristics of a government executory contract. Mr. Mason has given no bond or surety for the discharge of the obligations assumed by his acceptance. If, from any cause, he shall neglect or refuse a delivery of the guns at the times stipulated, the government is without the means of obliging him to make it, and without any indemnity for his failure.

Law and sound policy alike forbid that the great national interests, which may be bound up with the faithful fulfilment of these contracts for arms, shall be exposed to the hazards of so loose and irresponsible a mode of dealing as this. These interests make it the duty of the government to demand the customary guarantees, and the very full prices to be paid justify the commission in determining that this demand shall be insisted on. It is therefore decided that the order to Mr. Mason be confirmed, subject to all its terms, to the extent of thirty thousand muskets, upon condition that he shall, within fifteen days after notice of this decision, execute bond, with good and sufficient sureties, in the form and with the stipulations prescribed by law and the regulations, for the performance of the contract, as thus modified, resulting from said order and acceptance, and, upon his failure or refusal to execute such bond, then the said order shall be declared annulled and of no effect.

We are, sir, very respectfully, your obedient servants,

J. HOLT,
ROBERT DALE OWEN,
Commissioners, &c.

Brigadier General J. W. RIPLEY,
Chief of Ordnance.

WILLARDS' HOTEL,
Washington, May 28, 1862.

GENTLEMEN: Your award respecting my contract with the War Department is so far short of what I had reason to hope and expect that I venture to ask a revision of it.

You infer from my statement that, by my original proposition made to Mr. Scott, I was to manufacture at my own establishment at Taunton every part of the arm, and that this was one of the main inducements both for the order for fifty thousand muskets and the right to extend it to one hundred thousand, as it held out the prospect of establishing an efficient armory to furnish arms for the government.

Permit me to correct the impression you have thus received. Certainly I did not expect or design to have all the several parts of the Springfield rifle muskets, which I undertook to furnish, made at my own works, so as to begin the deliveries during next month, nor did I even design to convey that impression to you or to the Secretary.

Indeed, it would have been exceedingly difficult, if not impossible, for me to have procured the necessary machinery and workmen. Besides, it was, as I supposed, well known to the Secretary and to you, gentlemen, that many of the parts of the musket are made in different places, and are brought together where the arm is finally assembled and finished. It is the course of the manufacture, and, so long as they are finished at the time, of the material, workmanship, and pattern required, I had not supposed it was material where they were made. Undoubtedly it was, and is, my purpose, progressively, to procure the required machinery, and have every part manufactured, under my immediate superintendence, in my own workshops, and thus establish a complete armory. But this must be the work of time, and grow out of my success, and that success must mainly depend on my getting contracts which will enable me to make these arrangements; and this was one of the considerations with me to accept this order, inasmuch as I knew, until I could get the machinery myself, I could have the article supplied under my own direction.

Indeed, there are very few extensive manufactories in this country in which the whole machine in all its parts, if it consists of many parts, is made. Such, I know, is the case with most, if not all the manufacturers of locomotive and cotton machinery, &c. My great object, I have already stated, was to establish a manufactory or armory for fire-arms, but I never contemplated its being done before I commenced the manufacture, understanding then, as I do now, that it would be a full compliance with my contract if I supplied the arms, principally made by myself, at the times and according to the stipulations of my contract.

I am the more desirous that this shall be clearly understood because, however undesignedly, the award seems to impute to me a breach of faith in my representations of my objects and ability to execute the order. To show that my meaning has been misapprehended, you have but to consider the fact, that to execute that order, as I have already stated to you, I have, including the moneys already expended and the responsibilities I have incurred, embarked in this business about six hundred thousand dollars, and still my machinery is incomplete for the making of each several part of the musket, and a larger outlay will yet be required to enable me to turn them out so as to furnish the supply at the time stipulated. I do not mean to say that all this machinery and outlay would be lost if the contract were now taken from or refused me, but I do mean to say I have incurred it for the purpose and with the view of fully complying with the terms of my engagement, and the loss must be very great. Nor do I at present see how it can be covered, and give me any reasonable remuneration if I am even saved from loss, if it shall be reduced to thirty thousand muskets as proposed by you.

This expenditure has been incurred in perfect good faith. I have been led into it by the authorized agents of the government, and upon their promise I have undertaken to make an armory which shall be national in its character. It is not a manufacture to be supported by trade and the demands of business, furnishing articles or machinery in common use, but, from its very nature and the implements it is intended to produce, must, in a great degree, depend on government patronage; and for these and like reasons I submit for your further consideration whether it be just and fit for the government to reduce their order so as, in a great measure, to defeat the main object of both parties when that order was given, and which I am in good faith devoting my capital and energies to the execution of my part of it. A fair and close calculation has been made of the cost of production of the muskets, delivered, and there is no margin for a reduction of the order below seventy-five thousand. Above that my profits would be no more than a fair and just compensation for the time, labor, care, and capital required to a faithful execution of the order. Below that number I cannot receive a reasonable recompense. I do not, in the midst of the pressure now existing and that which is to come upon the people of this country, make any appeal to the liberality of the government, but I do ask even-handed justice.

You have yourselves by your award settled the question whether, under the circumstances, the government ought to give me a contract, but, under a misapprehension of the facts, have reduced it so low as to render it not only useless, but probably a loss to me, and I have endeavored to correct that misapprehension.

"I observe in your award," you say, "that the order to Mr. Mason be confirmed, *subject to all its terms*, to thirty thousand muskets." If by this is meant that every part or piece employed in the musket is to be made in my workshops in Taunton, it is what has never been required from any manufacturer in the country, and certainly it was not contemplated by Mr. Scott when he gave the order, or by myself when I accepted it.

The terms used in the postscript, "if manufactured in your establishment in Taunton," mean that the barrels, stocks, and all the material parts, be made under my direction, and put together there; that the musket shall be my musket, just as a locomotive would be manufactured by me, although the flues, axles, tires, &c., should be made to my order, brought to my workshops, and then fitted and set up with the residue of the machine. This is what General

Ripley meant: that the musket should be made under my direction and super-intendence, assembled and completed in my works. It was to avoid the possi-bility of my palming off an inferior article on the government, and, as such, I was and am willing to accept and comply with the terms. I am already pre-pared with the machinery for finishing barrels at the rate of two hundred and fifty in ten hours, and my stocking machinery is nearly completed. The most of my ramrod machinery is at work, and all parts of the musket is in progress under my direction and control.

It may not be irrelevant for me to say, that when the order for fifty thousand muskets was offered to me, I declined it, and would not have taken it without the postscript added by General Ripley; and if he had intimated that each and every part of the gun was to be made in my workshops, I would not have hesi-tated a moment to reject it. I knew that most, if not all, gun-makers (not even excluding the Springfield armory) get some parts made outside, and I intended to avail of the same artisans until I could get improved machinery to do the work; and it is in this very effort I have expended so much. Were it otherwise, and I was not involved, an order for seventy-five thousand would not induce me to undertake another such task.

Now, after having embarked so much capital in it, and being satisfied that I can turn out an implement fully equal, if not superior, to any I have seen, I am willing to have my order reduced to seventy-five thousand muskets.

I have the honor to be, gentlemen, your obedient servant,

WM. MASON.

Hon. JOSEPH HOLT and ROBERT DALE OWEN, *Commissioners.*

JUNE 10, 1862.

Considered by the commission, and it is decided that the number of arms as-signed to Mr. Mason is as large as the commission think it proper at this time to assign to one contractor at the price of $20.

J. HOLT,
ROBERT DALE OWEN,
Commissioners.

CASE No. 73.

BURNSIDE RIFLE COMPANY.

PROVIDENCE, RHODE ISLAND, *February* 7, 1862.

SIR: In compliance with general order requiring all persons "claiming to have any contract, bargain," &c., with the War Department or "any bureau thereof," to give written notice of such, and its purport, the Burnside Rifle Company of this city respectfully submit the following copies of contracts and orders, and also their acceptances of the same.

Under these contracts and orders, we have delivered to Captain Rodman, in accordance with the order of November 1, 580 carbines, as per inspector's receipt, dated December 11. The balance of that order, 60 carbines, are now ready for inspection. The whole number of carbines which we will be able to deliver in this and the first part of next month is 1,130, of which 60 belong to order of November 1; 520 should go to complete a contract made with the State of In-diana early in the summer, and since assumed by the government; 480 under that contract having been already delivered. The remainder, say 550, will be our first delivery under contract of August 27.

No lack of money or individual exertion has prevented a strict compliance with that contract.

We have accomplished all that was possible for us. Since July last we have built and nearly equipped an armory of sufficient capacity to turn out from 25,000 to 30,000 rifles per annum, and by the month of April next will produce at that rate. Exclusive of the 1,130, we have now in process about 6,000 carbines which we shall begin to deliver in the month of April next.

Respectfully, your obedient servant,

ISAAC HARTSHORN, *Agent.*

Hon. EDWIN M. STANTON,
Secretary of War, Washington, D. C.

ORDNANCE OFFICE,
Washington, July 16, 1861.

SIR: There are required immediately by this department eight hundred of Burnside's carbines, for which the same price last paid will be allowed. Please inform me of the shortest time possible you are prepared to furnish them.

Respectfully, your obedient servant,

JAMES W. RIPLEY,
Brevet Brigadier General.

CHARLES JACKSON, Esq.,
Treasurer of the Burnside Fire-arms Company,
Providence, Rhode Island.

Extract from letter of acceptance of foregoing order.

PROVIDENCE, *July 18, 1861.*

SIR: I have your letter of the 16th instant, ordering eight hundred Burnside carbines. In reply, I beg to say that, having perfected the arm during the last two years, I have recently reorganized, under the name of the Burnside Rifle Company, Isaac Hartshorn, agent. We will take your order for the eight hundred carbines, to be delivered in December next, in whole or in part, probably the whole. This is the earliest moment that we can safely promise them.

I am, very respectfully, your obedient servant,

CHARLES JACKSON,
Treasurer of the Burnside Fire-arms Company.

Brigadier General J. W. RIPLEY,
Chief of Ordnance, Washington, D. C.

ORDNANCE OFFICE,
Washington, November 5, 1861.

SIR: Please have ready for Governor Sprague, as soon as possible, 632 carbines, on account of the order to you of the 27th August last. Inform Captain Rodman, at Watertown arsenal, Massachusetts, when they are ready for inspection, and he will be directed to have them inspected, and to give you the certificates and receipts to accompany your bills for payment.

Respectfully, your obedient servant,

JAMES W. RIPLEY,
Brigadier General.

ISAAC HARTSHORN, Esq., *Providence, Rhode Island.*

A verbal permission was given on the 19th of November to substitute the order of July 16 for the foregoing, and under that order there were inspected and delivered to Captain Rodman five hundred and eighty carbines, as per in-

Ex. Doc. 72——21

spector's receipt sent to the Ordnance department under date of December 11. The remainder of the order is about ready for delivery.

ORDNANCE OFFICE,
Washington, August 27, 1861.

SIR : By direction of the Secretary of War, I offer you an order for seven thousand five hundred Burnside's carbines, on the following terms and conditions, viz :

The carbines to have steel barrels, twenty-one inches long, to be half stocked, bore .54 inch, weight from seven and a quarter to seven and an eighth pounds. The carbines, with appendages, are to be delivered at the United States arsenal on Governor's island, New York. The first one thousand in January, 1862 ; twelve hundred in February, 1862; and fifteen hundred in each succeeding month, until the whole 7,500 are delivered. The arms and appendages are to be subject to inspection by such officer as this department may designate for the purpose. In case of a failure to deliver in or within the terms before specified, the government is to be under no obligation to take the arms or appendages, but may or may not do so, at its option. Payments are to be made in such funds as the Treasury Department may provide, on certificates of inspection and receipt by the United States inspecting officer, at the rate of thirty-five dollars ($35) for each carbine, including appendages, which are to be one wiping thong and brush, one spare cone, one screw-driver and wrench for each arm, and one spring vise and one bullet mould for every ten arms.

Please signify, in writing, whether you accept the foregoing order on the terms and conditions specified herein.

Respectfully, your obedient servant,
JAMES W. RIPLEY,
Brigadier General.
ISAAC HARTSHORN, Esq., *Agent, Washington, D. C.*

ORDNANCE OFFICE,
Washington, August 28, 1861.

SIR : By direction of the Secretary of War, I offer you an order for one thousand Burnside's infantry rifle muskets, on the following terms and conditions, viz :

The muskets to have angular bayonets, steel barrels 37 inches long, full stocked, weight from 9 to 9½ pounds. The muskets, with appendages, are to be delivered at the United States arsenal on Governor's island, New York, during the year 1862. The arms and appendages are to be subject to inspection by such officer as this department may designate for the purpose. In case of failure to deliver in the time before specified, the government is to be under no obligation to take the arms or appendages, but may or may not do so, at its option. Payment is to be made in such funds as the Treasury Department may provide, on certificates of inspection and receipt by the United States inspector, at the rate of thirty-eight and a half dollars ($38 50) for each musket, including appendages, which are to be one wiping thong and brush, one spare cone, one screw-driver and wrench for each arm, and one spring vise and one bullet mould for every ten arms.

Please state, in writing, whether you accept the foregoing order on the terms and conditions stated herein.

Respectfully, your obedient servant,
JAS. W. RIPLEY, *Brigadier General.*
ISAAC HARTSHORN, Esq.,
Agent, Washington, D. C.

PROVIDENCE, *August* 31, 1861.

SIR: Your two letters of the 27th and 28th instant—the first offering us a contract for 7,500 Burnside breech-loading carbines, and the second a contract for 1,000 Burnside breech-loading infantry rifle muskets with angular bayonets— are received.

I accept both offers, in behalf of our company, on the terms stated in your letters.

Very respectfully, your obedient servant,

For BURNSIDE RIFLE COMPANY,

ISAAC HARTSHORN, *Agent.*

General JAMES W. RIPLEY,
Chief of Ordnance, Washington, D. C.

ORDNANCE OFFICE, *Washington, November* 21, 1861.

SIR: By direction of the Secretary of War, I offer you an order for twenty-five hundred (2,500) Burnside's breech-loading rifles, with sabre bayonets, Harper's Ferry rifle length, calibre .58 inch, on the following terms and conditions, viz: these arms, with appendages, are to be delivered for inspection by the 15th day of August next, or earlier if possible, and are to be subject to inspection by such officers as this department may designate for the purpose. In case of failure to deliver in the time before specified, the government is to be under no obligation to receive or pay for any of the 2,500 arms or appendages remaining undelivered at the time of such failure, and is authorized to cancel and annul this order as regards those arms. Payments are to be made in such funds as the Treasury Department may provide, on certificates of inspection and receipt by the United States inspector, at the rate of thirty-eight and a half dollars ($38 50) for each arm, including appendages, which are to be one wiping rod and brush, one spare cone, and one screw-driver and wrench for each arm, and one spring vise and one bullet mould for every ten arms.

Please signify your acceptance or non-acceptance of this order on the terms and conditions herein stated.

Respectfully, your obedient servant,

JAMES W. RIPLEY,

Brigadier General.

ISAAC HARTSHORN, Esq.,
Providence, Rhode Island.

PROVIDENCE, *December* 11, 1861.

SIR: Your order, dated November 21, for 2,500 Burnside breech-loading rifles was duly received. We accept it.

The only question as to its acceptance has been in regard to the time of delivery, which is short, considering the number of arms to be delivered by us previous to the date named.

We will make every exertion to meet your requirements.

Very respectfully, your obedient servant,

For BURNSIDE RIFLE COMPANY,

ISAAC HARTSHORN, *Agent.*

General JAMES W. RIPLEY,
Chief of Ordnance, Washington, D. C.

PROVIDENCE, R. I., *April* 7, 1862.

SIR: In reply to your letter of the 29th ultimo, referring to our communication to the honorable Secretary of War, dated February 7, we respectfully submit that in said communication we explained somewhat the extent of our preparations for making rifles. The same difficulties that have stood in the way of other contractors for the delivery of arms have obstructed our progress. It seems that all have underrated the preliminary difficulties inherent to a new business. We have suffered, and do now suffer, from the failures of contractors in the delivery of machinery, and in many instances could not anticipate our own wants so as to order it in time. When the machines are delivered, the infinite variety of small tools required before they can be successfully operated is entirely beyond ordinary experience in business.

Gun-making is, comparatively, a new business in this country. Competent workmen are scarce, and so great is the demand for them that wages have advanced from two to three dollars per day. Notwithstanding all this, we hope we may have credit for some activity. The first order from the Ordnance department for rifles, dated July 16, 1861, a copy of which is enclosed, was entirely unexpected, and found us unprepared to execute. On the 22d day of the same we began to excavate for the foundations of our new armory buildings; they are now complete and in successful operation, but will yet require time to perfect them in the details of the several departments.

On the 13th of December we delivered to L. Leonard, the military storekeeper at Watertown arsenal, 580 carbines, and on the 10th of February we delivered the same officer 60 more—making in all 640—the amount called for at the time under the order of July 16. Copies of the storekeeper's receipts for said arms we herewith enclose. On the 13th of March we delivered Governor Sprague, as per order dated November 1, 1861, a copy of which is herewith enclosed, 260 carbines. We enclose a copy of Quartermaster General Frieze's receipt for the same. On the 20th of March we had ready for inspection 800 carbines. These are now being inspected under order of Major Balch, of the Springfield armory. We have also in process, in various stages of completion, 6,000 carbines—some of which are far advanced. Thus it will be perceived that we have endeavored to carry out our verbal engagement with the honorable Secretary of War, viz: that we would build and equip, in the shortest space of time, an armory of large productive capacity, and would perfect and cheapen the cost of the arm to the utmost of our ability.

We have effected great improvements in the simplicity and efficiency of the arm, and are authorized by Captain Rodman, of Watertown, to whom they have been submitted, to use his name in reference to them. These improvements, with the permission of the department, will be ingrafted upon the arm in a few weeks.

The undersigned will have the honor to present himself in a few days to the honorable commission, when he will be happy to make any further explanations that may be required.

Very respectfully, your obedient servant,

For BURNSIDE RIFLE COMPANY,
ISAAC HARTSHORN, *Agent.*

P. V. HAGNER,
Major of Ordnance, Washington, D. C.

ORDNANCE OFFICE, *Washington, March* 29, 1862.

SIR: In answer to your note of this morning, I have to state that I have not the means of estimating the cost of the Burnside carbine, and cannot, therefore, say what price will afford a fair profit to the manufacturers.

Respectfully, your obedient servant,

JAS. W. RIPLEY, *Brigadier General.*

J. WISE, Esq., *Secretary to Commission, &c.*

Before commission, April 21, 1862.

Mr. Hartshorn, of Burnside Rifle Company, states: We have orders for 7,500 carbines, at $35; 2,500 breech-loading rifles, at $38 50; 1,000 muskets, at $38 50. The times of delivery are, for the carbines, 1,000 in January, and 1,500 per month thereafter; rifles, prior to August 15; muskets, during 1862.

We have done nothing as yet on the rifles and muskets. We have 800 carbines now ready, with malleable iron band and sight seat; 530 of these have been inspected, and the malleable parts have been changed to meet the order of the inspector. This change we are to make in all as soon as possible. It will require at least four weeks. The reason that this happens is, that the band is an addition not heretofore used. The base of the sight has long been made of malleable iron. 520 of these arms have been made upon the order of Indiana, but they have been assumed by the government and inspected by its officers. The product of our establishment can be readily increased, so that in a short time we could deliver from 30,000 to 40,000 per annum. We have a large armory and an investment of $235,000. I understand the order for 520 from Indiana is in addition to our order for 7,500 from the government. The original order from Indiana was for 1,000; of this we delivered 480 in October, and the 520 completes the number. We would wish to deliver 600 besides the 800 of the old pattern, and then proceed with the new.

WASHINGTON, *May* 14, 1862.

It has been suggested to the undersigned that the contract price for the Burnside carbine is objected to as being greater than what is paid for other breech-loading carbines, and that the reduced price of $30 per gun would be acceptable; he submits to those suggestions, and respectfully requests you to confirm the contract for seventy-five hundred carbines, at $30 each.

While yielding to your wishes, we beg to submit that we have been stimulated, by the exigency of the government, to expensive and overstrained exertions to manufacture arms rapidly; that we have lost about three months' time in our endeavors to perfect certain improvements; that these will yet require more time; we respectfully request, therefore, that you indulge us with such extension as you have granted those who manufacture the Springfield musket.

We would like to deliver these carbines at the rate of one thousand per month, commencing with the month of June. The first two deliveries will be the most difficult of execution. Such indulgence will enable us to fulfil all our obligations. One to the Navy Department.

May the undersigned be permitted to request as early a decision in his case as is practicable?

Very respectfully,

ISAAC HARTSHORN.

The honorable COMMISSION ON CONTRACTS, &c.

COMMISSION ON ORDNANCE AND ORDNANCE STORES,
Washington, May 15, 1862.

GENERAL: The commission have the honor to report as follows:

CASE No. 73.—ISAAC HARTSHORN, Agent Burnside's Rifle Company.

Order given by direction of the Secretary of War, dated August 27, 1861. Page 182, Ex. Doc., No. 67. Referred by direction of the Secretary of War.

To furnish 7,500 Burnside's carbines, subject to inspection, at $35 each, with appendages. Deliveries to be made as follows: 1,000 in January, 1,200 in February, and 1,500 monthly thereafter. In case of failure to deliver in or within the times specified, the government is to be under no obligation to take the arms and appendages, but may or may not do, so at his option.

The commission find that no deliveries have yet been made under the above orders, although the company have been engaged in extending their works and in improving the model of their carbine, and are now nearly prepared to proceed vigorously with their work, having essentially improved it in several particulars. Under the condition stipulated in the order the government is not bound to receive the carbines; as the price is deemed unreasonably high, the commission called upon Mr. Hartshorn, the agent of the company, to make a proposition based upon a price not exceeding thirty dollars for each, including appendages.

Mr. Hartshorn has appeared before the commission, and agreed to furnish the arms at thirty dollars each, including appendages, provided the order be confirmed as to the number, and the first delivery of 1,000 be not required before June, 1862.

The commission accept the above, and direct that the terms and conditions of the original order, dated August 27, be confirmed, allowing only $30 per carbine, including appendages accepted after inspection, instead of $35, and stipulating that the first delivery of 1,000 shall be made in June, 1862, and the second, of at least 1,000, in July, 1862, and that 1,500, and more, if possible, be delivered monthly thereafter, until the whole 7,500 be delivered; which acceptance is upon condition that he shall, within fifteen days after notice of this decision, execute bond, with good and sufficient sureties, in the form and with the stipulations prescribed by law and the regulations for the performance of the contract, as thus modified, resulting from said order and acceptance; and upon his failure or refusal to execute such bond, then the said order shall be declared cancelled and of no effect.

We are, sir, very respectfully, your obedient servants,

J. HOLT,
ROBERT DALE OWEN,
Commissioners, &c.

P. V. HAGNER,
Major Ordnance, Assistant to Commission.

General J. W. RIPLEY,
   Chief of Ordnance.

CASE No. 74.

BURNSIDE RIFLE COMPANY.

COMMISSION ON ORDNANCE AND ORDNANCE STORES,
Washington, May 15, 1862.

GENERAL: The commission have the honor to report as follows:

CASE No. 74.—ISAAC HARTSHORN, Agent Burnside Rifle Company.

Order by direction of the Secretary of War, dated August 28, 1861.— (See page 69, Ex. Doc No 67.) Also, order by same direction, dated November 21, 1861.— (See page 139, Ex. Doc. No. 67.) Referred by direction of the Secretary of War.

To furnish 1,000 Burnside infantry rifle muskets during the year 1862, at the rate of $38 50 for each musket, including appendages. In case of failure to deliver as specified, the government may or may not receive the guns, at its option.

To furnish 2,500 Burnside breech-loading rifles, with sabre bayonets, prior to August 15, 1862, at the rate of $38 50, including appendages. Same provision as above, in case of failure to deliver.

The commission find that the above orders were given after the remonstrance of the chief of ordnance, who, in reference to the offer of this company, stated, under date of July 24, "that the acceptance is objectionable on account of the prices charged, of the remote periods of delivery, and of the introduction of rifles and muskets requiring special ammunition." Mr. Hartshorn, agent of the company, has appeared before the commission, and states that no work has been done upon either of these orders, as the company have been fully occupied in working for the government upon the order given them for 7,500 carbines. He has further agreed that, as the commission has confirmed the order for carbines, and thus given employment for his factory, and as he is anxious to gain further experience before undertaking new patterns of arms, he will surrender these two orders, if desired by the commission. The commission accept this offer, and therefore direct that the two orders above be revoked and annulled.

Very respectfully, your obedient servants,

J. HOLT,
ROBERT DALE OWEN,
Commissioners, &c.
P. V. HAGNER,
Major of Ordnance, Assistant to Commission.

General J. W. RIPLEY,
Chief of Ordnance.

CASE No. 75.

C. B. HOARD.

WASHINGTON CITY, *December* 9, 1861.

SIR: I understand that the honorable C. B. Hoard, of the State of New York, has before you an application for a contract for manufacturing arms for the government. Mr. Hoard is believed to be a gentleman of sufficient pecuniary means, of mechanical skill, and of great integrity; and the success of the object he has in view would subserve the public interest, and be highly appreciated by our people in his section of our State. I therefore strongly recommend his application to your favorable consideration and approval.

I have the honor to be, with great respect, your most obedient servant,

E. D. MORGAN.

Hon. SIMON CAMERON,
Secretary of War.

Senator King's letter.

WASHINGTON, *December* 4, 1861.

DEAR SIR: The honorable Charles B. Hoard has an extensive steam-engine manufactory at Watertown, New York, and proposes to enter upon the manufacture of arms. He is a gentleman of character, skilful business qualifications, and responsibility. I suppose arms are purchased or contracted for where they can be obtained of the best quality for the smallest price. Mr. Hoard proposes to compete for furnishing arms. I think he can be relied upon to perform any agreement he will undertake to perform.

Very respectfully,

PRESTON KING.

Hon. SIMON CAMERON,
Secretary of War.

December 5, 1861.—C. B. Hoard, of New York.—Proposal to furnish 50,000 Springfield rifled muskets.

WASHINGTON CITY, *December 4, 1861.*

The undersigned, a resident of New York, desires to obtain a contract to manufacture for the government fifty thousand stand of the Springfield rifled musket upon the same terms as to quantity, price, and time for delivery, given to other parties having similar contracts.

Very respectfully,

C. B. HOARD.

Hon. SIMON CAMERON,
　　Secretary of War.

C. B. Hoard.—Proposal to make arms.

WASHINGTON, *December 2, 1861.*

We understand that Mr. C. B. Hoard, of New York, desires to procure a contract from the government for making the Springfield arms, and we are informed that New York has had but very little of that kind of patronage, whilst it must be conceded that she is entitled to a liberal share. We considered Mr. Hoard (who, we understand, has a large manufacturing establishment now entirely idle, his business having been cut off by this unfortunate rebellion) entitled to a favorable consideration, and shall be gratified if a contract is awarded to him.

A. S. DIXON.
IRA HARRIS.
THEO. M. POMEROY, 25th Dist., N. Y.
BURT VAN HORN, 31st Dist., N. Y.
WILLIAM WALL, 5th Dist., N. Y.
A. B. OLIN, 13th Cong. Dist.
R. CONKLING.
W. A. WHEELER, 16th Dist., N. Y.
R. FRANCHOT, 19th Dist., N. Y.
S. N. SHERMAN, 17th Dist., N. Y.
C. B. SEDGWICK, 24th Dist.
M. F. ODELL, 2d Dist.
EDW. HENRY SMITH, 1st Dist.

J. P. CHAMBERLAIN, 20th Dist.
E. G. SPAULDING.
ERASTUS CORNING.
EDWARD HAIGHT, 9th Dist.
JOHN B. STEELE, 11th, N. Y.
R. H. DUELL, 21st, N. Y.
JAMES B. MCKEAN, 15th N. Y.
R. E. FENTON, 33d, N. Y.
ELIJAH WARD, 7th, N. Y.
STEPHEN BAKER, 12th, N. Y.
W. E. LANSING, 22d, N. Y.
AUGUSTUS FRANK, 30th Dist., N. Y.
R. B. VAN VALKENBURGH, 28th Dist.

Hon. SIMON CAMERON,
　　Secretary of War.

Mr. Hoard's letter to Senator Simmons.—The city representatives ask contract for Hoard.

DECEMBER 17, 1861.

DEAR SIR: The governor has gone into Virginia to-day to review the New York troops, and for that reason I could not get his letter this morning. It shall be duly filed. The remaining names, with unimportant exceptions, of members of Congress from New York can be obtained, if desired by the department. But for the adjournment over till Monday they would have been obtained yesterday. The list now embraces Corning, of Albany; Conkling, of Utica; Sedgwick, of Syracuse; Spaulding, of Buffalo; Olin, of Troy; Sherman, of Ogdensburg, representing Herkimer county; and part of the city members.

Senators Harris and King have both given their names. I am anxious to get away, and since Colonel Scott has kindly offered to give me a contract for 25,000, it appears to me that his sense of justice will carry him the rest of the way; for why should I, an applicant from New York, be less favored than those of other States?

If he could give me 25,000, with the privilege of making what I could in two years, I would be content with that, for I intend to get myself in condition to compete with all other bidders for any future contracts.

Truly yours,

C. B. HOARD.

Hon. Mr. SIMMONS.

TREASURER'S OFFICE, *December* 10, 1861.

DEAR SIR: Having been informed that honorable Charles B. Hoard has it in contemplation to commence the manufacture of arms, and believing, from a full knowledge of the man and his means, that he would be able to furnish a supply to the government perhaps sooner than any other person who is not already engaged in the manufacture of arms, I would most respectfully but earnestly recommend that a contract be given him.

I have the honor to be, very respectfully, your obedient servant,

F. E. SPINNER.

Hon. SIMON CAMERON,
Secretary of War, Washington, D. C.

ORDNANCE OFFICE, *Washington, December* 24, 1861.

SIR: By direction of the Secretary of War, I offer you an order for fifty thousand (50,000) muskets, with appendages, of the Springfield pattern, on the following terms and conditions, viz: These arms are to be furnished with the regular appendages, and are to be in all respects identical with the standard rifle muskets made at the United States armory at Springfield, Massachusetts, and are to interchange with it and with each other in all their parts; they are to be subject to inspection by the United States inspectors, in the same manner that the Springfield arms are inspected, and none are to be received or paid for but such as pass inspection and are approved by the United States inspectors. These fifty thousand (50,000) arms and appendages are to be delivered at your armory as follows, viz: Not less than one thousand (1,000) in each of the months of July, August, and September, 1862; not less than two thousand (2,000) in each of the months of October and November, 1862; not less than three thousand (3,000) in December, 1862; and not less than four thousand per month thereafter, until the entire fifty thousand shall have been delivered; and you are to have the right to deliver more rapidly than according to the number of arms before specified, if you can do so. In the case of any failure to make deliveries to the extent and within the times before specified, you are to forfeit the right to deliver whatever number may be deficient in the specified number for the month in which the failure occurs. All these arms and appendages are to be delivered by you, and this order, if transferred to another party, is to be thereby forfeited. Payments are to be made in such funds as the Treasury Department may provide, for each delivery, on certificates of inspection and receipt by the United States inspectors, at the rate of twenty dollars ($20) for each arm, including appendages. All these arms and appendages are to be packed by you in boxes of the regular pattern, with twenty (20) muskets and appendages in each box, for which a fair price, to be determined by the United States inspectors, will be allowed.

Please signify in writing, your acceptance or non-acceptance of this order, on the terms and conditions before stated herein.

Respectfully, your obedient servant,

JAS. W. RIPLEY, *Brigadier General.*

C. B. HOARD, *New York, N. Y.*

WATERTOWN, *N. Y., January* 11, 1862.

SIR: I hereby accept the order, dated December 24, 1861, for fifty thousand muskets, on the terms and conditions stated in the said order, which was mailed to me at Washington on the 7th January, instant.

Very respectfully, your obedient servant,

C. B. HOARD.

Brigadier General JAS. W. RIPLEY, *Washington, D. C.*

Memorandum.

I went to Washington, on the 28th or 29th December, to get this order, but Colonel Scott, to whom General Ripley delivered it, was in Philadelphia, and I could not get it from any of the clerks, but they telegraphed to Colonel Scott, and he replied that he would send it to me when he returned; so I got a copy from General Ripley's book. I could not, therefore, accept it till received, which was on the night of 10th January, 1862.

C. B. HOARD.

Copy of a letter to honorable P. King.

WATERTOWN, *January* 25, 1862.

MY DEAR SIR: Under a contract or an order from the War Department, dated December 24, 1861, I have incurred large liabilities for machinery and tools to manufacture guns (rifle muskets) at the price of $20 for each gun and appendages. In regard to the price, whatever impressions may have been made upon the popular mind, or on the mind of individuals, I assure you that these guns do not yield an ordinary manufacturing per cent. of profit; certainly, not so much by 10 per cent. as I have always made upon the manufacture of steam-engines; not so much as is made on locomotives, on printing presses, on pistols. But it was not to speak of the price, further than to contradict the error that I know exists to some extent in that regard, but to ask you—having said that I have, on the faith of the order given me, incurred liabilities that would be a very serious embarrassment to me if the government should repudiate the act of the department—to see the Secretary of War, or other proper officer, and advise me if there is any such purpose.

I suppose that there are outstanding orders, given to parties not manufacturers, and who have made no preparations to manufacture, which cannot be executed according to their tenor, and which, unless extended or modified, would be void. I have seen a copy of an order, conditioned for the delivery of a definite number at stated times, which I suppose would be broken on the first failure to deliver at the time specified, but no responsible manufacturer who intended to execute his order would make any outlay on one of that kind, for it would be impossible to comply with it.

The order under which I have incurred liabilities provides that if I fail to deliver in any month, the deficiency is to be deducted from the whole number in the contract. Thus you see that if by flood, or fire, or strike of hands, or any other thing working a disability to deliver in any given month, it does not affect the future instalments of the contract. There is also a clause declaring the contract forfeited if it shall be transferred. I mention this to show that it is not a thing to be offered for sale, but was given and taken in good faith.

I represented myself to the department as a responsible manufacturer, and it was because of that representation and on that ground, as I believe, that the contract was given to me. Now, I am not willing to be ranked with men who would take advantage of the necessities of the government, if they could, to profit therefrom. If the government does not need the guns certainly I do not desire to make any;

but if it does need them, and they are to be made by some one, at a fair price, then I, having a large factory idle, which can be converted into an armory, would like to put its wheels in motion which have been stopped by this rebellion much to my injury, and convert it to that use. If the government desire to arrest these bona fide contracts, let it give notice that it will relieve the contractors from damages, and tell them to stop. All orders for machinery could then be countermanded, and the damages arrested at this point. This is a matter of so great importance to me, that I hope I may count upon your giving it your attention at the earliest convenient day; for, in the meantime, I must go on with my preparations, relying upon the faith, until some action is had in the opposite direction on which I can rely.

Very respectfully, yours,

C. B. HOARD.

Hon. PRESTON KING, *Washington.*

C. B. Hoard submits copy of contract to furnish 50,000 Springfield muskets at $20:

WATERTOWN, *New York, February* 4, 1862.

SIR: My brother, Mr. Samuel Hoard, is hereby authorized to make any statements in relation to an order for guns given to me and the proceedings taken under it that you may desire, and he has been furnished by me with the necessary data.

Very respectfully,

C. B. HOARD,

The SECRETARY OF WAR, *Washington.*

WASHINGTON, *February* 8, 1862.

SIR: Having received an order from the War Department, bearing date 24th of December last, to furnish 50,000 muskets of a specific description, and noticing in the New York Herald, of the 29th of January, what was styled "an important order from the Secretary of War," though without signature, which required:

1st. That no further contract be made by this department, or any bureau thereof, for any article of foreign manufacture.

2d. All outstanding orders, &c., for the purchase of arms, clothing, or anything else in foreign countries, &c., are revoked and annulled.

3d. All persons claiming to have any contract, &c., with this department, &c., for furnishing arms, &c., are required, within fifteen days from this date, to give written notice of such contract and its purport, with a statement, in writing, of what has been done under it, and to file a copy with the Secretary of War.

4th. All contracts, &c., of which notice and a copy is not filed in accordance with this order within the period mentioned, shall be deemed and held to be *prima facie* fraudulent and void.

Assuming this order, thus published and without your official signature, to be an official document, and applicable to the order issued to me as above indicated, it becomes my duty to comply with its requirements. Under the conviction that it was issued in good faith by the department, and that it would be complied with in like faith, I accepted it. My belief was that the arms were necessary to an efficient prosecution of the war, and were especially required for the security of the nation in any future conflict to which, like all others, it is exposed, and for which it should be prepared. Perhaps to the want of arms, more than to any other cause, may be attributed the procrastination of the conflict in which we are now so unhappily engaged, and the vast expenditure required to carry on the war.

The documents on file in your department, respecting my character and responsibility, signed by the governor, United States senators, and twenty-four members of Congress from New York, will, I trust, satisfy you that I am not to be ranked among that class of peculating contractors who are fattening upon the life blood of the nation in this her great struggle for national existence. Unless the government wants the arms, and they are required for its safety and success, I, most assuredly, do not desire to make them. The price at which I have agreed to deliver them, taking into consideration the great outlay for machinery and its prospective depreciation after the order shall have been filled, is so low that it does not yield the ordinary manufacturer's profit on engines, printing presses, locomotives, and many other articles permanently required for ordinary pursuits, and, consequently, the manufacturer's loss upon machinery not nearly so great. If, however, the government does want the arms, then I do desire to manufacture them, for I have a large factory idle, and have an honest pride and pleasure in making a good article at a simply fair remunerative price.

The order alluded to, published in the New York Herald of the 29th of January, requires that a statement be made of what has been done under any orders issued by your department, and in compliance with such requirement, I would say that I own a large factory, which, until the breaking out of this war, was extensively used in manufacturing steam-engines. That, on receiving the order referred to, I immediately proceeded to take active measures to comply with its terms. I began remodelling my factory, changing and altering my machinery, building such new kinds as I could manufacture in time to meet my contract. That I also bought, at an expense of $8,000, an undivided half of a factory engaged in making agricultural implements, one-half of which I previously owned. That the half which I purchased was owned by the person who managed the business, and that if this contract should be annulled I should have this factory on my hands unoccupied and comparatively useless. This establishment is designed to be used for manufacturing the stocks of the muskets. That I have employed a very considerable number of hands in the alterations and changes of my machinery from one object to the other. That I have at some expense succeeded in obtaining a foreman of experience and skill in the manufacture of arms at a high salary, whose services would be useless unless I proceed to fill the order. That I have expended in travelling expenses, telegraphing, and otherwise, in making my contracts, about $500. Thus it will cost about $40,000 to make such machinery as I shall manufacture at my proposed armory, consisting of drops, drilling machines, milling machines, lathes, &c. That I have contracted with Messrs. Robert Hoe & Co , of New York, for one barrel-tapping machine, six rifling machines, six barrel-boring machines, (two augers, each,) one profiling machine for triggers, one profiling stock machine, one band biddery machine, one breech-pin threading machine, four clamp milling machines, two profiling machines for lock-plates, one butt shaping machine, one machine for turning between bands, which are to be made at prices amounting to about $25,000, and are all to be completed for delivery on or before the 1st of June next. I have also contracted with the American Machine Works, at Springfield, Massachusetts, for the following machinery, viz: two barrel bedding machines; three second-turners barrel machines; ten milling machines; one ramrod and band-spring fitting machine; one machine for splitting for bearings; one lock bedding machine; one butt-plate bedding, boring, and tapping machine; one guard-plate bedding machine with side apparatus for boring for screws; all of which are to cost $21,300, and on account of which I paid $1,500 dollars in advance, and am to pay $1,500 monthly until completed, which is to be on the 1st of June, 1862, when all are to be paid for. I have likewise contracted with Mr. N. Washburn, of Worcester, Massachusetts, for 50,000 gun barrels, cone-seated, at $1 50 each, 1,000 to be delivered 1st of May, 1,000 1st of June, 2,000 1st of July, and thereafter as rapidly as may be desired, not exceeding 5,000 per month. Terms, cash on delivery.

I have also made a contract with Mr. C. C. Chaffee, of Springfield, Massachusetts, for 50,000 musket cones, at 9 cents each, to be delivered, 1,500 July 1, 1862; 1,500 August 1, 1862; 1,000 September 1, 1862; 2,000 October 1, 1862; 3,000 December 1, 1862, and 4,000 on the first day of each month thereafter, until all are delivered.

I have also employed an agent to visit Springfield armory and make all necessary plans, drawings, and specifications, to obtain all required instructions to make all the various parts of guns, whose services I expect will cost me about $500.

I have likewise employed men to make the different gauges and dies for the various parts composing a gun, so that they can be made with that required perfection to interchange with each other and the muskets manufactured at the Springfield armory. These gauges and dies will cost from $1,000 to $2,000.

Should this order be immediately annulled, it is probable that my own actual damages would not exceed $10,000. What I should be compelled to pay Messrs. Hoe & Co., the American Machine Works, Mr. Washburn, and Mr. Chaffee, you are as competent to determine as myself. If the order is to be revoked, it is most apparent that it should be done instantly, so that as little sacrifice as possible should be suffered either by myself or the government.

You will find accompanying this communication a copy of the order issued to me on the 24th December, 1862, with my acceptance, and a memorandum explanatory of the delay of acceptance. You will also find a copy of a letter addressed to the Hon. Preston King, senator from New York, on the 25th January, in the hope that something of the character of your order of 29th January might be done to satisfy the public mind in regard to contracts, and relieve those who were endeavoring to carry them out in good faith from the doubt and anxiety arising from newspaper comments and otherwise as to the desire and intention of the government.

I have authorized my brother, Mr. Samuel Hoard, to act in my behalf in making these statements, and you will confer a favor by communicating to him your wishes and intentions at your earliest convenience, the importance and magnitude of the subject, in my opinion, requiring it.

I have the honor to be, with respect, your obedient servant,

C. B. HOARD,
Per SAM'L HOARD.

Hon. E. M. Stanton,
    Secretary of War.

N. B.—Mr. Hoard will remain at Willards' until he shall be honored with your reply.

Washington, *February* 13, 1862.

Sir: You will remember that I called yesterday to obtain a sight of the communication made to the War Department in relation to what had been done under an order to me to furnish 50,000 muskets; that you expressed a wish that *personal* interviews should not be asked when written communications could accomplish the object. I desired to see my statement, believing, from my memoranda, that I had omitted to mention one contract, made with Mr. Crompton, for two stock-turning machines, the contract price for which is $2,400, I furnishing the castings. You promised to send the paper to Willards', but I presume, from the multiplicity of duties devolving upon you, the promise has escaped your memory. As I desire that the statement should be perfect, and as this is the last day for filing papers under the provisions of the order from the Secretary of War in regard to contracts, and fearing you may not bring to mind your promise in season to enable me to make the addition to my statement,

if, as I believe, it was omitted in that filed on the 8th instant, I herewith send it to be placed with the other alluded to, and to be considered as a part thereof.
Very respectfully, your obedient servant,

C. B. HOARD,
Per SAM'L HOARD.

P H. WATSON,
Assistant Secretary of War.

N. B.—I will remain at the door to be informed that Mr. Watson has placed the additional statement on file.   S. H.

WASHINGTON, *February* 13, 1862.
Samuel Hoard, esq., asks relief from loss caused by rejection of C. B. Hoard's contract for making 50,000 Springfield patent muskets; asks the President to confer with the Secretary of War about the case. Referred to the ordnance commission.

WASHINGTON, *February* 13, 1862.
SIR : Knowing how much your time, thoughts, and patience are taxed by the grave and important duties of your station, and particularly at a time when your family demands so much of your solicitude, I should not have taken the liberty of addressing you, but from the fact that I have been intrusted with some important business which compels me to ask your official action. I will endeavor to state the case as briefly as possible, and at the same time give you a clear understanding of the affair.

My brother, Hon. C. B. Hoard, of New York, received an order on the 24th of December last to manufacture 50,000 muskets, Springfield pattern. They were to be made in all their parts to interchange with each other and with the Springfield gun. They were to be inspected by government officers in the same manner as government guns are inspected, and delivered monthly : 1,000 in each of the months of July, August, and September; 2,000 in each of the months of October and November; 3,000 in December; and 4,000 monthly thereafter, until all were delivered. They were to be paid for in such funds as the Secretary of the Treasury provided for the respective months in which they were delivered. A failure to deliver, in consequence of fire, flood, strike of hands, or any other causes, for any one month, was a forfeiture of a right to deliver such number of guns on the contract as were deficient in that month. The order was not transferable, and was given on the assurance of my brother's respectable character as a man and manufacturer, and his responsibility. This recommendation was signed by the governor of New York, by the United States senators, and by twenty-four members of Congress from that State. Under this order my brother proceeded to act most efficiently. He owned a large factory for making steam-engines, and half of another factory for making agricultural implements. The former was thrown out of business in consequence of the rebellion, and, with some hundreds of men employed by him, was idle. He immediately commenced changing this factory into an armory, and has spent several thousand dollars in making such alterations. He bought the undivided half of the agricultural implement manufactory at an expense of $8,000. He commenced making such tools and machinery as could be made in time at his factory, and has already expended large sums in making drops, drills, milling machines, &c., which will be worth from $40,000 to $50,000 when completed. He has also spent about $500 in travelling expenses, telegraphing, securing hands, making contracts, obtaining models, plans, and specifications. He has contracted with Robert Hoe & Co., of New York, for making a variety of machinery amounting to about $25,000. He has contracted with the American Machine Works for other necessary machinery to the amount of $21,300; with Mr. George Crompton for $2,400 worth of machinery; with Mr. N. Washburn, of Worcester, Massachusetts, for $75,000 worth of gun barrels. He has employed agents to make dies and gauges, which will cost between one and two thousand dollars, and he has employed other agents at considerable expense to forward the enterprise. The expenditures and liabilities already made and incurred amount to over $150,000. Reports having been circulated that it was intended to annul all contracts made by Mr. Cameron as early as the 25th of January last, my brother addressed Hon. P. King, requesting him to ascertain the truth of these reports, informing him that the order might at that time be annulled without any serious loss if the government desired or intended to do so, but that any delay would be attended with a daily increase of loss of perhaps thousands of dollars. That unless the government wanted the guns, he did not desire to make them. This letter Mr. King handed to Mr. Simmons, a mutual friend, who wrote my brother that there could be no doubt as to the intentions of the government fulfilling all contracts made, as his was, in good faith. This was considered sufficient; but on the 29th of January a notice appeared, from the Secretary of War, in the New York Herald, ordering copies of all contracts to be filed with the Secretary of War, and statements made of what had been done under them. For this purpose I came to Washington, at my brother's request, to comply with the terms of this order, and on filing them was informed by Mr. Watson, Assistant Secretary of War, that such contracts would probably be annulled. I expressed surprise, and hope, if so, provision would be made for payment of damages, as it would be about tantamount to a loss of all to be compelled to seek relief by a petition to Congress. To this Mr. Watson replied that that was purely a *personal matter;* that contracts were made with such a possibility before the contractor, &c. The order under which my brother acted is explicit, and does not reserve the right of annulling it or revoking. it, for no man of prudence would accept an order involving so large expenditures for machinery, &c., under such contingencies. Admitting, for a moment, the power to annul an order given and accepted in good faith exists in the Secretary of War, such power is certainly not derived from the spirit or letter of our laws, and its exercise would tend to destroy confidence and respect for our institutions, rather than a determination to honor and maintain them. Senator Simmons informs me that he called upon you on this subject, and that you expressed a determination not to allow an act of such injustice while the administration was in your charge. This declaration is only such as was relied upon by all who know your innate sense of justice and your life-long guidance by its principles. My main object in addressing this communication is to ask that you will personally consult with Secretary Stanton before he makes any decision, because if Mr. Watson has foreshadowed his views, a decision might be made which your sense of right and justice, as well as national honor, would lead you to disapprove.

I have copied for your inspection as tending, in my opinion, to show the policy of the Secretary of War in issuing this and like orders, and evincing the motives which induced its being given and accepted.

With warm sympathy for your family affliction, and the hope that it will soon pass away, I am, with great respect, your obedient servant,

SAMUEL HOARD.

His Excellency ABRAHAM LINCOLN,
President of the United States.

*Copy of closing remarks accompanying statement of what had been done under
order to C. B. Hoard for 50,000 muskets.*

In closing my statement I do not deem it irrelevant to say that I have made
inquiries, at the proper department, to ascertain the exact cost of the Springfield
armory, and the number of guns annually manufactured at that establishment;
and though a perfectly correct answer could not be given, without involving
more labor and time than were now at the command of that bureau, yet I was
informed that the supposed cost was about two millions of dollars for structures,
land, and machinery, and that the number of guns annually produced would
vary from 8,000 to 20,000, making an average of 14,000 per annum. Upon
this data as a basis—and I believe it is very near the truth—it will appear
that the annual interest, at six per cent., is $120,000
Assuming that the machinery cost one-half of the outlay—which
  is not far from the fact—and that the natural wear and loss on
  machinery is ten per cent. per annum—which, where work is prosecuted only during the day, is the rate calculated upon by manufacturers, and double that when night and day work is performed—the
  loss at the lowest rate would be, on one million of dollars....... 100,000
The cost estimated for the present production of a musket and
  appendages is $14 for each gun, which would make the cost of
  14,000 to be............................. 196,000

                                                          416,000

Showing the actual cost of every gun, by this calculation, to be $29 71,
which is probably below the real cost to the United States.

I make this estimate to show that I believed the government was acting upon
economical principles when it gave the order for guns at $20 each, and that,
wanting the guns, such order was issued in good faith. I believe also that
other considerations, of an important character, had weight with your predecessor to induce the issuing of this and like orders. Under the belief that it
was indispensable to the safety and security of the nation that from one to two
millions of arms should always be in the arsenals of our country, and that this
could be most speedily accomplished through the establishment of private
armories, which should be required to produce the exact counterpart, in all
respects, of the Springfield musket, he gave contracts to individuals which would
secure the result. He considered, in my estimation, that the several States
would probably order small arms hereafter, and that it was very desirable such
arms should be made to interchange with those manufactured by the United
States government; that such armories, being owned by different persons, and
out of employ after the fulfilment of their orders, would be able and their owners
willing to supply guns at even a less price than they actually cost the United
States, and thus, while the government was supplying itself at a reasonable
price, the nation might and probably would be benefited.

I have said this much as supposititious for the good faith of the War Department, and as to my own I have referred for character and responsibility to papers
on file in your department and to my acts under the order. As soon as any
doubt arose as to the possibility of an abrogation of the contract, or a desire on
the part of the government to revoke it, I sought to know the wishes of yourself
on this subject, that as little loss should take place as possible; thus again
showing that I was not only willing but desirous of having the order annulled
if the government did not want the arms. As it appears by my statement that
I have made contracts and expenditures involving liabilities to the amount of
over one hundred and fifty thousand dollars, with the utmost confidence in the

integrity of those administering a government based upon principles of justice and equity; that I have been acting under an order which by its terms does not admit of revocation; that I have again and again expressed a willingness that it should be revoked upon payment of *actual* not penal damages, therefore I appeal to you, as a high-minded, honorable man, not to place me, if it be in your power to do so, side by side with peculators and fraudulent contractors, if such there be, and oblige me to seek relief by petition to Congress, which, in my estimation, would be a virtual denial of justice, and nearly tantamount to a loss of all the expenditures I have made and the liabilities I have incurred.

I have the honor to be, with respect, your obedient servant,

C. B. HOARD,
Per SAMUEL HOARD.

Addenda to statements filed by C. B. Hoard February 8, 1862.

WASHINGTON, *February* 13, 1862.

I have also contracted with Mr. George Crampton, of Worcester, Massachusetts, for the manufacture of two stock-turning machines for the first turning of Springfield musket stocks, one for turning above the bands and one for turning below the bands. I am to furnish the castings and to pay twelve hundred dollars each for making the machines, three hundred dollars to be paid monthly while they are making, and the balance on completion. The machines to be made within four months from the delivery of the castings, which were delivered nearly a month since. The contract was made on the 17th of January last, and the castings delivered soon after.

In closing my statements I do not deem it irrelevant to say that I have made inquiries at the proper department to ascertain the exact cost of the Springfield armory, and the number of guns annually manufactured at that establishment; and although a perfectly correct answer could not be given without involving more time and labor than was now at the command of that bureau, yet I was informed that the supposed cost was about two millions of dollars for structures and machinery; and that the number of guns annually produced would vary from 8,000 to 20,000, making an average of 14,000 per annum. Upon this data as a basis, and I believe it is very near the truth, it would appear that the annual interest at 6 per cent. on the cost is...................... $120,000

Assuming that the machinery cost one-half of the outlay, which is not far from the fact, and that the natural wear and loss of machinery is ten per cent., and when work is prosecuted only during the day, and this is the rate usually calculated upon by manufacturers, and double that when night and day work is performed, the loss on one million of dollars would be annually........................... 100,000

The cost estimated for the present production of a musket is $14 each, which would be for 14,000 muskets........................... 196,000

416,000

Showing the actual cost to the government, upon this calculation, believed to be even below the truth, to be $29 71, (twenty-nine dollars and seventy-one cents.)

I make this estimate to show that I believed the government was acting upon economical principles when it gave the order under which I have been acting, and that, wanting the guns, such order was given in good faith when it was issued. I believe, also, that other considerations of an important character had weight with your predecessor to induce the issuing of this and like orders. Under the conviction that it was indispensable to the safety and security of the nation that from one to two millions of small arms should always be in the arsenals of our country, and that this could be most speedily accomplished through the establishment of private armories, which should be required to produce the exact counterparts in all respects of the Springfield muskets, he gave contracts to individuals that would effect this result. He considered, in my estimation, that the several States would hereafter order small arms, and that it was very desirable that such arms should be so made as to interchange in all their parts with those manufactured for the United States. That such armories being owned by different parties, and probably out of employ after their contracts were filled, would be able to supply guns in all respects equal to those of the United States at even less than the actual cost to the government; and thus while the United States was obtaining a supply at a reasonable price the whole nation might, and probably would, be benefited. I have supposed thus much as evincing my own belief that the government acted in good faith on its part, and as to my own I have referred you to papers on file in your office, which I presume are satisfactory as to my character and responsibility. As soon as any possibility or doubt arose as to the abrogation or revocation of the order, I sought, as I have shown you by my letter to Mr. King, to ascertain the wishes of yourself on this subject, that as little loss might be sustained as was possible under the circumstances; thus evincing that I was not only willing but desirous that the order should be revoked if the government did not want or need the arms. As appears by my statement, I have made contracts and expenditures involving liabilities to the amount of one hundred and fifty thousand dollars.

I have done this in the utmost confidence of the integrity of the executive department of the government, believing that while it is administered on principles of justice and equity only can it secure the confidence and respect of the people. I have again and again expressed a willingness that the order should be revoked upon payment of actual and not penal damages; but I cannot consent to be nor do I believe that an honorable minded man, such as you have the established reputation of being, would willingly place me side by side with peculators and fraudulent contractors, if such there be, and compel me to seek relief for damages by a petition to Congress, which in my estimation would be a virtual denial of justice and nearly or quite tantamount to an actual loss of all the damages I should sustain. The order on its face does not contain the right of revocation, and if by any implication such a right pertains to your official position its existence is unknown to me. I do not, however, wish to place myself in antagonism of that supposed right, but simply appeal to your sense of justice not to attempt such a revocation without previously providing for a liquidation of all just damages.

I have the honor to be, with respect, your obedient servant,

C. B. HOARD,
Per SAM'L HOARD.

C. B. Hoard's contract for 50,000 Springfield rifles.

WATERTOWN, N. Y., *March* 10, 1862.

DEAR SIR: I hope that the justice and propriety of the request I am about to make will be so apparent, and require so little time or thought, that you will feel it consistent with your duties of a more public nature to give it a moment's attention.

The action which you felt it your duty to take in regard to contracts for guns has caused embarrassment to some parties who had honestly entered into such contracts, and before your notice was published, and even before you came into office, had entered in good faith, and at great cost upon the execution of them. I am one of those suffering under such embarrassments, and whilst I do not desire you at this time to decide upon any particular case, I do desire and request that you will cause me to be informed by letter of the rules by which you intend to be guided in your action in relation to the rights of those contractors.

In a conversation I had with you some weeks ago, and in a later one that my brother had with you on this subject, we understood you to say that you should not interfere with the legal rights of parties whose contracts were made in good faith, and who had machinery and were preparing honestly to fulfil them. Of course I do not ask you to say what my legal rights under my contract are, but only whatever they are you do not intend to disregard or violate them.

Very respectfully, your obedient servant,

C. B. HOARD.

Hon. E. M. STANTON, *Secretary of War.*

WATERTOWN, *New York, March* 21, 1862.

GENTLEMEN: I have read the order of the Secretary of War, dated 13th instant, appointing you commissioners for certain purposes named in said order, and also an order dated 17th instant, signed by J. Wise, secretary, in relation to subjects mentioned therein.

I have a contract, dated December 24, 1861, for the manufacture of 50,000 Springfield rifle muskets, upon which no delivery of guns is to be made till next July; but I have been ever since the contract was issued preparing in good faith to execute it, and I have incurred large liabilities and made large expenditures in preparations to make guns. I am a manufacturer, and have had a large manufacturing establishment at this place for many years past, which was thrown out of business by the rebellion. I applied as a manufacturer for the contract which was awarded to me, and the papers on file in the War Department will fully show the character of my application; and the signature of the governor of New York, the two senators, and most of the members of Congress from my State, recommending me as a suitable person to receive such contract, will, I trust, protect me from being classed with those who have obtained contracts for speculative purposes. The papers on file in the department, in response to the first order of the Secretary of War in relation to contracts for arms, will show what had been done up to that time, and since then I have proceeded with all possible energy in preparations to manufacture the guns.

The principal object, however, of this letter is to inquire whether as commissioners you intend to take any action upon such inchoate contracts, unless they are found within the third subdivision of the Secretary's order of the 13th, and if so, what action, and what you desire me to do, if anything.

I am, very respectfully, your obedient servant,

C. B. HOARD.

Hon. JOSEPH HOLT and ROBERT DALE OWEN,
Commissioners, Washington, D. C.

WASHINGTON, *April* 8, 1862.

The papers which I filed on the 8th of February show that I had then contracted for machinery for manufacturing guns as follows:

Gun machinery, (has patterns and has made same for government.)—Of Messrs. R. Hoe & Co., New York city, 25 different machines, to cost from $20,000 to $25,000 .... $22,500

Stocking machines and heavy milling machines.—Of the American machine works, Springfield, Massachusetts, 19 different machines, to cost 21,300

Furnishing letters.—Of Mr. George Crampton, Worcester, Massachusetts 2 machines, to cost about 2,500

————————

46,300

Barrels warranted to pass inspection.—That I had contracted with
Mr. Washburne, of Worcester, for 50,000 barrels, computed to cost .. $75,000

Cones, (he is to get these cones made.)—That I had contracted with
C. C. Chaffee, of Springfield, Massachusetts, for 50,000 cones....... 4,500

Real estate.—That I had purchased the agricultural buildings owned
by myself and J. McSwaney, to insure me sufficient shop room and
water power to carry on my work, in addition to my engine shop, at
cost of 8,000

That I was converting my buildings into an armory, and making
machinery myself for the manufacture of guns, in addition to that contracted for as above, which, with what I had on hand in my engine
building factory when altered, would be worth some.............. 40,000

Since that statement was made I have had from forty to sixty men at work
making the alterations and constructing new machinery, viz:

Six heavy drops, nine drilling machines, thirty-five milling
machines, twenty-five fires for blacksmiths, which when done
will be worth, say...................................... $10,500
And it will cost to complete about 3,000
                                       ————
                                       7,500

Stocks.—I have contracted with Thomas Wait for 50,000 black
walnut stocks, worth, delivered at Watertown, say................ 10,000

Bayonets.—I have negotiation going on (was not closed when I left
but, I presume, will be soon) for 10,000 to 20,000 bayonets with the
cutlery establishment at Rochester, to cost ....16,400 to 32,800

New buildings.—I have purchased stones, bricks, and timber and
lumber for a blacksmith shop 100 feet long; a dry house 32 feet by
24 feet, and the foundations of the dry house are now being laid if the
weather there will permit; say now expended and liable for........ 2,000

Mr. Tyler at the arm machine works has several men making
gauges for me from the government gauges there, but I am not advised
how nearly done they are. They will cost, I think, $1,000, and I
suppose are pretty well advanced.

Hon. J. HOLT and R. D. OWEN, *Commissioners.*

Before commission, April 8, 1862.

Mr. C. B. Hoard states:

I have a contract for 50,000 Springfield muskets. I was a manufacturer of
steam-engines. I propose to make eventually all the parts of the arm at my
own establishment except the barrels. I will not roll barrels. I have a contract for all barrels in the rough. I want at first to buy a few locks, bayonets,
and finished barrels. I am about closing a contract with Mr. Barton, of Rochester, of New York, for bayonets. I want but 10,000, and he wishes me to take
20,000. I purpose contracting for locks with Norris, of Springfield, Hewlitt,
agent, or a man at Milbury, Massachusetts, named Watts, who has made arms
for the government. I only want a few locks for accommodation, as I will make
locks eventually myself. All the steps have been taken to secure machinery
set forth in my papers. (See letter in response to the order of the 29th of January.) I have contracted for cones to be made at Springfield. Mr. Tyler supervises gauge making for me; he has my men under his superintendence. All
my machinery will be delivered, when made, at New York or Springfield. My
inspection commences on the 1st June. My foreman is named W. A. Roberts,
a man who has worked for Remington. I have made contracts to the extent of

$130,000 to $140,000. Mr. Chaffee gets my cones for me; I am aware that he is a "middle man," but I feel certain about his furnishing them. Washburne, I think, is under obligations to furnish me iron, the same as is furnished the government, warranted to pass inspection. Washburne stated to me that he is engaged to furnish 300,000 barrels to contractors. I will assemble my guns at Watertown and devote my own personal attention to creating an armory; I have no engagements to prevent this. I wrote to Washington, as soon as I heard rumors about contracts being too numerous, expressing a willingness to give up my contract in case the guns were not needed by the government. I could then have gotten out of it for $10,000, but could not now for less than $60,000, unless the government would take our machinery, &c., off our hands. I could not accept of less than 50,000 guns at the price named. I suppose that I would have 20 per cent. profit upon the contract, but I am now unable to make any satisfactory estimate, and greatly fear that the delays and doubts in the way will considerably reduce the profits.

WATERTOWN, *New York, April* 23, 1862.

375.—C. B. Hoard is embarrassed in relation to his contract to furnish arms. Machinery nearly ready.

ORDNANCE OFFICE, *April* 28, 1862.

Respectfully referred to the commission on contracts, before which Mr. Hoard's case is supposed to be pending.

JAMES W. RIPLEY,
Brigadier General.

WATERTOWN, *New York, April* 23, 1862.

DEAR SIR: When I was last in Washington I went before the commissioners Holt and Owen to answer such questions and give them such information as they desired in regard to my contract to furnish arms, and after giving them such information as they desired I was informed that proper action would soon be taken to remove the embarrassments which the action of the War Department had thrown in the way of parties who were proceeding in good faith, and at great expense, to fulfil their contracts; and I was told, verbally, to proceed with my arrangements the same as if the order of the Secretary of War of 29th January last had not been issued, until their report should be made, which would only require a few days, when some proper notification would be given to me by the Ordnance department. The machinery for making the arms which I contracted for in the fore part of January is nearly ready to be delivered, when I must make large payments, and to do so must satisfy parties or banks, where I may apply for money, that my contract is not to be annulled or interfered with unless broken on my part. The delay in the payments to government creditors, which has for the last year been unavoidable, makes capitalists hesitate to furnish money to prosecute any enterprise for the government; and if to this is superadded the embarrassment before alluded to it may destroy men whose misfortune it will have been to accept and endeavor to execute faithfully a contract offered to them by their government.

The embarrassment is so palpable, and my right to relief so just and necessary, that I hope I may count on your aid to grant the relief sought without delay, as I presume the commissioners must have reported before this time.

Very respectfully, your obedient servant,

C. B. HOARD.

General J. W. RIPLEY. *Washington.*

COMMISSION ON ORDNANCE,
Washington, May 31, 1862.

GENERAL: The commission direct me to request that you will return their decision in the case of C. B. Hoard.

One of the contractors has objected to signing the bond prescribed on account of the use of the words "in case the parties of the first part shall in any respect fail to perform this contract on their part," unless the idea be specially excluded that a failure in a monthly delivery (previously provided for in the contract) does also render liable a *total forfeiture* "at the option of the United States."

The commission, therefore, respectfully recommend the introduction, in a parenthesis, after the words above quoted " on their part," as follows : (" Except as to the number of any monthly delivery.") This will remove the only objection, that has been made known to them, to the form of the contract for ordnance stores.

Very respectfully, your obedient servant,

P. V. HAGNER,
Major of Ordnance.

General J. W. RIPLEY,
Chief of Ordnance.

ORDNANCE OFFICE,
War Department, Washington, May 31, 1862.

SIR : As requested in Major Hagner's letter of this date, I return herewith the decision (No. 75) in the case of C. B. Hoard, with the accompanying papers.

Respectfully, your obedient servant,

JAS. W. RIPLEY,
Brigadier General, Chief of Ordnance.

J. WISE, Esq.,
Secretary to Commission on Ordnance and Ordnance stores,
Washington City.

WASHINGTON, *May* 31, 1862.

GENTLEMEN : In a conversation which I had the honor of holding yesterday with Mr. Holt in regard to gun contracts, he made the avowal that it was not the desire or intention of the commissioners to utterly ruin all who had taken such contracts in good faith, and had been honestly and efficiently endeavoring to execute them, and that he did not believe it was the intention of the government to do so. This was the first and only gleam of light, from any connected with the War Department, since the induction of the present incumbent as Secretary ; all else has been impervious darkness. I have a contract to make 50,000 rifle muskets, at twenty dollars each. This contract was given and accepted in good faith, and in conformity with the general action of the Ordnance department. In endeavoring to execute it, I have expended and incurred liabilities exceeding $300,000, and must increase that sum at least $75,000 more, before I can expect any return from the government. I have contracted with workmen to make the various parts of the 50,000 muskets. These workmen, skilled in the business, have been obtained from all parts of the country at large expense, and have removed with their families to Watertown, under my agreement that they should have permanent employment at good wages ; and, to save myself from utter ruin or immense loss, I must manufacture the number of guns I have contracted in good faith to deliver, and also to save myself, and make a reasonable profit for my outlays, use of tools and machinery, use of capital, and great loss on the value of the tools and machinery after my contract expires, I ought not to accept less than twenty dollars each for the entire number of guns contracted for. I have repeatedly proposed to surrender this contract by simply being reimbursed for the loss I might actually suffer, as the commissioners must have learnt, if they have examined the papers in my case. In this spirit, and not because I consider it just or right to surrender a contract made and attempted to be executed in good faith, I now consent that my contract shall be modified as follows : The original contract shall be confirmed in all its terms and conditions, except as to price, which I consent shall be twenty dollars each for the first 25,000, and for the balance a fair and equitable price, not less than sixteen dollars for each musket and appendages, delivered according to contract. I consider the modification of my contract, as proposed by the commissioners, wholly inacceptable. It could not be complied with; it proposes a bond which wholly changes the nature and spirit of the contract. It puts the contractor in the power of the government to ruin him beyond the possibility of escape; and, if they do not intend to ruin him, why ask such power? It, in fact, enables the government to fix its own price for the guns, or to declare the contract void. With my experience in gun contracts, I must, therefore, utterly decline to accept the decision of the commissioners, and have now made the only proposition I have to offer. I make this proposal to surrender one hundred thousand dollars of my just rights, to ascertain if the War Department is willing to adopt any course not utterly ruinous to contractors, like myself, who have risked much on the good faith of the government.

CHARLES B. HOARD.

By his attorney, SAM'L HOARD.

Hon. J. HOLT and R. DALE OWEN,
Commissioners.

COMMISSION ON ORDNANCE, *May* 31, 1862.

SIR : In reply to your note just received, I have to state that it is the purpose of the commission to confirm the order to your brother, C. B. Hoard, for the remaining 25,000 muskets not embraced in their former decision, which confirmation will be on the basis which you, as attorney in fact of your brother, have proposed, viz: at the price of $16 per musket, instead of $20, as mentioned in the original order.

Respectfully, &c.,

J. HOLT, *Commissioner.*

Mr. SAMUEL HOARD, *Washington.*

WASHINGTON, *May* 31, 1862.

DEAR SIR : My brother remains sick; I ought to return. If you will address me a note saying that you will recommend a compliance with my proposition, and that the bond shall be made conformable to our understanding, I will not move further in the matter, avoiding the troubling of the President or members of Congress; and I will say also that, having an armory established complete and perfect in all its parts, I shall be willing to supply the Springfield musket hereafter at $16 each, and should be willing to make contracts at that price for any number the government may want, and I may be able to make what would be at the rate of nearly 50,000 annually.

Respectfully yours,

CHARLES B. HOARD,
Per SAMUEL HOARD.

Hon. J. HOLT, *Commissioner.*

N. B.—An answer can be sent to Willards'. If I leave to-day, it must be in the 5 o'clock train.

COMMISSION ON ORDNANCE,
Washington, June 2, 1862.

SIR: The commission, as above, are prepared to confirm your order for Springfield muskets upon the conditions proposed to them by your brother and attorney in fact, Mr. Samuel Hoard, viz: 25,000 guns to be delivered under the said order at $20 per gun, and 25,000 guns at $16 per gun, deliveries to be made on the terms stipulated in your original order, and bond to be given, &c. If this be satisfactory to you, please inform the commission by return mail.
Very respectfully, &c.,

J. WISE, *Secretary.*
Mr. C. B. HOARD, *Watertown, N. Y.*

COMMISSION ON ORDNANCE,
Washington, June 3, 1862.

SIR: As it is necessary to preserve record evidence of the authority under which you acted in behalf of your brother before the commission, as above, you will please hand him the enclosed note, for his early consideration.
Very respectfully, &c.,

J. HOLT, *Commissioner.*
Mr. SAMUEL HOARD, *Watertown, N. Y.*

WATERTOWN, *Jefferson County, N. Y., June* 6, 1862.

GENTLEMEN: Your communication of the 3d instant is received, requesting that record evidence should be furnished of my authority to act in my brother's behalf. This request has been communicated to him, and I am happy to say that his health is so far recovered that he has started for Washington, so that when he reaches there he will be able to answer your interrogatories in person. He expects, necessarily, to be delayed somewhat in his journey to your city, and possibly may not arrive till the last of the ensuing week. Under his state of health you will, of course, see the propriety and necessity of deferring all action in his case until he reaches Washington.
Very respectfully, yours,

SAMUEL HOARD
Messrs. J. HOLT and ROBERT DALE OWEN,
Commissioners, &c., Washington, D. C.

Before commission, June 10, 1862.

Mr. C. B. Hoard appeared before the commission, and expressed his willingness to adjust his contract with the government on the conditions of the confirmation of his contract to its full extent of 50,000 guns, 25,000 at $16, and 25,000 at $20, *and* an expression by the commission of their belief that $16 per gun would be a fair price for all over 25,000 guns.

He subsequently requested that in the confirmation of his order the 25,000 guns first to be delivered should be paid for at the rate of $16 each, and the 25,000 last delivered at the rate of $20 each, in order that all his forfeitures for non-delivery should be of the guns at $16 each.

P. V. HAGNER,
Major of Ordnance.

COMMISSION ON ORDNANCE AND ORDNANCE STORES,
Washington, June 10, 1862.

GENERAL : The commission have the honor to report as follows :

CASE No. 75.—C. B. HOARD, Watertown, New York.

Order by direction of the Secretary of War, dated Dec. 24, 1861.— (See page 155, Ex. Doc. No. 67) Referred by direction of the Secretary of War.

To furnish 50,000 muskets, with appendages, of the Springfield pattern, at the price of $20 per gun. Deliveries to be made of not less than 1,000 in each of the months of July, August, and September, not less than 2,000 in each of the months of October and November, not less than 3,000 in December, and not less than 4,000 per month thereafter.—(See case No. 72.)

The commission find that the above order was not given in accordance with the law and regulations, and that it is not therefore a contract of legal force, inasmuch as it does not contain the express requirements of the law, and was not made " after previous advertisement for proposals respecting the same," nor can it be regarded as an " open purchase," being for articles which did not require " immediate delivery," but which were stipulated to be manufactured and delivered at prescribed distant periods.

In accordance with the principles set forth in Mason's case, No. 72, the commission have sought to so modify the number or price of the arms, that Mr. Hoard could proceed with his work, sufficiently secured against loss, and also that the government should receive a fair and just return for the large outlay required to be made.

After consultation with Mr. Hoard, who has appeared in person before the commission, it has been determined, in accordance with his proposition, to leave the number of arms unchanged, provided the first 25,000 of the order should be furnished at the price of $16 each gun, the sum at which responsible manufacturers have agreed to deliver arms of this pattern, and which the commission have ascertained and believe to be a reasonable price, it being Mr. Hoard's wish that this reduction of price, to which he has agreed, shall apply to the first instead of the second 25,000 stipulated to be delivered.

The commission therefore decide that the original order, dated December 24, 1861, to Mr. C. B. Hoard, be confirmed, subject to all its terms to the extent of 50,000 guns, 25,000 of which, last to be delivered, are to be paid for at the rate of twenty dollars ($20) each gun, irrespective of any tax levied thereon, and the first 25,000 at the rate of sixteen dollars ($16) per gun, to which price of $16 is to be added any tax which may be imposed on the same by Congress ; which confirmation is upon condition that he shall, within fifteen days after notice of this decision, execute bond with good and sufficient sureties, in the form and with the stipulations prescribed by law and the regulations for the faithful performance of the contract, as thus modified, resulting from said order and acceptance, and upon his failure or refusal to execute such bond, then the said order shall be declared cancelled and of no effect.

The commission further decide that the deliveries under the contract to be executed shall be required at or within the periods stipulated in the original order.

We are, sir, very respectfully, your obedient servants,

J. HOLT,
ROBERT DALE OWEN,
Commissioners, &c.
P. V. HAGNER,
Major of Ordnance, Assistant to Commission.
General J. W. RIPLEY, *Chief of Ordnance.*

CASE No. 76.

J. D. MOWRY.

ORDNANCE OFFICE,
Washington, December 26, 1861.

SIR: By direction of the Secretary of War I offer you an order for thirty thousand (30,000) muskets, of the Springfield pattern, on the following terms and conditions, viz: These arms are to be furnished with the regular appendages, and are to be in all respects identical with the standard rifle musket made at the United States armory at Springfield, Massachusetts, and are to interchange with it and with each other in all their parts.

They are to be subject to inspection by United States inspectors in the same manner that the Springfield arms are inspected, and none are to be received or paid for but such as pass inspection and are approved by the United States inspector.

These thirty thousand (30,000) arms and appendages are to be delivered at your armory as follows, viz: Not less than two thousand (2,000) in the month of July, 1862, and monthly deliveries of not less than two thousand (2,000) thereafter until the entire thirty thousand (30,000) shall have been delivered. And you are to have the right to deliver more rapidly than according to the number of arms before specified if you can do so.

In case of any failure to make deliveries to the extent and within the time before specified, you are to forfeit the right to deliver whatever number may be deficient in the specified number for the month in which the failure occurs. All these arms and appendages are to be delivered by you, and this order, if transferred to another person, is to be thereby forfeited.

Payments are to be made in such funds as the Treasury Department may provide for each delivery on certificate of inspection and receipt by the United States inspector at the rate of twenty dollars ($20) for each arm, including appendages.

All these arms and appendages are to be packed by you in boxes of the regular pattern, with twenty (20) muskets and appendages in each box, for which a fair price, to be determined by the United States inspector, will be allowed.

Please signify in writing your acceptance or non-acceptance of this order on the terms and conditions herein stated.

Respectfully, your obedient servant,

JAMES W. RIPLEY,
Brigadier General.

JAMES D. MOWRY, Esq., *New York.*

NORWICH, CONNECTICUT,
February 10, 1862.

James D. Mowry submits copy of contract to furnish 30,000 Springfield rifles at $20.

NORWICH, CONNECTICUT,
February 10, 1862.

SIR: In pursuance of an order of the War Department, dated Washington, June 29, 1862, I have to report:

First. That I have an order from the Ordnance department, dated December 26, 1861, and accepted by me, authorizing me to manufacture for the government thirty thousand rifles, of the Springfield pattern, at twenty dollars each, and delivered as follows, viz: "Not less than 2,000 in the month of July, 1862, and monthly deliveries of not less than 2,000 thereafter until the entire 30,000 is delivered."

Second. I have to report that I am making such arrangements for the delivery of said arms as I think will enable me to deliver them promptly within the time stipulated, and trust I shall be able to anticipate the time materially.

Third. I enclose a copy of said order to be filed in the department.

Very respectfully, yours,

JAMES D. MOWRY.

Hon. EDWIN M. STANTON,
Secretary of War.

NEW YORK, *April* 15, 1862.

GENTLEMEN: Your communication of the 2d instant was not received by me until yesterday. In answer thereto I beg to say that I have made such arrangements as are necessary to complete the arms at an early day, expecting to anticipate the stated deliveries materially.

I trust to be able early in June to furnish a complete arm for inspection as a pattern indicative of the future deliveries. The deliveries will be made in the city of New York.

I have not agreed to furnish any other contractor with any parts. I can, I think, furnish locks and stocks, if required, at a fair price. I shall probably visit Washington shortly, and will then communicate personally with the commission on all matters on which they may require information.

Very respectfully, yours,

JAMES D. MOWRY.

The COMMISSION ON ORDNANCE AND ORDNANCE STORES.

NEW YORK, *April* 25, 1862.

MY DEAR SIR: Allow me to introduce to you my friend, Mr. James W. Mowry, who visits Washington in regard to his contract with the Ordnance department for thirty thousand United States rifled muskets.

Mr. Mowry and his partners assure me that they will deliver the muskets within the time specified by the contract.

I have told Mr. Mowry that I was sure you would give him any information that he might desire that you could consistently.

I remain, my dear sir, very truly, your friend,

CYRUS W. FIELD.

Major P. V. HAGNER, *Washington, D. C.*

NEW YORK, *May* 1, 1862.

DEAR SIR: Mr. Cyrus W Field kindly gave me the accompanying letter of introduction to yourself, which I hoped to have presented in person, but unforeseen circumstances prevent.

I therefore take the liberty to hand it with this to Mr. F. W. Cammann, of New York, who is, and has been from the first, interested with me in my gun contract. He goes to Washington for the purpose of having the contract confirmed by the ordnance committee.

I trust there will be no difficulty in responding to what will be required.

Very truly, yours,

JAMES D. MOWRY.

Major P. V. HAGNER, *Washington.*

NEW YORK, *May* 6, 1862.

GENTLEMEN : In pursuance of my promise to you to make a written proposal in regard to the reduction in the number of arms in the order granted to furnish thirty thousand Springfield rifles to the government, I beg respectfully to suggest that such reduction, if any, should not exceed in number five thousand.

I trust no material variation from the foregoing will be required by the government; and I feel from the impression received by myself when personally present before the committee, that they will do all they consistently can do to meet my views.

May I ask the favor of an answer by return mail, as my arrangements are for the whole number in the order.

I am, very respectfully,

JAMES D. MOWRY,
Per FREDERICK W. CAMMANN.

The COMMISSION ON ORDNANCE AND ORDNANCE STORES.

NEW YORK, *May* 10, 1862.

MY DEAR SIR : Allow me to introduce to you my friend, Frederick W. Cammann, esq., partner with Mr. James D. Mowry in his contract with the United States government for thirty thousand rifled muskets.

Mr. Cammann informs me that he has not yet received a confirmation of his contract, and that he visits Washington for that purpose, and hopes not to be detained there, as he is anxious to push forward the contract as rapidly as possible.

I remain, my dear sir, very truly, your friend,

CYRUS W. FIELD.

Major P. V. HAGNER, *Washington, D. C.*

Before commission, May 3, 1862.

Mr. Cammann appeared and stated:

I am interested with Mr. Mowry in the order for 30,000 Springfield muskets. We have made arrangements to have everything made for us except the stocks. We propose to have a full suit of stocking machines, and to have the stocks made in New York. The finished arms are to be assembled in Springfield under the supervision of Mr. Norris. Stocks can be made, I think, at $1 30; we are charged $2 for them. We have not definitely arranged about *barrels;* we have offers from two parties, but, by Mr. Norris's advice, have declined to close with either as the price seems too high, and we are assured that Mr. Washburne can supply us at a less rate—not over $5. *Locks.*—We can get these of Williams & Co., of Philadelphia, at $2 25. Mr. Bateman, of New York, has offered us locks at $2, but I do not know how far he has advanced in this work. Mr. Congdon, an importer of English hardware, in New York, has recently received a sample of English barrel skelps, which he has just taken to Springfield to have tried. He thinks it is superior to the Marshall iron; if it answers, he says the barrel can be furnished at a little over $4. *Mountings.*— Mr. Norris has agreed to supply all the small parts; everything but locks, stocks, and barrels; and to assemble the arms, and be responsible for the inspection. Unless I can do better, I will accept this offer. I have had three offers from manufacturers to make these guns complete at their risk; these offers were from $17 to $18 50. I have also offers for each part, at the risk of the maker. In every case the party offering requires an advance of from $40,000 to $50,000. My disbursements have thus far been small, and Mr. Mowry's also. He has gotten some machines, I think. He is a paper manufacturer, but his father has a machine shop in Norwich, Connecticut, and Mr. Mowry expected, at first, to make there himself most of the parts of the gun. He applied for 50,000 guns, but as he only got 30,000 he decided not to make much—only a part of the work. The stocking machinery in New York belongs exclusively to Mr. Mowry and myself, and is to be used solely upon his orders, unless we find that we can make more than we want. There are parties abundantly able and willing to furnish us ample means to carry out this contract, and they will give any desired security. We think we can make our first delivery in July; this would make the gun cost us higher, but we can do it I hear, and would undertake it. I have received from England samples of barrels, one in the rough, one rough turned and bored, one smooth bored and ground. 4,000 per month of either kind are offered after June 1, 1862. This, I think, would enable us to deliver guns in July.

P. V. HAGNER,

Assistant Major of Ordnance.

COMMISSION ON ORDNANCE AND ORDNANCE STORES,

Washington, May 16, 1862.

GENERAL: The commission have the honor to report as follows :

CASE No. 76.—J. D. MOWRY, New York.

Order by direction of the Secretary of War, dated Dec'r 26, 1861.— (See page 168, Ex. Doc. No. 67.) Referred by direction of the Secretary of War.

To furnish 30,000 muskets, with appendages, of the Springfield pattern, at the price of $20 per gun. Deliveries to be made of not less than 500 in each of the months of July, August, and September, and not less than 1,000 in each of the months of October and November, and not less than 1,500 in December, 1862, and not less than 2,000 per month thereafter.—(See case No. 72.)

The commission find that the above order was not given in accordance with the law and regulations; that it is not, therefore, a contract of legal force, inasmuch as it does not contain the express requirements of the law, and was not made "after previous advertisement for proposals respecting the same;" nor can it be regarded as an "open purchase," being for articles which did not require "immediate delivery," but, as stipulated, to be manufactured and delivered at prescribed distant periods.

They further consider that the number of arms ordered is larger than the wants of the government justify in this case, at the price fixed; and therefore, according to the principles set forth in Mason's case, No. 72, they decide that the order to Mr. Mowry be confirmed, subject to all its terms, to the extent of 20,000 muskets, upon condition that he shall, within fifteen days after notice of this decision, execute bond, with good and sufficient sureties, in the form and with the stipulations prescribed by law and the regulations, for the performance of the contract as thus modified, resulting from said order and acceptance; and upon his failure or refusal to execute such bond, then the said order shall be declared cancelled and of no effect.

The commission further decide that the deliveries under the contract to be executed shall be required at or within the periods stipulated in the original order, but that the number specified may be reduced proportionately to the reduction of the whole number, so that the contract shall be completed within the time allowed in the original order.

We are, sir, very respectfully, your obedient servants,

J. HOLT,
ROBERT DALE OWEN,
Commissioners, &c.
P. V. HAGNER,
Major of Ordnance.

General J. W. RIPLEY,
Chief of Ordnance.

CASE No. 77.

EAGLE MANUFACTURING COMPANY.

EAGLE MANUFACTURING COMPANY OFFICE,
Mansfield, Connecticut, February 6, 1862.

SIR: In compliance with your order of January 29, we beg leave to state that this corporation received an order for the manufacture of twenty-five thousand (25,000) muskets of the Springfield pattern, dated December 26, 1861, and signed by Brigadier General Ripley.

The terms and conditions of the order were as follows: "These arms are to be furnished with the regular appendages, and are to be, in all respects, identical with the standard rifle musket made at the United States armory at Springfield, Massachusetts, and are to interchange with it and with each other in all their parts. They are to be subject to inspection by United States inspectors, in the same manner that the Springfield arms are inspected, and none are to be received or paid for but such as pass inspection and are approved by the United States inspectors." These twenty-five thousand arms and appendages are to be delivered at our armory as follows: Not less than five hundred (500) in each of the months of July, August, and September, 1862; not less than one thousand (1,000) in each of the months of October and November, 1862; not less than fifteen hundred (1,500) in December, 1862; and not less than two thousand (2,000) per month thereafter, until the entire twenty-five thousand shall have been delivered; and we are to have the right to deliver more rapidly if we can do so. The price to be paid for these arms, on certificate of inspection, is to be twenty dollars for each arm, including appendages.

This order was accepted by us without reservation, and is on file at the department.

Yours, respectfully,

EAGLE MANUFACTURING COMPANY,
Per A. H. ALMY, *Treasurer.*

Hon. E. M. STANTON,
Secretary of War.

P. S.—This company have built an armory, and have made contracts for the machinery necessary for the prompt carrying out of this contract, and will be prepared to make the first delivery of guns at the time stipulated.

A. H. ALMY, *Treasurer.*

FEBRUARY 18, 1862.

In December last I introduced to Assistant Secretary T. Scott a shareholder of the Eagle Manufacturing Company, of Connecticut, who represented its capacity to manufacture muskets on the Springfield pattern, and solicited an order for 50,000. Having taken three or four weeks to consider the application, Mr. Scott deemed it to come within the rule which was established about that time by the Secretary of War, that contracts for fire-arms should thereafter be made with manufacturers having shops, machinery, and motive power, and directed an order to be issued by General Ripley to the company but for 25,000 muskets only.

On the representations to me, by letter, of the company's manager, that that number would not build and set in motion the costly tools required for fine gun-making, I asked Mr. Scott to increase the order. The policy of placing this manufacture in the hands of professional mechanics, and on larger orders, so as to insure the fulfilment of contracts, having acquired strength in Mr. Cameron's mind, my request was promptly granted, and I was told to assure the company that the additional order would be given them, but to go ahead on the one they had.

Within ten days I went for this additional order. The press of business had been so great that it was not made out. I then got engrossed in the business of my paper; indeed, I confess that I wholly forgot the muskets, and forgot the Eagle Manufacturing Company till the day when Mr. Cameron told me he was going out of the cabinet. Then I saw the danger to which I had exposed friends who had unluckily selected me as an agent. I immediately asked Mr. Cameron if he felt at liberty, before retiring, to direct Mr. Ripley to issue the order. He asked me if I would do so at such a moment. I frankly said I would not, and there the matter rested.

But in the meantime the company, upon the positive assurance of the Assistant Secretary that the second order for 25,000 muskets should be given to it, entered into contracts for more than fifty thousand dollars' worth of the costly gun tools, to be delivered before April; engaged for the alteration of their present establishment, and the erection of new buildings and new machinery, to the amount of one hundred thousand dollars more; have hired experts in this gun manufacture at high wages; have secured for a superintendent the mechanic who set up the Springfield-made machinery used in the Enfield rifle factory in England, and "are in for it" every way.

The company is entitled to the additional order, and a great wrong would be done them, and a crushing injury inflicted, if it were withheld.

I beg the department to enable me to send it to them.

SAMUEL WILKESON.

Hon. E. M. STANTON,
  Secretary of War.

WILLARDS' HOTEL, *Washington, January* 29, 1862.

SIR: Having an order from the War Department for the manufacture of 25,000 Springfield rifle muskets, and having so far completed my arrangements as to insure a prompt delivery in July next, as specified in the order, I beg an interview on the subject. Major Dyer, of the Springfield armory, has given us a model arm, and knows something of our preparations, involving a large expenditure, and to him I would refer you.

  Very respectfully,

A. H. ALMY,
  Treasurer Eagle Manufacturing Co., Mansfield, Conn.

Hon. E. M. STANTON,
  Secretary of War.

HEADQUARTERS CONNECTICUT,
137 *Broadway, New York, March* 24, 1862.

MY DEAR SIR: Will you allow me to introduce to you my brother, Mr. A. H. Almy, treasurer of Eagle Manufacturing Company? In December last he received an order from General Ripley for 25,000 Springfield muskets, to be delivered in certain quantities, commencing in July next, and monthly until the order is completed. He has, in good faith, taken measures to establish an armory at great expense in order to comply with the conditions of his contract. He is very anxious to know what government intends to do with such contracts, and any information or assistance you may give him will be appreciated by myself.

For courtesies on many occasions to myself, personally, I wish to express my sincere acknowledgments.

I am, very truly, yours,

J. H. ALMY,
Assistant Quartermaster General Com'd'g.

Major HAGNER.

HEADQUARTERS CONNECTICUT,
137 *Broadway, New York, April* 19, 1862.

MY DEAR SIR: The Eagle Manufacturing Company, represented by my brother, A. H. Almy, treasurer, immediately after his interview with you at Washington, recommenced their suspended operations, and they are fully prepared to complete the contract for 25,000 Springfield muskets, if they can have said contract confirmed.

I learn from him to-day that he has received no notice from the committee of its confirmation. Other parties, however, report that their contracts have passed the ordeal, and that a full recognition of their validity has been given. May I ask of you the favor to call the attention of the committee to the fact, and, if possible, have an early certification of the validity of the contract, as the want of the same embarrasses my brother greatly. I trust you will pardon me for thus troubling you, but my brother's interests are hazarded by the delay in confirming his contract, and I would be greatly obliged if you will refer the case when you meet the committee.

Very truly, your obedient servant,

J. H. ALMY,
Assistant Quartermaster General, Connecticut.

Major HAGNER.

WILLARDS' HOTEL, *May* 15, 1862.

GENTLEMEN: Soon after the Eagle Manufacturing Company received their order for the manufacture of 25,000 guns, they notified the government that they could not, without loss, build the costly machinery for such purpose unless they could have the order increased.

Messrs. Colt, Lamson, Goodnow & Co., and other contractors, gave the same notice, and their orders were increased. The same was promised us by the War Department, and on that assurance we embarked in the enterprise. Mr. Cameron's retirement, a short time after, made it impossible to get it officially increased, and the record only shows a contract of 25,000. Now if, as Major Hagner says, you will reduce all the contracts a certain amount, we would respectfully represent that equal and exact justice could not be made to us unless these facts are considered, and this is the apology which I offer for this note.

We have been acting on the faith of the government that our order was good for 50,000 arms.

Yours, respectfully,
EAGLE MANUFACTURING COMPANY,
Per A. H. ALMY, *Treasurer.*

Messrs. HOLT and OWEN,
Commissioners on Ordnance Contracts. Washington.

Before commission, March 26, 1862.

Mr. Almy, treasurer of the Eagle Manufacturing Company, appeared before the commission: States that he has invested to a very large extent in buildings and machinery for this work; that he cannot now give up his order without serious loss; that he proposed to make stocks or finish barrels at his shops; he had commenced getting up stocking machinery.

May 15.—Mr. Almy again appeared before the commission: States that his actual engagements are such that he cannot reduce his order below 20,000 without serious loss to him; that if the order be confirmed for that number he will be able to go on safely.

P. V. HAGNER, *Major Ordnance.*

COMMISSION ON ORDNANCE AND ORDNANCE STORES,
Washington, May 16, 1862.

GENERAL: The commission have the honor to report as follows:

CASE No. 77.—EAGLE MANUFACTURING COMPANY.

Order by direction of the Secretary of War, dated Dec. 12, 1861.—(See page 165, Ex. Doc. No. 67.) Referred by direction of the Secretary of War.
To furnish 25,000 muskets, with appendages, of the Springfield pattern, at the price of $20 per gun. Deliveries to be made of not less than 500 in each of the months of July, August, and September, 1862; not less than 1,000 in each of the months of October and November, 1862; not less than 1,500 in December, 1862; and not less than 2,000 per month thereafter.—(See case No. 72.)

The commission find that the above order was not given in accordance with the law and regulations; that it is not therefore a contract of legal force, inasmuch as it does not contain the express requirements of the law, and was not made "after previous advertisement for proposals respecting the same," nor can it be regarded as an "open purchase." being for articles which did not require "immediate delivery," but as stipulated to be manufactured and delivered at prescribed distant periods.

They further consider that the number of arms ordered is larger than the wants of the government justify in this case, at the price fixed; and therefore, according to the principles set forth in Mason's case, No. 72, they decide that the order to the Eagle Manufacturing Company be confirmed, subject to all its terms, to the extent of 20,000 muskets, upon condition that they shall, within fifteen days after notice of this decision, execute bond, with good and sufficient sureties, in the form and with the stipulations prescribed by law and the regulations for the performance of the contract, as thus modified, resulting from said order and acceptance, and upon their failure or refusal to execute such bond, then the said order shall be declared cancelled and of no effect.

The commission further decide that the deliveries under the contract to be executed shall be required at or within the periods stipulated in the original order, but that the numbers specified may be reduced proportionately to the re-

Ex. Doc. 72——23

duction of the whole number, so that the contract shall be completed within the time allowed in the original order.

We are, sir, very respectfully, your obedient servants,

J. HOLT,
ROBERT DALE OWEN,
Commissioners, &c.
P. V. HAGNER,
Major of Ordnance, Assistant to Commission.

Brigadier General J. W. RIPLEY,
Chief of Ordnance.

CASE No. 78.

JAMES T. HODGE.

NEW YORK, *February* 8, 1862.

SIR : In response to your order of January 29, I beg respectfully to state :

I. That I have contracted with the ordnance department to manufacture 50,000 muskets, of the Springfield pattern, for $20 each. The first delivery to be made in July next. The order bears date December 26, 1861, a copy of which is herewith enclosed. This order I duly accepted.

II. In connexion with James T. Hodge, esq., (but avoiding a partnership,) who holds an order for a like number of muskets, and with the same terms and conditions as mine, and mutually to lessen the burden, I leased on the 13th of January the extensive and well-known factories, shops, power, and machinery of the Trenton Locomotive and Machine Manufacturing Company of Trenton, New Jersey.

I have, in connexion with Mr. Hodge, contracted with this company to furnish me all of my labor, and to provide me with such gun machines and tools as they are themselves capable of manufacturing. All of the additional machinery I have bought, or am now engaged in ordering and buying for cash to the extent already of sixty thousand dollars. I have thus far procured more than forty-five principal and distinct machines, and am daily adding to the number. In two weeks I can produce from our own factory many parts of the musket com plete. All of the different parts, except the rough barrels for the earlier deliveries, I expect to manufacture in our own shops.

If energy and the expenditure of a large capital on my part, and skill on the part of my employés, are criterions by which to judge, I shall meet the requirements of my contract.

As the number of muskets to be delivered increases from month to month, I shall increase my machinery, and when the last delivery is made, the company above mentioned, Mr. Hodge and myself, will possess an armory second only to that at Springfield, and which may prove of essential service to the government.

My order, as well as Mr. Hodge's, prohibits any transfer of the order under the penalty of forfeiture. Doubting as to the meaning of this, or to what extent it reaches, and fearing to risk so large a capital and such heavy liabilities as we are under, we have preserved our interests separate with much difficulty and inconvenience. A simple partnership, including Mr. Hodge, myself, and two or three capitalists who have aided us, would simplify the business details of our manufacture nearly one-half, as must be evident to you.

Is there any objection to allowing these contracts to stand in the name of Burt, Hodge & Co.? It could work no injury to the government and would greatly relieve us.

As soon as the machinery already purchased shall be put up, we invite the examination of an ordnance officer, to be detailed by the department, who shall examine as to our progress and probable success, and thoroughly scrutinize in detail the facts stated generally in this report.

I have the honor to be, your obedient servant,

ADDISON M. BURT.

Hon. E. M. STANTON, *Secretary of War.*

NEW YORK, *February* 10, 1862.

SIR: In pursuance of your order of January 29, 1862, I have the honor to report that I am a contractor with the government of the United States through the ordnance department, by virtue of the order of December 26, 1861, (a copy of which is herewith enclosed,) which order I have duly accepted.

Upon the receipt and acceptance of the said order, I entered upon arrangements for fulfilling it. In connexion with Addison M. Burt, esq., I have leased the works, power, machinery, &c., of the Trenton Locomotive and Machine Manufacturing Company, at Trenton, New Jersey, and am now engaged in adding machines which I think will enable me to fulfil my contract. As these arrangements are so entirely upon the same basis, although we are acting independently of each other, I append a copy of Mr. Burt's report, which will give you the precise state of the case. And I beg to add the expression of my desire that you will comply with Mr. Burt's request contained in his report, if compatible with the public interest.

I have the honor to be, very respectfully, your obedient servant ,

JAMES T. HODGE.

Hon. E. M. STANTON, *Secretary of War.*

ORDNANCE OFFICE, *Washington, December* 26, 1861.

SIR: By direction of the Secretary of War I offer you an order of fifty thousand (50,000) muskets, with appendages, of the Springfield pattern, on the following terms and conditions, viz: These arms are to be furnished with the regular appendages, and are to be in all respects identical with the standard rifle musket made at the United States armory at Springfield, Massachusetts, and are to interchange with it and with each other in all their parts. They are to be subject to inspection by United States inspectors in the same manner that the Springfield arms are inspected, and none are to be received or paid for but such as pass inspection, and are approved by the United States inspector. These fifty thousand (50,000) arms and appendages are to be delivered at your armory as follows, viz: Not less than one thousand (1,000) in each of the months of July, August, and September, 1862; not less than two thousand (2,000) in each of the months of October and November, 1862; not less than three thousand (3,000) in December, 1862; and not less than four thousand (4,000) per month thereafter until the entire fifty thousand (50,000) shall have been delivered. And you are to have the right to deliver more rapidly than, according to the number of arms, before specified, if you can do so.

In case of any failure to make deliveries to the extent and within the times before specified, you are to forfeit the right to deliver whatever number may be deficient in the specified number for the month in which the failure occurs.

All these arms and appendages are to be delivered by you, and this order, if transferred by you to another party, is to be thereby forfeited.

Payments are to be made in such funds as the Treasury Department may provide for each delivery, on certificates of inspection and receipt by the United States inspectors, at the rate of twenty ($20) dollars for each arm, including appendages.

All these arms and appendages are to be packed by you in boxes of the regular pattern, with twenty (20) muskets and appendages in each box, for which a fair price, to be determined by the United States inspectors, will be allowed.

Please signify, in writing, your acceptance or non-acceptance of this order on the terms and conditions before stated herein.

Respectfully, your obedient servant,

JAS. W. RIPLEY,
Brigadier General.

JAMES T. HODGE, *New York.*

NEW YORK, *April* 10, 1862.

SIR: I have received your communication of April 2, 1862, directing me to inform the commission of the present condition of each branch of my work upon the contract to furnish 50,000 Springfield arms, on whom I rely for the parts, and when I shall be able to furnish a complete gun, ready for the inspector; where my arms are to be finally assembled, and whether I shall be able to furnish any other contractor with any finished parts, and whether I have promised any, and to whom? In reply permit me to refer you particularly to my report in answer to the order of the Secretary of War, a copy of which is enclosed, which will fully explain the *status* of my business, no change having since been made.

The work is being vigorously prosecuted at the factory taken by Mr. A. M. Burt and myself, at Trenton, New Jersey. Every portion of the machinery is progressing rapidly. The machinery and tools are contracted for with competent and responsible persons, and are being daily delivered. The contracts for these now exceed $65,000 in cash and will soon reach $120,000. This machinery and these tools are as far advanced as it was possible to make them with ready money and untiring energy. I think I shall be able to furnish a finished musket by the 31st day of July next. In case I shall be disappointed in the delivery of the machinery for some of the parts, and the government shall hold me strictly to my contract, I am assured that the parts wanting for the first delivery, in addition to those manufactured at the factory, can be procured by me.

I rely solely upon the factory for all of the parts, except in the above contingency, and the rough barrels which I shall purchase outside. Three different concerns offer to sell me the rough barrels, and I am still undetermined from which to take them, viz: N. Washburne, Worcester, Massachusetts; the Trenton Iron Company, Trenton, New Jersey; and Messrs. Morris, Tasker, & Co., Philadelphia.

The arms will be assembled in the factory at Trenton. I have no engagements to furnish any parts to any other contractor, but could furnish some. None are promised, and I think it most prudent to make no engagement of the kind.

The accompanying report to the Secretary of War will explain my relations with Addison M. Burt, who is carrying on a contract in the same factory with mine. He principally manages the factory, but has received no notice from the commission. I have no pecuniary interest in his contract, but desire to say that both operations are progressing together.

Yours respectfully,

JAMES T. HODGE

J. WISE, Esq.,
Secretary of Commission.

COMMISSION ON ORDNANCE AND ORDNANCE STORES,
Washington, May 16, 1862.

GENERAL: The commission have the honor to report as follows:

CASE No. 78.—J. T. HODGE, of New York.

Order by direction of the Secretary of War, dated ———— —(See page —. Ex. Doc. No. 67.) Referred by direction of the Secretary of War.

To furnish 50,000 muskets of the Springfield pattern, with appendages, at the price of $20 per gun. Deliveries to be made of not less than 1,000 in each of the months of July, August, and September; not less than 2,000 in each of the months of October and November; not less than 3,000 in December, and not less than 4,000 per month thereafter.— (See case No. 72.)

The commission find that the above order was not given in accordance with the law and regulations; that it is not therefore a contract of legal force, inasmuch as it does not contain the express requirements of the law, and was not made "after previous advertisement for proposals respecting the same;" nor can it be regarded as an open purchase, being for articles which did not require "immediate delivery," but, as stipulated, to be manufactured and delivered at prescribed distant periods.

They further consider that the number of arms ordered is larger than the wants of the government justify in this case, at the price fixed, and therefore, according to the principles set forth in Mason's case, (No 72,) they decide that the order to Mr. Hodge be confirmed, subject to its terms to the extent of 25,000 muskets, upon condition that he shall, within fifteen days after notice of this decision, execute bond, with good and sufficient sureties, in the form and with the stipulations prescribed by law and the regulations for the performance of the contract as thus modified, resulting from said order and acceptance; and upon his failure or refusal to execute such bond, then the said order shall be declared cancelled and of no effect.

The commission further decide that the deliveries under the contract to be executed shall be required at or within the periods stipulated in the original order, but that the numbers specified may be reduced proportionately to the reduction of the whole number, so that the contract shall be completed within the time allowed by the original order.

We are, sir, very respectfully, your obedient servants,

J. HOLT,
ROBERT DALE OWEN,
Commissioners, &c.

P. V. HAGNER,
Major of Ordnance, Assistant to Commissioners.

Brigadier General J. W. RIPLEY,
Chief of Ordnance.

(See case No. 79.)

CASE NO. 79.

A. M. BURT.

NEW YORK, *February* 10, 1862.

SIR: In pursuance of your order of January 29, 1862, I have the honor to report that I am a contractor with the government of the United States, through the ordnance department, by virtue of the order of December 26, 1861, a copy of which is herewith enclosed, which order I have duly accepted.

Upon the receipt and acceptance of the said order, I entered upon arrangements for fulfilling it.   In connexion with Addison M. Burt, esq., I have leased the works, power, machinery, &c., of the Trenton Locomotive and Machine Manufacturing Company, at Trenton, New Jersey, and am now engaged in adding machines which I think will enable me to fulfil my contract.   As these arrangements are so entirely upon the same basis, although we are acting independently of each other, I append a copy of Mr. Burt's report, which will give you the precise state of the case.   And I beg to add the expression of my desire that you will comply with Mr. Burt's request, contained in his report, if compatible with the public interest.

I have the honor to be, very respectfully, your obedient servant,

JAMES T. HODGE.

Hon. E. M. STANTON,
    Secretary of War.

NEW YORK, *February* 8, 1862.

SIR : In response to your order of January 29, I beg respectfully to state :

I. That I have contracted with the ordnance department to manufacture 50,000 muskets, of the Springfield pattern, for $20 each.   The first delivery to be made in July next.   The order bears date December 26, 1861, a copy of which is herewith enclosed.   This order I duly accepted.

II. In connexion with James T. Hodge, esq., (but avoiding a partnership,) who holds an order for a like number of muskets, and with the same terms and conditions as mine, and mutually to lessen the burden, I leased on the 13th of January the extensive well-known factories, shops, power, and machinery of the Trenton Locomotive and Machine Manufacturing Company of Trenton, New Jersey.

I have, in connexion with Mr. Hodge, contracted with this company to furnish me all of my labor, and to provide me with such gun machines and tools as they are themselves capable of manufacturing.   All of the additional machinery I have bought, or am now engaged in ordering and buying for cash, to the extent already of sixty thousand dollars.   I have thus far procured more than forty-five principal and distinct machines, and am daily adding to the number.

In two weeks I can produce from our own factory many parts of the musket complete.   All of the different parts, except the rough barrels for the earlier deliveries, I expect to manufacture in our own shops.

If energy and the expenditure of a large capital on my part, and skill on the part of my employés are criterions by which to judge, I shall meet the requirements of my contract.

As the number of muskets to be delivered increases from month to month, I shall increase my machinery, and when the last delivery is made, the company above mentioned, Mr. Hodge and myself, will possess an armory second only to that of Springfield, and which may prove of essential service to the government.

My order, as well as Mr. Hodge's, prohibits any transfer of the order under penalty of forfeiture.

Doubting as to the meaning of this, or to what extent it reaches, and fearing to risk so large a capital and such heavy liabilities as we are under, we have preserved our interests separate with much difficulty and inconvenience.   A simple partnership, including Mr. Hodge, myself, and two or three capitalists who have aided us, would simplify the business details of our manufacture nearly one-half, as must be evident to you.

Is there any objection to allowing these contracts to stand in the name of Burt, Hodge & Co. ?   It could work no injury to the government and would greatly relieve us.

As soon as the machinery already purchased shall be put up, we invite the examination of an ordnance officer, to be detailed by the department, who shall examine as to our progress and probable success, and thoroughly scrutinize in detail the facts stated generally in this report.

I have the honor to be, your obedient servant,

ADDISON M. BURT.

Hon. E. M. STANTON, *Secretary of War.*

ORDNANCE OFFICE, *Washington, December* 26, 1861.

SIR: By direction of the Secretary of War I offer you an order for fifty thousand (50,000) muskets and appendages, of the Springfield pattern, on the following terms and conditions, viz:

These arms are to be furnished, with the regular appendages, and are to be in all respects identical with the standard rifle musket made at the United States armory at Springfield, Massachusetts, and are to interchange with it and with each other in all their parts. They are to be subject to inspection by the United States inspectors, in the same manner that the Springfield arms are inspected, and none are to be received and paid for but such as pass inspection and are approved by the United States inspectors.

These fifty thousand (50,000) arms and appendages are to be delivered at your armory as follows, viz: Not less than one thousand (1,000) in *each* of the months of July, August, and September, 1862; not less than two thousand (2,000) in each of the months of October and November, 1862; not less than three thousand (3,000) in December, 1862; and not less than four thousand (4,000) per month thereafter until the entire fifty thousand (50,000) shall have been delivered; and you are to have the right to deliver more rapidly than, according to the number of arms, before specified, if you can do so.

In case of any failure to make deliveries to the extent and within the times before specified, you are to forfeit the right to deliver whatever number may be deficient in the specified number for the month in which the failure occurs.

All these arms and appendages are to be delivered by you, and this order, if transferred by you to another party, is to be thereby forfeited.

Payments are to be made in such funds as the Treasury Department may provide for each delivery, on certificates of inspection and receipt by the United States inspectors, at the rate of twenty dollars ($20) for each arm, including appendages.

All these arms and appendages are to be packed by you in boxes of the regular pattern, with twenty (20) muskets and appendages in each box, for which a fair price, to be determined by the United States inspectors, will be allowed.

Please signify, in writing, your acceptance or non-acceptance of this order on the terms and conditions before stated herein.

Respectfully, your obedient servant,

JAMES W. RIPLEY,
Brigadier General.

ADDISON M. BURT, Esq., *New York,*

NO. 20 EXCHANGE PLACE,
New York, April 12, 1862.

DEAR SIR: I have this moment received your letter of the 4th instant. From the fact that Mr. Hodge duly received his of the same date, I have been at a loss to account for my not hearing from you, as I was under the impression that my address, as above, was given on my papers referred to the commission. However, an advertised letter in this morning's list for "A. W. Burt, New York," proves to be your favor of the 4th instant; and with this explanation of my apparent neglect, I proceed to give you the information required.

Respectfully referring to my report to the War Department, under the general order of 29th January last. a copy of which is herewith enclosed, I have to say that the design therein explained of establishing at Trenton a complete armory for the manufacture of arms in all their parts has been diligently prosecuted, and is now as far advanced toward completion as could possibly be accomplished by sufficient capital and the best mechanical skill. The machinery and tools required have been purchased or contracted for. A considerable part are already delivered and the remainder nearly ready for delivery. The purchases and contracts amount now to upwards of $80,000, for all which the cash is paid on delivery, except in some cases where it had to be paid in advance.

The following is a list of the bills thus far :

Bement & Dougherty, Philadelphia	$23,435 00
Hughes & Phillips, Newark, New Jersey	2,650 00
Brown & Sharpe, Providence, Rhode Island	1,449 50
James S. Brown, Pawtucket	2,100 00
Wood, Light & Co., Worcester, Massachusetts	1,050 00
George Crompton, Worcester, Massachusetts	5,500 00
William Mason, Taunton, Massachusetts	364 00
Am. Machine Works, Springfield	15,000 00*
Hope Iron Company, Providence	3,755 00
W. A. Wheeler, Worcester	4,030 00
Charles Parker, Meriden, Connecticut	100 00
—— Ames, Chicopee	5,000 00
Massachusetts Arms Company, Chicopee Falls	775 00
George S. Lincoln & Co., Hartford	452 25
Trenton Locomotive Works, Trenton, New Jersey	15,791 00
Total	81,451 75

* NOTE.—This item is for the stock machines. In addition, the same concern is making, by days' work, the *gauges*, amounting to, say 5,000 00

Making a total of................................. 86,451 75

This amount is to be increased as rapidly as the machinery can be procured till it will reach about $120,000.

I am not getting guns together in parts made at different shops, but rely for the complete gun upon the armory at Trenton, when I expect to be able to furnish arms ready for the inspector by the end of July next, though it is possible that some unlooked for delay may render it necessary, in order to make my first delivery, to purchase some of the parts from other manufacturers. This, however, I shall find no difficulty in doing. From the foregoing you will see that my arms are to be finally assembled at Trenton.

In answer to your inquiry, " Will you be able to furnish any other contractor with any finished parts, and have you promised any, and to whom?" I beg leave to say that, as stated in my enclosed report, and also in that of Mr. James T. Hodge, we leased the same factory without, however, becoming partners, and our contracts are progressing with equal steps. This plan was adopted for mutual benefit, and with the view, while fulfilling our contracts with the government, to be able to command a business hereafter not only with our own government but with all other customers.

We applied to the Secretary of War in our respective reports to consolidate our contracts. The legislature of New Jersey have chartered an arms company which Mr. Hodge and I control, with a capital of $400,000. If our contracts were united, this company would possess the whole capital for our work, free from debt, with material property, amounting to $200,000, and the balance in cash. I see no reason, if the government want these arms, and the commission are satisfied of the facts herein stated, the evidence of which I am ready to lay before them, why this request should not be granted, and I respectfully ask the aid of the commission in this matter. I have not promised, nor do I expect to promise, any parts to any other person. All the several parts are to be manufactured, from the raw material up to completion, in our own factory, with the exception of barrels in the rough, which will be purchased probably from one or all of the following manufacturers, viz: Washburn, of Worcester, the Trenton Iron Company, and Morris, Tasker & Co., of Philadelphia. All these establishments have offered to supply the rough barrels, and are abundantly able to do it.

As to the necessary labor and skill, we already have it offered to us in great abundance by mechanics of large experience.

I believe I have now communicated all the information called for by your letter, and I beg to subscribe myself, very respectfully, yours, &c.

ADDISON M. BURT,
20 Exchange Place.

J. WISE, Esq., *Secretary, &c.*

OFFICE, Trenton, New Jersey, April 19, 1862.

GENTLEMEN : I beg to inform the commission and Major Hagner, with reference to our interview of yesterday, that Mr. Vancleve will proceed on Monday to visit all the shops where our machinery is being made, and, after personally inspecting the condition of the several machines, will appear before you and give you the positive information desired. It will take him about four days to make the tour, so that it may be the last of next week before he reaches Washington.

Very respectfully,

A. M. BURT.

Hon. JOS. HOLT and ROBERT DALE OWEN,
Commission, &c.

20 EXCHANGE PLACE,
New York, April 25, 1862.

DEAR SIR: I beg leave to say that, owing to imperative business, Mr. Vancleve has not been able to make his proposed tour of the shops in season to appear before you this week as I promised.

He starts to-day or to-morrow, however, and will certainly be in Washington, able to give all desired information with regard to my machinery, &c., next week.

Very respectfully,

A. M. BURT.

Hon. JOSEPH HOLT and ROBERT DALE OWEN,
Commission, &c., Washington.

PHILADELPHIA, April 24, 1862.

DEAR SIR: In reply to your inquiry for 20,000 gun locks, we have to say that we expect to complete arrangements this week for increasing our present capacity to such an extent as to enable us to fill your order, to commence delivering to you in August, possibly sooner.

Accompanying this we send you one of our locks which has passed inspection at the Springfield armory, together with a copy of a letter from an eyewitness, through whose influence the inspection was made for us.

We took *four* of our locks, which, in the presence of Major Dyer and Mr. Allen, the master armorer, were taken entirely to pieces and mixed up with a corresponding number of parts of the Springfield make. They were then reassembled, the whole coming together and fitting and working perfectly to the entire satisfaction of the above-named parties. We should be pleased to have your order for ramrods and cones, which we can supply considerably in advance of the locks. Be kind enough to return to us the lock we now send you as *we* value it far above its intrinsic worth.

Let us know of the confirmation of your contract as soon as you get it, and oblige

Yours, truly,

C. H. WILLIAMS & CO.

A. G. M. Prevost, Esq.,
    Director Trenton Locomotive and Machine Manufacturing Company.

Springfield, Massachusetts,
April 1, 1862.

Gentlemen: I am very happy to say I had the pleasure of seeing the locks brought by your Mr. Prevost examined rigidly by the superintendent and master armorer of the United States armory in this place, and I congratulate you on the very satisfactory result which Mr. Prevost will report. The locks were interchanged with all the parts of the locks manufactured here and were found to work as well as they did before, in fact perfectly.

I think you will have no cause to fear inspection of your work, if the locks you manufacture are as perfect as these. I should also say they fit the gun stock most perfectly.

Truly yours,

SAMUEL NORRIS.

Messrs. C. H. Williams & Co., *Philadelphia.*

Machines contracted for by Trenton Arms Company.

MILLING MACHINES.

10 finished, 6 of them in the mill.
24 to be delivered May 15.
10 to be delivered May 20.
1 clamp miller for muzzles, to be finished July 1.
2 small clamp millers, now finished.
2 small clamp millers, to be finished July 20.
1 universal milling machine, to be finished July 1.
1 index milling machine, now at work.
1 tap milling machine, now at work.
1 gear cutting machine, now at work.
1 index milling machine, to be finished June 1.
1 breaching machine for bands, now finished.
1 complete set milling tools for barrels.

DRILLS.

3 four-spindle drills, finished and in mill.
2 four-spindle drills, to be delivered May 15.
3 three-spindle drills, finished and at work.
1 light drilling machine, finished and in mill.

RIFLING MACHINES.

1 two-spindle, finished and in mill.
The manufacturer can deliver others in July.

BORING MACHINES.

1 nut boring machine, finished and in mill.
2 nut boring machines, will be finished June 20.
1 quick boring machine, finished and in the mill.
2 quick boring machines, will be finished June 20.
1 smooth boring machine, finished and in mill.
4 quick boring machines, will be finished June 20.

SCREW MACHINES.

3 revolving head-screw lathes, finished and in mill.
1 tapping lathe, finished and in mill.

BARREL TURNING LATHE.

6 taper turning lathes, to be delivered June 1.
2 octogon turning lathes, to be delivered June 1.
1 barrel tapping machine, to be delivered August 1.
1 screw breech-pin machine, to be delivered August 1.

FORGING MACHINES.

2 drops, now in mill.
2 drops, to be delivered July 1.
9 trip hammers, to be delivered July 1.
3 trip hammers, now at work in mill.

VICES.

27 filer's vices, now in shop.
30 large tool vices, now in shop.

STOCKING MACHINES.

1 slubbing and sawing-off machine, finished July 10.
1 centring for turning, finished July 10.
2 first turning machines, to be delivered July 1.
3 second turning machines, to be delivered July 1.
1 spotting machine, for bearing points, to be delivered July 1.
1 bedding machine for bands, to be delivered July 1.
1 bedding machine for locks, to be delivered August 1.
1 bedding machine for guard plate, to be delivered August 1.
1 grooving machine for ramrods, and letting in band spring, to be delivered August 1.
1 machine for turning between band, to be delivered August 1.
1 machine for turning bands, to be delivered August 1.
1 profiling machine, three cuts, to be delivered August 1.
1 machine for cutting butt plates, to be delivered July 20.
1 machine for cutting, boring, and tapping for butt plates, to be delivered August 1.

Investment in machines for Trenton Arms Company machinery, &c., &c., now in hand at armory at Trenton.

6 sets rotary edging machines	$3,600
6 sets fixtures	500
5 4-spindle upright drills	1,500
2 3-spindle upright drills	400
10 sets castings for small millers	845
1 gear cutter	330
1 muzzle clamp miller	325
1 sight drilling machine	100
5 miller's drilling machines	750
1 rifling machine	750
1 3-spindle drill	175
1 nut-boring machine	300
1 quick boring machine	125
1 finishing machine	300
1 large revolving head-screw lathe	300
2 small revolving head-screw lathes	570
1 tapping machine	100
2 sets castings for nut-boring machine; 2 sets castings for quick boring machine; 4 sets castings for finished machine	600
1 set barrel fixtures; 1 set castings for smith's forge; 1 set castings for profile machine; 1 set castings for bayonet-milling tools	1,950
1 large drop, complete, with hammer	300
1 small drop, complete, with hammer	275
27 vices	100
1 index-milling machine	452
7 hand lathes	1,155
1 engine lathe, 13 feet shears	640
1 engine lathe, 17 feet 6-inch shears	530
1 engine lathe, 10 feet shears	480
1 engine lathe, 9 feet shears	421
1 engine lathe, 9 feet shears	300
1 engine lathe, 10 feet shears	300
1 engine lathe, 8 feet shears	230
1 engine lathe, 9 feet 6-inch shears	375
2 engine lathes, 12 feet and 15 feet shears	1,250
1 engine lathe, 15 feet shears	250
2 shoping machines	1,000
1 slotting machine	825
1 upright drill	190
1 upright drill	310
1 upright drill	100
1 planer, 10 feet long	530
1 planer, 10 feet long	450
4 grindstones	140
Hoisting apparatus	300
1 punching and shearing machine	492
1 punching and shearing machine	200
1 trip hammer	250
1 fan-blower	100
Shafting, pullies, and belts	1,000
6 smiths' fires	198
Polishing machine	75

10 milling machines	$3,250
1 small top milling machine	200
1 large top milling machine	250
Finishing ten milling machine castings	750
Nut boring, smooth boring, and quick reaming	550
2 polishing machines	1,300
Shafting, 300 feet, with pulleys, at $2 50	750
Finishing a set of barrel fixtures, fitting up smiths' forge, fitting up castings for profiling machines, fitting up castings for bayonet-milling tools	1,000
Work on dies, gauges, and fixtures in shop	2,000
	36,788

Before commission, April 18, 1862.

Mr. A. M. Burt, of New York, No. 20 Exchange Place, states :

Mr. Hodge and myself, having each orders for fifty thousand Springfield guns, have united, (without partnership,) and leased the Trenton Locomotive Works. We intend to make the entire arm except the rough barrels. Up to April 12 we had ordered tools, machinery, &c., to the extent of $86,000, and upon it we agreed to pay one-third advance. We have actually paid already for tools and machinery $42,000. We have leased the machine shops, and have made a contract with the company to furnish all the labor and material. I am to supply all the machinery, and I have agreed with Mr. Hodge to make his guns on my machines. This is equivalent to having my monthly deliveries doubled. I have applied for permission to consolidate our contracts, so that they may be carried out in the name of Burt, Hodge & Co., fearing to do anything in this way without special permission, as our orders forbid transfers. My pledge to Mr. Hodge is to comply with the terms of his agreement, if possible. I mean to give him an equal share in the product of the works, so that his agreement shall be filled if mine is.

I hand in a list of machines now in shop, valued at $36,700, and also a statement showing total of orders for machines, part of which have been delivered, and are included in the first. Since the date of the statement 12th April, I have ordered and purchased about $6,000 worth of machines, not included in that statement, making the whole orders, up to date, $92,000.

I have myself heretofore had direction of a manufacturing company in Richmond making car springs, and I was obliged to break up in March and leave all my property there. I am not a mechanic myself; I attend to the financial branch of the business. I have secured an experienced foreman and good laborers to carry on the work.

Our machines will, we think, be capable of furnishing 9,000 guns per month ; if they are not, we must order more, as our investment is made with a view to establishing an armory of that capacity at Trenton, and we must now go on, no matter at what cost. We can get money enough.

The first delivery of 2,000 on the two orders is to be made in July. We do not expect to manufacture all the parts of the arm for this delivery; we shall make some of the parts and purchase the rest.

Redfield & Co., of New York, have offered to furnish the whole 100,000 stocks. I have not seen their establishment, but one Mr. Prevost and, I think, Mr. Van Clieve have seen it, and think he can be relied upon to furnish what may be wanted. We intend, however, to make our own stocks in the main, and we have ordered our stocking machines.

I consider that there has been no " transfer," so to speak, as forbidden by the order, either by Mr. Hodge or by myself. I have shops and machines, and make contracts with the locomotive company to furnish labor and do the work. Mr. Hodge makes contracts with me and with the locomotive company to do his work. He has leased, also, a part of the shop, which may be used in some of the details of the work.

All our barrels in the rough are to be furnished us either by Washburne, by Morris, Tasker & Co., or by the Trenton Iron Company. All have offered, but we have as yet given no orders.

Locks we can obtain, as I hear, in Philadelphia, of Williams & Co., or, at Windsor, locks from Dinslow & Chase, where Muir & Co. are to get theirs. My brother is a partner in the firm of Muir & Co.

I have not acquainted myself with all the details of the work, but will, if the commission desire it, send Mr. Van Clieve or Mr. Prevost. At first I expected to spend only $60,000, and estimated a profit of $2 to $2 50 per gun. I now foresee greatly increased expenditure, and I am unable to say whether I will do as well or even whether I will clear anything or not. Mr. Hodge puts in no capital, but he pays me so much per gun for what I do for him. He only pays for guns which pass inspection, after payment to him by the government.

Before commission, May 2, 1862.

Mr. H. M. Burt states :

My actual disbursements have been increased, up to this day, to $48,000. The stocks are to be furnished by the Empire Works, and not by Redfield. I have seen the stocking machines. All are said to be complete, except that for fitting at the bands. I saw the parts for this machine in the lathes, which they said would be finished this week. They have actually finished a few stocks, one of which they gave to Mr. Esler, of Philadelphia, to show to the commission, and they also promised to send one next week. They have, it is said, 10,000 stocks partly finished. They are to make nothing but stocks; they have a large establishment, and offer to deliver by July 1. I hear that Robins & Co., of Hartford, will be able to manufacture next week. Mr. Van Clieve has just visited the machine shops at Milbury, near Worcester, Massachusetts. They are making bayonets and rods for the armory at Springfield, and the proprietor offers to deliver us, by August 1st, at the rate of 2,000 per month.

COMMISSION ON ORDNANCE AND ORDNANCE STORES,
Washington, May 14, 1862.

SIR : I am directed by the commission as above to state to you that your proposal of yesterday to reduce the number of guns to be manufactured by you to 25,000 has been accepted and the same number will be confirmed to your associate Mr. Hodge.

The report of the confirmation of your contract and that of Mr. Hodge in that modified form will be made to the chief of ordnance, so that you may proceed with confidence in carrying it out.

Very respectfully, &c.,
P. V. HAGNER,
Major of Ordnance.

Mr. A. M. BURT.

COMMISSION ON ORDNANCE AND ORDNANCE STORES,
Washington, May 16, 1862.

GENERAL : The commission have the honor to report as follows :

CASE No. 79.—A. M. BURT, of New York.

Order by direction of the Secretary of War, dated   .—(See page   , Ex. Doc. No. 67.) Referred by direction of the Secretary of War.

To furnish 50,000 muskets, with appendages, of the Springfield pattern, at the price of $20 per gun. Deliveries to be made of not less than 1,000 in each of the months of July, August, and September; not less than 2,000 in each of the months of October and November; not less than 3,000 in December; and not less than 4,000 per month thereafter.—(See case No. 72.)

The commission find that the above order was not given in accordance with the law and regulations ; that it is not therefore a contract of legal force, inasmuch as it does not contain the express requirements of the law and was not made "after previous advertisement for proposals respecting the same," nor can it be considered as an "open purchase," being for articles which did not require "immediate delivery," but, as stipulated, to be manufactured and delivered at prescribed distant periods.

They further consider that the number of guns ordered is larger than the wants of the government justify in this case at the price fixed, and therefore, according to the principles set forth in Mason's case, No. 72, they decide that the order to Mr. Burt be confirmed, subject to all its terms, to the extent of 25,000 muskets, upon condition that he shall within fifteen days after notice of this decision, execute bond with good and sufficient sureties, in the form and with the stipulations prescribed by law and the regulations for the performance of the contract as thus modified, resulting from said order and acceptance, and upon his failure or refusal to execute such bond, then the said order shall be declared cancelled and of no effect.

The commission further decide that the deliveries under the contract to be executed shall be required at or within the periods stipulated in the original order, but that the numbers specified may be reduced proportionately to the reduction of the whole number, so that the contract shall be completed within the time allowed by the original order.

We are, sir, very respectfully, your obedient servants,

J. HOLT,
ROBERT DALE OWEN,
Commissioners, &c.
P. V. HAGNER,
Major of Ordnance, Assistant to Commission.

Brigadier General J. W. RIPLEY,
Chief of Ordnance.

CASE No. 80.

W. W. WELCH.

ORDNANCE OFFICE,
Washington, November 6, 1861.

SIR : By direction of the Secretary of War, I offer you an order for eighteen thousand (18,000) rifle muskets and appendages, on the following terms and conditions, viz : These arms are to be in all respects identical with the standard rifle muskets made at the United States armory at Springfield, Massachusetts, and are to exchange with it and with each other in all their parts; they are to be subject to inspection by United States inspectors in the same manner that the Springfield arms are inspected, and none are to be received or paid for but such as pass inspection and are approved by the United States inspector. These 18,000 rifle muskets and appendages are to be delivered for inspection at Norfolk, Connecticut, as follows, viz:

Five hundred (500) on or before...................... April 6, 1862.
One thousand (1,000) on or before.................... May 6, 1862.
Fifteen hundred (1,500) on or before...... .... June 6, 1862.
Fifteen hundred (1,500) on or before.................. July 6, 1862.
Sixteen hundred (1,600) on or before.................. August 6, 1862.
Sixteen hundred (1,600) on or before.................. September 6, 1862.
Sixteen hundred (1,600) on or before.................. October 6, 1862.
Seventeen hundred (1,700) on or before................ November 6, 1862.
Seventeen hundred (1,700) on or before................ December 6, 1862.
Eighteen hundred (1,800) on or before................. January 6, 1863.
Seventeen hundred (1,700) on or before................ February 6, 1863.
Eighteen hundred (1,800) on or before................. March 6, 1863.

In case of failure to make any one of the deliveries in or within the times before specified, the government is to have authority to revoke and annul this order immediately. Payments for each delivery are to be made in such funds as the Treasury Department may provide, on certificates of inspection and receipt by the United States inspector, at the rate of twenty dollars ($20) for each arm, including appendages. All these arms and appendages are to be packed by you in boxes of the regular pattern, with twenty muskets and appendages in each box, for which a fair price, to be determined by the United States inspector, will be allowed. Please signify in writing your acceptance or non-acceptance of this order on the terms and conditions herein stated.

Respectfully, your obedient servant,

WILLIAM MAYNADIER,
Lieut. Colonel of Ordnance.

W. W. WELCH, Esq., *Washington, D. C.*

ORDNANCE OFFICE, *March* 31, 1862.

True copy.

JAS. W. RIPLEY, *Brig. General.*

WASHINGTON, D. C., *February* 3, 1862.

SIR: I propose to submit for your consideration the enclosed statement, setting forth the facts briefly upon which my application for an extension of forty-five days from April 6, 1862, of my order from the War Department for the delivery of 18,000 rifled muskets and appendages is based.

The assurance that it was the policy of the government to encourage private enterprise in the manufacture of its most approved arm, with the fact that I had, with my associates in the execution of my order, a somewhat extensive manufactory there but partially employed, induced me to accept the enclosed order and undertake its execution.

Our manufactory in Norfolk, Connecticut, with the machinery now in it, has cost about $70,000, and furnishes the capacity in power and room for the annual production of a large amount of fire-arms.

The plan adopted to execute my order in the short time specified, to wit, five months, was to manufacture as much of the rifle as we believed we could complete in the prescribed time. We decided to bring out the barrels ready to attach to gun, and to make the ramrods and some other small attachments in our shop.

I at once contracted with first-class manufacturers for most of our gun ma chinery, and have employed from twenty to thirty mechanics in our manufactory to this time in making tools and fixtures required to do our work. We have in our manufactory nearly all the machinery required to finish sixty barrels and ramrods per day, and mechanics capable of doing our work according to contract. In obtaining a part of our machinery we have been delayed more than one month, and shall not receive before the last week in March next our entire machinery, which by contract should have been delivered by February 20, 1862. We have been somewhat delayed by our gauges, made in our shop by the pattern barrel furnished us at Springfield armory, not corresponding with the standard armory gauges. To avoid this delay no effort or expense has been spared.

We have in our shop nearly six hundred barrels bored, ground, and turned; but imperfect material renders it necessary to discard a part of these barrels, which occasions delay.

The various parts of the gun produced by contract are being manufactured by reliable and responsible parties, who have given and received satisfactory sureties for the execution of contracts.

My positive obligations incurred in the execution of the enclosed order with the War Department are more than $48,000, not including contingent liabilities for damages that may be sustained by my non-fulfilment of my contracts to receive and pay for various parts of the gun on their receipt by the War Department. With knowledge of the material facts in the case, I fully believe if an extension of my order enclosed, for forty-five days, is granted from April 6, 1862, it will be executed to the satisfaction of the War Department. I engaged in the execution of my order in good faith, and have spared no effort or expense believed necessary to complete it.

I respectfully submit to your consideration and decision the within application for an extension of forty-five days from April 6, 1862, of the enclosed order.

I am, very respectfully, yours,

WM. W. WELCH.

Hon. E. M. STANTON, *Secretary of War.*

WAR DEPARTMENT, *April* 3, 1862.

GENTLEMEN: The original papers in the case of W. W. Welch's alleged contract for muskets are supposed to have been sent, with others, to you. It is represented that they cannot be found, and Mr. Welch has furnished certain papers, herewith enclosed, which he represents to be in part true copies, and in part only an approximation to copies.

Very respectfully, your obedient servant,

P. H. WATSON,
Assistant Secretary of War.

Hon. JOSEPH HOLT and ROBERT D. OWEN,
Special Commissioners.

Copy of indorsement on a letter from William W. Welch to the Secretary of War, asking for an extension of time for delivery of arms.

"ORDNANCE OFFICE, *February* 7, 1862.

"Respectfully returned. I believe that Mr. Welch has made arrangements, as far as in his power, for fulfilling his contract, and that he intends to fulfil it

Ex. Doc. 72- ——24

in good faith, and I recommend that the extension of sixty days, which he applies for, be granted.

"JAMES W. RIPLEY,

"*Brigadier General.*"

SENATE CHAMBER, *Washington, D. C., March* 31.

This will introduce to you Hon. W. W. Welch, of Norfolk, Connecticut, a gentleman of *standing* and *character*, entirely reliable, and faithful to the interests of the government.

Mr. Welch is a *manufacturer*, and is, at a great expense and in good faith, preparing to make for the government, according to his contract, the most approved arm of the military service, viz : the "*Springfield rifle,*" parts interchangeable.

The Ordnance department has recommended and approved of his application for a short extension of time. We shall feel obliged to have it granted, as we feel entire confidence in the result, both as to the success of Mr. Welch as a manufacturer and the arm he proposes to make.

We are, very truly and respectfully, yours, &c.,

S. C. POMEROY,

United States Senator.

I cordially concur in the above.

JAMES DIXON,

United States Senator.

Messrs. HOLT and OWEN, *Commissioners, &c.*

Before commission, April 3, 1862.

W. W. Welch, esq., of Norfolk, Connecticut, before commission, states :

I have a contract for 18,000 Springfield guns. The first delivery is due April 6. I have applied for an extension of sixty days from February 3, 1862. The extension has been recommended by the chief of ordnance. I now think I will need an extension of forty-five days from April 6, 1862. The War Department has done nothing in my behalf. I came to Washington with a letter asking for the first extension of time, and saw Mr. Stanton, who was very much pressed with business. My letter was referred to the Ordnance department, and General Ripley recommended the extension of time. A copy of this recommendation is now before the commission.

My stocks and locks are contracted for with Essler & Bro., Philadelphia. The locks for the first 500 are complete to-day. The stocks are not yet complete, but Essler & Bro. are under obligations to furnish them. A guarantee is responsible in money if the stocks are not furnished as soon as I am ready for them. Essler & Co. have no stocking machinery, but they have contracted with other parties who have. Mr. Essler says stocks will be ready to be turned out by the 15th April. He devotes his own time and attention to the manufacture of stocks, and says there will be no difficulty about them.

I will make the barrels myself. I will get them in the rough from Washburn, who has delivered some 600, which I am now turning out. Some of these are imperfect; I do not know what proportion. The barrels are, I believe, of semi-steel, such as Mr. Washburn has furnished at Springfield. I do not know where this is made, but Washburn guarantees to me an article warranted to answer.

I have most of my machinery, but I need more machines to be made before I can give the full product, sixty per day. I have to obtain one more rifling machine. My milling machines and tools for butts of barrels are finished. I had not received my polishing machines when I left, but I suppose they may be at my establishment to-day. H. Bigelow, of New Haven, will furnish me with butt plates, guard, and trigger; Richardson & Barnum will furnish bands, appendages, and implements; ramrods I will make myself. Five hundred bayonets will be ready next week, made by Mr. Gatchell, of Rahway, New Jersey. Sights are made by Mr. Charlton, of Newark. Every sub-contractor will be ready as soon as I will, and they are responsible to me in general terms for their failure. The maximum profit on Springfield guns will not, I think, exceed $3. I think all my sub-contractors will be up to time. I used no political influence to get my contract.

Before commission, April 8, 1862.

Mr. Robert Essler, of C. H. Williams & Co., of Philadelphia, states:

We have been manufacturers of gun-locks since September 1, 1861. We were sawyers of wood, mouldings, &c. We have a full suit of machines for locks, and we have already finished 500 for Mr. Welch, of Connecticut, 500 for A. M. Burt, of New York, and 500 for John Rice. We have in hand about 6,000 locks, intended for the above parties. Mason, of Taunton, Massachusetts, has applied to us for 50,000 locks, and we have agreed to furnish them according to the terms of his contract. This agreement has not yet been signed. We cannot extend the quantity above required of us without increasing our machinery; this we purpose doing.

Mr. Bodine, Mr. Muir, and Mr. Gallaher have all spoken to us about locks, but we are under no obligations to manufacture for them. We have fifty men employed, and our capacity is about 250 locks per day. In three weeks we will have day and night parties better arranged, and then we will make 300 per day, at least. We also make cones. We have engaged to make for the same parties as above, probably 50,000. We can make more of these and can sell them at $7 50 per gross. We have agreed to furnish 18,000 stocks complete to Mr. Welch; we are to get them from the Empire Works. Mr. Redfield, I believe, is in this concern, but E. W. Wright is the working man. I have been to the shop every day for ten days and have seen the machines up and at work; have seen 800 stocks partly finished, some to the last turning; these are for us, and are to be delivered to us in New York, on the 18th, to meet our engagements with Mr. Welch. We have no other obligations for any work. Our lock has just been taken to the Springfield armory and tried by Mr. Williams in their gauges; it is pronounced a perfect success. We rate the value of lock and stock at $5 35; we cannot furnish for less at present.

COMMISSION ON ORDNANCE AND ORDNANCE STORES.

Washington, May 17, 1862.

GENERAL: The commission have the honor to report as follows:

CASE NO. 80.—W. W. WELCH, Norfolk, Connecticut.

Order by direction of the Secretary of War, dated Nov. 6, 1861.—(See Ex. Doc. No. 67, page 134.) Referred by direction of the Secretary of War.

To furnish 18,000 rifled muskets, in all respects identical with the standard rifle musket, at the price of $20 each, including appendages; deliveries to be made within one year, on or before March 6, 1863.—(See Case No. 72.)

The commission find that the above order was not given in accordance with the law and regulations; that it is not, therefore, a contract of legal force, inasmuch as it does not contain the express requirements of the law, and was not made "after previous advertisement for proposals respecting the same ;" nor can it be regarded as an "open purchase," being for articles which did not require "immediate delivery," but stipulated to be manufactured and delivered at prescribed distant periods.

They further consider that the number of arms ordered is larger than the wants of the government justify in this case, at the price fixed, and therefore, according to the principles set forth in Mason's case, No. 72, they decide that the order to Mr. Welch be confirmed, subject to all its terms, to the extent of 16,000 muskets, upon condition that he shall, within fifteen days after notice of this decision, execute bond, with good and sufficient sureties, in the form and with the stipulations prescribed by law and the regulations for the performance of the contract as now modified, resulting from said order and acceptance ; and upon his failure or refusal to execute such bond, then the said order shall be declared cancelled and of no effect.

The commission further decide that the whole number of 16,000 be delivered within one year from April 6, 1862, commencing in June with 500 and 1,000 in July, and not less than 1,600 monthly thereafter; and in case of failure to deliver as above prescribed in any one month, the right to deliver the number that may be deficient for that month in which the failure occurs may or may not be forfeited, at the option of the government.

We are, sir, very respectfully, your obedient servants,

J. HOLT,
ROBERT DALE OWEN,
Commissioners, &c.
P. V. HAGNER,
Major of Ordnance, Assistant to Commission.
Brigadier General J. W. RIPLEY,
Chief of Ordnance.

CASE No. 81.

W. C. FREEMAN.

WASHINGTON, *August* 28, 1861.

SIR: I propose to make two thousand revolving pistols, Joslyn's patent, army size, at twenty-five dollars ($25) each, and deliver the same within three months from the making of the order therefor.

Very respectfully,

WILLIAM C. FREEMAN.

Hon. SIMON CAMERON,
Secretary of War.

Referred to the chief of ordnance.

SIMON CAMERON.
Secretary of War.

The Secretary, since writing the above, has authorized me to say that a contract shall be made for five hundred (500) pistols, provided they are delivered within thirty days from this date, subject to the inspection and approval of the Ordnance department.

THOS. A. SCOTT,
Assistant Secretary.

ORDNANCE OFFICE,
Washington, August 28, 1861.

SIR: By direction of the Secretary of War, I offer you an order for five hundred revolver pistols, Joslyn's patent, with appendages. These pistols are to be subject to inspection by such officer as this department may designate for the purpose. They are to be delivered at the New York arsenal, Governor's island, in thirty days from this date. In case of a failure to deliver in or within the time specified, the government is to be under no obligation to take the pistols or appendages, but may or may not do so, at its option. Payment is to be made in such funds as the Treasury Department may provide, on certificates of inspection and receipt by the United States inspectors, at the rate of twenty-five dollars ($25) per pistol, including appendages, which are to be one screw-driver and cone wrench, one bullet mould, and one extra cone for each pistol.

Please signify, in writing, whether you accept the foregoing offer, on the terms and conditions stated herein.

Respectfully, your obedient servant,

JAMES W. RIPLEY,
Brigadier General.

W. C. FREEMAN, *Washington, D. C.*

WASHINGTON, *September* 6, 1861.

SIR: In answer to your favor of the 28th ultimo, I have to say that I accept the order for five hundred of Joslyn's pistols, therein given, according to the terms and conditions therein stated, and will use my best exertions to have the same delivered within the time specified.

Very respectfully, yours, &c.,

W. C. FREEMAN.

Brigadier General J. W. RIPLEY.

NATIONAL HOTEL, *Washington, May* 2, 1862.

DEAR SIR: You will oblige by informing me whether you will receive the 500 Joslyn revolving pistols ordered last August.

The delivery has been delayed by our desire to give the government a good article, (the pistols then on hand not being in all respects what the government needed;) also from disappointment in receiving machinery ordered as early as April and May of last year, the same having been sold to the government for its works at Springfield, to meet the urgent demands of the government at that time.

We can now deliver the pistols within a few days, if required.

Very respectfully, yours, &c.,

WILLIAM C. FREEMAN.

Hon. E. M. STANTON,
Secretary of War.

ORDNANCE OFFICE,
Washington, May 5, 1862.

SIR: The enclosed paper was handed to me this morning by Mr. J. S. Williams, with a statement that you desired a report thereon.

All the circumstances connected with the contract for pistols to which it refers may be found in Ex. Doc. No. 67, present Congress, page 196, and the case is before the commission on ordnance and ordnance stores for their consideration and decision.

Respectfully, your obedient servant,

JAMES W. RIPLEY,
Brigadier General.

Hon. E. M. STANTON,
Secretary of War, Washington, D. C.

———

COMMISSION ON ORDNANCE AND ORDNANCE STORES,
Washington, May 17, 1862.

GENERAL : The commission have the honor to report as follows :

CASE No. 81.—W. C. FREEMAN, Agent.

Order by direction of the Secretary of War, dated Aug. 28, 1861.— (See pages 196, 197, Ex. Doc. No. 67.)

To furnish 500 revolver pistols, Joslyn's patent, with appendages. To be delivered within thirty days from date of order, at the price of $25 per pistol, including appendages. In case of failure to deliver in or within the time specified, the government is to be under no obligation to take the arms, but may or may not do so, at its option.

No deliveries made under the above order.

A letter of May 2, 1862, from W. C. Freeman, agent, to Hon. E. M. Stanton, Secretary of War, has been specially referred to the commission in connexion with this case, offering now to deliver the 500 revolvers.

The commission find that, as specially stipulated and accepted at the date of the order of the 28th August, the government is under no obligation to receive these pistols, the order being forfeited by non-compliance. As the price is unreasonably high, according to the prices paid for like arms, the commission decide that the original order be considered annulled and withdrawn. Future purchases of these revolvers in open market should be at prices not exceeding $15.

We are, sir, very respectfully, your obedient servants,

J. HOLT,
ROBERT DALE OWEN,
Commissioners, &c.
P. V. HAGNER,
Major of Ordnance, Assistant to Commission.

Brigadier General J. W. RIPLEY,
Chief of Ordnance.

———

CASE No. 82.

J. W. SCHMIDT & Co.

68 BROAD STREET, NEW YORK, *January* 30, 1862.

SIR : Observing in the newspapers this morning your recent order requiring those holding contracts or orders from the government for army supplies to file in your office notice of the same, with what has been done under such contracts or orders, although not quite sure that such transactions as our recent sale to the government of Holberg lead come under the provisions of the said order, the sale being single and entire, yet, as they possibly may do so, we beg respectfully to submit a copy of the correspondence relating to the matter, which you will please find on the following pages.

We beg to add that the recent storms have delayed the arrival of the different vessels having the lead on board. You will, however, see from the correspondence that the deliveries of four hundred tons have already commenced, and are being made to the satisfaction of the ordnance officers. Believing that the sale of this lead and the terms of payment embraced in our proposal will meet your approbation, we beg to be informed to that effect.

To-day four hundred tons.

Very respectfully, your most obedient servants,

J. W. SCHMIDT & CO.

Hon. E. M. STANTON,
Secretary of War, Washington, D. C.

Copy of correspondence.

NEW YORK, *December* 19, 1861.

SIR : We beg to offer you, subject to your reply to-morrow or Saturday, 1,000 or 1,500 tons Holberg lead, part shipped and part intended to be shipped from Europe, at the price of 7¼ cents per pound; payment, cash on delivery in bond of each parcel, subject to arrival.

Of the above lead, according to our last dates from Europe, 450 tons were already shipped from Europe in November, as follows : 100 tons per Coriolan, 100 tons per Caroline, 100 tons per Meridian, from Bremen; 150 tons per Arctic, from Antwerp; and further, 200 tons were in course of shipment by Belgian steamer Stella, to sail from Antwerp on the 10th of December; the balance of 400 to 900 tons was intended to be shipped in December and January from Antwerp, Rotterdam, Bremen, and Hamburg.

The price of Galena lead here, to-day, is 7¼ cents, and the market almost bare and daily advancing.

J. W. SCHMIDT & CO.

Hon. SIMON CAMERON,
Secretary of War, Washington, D. C.

Reply by telegraph.

WASHINGTON, *December* 23, 1861.

Your proposition for 1,500 tons is accepted. Deliveries to be made to ordnance officers.

SIMON CAMERON.

J. W. SCHMIDT & CO., *New York.*

NEW YORK, *December* 31, 1861.

SIR : We beg to refer to our respects of December 19, offering you from 1,000 to 1,500 tons of lead, part shipped, part to be shipped from Europe, to which we have received your acceptance by telegram, of December 23, *not by mail thus far.*

As we may expect, before long, the arrival of some of the vessels with part of the above lead, we beg you will send us an order for the collector to admit the same to free entry as it arrives, in order that we may deliver it as soon as discharged with the least possible delay; and we would also request you to designate to us the ordnance officer to whom the deliveries are to be made.

J. W. SCHMIDT & CO.

Hon. SIMON CAMERON,
Secretary of War, Washington, D. C.

Reply.

ORDNANCE OFFICE,
Washington, January 4, 1862.

GENTLEMEN : Your letter of 31st ultimo, respecting the delivery of pig lead, has been referred from the War Department to this office.

The ordnance officers designated to receive the lead were Major R. H. K. Whiteley, at Governor's island, and Major P. V. Hagner, No. 35 White street, New York. Please see them on the subject.

J. W. RIPLEY,
Brigadier General.

Messrs. J. W SCHMIDT & Co., *New York.*

NEW YORK, *January* 24, 1862.

SIR : The Caroline, Stricker, master, with 1,600 pigs (100 tons) Holberg lead, on account of government contract, has arrived. We beg to enclose bill of lading, and shall thank you to give us free permit and instructions where to deliver the lead.

J. W. SCHMIDT & CO.

Major P. V. HAGNER,
United States Ordnance Officer.

NEW YORK, *January* 29, 1862.

SIR : The Arctic, Toft, master, from Antwerp, is below with our second delivery of 2,428 pigs, or about 150 tons of lead. We beg to enclose bill of lading, and shall thank you for a free permit and order of delivery for the same.

January 30.—Further, 150 tons—South Carolina—arrived from Antwerp.

J. W. SCHMIDT & CO.

Major P. V. HAGNER,
United States Ordnance Officer.

NEW YORK ARSENAL,
January 25, 1862.

GENTLEMEN : Have you on hand any quantity of the lead named in your letter of December 19, 1861, to the Secretary of War? Please advise me the number of pigs and of pounds of each lot in store, for I am instructed by General Ripley, chief of ordnance department, Washington, to keep Major N. A. Thornton, Watervleit arsenal, well supplied. Therefore, forward to Watervleit arsenal, by rail, such as you may have in store, described in the above-mentioned letter, marking the pigs with and sending bill of lading and bill of lead to Major Thornton's address. Please send the lots as they arrive to the same address, advising me each shipment the number of pigs and pounds forwarded.

R. H. K. WHITELEY,
Major of Ordnance.

Messrs. J. W. SCHMIDT & Co.,
New York City.

Reply.

68 BROAD STREET, *January* 27, 1862.

SIR: In reply to your favor of 25th, we beg to say that the lead contracted for with the government is to arrive from Europe, of which 1,600 pigs, equal to 100 tons, is now in port on board the Caroline, from Bremen, and will be discharged to-morrow. Several vessels are due and may arrive *every day*, viz:

Coriolan, 100 tons; Meridian, 100 tons, from Bremen; South Carolina, 150 tons; Thusnelder, 50 tons; Arctic, 150 tons; Elizabeth, 150 tons, from Amsterdam. Further quantities were in course of shipment. Regarding the delivery of the lead contracted for, it has to be made to the United States officers *in this city* when discharged from board, according to terms of contract. Colonel Tompkins, United States assistant quartermaster, has already been instructed by Major Hagner to provide transportation to the Watervleit arsenal for the 1,600 pigs—Caroline—and he has arranged to receive the same when landing. It is very unfortunate that the above-named vessels have been delayed so much by contrary winds, but we have no doubt they will all come in *now very fast*. Should the Watervleit arsenal, however, want more lead for immediate use, we offer to purchase on your order, aside of our contract, lead of the quality required for the bullet machines, although such is very scarce.

J. W. SCHMIDT & CO.

Major R. H. K. WHITELEY,
Governor's Island.

NEW YORK ARSENAL,
January 28, 1862.

GENTLEMEN: I have received your note dated yesterday. I was not aware you had instructions from Major Hagner in regard to the lead you sold to the United States to arrive from Europe, or I would not have written you on the subject. The quantity (100 tons) you state in port will be sufficient for the want of the arsenal until other lots arrive. Please report them to Major Hagner for instructions as fast as they arrive.

R. H. K. WHITELEY,
Major of Ordnance.

Messrs. J. W. SCHMIDT & Co.,
68 *Broad Street.*

WATERVLEIT ARSENAL, *April* 30, 1862.

GENTLEMEN: Your note of the 15th instant and the two pigs of lead were duly received, and, pursuant to your request, I have made a trial of them.

The *Italian* lead is too hard for easy working in our bullet machines. The English lead is softer, and consequently is more readily moulded by the ball press into the form required for the balls.

Respectfully, I am, sir, your obedient servant,

W. A. THORNTON,
Major of Ordnance, Commanding Arsenal.

J. W. SCHMIDT & Co., 68 *Broad Street, New York.*

NEW YORK, *May* 9, 1862.

SIR: Since we understand from our Mr. Leop. Schmidt that the War Department can only use the *very best refined* and *softened* lead, we have to modify our last proposition for a further supply, as follows:

We offer to furnish 2,000 to 2,500 tons of the desired description of lead, suitable for Major Thornton's bullet machines, viz: *Holberg*, very soft, *English*, and *German*, at the price of $6\frac{3}{8}$ cents in bond for Holberg, and $6\frac{1}{4}$ cents for the English and German—180 tons English already in store here—about 700 tons of the three kinds already shipped or in course of shipment from Europe, and the balance intended to be shipped in May, June, and July.

The larger portion of the above offer we hope to be able to deliver in Holberg lead; and with regard to the English and German, we beg to observe that previously to Mr. Leop. Schmidt's return we had already sent to Major Thornton a sample of the English in store here, which was found satisfactory, as per *annexed report*.

The political state of Europe is so unsettled that we may possibly have serious complications there in the course of the summer, and as in that case the exportation of lead may again be prohibited, we respectfully request your *earliest possible* decision, to enable us to make our arrangements in Europe without further loss of time.

We remain, sir, yours, very respectfully,

J. W. SCHMIDT & Co., 68 *Broad Street.*

Gen. JAS. W. RIPLEY, *Chief of Ordnance, Washington, D. C.*

ORDNANCE OFFICE, *May* 13, 1862.

SIR : In view of the large amount of lead required to meet the demands of the service and the difficulty of always procuring it in this country as it is wanted, I recommend that the offer of Messrs. J. W. Schmidt & Co., of New York, and herewith enclosed, be accepted, viz :

To supply this department with twenty-five hundred tons of Holberg and soft English and German leads, at the rate of $6\frac{3}{8}$ cents per pound for the Holberg, and $6\frac{1}{4}$ cents per pound for the soft English and German leads. The acceptance of the soft German lead to depend upon the favorable report of a trial to be made of it at the Watervliet arsenal. The whole of the 2,500 tons to be delivered to the agent of this department in the city of New York before the 1st of September next.

Respectfully, your obedient servant,

JAS. W. RIPLEY, *Brigadier General.*

Hon. E. M. STANTON, *Secretary of War, Washington, D. C.*

COMMISSION ON ORDNANCE AND ORDNANCE STORES,
Washington, May 17, 1862.

SIR: The commission have the honor to report as follows:

CASE NO. 82.—J. W. SCHMIDT & CO.

Offer to supply lead, in letter dated May 9, 1862, and recommended in letter from chief of ordnance, dated May 13, 1862.

Offers Holberg lead at the rate of $6\frac{3}{8}$ cents per pound in bond, and very soft English and German at the rate of $6\frac{1}{4}$ cents per pound in bond. 2,500 tons are required for the service, to be delivered in the city of New York before the 1st of September next. Referred to the commission by the special direction of the Secretary of War, dated May 14, 1862.

The commission respectfully recommend that no further acceptances of foreign lead be made without public advertisement, as the prices offered in the above proposal seem to be unreasonably high, judging from the latest prices current accessible to them. Cincinnati papers of the 14th instant quote pig lead at $6\frac{1}{4}$ to $6\frac{3}{4}$ cents, and New York papers $6\frac{1}{2}$ to 7 cents. The cost to the government under Mr. Schmidt's proposal would be, with duties added, $8\frac{12}{100}$ and $8\frac{28}{100}$ cents.

As so large an amount as 2,500 tons is required, and so distant a date as September can be granted within which to deliver, the commission consider that the few days' delay requisite for advertising in St. Louis, Cincinnati, Chicago, Galena, and New York, might be allowed without inconvenience, and, if absolutely necessary to obtain earlier a small supply, it might be purchased in New York, after two or three days' advertisement, only.

The commission are the more convinced of the necessity of ceasing to accept private proposals for delivering foreign lead, as the state of the market is such, owing to the decrease of consumption in the arts, that competition between holders of this stock is particularly necessary in order to secure a fair market price; and native lead of the best quality for military use can now be obtained in considerable quantity.

We are, sir, very respectfully, your obedient servants,

J. HOLT,
ROBERT DALE OWEN,
Commissioners, &c.
P. V. HAGNER,
Major of Ordnance, Assistant to Commission.

Hon. E. M. STANTON, *Secretary of War.*

CASE No. 83

SARSON & ROBERTS.

OFFICE OF SARSON & ROBERTS,
No. 11 *Platt street, New York, February* 8, 1862.

SIR: In compliance with your order published the 29th ultimo, we beg leave to append a copy of a contract for the furnishing to your department twenty-five thousand Springfield rifle muskets made with us December 26, 1861.

To fulfil the terms of this contract we had previously purchased sufficient material to make the whole number of stocks; we have built the machinery to manufacture the same in accordance with the prescribed model, and it is now all in running order; we have also had the machinery built for making the rough barrels; a sufficient quantity of iron of a suitable quality has been obtained for their manufacture, and the first lot was made satisfactorily this week, and are now being finished. Our finishing machinery is now all in running order; our machinery for the locks is quite finished, and we have a small lot completed. The machinery for the remainder of the gun is all in forwardness and nearly ready, and we entertain a confident expectation of being able to make complete guns ready for delivery considerably in advance of the period specified in the contract.

In doing this work we beg leave to say we have met with many great and unexpected difficulties; it has been very difficult to obtain the machinery and the material for the stocks and barrels, in consequence of the extraordinary demand for the same, and the price has been so greatly enhanced by competition as to make our original calculations in regard to cost much below the actual fact.

We shall be ready to deliver the guns in accordance with the stipulations of the contract, and have no doubt that we shall be able to do so before the time specified.

We have the honor to be, sir, your obedient servants,

SARSON & ROBERTS.

Hon. EDWIN M. STANTON,
Secretary of War, Washington.

ORDNANCE OFFICE, *Washington, December* 26, 1861.

GENTLEMEN: By direction of the Secretary of War, I offer you an order for twenty-five thousand (25,000) muskets of the Springfield pattern, on the following terms and conditions, viz: These arms are to be furnished with the regular appendages, and are to be in all respects identical with the standard rifle musket made at the United States armory at Springfield, Massachusetts, and are to interchange with it and with each other in all their parts.   They are to be subject to inspection by the United States inspectors in the same manner that the Springfield arms are inspected, and none are to be received or paid for but such as pass inspection, and are approved by the United States inspectors. These twenty-five thousand (25,000) arms and appendages are to be delivered by your armory as follows, viz: Not less than five hundred (500) in each of the months of July, August, and September, 1862; not less than one thousand (1,000) in each of the months of October and November, 1862; not less than fifteen hundred (1,500) in December, 1862, and not less than two thousand (2,000) per month thereafter, until the entire twenty-five thousand (25,000) shall have been delivered, and you are to have the right to deliver more rapidly than according to the number of arms before specified, if you can do so.   In case of any failure to make deliveries to the extent and within the time before specified, you are to forfeit the right to deliver whatever number may be deficient in the specified number for the month in which the failure accrues.

All these arms and appendages are to be delivered by you, and this order, if transferred to another person, is to be thereby forfeited.

Payments are to be made, in such funds as the Treasury Department may provide, for each delivery, on certificates of inspection and receipt by the United States inspectors, at the rate of twenty dollars ($20) for each arm, including appendages.

All these arms and appendages are to be packed by you in boxes of the regular pattern, with twenty (20) muskets and appendages in each box, for which a fair price, to be determined by the United States inspector, will be allowed.   Please signify, in writing, your acceptance or non-acceptance of this order, on the terms and conditions herein stated.

Respectfully, your obedient servant,

JAMES W. RIPLEY,
Brigadier General.

Messrs. SARSON & ROBERTS, *New York.*

OFFICE OF SARSON & ROBERTS,
No. 11 *Platt Street, New York, April* 3, 1862.

SIRS: In compliance with an order of the Secretary of War, dated 29th January last, we made a statement of our proceedings in fulfilment of a contract for twenty-five thousand Springfield rifle muskets, issued to us December 26 1861.   Since that time we have brought the matter nearly to a state of completion.   Of many parts we have now a large stock, and shall deliver guns considerably before the period specified in the contract.

We would now beg leave to inquire if it is necessary that we should send you a copy of the contract, with a statement of our progress, or shall we be justified in going on as at present, to make our deliveries as rapidly as possible ?

Requesting the favor of a reply, we remain, your obedient servants,

SARSON & ROBERTS.

Hon. ROBERT DALE OWEN and JOSEPH HOLT,
Washington.

Before commission, April 7, 1862.

Messrs. Sarson & Roberts, relative to their contract for Springfield guns, state:

We have a full suit of stocking machinery.   It was built by Mr. Pusey from Springfield models.   It has been finished about two months, and we have two hundred stocks completed.   Our barrel machinery is completed under the name of A. & F. Brown. Pusey's stocking shop is at the corner of Elm and Pearl streets. Jenks & Sons have agreed to make everything for us except stock, barrel, and sight. Our sights will be made by Brown. We have made one gun from our own parts and those obtained from Jenks. Rough barrels are obtained from Morris, Tasker & Co. We are losing 50 per cent. on our own inspection. We have some barrels free from flaws and cracks. There is no question about our filling our contract except as regards barrels. We have compared the gauges for barrels made by A. & F. Brown. The iron we now use is made at Reading, Pennsylvania, by Craig & Koch. We have ordered 1,000 barrels in England of the Marshall iron, but we are not entirely sure about getting them.

OFFICE OF SARSON & ROBERTS,
No. 11 Platt Street, New York, March 31, 1862.

SIR: Having a considerable number of barrels, some quite and others nearly ready for proving, we should feel obliged by your informing us where we may apply for a proper person to superintend the proving, such being, as we are informed, necessary. We have built a proper place for proving the barrels in this city, and awaiting your reply, remain, respectfully, your obedient servants,

SARSON & ROBERTS.

Brigadier General JAMES W. RIPLEY,
Chief of Ordnance, Washington.

OFFICE OF SARSON & ROBERTS,
No. 11 Platt Street, New York, April 18, 1862.

SIR: On the 31st day of March last we addressed you in reference to information as to where we would apply for a proper person to superintend the proving of our barrels. We now have a quantity ready, and await your reply.

Very respectfully, your obedient servants,

SARSON & ROBERTS.

Brigadier General JAMES W. RIPLEY,
Chief of Ordnance, Washington.

NEW YORK, *May* 1, 1862.

SIR: We had the honor to address you on the 31st March and 18th ultimo, in reference to what inspection might be required in proving barrels for the Springfield rifle musket, and to which we have received no reply.

We now beg leave to state that we have a number ready for proof, and in order that we may not be compelled to stop our machines we propose to prove two hundred barrels to-morrow, in accordance with the direction as found in the Manual of Ordnance. Awaiting your further directions, remain, very respectfully, your obedient servants,

SARSON & ROBERTS,

Brigadier General JAMES W. RIPLEY,
Chief of Ordnance, Washington.

ORDNANCE OFFICE, *Washington, May* 5, 1862.

GENTLEMEN: I have to acknowledge your letters of 31st March, 18th April, and 1st instant, and, in reply, to inform you that the Secretary of War has referred to a commission, appointed for the purpose, all matters in relation to contracts made by the War Department for ordnance and ordnance stores.

As soon as the decision of the commission in your case is communicated to this office you will be duly advised, and such instructions will then be given as may be necessary.

Respectfully, your obedient servant,

JAMES W. RIPLEY,
Brigadier General.

Messrs. SARSON & ROBERTS,
No. 11 *Platt Street, New York.*

OFFICE OF SARSON & ROBERTS,
No. 11 *Platt Street, New York, April* 23, 1862.

SIR: We have a number of barrels now ready for proof, and beg leave to address you in regard to their inspection.

Will you have the goodness to inform us of the weight of charges of powder, ball, &c., and if we can be allowed to prove them ourselves, or if it is necessary to wait for an official inspector, and oblige,

Very respectfully, your obedient servants,

SARSON & ROBERTS.

Major A. B. DYER,
United States Corps of Ordnance, Springfield.

SPRINGFIELD ARMORY, *April* 24, 1862.

GENTLEMEN: Your letter of the 23d is received. The musket barrels are required to be proved as follows, viz: First charge, 280 grains of powder, one ball weighing 500 grains, and two wads. Second charge, 250 grains of powder, one ball weighing 500 grains, and two wads.—(See Ordnance Manual, page 184.) You should report to the chief of ordnance, at Washington, that you have barrels ready for proof, and ask for instructions. I have been ordered to have barrels proved for some of the contractors.

Very respectfully, your obedient servant,

A. B. DYER,
Captain of Ordnance.

Messrs. SARSON & ROBERTS,
No. 11 *Platt Street, New York.*

OFFICE OF SARSON & ROBERTS,
No. 11 *Platt Street, New York, May* 6, 1862.

SIRS: We beg leave to refer to the enclosed copies of correspondence between Brigadier General James W. Ripley, Major A. B. Dyer, and ourselves, in reference to proving musket barrels.

In accordance with General Ripley's directions we would beg leave to ask you for instructions in respect to the same, and also with regard to the inspection of stocks, and the barrels in their various stages of forwardness, and remain,

Respectfully, your obedient servants,

SARSON & ROBERTS.

Hon. JOSEPH HOLT and ROBERT DALE OWEN,
Commissioners on Ordnance and Ordnance Supplies, Washington.

COMMISSION ON ORDNANCE AND ORDNANCE STORES,
Washington, May 8, 1862.

GENERAL: The commission direct me to inform you that they will assign and confirm to Sarson & Roberts a certain proportion of the number of arms in their order, (not to exceed 20,000,) and therefore request that such steps as you may think proper to enable them to have their barrels proved and to go on with their work may be taken without further delay. The commission have received from Messrs. Sarson & Roberts copies of letters from them to you and your answer, and, with the desire not to arrest the completion of any proper work, impart to you their intentions in this case before they have ready for issue their final decision in this class of cases.

Very respectfully, your obedient servant,

P. V. HAGNER,
Major of Ordnance.

General J. W. RIPLEY,
Chief of Ordnance.

COMMISSION ON ORDNANCE AND ORDNANCE STORES,
Washington, May 17, 1862.

GENERAL: The commission have the honor to report as follows:

CASE No. 83.—SARSON & ROBERTS, New York.

Order by direction of the Secretary of War, dated December 26. 1861 Ex Doc. No. 67. pages 52 and 167. Referred by direction of the Secretary of War

To furnish 25,000 rifle muskets of the Springfield pattern, with appendages, at the price of $20 per gun, including appendages. Deliveries to be made of not less than 500 in each of the months of July, August, and September, 1862, and not less than 1,000 in each of the months of October and November, 1862, not less than 1,500 in December, and not less than 2,000 per month thereafter. (See Case No. 72.)

The commission find that the above order was not given in accordance with the law and regulations, and that it is not therefore a contract of legal force, inasmuch as it does not contain the express requirements of the law, and was not made "after previous advertisement for proposals respecting the same;" nor can it be regarded as an "open purchase," being for articles which did not require "immediate delivery," but, as stipulated, were to be manufactured and delivered at prescribed distant periods.

They further consider that the number of arms ordered is larger than the wants of the government justify in this case, at the price fixed, and therefore, according to the principles set forth in Mason's case, (No. 72,) they decide that the order to Sarson & Roberts be confirmed, subject to all its terms, to the extent of 20,000 muskets, upon condition that they shall, within fifteen days after notice of this decision, execute bond, with good and sufficient sureties, in the form and with the stipulations prescribed by law and the regulations for the performance of the contract, as thus modified, and resulting from said order and acceptance; and upon his failure or refusal to execute such bond, then the said order shall be declared cancelled and of no effect.

The commission further decide that the deliveries under the contract to be executed shall be required at or within the periods stipulated in the original order, but that the numbers specified may be reduced proportionately to the reduction of the whole number, so that the contract shall be completed within the time allowed in the original order.

We are, sir, very respectfully, your obedient servants,

J. HOLT,
ROBERT DALE OWEN,
Commissioners, &c.
P. V. HAGNER,
Major of Ordnance, Assistant to Commission.

Brigadier General J. W. RIPLEY,
Chief of Ordnance.

COMMISSION ON ORDNANCE AND ORDNANCE STORES,
June 26, 1862.

Respectfully referred back to the War Department.

The requirement of sureties in the bond referred to in the within is in accordance with the law and regulations of the department, and should not, in the judgment of the commission, be waived in this or any other case.

J. HOLT.

ROBERT DALE OWEN.

Indorsement upon request to dispense with executing a contract and giving sureties.

P. V. HAGNER,
Major of Ordnance.

CASE No. 84.

ELI WHITNEY.

WASHINGTON, *December* 17, 1861.

I propose to furnish government forty thousand stand of Springfield muskets of the latest model, viz., 1861, equal in every respect to the guns made, with bayonets and all usual implements complete, at Springfield armory, and agree that the work shall be interchangeable and be done as well as the work is now done at said armory, at the following periods, viz:

First delivery, 2,000 in six months; second delivery, 2,000 in seven months; third delivery, 2,000 in eight months; fourth delivery, 2,000 in nine months; fifth delivery, 2,000 in ten months; sixth delivery, 2,000 in eleven months; seventh delivery, 2,000 in twelve months; eighth delivery, 2,000 in thirteen months; ninth delivery, 2,000 in fourteen months; tenth delivery, 2,000 in fifteen months; eleventh delivery, 2,000 in sixteen months; twelfth delivery, 2,000 in seventeen months; thirteenth delivery, 2,000 in eighteen months; fourteenth delivery, 2,000 in nineteen months; fifteenth delivery, 2,000 in twenty months; sixteenth delivery, 2,000 in twenty-one months; seventeenth delivery, 2,000 in twenty-two months; eighteenth delivery, 2,000 in twenty-three months; nineteenth delivery, 2,000 in twenty-four months; twentieth delivery, 2,000 in twenty-six months; with bayonets and usual fixtures complete. The price per musket, twenty dollars. Payment to be made upon delivery of guns in lots of 100 and upwards, after a full inspection, in such funds as the treasury may provide.

Yours, very respectfully,

ELI WHITNEY.

Hon. SECRETARY OF WAR.

ORDNANCE OFFICE, *Washington, December* 24, 1861.

SIR: By direction of the Secretary of War, I offer you an order for forty thousand (40,000) muskets, with appendages, of the Springfield pattern, on the following terms and conditions, viz:

These arms are to be furnished with the regular appendages, and are to be in all respects identical with the standard rifle musket made at the United States armory at Springfield, Massachusetts, and are to interchange with it and with each other, in all their parts; they are to be subject to inspection by United

States inspectors in the same manner that the Springfield arms are inspected, and none are to be received or paid for but such as pass inspection, and are approved by the United States inspectors. These forty thousand (40,000) arms and appendages are to be delivered at your armory as follows, viz : Not less than one thousand (1,000) in *each* of the months of July, August, and September, 1862 ; not less than two thousand (2,000) in *each* of the months of October and November, 1862 ; not less than three thousand (3,000) in December, 1862 ; and not less than four thousand per month thereafter, until the entire forty thousand (40,000) shall have been delivered ; and you are to have the right to deliver more rapidly than according to the number of arms before specified, if you can do so. In case of any failure to make deliveries to the extent and within the times before specified, you are to forfeit the right to deliver whatever number may be deficient in the specified number for the month in which the failure occurs.

All these arms and appendages are to be delivered by you, and this order, if transferred to another party, is to be thereby forfeited. Payments are to be made in such funds as the Treasury Department may provide, on certificates of inspection and receipt by the United States inspectors, at the rate of twenty dollars ($20) for each arm, including appendages.

All these arms and appendages are to be packed by you in boxes of the regular pattern, with twenty (20) muskets in each box, for which a fair price, to be determined by the United States inspector, will be allowed.

Please signify, in writing, your acceptance or non-acceptance of this order, on the terms and conditions before stated herein.

Respectfully, your obedient servant,

JAMES W. RIPLEY,
Brigadier General.

ELI WHITNEY, Esq., *Whitneyville, Conn.*

OFFICE OF WHITNEYVILLE ARMORY,
Whitneyville, (near New Haven, Conn.,) February 4, 1862.

SIR : In accordance with your notice given, I send you a copy of the order I received from your department for 40,000 Springfield muskets and appendages. I have made great advances towards filling the contract, and have engaged all the additional machinery to be completed April 1, 1862.

The 40,000 barrels are contracted for, and are being made at Mr. Washburn's, of Worcester, the same party that furnishes gun-barrel iron to the Springfield armory. Mr. Washburn's rolls are up and running, and he has sent me sample barrels. I have built, within the year, a large armory of brick, and expect to have another large factory completed by April 1, 1862, it now being in process of construction. I have a long line of new shafting completed for the new factory, and a water-wheel of iron 30 feet in diameter. I shall have 16 rifling machines, to be done April 1 ; 10 smooth boring ; 7 barrel lathes ; 2 barrel-bedding machines for stocks, &c. Have contracted for large amounts of stocks ; have tools all made for locks and mountings, and stocks and barrels, &c.

I have made several thousand Springfield muskets this last summer.

Yours, very respectfully,

ELI WHITNEY.

Hon. E. M. STANTON,
Secretary of War, Washington, D. C.

Ex. Doc. 72——25

Before commission, April 11, 1862.

Mr. Eli Whitney states:

I have a contract for 40,000 Springfield arms. I have built, since I received the order, a new factory. This is now finished. I have a full suit of all machinery in my shops, except that for bayonets and ramrods. I get my barrels in the rough from Washburn. I have had samples from him; some do not turn out well, but being a very responsible man, I feel sure of his success. He is to make his first delivery to me very soon. I will finish all barrel work, and I have all the machines necessary for a few barrels, but I will put in more, so as to finish from 100 to 150 per day. I have made no arrangements to supply other parties. I have been applied to by many, but have always declined. I have rough stocks on hand to a considerable amount—5,000 to 10,000 fit to work. I have four kilns for drying them. The loss in seasoning them is very great—nearly 50 per cent. This is the experience of the Springfield and other large establishments. We have sufficient machines ready (except one barrel-bedding machine) to turn out 150 per day. We have yet to deliver 2,000 arms (nearly of Springfield pattern) to the State of Connecticut; I have delivered already 3,600, and get $18 each for them; they have the Enfield bayonet. I can make the gun cheaper, because I imported the bayonets, which I am permitted to use, and which cost only from $1 to $1 75, while we will have to pay $2 25 for the Springfield bayonet: at this price, I learn, the manufacturers expect 10 per cent. profit. I do not think this is too much, considering the risk of inspection; some parties have made agreements at $1 83. The Collins Axe Company make mountings for me. I am not yet ready to make sights, as I have been using, for the State work, sights of another pattern. I am now forging the Springfield pattern. I will make appendages myself; I have commenced on some. My bayonets are from the Collins Axe Company. They have already many forged, and they have ten or twelve milling machines. They are to deliver to me in May, June, and July, so that I may be ahead of my contracts. These are to pass the United States inspection, and for those only which pass I pay $2 25. W. A. Ives, a neighbor of mine, furnishes my ramrods. He has already furnished many, and has milling machines ready, or nearly so. He makes for me and for Colt only. He can probably furnish nearly 4,000 per month. The terms are the same as with the Collins Axe Company, as to pay and inspection. I have my gauges complete, or nearly so. I am making locks myself, and can furnish 100 to 160 per day of ten hours. I expect to be more particular in my government work than in my State work, as the State inspection is not with gauges. The inspector only examines the finished gun, which we agree to furnish good and serviceable. I have now 200 men employed, can increase to 325, and have everything so arranged that I can turn out government work at any time. I will certainly make my first delivery as promised, unless prevented by accident. I do not think the price, $20, too high, considering the expedition required, and the conditions of payment. I do not think the government will obtain over one quarter of the guns ordered, taking all together, and enforcing stipulations as to time. I would take 12½ per cent. and surrender my contract.

CASE No. 84.

COMMISSION ON ORDNANCE AND ORDNANCE STORES,
Washington, May 17, 1862.

GENERAL : The commission have the honor to report as follows :

CASE No. 84.—ELI WHITNEY, of New Haven.

Order by direction of the Secretary of War, dated December 24, 1861 Ex. Doc. No 67, page 162. Referred by direction of the Secretary of War.

To furnish 40,000 rifle muskets of the Springfield pattern, with appendages, at the price of $20 each gun, including appendages.

To be delivered not less than 1,000 in each of the months of July, August, and September, and not less than 2,000 in October and November, not less than 3,000 in December, 1862, and not less than 4,000 per month thereafter.—(See Case No. 72.)

The commission find that the above order was not given in accordance with the law and regulations, and that it is not, therefore, a contract of legal force, inasmuch as it does not contain the express requirements of the law, and was not made "after previous advertisement for proposals respecting the same," nor can it be regarded as an "open purchase," being for articles which did not require "immediate delivery," but, as stipulated, were to be manufactured and delivered at distant prescribed periods.

They further consider that the number of arms ordered is larger than the wants of the government justify in this case at the fixed price; and therefore, according to the principles set forth in Mason's case, No. 72, they decide that the order to Mr. Whitney be confirmed, subject to all its terms, to the extent of 25,000 muskets, upon condition that he shall, within fifteen days after notice of this decision, execute bond, with good and sufficient sureties, in the form and with the stipulations prescribed by law and the regulations for the performance of the contract, as thus modified, resulting from said order and acceptance, and, upon his failure or refusal to execute such bond, then the said order shall be declared cancelled and of no effect.

The commission further decide that the deliveries under the contract to be executed shall be required at or within the periods stipulated in the original order, but that the numbers specified may be reduced proportionately to the reduction of the whole number, so that the contract shall be completed within the time allowed in the original order.

We are, sir, very respectfully, your obedient servants,

J. HOLT,
ROBERT DALE OWEN,
Commissioners, &c.
P. V. HAGNER,
Assistant to Commission.

Brigadier General J. W. RIPLEY,
Chief of Ordnance.

CASE No. 85.

W. MUIR & CO.

NEW YORK, *February* 10, 1862.

DEAR SIR : In compliance with the third section of your general order of the 29th ultimo, we have the honor to report that on the 7th day of December last the then honorable Secretary of War issued an order to William Muir for thirty thousand (30,000) Springfield muskets for the United States government; that on the 10th day of January the said order was amended, so as to read William Muir & Co., and that under that amended order the present company was formed.

We enclose copies of the orders referred to. We have the honor further to report that these arms are being assembled at Windsor Locks, Connecticut, and that there has been already expended the sum of $50,000, and a further liability incurred of $21,000 under contract for machinery, to be delivered and paid for within the next sixty days.

There is also a large amount of machinery, incidental to the manufacture of these arms, which has been diverted from the purposes for which it was originally intended, the value of which has not been included in the foregoing statement.

We shall, in all reasonable probability, be able to deliver these arms promptly, according to the requirements of our contract.

Respectfully,

WILLIAM MUIR & CO.,
By T. C. K., 272 *Broadway*.

Hon. EDWIN M. STANTON,
Secretary of War.

ORDNANCE OFFICE,
Washington, December 7, 1861.

SIR: By direction of the Secretary of War, I offer you an order for thirty thousand (30,000) muskets and appendages of the Springfield pattern on the following terms and conditions, viz:

These arms are to be in all respects identical with the standard rifle musket made at the United States armory at Springfield, Massachusetts, and to interchange with it and with each other in all their parts. They are to be subject to inspection by the United States inspector in the same manner that the Springfield arms are inspected, and none are to be received and paid for but such as pass inspection, and are approved by the United States inspector. These thirty thousand arms and appendages are to be delivered as follows, viz: Not less than 1,000 on the 1st of May, 1862, not less than 1,000 on the 1st of June, 1862, and not less than 2,000 per month thereafter, until the whole 30,000 shall have been delivered.

In case of any failure to make the deliveries to the extent and within the times before specified, all the obligations of the United States to receive or pay for any muskets or appendages than deliverable under this order shall be cancelled and become null and void. Payments are to be made for such delivery in such funds as the Treasury Department may provide, on certificates of inspection and receipt by the United States inspectors, at the rate of twenty dollars for each arm, including appendages. All these arms and appendages are to be packed by you in boxes of the regular pattern, with twenty muskets and appendages in each box, for which a fair price, which shall be determined by the United States inspector, will be allowed.

Please signify, in writing, your acceptance or non-acceptance of this order on the terms and conditions herein stated.

Respectfully, your obedient servant,

JAMES W. RIPLEY,
Brigadier General.

Mr. WILLIAM MUIR,
372 *Broadway, New York.*

Which order was accepted by the said William Muir in the words following, to wit:

WASHINGTON, *December* 19, 1861.

SIR: I have the pleasure of acknowledging the receipt of an order from the honorable Secretary of War for the manufacture of thirty thousand Springfield muskets, and herewith signify my acceptance of the same in accordance with the specifications of my contract.

Yours, respectfully,

WILLIAM MUIR.

General JAMES W. RIPLEY,
Ordnance Office, Washington, D. C.

ORDNANCE OFFICE,
Washington, January 10, 1862.

GENTLEMEN: The order given from this office on the 7th December, 1861, to Mr. William Muir, for thirty thousand (30,000) muskets and appendages, of the Springfield pattern, has been sent to this office with the following indorsement, dated to-day, and signed by Thomas A. Scott, Assistant Secretary of War, viz: "There is no objection to Mr. Muir associating capitalists with him to carry out his agreement under the name or firm of William Muir & Co. Give the firm the same terms in relation to forfeiture that is given to other contractors." The order given to William Muir, of the 7th December, 1861, is therefore now given to William Muir & Co., with the same terms and conditions, excepting only that in relation to forfeiture, which is so modified as to read as follows, viz: In case of any failure to make deliveries to the extent and within the terms specified in the order of December 7, 1861, you are to forfeit the right to deliver whatever number may be deficient in the specified number for the month in which the failure occurs. All these arms are to be delivered by you; and this order, if transferred to another party, is to be thereby forfeited.

You will please signify, in writing, whether you accept or not, in your corporate capacity, this modified order in the place of that given to Mr. William Muir on the 7th December, 1861, it being distinctly understood that the total number of arms and appendages to be received by the government is not to exceed thirty thousand.

Respectfully, your obedient servant,

JAMES W. RIPLEY,
Brigadier General.

Messrs. WILLIAM MUIR & CO.,
372 *Broadway, New York.*

NEW YORK, *January* 19, 1862.

SIR: We herewith acknowledge the receipt of an order given by the honorable Secretary of War to William Muir & Co. January 10, 1862, said order being an amendment of an order given to William Muir December 7, 1861, so amended as to read William Muir & Co. We note also the modification that has been made in the clause relating to forfeiture. And we do hereby signify our acceptance of the order given to William Muir & Co., in accordance with the specifications of that order.

Yours, respectfully,

WILLIAM MUIR & CO.

General JAMES W. RIPLEY,
Chief of Ordnance, Washington, D. C.

Before the commission, April 3, 1862.

Mr. Wm. Muir, of New York, appeared before the commission, and says :

That he has a contract for 30,000 Springfield guns; has made advances to Dinslow & Chase, Windsor Locks; first advance, $7,500; they undertook to furnish barrels; contracted for other machinery to be furnished them; barrels in rough I get from Washburn; Dinslow & Chase made the contract with Mr. Washburn; Dinslow & Chase are responsible to me, and Washburn to Dinslow & Chase; I only pay for those that pass inspection; stocks made at Hartford by Mr. H. E. Robbins, taken subject to inspection, to be delivered at Windsor Locks, where guns will be assembled; I have a shop there; the whole responsibility of the stocks is on Mr. Robbins; we have ample money security; Parker, Snow, Brooks & Co. make guard, plate, and lock; Peck & Smith, of Plattville, furnish butt plate; Washington Medallion Pen Company, of New York, furnish sight and band springs; Humphreyville Manufacturing Company, Seymour, Connecticut, furnish bayonet and ramrod; Dwight & Chapin furnish appendages and cone and barrels; securities and counter securities given; all the work has been arranged for; all sub-contractors required to keep fifteen days in advance of contractor's deliveries; 4,000 locks engaged of Esler & Bro., Philadelphia; I have provided against failures by contractors by securities, when the contractors are not responsible; I have seen all the factories; Mr. Robbins will give perfect stocks on the 15th of April; must deliver 1,000 on that day; I have seen his machinery within ten days; all his machinery is nearly done; Robbins has not turned out anything yet; I cannot estimate the cost of the gun; it will cost more than $15; Mr. Andrews supervises the assembling from Windsor Locks; he has had experience from his representations; I have asked no inspection; I have seen Major Dyer at Springfield several times, and was told I must inspect my own barrels, (fire test;) Mr. Parker, of the firm of Parker, Snow, Brooks & Co., was a foreman at Springfield, and knows all about locks; we are involved to the extent of our advances, and also bound to take from sub-contractors all work made according to contract; the maximum profit desirable from the contract in our opinion cannot exceed $3 50 per gun; it may be much less, and will be so if our advances have to be greatly increased before a payment is made; contracts with sub-contractors embody both orders from government; sub-contractors are bound to contractors as contractors are bound to the government; all the parts of the gun are now under way to be finished; Washburn has delivered barrels; no bayonets have been delivered yet.

372 BROADWAY, *New York, April* 12, 1862.

DEAR SIR: In reply to your request, made to me when at your office in Washington, to give you a statement of the progress of Wm. Muir & Co. in carrying out their contract with the United States government to furnish 30,000 rifled muskets, I have the honor to submit for your consideration letters from Messrs. Dinslow & Chase, of Windsor Locks, Connecticut; Parker, Snow, Brooks & Co., of Meriden, Connecticut; the Humphreyville Manufacturing Company, of Seymour, Connecticut; and H. E. Robbins, esq., of Hartford, Connecticut.

There is no doubt that we shall be in time in our deliveries.

Messrs. Wm. Muir & Co. have expended thus far in cash $28,000, and are under contract for machinery, &c., to be paid for almost immediately to the amount of $13,000, and have assumed a further liability under contract of an amount nearly equalling the cost of the guns.

Please place these letters on file with the commission.

Yours, truly,

WILLIAM MUIR.

Major P. V. HAGNER, *Washington, D. C.*

OFFICE OF PARKER, SNOW, BROOKS & CO.,
West Meriden, Connecticut, April, 1862.

GENTLEMEN: In relation to our ability to manufacture the thirty thousand locks contracted for with you, we have no doubt we shall be able to do so at the times and in the quantities called for by our contract. We are progressing with our machinery and tools as fast as possible, and shall undoubtedly be on time in our deliveries. Our capacity will be for 200 locks per day, to be increased as we may need for our contracts; and as your contract has precedence over any other, you need not have any fears of our allowing any other to interfere with it.

In relation to our mechanical skill and knowledge of making locks, we will say that one, Mr. Snow, was educated to the manufacture of arms and understands the business fully. Our arrangements for labor are with some of the most experienced men from the armories of Springfield and Hartford, and the quality of our work we know will be all you will require. The guard plates we shall get out soon, and they will be all that the government will require as to quality.

Respectfully, your obedient servants,

PARKER, SNOW, BROOKS & CO.

Messrs. WILLIAM MUIR & CO.

OFFICE OF THE HUMPHREYVILLE MANUFACTURING COMPANY,
No. 5 Gold Street, New York, April 7, 1862.

GENTLEMEN: In reply to your inquiry about our facilities and capacity for manufacturing bayonets and ramrods, we will say that we are fitting up machinery, and have the room and power necessary to turn out five hundred to six hundred per day of each bayonets and ramrods.

We expect to turn out the first lot finished of the Springfield pattern within two weeks from this date, and shall be able to make the delivery to you of one thousand this present month, and the balance as called for by our contract with you.

Thus far we have only taken contracts from yourselves and Mr. John Rice, of Philadelphia, so you need have no fear of our not being able to make our deliveries promptly. We shall not close other contracts (now being offered us) until we ascertain our capacity to deliver beyond question.

You ask us the amount of capital we have invested in this branch of our business. We have diverted from other uses, in the shape of buildings, power, &c., and put in new, and altered old, machinery to adapt it to this business—property that I estimate has cost us fully fifty thousand dollars.

Respectfully, yours,

W. H. MARSHALL,
Treasurer Humphreyville Manufacturing Company.

Messrs. WILLIAM MUIR & CO.

WINDSOR LOCKS, *April* 11, 1862.

GENTLEMEN: In reply to your inquiry about our capacity for the manufacture of barrels for the Springfield musket, we will say that we have our machinery nearly completed to turn out one hundred barrels per day. Our vent-boring, reaming, and turning lathes are now complete, and we are now at work turning the barrels ready for proving, and are ready for you to send us an inspector to prove them, which we hope you will do by *Tuesday of next week,* as they must be proved before we can finish them. Our milling machines for milling are being put up, and our rifling machines are now having the belts put on ready for work.

We shall be able, with our tools complete, to turn out finished barrels this month, and shall be fully able to turn out barrels, as called for by our contract with you, to the full extent after this month. We do not expect to get out the full number for this month's delivery, but if we can get 200 or 500 barrels inspected by Tuesday next, we shall try hard to get out 400 or 500 for this month's delivery. The cost of our machinery for the fulfilment of our contracts with you, independent of buildings and power, will be about $25,000. The buildings, power, &c., diverted from another purpose to this business are worth about $15,000, making our investment for the fulfilment of our contract with you about $40,000. We have experienced, practical workmen, most or all of whom have worked only in armories, either Springfield, Sharpe's, or Colt's, and with the same kind of machinery and tools used at Springfield armory in producing barrels there, and men who are perfectly skilled in doing this same work there. We have no doubt of being able to make as good and perfect barrels as those produced at Springfield armory.

We are having barrels rolled by Mr. Washburn, of Worcester, from a very superior class of iron, or semi-steel, which is made at the works of the Damascus Steel and Iron Company, on Staten Island, and, from those we have thus far tested, we think they will be superior to any barrels ever before made. We have made some of these barrels by drilling the hole in the solid piece, but experiments made show that the hole can be got by rolling over a mandril more economically, and we expect to produce *the best musket barrel ever made*. We have one other contract besides yours, with Mr. O. T. Burt, for 25,000 barrels, commencing delivery first of August next, but our capacity will be, before that time, fully equal to the fulfilment of both. We could hardly afford to put up machinery for making less than 50,000 barrels, as the outlay necessary to make *one barrel* gives us a capacity to make a large quantity. By adding a little to the set we have of some few tools enables us to turn out easily the quantity we have contracted for, and by running night and day our capacity would be doubled, or equal to two hundred barrels per day.

Your contract has priority over the other, but we expect to fulfil both.

Yours, respectfully,

DINSLOW & CHASE.

Messrs. WILLIAM MUIR & CO.

HARTFORD, *April* 10, 1862.

GENTLEMEN: In response to your inquiry relative to my capacity for making Springfield musket stocks, I respectfully reply, I have completed and am completing (to be done about the 20th of this month) a full set of all the proper machinery, mostly from pattern furnished by the Springfield armory. Our lathes are of Blanchard's patent, with improvements, and duplicates of those used at Springfield. The letting-on machine for the lock is a fine slide machine, with double parallel bed. The barrel-bedding machine was cast at Chicopee, from patterns furnished by the armory. The capacity of these machines is, at the lowest estimate, six thousand stocks per month of ten hours per day. I have three contracts in process, amounting in all to one hundred and five thousand. Yours having the priority and preference, I have contracted with reliable parties for the best walnut to be had, and am already in receipt of a portion of the same, a duplicate lot being shipped, under inspection, to the army. My factories I have located at Unionville, (near this city,) for economy of power and safety from fire. My help are experienced in stock-making at other armories, and my means and resources ample to complete satisfactorily the contracts that I have undertaken. When my works are complete, I shall have made an investment of from twenty to twenty-five thousand dollars; and I respectfully solicit your examination of the works I have erected, in corroboration of my statement.

Yours, respectfully,

W. E. ROBBINS.

Messrs. WILLIAM MUIR & Co.,
New York.

HARTFORD, *April* 11, 1862.

I consider Mr. Robbins a reliable person, and fully able to carry out the above agreement.

W. H. D. CALLENDER.

No. 372 BROADWAY, *New York, May* 2, 1862.

GENTLEMEN: Enclosed we hand you copy of a letter from Messrs. Dinslow & Chase, our agents at Windsor Locks, Connecticut, referring to an accident to our works, arising from the unprecedented freshet in the Connecticut river. This untimely accident will prevent our making our first of May delivery of muskets, according to contract. We now expect to be able to make the delivery by the twenty-fifth of this month, but would like to throw the May delivery into August, making the June and July deliveries as called for under the contract. Please recommend to the proper authority to make this change.

We have a few guns assembled, and expect to be in Washington in a few days, when we will show you one.

Respectfully, yours,

WILLIAM MUIR & CO.

Messrs. JOSEPH HOLT and ROBERT DALE OWEN,
Commissioners on Contracts, Washington, D. C.

WINDSOR LOCKS, *April* 23, 1862.

GENTLEMEN: We regret exceedingly to be obliged to notify you of an accident to our works.

Last night the high water of the Connecticut river washed away several thousand feet of the embankment of the canal from which we draw our supply of water. This accident completely stops our works for the present. The superintendent of the water-works informs us that as soon as the water subsides sufficiently a coffer-dam will be built around the breach, in such a manner as to give us all the water we need, but that we cannot expect to get under way again for at least three weeks from this date.

We have had our barrels proved at Springfield, the proof being highly satisfactory. We have since finished them up, and are much pleased with them. Had it not been for this untimely accident, we should have had our delivery ready. We regret it as much as you possibly can, and shall use our every exertion to get in running order again with the least possible delay.

Truly yours,

DINSLOW & CHASE.

Messrs. WILLIAM MUIR & Co.

372 BROADWAY, *New York, May* 19, 1862.

GENTLEMEN : After reviewing our position we conclude to offer proposal for twenty-five thousand muskets, as 20,000 will not protect us against loss.

We have conferred with some of our sub-contractors, and they all decline to compromise with us at 20,000, but the most of them will accept at 25,000. At even this number it is very doubtful whether we can make ourselves whole, still we think and hope it may. It is but little we ask, being but an additional 5,000, and we would not insist upon this, did we not see that on a less number we should lose on our investment.

We have made the reservation in regard to the use of malleable iron for butt plates and tips, as at Springfield, as we cannot afford, under the change, to put up the new machinery necessary to manufacture them from wrought iron, and the clause in relation to forfeiture, to guard against accidents, not from any doubt of our ability to fulfil, as we confidently hope to be able to deliver 1,500 by the 15th June. We have made the within proposal in the name of Muir & Co., merely to distinguish the new transaction from the old, as the entire business will have to be reconstructed and new contracts made to agree with the change in the deliveries, but in this proposal we do not ask any more time than is called for under the contract of January 10, 1862, with William Muir & Co.

We understand that the government really needs and is likely to need these arms as rapidly as they can be manufactured; and you should remember that, when this rebellion broke out, the country was entirely destitute of the facilities for manufacturing arms, except at the national armories, and that the government ought to endeavor to foster an interest which may at some future day be indispensable to its own protection. We enclose this matter to you for your consideration, fully trusting that you are disposed to deal fairly with all contractors. We think we are entitled to a little more consideration than most contractors, and, although we were the last in the field, we bid fair to be among the first to make deliveries, and hope, within a day or two, to send you all the parts of a gun of our own manufacture, in such a state of progress as will convince you of our ability to perform all we contract. If this proposal meets your approbation, you will please recommend it to the Hon. Secretary of War, that we may take out our new contract as soon as possible, as this state of uncertainty delays our work, and adds very materially to our expenses.

Very respectfully, yours,

WILLIAM MUIR.

Messrs. JOSEPH HOLT, ROBERT DALE OWEN, and Maj. P. V. HAGNER,
Washington, D. C., Commissioners of Ordnance.

WASHINGTON, D. C., *June* 25, 1862.

GENTLEMEN : Having all our parts for a Springfield musket now ready to commence finishing and assembling, we think we can consistently ask you to give us the amount our order called for, viz: 30,000. Our expenditure is made for machinery, and our sub-contracts are made for 30,000 bayonets and locks, and we shall be obliged to take them.

Under these circumstances we would make the extra 10,000 at $18 extra, rather than have the parts thrown upon our hands; or if you prefer to give us 25,000 at $20 extra, and 5,000 at $16 each, we would take that. Waiting your favorably reply, we are,

Yours, very respectfully,

WILLIAM MUIR & CO.,
58 *Liberty street, New York.*

The above quantity to be all delivered in the time called for by your last decision.

Hon. JOSEPH HOLT and ROBERT DALE OWEN,
Commissioners.

CASE NO. 85.

COMMISSION ON ORDNANCE AND ORDNANCE STORES,
Washington, May 19, 1862.

GENERAL : The commission have the honor to report as follows :

CASE No. 85.—WILLIAM MUIR & Co., New York.

Order by direction of the Secretary of War, dated December 7, 1861.—(See page 147, Ex. Doc. No. 67.)

Referred by order of the Secretary of War.

To furnish 30,000 muskets and appendages of the Springfield pattern, at the price of $20 for each gun, including appendages. Deliveries to be made as follows :

Not less than 1,000 on 1st May, 1862; not less than 1,000 on 1st June, 1862; and not less than 2,000 per month thereafter.

" In case of any failure to make the deliveries to the extent and within the time before specified, all the obligations of the United States to receive or pay for any muskets and appendages then deliverable under this order shall be cancelled, and become null and void."

The commission find that this order, under the condition above quoted, may now be declared cancelled, as no delivery has yet been made under it (May 17) and none can probably be made this month. But as it appears to the satisfaction of the commission that obligations have been incurred by the parties in their efforts to comply with the order, and that the work is now in actual progress, and a portion will soon be ready for the inspectors, they decide that the question of total forfeiture be waived, and that the order to Messrs. Muir & Co. be confirmed, subject to all its terms to the extent of 20,000 muskets, upon condition that they shall, within fifteen days after notice of this decision, execute bond with good and sufficient sureties, in the form and with the stipulations prescribed by law and the regulations for the performance of the contract, as thus modified, resulting from said order and acceptance; and upon their failure or refusal to execute such bond, then the said order shall be declared cancelled and of no effect.

The commission further decide that the deliveries under the contract to be executed shall be required at or within the periods stipulated in the original order, except those in May and June, but that the numbers specified may be reduced proportionally to the reduction of the whole number, so that the contract shall be completed within the time allowed in the original order.

We are, sir, very respectfully, your obedient servants,

J. HOLT,
ROBERT DALE OWEN,
Commissioners, &c.

P. V. HAGNER,
Major of Ordnance, Assistant to Commission.

Brigadier General J. W. RIPLEY,
Chief of Ordnance.

Postscript, June 25, 1862.—Upon further showing being made to the commissioners in this case by William Muir & Co., it is directed that the order be confirmed for thirty thousand guns, of which twenty-five thousand only shall be paid for at the rate of twenty dollars and five thousand at the rate of sixteen dollars, the said reduction in price to sixteen dollars for all the guns over twenty-five thousand being in accordance with a written proposal of this date made by said William Muir & Co.

> J. HOLT,
> ROBERT DALE OWEN,
> *Commissioners, &c.*
> P. V. HAGNER,
> *Major of Ordnance, Assistant to Commission.*

CASE No. 86.

A. O. LEONHARDT.

WAR DEPARTMENT, *October* 25, 1861.

SIR: Your communication of the 18th instant, asking for information in reference to bills for supplies furnished volunteer forces upon the order of Brigadier General Lyon, has been received.

In reply, you are respectfully informed that you can forward the bills in duplicate, properly certified, to the War Department, and, upon examination and approval, the chiefs of the different bureaus will order the payment.

I transmit herewith, for your information, copies of blank forms, such as are required by the quartermaster and commissary departments.

The important points essential to be stated are—

1. That the items were necessary, and were furnished;
2. That the account has not been paid; and, if possible, in all cases,
3. That the items were issued and expended on government account for such and such troops, stating which regiment, &c.

> Very respectfully,
>
> SIMON CAMERON,
> *Secretary of War.*

AMOS P. FOSTER,
> *Barnum's St. Louis Hotel, St. Louis.*

(Three enclosures.)

PAYMASTER'S DEPARTMENT MISSOURI STATE MILITIA,
St. Louis, Missouri, February 13, 1862.

SIR: I forward you an account for payment, as per instructions of late Secretary Cameron's letter to me, which I enclose. The account has been mislaid in some of the offices here, and was only found a short time since. Mr. Leonhardt needs his pay *very* much, and I hope it will be attended to immediately, as he has been kept out of his money for a long time. It is also indorsed by Hon. F. P. Blair, M. C.

> Respectfully,
>
> AMOS P. FOSTER,
> *Deputy Paymaster Missouri State Militia.*

Hon. E. M. STANTON,
> *Secretary of War, Washington City, D. C.*

ORDNANCE OFFICE, *February* 25, 1862.

Respectfully submitted to the Secretary of War for instructions as to whether the enclosed account of A. C. Leonhardt ($506 40) for accoutrements furnished to Colonel J. W. Owens's regiment of Missouri troops in July, 1861, shall be paid.

The instructions from the War Department to the commission for the examination of claims against the department of the west contemplated that all claims originating prior to the 14th of October last should be passed upon by the commission, and it was so published throughout the State of Missouri. But, by the letter from the Secretary of War to Mr. Foster, herewith, it appears that a course was pointed out to be pursued, in this case, which has been done, and it is in view of these facts that the case is submitted for instructions. The articles have been furnished, and the prices charged for them are reasonable.

JAMES W. RIPLEY,
Brigadier General.

OFFICE OF THE PROVOST MARSHAL GENERAL,
Department of the Mississippi, St. Louis, May 2, 1862.

DEAR SIR : I have written several times relative to an account for ordnance in favor of Aug. O. Leonhardt that I sent to you some four months ago. I would like much to know *why* the payment of said account is so *long* delayed.

Most respectfully, your obedient servant,

AMOS P. FOSTER.

Hon. E. M. STANTON, *Secretary of War.*

Before commission.

Copy of certificates on account of A. O. Leonhardt, dated July, 1861, *amounting to* $506 40.

The articles herein named were purchased and furnished to my command as stated, because this department at that time could not furnish me with any, and it was absolutely necessary that my men should be thus furnished, as they were distributed along the main line and southwest branch of the Pacific railroad guarding bridges, and it was impossible to keep ammunition so it could be used without them, as we had no tents. They were distributed amongst companies C, D, and F, of my command. They have been properly accounted for, and the bill for the same has not been paid.

JAMES W. OWENS,
Col. of Franklin Co. Reg't, U. S. Reserve Corps.

I certify that the above account is correct and just, amounting to five hundred and six dollars and forty cents.

AMOS P. FOSTER,
Quarterm'r Franklin Co. Reg't, U. S. Reserve Corps.

True copy.

P. V. HAGNER, *Major of Ordnance.*

COMMISSION ON ORDNANCE AND ORDNANCE STORES,
Washington, May 19, 1862.

GENERAL : The commission have the honor to report as follows :

CASE No. 86.—AUGUSTUS O. LEONHARDT, St. Louis.

Claim for payment of voucher dated July 12, 1861. Referred by special directions of the Secretary of War.

Account rendered for infantry accoutrements furnished to Colonel James W. Owens, regiment of Franklin county, Missouri, and issued by Amos P. Foster, A. Q. M. of the regiment, to companies C, D, and F. Amount, $506 40.

The commission find that the articles are ordnance stores, and according to law should have been purchased under directions of the chief of ordnance, and also that the account should have been rendered at an earlier date, so that the examination could have been made by the commission in St. Louis, as was directed for this class of claims; but as it appears by the certificate of Colonel James W. Owens, on the face of the voucher, that the accoutrements were absolutely necessary for the use of his regiment, then in the field, that none could be obtained by him from other sources at the time; that they were actually received, as acknowledged by A. P. Foster, A. Q. M., and issued to companies duly mustered into service; and as the prices are reasonable, the commission decide that the account be examined and audited, as usual, without objection on account of informality.

We are, sir, very respectfully, your obedient servants,

J. HOLT,
ROBERT DALE OWEN,
Commissioners, &c.
P. V. HAGNER,
Major of Ordnance, Assistant to Commission.

Brigadier General J. W. RIPLEY,
Chief of Ordnance.

CASE No. 87.

C. A. EATON.

Before commission.

Copy of certificate to the account of Charles A. Eaton, of Chicago, amounting to $9 30, dated

"CAMP DOUGLAS,
"*Chicago, February* 20, 1862.

" I certify that the above requisition is correct and just, and that the articles are absolutely necessary for the public service, to guard the prisoners sent up from the south.

" Mr. Charles A. Eaton will furnish the articles specified. I have received the above, and recommend payment.

"A. VOSS,
"*Colonel Commanding Post.*"

COMMISSION ON ORDNANCE AND ORDNANCE STORES,
Washington, May 20, 1862.

GENERAL: The commission have the honor to report as follows:

CASE No. 87.—CHARLES A. EATON, Chicago, Illinois.

Claim for payment of a bill dated February 20, 1862. Referred by special direction of Secretary of War.

Bill for powder and cannon primers, amounting to $9 30, ordered by Colonel Voss, commanding Camp Douglas.

The commission find that the order to furnish the above-named ordnance stores was given by Colonel Voss, commanding officer at Camp Douglas, to the claimant upon receipt of information that a large number of prisoners had been ordered to his camp, part of which were to arrive the next day; and being without any ammunition for his gun, and unable to obtain any in time by the course prescribed by law and regulations, has felt compelled to procure a small quantity as above.

The prices charged in the account are high; but as the quantity is small, and the article may have been scarce in Chicago, the commission decide that the account be examined and audited, as usual, without objection on account of informality or the price of the items.

We are, sir, very respectfully, your obedient servants,

J. HOLT,
ROBERT DALE OWEN,
Commissioners, &c.
P. V. HAGNER,
Major of Ordnance, Assistant to Commission.

Brigadier General J. W. RIPLEY,
Chief of Ordnance.

CASE No. 88.

E. A. STRAW, Agent.

AMOSKEAG MANUFACTURING COMPANY,
Manchester, New Hampshire, February 11, 1862.

SIR: The Amoskeag Manufacturing Company of Manchester, New Hampshire, are at work under an order from the Ordnance office upon "ten thousand muskets, with appendages, of the Springfield pattern." The order is dated January 7, 1862.

We have contracted for all the materials required in the manufacture of the above muskets, some of which we have received and are at work upon; and we are changing as rapidly as possible the fixtures upon our gun tools, so as to adapt them to the Springfield pattern musket.

Accompanying this please find copies of the official order and my acceptance thereof, all of which is respectfully submitted in compliance with your published orders dated January 29, 1862.

Respectfully, your most obedient servant,

E. A. STRAW, *Agent.*

Hon. EDWIN M. STANTON,
Secretary of War.

ORDNANCE OFFICE,
Washington, January 7, 1862.

By direction of the Secretary of War, I offer you an order for ten thousand (10,000) muskets, with appendages, of the Springfield pattern, on the following terms and conditions, viz: These arms are to be furnished with the regular appendages, and are to be in all respects identical with the standard rifle musket made at the United States armory at Springfield, Massachusetts, and are to interchange with it and with each other in all their parts. They are to be subject to inspection by United States inspectors in the same manner that the Springfield arms are inspected, and none are to be received or paid for but such as pass inspection, and are approved by the United States inspectors. These ten thousand (10,000) arms and appendages are to be delivered at your armory as follows, viz: Not less than one thousand (1,000) of these arms and appendages in the month of May, 1862, and not less than one thousand per month thereafter (for the nine consecutive months) until the entire ten thousand shall have been delivered, and you are to have the right to deliver more rapidly than according to the number of arms before specified, if you can do so. In case of any failure to make deliveries to the extent and within the times before specified, you are to forfeit the right to deliver whatever number may be deficient in the specified number for the month in which the failure occurs. All the arms and appendages are to be delivered by you, and this order, if transferred to another party, is to be thereby forfeited. Payments are to be made in such funds as the Treasury Department may provide for each delivery, on certificate of inspection and receipt by the United States inspectors, at the rate of twenty dollars ($20) for each arm, including appendages. All these arms and appendages are to be packed by you in boxes of the regular pattern, with twenty (20) muskets and appendages in each box, for which a fair price (to be determined by the United States inspectors) will be allowed.

Please signify, in writing, your acceptance or non-acceptance of this order on the terms and conditions before stated herein.

Respectfully, your obedient servant,

JAMES W. RIPLEY,
Brigadier General.

The AMOSKEAG MANUFACTURING COMPANY,
Per E. A. Straw, agent, Manchester, N. H.

AMOSKEAG MANUFACTURING COMPANY,
Manchester, New Hampshire, January 10, 1862.

SIR: I am in receipt of your order under date of January 7, 1862, for "ten thousand (10.000) muskets, with appendages, of the Springfield pattern."

We accept the order on the terms and conditions stated therein, and shall proceed to execute it at once. Please forward me your order for a model gun from the Springfield armory.

Allow me to add that we have considerable facilities for doing work of this character. We have an abundance of shop-room, a large number of tools recently completed specially for this work, and shall be pleased to accept further orders from your department, and trust to be able to execute them promptly and to your entire satisfaction.

Respectfully, your most obedient servant,

E. A. STRAW, *Agent.*

General JAMES W. RIPLEY,
Ordnance Department, Washington, D. C.

AMOSKEAG MANUFACTURING COMPANY,
Manchester, New Hampshire, April 9, 1862.

SIR: I am in receipt of your letter of the 3d instant, referring to our contract for 10,000 Springfield rifled muskets.

In reply, I have to state that we are prepared to make, in our own workshops, all parts of the musket, and rely upon no other parties for anything except materials in the rough. The arms will finally be assembled in our own armory.

Our contract, made in January last, calls for deliveries in May next, and I now feel confident that we shall have a completed gun ready for the inspector before the 1st of June, and shall be able to finish 1,000 muskets during that month.

We have already *paid out*, for labor and materials in connexion with this work, more than $30,000. The iron and steel for the whole contract is in hand. The barrels in the rough are to be furnished by Washburn, of Worcester, Massachusetts, who has commenced deliveries, and we are now at work boring and turning. All the necessary fixtures to our tools to adapt them to the Springfield model are now *very nearly* ready for the workmen to begin work upon all other parts of the gun. The blocks for the stocks are all sawed out and are drying.

I suppose we might furnish some finished parts to other contractors, but have promised none and did not intend to do so. We have a large machine shop, usually employing about 600 men, and an armory which, when fully arranged, will, in connexion with our shop, be able to complete 1,500 muskets per month, but as I understand we can deliver to the government as fast as the arms are completed I have declined all offers for finished parts.

I should be pleased to appear before the commission in person at any time, and will do so at once if it can be done without my being detained in Washington more than two days.

Very respectfully, your obedient servant,

E. A. STRAW, *Agent.*

J. WISE, Esq.,
Secretary to Commission on Ordnance and Ordnance Stores.

WASHINGTON, *November* 14, 1861.

SIR: I am authorized to offer to contract to make 10,000 rifled muskets, Springfield pattern, (new,) to commence delivering in ten weeks from date of contract, at the rate of 200 per week—price equal to that paid by government to other contractors—not less than $20.

The contractors proposed are the Amoskeag Manufacturing Company of Manchester, New Hampshire—a highly responsible company, having $3,000,000 capital, and fully capable of executing the above contract to your satisfaction. I respectfully ask an early reply.

Very truly, your obedient servant,

C. H. DALTON.

General RIPLEY, *United States Army.*

Address at Willards' till 16th instant, then Boston.

ORDNANCE OFFICE, *November* 18, 1861.

Respectfully submitted to the Secretary of War. In the opinion of this department orders and contracts for arms on prospective deliveries have already been given to a sufficient extent. Any arms of a kind and quality suitable for the military service, which are offered to our agent in New York, will be bought by him at a fair price.

JAMES W. RIPLEY,
Brigadier General.

COMMISSION ON ORDNANCE AND ORDNANCE STORES,
Washington, May 21, 1862.

GENERAL: The commission have the honor to report as follows:

CASE No. 88.—E. A. STRAW, agent of the Amoskeag Manufacturing Company, Manchester, New Hampshire.

Order by direction of the Secretary of War, dated January 7, 1862.—(See page 173, Ex. Doc. No. 67.) To furnish 10,000 rifled muskets, in all respects identical with the standard Springfield musket, at the price of $20 per gun, including appendages. Deliveries to be made as follows: Not less than 1,000 in May, 1862, and not less than 1,000 monthly thereafter until all are delivered.

The commission find that the above order was not made in accordance with the law and regulations, and that it is not therefore a contract of legal force, inasmuch as it does not contain the express requirements of the law, and was not made "after previous advertisements for proposals respecting the same;" nor can it be regarded as an "open purchase," being for articles which did not require "immediate delivery," but were stipulated to be manufactured and delivered at prescribed distant periods.

The commission decide (as the number ordered in this case is not large, and as the parties have shown that they have much of the work in full progress) that the order to Mr. Straw be confirmed, subject to all its terms, upon condition that he shall, within fifteen days after notice of this decision, execute bond, with good and sufficient sureties, in the form and with the stipulations prescribed by law and the regulations for the performance of the contract, resulting from said order and acceptance, and upon his failure or refusal to execute such bond, then the said order shall be declared cancelled and of no effect.

We are, sir, &c.,

J. HOLT,
ROBERT DALE OWEN,
Commissioners, &c.
P. V. HAGNER,
Major of Ordnance, Assistant to Commission.

Brigadier General J. W. RIPLEY,
Chief of Ordnance.

CASE No. 89.

GREEN KENDRICK.

WATERBURY, CONN., *February* 6, 1862.

DEAR SIR: In compliance with your order, No. 11, "in respect to army contracts," dated January 29, 1862, I herewith enclose a copy of an order for Springfield muskets, given me by order of the Secretary of War on the 10th day of January last. I also enclose a copy of my letter accepting said order, dated January 17, 1862.

In further compliance with your order, requiring that I should state "what had been done under said order," I would state that I have made as much progress as could have been expected in the few days that have elapsed since I received the order. A part of the machinery and tools for making the guns are made and ready for use, and a still larger portion are in progress, and no efforts will be spared to comply in all respects with the times and conditions of the order.

I shall very soon stand in need of a *sample musket*, and you will greatly oblige me by causing an order to be sent to the superintendent of the armory at Springfield to deliver me a *musket* and *appendages* of the kind I am to make.

Very respectfully, &c.,

GREEN KENDRICK.

Hon. EDWIN M. STANTON,
Secretary of War, Washington City.

ORDNANCE OFFICE,
Washington, January 10, 1862.

SIR: By direction of the Secretary of War I offer you an order for twenty-five thousand (25,000) muskets, of the Springfield pattern, on the following terms and conditions, viz: These arms are to be furnished with the regular appendages, and are to be in all respects identical with the standard rifle musket made at the United States armory at Springfield, Massachusetts, and are to interchange with it and with each other in all their parts; they are to be subject to inspection by United States inspectors in the same manner that the Springfield arms are inspected, and none are to be received or paid for but such as pass inspection and are approved by the United States inspector. These twenty-five thousand (25,000) arms and appendages are to be delivered at your armory as follows, viz: Not less than five hundred (500) in *each* of the months of July, August, and September, 1862; not less than one thousand (1,000) in *each* of the months of October and November, 1862; not less than fifteen hundred (1,500) in December, 1862; and not less than two thousand (2,000) per month thereafter until the entire twenty-five thousand (25,000) shall have been delivered; and you are to have the right to deliver more rapidly than according to the number of arms before specified, if you can do so. In case of any failure to make deliveries to the extent and within the time before specified, you are to forfeit the right to deliver whatever may be deficient in the specified number for the month in which the failure occurs.

All these arms and appendages are to be delivered by you, and this order if transferred to another party is to be thereby forfeited. Payments are to be made, in such funds as the Treasury Department may provide, for each delivery, on certificate of inspection and receipt by the United States inspector, at the rate of twenty dollars ($20) for each arm, including appendages.

All the arms and appendages are to be packed by you in boxes of the regular pattern, with twenty (20) muskets and appendages in each box, for which a fair price, to be determined by the United States inspector, will be allowed.

Please signify, in writing, your acceptance or non-acceptance of this order, on the terms and conditions herein stated.

Respectfully, your obedient servant,

JAMES W. RIPLEY,
Brigadier General.

GREEN KENDRICK, *Waterbury, Connecticut.*

WATERBURY, *January* 17, 1862.

DEAR SIR: I have received the order for twenty-five thousand Springfield muskets, which you gave me the 10th instant, by order of the Secretary of War, and accept the same on the terms and conditions therein contained.

Very respectfully, yours,

GREEN KENDRICK.

General JAMES W. RIPLEY,
Chief of Ordnance Department, Washington City.

WATERBURY, *Connecticut, April* 7, 1862.

GENTLEMEN: Yours of the 2d instant, relative to arms contract between the War Department and Green Kendrick for 25,000 Springfield muskets, is received.

Mr. Kendrick (my father) is at present very seriously ill, and entirely unable either to answer your communication himself or to dictate an answer. Should he not within a short time be able to respond, I will obtain the information necessary to give explicit answers to your inquiries. In the meantime all I know is that he has concluded arrangements for the manufacture of the guns.

Very respectfully, your obedient servant,

JOHN KENDRICK,
For GREEN KENDRICK.

The COMMISSION ON ORDNANCE AND ORDNANCE STORES,
Washington, D. C.

WATERBURY, *April* 11, 1862.

GENTLEMEN: My father, (Green Kendrick,) who is still confined by sickness, requests me to say to your honorable commission in regard to the contract for 25,000 Springfield muskets, between the War Department and himself, that he has arranged with O. Y. Burt, esq., a partner of Wm. Muir, to have the guns manufactured with theirs, as by making contracts together for the various parts they were enabled to present such extent of orders as to secure the most desirable manufactures and terms.

The same parties who are making the parts for Messrs. Muir & Co. are making his.

All the parts are in forward progress, and as he learns that your honorable commission has received a statement in detail from Messrs. Muir & Co., you are in possession of all the facts bearing on this point.

The sub-contractors are Parker, Snow, Brooks & Co., locks and guard plate; Humphreysville Manufacturing Company, bayonets and ramrods; Dunlow & Chase, barrels and finishing; A. Granger, sights and band springs; Dwight, Chapin & Co., appendages; H. E. Robbins, stocks.

His arms are to be finally assembled at Windsor Locks, Connecticut, by Mr. E. W. Andrews.

He has not promised to furnish any other contractors with any parts, though he *presumes* that the parties whom he had employed to make his parts would be willing to contract further on the same terms.

Your obedient servant,

JOHN KENDRICK,
For GREEN KENDRICK.

The COMMISSION ON ORDNANCE AND ORDNANCE STORES,
Washington, D. C.

WATERBURY, *May* 29, 1862.

GENTLEMEN : I have not yet received from General Ripley the papers confirming my order for Springfield muskets, at 20,000 instead of 25,000, as originally given to me. I have to-day written to General Ripley on the subject, and should be glad to receive the papers, in order that the matter may be settled according to your decision when I was at Washington last week.

Very truly yours,

GREEN KENDRICK.

The COMMISSION ON ORDNANCE, &C.,
Washington City.

COMMISSION ON ORDNANCE AND ORDNANCE STORES,
Washington, May 17, 1862.

GENERAL : The commission have the honor to report as follows :

CASE No. 89.—GREEN KENDRICK, Waterbury, Connecticut.

Order by direction of Secretary of War, dated January 10, 1862.—(See p. 175, Ex. Doc. No. 67.)   To furnish 25,000 muskets of the Springfield pattern, with appendages, at $20 each; to be delivered not less than 500 in each of the months of July, August, and September, 1862; and not less than 1,000 in each of the months of October and November; not less than 1,500 in December, and not less than 2,000 per month thereafter.—(See Case No. 72.)

The commission find that the above order was not given in accordance with the law and regulations, and that it is not, therefore, a contract of legal force, inasmuch as it does not contain the express requirements of the law, and was not made " after previous advertisement for proposals respecting the same," nor can it be regarded as an " open purchase," being for articles which did not require "immediate delivery," but were stipulated to be manufactured and delivered at prescribed periods.

They further consider that the number ordered is larger than the wants of the government justify in this case, at the fixed price, and therefore, acccording to the principles set forth in Mason's case, No. 72, they decide that the order to Mr. Kendrick be confirmed, subject to all its conditions to the extent of 20,000 muskets, upon condition that he shall, within fifteen days after receiving notice of this decision, execute bond with good and sufficient sureties, in the form and with the stipulations prescribed by law and the regulations for the performance of the contract, as thus modified, resulting from said order and acceptance, and upon his failure or refusal to execute said bond, then the said order shall be declared cancelled and of no effect.

The commission further decide that the deliveries under the contract to be executed shall be required at or within the periods stipulated in the original order, but that the numbers specified may be reduced proportionately to the reduction of the whole number, so that the contract shall be completed within the time allowed in the original order.

We are, sir, very respectfully, your obedient servants,

J. HOLT,
ROBERT DALE OWEN,
Commissioners, &c.
P. V. HAGNER,
Major of Ordnance, Assistant to Commission.

Brig. Gen. J. W. RIPLEY,
Chief of Ordnance.

CASE No. 90.

J. MULHOLLAND.

READING, *February* 19, 1862.

SIR : I have the honor to enclose you herewith copy of an offer for an order for 50,000 muskets of the Springfield pattern, which was addressed to me on the 7th of January last by General Ripley, of the United States Ordnance department, together with a copy of a letter which he wrote me on the 13th of this month. This letter contained an order for a sample of a Springfield United States musket, asked for by me before I could accept of the aforesaid order, and for which I have waited ever since.

As soon as practicable after the receipt of said sample musket, (say on the 17th instant,) I notified to General Ripley my acceptance of the order under the conditions named, and I concluded all my arrangements for the efficient manufacture of them.

I am, very respectfully, your obedient servant,

JAMES MULHOLLAND.

Hon. EDWIN M. STANTON,
Secretary of War, Washington, D. C.

ORDNANCE OFFICE, *Washington, January* 7, 1862.

SIR : By direction of the Secretary of War I offer you an order for fifty thousand (50,000) muskets, with appendages, of the Springfield pattern, on the following terms and conditions, viz : These arms are to be furnished with the regular appendages, and are to be in all respects identical with the standard rifle musket made at the United States armory at Springfield, Massachusetts, and are to interchange with it, and with each other, in all their parts; they are to be subject to inspection by United States inspectors in the same manner that the Springfield muskets are inspected, and none are to be received or paid for but such as pass inspection and are approved by the United States inspector.

These fifty thousand (50,000) arms and appendages are to be delivered at your armory as follows, viz: Not less than one thousand (1,000) in each of the months of July, August, and September, 1862; not less than two thousand (2,000) in each of the months of October and November, 1862; not less than four thousand per month thereafter until the entire fifty thousand (50,000) shall have been delivered; and you are to have the right to deliver more rapidly than according to the number of arms before specified, if you can do so. In case of any failure to make deliveries to the extent and within the time before specified you are to forfeit the right to deliver whatever number may be deficient in the specified number for the months in which the failure occurred. All these arms and appendages are to be delivered by you, and this order if transferred to another party is to be forfeited.

Payments are to be made in such funds as the Treasury Department may provide for each delivery, on certificate of inspection and receipt by the United States inspector, at the rate of twenty dollars ($20) for each arm, including appendages. All these arms and appendages are to be packed by you in boxes of the regular pattern, with twenty (20) muskets and appendages in each box, for which a fair price, to be determined by the United States inspector, will be allowed.

Please signify, in writing, your acceptance or non-acceptance of this order, on the terms and conditions hereinbefore stated.

Respectfully, your obedient servant,

JAMES W. RIPLEY,
Brigadier General.

JAMES MULHOLLAND, Esq.,
Reading, Pennsylvania.

ORDNANCE OFFICE, *Washington, February* 13, 1862.

SIR: The superintendent of the Springfield armory has been instructed to let you have a pattern musket, and the —— parts of one musket, on the presentation of your contract to him and your payment of the cost to the United States.

Respectfully, your obedient servant,

JAMES W. RIPLEY,
Brigadier General.

Mr. JAMES MULHOLLAND,
Reading, Pennsylvania.

READING, *February* 17, 1862.

SIR: I have duly received your favor of the 13th instant, informing me that the superintendent of the Springfield armory had been instructed to let me have a pattern musket, for which I have been waiting for since I came in possession of your favor of the 7th of January last. I have now the honor to inform you that I have, in consequence, completed all my arrangements to furnish the War Department with fifty thousand muskets of the Springfield pattern, under the conditions detailed in your said favor to me of the 7th of January, and in all respects like the sample musket.

Very respectfully,

JAMES MULHOLLAND.

Brigadier General JAS. W. RIPLEY,
Washington, D. C.

WASHINGTON, D. C., *March* 24, 1862.

GENTLEMEN : By order of the honorable Edwin M. Stanton, Secretary of War, under date of March 13, 1862, I have the honor to report to you that, on the 7th of January last, Brigadier General James W. Ripley issued to me, by order of the Secretary of War, an order to furnish the government of the United States fifty thousand muskets of the Springfield pattern, as will more fully appear by a copy herewith appended, marked A. I immediately, upon receipt of said order, commenced making arrangements for machinery and such facilities as were necessary to enable me to fulfil the stipulations of said order. On the 13th of Feburary the said Brigadier General James W. Ripley issued to me an order for a sample musket, which had been promised me some time previous, a copy of which is herewith filed, marked A A. As soon as I received said order for the sample of what I was to manufacture, I immediately, on the 17th day of February, (four days after said order was issued to me,) accepted said order, a copy of which is herewith filed, marked B. I had, before making my acceptance, completed my arrangements to produce the arms at the time and in the quantities called for by said order. On the 19th of February my attention was called to an order of the honorable Edwin M. Stanton, dated at Washington on the 29th of January, requiring that all parties holding contracts for arms from the government should file a copy of their order and of their acceptance of the same within fifteen days from the date of said order. I immediately, by first mail, sent the honorable Secretary of War a copy of my contract and of my acceptance, a copy of which is herewith filed, marked B, but the fifteen days expired *the day after the order was issued to me for said sample musket and before I had received said order from the department.*

This being a plain statement of facts, will the honorable commissioners please inform me whether the report I made under the order of the honorable Secretary of War is not strictly in accordance with the intent of said order, and such as to entitle me to a full recognition of my rights under said order.

All the machinery necessary to manufacture said arms is in process of manufacture, and as soon as the honorable commissioners will inform me that my report is such as entitles me to the full benefit of said order, I shall ask to have a proper person designated to inspect said works and machinery, to know that I have done eveything in good faith to fulfil said order, and that I have the ability to do so.

The honorable commissioners will see, that having made such arrangements and engagements to furnish these arms to the government as stipulated by them, a failure on their part to acknowledge said order would entail upon me very serious consequences.

Very respectfully, your obedient servant,

JAMES MULHOLLAND.
Reading, Pennsylvania.

Hon. JOSEPH HOLT and ROBERT DALE OWEN,
Commissioners.

Before commission, March 24, 1862.

James Mulholland states :

I have a contract for 50,000 Springfield guns. I am superintendent of the Reading railroad. My locks will be made in Philadelphia, by Williams & Co., or at Meriden; the bayonets will be made by myself at Meriden—they are not yet commenced; mountings at Meriden; barrels at Worcester, Massachusetts, or at Meriden, and ramrods at Meriden. I have thus far only arranged for making machines at Meriden; some are finished; I do not know how many. They are to made by Perkins, Snow, Brooks & Co.

READING, *Pennsylvania, April* 15, 1862.

GENTLEMEN : In compliance with your suggestion to me, I have the honor to enclose you various letters from the parties who are engaged by me to fulfil my contract for furnishing the government with 50,000 Springfield pattern rifled muskets. I am satisfied that I shall be able to make my deliveries as called for by my contract, and I wish to make a special request that you will do me the favor to give me an official notice that I have made my report, and that is all you require and satisfactory, or otherwise.

Parties that I have employed on this government work report to me constantly that it is rumored that contracts for these arms are to be annulled, and, if at all compatible with your duty, I should feel greatly obliged to have these annoyances silenced by your report.

Very respectfully, your obedient servant,

JAMES MULHOLLAND.

Hon. JOSEPH HOLT and ROBERT DALE OWEN.
Commissioners.

OFFICE OF THE HUMPHREYSVILLE MANUFACTURING COMPANY,
No. 5 Gold street, New York, April 14, 1862.

GENTLEMEN : We now expect to get out our first lot of bayonets and ramrods of the Springfield pattern in about ten days, and we are satisfied that we shall be able to give you all you will need for your contract for 50,000, commencing your delivery in June or July, as you may wish.

The contracts we have with Messrs. Rice, and Muir & Co. will not at any time call for more than 250 per day, and our estimated capacity will be equal to 500 to 600 per day.

As you stand next on our list to Messrs. Rice, and Muir & Co., we think you can feel safe in getting all you require from us.

Yours, respectfully,

WILLIAM H. MARSHALL,
Treasurer and Agent Humphreysville Manufacturing Co.
Messrs. PARKER, SNOW, BROOKS & CO.,
West Meriden, Connecticut.

MIDDLETOWN, *April* 8, 1862.

DEAR SIR : In answer to yours of the 5th instant, in reference to your connexion with Messrs. Parker, Snow, Brooks & Co., of Meriden, for the purpose of manufacturing 50,000 Springfield rifles under a contract with the government, I can confidently say that those gentlemen have ample means and facilities for fulfilling any contract they may undertake. One of the firm (Mr. Snow) is a practical gun-maker, having worked at the business about fourteen years, and they have been doing a large business manufacturing gun machinery, and being gentlemen of high character and ample means, I have no hesitation in recommending them.

I am your obedient servant,

EDWARD SAVAGE.

JAMES MULHOLLAND, Esq., *Philadelphia.*

OFFICE OF THE WOODRUFF & BEACH IRON-WORKS,
Hartford, April 14, 1862.

GENTLEMEN : Yours of the 12th instant is received. We expect to have the barrel lathes finished ready to deliver next week, and the nut-boring and reaming machines the week following. We have no doubt of being able to complete all you may require in six or eight weeks from this time.

Yours truly,

H. B. BEACH.

Messrs. PARKER, SNOW, BROOKS & CO.,
West Meriden.

HARTFORD, *April* 10, 1862.

GENTLEMEN : In response to your inquiry relative to my capacity for making Springfield musket stocks, I respectfully reply : I have completed, and am completing, (to be done about the 20th of this month,) a full set of all the proper machinery, mostly from patterns furnished by the Springfield armory. Our lathes are of Blanchard's patent, with improvements and duplicates of those used at Springfield. The letting-in machine for the lock is a fine slide machine with double parallel bed. The barrel-bedding machine was cast at Chicopee from patterns furnished by the armory. The capacity of these machines is, at the lowest estimate, six thousand stocks per month of ten hours per day. I have in process your contract and two others, amounting in all to one hundred and five thousand. I have contracted with reliable parties for the best walnut to be had, and am already in receipt of a portion of the same, a duplicate lot being shipped under inspection to the armory. My factories I have located at Unionville, (near this city,) for economy of power and safety from fire. My help are experienced in stock making at other armories, and my means and resources ample to complete satisfactorily the contracts I have undertaken. When my works and machinery are all complete I shall have made an investment in them of from twenty to twenty-five thousand dollars. I shall not take any more contracts than what I have named, although I might safely do so by running my works night and day.

Yours, respectfully,

H. E. ROBBINS.

Messrs. PARKER, SNOW, BROOKS & CO.

WEST MERIDEN, *April* 14, 1862.

DEAR SIR : In reply to your inquiries, we have thought best to give you letters from parties who are to furnish some parts of the muskets we have contracted to make, as well as a portion of the machinery. The time is too short for us to get up an entire armory to make all parts of the musket for delivery in July. We shall get ready to make the locks, barrels, guard and trigger plates, screws and other trimmings, but have been obliged to get the bayonets, ramrods, and stocks under contract with other parties. By this means we shall be able to deliver the arms at times called for in your contract. We are having our gauges made by Messrs. Smith & Wesson, at Springfield, and verified by the standard gauges at the armory, They are nearly completed. We are pushing along our small tools as fast as possible, so as to be ready to go to work as soon as our large tools are finished.

If it is possible for you to get the commissioners on contracts or the honorable Secretary of War to say that your contract stands fair and unprejudiced in the department, it will be a great satisfaction to us and to those you employ, for the rumors that are afloat that the commissioners are annulling all gun contracts operates very seriously against us. It injures our credit and cripples us in our resources, and delays our work. Our bank officers are constantly reminding us of these rumors, and we ought to be able to silence them. We have more faith in our government than to suppose that she will repudiate her contracts, or injure those who are honestly endeavoring to serve her.

Respectfully, yours,

PARKER, SNOW, BROOKS & CO.

JAMES MULHOLLAND, Esq.

Before commission, April 16, 1862.

Mr. Andrews states :

I was the managing agent of steel works on Staten island. I intend devoting myself to perfecting the barrels for Mr. Mullholland's order. I have no connexion with Mr. Mulholland. Parker, Snow, Brooks & Co., of Meriden, Connecticut, have a contract with Mr. Mulholland to deliver to him the finished arm, and I have a written contract with them to supply the rough barrels.

I am also furnishing in the Muir contract, having made a contract in the same way with Muir & Co. for 30,000 barrels. This gives me 80,000 barrels to furnish. The steel works can furnish three times as many, but no more have yet been agreed upon.

I have delivered a few barrels to Messrs. Muir & Co. on their order; these have worked well. I had two barrels tried at Springfield last week; they were tried in the gauges, and also by firing. Both were satisfactory, and I am now to furnish at the rate of forty per day on the Muir order, and to increase as fast as needed.

READING, PENNSYLVANIA, *April* 23, 1862.

GENTLEMEN : Messrs. Parker, Snow, Brooks & Co., who are at work for me to enable me to fulfil my contract with the government for furnishing fifty thousand rifled muskets, inform me that they are greatly embarrassed in their operations by the uncertainty that exists in the public mind about your action on their gun contracts; that machinists who are building machinery are loth to push forward their work until I know how my contract is to be treated by you; that the banks are discouraging the preparations they are making, and they are sadly perplexed to know what to do: to stop would incur great loss; and if your action should be favorable to my contract, these embarrassments are delaying them so much that the first delivery will be utterly out of the question without they can have an early assurance of your favorable decision.

I did not ask for this contract, but after consenting to take it and having promised to fulfil it, and having enlisted capital and got machinery built and being built, and incurred large responsibilities to enable me to be faithful in fulfilling my engagements, am I asking too much of you in urging your favorable, prompt reply ?

Very respectfully, your obedient servant,

JAMES MULHOLLAND.

Hon. JOSEPH HOLT, ROBERT DALE OWEN, and Major P. V. HAGNER,

Commissioners.

COMMISSION ON ORDNANCE AND ORDNANCE STORES,
Washington, May 17, 1862.

GENERAL: The commission have the honor to report as follows:

CASE No. 90.—JAMES MULHOLLAND, Reading, Pennsylvania.

Order by direction of the Secretary of War, January 7, 1862.—(See page 171, Ex. Doc. No. 67.)

To furnish 50,000 muskets, with appendages, of the Springfield pattern. To be delivered not less than 1,000 in each of the months of July, August, and September, 1862; not less than 2,000 in each of the months of October and November; not less than 3,000 in December; and not less than 4,000 per month thereafter, at $20 each.—(See case No. 72.)

The commission find that the above order was not given in accordance with the law and regulations, and that it is not, therefore, a contract of legal force, inasmuch as it does not contain the express requirements of the law, and was not made "after previous advertisement for proposals respecting the same;" nor can it be regarded as an "open purchase," being for articles which did not require "immediate delivery," but were stipulated to be manufactured and delivered at prescribed distant periods.

They further consider that the number ordered is larger than the wants of the government justify in this case at the price fixed, and therefore, according to the principles set forth in Mason's case, No. 72, they decide that the order to Mr. Mulholland be confirmed, subject to all its terms, to the extent of 25,000 muskets, upon condition that he shall, within fifteen days after receiving notice of this decision, execute bond, with good and sufficient sureties, in the form and with the stipulations prescribed by law and the regulations, for the performance of the contract, as thus modified, resulting from said order and acceptance; and upon his failure or refusal to execute such bond, then the said order shall be declared cancelled and of no effect.

The commission further decide that the deliveries, under the contract to be executed, shall be required at or within the periods stipulated in the original order, but that the numbers specified may be reduced proportionately to the reduction of the whole number, so that the contract shall be completed within the time allowed in the original order.

We are, sir, very respectfully, your obedient servants,

J. HOLT,
ROBERT DALE OWEN,
Commissioners, &c.
P. V. HAGNER,
Major of Ordnance, Assistant to Commission.

Brigadier General J. W. RIPLEY,
Chief of Ordnance.

READING, *June* 5, 1862.

GENTLEMEN: I have received a notice from General James Ripley, of the 28th of May, saying that my contract to build fifty thousand muskets of the Springfield pattern has been reduced by you to twenty-five thousand, and you inform me that I can go on and manufacture said twenty-five thousand muskets within the time stipulated in the order of January 7, 1862.

You have also sent me a bond to have executed and returned to you, containing the same terms and conditions as those contained in the original order from the Ordnance office of January 7, 1862, viz: "that in case of any failure to make delivery to the extent, and within the time specified, you are to forfeit the right to deliver whatever may be deficient in the specified number for the month in which the failure occurs."

You have added another clause, providing that, in case I fail to make my delivery, or in any respect to fulfil the contract, that I shall pay you damages not exceeding twenty-five thousand dollars, and further, that you shall have the privilege at your option in any such failure to make it null and void. These are terms and conditions that I never would have consented to, and such as does not seem right for you to ask. I am willing and ready to give bonds for any reasonable amount to faithfully perform the contract for twenty-five thousand muskets, according to the terms and conditions contained therein.

The uncertainty of the action of the commissioners upon my order of January 7, 1862, with their assertion that the contract was looked upon by them as *void* for want of legality, has prevented me for months in progressing as I otherwise should in my preparations to manufacture the muskets, and your decision to give but twenty-five thousand instead of fifty thousand has verified my fears that I should have been ruined if I put up all the machinery necessary to fulfil my contract as stipulated with the government. At this late moment I am informed that my contract is confirmed for twenty-five thousand muskets, and that I must deliver five hundred in sixty days or give the government the privilege to annul the contract altogether, and be subject to damages not exceeding twenty-five thousand dollars.

I cannot see the justice of asking me to execute such a bond, and think, upon bringing these facts to your notice, you will have it so modified as to cover simply the terms and conditions under which I agreed to take the contract. I should like to make another request, and that is, that you will so far modify, in relation to deliveries, that I shall have the right to deliver within the months of July, August, and September, fifteen hundred instead of five hundred in each month. I think I am entitled to this, from the uncertainty I have been obliged to labor under in respect to your final decision. I expect to be able by the 10th of August to turn out the arms finished, but I cannot, probably, much before that time, but can furnish in the three months the amount called for, viz: fifteen hundred.

Your prompt answer to my request will greatly oblige your humble servant,

JAMES MULHOLLAND.

Hon. Jos. Holt and Robert Dale Owen,
Commissioners.

Before commission.

Mr. Mulholland informed that the contracts are not intended to declare total forfeiture for failure in a monthly delivery, and that no other liability attaches to such failures than the forfeiture of the number due and not delivered.

All contracts are so altered upon application to the chief of ordnance.

P. V. HAGNER,
Major of Ordnance.

CASE No. 91.

F. L. BODINE.

PHILADELPHIA, *February* 1, 1862.

Sir: In accordance with the published order of you department, I have the honor to enclose herewith copies of the order of the Ordnance department for 25,000 Springfield rifle muskets, as contained in papers marked A, together with my replies and letters thereto relating, as contained in papers marked B.

I have made the necessary arrangements for the manufacture and delivery of the arms as specified in the contract, but hope and expect to commence the delivery earlier than required.

Recent newspaper articles have canvassed the possibility of annulling some of the contracts. Having acted in entire good faith in the matter, I do not believe I shall find aught different on the part of the government, and yet, from my large outlays and risks, an assurance from you to that effect would be a satisfaction.

Respectfully, your obedient servant,

F. L. BODINE.

Hon. EDWIN M. STANTON,
Secretary of War, Washington, D. C.

ORDNANCE OFFICE, *Washington, December* 12, 1861.

SIR: By direction of the Secretary of War I offer you an order for twenty-five thousand rifle muskets and appendages, on the following terms and conditions, viz: These arms are to be in all respects identical with the standard rifle musket made at the United States armory, Springfield, Massachusetts, and are to interchange with it and with each other in all their parts; they are to be subject to inspection, by United States inspectors, in the same manner that the Springfield arms are inspected, and none are to be received and paid for but such as pass inspection and are approved by the United States inspector. These twenty-five thousand arms and appendages are to be delivered at the United States arsenal, Bridesburgh, Pennsylvania, as follows, viz: Two thousand (2,000) in five months from this date; two thousand (2,000) more in six months from this date; and three thousand (3,000) additional per month thereafter, until the whole twenty-five thousand are delivered. In case of failure to make any of the deliveries in or within the times before specified, the government is to have authority to revoke and annul this order immediately, so far as regards the arms and appendages remaining undelivered at the time of such failure. Payments for each delivery are to be made, in such funds as the Treasury Department may provide, on certificate of inspection and receipt by the United States inspector, at the rate of twenty dollars ($20) for each arm, including appendages. All these arms and appendages are to be packed by you in boxes of the regular pattern, with twenty muskets and appendages in each box, for which a fair price, to be determined by the United States inspector, is to be allowed.

Please signify your acceptance or non-acceptance of this order, on the terms and conditions herein stated.

Respectfully, your obedient servant,

JAS. W. RIPLEY,
Brigadier General.

F. L. BODINE, Esq.,
Box 2,242, Philadelphia, Pennsylvania.

PHILADELPHIA, *December* 14, 1861.

SIR: Your favor of 12th instant, concerning order for arms and appendages, is at hand and noted. My proposition, as accepted by the Secretary of War, differs in two points from the order just received. These are, first, the government to inspect and pay for arms in lots of 100 or upwards, as I am ready to deliver. Secondly, your order provides for authority on part of government, on my failure to deliver any of the lots specified, to cancel the whole remaining order. My proposition is, only to cancel the undelivered part of the month's quota in which such failure may occur, but in nowise to affect any other portion of the order. This clause is only intended to protect me in case of failure arising from unavoidable causes. With these modifications I accept the order. Please forward at your early convenience an order embodying the above.

Respectfully, your obedient servant,

F. L. BODINE.

Brigadier General JAMES W. RIPLEY, •
    Ordnance Department, Washington, D. C.

N. B.—The two last words of the third line from the last cannot be certainly read from the copy, but they convey about the sense.

ORDNANCE OFFICE,
Washington, December 27, 1861.

SIR: In answer to your letters respecting the orders to you of the 12th instant for 25,000 rifle muskets and appendages, I have to state that there will be no difficulty in regard to the inspections and payments for the arms as the order now stands. Whenever you are ready for an inspection, and so notify this office, it will be attended to as soon as possible, consistently with the public interest, but the separate inspection of parcels so small as one hundred would involve much unnecessary trouble and expense. You are hereby authorized to substitute for the provision respecting failure to deliver, contained in the order of the 12th instant, the following, viz: "In case of any failure to deliver to the extent and within the times specified, you are to forfeit the right to deliver whatever number may be deficient in the specified number for the month in which the failure occurs." The arms to be furnished under your order must conform in all respects to the samples from the United States armory.

Respectfully, your obedient servant,

JAS. W. RIPLEY,
Brigadier General.

F. L. BODINE, Esq.,
    Philadelphia, Pa.

PHILADELPHIA, *January* 15, 1862.

SIR: I find, in common with other manufacturers of arms for government, that it is impossible to furnish gunstocks of weather-seasoned timber, and to fill the order of government of 12th December ultimo I will be obliged to use kiln-dried wood. This is now being done at the armory at Springfield. As my contract only impliedly covers this case, I desire the permission of the department to use kiln-dried wood, provided those furnished equal in manufacture those now made at the Springfield armory.

Your early reply will much oblige your obedient servant,

F. L. BODINE.

Brigadier General JAS. W. RIPLEY,
    Chief of Ordnance Department U. S., Washington, D. C.

ORDNANCE OFFICE,
Washington, January 17, 1862.

SIR: I have received your letter of the 15th instant, respecting stocks for the Springfield muskets, to be delivered under your order. In answer I have to state that stocks equal in quality and finish to those made at the Springfield armory will be accepted, whether made of weather-seasoned or kiln-dried wood. The former is preferable if it can be obtained; but either kind must be thoroughly seasoned.

Respectfully, your obedient servant,

JAS. W. RIPLEY,
Brigadier General.

F. L. BODINE, Esq.,
Philadelphia, Pa.

Before commission, May 2, 1862.

Mr. F. L. Bodine states:

Mr. Mason, of Taunton, Massachusetts, furnishes my barrels, and he is responsible for their delivery in time to make good my order. He should have delivered 2,000 about a month since, but he has not yet done so. I cannot hold him responsible for his failure in the first month's delivery, am not sure that I could for the second, but I am sure that I can for the third. The reason of this indeterminativeness is, that he agreed in writing to have the barrels in time for the other work. In conversation I have stated that I did not expect to be ready, as some of the other work is not ready for first delivery. I am sure that he feels bound to deliver this month, and I can hold him responsible for failure if he does not. Mr. Redfield, of New York, has contracted to deliver my stocks. He is bound the same as Mr. Mason. In conversation with him he has stated that if I had demanded stocks for the first delivery he could have furnished them. As neither party was ready, however, that delivery has been postponed, I expect the delivery in time for my second lot, and will hold him responsible for failure.

I have made no definite arrangement about mountings, but I have made inquiries so as to get them with the least delay as soon as the commission make their decision.

My locks are to be made by Williams & Co., of Philadelphia, although my contract was made with E. P. Coleman, who has since joined the Messrs. Williams & Co. They are ready to deliver to me. Mr. Coleman is responsible to me for rods, and he is now ready to deliver to me.

My actual disbursements have only been for expenses in travelling, &c., but my obligations to sub-contractors are absolute, and must be met by me. I have made no arrangements as yet for my bayonets. My sights are to be made by Gillingham, Bowling & Co., of Trenton. They are ready for their first delivery.

Mr. Norris, of Springfield, has agreed to furnish my appendages. I have not seen or heard from him, but I presume he is ready.

In all the sub-contracts I have made I presume I must bear such responsibility as can be shown to result actually from any refusal I may make to accept when offered.

The makers of sights and locks have both reported to me that they were ready to deliver whenever I was ready to receive. I look upon this as a formal notice of compliance on their part, and I suppose it will be so considered by them. They all know of the existence of the commission, and they are all awaiting its actions.

I applied to Mr. Mason to know if he would release me of my obligations to him. He said he supposed he could do so, but he has since said that if the stoppage of arms making is to be so general as to cause him loss for his preparations, he should have to hold all parties to their bargains with him.

PHILADELPHIA, *May* 5, 1862.

SIRS: Having understood that it is desirable to the government to reduce the contracts for Springfield muskets, I would be willing, if you so desire, that my contract of 12th December, 1861, be changed from 25,000 to 20,000 rifled muskets, with an extension of time of commencement of deliveries to 2,000 during July.

In addition, I would only repeat for your consideration that at the start inducements were held out of a duplicate contract, when I could report my ability to fill it; but that now this cannot be, and that the difficulties of filling the small order are greater even than for a small one.

Hoping you will deem this fair and liberal, and for your early reply hereto, I am, with great respect, your obedient servant,

F. L. BODINE, P. O. Box 2.242.

Hon. JOSEPH HOLT and ROBERT DALE OWEN,
    Commission on Ordnance and Ordnance Stores.

PHILADELPHIA, May 13, 1862.

GENTLEMEN: On the 5th instant I wrote you, with proposition, concerning my contract for Springfield rifle muskets, which I trusted would be acceptable, and had hoped for reply by this time. Permit me to request your earliest attention, or, if the delay is at Ordnance office, having been passed by you, can you not influence an early reply? Four months of delay have now elapsed, and, as you can conceive, have been attended with serious detriment.

Very respectfully, your obedient servant,

F. L. BODINE.

Hon. JOS. HOLT and ROBERT DALE OWEN,
    Commission on Ordnance and Ordnance Stores.

NEW YORK, June 4, 1862.

SIRS: I came over yesterday from Philadelphia, hoping to meet your Mr. Owen here, but was too late. At an interview with him about ten days since, I was informed that my contract had been reported at 20,000, and he *thought* with the extension for first deliveries to August, as asked for; and, also, that my papers would probably meet me on my return home. I have not yet received them, but yet am acting on the above statement.

As Mr. Owen did not positively remember as to the extension for first delivery, permit me to urge upon your attention further that this point is essential, and but equitable alike from the delays occasioned by the department, from the reduction proposed in the contract, and from the unexpected difficulties affecting me, as all others, engaged in these matters.

With the proposed extension I do not object to the change in the number to 20,000, nor will it in any measure diminish my efforts to deliver the guns as rapidly as possible.

Hoping for your favorable consideration of these points, if not already settled in accordance therewith, and for your early reply hereto, I am, with great respect, your obedient servant,

F. L. BODINE.

Hon. JOSEPH HOLT and ROBT. DALE OWEN,
    Commission on Ordnance and Ordnance Stores, Washington, D. C.

WASHINGTON, June 10, 1862.

SIRS: My contract, as modified and received from Ordnance department, requires deliveries of 1,600 in each of the months of June and July, &c. I desire a modification, that " in case of failure to deliver all or part of the first two months' deliveries, I do not forfeit the right to deliver afterwards, provided the same are delivered within the whole time named for the delivery of the 20,000."

This extension will in no degree affect the energy with which I shall strive to fill my contract, but, on the contrary, my effort and expectation will be to finish deliveries earlier than the contract requires.

This change seems proper, because it is only within a few days that I have received the contract, and June is almost gone, and also some little margin to be allowed in prosecuting an undertaking proved to be so very difficult, and the great damage to result if disappointed in our expectations.

If the above meets with your favor, please request the chief of ordnance to so notify me at as early day as possible; and with this provision I accept the reduction to 20,000.

Very respectfully, your obedient servant,

F. L. BODINE.

Hon. Jos. Holt and Robt. Dale Owen,
Commission on Ordnance and Ordnance Stores.

Washington, *May* 17, 1862.

General: The commission have the honor to report as follows:

Case No. 91.—F. L. Bodine, Philadelphia, Pennsylvania.

Order by direction of the Secretary of War, dated December 12, 1861.—(See page 150, Ex. Doc. No. 67.)

To furnish 25,000 rifled muskets and appendages, in all respects identical with the standard Springfield arm, at the price of $20 for each gun, including appendages. Deliveries to be made as follows: 2,000 in five months from date, May 12; 2,000 in six months from date, June 12; 3,000 additional per month thereafter, until all are delivered.—(See case No. 72.)

The commission find that the above order was not given in accordance with law and the regulations, and that it is not therefore a contract of legal force, inasmuch as it does not contain the express requirements of the law, and was not made "after previous advertisement for proposals respecting the same;" nor can it be regarded as an "open purchase," being for articles which did not require "immediate delivery," but were stipulated to be manufactured and delivered at distant prescribed periods.

They further consider that the number ordered is larger than the wants of the government justify in this case, at the fixed price, and therefore, according to the principles set forth in Mason's case, No. 72, they decide that the order to Mr. Bodine be confirmed, subject to all its terms, to the extent of 20,000 muskets, upon condition that he shall, within fifteen days after receiving notice of this decision, execute bond, with good and sufficient sureties, in the form and with the stipulations prescribed by law and the regulations, for the performance of the contract as thus modified, resulting from said order and acceptance; and, upon his failure or refusal to execute such bond, then the said order shall be declared cancelled and of no effect.

The commission further decide that the deliveries under the contract to be executed shall be made at the rate of 1,600 in the month of July, 1,600 in the month of August, and 2,250 per month thereafter.

We are, sir, very respectfully, your obedient servants,

J. HOLT,
ROBERT DALE OWEN,
Commissioners, &c.

P. V. HAGNER,
Major of Ordnance, Assistant to Commission.

Brigadier General J. W. Ripley,
Chief of Ordnance.

Ex. Doc. 72——27

CASE No. 92.

E. J. DuPont & Co.

COMMISSION ON ORDNANCE AND ORDNANCE STORES,
Washington, May 26, 1862.

GENERAL: The commission have the honor to report as follows:

CASE No. 92.—Messrs. E. J. DuPont & Co., Wilmington, Delaware.

Account of purchase and shipment of saltpetre on account of the United States. Abstract of expenses, dated March 31, 1862. Final account current, closed by receipt of assistant treasurer of United States for balance, dated April 2, 1862.

By the concurrent action of the Secretary of State, Assistant Secretary of War, and Secretary of the Treasury, Mr. Lammont DuPont, of the above firm, visited England twice, furnished with a credit of £82,800 7s. 1d., upon the Messrs. Baring Brothers, and purchased and shipped saltpetre at a cost of £79,699 16s. 8d.

Referred by special direction of the Secretary of War, May 22, 1862.

The commission find that the transaction above was not conducted in exact accordance with the terms of the law and regulations, but that, in the opinion of the high officers of the government named, the course pursued was necessary and prudent; that Mr. Lammont DuPont conducted the affair satisfactorily and advantageously, and has rendered a full and formal account of the disbursement of the funds intrusted to him, supported by sub-vouchers, and closed by the receipt, for the unexpended balance, of the assistant treasurer of the United States at Philadelphia. The commission therefore direct that the accounts be examined and audited as usual, without objection on account of informality in ordering the purchase.

We are, sir, very respectfully, your obedient servants,

J. HOLT,
ROBERT DALE OWEN,
Commissioners, &c.

P. V. HAGNER,
Major of Ordnance, Assistant to Commission.

Brigadier General J. W. RIPLEY,
Chief of Ordnance.

CASE No. 93.

WARREN FISHER, Jr.

HOUSE OF REPRESENTATIVES,
Washington, April 24, 1862.

DEAR SIRS: Permit me to introduce to you the bearer, Warren Fisher, jr., esq., of Boston, Massachusetts, who is one of my constituents, and well known to me as a gentleman of great respectability.

Mr. Fisher wishes to see you in reference to some business that he will explain, and my object in writing this note is to assure you that any statement he may make is entitled to your confidence and consideration.

With great respect, I have the honor to be, your obedient servant,

J. HOOPER, *M. C.*

Hon. JOSEPH HOLT and ROBERT DALE OWEN.

BOSTON, *March* 22, 1862.

SIR: Understanding through our papers that the Secretary of War, honorable E. M. Stanton, has appointed honorables Joseph Holt and Robert Dale Owen commissioners to examine contracts with government for furnishing arms and ammunition, I have taken the liberty to forward to them, through you, all documents relating to our contract in order to assist them in their labors. I will consider it a favor if you will please hand the enclosed documents, as directed, to Messrs. Holt and Owen at your earliest convenience, for which trouble I shall be under many obligations. I am desirous that the documents reach the parties at as early date as possible. If I send direct to them there will be no acknowledgment of their receipt, hence I am obliged to trouble you; will thank you to advise me of their delivery.

I remain, respectfully yours,

WARREN FISHER, JR.

Hon. ALEXANDER H. RICE, *Washington.*

OFFICE OF THE SPENCER REPEATING RIFLE COMPANY,
Boston, Massachusetts, May 27, 1862.

GENTLEMEN: On the 26th of December, 1861, I received from General James W. Ripley, chief of ordnance, an order for ten thousand Spencer repeating rifles, on certain conditions as to price, mode of manufacture, and time of delivery, all of which conditions were assented to; and on the 31st of the same month the order formally accepted by me, as one of the owners of the rifle authorized to act for the others. With this acceptance the contract was perfected, and, as we understood it, made mutually and honorably binding. We at once organized ourselves, under the statutes of Massachusetts, as the "Spencer Repeating Rifle Company," and proceeded without a day's delay to perform our part of the contract, and in so doing expended a large sum of money within a very brief period, and the outlay has continued steadily ever since, until the sum actually paid out has reached an aggregate of $132,647 58. With contracts, obligations, and purchases already made, but not yet fulfilled and delivered, our gross expenditures foot up to the sum of over $198,000. We occupy as an armory a building whose value is not less than $200,000, and have added thereto large improvements of a permanent character at great cost, and with the exception of the United States armory, at Springfield, and Mr. Colt's establishment, at Hartford, we claim to have the most extensive and completely fitted armory in the country, amply prepared to manufacture every part of our arm in the most superior style. All these outlays, purchases, and improvements have been made directly in consequence of our contract with government. I enclose herewith, on sheet marked A, a copy of General Ripley's order for the rifles, together with copies of my proposition to furnish them, and my acceptance of the terms enjoined by him.

In addition to the assurance of validity conveyed in an order coming to us directly over the signature of General Ripley, and by express direction of the Secretary of War, we have received from time to time the most satisfactory confirmations, both expressed and implied, that our contract was recognized by the War Department as of full force and effect. Shortly after the retirement of Mr. Cameron from the cabinet, feeling somewhat anxious on account of the newspaper and congressional comments on the mode in which contracts for arms had been issued, I caused an inquiry to be made at the War Department in regard to our order, and on the 25th of January received from the Assistant Secretary a written assurance that he "had heard of no reason why the contract should be rescinded; that the gun is a good one and needed for our sharpshooters—an arm of the service for which it is intended."

On the 29th of January Secretary Stanton issued a public notice requiring all contractors for arms to furnish copies of their contracts, and with this order we promptly complied, by mailing duplicates of our contract to the Secretary on the 4th and 5th of February, accompanying each with an explanatory note, a copy of which is enclosed on sheet marked B. As we received no reply from the war office, our natural and only inference was that our contract and our progress and expenditures under it were in all respects satisfactory to the department.

Still further, when your honorable commission was organized I forwarded to you a copy of our contract, with a statement of our proceedings under it; and, to be entirely assured that you should duly receive it, I enclosed it to honorable A. H. Rice, representative in Congress from this district, requesting that he deliver it in person, which he subsequently informed me he had done. I enclose a copy of what I then sent to you, on sheet marked C. You will observe that I respectfully requested to be summoned by you if there was need of my personal presence, and not receiving such summons was naturally construed by me as an additional assurance that our contract could in no respect call for change or modification at your hands, and that the large expenditures which I informed you we had made and were making under it received your sanction and approbation.

On the 24th of April, being in Washington for the purpose of laying our pattern rifle before General Ripley, (see letter to General Ripley, sheet marked D,) as required by his order, I called upon your commission and made a request in writing to the effect that we might be allowed to deliver all the rifles covered by our order, provided we did so within the period originally assigned for the completion of the whole number. This request was made upon the admission that the deliveries required in the first few months could not be made, and by strict construction of our contract the right to deliver for those months would be forfeited. In a personal interview of more than an hour's duration, no hint was given me of an intention to abridge in any way our rights under the contract, and I left with the impression that the request which I had submitted in writing would in due season be granted, and with the specific assurance that I should hear from you promptly through the Ordnance office. For copy of the request see sheet marked E.

After these repeated and significant recognitions of the validity of a contract originally obtained in the most direct and open manner, you can conceive my surprise when, on the 15th instant, being again in Washington for the purpose of exhibiting our carbine, I received an intimation from your commission of an intention to change the nature of the contract and very essentially to modify its terms. As we have been well nigh five months at work for government, and have made a vast outlay solely and directly in consequence of the order from General Ripley, you can appreciate the grave embarrassment and anxiety caused by your verbal communications to me on the 15th. Our machinery is of the best and most expensive character, and most of it made with special adaptation to our own gun, and we could not enter upon the manufacture of any other species of arm without commencing *de novo*. Indeed, the machinery and tools particularly adapted to our rifle and utterly useless even for our small carbine, have cost us at least $75,000, and if the manufacture of the rifle should be abandoned by your order, this machinery and these tools would be a total loss upon our hands. With the sense of justice which I know must govern your proceedings, I am quite sure that you would not throw this loss upon us, and I therefore rest confidently in the belief that whatever modification you may make in our contract, you will protect us by an allowance for an outlay made in entire good faith and in pursuance of an order from government.

If, however, it has been resolved, as you intimated to me, to prohibit the introduction of any breech-loading arm in the infantry service, it becomes of course necessary to make such a modification and compromise of our contract as will release the government from all obligation to receive an arm which it has been determined not to use, and at the same time shield us from ruinous loss. I therefore cheerfully comply with your request to submit a proposition which may form the basis of an equitable adjustment of all the questions at issue between the government and our company. I propose, therefore, the following:

1. That the government pay us the amount expended for machinery and tools specially adapted to our rifle, and which will be useless if the manufacture of that arm is abandoned; the amount to be ascertained by appraisal, from actual examination and inspection and the production of vouchers.

2. That the government change our order from rifles to carbines for the cavalry service—6,500 carbines of the large size, weighing about nine pounds; 6,500 of the smaller size, say, six and a half pounds. The uniform price to be $30; deliveries to be at the rate of 1,000 per month, commencing in August next. If any failure occurs in any month, right to deliver deficiency for said month forfeited.

As to the merit of our arm, I think there is a general concurrence of favorable opinion on the part of those who have given it a critical examination. I can refer with special satisfaction to the written judgment of Major Dyer, of the Springfield armory; Colonel Kingsbury, of General McClellan's staff; Captain Dahlgren, of the navy; and to the report of the board of examination specially appointed by General McClellan to test the arm. These several opinions are on file in the Ordnance office. I should be glad to submit the arm to any further examination you may desire, with special reference to its uses and advantages for cavalry service. In respect to strength and compactness of construction, security against getting out of order, safety, accuracy, range, and rapidity in firing, I should be glad to have it compared with any other arm in service. It can be used indifferently as a "repeater" or "single-loader," and, I respectfully submit, is unsurpassed for efficiency in either capacity. Its peculiar merit is as a "repeater;" but without this feature I think it will stand a successful comparison with any other breech-loading arm yet invented.

In addition to the disastrous loss to be entailed upon us by the suspension of our contract, the numerous artisans in our employment would, with their families, suffer the keenest deprivation. Many of these workmen have been induced by us, on account of their superior skill, to come from distant parts of the country, and to give up situations in which they might have continued had we not made them offers of permanent employment and liberal compensation, based on our confidence in our contract with the government. Were we to cease operations these men would be thrown out of employment at a time when it would be difficult, if not impossible, to procure labor. I offer this consideration as one appealing alike to your sense of humanity and justice. The loyal people are making all needful sacrifices to sustain the government, and, in turn, those who represent the government will, I know, deal magnanimously, and not harshly, with the people.

It may not be out of place for me to remark that our arm is not in speculative or adventurous hands. The gentleman who invented it, and whose name it bears, is directly interested in its manufacture under the present contract, and those only share with him who advanced the requisite means for perfecting the invention and securing the patent both at home and abroad. Having incurred all the risk and outlay, they only ask a share of the profits, if any shall accrue.

In closing it may be proper to say, lest silence on that point should be misconstrued, that our contract was obtained in the most direct and business-like manner, without the aid or intervention of any agent, attorney, or "middle-man," and that our company have not paid, and have not agreed to pay, a single dollar to any outside person; nor was congressional or political influence used or evoked in any manner, direct or indirect, near or remote.

Such a contract, obtained in the most open and honorable manner, and faithfully executed to the very best of our ability thus far, with so large an expenditure of our private means, is submitted to your judgment, with the confident belief, already expressed, that however you may feel called upon to modify it, you will, at least, protect us from loss, and preserve to us those rights to which we think we are entitled by the plainest principles of equity.

I am ready to come to Washington to confer with you at any moment you may summon me; and in the meantime we shall continue to perfect the machinery and tools necessary to carry out the contract, whose obligations are still upon us. I may be allowed to suggest that it is exceedingly desirable for us to have the matter adjusted at the earliest day your official engagements will allow.

I remain, very respectfully, your obedient servant,

WARREN FISHER, JR.,
Treasurer of Spencer Repeating Rifle Company.

Hon. JOSEPH HOLT and ROBERT DALE OWEN,
Commissioners, &c.

A.

WASHINGTON, *December* 18, 1861.

SIR: The proprietors of the Spencer repeating rifle propose to contract with the United States for the manufacture and delivery of 10,000 of said arms, with triangular bayonets and the usual appendages for service, at the rate of forty dollars ($40) for each rifle, complete.

The whole number of rifles to be delivered for inspection, at the manufactory in Boston, within the year 1862, as follows:

500 in the month of March.

1,000 in each of the months of April, May, June, July, August, September, October, and November.

1,500 in the month of December.

Your obedient servant,

WARREN FISHER, JR.
One of the Proprietors of the Spencer Repeating Rifle.

Hon. SIMON CAMERON,
Secretary of War.

ORDNANCE OFFICE,
Washington, December 26, 1861.

SIR: By direction of the Secretary of War, I offer you an order for ten thousand (10,000) Spencer breech-loading magazine rifles, with angular bayonets, and appendages, on the following terms and conditions, viz: These rifles are all to be of the same pattern, and of the calibre .58 inch, and are to be subject to inspection and proof by such inspectors as this department may designate for the purpose. They are to be made according to a pattern to be previously submitted by you for examination, and approved at this office, and to serve as a standard in the inspection; and none are to be received or paid for but such as are approved by the United States inspectors as, in all respects, like and equal in quality to the standard. These rifles are to be delivered by you, at your armory, as follows, viz: not less than five hundred (500) in March, 1862, and not less than one thousand (1,000) per month thereafter, until the whole ten thousand (10,000) shall have been delivered; and you are to have the right to deliver more rapidly than according to the number of arms before specified, if you can do so. In case of any failure to make deliveries to the extent and within the times before specified, you are to forfeit the right to deliver whatever number may be deficient in the specified number for the month in which the failure occurs. All these arms and appendages are to be delivered by you, and this order, if transferred by you to another party, is to be thereby forfeited. Payments are to be made in such funds as the Treasury Department may provide for each delivery, on certificates of inspection and receipts by United State inspectors, at the rate of forty dollars ($40) for each arm complete, including appendages. All these arms and appendages are to be packed by you in good boxes, with twenty (20) rifles and appendages in each box, for which a fair price, to be determined by the United States inspectors, will be allowed.

Please signify, in writing, your acceptance or non-acceptance of this order, on the terms and conditions herein stated.

Respectfully, your obedient servant,

JAMES W. RIPLEY,
Brigadier General.

WARREN FISHER, Jr., Esq., *Boston, Mass.*

BOSTON, *December* 31, 1861.

DEAR SIR: Yours is received as follows:

"ORDNANCE OFFICE,
" *Washington, December* 26, 1861.

"SIR: By direction of the Secretary of War, I offer you an order for ten thousand (10,000) Spencer breech-loading magazine rifles, with angular bayonets and appendages, on the following terms and conditions, viz: These rifles are all to be of the same pattern, and of the calibre .58-inch, and are to be subject to inspection and proof by such inspectors as this department may designate for the purpose. They are to be made according to a pattern, to be previously submitted by you for examination and approval at this office, and to serve as a standard in the inspection; and none are to be received or paid for but such as are approved by the United States inspectors, as in all respects like and equal in quality to the standard. These rifles are to be delivered by you, at your armory, as follows, viz: Not less than five hundred (500) in March, 1862; and not less than one thousand (1,000) per month thereafter, until the whole ten thousand (10,000) shall have been delivered; and you are to have the right to deliver more rapidly than according to the number of arms before specified, if you can do so. In case of any failure to make deliveries to the extent and within the times before specified, you are to forfeit the right to deliver whatever number may be deficient in the specified number for the month in which the failure occurs. All these arms and appendages are to be delivered by you; and this order, if transferred by you to another party, is to be forfeited. Payments are to be made in such funds as the Treasury Department may provide for each delivery, on certificates of inspection and receipts by the United States inspectors, at the rate of forty dollars ($40) for each arm complete, including appendages. All these arms and appendages are to be packed by you in good boxes, with twenty (20) rifles and appendages in each box, for which a fair price, to be determined by the United States inspectors, will be allowed.

"Please signify, in writing, your acceptance or non-acceptance of this order, on the terms and conditions herein stated.

"Respectfully, your obedient servant,

"JAMES W. RIPLEY,
" *Brigadier General.*

" WARREN FISHER, Jr., Esq.,
" *Boston, Massachusetts.*"

I hereby signify, in writing, my acceptance of the order therein referred to, on the terms and conditions therein stated

Respectfully, your obedient servant,

WARREN FISHER, JR.

Brigadier General J. W. RIPLEY.

B.

[Duplicate.]

OFFICE OF THE SPENCER REPEATING RIFLE COMPANY,
Boston, February 4, 1862.

SIR: In response to your order of the 29th of January, I have the honor to enclose you a copy of an order from the Ordnance office, by direction of the Secretary of War, dated December 26, 1861, for ten thousand Spencer repeating rifles. On the 31st of the same month the order was formally accepted by me, in writing, on the terms and conditions therein stated.

The contract thus made will be carefully and faithfully executed by the company represented by the undersigned, with the exception of the first month's delivery, afterwards the arms will be furnished, I trust, even more rapidly than the order directs. Already a large sum of money, exceeding one hundred thousand dollars, ($100,000,) has been expended in filling the order, and no effort or outlay will be spared in completing it at the earliest practicable period.

I remain, very respectfully, your obedient servant,

WARREN FISHER, JR.,
Treasurer Spencer Repeating Rifle Company.

Hon. E. M. STANTON,
Secretary of War.

C.

SPENCER REPEATING RIFLE COMPANY,
Chickering's Building, Tremont street, Boston, March 22, 1862.

GENTLEMEN: I notice by our newspaper reports that you are appointed commissioners by the Secretary of War (Hon. E. M. Stanton) to examine the contracts of the government for arms and ammunition, and I have taken the liberty, in hopes of giving what little aid I can to your labors, to send you copies of my letters and contract with the government for the Spencer repeating rifle. The manufacture of the rifles is being vigorously pressed at our armory, Chickering's building, Boston, and the pattern rifle as standard, as directed by General Ripley in his order, will be forwarded to the department in a few days.

If you should desire to see me personally, please give me a few days' notice, as I am very much engaged in active duties. Please address me at this city.

I remain, very respectfully, your obedient servant,

WARREN FISHER, JR., *Treasurer.*

Hons. JOSEPH HOLT and ROBERT DALE OWEN,
Washington.

D.

SPENCER REPEATING RIFLE COMPANY,
Chickering's Building, Tremont street, Boston, April 23, 1862.

SIR: Herewith I lay before you a Spencer repeating rifle as a pattern by which those ordered in your letter of December 31, 1861, will be manufactured.

Some unexpected but unavoidable delays in the requisite perfection of our machinery postpone somewhat the earlier delivery we had hoped to make, but we feel entirely assured of our ability to furnish the whole number within the period assigned by you.

I have the honor to remain, very respectfully, your obedient servant.

WARREN FISHER, JR.,
Treasurer.

Brigadier General JAMES W. RIPLEY,
Chief of Ordnance, War Department.

E.

WASHINGTON, *April* 24, 1862.

GENTS : Under date of 22d ultimo, from Boston, I conveyed to you a copy of the contract made by the ordnance bureau for the manufacture of ten thousand Spencer repeating rifles. The letter and accompanying documents were handed to you by the Hon. A. H. Rice, M. C. Owing to some unexpected, and, to our company, very expensive delays in perfecting the machinery in our armory, we are unable to make the deliveries called for in the first four months, and, according to the letter of the contract, we lose the right to deliver the number of rifles required in those months. In consideration, however, of our very large outlays, amounting already to some $135,000, and of the good faith with which we have labored to fill the contract, we respectfully ask that we may have the right to furnish the whole ten thousand rifles, provided we do it within the period originally assigned in the order from the Ordnance office.

I remain, respectfully, your obedient servant,

WARREN FISHER, JR.,
Treasurer Spencer Repeating Rifle Company.

Hon. JOSEPH HOLT and ROBERT DALE OWEN,
Commissioners, &c.

WAR DEPARTMENT, *December* 10, 1861.

SIR: Please examine the reports heretofore made upon the Henry and Spencer gun, and (in connexion with your own examination of the gun) report to this department your opinion upon its merits as an arm such as is needed by the government.

Respectfully,

THOMAS A. SCOTT,
Assistant Secretary.

General RIPLEY,
Chief of Ordnance.

ORDNANCE OFFICE, *Washington, December* 11, 1861.

SIR: As directed from the War Department, I have examined the reports upon the Henry and Spencer guns, accompanying the propositions to furnish those arms to the government, and have also examined the arms. Both of them are magazine arms; that is to say, they have the cartridges for use carried in a magazine attached to or forming part of the arm, and fed out by a spiral spring. They require a special kind of ammunition, which must be primed or have the fulminate in itself. The reports heretofore made are favorable, so far as the limited trials went; but they do not go further than to suggest or recommend the procurement of a sufficient number to place in the hands of troops in the field for trial. Indeed it is impossible, except where arms are defective in principle, to decide, with confidence, in advance of such practical trials, on their value, or otherwise, as military weapons. I regard the weight of the arms, with the loaded magazine, as objectionable, and also the requirement of a special ammunition, rendering it impossible to use the arms with ordinary cartridges, or with powder and ball. It remains to be shown by practical trial what will be the effect on the cartridges in the magazine of carrying them on horseback, when they will be exposed to being crushed or marred, possibly to such extent as to interfere with their free passage into the barrel; and whether they will be safe in transportation with the fulminate in the cartridge; also, what will be the effect on the spiral spring of long use and exposure in the field. I do not discover any important advantage of these arms over several other breech-loaders, as the rapidity of fire with these latter is sufficiently great for useful purposes, without the objection to increased weight from the charges in the arm itself, while the multiplication of arms and ammunition of different kinds and patterns and working on different principles is decidedly objectionable, and should, in my opinion, be stopped by the refusal to introduce any more, unless upon the most full and complete evidence of their great superiority.

In view of the foregoing, of the very high prices asked for these arms, and of the fact that the government is already pledged on orders and contracts for nearly 73,000 breech-loading rifles and carbines, to the amount of two and a quarter millions of dollars, I do not consider it advisable to entertain or accept either of the propositions for furnishing these arms.

Respectfully, your obedient servant,

JAS. W. RIPLEY,
Brigadier General.

Hon. SIMON CAMERON,
　Secretary of War.

ORDNANCE OFFICE,
Washington, D. C., April 26, 1862.

SIR: I have to acknowledge the receipt of Major P. V. Hagner's letter of the 26th instant, in relation to the Spencer magazine rifles. I enclose herewith my letter to the Secretary of War, dated December 9, 1861, on this subject, which gives my views in reference to the propriety of introducing such an arm into the service.

I am unable to find in the records of this office any reports on this arm. Those referred to in my letter of December 9 must have been returned to the War Department.

With regard to the sample arm furnished by the contractors, it appears to be well finished, but as I consider the use of malleable iron mountings as decidedly objectionable, and as a portion of the parts of this gun are made of this material, I should not be willing to sanction its use as a model by which to make other guns.

Respectfully, your obedient servant,

JAMES W. RIPLEY,
Brigadier General.

J. WISE, Esq.,
　Secretary Commission on Ordnance Stores.

Before the commission, April 25, 1862.

Warren Fisher, jr., came before the commission relative to contracts for Spencer repeating rifles, and having been sworn, says:

That under agreement 500 guns were due in March and 1,000 in April. We have none ready, and can have none prior to July. The sample arm required by our order has been presented to the Ordnance office yesterday, but is not as yet approved. It has not been inspected at all nor subjected to any proof. We have all the machinery requisite to make a gun according to this pattern, which itself was made by this machine, and we have working and standard gauges for all parts of the gun. We have some few parts forged, but cannot go on until the pattern is approved. We have put our men to work on tools, and have about 130 so employed. We have intended to turn out fifty guns per day of ten hours, when under full headway, and do all the work in our own shops. We intend using solid steel bars for barrels, and to bore them at our shops; barrel turning and milling all smaller machines also as above. We have been delayed also by the machinists. The navy have 700 to be delivered by us first. As we have invested, actually disbursed, and contracted for $135,000 or more in this business, we request that the full number of 10,000 may be furnished to the army, provided all can be delivered by us within the same ultimate period originally stipulated, prior to January 1863. We can make no proposition to reduce the price, nor change the order to the Springfield pattern.

COMMISSION ON ORDNANCE AND ORDNANCE STORES,
Washington, April 26, 1862.

GENERAL: Should there be any reports in your office relative to the Spencer magazine rifle the commission request that they be sent to them, as well as your own views in reference to the propriety of introducing such an arm into service. They would also desire to know whether the sample arm furnished by the contractor is satisfactory to the department.

Very respectfully, your obedient servant,
P. V. HAGNER,
Major of Ordnance.

General J. W. RIPLEY, Chief of Ordnance.

ORDNANCE OFFICE,
War Department, Washington, June 9, 1862.

SIR: Referring to my letter of the 26th April on the subject of the model Spencer breech-loading rifle presented for the approval of this office, and in which objection was made to the model on account of some parts of the gun having the appearance of being made of malleable iron, I have now to say that if these parts prove to be made of wrought iron I see no objection to accepting the gun as the model arm for this contract.

Respectfully, your obedient servant,
JAMES W. RIPLEY,
Brigadier General.

J. WISE, Esq.,
    Secretary Commission on Ordnance Stores, Washington, D. C.

WASHINGTON, June 9, 1862.

GENTLEMEN: Having been informed by your honorable commission that our contract for the Spencer repeating rifle has been confirmed, by your giving us the right to deliver seventy-five hundred (7,500) rifles, commencing in the month of June for the first delivery, and owing to some unexpected delays on the part of the Ordnance department in not notifying us of the acceptance of the pattern rifle presented to them by us in the month of April, thereby causing an unavoidable delay on our part in the manufacture of the rifle, we respectfully ask of your honorable commission that you extend the time of our first delivery to the month of August.

I remain, respectfully, your obedient servant,

WARREN FISHER, Jr.,
Treasurer Spencer Repeating Rifle Company.

Hon. JOSEPH HOLT and ROBERT DALE OWEN,
Commissioners, &c.

WASHINGTON, *June* 10, 1862.

GENTLEMEN : In consideration of the very extra heavy expense necessary to carry out our contract for the manufacture of the first one thousand Spencer repeating rifles (caused by the delay in not accepting of pattern rifle deliveries in the month of April) to be delivered in the month of July, which delivery we intend to make, we propose to your honorable commission by your granting us the extension asked for in my favor of the 9th instant, making the first month delivery in August instead of July, to deduct from the price of the first month's delivery five dollars per rifle on all rifles delivered in said month of August, thereby giving to government that portion of extra cost which must necessarily fall upon us. We would add it is our intention to deliver the whole 7,500 rifles by working extra time. We think, without doubt, we shall make the first delivery in July, but would prefer to make the deduction to government on the first month's delivery, providing such a proposition will meet with your favor and you grant us our request.

I remain, respectfully yours,

WARREN FISHER, Jr.,
Treasurer of Spencer Repeating Rifle Company.

Hon. JOSEPH HOLT and ROBERT DALE OWEN,
Commissioners, &c.

COMMISSION ON ORDNANCE AND ORDNANCE STORES,
Washington, May 31, 1862.

GENERAL: The commission have the honor to report as follows:

CASE No. 93.—WARREN FISHER, Jr., Agent, Boston, Massachusetts.

Order by direction of the Secretary of War, dated December 26, 1862.—(See Ex. Doc., page 168.) Referred by order of the Secretary of War. In case of any failures to make deliveries as stipulated, the right to deliver the deficient number to be forfeited.

To furnish 10,000 Spencer breech-loading magazine rifles with angular bayonets and appendages. To be made according to a pattern to be previously submitted for examination and approved at the Ordnance office, and to serve as a standard in the inspection. To be delivered not less than 500 in March, 1862, and 1,000 per month thereafter. Payment to be made at the rate of $40 for each arm complete including appendages for such as are approved as in all respects like and equal in quality to the standard.

The commission find that the above order was given by direction of the Secretary of War after some trials of the arm by officers, which were so far satisfactory that they recommended the procurement of a few for trial in the field. The chief of ordnance made report by special order of the Assistant Secretary of War, after examining all of these reports of trials, that though they were favorable as far as the limited trials went, none go further than a recommendation of trial in the field; that in his opinion the weight of the arms, the requirement of a special ammunition with fulminate enclosed in it, the principle of carrying spare charges in the stock, and the little advantage to be derived from so doing (considering the rapidity of discharge now attainable from all breech loaders, and the inconvenience from their weight in the ordinary use of this gun,) and the high price charged for it, all combined to show that it was not advisable to accept the proposal made for supplying these arms.

The commission are fully convinced that the interests of the government, as well as a proper prudence, make it necessary to have more extensive and satisfactory trials with this arm before intrusting it in the hands of any large number of troops, and that its success should be complete and its advantages very great to justify the purchase at so high a price. They were therefore anxious that, if possible, with due regard to the equitable rights of the manufacturers, the number should be reduced or the order modified so as to suspend the present manufacture of more than 1,000.

In accordance with the principles decided in case No. 72, the order not having been given in conformity with the law and regulations, could not be regarded as a contract binding upon the government.

The president and treasurer of the company, Mr. Warren Fisher, jr., in whose favor the original order was given, having appeared before the commission, these views were explained to them and a request made that they would consider whether any satisfactory arrangement could be suggested in accordance therewith. The commission has since received a reply proposing 1st, that the government should pay for all the machinery and tools they have prepared special to this rifle, supposed to be of the value of $75,000; and 2d, that Spencer *carbines* to the extent of 13,000 in number be ordered (in place of the *rifles*) at $30 each.

These propositions are not of the kind suggested by the commission and they do not consider their acceptance advisable.

The commission find that the deliveries stipulated to be made in the months of March, April and May, amounting to 2,500 guns, have not been made in whole or in part, and that the right to make them is by this default forfeited. In view of the extravagant price agreed to be paid for these arms, of which an early delivery was undoubtedly an element, and of their undesirableness for the service, it is decided that the said twenty-five hundred thus forfeited shall not hereafter be received, but that the contract for the remaining seven thousand five hundred shall be confirmed, and that the deliveries under this confirmation shall be made in accordance with its terms as follows, viz: one thousand in the month of June, 1862, and one thousand monthly thereafter until the whole number of 7,500 shall have been delivered. A failure to deliver the whole amount due for any month or months shall work a forfeiture of the right to deliver the guns due in said month or months, which shall not thereafter be received. This confirmation however is upon condition that the said Warren Fisher, jr., agent, shall, within fifteen days after notice of this decision, execute bond with good and sufficient sureties in the form and with the stipulations prescribed by law and the regulations for the performance of the contract, as thus modified, resulting from said order and acceptance, and upon his failure or refusal to execute such bond, then the said order shall be declared cancelled and of no effect.

We are, sir, very respectfully, your obedient servants,

J. HOLT,
ROBERT DALE OWEN,
Commissioners, &c.
P. V. HAGNER,
Major Ordnance, Assistant to Commission.

Brigadier General J. W. RIPLEY,
Chief of Ordnance.

JUNE 9, 1862.

It having been shown to the satisfaction of the commission that a delay has occurred not ascribable to the contractors in obtaining the approval of the ordnance department to their sample gun, the commission decide that the times of delivery stated in their decision shall be changed as follows: Instead of "one thousand in the month of June, 1862," it shall read, "one thousand in the month of July, 1862." The monthly deliveries thereafter to be at the rate specified, viz: "one thousand per month thereafter, until the entire seven thousand five hundred shall have been delivered."

Very respectfully, your obedient servants,

J. HOLT,
ROBERT DALE OWEN,
Commissioners, &c.
P. V. HAGNER,
Major of Ordnance, Assistant to Commission.

CASE No. 94

MERRILL, THOMAS & CO.

BALTIMORE, *February* 13, 1862.

DEAR SIR: In reply to your circular requiring copies of all contracts made with the War Department before your accession thereto to be sent to you, we beg leave respectfully to hand the enclosed copy, with the information that we have fulfilled our part to this time, and have, at a very large outlay, prepared ourselves to carry out the entire contract in due season, and, indeed, increase it, if the government shall require us to do so.

Very respectfully,

MERRILL, THOMAS & CO.

Hon. EDWIN M. STANTON,
Secretary of War, Washington, D. C.

ORDNANCE OFFICE,
Washington, December 24, 1861.

GENTLEMEN: By direction of the Secretary of War, I offer you an order for five thousand (5,000) of your breech-loading carbines, with appendages, on the following terms and conditions, viz: These carbines are all to be of the same pattern and calibre, and are to be subject to inspection and proof by such inspectors as this department may designate for the purpose. They are to be made according to a pattern to be previously submitted by you for examination and approval at this office, and to serve as a standard in the inspection; and none are to be received or paid for but such as are approved by the United States inspector as in all respects like and equal in quality to the standard. These carbines and appendages are to be delivered by you at your armory as follows, viz: Not less than five hundred in thirty days, and not less than five hundred more in sixty days from this date, and not less than one thousand per month thereafter, until the whole five thousand shall have been delivered. You are to have the right to deliver more rapidly than according to the number of arms before specified if you can do so. In case of any failure to make delivery to the extent and within the times before specified, you are to forfeit the right to deliver whatever number may be deficient in the specified number for the month in which the failure occurs. All these arms and appendages are to be delivered by you; and this order, if transferred to another, is to be thereby forfeited. Payments are to be made, in such funds as the Treasury Department may provide, for each delivery, on certificates of inspection and receipt by the United States inspectors, at the rate of thirty dollars ($30) for each arm, including appendages. All these arms and appendages are to be packed by you in boxes, with twenty carbines and appendages in each box, for which a fair price, to be determined by the United States inspector, will be allowed.

Please signify, in writing, your acceptance or non-acceptance of this order, on the terms and conditions herein stated.

Respectfully, your obedient servant,

JAS. W. RIPLEY, *Brigadier General.*

Messrs. MERRILL, THOMAS & CO.,
  Baltimore, Maryland.

          BALTIMORE, *February* 18, 1862.

DEAR SIR: We are greatly obliged by receipt of the circular of the Secretary of War from you, with the notice of our omission; but thought that in furnishing him with a copy of the contract, and stating that we had complied with it to the time specified, was sufficient.

We now beg leave to state that of the first five hundred carbines made under the contract two hundred have been delivered at the Washington arsenal, on requisition of General Stoneman, through ordnance department; and we believe Colonel Dickel, of 1st New York mounted rifles, has them. Two hundred were delivered to Major General Dix, here, by order of ordnance department. The other one hundred are here, awaiting orders from ordnance department.

Should anything further be required from us, please let us know, and oblige yours, respectfully,

         MERRILL, THOMAS & CO.

P. H. WATSON, Esq.,
 Assistant Secretary of War, Washington, D. C.

      HEADQUARTERS, *Baltimore, January* 31, 1862.

SIR: Colonel McMillan, of the 21st regiment of Indiana volunteers, is desirous of procuring Merrill's rifles for his regiment. I know the arm, and think very highly of it. The government has a contract with Merrill & Thomas for 5,000 rifled carbines constructed on the same principle. If 566 of these (enough for the 21st Indiana regiment) could be exchanged for the larger arm, by arrangement with the Ordnance department, I would recommend it.

Colonel McMillan has 192 of these rifles already and 242 Enfield rifles. The residue of his arms are Belgian and Prussian, for the most part unfit for service and diverse in construction.

I am, very respectfully, your obedient servant,

        JOHN A. DIX, *Major General.*

Hon. EDWIN M. STANTON, *Secretary of War.*

      [Indorsements]

          FEBRUARY 1, 1862.

The chief of ordnance will report immediately whether the exchange within mentioned can be made.

     EDWIN M. STANTON, *Secretary of War.*

ORDNANCE OFFICE, *February* 1, 1862.

Respectfully returned. I see no objection to making the exchange of arms recommended by General Dix, if Merrill & Thomas will deliver the rifles instead of carbines, under their contract. It will delay the work on carbines for a short time.

JAS. W. RIPLEY, *Brigadier General.*

The chief of ordnance will ascertain whether they will agree to the exchange or not.

EDWIN M. STANTON, *Secretary of War.*

ORDNANCE OFFICE, *February* 1, 1862.

Messrs. Merrill & Thomas will please inform me whether they will agree to the exchange ; *and return this paper.* What will be the price for the rifles ?

JAS. W. RIPLEY, *Brigadier General.*

ORDNANCE OFFICE, *February* 4, 1862.

Respectfully transmitted to the Secretary of War. Messrs. Merrill & Thomas will agree to the exchange, charging $45, each, for the rifles. The price of the carbines is $30. I think the charge for rifles too high.

JAS. W. RIPLEY, *Brigadier General.*

MARCH 12, 1862.

Let the exchange be made if *now* desired or approved by General Dix ; but let him be telegraphed, and obtain his answer previous to making the exchange.

EDWIN M. STANTON, *Secretary of War.*

ORDNANCE OFFICE, *Washington, March* 14, 1862.

SIR : Please return the enclosed papers to this office, with your answer as to whether you now desire or approve the exchange therein mentioned. As the subject is of old date I cannot make it entirely intelligible to you by tele-graphing, and therefore send the papers.

Respectfully, your obedient servant,

JAS. W. RIPLEY, *Brigadier General.*

Major General JOHN A. DIX, *Baltimore, Md.*

HEADQUARTERS, *Baltimore, March* 21, 1862,

GENERAL : In reply to the enclosed communication of Merrill, Thomas & Co., I am directed by Major General Dix to say that his approval of the pro-posed exchange of the Merrill carbine for the Merrill rifle, to be issued to the 21st regiment Indiana volunteers, was indorsed upon a paper attached to the papers relating to the subject forwarded to him by you. He directs me to repeat his approval and recommendation of the proposed exchange.

I am, very respectfully, your obedient servant,

WM. H. LUDLOW, *Major and A. D. C.*

Brig. Gen. J. W. RIPLEY, *Chief of Ordnance.*

ORDNANCE OFFICE, *Washington, February* 28, 1862.

GENTLEMEN : Be pleased to send to Colonel W. A. Barstow, 3d Wisconsin cavalry, Janesville, Wisconsin, 200 carbines and appendages, and 40,000 cart-ridges for the same. This in addition to the order issued from this office on the 25th of February.

I will thank you to turn these stores over to Major Belger, quartermaster at Baltimore, for transportation, to the above address.

Respectfully, your obedient servant,

JAS. W. RIPLEY, *Brigadier General.*

Messrs. MERRILL, THOMAS & CO.,
Baltimore, Maryland.

ORDNANCE OFFICE, *Washington, February* 25, 1862.

GENTLEMEN : Be pleased to send to Colonel W. A. Barstow, 3d Wisconsin cavalry, Janesville, Wisconsin, 200 carbines and appendages, and 40,000 cartridges for the same.

I will thank you to turn these stores over to Major Belger, quartermaster at Baltimore, for transportation, to the above address.

Respectfully, your obedient servant,

JAS. W. RIPLEY, *Brigadier General.*

Messrs. MERRILL, THOMAS & CO.,
Baltimore, Maryland.

ORDNANCE OFFICE, *Washington, May* 13, 1862.

SIR : I have to acknowledge your letter of the 12th instant, asking for certain information in relation to the purchase of Enfield rifles and orders for Merrill's carbines, and, in reply, to state that the orders of the 27th March to Captain Crispin to purchase Enfield rifles from Howland & Aspinwall and Naylor & Co. were in pursuance of special authority from the Secretary of War. Copies of the applications made by the parties, and of the action thereon, are herewith enclosed, (marked 1 and 2.) At the time these letters were submitted to the Secretary of War, Enfield rifles were much wanted ; and it is believed the commission had not, at that time, taken definite action in cases affecting arms of that kind, *in part and ready for delivery.* The purchase thus made of Howland & Aspinwall was in completion of their original order of July, 1861, for 17,000 arms.

I enclose also, herewith, copies of the letters to Merrill, Thomas & Co., (Nos. 3 and 4,) of 25th and 28th February, 1862, asked for by you, and have to state that these letters are not considered as orders for arms in addition to the 5,000 to be delivered by them under their contract of 24th December last, but merely as orders to deliver so many of these arms to particular officers ; and these letters were erroneously reported as orders on the weekly report of obligations, &c.

My opinion on the subject of multiplying the already too great variety of arms in the hands of troops is so well known that I deem it unnecessary to repeat it here. In this particular case application was made directly to the Secretary of War, who, after duly considering the matter, finally directed the issue to be made. General Dix's letter (copy) on the subject, with the various indorsements upon it, is herewith enclosed (marked No. 5.)

Respectfully, your obedient servant,

JAS. W. RIPLEY, *Brigadier General.*

J. WISE, Esq., *Secretary to the Commission, &c.,*
Washington City.

COMMISSION ON ORDNANCE AND ORDNANCE STORES,
Washington, June 5, 1862.

GENERAL : The commission have the honor to report as follows :

CASE No. 94.—MERRILL, THOMAS & CO., Baltimore, Maryland.

Order by direction of the Assistant Secretary of War, dated December 24, 1862. Ex. Doc. No. 67, page 191.
To deliver 5,000 Merrill's breech-loading carbines, at $30 each, including appendages. Deliveries to be made not less than 500 in thirty days, and five hundred more in sixty days from date of order, and at the rate of 1,000 per month thereafter, until the contract is closed. In case of any failure to make deliveries to the extent and within the time stipulated, the government is to be under no obligation to take the number deliverable in any month in which such failure occurs.

The commission find that the stipulations as to the time of delivery have not been fulfilled by Messrs. Merrill, Thomas & Co., 200 only being ready instead of 500, as promised in January and February.

As the guns are represented to be of good quality, and of a kind needed in the service, and as the price is not unreasonable as compared with that paid at the time for like arms, they direct that the parties be permitted to continue their work under the terms of their order, and at the price named, but that such of the guns as have been or may be forfeited under the terms of the order be not received.

We are, sir, very respectfully, your obedient servants,

J. HOLT,
ROBERT DALE OWEN,
Commissioners, &c.
P. V. HAGNER,
Major of Ordnance, Assistant to Commission.

Brigadier General J. W. RIPLEY,
Chief of Ordnance.

CASE No. 95.

P. S. JUSTICE, Philadelphia, Pennsylvania.—700 *rifles, with sword bayonets,*
August 12, 1861.

ORDNANCE OFFICE,
Washington, July 13, 1861.

SIR : Mr. Philip S. Justice, of Philadelphia, will deliver to you, at Frankford arsenal, 1,000 rifles of the Enfield pattern, with sword bayonets. These rifles have been purchased by this department, to be taken and paid for, provided they are found, on inspection, to be good, serviceable arms, and fit, in all respects, for use in the field. You will please have these arms inspected, and furnish Mr. Justice with certificates of inspection, and with receipts for as many as are approved. The sword bayonets have leather scabbards with iron mountings. A sample will be sent to you from here.

Respectfully, &c.,

JAMES W. RIPLEY,
Brevet Brigadier General.

Lieutenant T. J. TREADWELL,
Frankford Arsenal.

P. S. JUSTICE, Philadelphia, Pennsylvania.—4,000 *foreign rifled muskets, calibre* *.69, August* 17, 1861.

FRANKFORD ARSENAL, *August* 13, 1861.

GENERAL: I have the honor to state that I have accepted the proposal of Mr. Justice, of Philadelphia, to furnish the United States 1,000 rifles, calibre .58, with sword bayonets—500 to be delivered in ten days, and the balance by the 1st of September—at the rate of $20 apiece, and $1 50 for packing boxes, to be inspected after a sample furnished. These, I think, are fine arms, and, in my opinion, much the best I have yet seen offered at so low a price.

I also enclose a proposition of Mr. Justice to furnish rifle muskets, calibre .69, and sabres. I have examined a sample of the musket, and it is a good, serviceable arm, calibre .69, clasp bayonet, long-range sight, original percussion barrel, and well finished. I think it would be desirable to secure these arms. Mr. Justice's proposition is explicit in point of time and numbers, and I respectfully submit it for your decision.

Some of the arms furnished by Mr. Ponder have no half cock; equal to the sample in other respects. Shall these be received or rejected?

Respectfully, &c.,

T. J. TREADWELL,
First Lieutenant of Ordnance.

General J. W. RIPLEY,
Ordnance Office, Washington, D. C.

PHILADELPHIA, *August* 12, 1861.

I propose to supply the Ordnance department of the United States with 4,000 rifled muskets, calibre .69 of an inch, similar in style and finish to the sample deposited with you, at $20 each.

In all the month of September I will deliver 1,000, and each month thereafter, until 1st January, 1862, I will deliver 1,000 of the above arms.

I will also engage to supply at least 500 cavalry sabres of best finish, subject to government inspection and approval, at $6 75 each, provided an order for at least 5,000 shall be given me at one time. If it is necessary that an increased quantity be produced each week, it can be done. I will want about two to three weeks' notice in commencing these sabres.

I have, to arrive by the steamer of 4th August from Southampton, six hundred and eighty (680) rifles of the Chasseur de Vincennes new pattern. They have the peculiar style of sabre blade usually attached to such arms, and are such as shown you. The barrels are thirty-one inches long, and the calibre, as usual, about .60 of an inch. These I will sell in bond at ($22 50) twenty dollars and fifty cents each. I shall have the same quantity, probably, shipped by steamer of 1st September, but of this I am not positively advised.

Very respectfully, &c.,

PHILIP S. JUSTICE.

Lieutenant T. J. TREADWELL.

ORDNANCE OFFICE, *Washington, May* 20, 1862.

SIR: In July and August last Lieutenant Treadwell was authorized to purchase 4,500 rifles and rifled muskets from P. S. Justice, of Philadelphia. In addition to these, many other arms of various kinds have been purchased from the same party. Complaints have reached me that some of the arms thus purchased from this person are not serviceable arms. I deem it my duty to withhold the payment of one of his vouchers, amounting to $19,071 25, until the matter could be investigated.

I now respectfully submit all the papers I have received on the subject, some of which are so conflicting, as to the number of arms reported upon, that I am induced to suggest that the whole matter be referred to the commission on contracts, who are able to take testimony, and therefore adjudicate the account of Mr. Justice on equitable terms.

Very respectfully, your obedient servant,

JAS. W. RIPLEY,
Brigadier General.

Hon. E. M. STANTON, *Secretary of War.*

A true copy.

CHAS. W. MORRIS,
Chief Clerk.

Referred to commission on ordnance by order of the Secretary of War.

P. H. WATSON,
Assistant Secretary.

CAMP HAMILTON, VIRGINIA,
Headquarters 58th Regiment Pennsylvania Volunteers.

SIR: I have the honor to report that the arms furnished to my regiment at Philadelphia prove, on trial, to be to a large extent, if not all, more or less defective.

From personal inspection, and the reports of the captains of my companies, I find that the sights are merely soldered on, though showing imitation screwheads, and come off at the gentlest handling. The screws to secure the locks are, many of them, merely stuck in, without sufficient thread, and fall out when the pieces are discharged. Many of the hammers, from weakness of the mainsprings or other causes, will not explode.

On the whole, I believe that an inspection of the arms by a competent ordnance officer would result in the condemnation of the whole issue.

Very respectfully, your obedient servant,

J. RICHTER JONES,

General RIPLEY.

Colonel 58th Regiment.

FORT MONROE ARSENAL, VA., *March* 20, 1862.

SIR: In compliance with verbal orders received from you, I have visited Camp Hamilton and inspected the arms of the 58th regiment, Pennsylvania volunteers, stationed at that post.

This regiment is armed with rifled muskets marked on the barrel "P. S. Justice, Philadelphia," and vary in calibre from .65 to .70.

I find many of them unserviceable and irreparable, from the fact that the principal parts are defective. Many of them are made up of parts of muskets to which the stamp of condemnation has been affixed by an inspecting officer. In many cases there is evidence of an attempt having been made to obliterate the letters "C" and "R." None of the stocks have ever been approved by an officer, nor do they bear the initials of any inspector. They are made of soft, unseasoned wood, and are defective in construction. A few of the barrels have been in service before, and bear the usual marks "V. P." and "U. S." Most of the rest, however, abound in flaws, and the rifling in nearly all is but a poor attempt. The grooves extend, in many cases, but a few inches from the muzzle, leaving the remainder of the barrel with a smooth bore. The sights are merely soldered on the barrel and come off with the gentlest handling; imitation screw-heads are cut on their bases.

The bayonets are made of soft iron, and, of course, when once bent remain "set." In some instances where the bayonets have been marked "C" deep indentations have been made in the attempt to erase this letter.

The locks are of very poor construction—screws, springs, and swivels being unserviceable.

The guard-bows are insecurely fastened and can be separated from the stock with ease.

There are no band springs, and when the stock is dry the bands drop off.

The thread of the screw on the rammer, is improperly cut.

On account of the difference of calibre existing in these arms, it is impossible to supply them with suitable ammunition.

I would respectfully recommend that the entire issue of these arms be condemned, and that these facts be made known to the parties who made the contract.

I have the honor to be, very respectfully, your obedient servant,

WILLIAM H. HARRIS,
Second Lieutenant of Ordnance.

T. G. BAYLOR,
First Lieutenant of Ordnance.

Respectfully forwarded.

T. G. BAYLOR,
First Lieutenant of Ordnance.

HEADQUARTERS DEPARTMENT OF VIRGINIA,
Fort Monroe, March 20, 1862.

Respectfully forwarded to the chief of ordnance, Washington, D. C., by command of Major General Wool.

WM. D. WHIPPLE,
Assistant Adjutant General.

ORDNANCE OFFICE,
Washington, March 24, 1862.

SIR: I have respectfully to request that you will cause payment to be stopped of the accounts of P. S. Justice, assigned to Drexel & Co. and G. M. Troutman, transmitted to you on the 28th ultimo and 19th instant, and of all previous accounts of Mr. Justice which may remain yet unpaid.

Respectfully, your obedient servant,

JAS. W. RIPLEY,
Brigadier General.

E. B. FRENCH, Esq.,
Second Auditor.

True copy.

CHAS. W. MORRIS,
Chief Clerk.

HEADQUARTERS MILITARY DEFENCES, NORTH OF THE POTOMAC.

[Special Order No. 18.]

Colonel Doubleday, of the 4th New York artillery, is hereby appointed inspector to inspect certain arms appertaining to the 88th Pennsylvania volunteers, and directed to report thereon to these headquarters without delay.

By order of Brigadier General A. Doubleday.

E. P. HALSTEAD,
Acting Assistant Adjutant General.

HEADQUARTERS FOURTH REGIMENT NEW YORK ARTILLERY,
Fort Carroll, March 25, 1862.

CAPTAIN: Pursuant to the above order, I held an inspection of the arms of the 88th regiment Pennsylvania volunteers March 24, 1862, and report as follows:

The arms which were manufactured at Philadelphia, Pennsylvania, are of the most worthless kind, and have the appearance of having been manufactured from old condemned muskets. Many of them burst, hammers break off, sights fall off when being discharged; the barrels are very light, not exceeding one-twentieth of an inch in thickness, and only rifled from four to nine inches from the muzzle; the stocks, many of them, are old ones newly mounted, and the balance made of green wood which has shrunk so as to leave the bands and trimmings loose; the bayonets are of so frail texture that they bend like lead, and many of them break off when going through the bayonet exercise. You could hardly conceive of such a worthless lot of arms; totally unfit for service, and dangerous to those using them.

I am, captain, very respectfully, your obedient servant,

THOMAS D. DOUBLEDAY,
Colonel Fourth Regiment New York Artillery.

Captain E. P. HALSTEAD,
Acting Assistant Adjutant General.

FRANKFORD ARSENAL, *March* 28, 1862.

GENERAL: I have the honor to enclose herewith copies of statements of the inspection of rifles and rifle muskets received at this arsenal from Mr. P. S. Justice, of Philadelphia.

The bulk of these arms were inspected by Mr. Wilson, late foreman (I think) at Harper's Ferry armory, and after he left his situation here, the inspection was made by Mr. Thomas Daffin who had previously assisted Mr. Wilson.

These statements show the manner in which the inspection was made, and the opinion of the inspectors as to their serviceableness and fitness for use in the field. My instructions to them were, to inspect the arms and reject all that, in their opinion, were not good and serviceable, and in all respects fit for use in the field. Having entire confidence in their ability and integrity, I think these instructions were complied with.

These arms were offered to me at a time when the demand for arms (especially rifled arms) was most imperative, and it was deemed desirable to accept them to meet in part the pressing demand.

Comparing the arms with those of our own manufacture, none would pass inspection, and it was not supposed they should be subjected to any such standard, but that all that were passed on inspection would prove good and serviceable was believed.

Examining two boxes of these arms in store, I do not find them to have the radical defects complained of, nor can I account for the very different report of their inspection at Camp Hamilton, and that made to me by my inspectors—especially, I cannot understand how the arms should gauge correctly here, and be found there to vary between .65 and .70 inch in calibre. I find the sights are soldered on, but on tapping twenty of them with a hammer sufficiently hard to dent them, some were found to come off or were started.

The letters enclosed with yours of the 24th instant are herewith returned.

Very respectfully, your obedient servant,

T. J. TREADWELL,
First Lieutenant of Ordnance.

General JAMES W. RIPLEY,
Chief of Ordnance, Washington, D. C.

Statement of Messrs. W. F. Wilson and Thomas Daffin, who inspected the rifles and rifled muskets received from Philip S. Justice, esq., of Philadelphia, at the Frankford arsenal.

BRIDESBURG, *March* 27, 1862.

DEAR SIR: The answer to your note of the 26th instant, in relation to the inspection of arms, rifle and rifle-musket, manufactured by Mr. Justice, is as follows:

1st. The bayonets were fitted on the guns.

2d. The bayonets were tested as follows: The angular, by springing them with the point on the floor; and the sword bayonet in a like manner, striking them occasionally over a round block.

3d. The ramrods were then examined to see that they were the proper length, and tapped to suit the appendages.

4th. The rifling of each barrel was examined, and the gun wiped out.

5th. The calibre of each barrel was tested by a parallel plug of proper size, which was passed through, all inspected by me.

6th. The vents were cleared, by exploding a cap or otherwise.

7th. The locks were examined, and found to be correct.

8th. The sights also examined, and found to be correct.

9th. The gun was then viewed, and, if no imperfections of sufficient importance were found, the guns were passed as serviceable.

I inspected some three thousand of these guns, referred to, and though they do not compare with the government standard, yet, in my opinion, every gun passed by me was in good condition, and, with proper care, is a safe and serviceable arm, and fit for use in the field.

Respectfully,

W. F. WILSON.

Lieutenant T. J. TREADWELL.

FRANKFORD ARSENAL, *March* 27, 1862.

SIR: At your request, I submit the following as a correct report of my inspection of the Justice arms:

The number inspected and received 1,311
The number inspected and rejected 392

The inspection was conducted in the following manner:

1st. The bayonets were fitted on the guns.

2d. The bayonets were tested as follows: The angular bayonets, by springing them with the point on the floor; and the sword bayonets, by springing them, also striking them over a round block.

3d. The ramrod was then examined, to see that it was of the proper length, and that the screw fitted the appendages.

4th. The rifling was examined, and the gun wiped out.

5th. The calibre was gauged with a plug of the proper size.

6th. The vent was cleared, by exploding a cap on each gun.

7th. The locks were examined, and found to be correct.

8th. The sights were examined, and found to be correct.

9th. The gun was then viewed, and, if no imperfections were found in the stock or barrel, it would be passed as serviceable.

In my opinion, every gun that passed my inspection was in a good condition, and, with proper care, a safe and serviceable arm, and fit for use in the field.

THOS. DAFFIN.

Lieutenant TREADWELL.

WASHINGTON, *April* 3, 1862.

SIR: I beg leave to inquire (as a creditor of the United States) whether it is possible for any department of this government to go behind, or annul, the certificates and vouchers of the regularly-appointed officers of your department, when such certificates, or evidences of debt, have been given for arms or supplies received and inspected within the government arsenals and buildings?

I ask this question without any reference whatever to the position in which the government may be placed, and its consequent liability where fraud or collusion may have been discovered on the part of its sworn officers, after such certificates as I have above alluded to may have been issued. An early reply to my address as below will confer a favor on

Yours, very respectfully,

PHILIP S. JUSTICE,
Willards' Hotel, Room 136.

Brigadier General J. W. RIPLEY,
Chief of Ordnance, War Department.

FORT MONROE ARSENAL, VA., *April* 4, 1862.

SIR: I return herewith the papers respecting Justice's arms. Colonel Jones has turned all of his arms over to me, and I have issued the Austrian rifles to him in their stead. I do not think that any regiment would be satisfied to take these (Justice's) arms, although some of them may be very good. If Mr. Justice has not been paid for these arms yet, I would suggest that the whole issue be rigidly inspected, and that he be required to replace every defective musket.

Very respectfully, your obedient servant,

T. G. BAYLOR,
First Lieutenant of Ordnance, Comd'g.

Brigadier General J. W. RIPLEY,
Chief of Ordnance, Washington, D. C.

WASHINGTON, D. C., *April* 9, 1862.

MAJOR: I have the honor to report that, in obedience to instructions from Brigadier General Wadsworth, I inspected yesterday the arms in the hands of the 91st regiment Pennsylvania volunteers, and found that the regiment has 800 guns CALLED Enfield rifles, furnished to the government by P. S. Justice, of Philadelphia.

I examined about seventy of these guns that had become unserviceable from various causes, each one showing some defect in material or manufacture. Many had burst; many cones had been blown out; many locks were defective; many barrels were rough inside from imperfect boring, and many had different diameters of bore in the same barrel.

These guns have been in the hands of the regiment about four months, and have been fired but little. At practice, with blank cartridges, one gun burst. At target practice so many burst that the men became afraid to fire them. At present it is with difficulty that the men are made to charge their arms for guard duty; those who do load them throw away part of the powder.

These arms seem to have been gotten up in a hurry from old material, and altered without any reference to service or safety. Most of the guns have the United States old musket lock, and in many cases only one of the screws for attaching it to the gun is used. Judging from what I saw of the guns, I pronounce them unserviceable and unsafe.

I am, very respectfully, your obedient servant,

JOHN BUFORD,
Assistant Inspector General.

Major T. TALBOT,
Assistant Adjutant General.

HEADQUARTERS MILITARY DISTRICT OF WASHINGTON,
Washington, D. C., April 16, 1862.

SIR: I have the honor to transmit herewith a requisition for arms for Colonel Gregory's 91st regiment Pennsylvania volunteers, also a report of my inspector general on the arms now in the hands of that regiment. Companies of the regiment are now rendering efficient service, and I desire to see them well armed, that they may undertake with confidence the performance of any duty that may be required of them.

I am, sir, very respectfully, your obedient servant,
JAMES S. WADSWORTH,
Brigadier General Commanding.

The CHIEF OF ORDNANCE CORPS,
Washington, D. C.

WASHINGTON, *April* 26, 1862.

SIR: Acknowledging receipt of your favor of this date, with copies of report and letter relative to rifled muskets furnished by me to your department, I beg leave to state that when I submitted to your inspection in July last the rifled musket which I proposed to make, and which was subsequently deposited and now exists in the arsenal at Frankford, I had no expectation of being able to make any better arm than the one offered, and I well knew that none inferior to it would be accepted. Upon this sample the order was issued from your department bearing date of August 17, 1861, for "4,000 muskets, to be equal in all respects to the sample deposited."

As I progressed in my manufacturing I found I could make many improvements, all of which your ordnance officers at Frankford acknowledged as such, and many of which were suggested by them. These, I discovered, had very materially increased the cost, but as they also added greatly to their value in the field as an efficient arm, I continued these improvements, hoping to obtain compensation for the same, or at least a continuance of my contract. Upon application to Lieutenant Treadwell for increased compensation, I was told that no power was vested in him to make any such allowance, but nevertheless I *did* continue these improvements, hoping, as I stated, for at least an enlargement of my contract. To prove the integrity of my intentions, I carefully stamped each gun with my name and address.

You are well aware of what the emergencies of the times at the period of the issuing of the contract to me led the government to—accepting in the way of arms of all kinds. Although an importer and manufacturer of sporting guns and rifles for nearly twenty years, I had no experience in *military* work. After much cost, I made the arrangements to manufacture the style of musket of which I showed you the sample. Knowing that I *could* make *such* arms, I felt *that if your judgment certified to its usefulness*, although it might not meet all your requirements, I was safe in pushing my manufacture to the utmost extent. Your judgment, as expressed through your officers, approved of it, and the order was given, and to this judgment I have always deferred and conformed, because I knew it was the only safe rule for me to follow.

The original arm shown you (and which, as stated, yet remains in the arsenal) was composed of a United States musket barrel, (condemned for short length, I think,) a United States bayonet of the old model, and a United States flint lock altered to percussion. The rest of the parts were all new.

You are well aware of the difficulty which then existed in obtaining arms or any portion of arms, and no attempt was made on my part to conceal how the gun was made, for I at once, in reply to your inquiry, stated how I had become possessed of these parts, and showed you how I had made the alterations.

I now assert, however, that in no instance have I ever allowed any defective barrels or parts to be used which could in any way vitiate the safety or usefulness of the arms made by me. As a proof of which, I have now a large amount of material condemned by my direction as unfit to use in the work in which I was engaged. It is, perhaps, almost superfluous to say that barrels, bayonets, and locks, excepting such as I have described above, have been entirely unattainable until within the past few weeks. I allude to this merely to show that I have never attempted to disguise how I made my guns, and I believed that the best recommendation I could have for my guns was the fact that they were made in part of government work.

You were pleased to add to my contract an order for 1,000 rifles with *sabre* bayonets, and on the completion of this order, Lieutenant Treadwell believing it to be a still more effective and serviceable weapon than the musket, and having greater requisitions for this style of arm, urged me to continue in its manufacture, and deliver them, as far as able, in lieu of the muskets. I finally assented to this, although I discovered they were costing me about $2 50 each more than the musket; but hoping to find my remuneration in a continuance of my work, if I mistake not, I delivered 1,469 more rifles than I was bound to do, and for which I received only the same price as the muskets, although costing me in the aggregate $3,672 50 more; but it kept my men at work in hard winter.

My muskets I have never invoiced or called as Enfield muskets, as charged, nor have I ever compared them to the Springfield musket, which I hold to be the best military arm extant. I do say emphatically, however, that as a handmade arm, it has been made by me *honestly* and *conscientiously* and as well as it could be made *with the opportunities offered, and is far better than the model in all its parts.* In summing up the charges made against me, therefore, I most emphatically declare—1. That it is entirely false that any musket ever made by me has been delivered to your department varying in calibre from $\frac{65}{100}$ to $\frac{70}{100}$ of an inch, as charged, as I have no machinery to make such variation unless at great expense, and therefore could not do it; and, further, because each barrel was twice gauged in my shops with standard gauges before the guns were packed for the arsenal; and, further, because many guns were returned to me for the fraction of $\frac{1}{100}$ part of an inch difference in calibres, showing how close the inspection was.

2. I deny that in *any* instance has any attempt been made to deface the stamps of rejection on any parts of the guns used by me, and I assert that in no instance have I allowed any imperfect or defective parts to be used where the strength or usefulness of the gun could be impaired by so doing.

4. I deny that I have ever used any other wood for the stocks than such as usually employed by the government, and that I have always taken especial care to purchase and use only the best seasoned stocks for which I have uniformly paid much higher prices than are paid by the government.

5. I deny that I have ever used barrels which have been in the service, as charged.

6. I utterly deny that I have ever made any muskets in which "the rifling was only cut for a few inches down from the muzzle," as charged, "and leaving the rest of the barrel smooth." I have no machinery which will do such work, and it could only be done at an extra expense; and the party making the charge must be extremely ignorant of gun-making, to believe that it can be readily effected. Each barrel was carefully examined twice before it was stocked. The unfairness of this charge is apparent.

7. I deny that "the sights will come off with the gentlest handling," as charged, but I fully acknowledge to the soldering of them (or the larger part of them) to the barrel by Lieutenant Treadwell's instruction; because both he and I knew it to be by far the safest and strongest (although not the cheapest way)

to secure the sights. The Enfield sights and most of those on other European arms are soldered on, for the simple reason that the single screw used to fasten the sight to the barrel is almost sure to loosen after repeated discharges; and when the screw is pressed down hard into the barrel, unless the utmost precision is used in the length of the screw and the tapping of the barrel, a small lump will be raised upon the inside of the barrel. Further, the tapping of the barrel weakens it, and when a hidden flaw exists it is apt to make the "lead" which often causes the gun to burst. I have tried, and the ordnance officers have tried in my presence, to *break* off these soldered sights, but have only been able to do so after we had destroyed them. The charge that I have cut a false screw-head on the plug used to fill up the countersink in the base of the sight, by which it is usually attached to the barrel, is on a par with the charge of soldering. There is a screw-head on this plug, and if the investigation had been pushed further, it would have been found that this plug had been originally a screw, and that the stem had been cut off, and merely the head soldered into the countersink to fill the hole neatly, in place of closing it up with solder. This whole charge seems to have been made without any real investigation or thought, and certainly without much knowledge.

8. I deny that "the bayonets are soft iron, and bend like lead," as charged. Each bayonet is a government-made bayonet, condemned for *pattern* only, being the old style lock bayonet, instead of the clasp bayonet now used. Each one has been tested by me, and afterwards still more seriously tested by your inspectors at the arsenal, as I know by the quantity returned, much to my cost. This charge of making them of soft iron has no more of truth or fairness in it than the rest, for there has been no attempt to erase the government proof-marks which still exist on them, and if any critical examination was made, they must have been discovered. I leave it to yourself to decide whether this government have ever made their bayonets in the manner charged.

9. The charge that the locks were poorly made is answered by my reply to the bayonet charge. They were all United States government locks, and principally of the latest construction of flint locks, if I remember right. These were all adapted to percussion, by inserting a dovetail wedge and then brazing a piece to fill the space occupied by the brass pan of the flint lock. The springs were lightened to prevent crushing the nipples by their extreme force (as the old flint lock springs are much heavier than the percussion) and hammers made of the best Norway iron were then attached. The charge that the screws were worthless and unserviceable, I am sure, is not correct; for having to take each lock to pieces, I had the opportunity of examining them, and I did not find that government work was made as charged. My special charge, however, to all my workmen was, uniformly, to condemn *all* parts not strictly serviceable. The rest of the charges, such as that "they had no springs to prevent the bands from falling off when loosened," is equally as just and fair as the charge against the "sights," for these guns were all made with the "Enfield" pattern band, which tightens with a screw, and has no band-spring like the old muskets.

I respectfully suggest that as it is natural that each soldier should desire to obtain the Springfield musket, whose qualities are so highly appreciated, they too often abuse the issue of other arms in the hope of condemning the same, and thus have a new chance offered them for obtaining what, perhaps, had been promised them by their officers, to secure their enlistment, as I am cognizant of the promise of Springfield arms having been made to the men in numerous cases of enlistment to aid the object which they were striving for. The results of such promises, when broken, are, abuse of the arms and the reputation of the maker. I had nearly been made a sufferer from this very cause, where a complaint was made that the stocks were "rotten," when, upon investigation, it was found the men had been using the muskets as seats, and thus broken stocks which were afterward acknowledged to be perfectly solid and seasoned.

I respectfully but earnestly protest against the gross injustice which would be done to me by now altering the standard by which my work is to be judged, when I honestly and faithfully conformed to all the requisitions of your own officers, and by their own admissions have made and delivered to them guns far superior to the sample gun by which I was instructed to work, and most of which have cost me, as before stated, $2 50 each above the cost of the sample gun. As I could have access to no higher authorities than your own officers to determine when my work was up to standard, I certainly cannot be morally or legally held liable to submit to requisitions of which I could have no means of ascertaining the character, or instructions from officers not in your department as to how my work should be made.

11. I respectfully but earnestly protest that it would be great injustice to oblige me to submit to an inspection of my arms after they have *passed entirely out of my possession*, and may have been submitted to influences of the most damaging character, entirely beyond my power to prevent. I therefore most decidedly protest against any inspection of my arms *after they have been issued for, or have been in service*, as a still greater act of injustice towards me.

12. I respectfully protest that gross injustice would be done to the public at large, and to many innocent parties, if the principle is established that any department of the government may at its pleasure go behind the acts of its own officers, and vitiate its own obligations of debt given, when these very obligations specify, as in my case, that each individual arm "has been examined in detail and found serviceable and fit for use in the field." For if such a precedent is established, then *all* government obligations become valueless to the capitalist, as he cannot possibly know which will be paid and which will be refused. In my own case not only will my means be entirely squandered in my efforts to aid the government I have always supported, and to feed several hundred of workmen during the past winter, but my character, which as a merchant and manufacturer has for twenty-five years been untainted, will also be ruined, as I shall hereafter be classed amongst the list of "contractors" whose main effort was to swindle the government they had sworn to support.

There is yet due me from this department about $80,000, some of which has remained unpaid since August last. I have in consequence been obliged to hypothecate all my vouchers with bankers and capitalists at a rate of interest which is rapidly eating away the principal, and I therefore trust that you will see fit at once to order my vouchers to be duly audited, and that I be thus saved from any further loss.

I am, sir, very respectfully, yours,

PHILIP S. JUSTICE.

Brigadier General RIPLEY, *Chief of Ordnance.*

I beg leave to remind you that the reply of Lieutenant Treadwell, (to whom it seems these charges against me were forwarded,) which was exhibited to me by you with other papers, is in itself a complete refutation of the whole matter, as the sworn certificate of his own inspectors shows that the arms were far more carefully examined even than I had supposed, and certainly much more critically than the charges against me bear evidence of having been.

P. S. J.

WAR DEPARTMENT,
Adjutant General's Office, Washington, April 29, 1862.

GENERAL: The chief of ordnance having been informed that the arms furnished the 58th Pennsylvania volunteers, Colonel Jones, are very defective, you are requested to cause a minute inspection to be made of them to ascertain their quality and condition; the report to be forwarded to this office as early as convenient.

I am, sir, very respectfully, your obedient servant,

L. THOMAS,
Adjutant General.

Major General Wool,
U. S. Army, Com'dg Dep't of Virginia, Fort Monroe, Va.

HEADQUARTERS DEPARTMENT OF VIRGINIA,
Fort Monroe, May 17, 1862.

Respectfully submitted to the adjutant general of the army.

WILLIAM D. WHIPPLE,
Assistant Adjutant General.

HEADQUARTERS DEPARTMENT OF VIRGINIA,
Fort Monroe, May 5, 1862.

Respectfully referred to First Lieutenant T. J. Baylor, Ordnance department, commanding Fort Monroe arsenal, who will comply with the within order from the War Department.

By command of Major General Wool.

WILLIAM D. WHIPPLE.

WASHINGTON, D. C., *May* 4, 1862.

GENERAL: In obedience to instructions of the Secretary of War, communicated from your office on the 28th ultimo, which, however, only reached me on the 2d instant, I yesterday inspected the arms of the 91st regiment of Pennsylvania volunteers, commanded by Colonel Gregory.

This regiment is now armed with the United States rifle musket, calibre .58, made at the Springfield armory in 1861. These arms, having been issued to the regiment on the 24th ultimo, are in fine order, and meet in all particulars the requirements of a good and serviceable weapon.

The "Justice musket" with which the 91st was, until recently, armed, having been inspected by Major Buford, assistant inspector general, and by him pronounced unserviceable, was returned into the Washington arsenal, and the regulation rifle musket issued in lieu thereof.

If the object of the inspection to be made by me was to determine whether or not payment should be made the contractor for the Justice musket, and I am led to infer that such was the object, would it not be advisable to have them inspected at the arsenal by a regularly appointed inspector?

As four-fifths of the 88th Pennsylvania volunteers were on detached service guarding the railroad to Manassas, I made no inspection of their arms yesterday, but will do so to-morrow, by which time the entire regiment will have returned to its encampment, near Cloud's mills.

I remain, general, very respectfully, your obedient servant,

R. JONES, *Assistant Inspector General.*

Brigadier General L. THOMAS,
Adjutant General U. S. Army, War Department, Washington.

[Special Order No. —.]

HEADQUARTERS 88TH REGIMENT PENNSYLVANIA VOLUNTEERS,
Acquia Creek, Virginia, May 9, 1862.

Captain Knabb and Lieutenant Wagner, of this regiment, are hereby detailed to proceed to Washington for the purpose of procuring arms and accoutrements for this command.

They are hereby authorized to draw arms and accoutrements, and receipt for the same. By order of

GEORGE P. McLEAN,
Colonel Commanding 88th Regiment Pennsylvania Volunteers.
J. S. STEEPLE, *Acting Adjutant.*

WASHINGTON, D. C., *May* 19, 1862.

SIR: Having destroyed the original copy of my report on the arms of the 88th regiment Pennsylvania volunteers, I am unable to give you an exact copy of it, but from recollection of the facts aided by the notes taken during the inspection, which fortunately have been preserved, I can without much error give the essence of the report.

The number of arms inspected was about seven hundred, all of which were stamped on the barrel "Justice, Philadelphia," except about 130, which were stamped on the lock "Remington, Ilion, New York."

Of these guns, 423 had the bayonet, and 401 the rammer either bent or broken; the bands of 262 were so loose as to fall from their places on discharging the guns; 140 had the sights loose, broken off, or otherwise injured; 158 locks were more or less injured, the mainsprings of many being too weak to explode a cap; 14 barrels were bent; and 22 had either burst or were dangerous to fire on account of flaws in the metal.

The stocks of 212 were broken or split, the injuries being mostly at the toe or heel of the butt, or around the lock, and quite a number were broken off at the small of the stock. It was noticed that the sights that had fallen off had been soldered on to the barrel and not secured by a screw; it was also observed that the rifling in many of the guns was so slight as to be scarcely perceptible to either the touch or sight.

The rammers and bayonets could be bent to take almost any angle, and this with but a slight effort in most cases.

I remain, general, very respectfully, your obedient servant,

R. JONES, *Assistant Inspector General.*
Brigadier General J. W. RIPLEY,
Chief of Ordnance.

FORT MONROE ARSENAL, *Virginia, May* 14, 1862.

SIR: In compliance with instructions received from you, I have inspected the rifle muskets marked P. S. Justice, Philadelphia, now in store for issue, and have to report the following:

The muskets are of a very inferior quality; but few would be passed if made in a government armory, the parts only fitting to the gun to which they are attached, with but few exceptions.

Many of the barrels have flaws and sand holes, and some have the marks of condemnation upon them. The rifling is very poor, in most cases either disposed to become soon leaded, or the grooves are hardly perceptible.

The stocks are not unfrequently made of unseasoned wood, and not well finished. The bands, in many cases, fit badly, and, having no springs, are apt to become loose in dry weather.

The rear sights, in all cases, are soldered to the barrel, and imitation screws made upon them. Many of the guns are without them, as they are easily knocked off. The same remarks may be said of the front sights, with few exceptions.

The bayonets are fitted only for the gun whose number they bear, and are of very inferior quality, possessing scarcely any elasticity, and are without clasps.

The locks are good, being of the model of eighteen hundred and twenty-two, (1822,) with new hammers—the locks that were put upon the old flint-lock musket, but the tumbler screw is often broken.

The screws and threads of the ramrods are poor.

The guard is poorly finished, and fits badly.

In consequence of the many defects of this arm, I respectfully recommend that they be not issued to troops, but be condemned.

I am, sir, your obedient servant,

R. M. HILL,
First Lieutenant of Ordnance.

J. G. BAYLOR,
First Lieutenant of Ordnance.

Respectfully forwarded.

J. G. BAYLOR,
First Lieutenant of Ordnance.

FORT MONROE ARSENAL, *Virginia, May 17, 1862.*

SIR: In compliance with instructions indorsed on letter from War Department, Adjutant General's office, Washington, April 29, 1862, sent to me from headquarters department of Virginia, Fort Monroe, May 5, 1862, I directed Lieutenant R. M. Hill, Ordnance department, to make a thorough and minute examination of the arms referred to, and I enclose herewith his report on the subject.

Very respectfully, your obedient servant,

J. G. BAYLOR,
First Lieutenant of Ordnance.

Colonel W. D. WHIPPLE,
Assistant Adjutant General, Department of Virginia, &c.

ADJUTANT GENERAL'S OFFICE, *May 22, 1862.*

Respectfully referred to the chief of ordnance.

E. D. TOWNSEND,
Assistant Adjutant General.

ORDNANCE OFFICE, *May 23, 1862.*

Respectfully referred to the commission on ordnance stores as a part of the paper in the "Justice" case.

JAMES W. RIPLEY,
Brigadier General.

COMMISSION ON ORDNANCE AND ORDNANCE STORES,
Washington, May 23, 1862.

GENERAL: The commission request that Major Laidley may be instructed to inspect some few of the "Justice arms," if he has any on hand, comparing them with the sample arm stated to be at the Frankford arsenal, and making a report of the result to the commission. Please direct his attention to the rifling, malleable iron hammers, thin barrels, or those with bad flaws; the condition of the stocks as to shrinkage, and consequent looseness of the bands, &c.; the temper and strength of the ramrods and bayonets. A box or two will be sufficient to examine.

The commission also request that some of the arms returned by the 91st or 88th Pennsylvania volunteers to the Washington arsenal may be examined there as to the rifling and any gross defects apparent, and report made. Please direct also that the sample gun may be sent here from the Frankford arsenal.

Very respectfully, your obedient servant,

P. V. HAGNER,
Major of Ordnance

Brigadier General J. W. RIPLEY,
Chief of Ordnance.

FRANKFORD ARSENAL,
Bridesburg, Pennsylvania, May 27, 1862.

GENERAL: I have the honor to report that, in obedience to your instructions of the 24th instant, I have examined two boxes of the arms furnished by Mr. Justice, and, having compared them with the sample arm, submit the following as the result of my examination.

I found three barrels which had flaws of considerable size. Several of the barrels were quite thin at the muzzle, but not of less thickness than the sample. The rifling is in almost all cases very slight, (about 0.05 inch,) and not as deep as in the sample arm.

I broke two hammers, which bent back and forth before yielding. I am of opinion that one, at least, is cast iron well annealed. Some of the workmen think both are. As I have known good judges to be much deceived in distinguishing between wrought iron and small pieces of cast iron carefully annealed, I am more cautious in expressing my opinion in a positive way on this point.

The rammers and bayonets are only slightly tempered, and take a set readily. I broke ten rammers in testing their temper from flaws and defects, caused by unskilful forging.

Some of the locks were rusted from the green wood and stocks, and the bands were, in some cases, loose, as they are on the sample arm.

With the exception of the rifling, and some flaws in the barrels, I regard the arms furnished by Mr. Justice that I have inspected equal to the sample arm.

I have this day forwarded by express to your address the sample arm, as requested by the commission.

Very respectfully, I am, general, your obedient servant,

T. T. S. LAIDLEY,
Brevet Major.

Brigadier General J. W. RIPLEY,
Chief of Ordnance.

ORDNANCE OFFICE, *May 28, 1862.*

Respectfully referred to the commission on ordnance and ordnance stores, as requested.

JAMES W. RIPLEY,
Brigadier General.

ARSENAL, *May 30, 1862.*

MAJOR: I received the sample Justice gun last evening, and but an indifferent sample at that. Is it to be understood that this gun is to be the standard, and that only similar guns are to be inspected?

There are here, marked "Justice," five varieties—two of muskets, and three of rifles.

Taking the value at twenty dollars, the gun is decidedly inferior; but, making the comparison with the sample, there is no great difference as to service qualities.

I write you in haste, and am very truly,

GEO. D. RAMSEY.

Major HAGNER, &c., &c., &c.

WASHINGTON ARSENAL, *May* 31, 1862.

SIR : When my inspection report was made, on the 27th instant, the sample "Justice" arm had not been furnished me. I have since then received it, re-inspected the arms, and now beg to make the following report :

There are at this arsenal five varieties of arms marked " Justice :"

1. Rifle musket, calibre .69, (like sample arm.)
2. Rifle musket, calibre .69, with iron mountings.
3. Short rifle, calibre .58, with sword bayonet and with brass mountings.
4. Short rifle, calibre .58, with sword bayonet and with iron mountings.
5. Short rifle, calibre .58, sword bayonet, without bands.

Under the first head, on comparison with sample, the locks vary in length from 0.5 to 0.9 inches, and the lock plates are variously patched to suit the cone seats. Unlike the sample arm, many of the locks are secured to the stock by two screws ; one or two are used, according to length of lock plate.

Barrels.—The rifling of the barrels varies from three to six grooves ; and some of the barrels are reduced by filing down the upper surface at butt to adapt them to the breech screws.

Sights.—Some are long, and others short. The long range sights are imperfectly secured, and readily move in the dove-tail seat ; (see sample arm.) The three leaf sights are coarsely riveted on the bands.

Ramrods.—Vary in size ; some are tempered, and some soft and easily bent.

Bayonets.—Like sample, without clasps. Supposed to be U. S. 1822.

The component parts of these arms are, apparently, with the exception of the brass mountings, of discarded armory work. These arms, in the average, cannot be said to be inferior to the sample arm furnished me, and now before the Commission on Ordnance and Ordnance Stores. They are far, however, from being a first class arm, and, in view of the contract price, $20, are decidedly of inferior quality.

The other varieties of the " Justice arms" on hand referred to are pretty much of same quality and diversity of parts. The rifles without bands have a coarse notch sight, and are the most inferior of the lot.

It is proper to add that all the " Justice arms" in store at the arsenal have been in the hands of troops, and have not since been repaired or cleaned. These arms were turned into the arsenal in exchange for others more reliable.

Very respectfully, I am, sir, your obedient servant,

GEORGE D. RAMSEY,
Lieutenant Colonel Commanding.

General J. W. RIPLEY,
   Chief of Ordnance.

ORDNANCE OFFICE,
War Department, Washington, June 3, 1862.

SIR : As requested in Major Hagner's letter of the 2d instant, I return the paper from P. S. Justice, therewith enclosed, (see letter ante-dated April 26, 1862,) on which I have to remark that the sample gun referred to in Mr. Justice's proposition of the 12th August, 1861, accepted by my letter to Lieutenant T. J. Treadwell of the 16th of that month, may, it is supposed, be obtained from the Frankford arsenal. As regards Mr. Justice's declarations, I have not the means of affirming or refuting them ; but see no reason why he should not have the benefit of them in any decision which the commission may make in his case, so far as they are not contradicted by other papers in the case before them. My own experience leads me to give weight to that part of Mr. Justice's remarks wherein he suggests that the hope and expectation of obtaining Springfield muskets may have led to a desire to condemn his arms, and to unfair treatment of them with a view to their condemnation and a consequent necessity for an exchange.

The copies of the orders referred to by Mr. Justice are to be found at pages 54 (No. 13) and 60 (No. 17) in Ex. Doc. No. 67, " Purchase of arms."

Respectfully, your obedient servant,

JAMES W. RIPLEY,
Brigadier General.

J. WISE, Esq.,
Secretary of Commission on Ordnance Stores, Washington, D. C.

COMMISSION ON ORDNANCE,
Washington, June 20, 1862.

GENERAL : The commission request that the papers in the case of P. S. Justice, with their report, may be returned to them.

Mr. Justice states that the table given page 14, Ex. Doc. No. 67, is incorrect in charging 700 sword bayonet rifles, of American manufacture, as delivered by him, and that the copies of orders published do not give the correct number or kind of arms delivered and ordered from him. He submits the enclosed statement, as showing the correct numbers of all arms manufactured by him delivered at the Frankford arsenal. This shows only 2,174 with angular bayonets, calibre .69, and 2,469 with sword bayonets, calibre .58.

The commission request that this statement be compared with the accounts, and report made to them if correct, and such differences stated as may exist. The reports of inspecting officers condemnatory of the "Justice arms" seem only to refer to those of calibre .69, with angular bayonets, (except in Colonel Ramsey's letter to Major Hagner;) and as Mr. Justice claims that the sword bayonet rifles of .58 calibre were not complained of in service, to his knowledge, the commission request that if any reports particularizing them have been made to the department they may be sent to the commission.

Very respectfully, sir, your obedient servant,

P. V. HAGNER,
Major of Ordnance.

General J. W. RIPLEY,
Chief of Ordnance.

Before commission, June 20, 1862.

Mr. P. S. Justice appeared before the commission, and presented a statement of the actual deliveries of arms made by him under the orders referred to the commission. He stated that the whole number ordered had not been delivered, as had been considered to be the case in the decision of the commission.

The commission replied that any error of that kind would be investigated and corrected by them.

Mr. Justice also complained that as his arms were accepted after inspection by government authority, the government could not justly decline to pay for all so accepted.

The commission replied that the purchase ordered was with the view of getting serviceable arms, and that deliveries and payments should be considered on account until the transaction was completed, if the government interests were better protected thereby; that the government had taken every precaution to have the exact quality of the arms delivered ascertained, and it had been shown that they were not of the kind expected, (viz, worth $20 at the time they were ordered,) and having used them to meet the exigencies of the moment, it was only incumbent upon the government to pay a fair market price for them; and this the commission decided to do.

ORDNANCE OFFICE,
War Department, Washington, June 24, 1862.

SIR: In compliance with the request of the commission of the 20th instant, I have to state that the tables in Ex. Doc. No. 67 do not contain any statement of arms delivered under contracts. Those tables were designed to show the number and kind of arms which had been contracted for, and also the number and kind which had been procured by open purchase. The aggregate, as recapitulated on page 21, shows the whole number for which provision had been made. The whole number procured from all sources, including those delivered under contracts, are stated in the annual report of contracts and purchases made to Congress, which is not yet printed.

The statement submitted by Mr. Justice to the commission, of rifles with sword bayonets, and of rifled muskets, delivered by him at Frankford arsenal, has been compared with his accounts on file in this office, and is found to be correct. 2,469 rifles, with sabre bayonets, and 2,174 rifled muskets, have been received at Frankford arsenal from him, all of which have been paid for, except those charged in the suspended account, which has not yet been settled by the Auditor. The statement submitted by Mr. Justice is herewith returned.

The reports of inspecting officers, condemnatory of the arms delivered by Mr. Justice, appear to refer to the rifled muskets alone, of which only 2,174 have been received by the United States. I am not aware of any complaints having been made respecting the quality of the rifles with sword bayonets.

Upon a re-examination of the records in this case, it appears that an error was made in stating the number of these rifles ordered. Instead of the two lots of 700 each, as stated in Nos. 12 and 13, page 34 of Ex. Doc. No. 67, the orders were for 1,000 rifles, with sword bayonets, afterwards conditionally increased by 500.

The report of the commission in the case of P. S. Justice, with all the papers relating to it, are herewith transmitted.

Respectfully, I am your obedient servant,

JAS. W. RIPLEY, *Brigadier General.*

J. WISE, Esq.,
Secretary of Commission on Ordnance Stores.

COMMISSION ON ORDNANCE AND ORDNANCE STORES,
Washington, June 6, 1862.

GENERAL: The commission have the honor to report as follows:

CASE No. 95.—PHILIP S. JUSTICE, of Philadelphia.

Letter dated Ordnance office, Washington, May 20, 1862. Referred by special direction of the Secretary of War, approving the recommendation of the chief of ordnance, May 20, 1862.

Letter of the chief of ordnance to the Secretary of War, in reference to Philip S. Justice, of Philadelphia, states that in July and August last Lieutenant Treadwell was authorized to purchase 4,500 rifles and rifle muskets from P. S. Justice, of Philadelphia. In addition to these, many other arms of various patterns have been purchased from the same person; and as complaints have been made by various officers that these arms were not serviceable, he has withheld payment of one of his accounts for $19,171 25, and sends the papers in the case, and asks that an investigation and decision be made by the commission.

The commission find that since this war commenced Mr. Justice, the claimant in this case, has sold to the government a large number of muskets and rifles, foreign and of his own make, at prices varying from $28 21 to $18; that he has also sold numbers of swords, sabres, and pistols; that being known to the department as a seller and maker of arms, on the 13th of July an order was given to Lieutenant Treadwell, commanding Frankford arsenal, to "inspect and accept, if found on inspection to be good serviceable arms, and fit in all respects for use in the field, 1,000 rifles, with sabre bayonets;" which order was conditionally increased July 18 by 500 more. August 13, Lieutenant Treadwell reports that he has accepted 1,000 under the above instructions, at $20 each, 500 to be delivered in ten days and the balance by the 1st of September; and also encloses to the chief of ordnance a proposition of Mr. Justice to furnish 4,000 rifle muskets, with angular bayonets. Lieutenant Treadwell states that the sample of these arms shown to him "is a good serviceable arm, calibre .69, clasp bayonet, long range sight, original percussion barrel, and well finished." August 16, 1861, the chief of ordnance authorized Lieutenant Treadwell to accept Mr. Justice's proposition, with the express condition "that the arms are to be delivered in or within the time specified, otherwise the government is to be under no obligation to take them, but may or may not do so at its pleasure." The times specified in the proposition were: "1,000 to be delivered in September, 1861, and 1,000 each month thereafter until January 1, 1862." The inspection certificates referred to the commission, and to which is attached the account of Mr. Justice, amounting to $19,171 25, the payment of which has been suspended by the chief of ordnance, embraces, with some sabres and revolvers, "350 rifles, with sword bayonets, and 472 rifled muskets, with angular bayonets." These are stated to have been purchased under the orders above referred to, and inspected "between January 27 and February 15, 1862."

No explanation has been given to the commission why so long a delay occurred in the delivery of the sword-bayonet rifles, due September 1st at latest; nor why the rifled muskets, with angular bayonets, were received after the expiration of the prescribed time.

It appears also that many varieties of pattern in both kinds ordered have been received, (five are now at the Washington arsenal,) and also that the pattern of the rifle musket deposited at the Frankford arsenal, and used as a standard for inspection, does not agree with the pattern shown to Lieutenant Treadwell by Mr. Justice, and described by him as having a "clasp bayonet." The standard has been examined by the commission, and has a bayonet of the model of 1822. These guns were issued, in part, to the 58th, 88th, and 91st Pennsylvania volunteers, and some remain in store at Fort Monroe and Frankford arsenal; all are stamped with Mr. Justice's name, as required by the Ordnance department, and can therefore be fully identified as those received under these orders.

Upon complaints of colonels of regiments and of department commanders, experienced officers, assistant inspectors Generals Jones and Buford, Colonel Doubleday, 4th New York artillery, and ordnance officers Lieutenants Hill and Harris, inspected with care and precision, at different times, the arms of the above-named regiments and others in the arsenal at Fort Monroe, and their reports before the commission concur in stating that they are unsafe and unserviceable, as well from special defects named as from the general character of the material and workmanship.

As these inspecting officers had no connexion with the regiments in whose hands the arms were, and as in two cases the arms were in store, not assigned to any regiment, the commission consider that the suggestion made by Mr. Justice that a desire for the new Springfield arms by the regiments caused a groundless prejudice against his arms, or produced the defects complained of by the bad treatment they received, cannot satisfactorily account for the defects reported.

The pressing demands upon the Frankford arsenal for arms made it necessary to hurry, as much as possible, the issue of these as soon as delivered, and the constant occupation of Lieutenant Treadwell prevented him from making personally any examination. He assigned the duty, however, to the best workmen he could obtain, experienced armorers, and, considering that a minute inspection of the arms was not possible at the time, directed them to handle each gun, and see that it was serviceable and equal to the sample. These workmen report that, in their opinion, none were passed which were not at the time in such condition.

As the inspectors did not examine the interior of the barrels, take off the locks, or try the temper of the rods and bayonets, except to judge whether they were equal to sample, which is itself of very inferior quality in these particulars, and as many of the defects complained of may be ascribable to the use of green wood for stocks, which could not be detected in new work, the commission consider that, except as to difference of calibre, (reported to exist by several officers and not discovered by the inspectors,) the reports of the workmen who received the arms do not necessarily invalidate or conflict with those made by the officers several months later, so far as the workmen profess to have examined, a new stock of *green* wood, causing, in time, the rusting of the lock and barrel, and the loosening of the bands and mountings by shrinkage, and the bad work in letting in the lock; the soft side-screws and ramrods, whose screw-threads would be soon deformed by use; the flaws in the barrel, and the bad rifling, and the hammers of malleable iron could not be easily detected by the inspection made at the arsenal. But these defects of material and manufacture were all necessarily known to Mr. Justice, or to his employers; and as Mr. Justice claims to be an experienced gunmaker of twenty years practice, the ill effects of such upon the efficiency and durability of the gun in service could not fail to be known to him.

The case, therefore, as presented to the commission, shows:

1st. That Mr. Justice did not comply with his original agreement in time of delivery.

2d. That he made use of improper and unsuitable material, which could not possibly produce a "serviceable" arm, such as was promised by him.

3d. That the sample proposed and approved by Lieutenant Treadwell, upon whose recommendation the order was given, was a more valuable gun than the sample used as a standard for the inspection.

4th. That many of the arms delivered do not equal the sample used as a standard, but were manifestly inferior to it in many particulars, and different from it in style of finish and appearance.

The character of the chief defects, as shown by the reports, are as follows:

1st. Many of the barrels were defective from flaws, from bad boring, and from insufficient rifling; many are so thin as to burst with the ordinary charge, and in one case with a blank cartridge.

2d. Many of the stocks are made of green wood, which rusted and made unserviceable the locks, and by shrinkage, after exposure, left the bands loose and the barrel illy secured, so as to be unsafe and untrue in actual service. The sample shown to the commission is of seasoned wood, and has not so shrunk from the bands nor rusted the locks.

3d. Ramrods and bayonets are unserviceable, being too weak and soft for use.

4th. The rear sights are soldered on without screws, thus exposed to being mal-placed and imperfectly secured when first put on, and to be easily lost or loosened when the heat of the firing weakens the hold of the solder. The bevelled mortise and screw used in the sample is evidently better, and is always adopted in good arms.

Major Laidley, now commanding at the Frankford arsenal, inspected, by request of the commission, forty of these arms, new and just as received from Mr. Justice, and his report leaves no room to doubt that in the above particulars most of these arms were so defective. He found three barrels with flaws of considerable size, several where the barrels were quite thin at the muzzle, (which is also the case in the sample,) the rifling in almost all cases very slight, the hammer, in his opinion, made of malleable iron in one case, (possibly in more,) ramrods and bayonets but slightly tempered, easily taking a set, and two rods breaking in the test, showing flaws and defects from unskilful forging.

Colonel Ramsey, commanding Washington arsenal, has likewise inspected, at the request of the commission, many of those turned in to him and replaced by other more reliable arms, and reports that he finds five varieties as to general finish, two of the musket and three of the short rifle; several different patterns of locks; that the rifling varies in number of groves from three to six; that many barrels are filed down at the breech to adapt them to the breech pins; sights differ in pattern, and all are badly attached; ramrods vary in size and quality; some are tempered and some soft; and bayonets all without clasps.

The commission consider it proved that Mr. Justice has not fulfilled his obligation to furnish a "serviceable arm" to the government, but has been paid at the rate of $20 a gun for arms not suitable in workmanship or material for the public service, and (judging) from the character of arms purchased at $20, and from the prices paid usually for inferior arms during the period of the delivery of these, that a price of $15 is an ample, if not excessive, equivalent for such arms.

In accordance with the principles set forth in Mason's case, (No. 72,) orders such as these given to Mr. Justice cannot be regarded in the light of contracts; but the legal principle that articles accepted and retained by the government should be paid for at their fair market value at the time they are so received must be the guide in establishing a proper price to be paid to Mr. Justice.

Postscript.

JUNE 25, 1862.

It appears by report from the chief of ordnance, dated June 24, just received by the commission, that 2,174 rifle muskets, calibre .69, and 2,469 rifles with sword bayonets, calibre .58, have been received at the Frankford arsenal upon the orders now before us; and of the 2,469 rifles with sword bayonets so received no complaints of inferiority have been made, except of one kind without bands, the number of which cannot now be accurately obtained. The commission decide that no deduction be made except on the first-named class of arms, and direct that the payments heretofore made to Mr. Justice for arms delivered at the Frankford arsenal be considered as "on account;" and that, in a closing settlement of his accounts, $15 per gun only be allowed for 2,174 rifle muskets, and $20 per gun for 2,469 rifles with sword bayonets, furnished under the above orders, as per statement signed by Mr. Justice, and hereto attached.

We are, sir, very respectfully, your obedient servants,

J. HOLT,
ROBERT DALE OWEN,
Commissioners.

P. V. HAGNER,
Major of Ordnance, Assistant to Commission.
Brigadier General J. W. RIPLEY, *Chief of Ordnance.*

Rifles and rifled muskets accepted by Lieutenant T. J. Treadwell at Bridesburg.

RIFLES—.58 BORE.		RIFLED MUSKET—.69 BORE.	
1861.		1861.	
August 27	166	September 14	35
September 14	225	October 10	206
October 10	242	October 25	171
October 25	300	November 18	241
November 18	331	November 30	192
November 30	142	December 19	95
December 19	147	December 31	252
December 31	343		
1862.		1862.	
January 18	182	January 18	247
January 31	41	January 31	263
March 20	350	March 20	472
Total	2,469	Total	2,174

Total amount accepted.............. 4,643 guns.

Total number delivered.................................. 5,035
Total number rejected.................................. 392

Accepted.................................. 4,643

PHILIP S. JUSTICE.

CASE No. 96.

A. K. EATON, New York.

NEW YORK, *February* 10, 1862.

SIR: Pursuant to your general order of the 29th ultimo, I beg respectfully to report that I am a contractor with the government for 50,000 Springfield muskets. My contract consists of an order from General Ripley, a copy of which is herewith enclosed, and my acceptance of the same, which was duly transmitted by mail.

Together with several gentlemen of capital and of well-known mechanical skill, I have organized a company, under the general manufacturing laws of this State, by the name of the Syracuse Fire-arms Company, which company, by the terms of its incorporation, have secured an available capital of $100,000, and are actively engaged in securing the necessary machinery and implements for the manufacture of these arms. From the large pecuniary means and high mechanical reputation of my associates in this company, I have no doubt whatever of being able to fulfil my contract according to its terms.

Respectfully,

A. K. EATON.

Hon. E. M. STANTON, *Secretary of War.*

ORDNANCE OFFICE,
Washington, December 24, 1861.

SIR: By direction of the Secretary of War, I offer you an order for fifty thousand (50,000) muskets, with appendages, of the Springfield pattern, on the following terms and conditions, viz: These arms are to be furnished with the regular appendages, and are to be in all respects identical with the standard rifle musket made at the United States armory at Springfield, Massachusetts, and are to interchange with it and with each other in all their parts. They are to be subject to inspection by United States inspectors in the same manner that the Springfield arms are inspected, and none are to be received or paid for but such as pass inspection and are approved by the United States inspectors. These fifty thousand (50,000) arms and appendages are to be delivered, at your armory, as follows, viz: not less than one thousand (1,000) in each of the months of July, August, and September, 1862; not less than two thousand (2,000) in each of the months of October and November, 1862; not less than three thousand (3,000) in December, 1862; and not less than four thousand (4,000) per month thereafter until the entire fifty thousand shall have been delivered; and you are to have the right to deliver more rapidly than according to the number of arms before specified, if you can do so. In the case of any failure to make deliveries to the extent and within the times before specified, you are to forfeit the right to deliver whatever number may be deficient in the specified number for the month in which the failure occurs. All these arms and appendages are to be delivered by you, and this order if transferred to another party is to be thereby forfeited. Payments are to be made, in such funds as the Treasury Department may provide, for each delivery, on certificates of inspection and receipt by the United States inspectors, at the rate of twenty dollars for each arm, including appendages. All these arms and appendages are to be packed by you in boxes of the regular pattern, with twenty (20) muskets and appendages in each box, for which a fair price, to be determined by the United States inspector, will be allowed.

Please signify, in writing, your acceptance or non-acceptance of this order on the terms and conditions before stated herein.

Respectfully, your obedient servant,

JAS. W. RIPLEY, *Brig. General.*

A. K. EATON, *New York, N. Y.*

Proposal of A. K. Eaton, of New York, to make 100,000 *muskets of the Springfield pattern.*

NEW YORK, *November* 15, 1861.

SIR: In view of the fact that our foreign relations may deprive the government of facilities for supplying itself with arms from abroad; and believing that the government cannot depend upon the manufactories, public and private, already existing for an adequate supply, even taking it for granted that the traitors now in arms are speedily subjugated; and knowing that the government will greatly prefer to look to its loyal citizens for the supply of arms, provided it can do so with full assurance that its orders will be filled rapidly, and with an arm equal in every respect to the best, I have, in connexion with eminent manufacturers in New England, New York, and New Jersey, been engaged for some time in preparing to offer to the government the following proposal:

1. I will contract to furnish the government of the United States, within one year, 100,000 Springfield muskets, equal in every respect to the model furnished me; the parts interchangeable, and subject to the rigid inspection of the department, for twenty dollars each, payable on delivery.

2. Within six months from the date of an order I will deliver 5,000, and the remaining 95,000 in seven equal monthly instalments.

I should prefer a larger order, fully to compensate me and my associates; the additional deliveries to commence after the expiration of the year above provided for.

I have for many years made the subject of arms, their improvement and efficiency, the subject of deep study and extensive practice, and I am thoroughly familiar, both theoretically and practically, with the whole subject.

The eminent foresight which characterizes the action of the War Department, and which, among other things, gives it the confidence of the whole country, cannot fail to appreciate the advantages of an organization such as I mention to the government, and which, while it places a magazine at the disposal of the government from which it can always draw, at the same time fosters the manufacturing ability of the country.

It is very important that I should have an order within forty days, if consistent with the views of the department.

I have the honor to refer to a number of eminent gentlemen whom you know by reputation, if not personally, as to my character and mechanical skill.

I have the honor to be your obedient servant,

A. K. EATON.

Hon. SIMON CAMERON, *Secretary of War.*

NEW YORK, *December 3, 1861.*

SIR: Permit me to introduce to your favorable attention my friend, A. K. Eaton, esq.

You will find Mr. Eaton to be a gentleman of high standing in this community, of high scientific attainments and great ingenuity and skill as a mechanic. I have also confidence in him as a man of honor and a gentleman.

Respectfully, your obedient servant,

PETER COOPER.

Hon. SIMON CAMERON, *Secretary of War.*

NEW YORK, *December 2, 1861.*

We take pleasure in certifying that A. K. Eaton, esq., has been for some time known to us, and that we have the highest opinion for his character as a reliable gentleman and man of the strictest probity. Mr. Eaton also stands in the front rank as a man of science, and is a thorough mechanic and an inventor of genius. He possesses, withal, an untiring energy, combined with great practical talent.

JOHN LORREY.

CUMMINS, ALEXANDER & GREEN,
20 *Exchange Place.*

COOPER, HEWITT & CO.

I take great pleasure in expressing my hearty concurrence in all that is stated above in relation to the character, position, and attainments of Mr. Eaton.

WILLIAM C. ALEXANDER.

I concur fully in the above.

J. F. BUTTERWORTH.

NEW YORK, *December 3, 1861.*

We take great pleasure in saying that we know Mr. A. K. Eaton to be a gentleman of uncommon mechanical skill in the department of fire-arms.

ROBERT L. MAITLAND.
JOHN AUCHINCLOSS.

NEW YORK, *May* 17, 1862.

GENTLEMEN : I enclose to you a copy of the report of my agent, Mr. W. R. Holbrook, who has contracted for the parts for me, and whom I have employed to aid me in assembling the guns. He is thoroughly acquainted with all those engaged in the manufacture of Springfield muskets, as well as with those who are manufacturing the several parts.

I have moved with the utmost care, and did not report earlier, as I expected to have the manufacture in a much more advanced state. I am confident, however, that I shall make my deliveries according to my contract.

Immediately after receiving my order, I perfected all my arrangements as proposed in my original application to the War Department, and I believe I was the first to suggest the plan of procuring the guns in parts. Just at this juncture I was prostrated by a severe attack of illness, (enclosed I send my physician's certificate,) and I was thus forced to make new arrangements with the Syracuse company, which I duly reported to the Secretary of War in reply to his general order. The Syracuse company, in consequence of this order, became alarmed as to the intentions of the government, and refused to comply with their agreement with me. I was then forced to return to my original method of procuring parts of the gun, in which I have been successful, and I shall fulfil the order according to its terms.

I am, respectfully, your obedient servant,

A. K. EATON.

The COMMISSION ON ORDNANCE AND ORDNANCE STORES.

If you desire more definite information than is conveyed by Mr. Holbrook's report, please advise me.

BROOKLYN, *May* 3, 1862.

This is to certify that I attended professionally Mr. A. K. Eaton during the months of January and February, 1862, and that he was confined to his bed by a severe attack of erysipelas, and unable to attend to business.

WM. SWIFT, *M. D.*

NEW YORK, *May* 16, 1862.

DEAR SIR : Referring to your agreement with me to contract, in your name, for the different parts of the Springfield muskets, and also the note from the commission of the 14th instant, I beg leave to say that if I had more fully understood the power and wishes of the commission, I should have reported in detail to you at a previous date. I supposed that they first wished to ascertain if your and all other contracts were properly obtained, which, of course, *you* only were to answer. Secondly, that they wished to know if you would be able to deliver according to the terms of your contract; that I understood you had already reported; therefore, I have only kept to work to secure your different parts in time. I have *no* doubt that you will be able to commence your deliveries in *August.* I have secured the principal parts—barrels, stocks, locks ; the other parts, I have no doubt, can be had *in time.* I am in daily communication with manufacturers of the other different parts, but have preferred not to positively close till I knew which of them would be the most certain to be in time.

Unless you think it of the last importance so as to make a *full* report to the commission, I should prefer not to sign and seal till about June 1st. If you find it essential, in making your report to the commission, to have their contracts signed, I can do so at once.

I regret that this misunderstanding should have existed, for if, through this, your contract is disturbed, I have placed you under heavy obligations to contractors, which must incur a serious loss in case the contract is not carried out. If you wish me to report more fully, please inform me.

Yours, truly,

W. R. HOLBROOK.

A. K. EATON, Esq.

COMMISSION ON ORDNANCE AND ORDNANCE STORES,
Washington, June 10, 1862.

GENERAL: The commission have the honor to report as follows:

CASE No. 96.—A. K. EATON, New York.

Order dated December 24, 1861. Specially referred by Secretary of War. Page 155, Ex. Doc. No. 67.

Order for 50,000 muskets, of the Springfield pattern, with appendages, at $20 each, to be delivered as follows: Not less than 1,000 in each of the months of July, August, and September, 1862; not less than 2,000 in each of the months of October and November, 1862; not less than 3,000 in December, 1862, and not less than 4,000 per month thereafter.—(See case No. 72.)

The commission find that the above order was not given in accordance with the law and regulations, and that it is not therefore a contract of legal force, inasmuch as it does not contain the express requirements of the law, and was not made "after previous advertisements for proposals respecting the same;" nor can it be regarded as an "open purchase," being for articles which did not "require immediate delivery," but were stipulated to be manufactured and delivered at prescribed distant periods.

They further consider that the number of arms ordered is larger than the wants of the government justify in this case, at the price fixed; and therefore, according to the principles set forth in Mason's case, No. 72, they decide that the order to Mr. Eaton be confirmed, subject to all its terms, to the extent of 25,000 muskets, upon condition that he shall, within fifteen days after notice of this decision, execute bond, with good and sufficient sureties, in the form and with the stipulations prescribed by law and the regulations for the performance of the contract, as thus modified, resulting from said order and acceptance; and upon his failure or refusal to execute such bond, then the said order shall be declared cancelled and of no effect.

The commission further decide that the deliveries under the contract to be executed shall be required at or within the periods stipulated in the original order, but that the numbers specified may be reduced proportionately to the reduction of the whole number, so that the contract shall be completed within the time allowed in the original order.

We are, sir, very respectfully, your obedient servants,

J. HOLT,
ROBERT DALE OWEN,
Commissioners, &c.

P. V. HAGNER,
Major of Ordnance, Assistant to Commission.

Brigadier General J. W. RIPLEY,
Chief of Ordnance.

CASE No. 97.

J. PIERPONT MORGAN.

[Indorsement.]

The within claim is referred to Hon. Joseph Holt and Robert Dale Owen, special commissioners, for investigation and report.

EDWIN M. STANTON,
Secretary of War.

The United States to J. P. Morgan, Dr.

ORDNANCE STORES.

1861.

August 7. 2,500 Hall's carbines, at $22............................	$55,000
5,000 screwdrivers, at 25 cents	1,250
5,000 wipers, at 20 cents..............................	1,000
500 spring vices, at 35 cents...........................	175
500 bullet moulds, at 50 cents.........................	250
125 packing boxes, at $4.............................	500
	58,175

The annexed named ordnance stores have been received in good order.

F. D. CALLENDER,
Captain of Ordnance, United States Army.

HEADQUARTERS WESTERN DEPARTMENT,
St. Louis, September 26, 1861.

The above ordnance was purchased by me for the troops under my command. Captain Callender, Ordnance department, will pay the account.

J. C. FRÉMONT,
Major General Commanding.

SEPTEMBER 26, 1861.

Not paid for want of funds.

F. D. CALLENDER,
Captain of Ordnance, United States Army.

56 BROADWAY, NEW YORK, *August* 5, 1861.

I have five thousand Hall's rifled cast-steel carbines, breech-loading, new, at twenty-two dollars, government standard, fifty-eight. Can I hear from you?
SIMON STEVENS.

J. C. FRÉMONT,
Major General Commanding, Cairo, Illinois.

HEADQUARTERS WESTERN DEPARTMENT,
St. Louis, August 6, 1861.

I will take the whole five thousand carbines. See agents Adams Express, and send by express, not fast freight. I will pay all extra charges. Send also ammunition.

Devote yourself solely to that business to-day.

J. C. FRÉMONT,
Major General Commanding

SIMON STEVENS.

ORDNANCE OFFICE,
Washington, June 6, 1861.

SIR: Your letter of the 5th instant is received. The instructions of the Sec
retary of War authorize the sale of the carbines "if all, of every quality or condition, are taken at the average of $3 50." You will thus see that you must buy
and pay for all before you can take away any. When you have paid for all,
there will be no objection to leaving at the arsenal, subject to delivery *there*, on
your order, such as you do not desire to take away immediately ; *provided* that
they can be stored there without inconvenience, of which the commanding officer
must judge and decide.

Respectfully, your obedient servant,

JAMES W. RIPLEY,
Lieutenant Colonel of Ordnance.

Mr. A. M. EASTMAN,
Manchester, New Hampshire.

ORDNANCE OFFICE, *Washington, June 20, 1861.*

SIR: Instructions have this day been given to the commanding officers of the
New York arsenal, Governor's island, New York harbor, and the Frankford
arsenal, near Philadelphia, *to sell to you* all the "Hall's carbines" of every
description (serviceable and unserviceable) on hand, at the rate of $3 50 apiece.
These arms are to be paid for at once, and to be at once taken away, *provided*
they can't be stored at the arsenal without inconvenience. of which the commanding officer must judge and decide.

Respectfully, your obedient servant,

JAS. W. RIPLEY,
Lieutenant Colonel of Ordnance.

Mr. A. M. EASTMAN,
St. Nicholas Hotel, New York City.

WASHINGTON CITY, *February* 15, 1862.

SIR: On the 9th of January and on several occasions previous and subsequent to that day, I requested you verbally, and you as often promised, to call
General Frémont to testify before your committee, or to address him a note of
inquiry as to whether he purchased the 5,000 Hall's carbines, alluded to in the
report of the committee, from me, or through me; and to state when, if at any
time, I acted for him in the purchase or forwarding of stores or supplies from
New York to St. Louis while he was in command of the western department.
As you have not complied with my requests by calling General Frémont to
testify to the matters above alluded to, I now make the request in writing, as I
am told General Frémont is about to leave the city.

I am, sir, very respectfully,

SIMON STEVENS.

Hon. C. H. VAN WYCK,
Chairman Committee to investigate Government Contracts.

HOUSE OF REPRESENTATIVES,
Washington City, February 20, 1862.

SIR: I desire to have a statement from you in writing, for the use of the House
of Representatives, as to whether you purchased the 5,000 Hall's carbines
alluded to in the report of the committee to investigate government contracts,
of which Mr. Van Wyck is chairman, from Simon Stevens, or through him, and
whether at any time Mr. Stevens was acting for you in the purchase or forward-

ing of ordnance stores to St. Louis during the time you were in command of the western department.

I have the honor to be, very truly, your obedient servant,

C. B SEDGWICK.

Major General J. C. FRÉMONT,
United States Army.

WASHINGTON, February 22, 1862.

SIR: In reply to your note of inquiry, dated 20th instant and received to-day, I have to say, that the Hall's carbines, concerning which question is made, were purchased by me directly from Mr. Stevens, and not through him, agreeably to the offer of sale received from him by telegram,

Subsequently, about the 18th August, Mr. Stevens was appointed to a post on my staff and instructed by me to occupy himself as might be directed, in procuring and forwarding arms and stores from New York, and consignments to me from Europe on account of the United States. In this capacity he continued to act until about the 26th of September.

With respect, yours truly,

J. C. FRÉMONT.

Hon. C. B. SEDGWICK,
House of Representatives.

No. 40 EXCHANGE PLACE,
New York, April 11, 1862.

GENTLEMEN: When last in Washington I had an interview with the Secretary of War, and without exhibiting to him the details of my claims upon his department, I simply stated the merits of the case, and desired him to direct its adjudication before your commission. In accordance with such direction I presented the papers to the Hon. Mr. Holt and was examined by him briefly as to the manner in which my house obtained the voucher, the amount of its advances on the strength of it, &c. Since my return, fearing that I may have omitted to call your attention fully to the essential points of my case, I now deem it proper to do so. In the first place, my house, in the usual course of its business, made the advance to Stevens on the contract between him and Frémont, the latter then being the acknowledged representative of the government in the department for which the arms were purchased. In making this advance we trusted entirely to the good faith of the government, only looking to satisfy ourselves that the arms had actually been ordered at a price sufficient to cover the amount of our advance, interest and commissions. That the government did so order them, through its recognized agent, is not disputed. We did all that any reasonable man would have deemed necessary for his own security. It was not in our province to investigate further, or to go behind the written order of the government.

In such a case any private individual would be compelled by the law to fulfil his contract, so far as we were concerned, unless he could show that we were in collusion with the party charged with defrauding him. No such suspicion has been breathed in this case, either in the report of the committee or in any of the evidence before it. Why then should the government avoid a responsibility which would attach legally to an individual in a similar case? Why should we be compelled to lose money which we have advanced in good faith upon the credit of the government because that government agent may have acted negligently or fraudulently towards his principal? In the second place: If our claim shall not be adjudicated upon the old and well-established principles of law; if our success in recovering the amount of our advance is made to depend upon the justice or injustice of Mr. Stevens's demand, I would respectfully ask whether there is anything in the testimony taken before the committee of the

House of Representatives which proves that the contract between Stevens and Frémont was not legally binding upon the government. The facts are undeniable that these arms were purchased by the government in a time of peace at the rate of $17 50; that they were entirely new and had never been issued when they were sold, unwisely, in the condition of the government at the time, by General Ripley to Mr. Eastman. The committee of the House say that they were so sold and bought in good faith. Then they are fairly and honestly in the market. Mr. Eastman sells them to Mr. Stevens. No fault is found with that. Mr. Stevens makes an alteration in them and sells them to General Frémont. If Mr. Stevens was really the owner, he had an undoubted right to sell them at any rate he might please, and this fact is not denied by the committee; but they seek to establish that Mr. Stevens, at the time of the purchase of these arms, was acting as an agent of the government under the authority of General Frémont. There is not a particle of evidence to show that any such relation existed on the 5th and 6th of August, 1861, at the time Stevens offered to sell and Frémont consented to buy. Stevens has a correct case *prima facie*. He purchased from Eastman in his own name, made the offer to sell in his own name; Frémont acknowledges in his letter to Hon. Mr. Sedgwick that the arms were sold to him by Mr. Stevens. What is there to overthrow this positive evidence? No positive proof; no proof strongly negative, even; nothing but surmises and conjectures. Such a defence cannot stand for a moment. The fact that Mr. Stevens made a large profit by the sale has nothing to do with either the legal or equitable merits of the case. It does not appear that Mr. Stevens sold them at any greater than market value to the government. That an arm made by the government and costing it $17 50 in time of peace, though not of the most approved pattern, should sell for $22 at a period when a most urgent necessity existed for any effective arms, is not of itself very astonishing. In closing these remarks, I deem it proper to state that it is by the immense sums which have been advanced by banks and bankers upon such vouchers as these that the government has been sustained, and without such advances the government could not have gone on and cannot now continue to do so. Verified certificates have been hitherto received as an undoubted security, we never dreaming that an attempt would be made to go behind them in our possession; and if it shall prove that the banker is liable to have the contract upon which these certificates are issued annulled or varied, then this source of relief to the government will terminate, because no one will be disposed to risk that liability.

With much respect, I remain, gentlemen, your obedient servant,
MORRIS KETCHUM,
Of KETCHUM, SON & CO.

Hon. Jos. HOLT and Hon. ROBERT DALE OWEN,
Commissioners, &c.

STATE OF NEW YORK, }
City and County of New York, } *ss.*

Be it remembered, that on this twelfth day of April, 1862, before me, Benjamin K. Phelps, notary public, duly commissioned and sworn, personally appeared Morris Ketchum, known to me to be one of the firm of Ketchum, Son & Co., bankers of the city of New York, and the individual who subscribed the foregoing instrument or letter, and made oath that the statement of facts therein contained is true and correct to the best of his knowledge, information, and belief.

In witness whereof, I have hereunto set my hand and affixed my notarial seal, [L. s.] at the city of New York, the day and year first above written.
BENJAMIN K. PHELPS,
Notary Public.

COMMISSION ON ORDNANCE AND ORDNANCE STORES,
Washington, April 19, 1862.

SIR: The commission are now ready to receive and consider any testimony which it may be the wish of yourself or others in interest to offer in reference to the actual value of the Hall's carbines, sold by Simon Stevens to the United States, and for a portion of the price of which a claim is now pending before us in the name of J. Pierpont Morgan.

The market value of these arms at the time of their sale by Mr. Stevens is a fact which it is deemed important to ascertain, and hence you are advised, in order that any evidence you may wish to introduce upon the point in behalf of the claimant, whose interests you have been representing before the commission, may be offered with as little delay as possible.

Very respectfully, your obedient servant,

J. HOLT.

Mr. MORRIS KETCHUM, *New York.*

OFFICE OF KETCHUM, SON & CO.,
No. 40 *Exchange Place, New York, no date, (probably May* 1, 1861,) 1860.

DEAR SIR: I was in hopes of sending the affidavits in relation to the value or market price of Hall's carbines at the time of purchase, which in your favor of the 19th ultimo you state is a fact deemed important to ascertain. I have, with as little delay as the case would admit of, procured the testimony of such manufacturers as are familiar with these arms, and who are now manufacturing arms for the government. Hall never having made the arms except for the government, it was impossible to obtain a market value except so far as it was fixed by the sale of these very arms, there being none other in the market.

I have, however, obtained several affidavits bearing on that point, which I trust will be satisfactory, and which will go forward by mail to-morrow.

Very respectfully, your obedient servant,

MORRIS KETCHUM.

Hon. JOSEPH HOLT,
Chairman of Commission on Ordnance and Ordnance Stores.

OFFICE OF THE ASSISTANT TREASURER OF THE UNITED STATES,
New York, March 28, 1862.

MY DEAR SIR: I have to-day written a letter of introduction to yourself for Morris Ketchum, esq., senior member of the well-known banking firm of Ketchum, Son & Co., of this city. I desire to say something more in his behalf than could, perhaps, with propriety be included in a mere letter of that character.

From the commencement of our difficulties to the present time the government has had no more influential, efficient, and courageous supporter in this community than Morris Ketchum. In the hours of greatest gloom and public depression he has been foremost in rallying capitalists to the support of the Treasury Department. His house, one of great wealth and extensive influence, both here and at the east, has by its energy and its boldness in offering for large amounts done more to facilitate the negotiations of our loans and sustain the credit of the government than any house in the country.

I know nothing of the merits of Mr. Ketchum's claim, he not having at all entered upon the subject with me. But I have a general confidence that he would not present any before you not founded in equity; and I presume that among your suitors there will not be many of whom I could speak in such strong terms of personal commendation.

I am ever, very faithfully yours,

JOHN J. CISCO.

Hon. JOSEPH HOLT,
&c., &c., &c., *Washington.*

OFFICE OF KETCHUM, SON & CO.,
No. 40 Exchange Place, New York, May 2, 1862.

SIR: I hand you herewith affidavits of Austin Baldwin, Edward Savage, James North, and W. W. Marston, in compliance with the suggestion of your letter of the 19th ultimo, of which I advised you yesterday.

Mr. Marston is a manufacturer of fire-arms of high standing and large experience; he is now executing a contract of arms for the government. Under an appointment by officers of the Ordnance department he has been and is now in the employ of the government as an inspector of arms imported from Europe. His testimony, therefore, we deem conclusive.

Mr. Edward Savage is one of the proprietors of the "Savage Revolving Fire-arms Company," and is now executing a contract for pistols for the government.

Mr. James North, who joins Mr. Savage in his affidavit, was for years a partner with Mr. Savage, and they, together with the late Colonel Simeon Nash. manufactured the carbines in question.

Mr. Austin Baldwin, who is proprietor of the "American European Express," was, some years ago, collector of the port of Middletown, Connecticut, and was also for several years military storekeeper, and, as such, received the carbines from the manufacturer.

All of these witnesses are gentlemen of high respectability and standing in their several lines of business, and, as I have before stated, this arm not having been manufactured for sale in the open market, but solely for the government, I do not know how more conclusive testimony can be furnished as to the value of these arms than that contained in these affidavits.

Very respectfully, your obedient servant,
MORRIS KETCHUM.

Hon. JOSEPH HOLT,
Chairman of Commission on Ordnance and Ordnance Stores.

NEW YORK, *May 2,* 1862.

STATE OF NEW YORK, *City of New York, ss:*

William W. Marston, of the city of New York, manufacturer of fire-arms, doing business corner 21st street and 2d avenue, in said city, being duly sworn according to law, deposes and says: That he is in the fortieth year of his age; that he has been engaged on his own account in the business of manufacturing fire-arms for the last fifteen years, and that for the last twelve years has had constantly in his employ upwards of fifty men, sometimes as high as two hundred and fifty, when business pressed; that he is familiar with the manufacture of fire-arms generally, particularly with pistols, carbines, rifles, and muskets; that he is well acquainted with the carbines known as Hall's carbines, manufactured at Middletown, Connecticut; that early in August, 1861, Mr. Simon Stevens called on this affiant at his factory and proposed to contract with this affiant for the rifling and chambering of 5,000 Hall's carbines, steel bands new; that he made a contract with Mr. Stevens to rifle and chamber the breech of 4,000 carbines, .58 bore, in a good and workmanlike manner; that he received the first thousand carbines, in pursuance of this agreement, from J. P. Morgan, on the 10th day of August, 1861, the second thousand on the 21st day of August, the third thousand on the 24th day of August, and the fourth thousand on the 29th day of August, 1861; that he executed the contract faithfully to the best of his ability, and in a good and workmanlike manner, and delivered them to the Adams' Express, upon the order of J. P. Morgan, as rapidly as possible; he finished and delivered the last lot to the Adams' Express on the ―― day of September, 1861; these four thousand carbines were all new, were of good material and workmanship; they all had upon them the inspector stamps of an ordnance officer and the stamp of the manufacturer, as well as the year in which they were made; they all had side levers with which to raise the breech; that, with the alterations referred to as made by affiant, he considers them a very good and effective weapon for military purposes.

This affiant has been engaged in the manufacture of fire-arms for over twenty-five years last past, and is now manufacturing arms for the United States government; that he personally inspected the work he did upon these Hall's carbines, and superintended their packing for shipment.

Some time in November this affiant was applied to by Major P. V. Hagner, United States army, to assist in the inspection of foreign arms; that this affiant complied with the request of Major Hagner, and did inspect about sixty thousand arms imported from Europe. The demand for fire-arms late in July and August, 1861, was greatly enhanced, and the prices were increased very much over prices in peace times.

This lot of Hall's carbines being new, improved, and effective, as described above, were, in the opinion of this affiant, well worth in the month of August, 1861, about $22; that rifles of the Enfield pattern then readily sold at about from $28 to $30. The same kind of rifles could have been purchased since at from $17 to $20 each.

W. W. MARSTON.

State of New York, *City and County of New York, ss:*

Be it remembered that on this 2d day of May, A. D. 1862, personally appeared before the undersigned notary public of the State of New York, residing in the city aforesaid, William W. Marston, who signed the above affidavit, and being duly affirmed according to law, declares and says that the facts therein stated are true, to the best of his knowledge and belief.

In testimony whereof, I have hereunto set my hand and affixed my notarial seal, at the city aforesaid, on the day and year aforesaid.

[L. S.]
AUGS. F. LEE,
Notary Public, City of New York.

State of Connecticut,
  City of Middletown, County of Middlesex, ss:

Edward Savage, of the town of Cromwell, county and State aforesaid, late of the firm of North & Savage, contractors with the government of the United States for the manufacture of the celebrated Hall's carbines, and now one of the proprietors of the Savage Revolving Fire-arms Company, located in the city of Middletown aforesaid, being duly sworn, deposes and says: That he is in the sixtieth year of his age; that he has been engaged in the manufacturing of fire-arms for the last twenty-five years; that he was the successor to his father's business, who was the associate of Colonel Simeon North, since deceased, who was the pioneer of government contractors for fire-arms.

This deponent is informed and believes that Colonel Simeon North commenced manufacturing fire-arms for the United States government in the year 1799, in the town of Berlin, State aforesaid; that in the year 1811, or thereabouts, said Simeon North removed his works to the town of Middletown aforesaid, at the request of the Secretary of War, and the government made large advances to Mr. North to enable him to remove to Middletown and to increase largely the capacity of his works, and at the same time gave him an order for about twenty thousand pistols. It was at this time that Colonel North introduced the system of making all the parts so they would change and interchange with each other with perfect accuracy; for this he was allowed a bonus of $1 per pistol. Subsequently, additional orders of many thousands were received and executed by Colonel North, who associated with him from 1811 the father of this affiant,

Josiah Savage. The said Josiah Savage died in 1831, and, after the settlement of his estate, this affiant, with Colonel Simeon North, was associated with James North, the son of Simeon aforesaid, and continued the manufacture of fire-arms. About the year 1829 or 1830 Hall's rifles and carbines were introduced into the United States service. The house of Colonel North and of North & Savage made, altogether, about thirty thousand. Only about two hundred and fifty of these arms were rifles; the remaining ones were carbines. They were all iron barrels, with the exception of about five or six thousand of those made in 1848, '49, '50, '51, '52, which were made of steel, with side levers for raising the breech, (Savage & North patent.) All of these arms were made in a superior manner, with the best of materials and possible workmanship, were all properly inspected by officers of the government appointed for the purpose, and the last five thousand referred to were received by Colonel Thornton for and in behalf of the United States.

Full particulars of government trials can be had by examining the reports of boards appointed for the purpose between 1830 and 1855. I consider this last lot of five thousand steel bands, when rifled and with breech enlarged, are now, and have always been, worth as much as any other carbines in use in the army of the United States.

EDWARD SAVAGE.

STATE OF CONNECTICUT, *City of Middletown, ss :*

James North, of the town of Middletown, State and county aforesaid, son of the Colonel Simeon North heretofore mentioned, being duly sworn, deposes and says that he was personally present when Edward Savage made the foregoing affidavit, and heard the same read, and that the facts therein stated are severally true, to the best of his knowledge and belief.

JAMES NORTH.

MIDDLETOWN, *April* 29, 1862.

STATE OF CONNECTICUT, *County of Middlesex, ss :*

Be it known that on this day personally appeared before me, the subscriber, a notary public in and for the State of Connecticut, residing in said Middletown, duly commissioned and sworn, Edward Savage and James North, personally known to me, and made oath that the affidavits hereunto subscribed by them to be true, according to their best knowledge and belief.

In testimony whereof, I have hereunto set my hand and affixed my notarial seal, at the city aforesaid, on the day and year above written.

[L. S.] GEO. W. HARRIS,
Notary Public.

STATE OF NEW YORK, *City and County of New York :*

Austin Baldwin, late of the city of Middletown, State of Connecticut, now doing business as one of the proprietors of the American European Express, at No. 72 Broadway, New York, being duly sworn, saith : That during the administration of President Harrison he was appointed and acted for some years as military storekeeper in said city of Middletown, and received arms manufactured in Middletown, from the contractors, for the government of the United States, upon the certificates of the inspectors ; and from his official position, as well as from an intimate acquaintance with the leading contractors, he became familiar with the operations of the manufacture of arms for the government; that the chief contractor and pioneer in the business of making arms for the government, Colonel Simeon North, since deceased, was the manufacturer of the then celebrated Hall's carbines, generally considered the most effective weapon of the kind in service; that these were made upon the principle introduced by Colonel North, and were distinguished by uniformity in all their parts, as well as for their superior workmanship, all having to stand the test of a most rigid inspection, and the slightest flaw or want of uniformity insuring their being condemned ; that none but the most perfect arms could have passed this inspection and thus become the property of the government; that the great item of expense in the manufacture of arms is the getting up and providing suitable machinery for doing the work in a manner to bear the inspection of the government, and for this reason the first contracts are usually higher than subsequent ones when the same machinery can be used; that according to the best recollection of this deponent the price paid for Hall's carbines was about ($20) twenty dollars each. In later years the price was reduced to as low as about $17 50, in consequence of continuance of large orders from the government, with the certainty of cash payments on inspection and delivery. These carbines were never, to the knowledge of this deponent, manufactured except for the government, consequently the parties manufacturing were not subject to charges and commissions necessary and incident to ordinary mercantile transactions. It is therefore impossible, in the opinion of this deponent, to fix any price as *their market value*, for market value must at all times be regulated by the supply and demand. The price, therefore, at which these 5,000 improved Hall's carbines were purchased from Mr. Stevens by the government is, in the opinion of this deponent, fair and reasonable at the time of purchase.

AUSTIN BALDWIN.

STATE OF NEW YORK, *City and County of New York, ss :*

Be it remembered that on this 26th day of April, in the year of our Lord one thousand eight hundred and sixty-two, personally appeared before me, the subscriber, a notary public in and for the State of New York, residing in the city and county of New York, Austin Baldwin, whose name is subscribed to the foregoing affidavit, and made oath to the truth of the said affidavit.

In testimony whereof, I have hereunto set my hand and affixed my seal of office this 26th day of April, 1862.

[L. S.]   EDGAR IRVING,
Notary Public.

56 BROADWAY, *New York, April* 24, 1862.

SIR : Mr. Ketchum has shown me your letter of the 19th instant, in which you ask to be furnished with evidence of the "market value" of Hall's carbines "in August, 1861."

By "market value" in this case I understand to be meant the price at which these weapons could be bought or sold. In this mercantile sense there could not be said to be a definite "market value," the supply and demand being both limited.

What their real value was I can easily show you, and will endeavor to do so in the early part of next week.

I am, sir, respectfully, &c., your obedient servant,

SIMON STEVENS.

Hon. JOSEPH HOLT,
Commissioner, &c., &c., Washington City, D. C.

COMMISSION ON ORDNANCE AND ORDNANCE STORES,
Washington, May 10, 1862.

SIR : Upon looking more carefully into the papers submitted in support of the claim for Hall's carbines sold by yourself to the government, we find the preparation on behalf of the claimant still incomplete in some of its details.

We have to request that you will without delay file with the commission the original accounts or vouchers showing the sale of the carbines by Eastman, and also the precise amounts expended for rifling and repairing them, and by whom and at what date.

These originals will be returned to you after the case shall have been disposed of.

Your obedient servant,

J. HOLT.

Mr. SIMON STEVENS.

NEW YORK, May 15, 1862.

SIR : I herewith send you the papers which I suppose are called for by your letter of the 10th instant, in which you say that "upon looking more carefully into the papers submitted in support of the claim for Hall's carbines sold by yourself to the government, we find the preparation on behalf of the claimant still incomplete in some of its details. We have to request that you will without delay file with the commission the original accounts or vouchers showing the sale of the carbines by Eastman, and also the precise amounts expended for rifling and repairing them, and by whom and at what date. These originals will be returned to you after the case shall have been disposed of."

1. A copy of my agreement with Mr. Eastman.
2. Agreements for rifling.
3. Accounts of the expense of rifling.
4. Other accounts of the expense of altering.

These papers I have no hesitation in sending, though I think it due to myself to add that I do not see upon what ground the United States can claim from me evidence of anything beyond my contract and ownership. My claim against the government is to be regarded as if it were a claim against any other corporation, that of the city of Washington, for instance. If I have a legal or equitable demand, the government should pay as any individual or corporation would pay me.

And I submit, with great deference, that this compliance with the request made by the commission should be considered as a matter of courtesy on my part, rather than as the concession of the right of the commission to enter into the history of my private transactions.

Respectfully, &c.,

SIMON STEVENS.

Hon. JOSEPH HOLT,
    Chairman of Commission on Ordnance and Ordnance Stores,
Washington, D. C.

The following are copies of the papers referred to :

Copy of agreement with Mr. Eastman.

Whereas A. M. Eastman, of Manchester, New Hampshire, has purchased of the United States government and is now the owner of five thousand carbines, known as "Hall's carbines;" and whereas Simon Stevens agrees to loan to said Eastman the sum of twenty thousand dollars within five days herefrom, and to have a lien upon said property as collateral security for the payment of said loan; and it is further agreed that said Simon Stevens so furnishing said sum of twenty thousand dollars, said Eastman agrees to sell to said Stevens said carbines, at the rate of twelve dollars and fifty cents each, deliverable on demand after the loan of the twenty thousand dollars is made. This agreement limited to twenty days from date.

Witness our hands this the first day of August, 1861, at Washington city, D. C.

ARTHUR M. EASTMAN.
SIMON STEVENS.

Copy of Marston's contract for rifling 1,000 carbines.

I hereby agree to rifle and enlarge the breech of the one thousand carbines (received of J. P. Morgan this day) in a good and workmanlike manner, of the government calibre of $\frac{58}{100}$ths inch, at seventy-five cents each, payable on delivery of such carbines completed to said J. P. Morgan, or his order.

W. W. MARSTON.

NEW YORK, *August* 10, 1861.

Copy of agreement with Taunton Locomotive Company for rifling 1,000 carbines.

I hereby agree to rifle the barrels and enlarge the breech of the one thousand carbines (received of J. Pierpont Morgan this day) in a good and workmanlike manner, of the government calibre of $\frac{58}{100}$ths inch, at the rate of one dollar each for those furnished on and previous to Saturday next, and seventy-five cents each for the remainder; payment to be made on delivery of such carbines completed to said J. P. Morgan, or his order.

HARRISON TWEED,
Treasurer of Taunton Locomotive Manufacturing Company.

TAUNTON, *Massachusetts, August* 16, 1861.

Copy of Marston's contract for rifling 1,000 carbines.

I hereby agree to rifle and enlarge the breech of the one thousand carbines (received this day from J. P. Morgan) in a good and workmanlike manner, of the government calibre of $\frac{58}{100}$ths inch, at seventy-five cents each, payable on delivery of said carbines completed to said J. P. Morgan, or his order.

S. MARSTON.

NEW YORK, *August* 21, 1861.

Copy of Marston's contract for rifling 1,000 carbines.

Received of J. P. Morgan one thousand carbines, to be rifled and enlarged as those previously received from him, and on the same terms, and when completed to be delivered solely to his order.

W. W. MARSTON.

NEW YORK, *August* 24, 1861.

Copy of Marston's agreement for rifling 1,000 carbines.

Received, New York, August 29, 1861, of J. P. Morgan, about one thousand carbines, say fifty cases supposed to contain twenty carbines each, to be rifled as those before received from him, and when completed delivered solely upon his order.

W. W. MARSTON.

Received from Simon Stevens a case containing one carbine.

W. W. MARSTON.

Copy of receipt of the Taunton Locomotive Manufacturing Company for rifling and enlarging breech, &c., 1,000 carbines.

J. Pierpont Morgan, esq., to Taunton Locomotive Manufacturing Company, DR.

1861.

August 23.—For rifling and enlarging breech of 92 carbines, at $1 ..	$92 00
For rifling and enlarging breech of 908 carbines, at 75 cents	681 00
Paid additional freight on carbines from New York.....	4 00
	777 00

Cash on delivery.

Taunton, August 29, 1861. Received payment.

TAUNTON LOCOMOTIVE MANUFACTURING CO.,

By HARRISON TWEED, *Treasurer.*

Copy of receipt of Davenport, Munroe & Co. for express charges, &c.

[Davenport, Munroe & Co.'s express between New York and New Bedford, Taunton, Nantucket, Mansfield, Foxboro, Norton, &c.]

Mr. J. Pierpont Morgan to Davenport, Munroe & Co., DR.

To freight on twenty-five cases guns.............................	$25 00
To expense carting to police station...........................	75
	25 75

Received payment for proprietors.

E. B. HARRINGTON.

NEW YORK, *September* 9, 1861.

Copy of account of J. P. Morgan with N. W. Wheeler & Co.—"Carbine account."

1861.

August 10.—To expenses of trip to Taunton.....................	$12 32
13.—To 3 days' services	15 00
15.—To cash paid for steam-tug	8 00
To incidental expenses	3 00
To expenses of second trip to Taunton.............	11 50
16.—To cash paid freight on 50 cases carbines............	20 00
17.—To car and stage expenses, &c.....................	3 00
To 1 day's services.............................	5 00
To 5 days' services in New York...................	25 00
21.—To telegraphing..................................	60
24.—To expenses of third trip to Taunton.................	11 50
To 2 days' services.............................	10 00
	124 92

Brought forward.......... $124 92

CR.

1861.
August   10.—By cash............................. $32 00
          15.—By cash.............................   21 00
              By cash.............................   28 00
       18, 21.—By cash.............................   10 50
          22.—By cash.............................   15 00
                                                    —————— 106 50

Balance due..   18 42

New York, September 3, 1861.   Pay to C. P. Dixon, or order.
                          NORMAN W. WHEELER.

Statement from folio 82.—*Copy of account of Simon Stevens, esq., with J.*
Pierpont Morgan.

DR.

1861.
September 9.—Paid Ketchum, Son & Co. for pay made by S. S. to
              W. W. Marston for rifling carbines........... $1,350 00
              Paid W. W. Marston, balance due him for rifling
              4,000 carbines.............................   1,650 00
              Paid Taunton Locomotive Manufacturing Company
              for rifling 1,000 carbines....................   777 00
              Paid Davenport, Munroe & Co. freight from Taun-
              ton 20 00
          14.—Paid commission, as trustee, for shipping, &c.....   5,400 00
              Paid interest in account......................   156 04

                                                             9,353 04

CR.

1861.
September 14.—By cash from S. S..........................   9,353 04

(E. E.)
                              J. PIERPONT MORGAN.
                              JAS. J. GOODWINE.
NEW YORK, *May* 13, 1862.

Copy of transportation account.

Hall's carbines to S. Stevens, DR.

1861.
August 10.—To paid barge for bringing 50 cases carbines from Gov-
              ernor's island to United States barge office—1½ hour,
              at $8................................... $12 00
          21.—To ....ditto.........ditto.........1 hour....   8 00
          24.—To ....ditto.........ditto..........ditto 8 00
          29.—To ....ditto.........ditto..........ditto 8 00

                                                             36 00

Paid.
                              SIMON STEVENS.

Copy of account.

Simon Stevens to Lucius B. Allen, Dr.

1861.

August 10.—To cartage and labor on 50 cases carbines from barge
office to factory of W. W. Marston, Twenty-second
street and Second avenue........................ $12 50

21.—To.........ditto.........ditto..........ditto 12 50

24.—To.........ditto.........ditto..........ditto 12 50

29.—To.........ditto.........ditto..........ditto 12 50

50 00

New York, October 2, 1861.   Received payment in full.

LUCIUS B. ALLEN.

Before commission, April 4, 1862.

Mr. Morris Ketchum states:

Mr. Morgan had not sufficient funds under his control to continue his advances, and made application to me. On the 26th September Mr. Morgan received pay for his first 2,500 guns. He took out his advance and paid the balance to me, as I had made subsequent advances. Morgan's advance was $26,343, mine was $46,226; total, $67,415. I dealt with Stevens on the strength of his despatches from General Frémont and a letter of introduction. I had no knowledge of the origin of the claim. I made my advance in good faith on the strength of the documents. I had no knowledge whether the purchases were legal or not, but I think there was no fraud.

ORDNANCE OFFICE,
Washington, April 17, 1862.

SIR: I have the honor to acknowledge your letter of the 16th instant, asking for information touching the sale of certain Hall's carbines to Mr. A. M. Eastman during the past summer, and on this subject have to reply: That on the 25th of August, 1857, in pursuance of instructions to that effect, Colonel Craig, then chief of ordnance, addressed a letter to the commanding officer of each arsenal, designating them, by authority of the Secretary of War, as inspecting officers to inspect and condemn unserviceable ordnance stores, agreeably to the requirement of the act of 3d March, 1825. (A copy of that letter is herewith enclosed.) By virtue of this appointment, each officer thus designated transmitted to this office a list of unserviceable ordnance stores and arms of obsolete pattern, all of which were embodied into one and submitted by Colonel Craig to the Secretary of War on the 5th November of same year, with a recommendation that all the arms, &c., embraced in the list be sold, except the muskets altered from flint to percussion, the sale of which he objected to at that time. This list embraced all the Hall's arms then belonging to the United States. The formality thus complied with fulfilled all the requirements of the law, and all articles embraced in the list submitted were thenceforward subject to sale whenever the Secretary of War thought proper to order their sale, it being understood that the official act of the Secretary carries the authority of the President. In virtue of this condemnation, most of the articles have been sold at various times. The regulations of the Ordnance department, part 94, 95, and 96, edition of 1852, provide that all condemned stores shall be sold at public auction; but if the prices offered are not deemed satisfactory they may be bid in, and may afterwards be sold at private sale, for prices not less than was offered for them at auction.

The Hall's carbines in question were sold to Mr. Eastman, under this provision of the regulations. He made an application to this office proposing to give $3 apiece for a certain number of them. The prices which had been realized for arms of this kind at previous sales of condemned stores ranged between one and two dollars, except in one case where a lot of *rifled carbines* sold somewhat higher; and as among the number then on hand there were many which were damaged, I recommended to the Secretary that the whole number on hand, including damaged ones, be sold to him for $3 50 each. This recommendation was approved, and Mr. Eastman was authorized to receive the arms upon his paying to the officers who had them in charge the price agreed upon. A copy of Mr. Eastman's offer, with my indorsement and the approval of the Secretary of War, is also enclosed herewith.

Very respectfully, your obedient servant,

JAMES W. RIPLEY,
Brigadier General.

Hon. J. HOLT,
   Com'r on Contracts for Ordnance and Ordnance Stores, Washington.

NATIONAL HOTEL,
Washington, May 28, 1861.

SIR: We find reported of Hall's carbines 5,184, and damaged, 1,240 additional. As they have been long ago condemned, and you decline any proposition to alter them, I now propose to purchase the entire lot at three dollars each for those entire in good order, and in proportion for the damaged, upon examination.

Payment therefor to be in cash on delivery, and all to be taken away within not exceeding ninety days.

To prepare our works to remodel and alter them, it is important that the whole number should be had, and you will oblige me by as early a reply as possible.

I am, sir, your obedient servant,

A. M. EASTMAN.

Colonel RIPLEY, &c., &c.

[Indorsement.]

ORDNANCE OFFICE, *May* 29, 1861.

Respectfully submitted to the Secretary of War. I consider the carbines worth $3 50 each, and recommend their sale, if all of every quality or condition are taken at the average of $3 50.

JAMES W. RIPLEY.
Lieutenant Colonel of Ordnance.

Approved.

SIMON CAMERON,
Secretary of War.

JUNE 1, 1861.

NATIONAL HOTEL, *Washington, June* 2, 1861.

DEAR SIR: Will you do me the favor of addressing a letter to me stating the terms on which I can have the Hall's fire-arms, and authorizing Colonel Whiteley to deliver the same to me in lots of one thousand or more, on being paid on delivery $3 50 each, and always having deposited in his hands five hundred dollars as a guarantee that the entire lot shall be called for before the expiration of ninety days?

As I have only a verbal arrangement with you, in case of any change of post, I might be much embarrassed by your successor.

And oblige, sir, your obedient servant,

A. M. EASTMAN,
Manchester, N. H.

Colonel RIPLEY.

ST. NICHOLAS HOTEL, *New York, June* 5, 1861.

SIR : I accept your proposition to sell me the Hall's fire-arms at three dollars and fifty cents ($3 50) each, and shall be ready to commence taking them within a few days. If you have not already sent to my home an order for delivery, you will oblige me by instructing Captain Whiteley to allow me to take them in lots, at intervals, as the loft where they are stored is otherwise nearly vacant, and so large a lot is unwieldy for us to handle at once.

I make this no condition of my acceptance, however, only as a business accommodation which I presume you will cheerfully grant.

I do not find the arms quite so valuable as I hoped.

Your obedient servant,

A. M. EASTMAN.

Please address me at Manchester, N. H.

Colonel J. W. RIPLEY.

MANCHESTER, N. H., *June* 11, 1861.

SIR : Your favor of 6th instant is received. I will be in Washington within a few days and settle the account for the purchase of the "Hall's carbines" of the government. As evidence of my ability to do so, I refer you to letter of Hon. Daniel Clark, United States senator from this State, to the Secretary of War, in my last.

I am, sir, respectfully, yours,

A. M. EASTMAN.

Colonel J. W. RIPLEY, *of Ordnance, &c., &c.*

MANCHESTER, N. H., *June* 18, 1861.

SIR : I am ready to receive and pay for the "Hall's carbines."

If you will oblige me with an order on the officers in command at the places of deposit, directed to me at the St. Nicholas Hotel, New York, I will pay the account as per our agreement, and take them at once. I suppose it is not necessary for me to go to Washington to conclude this business; if it is I will do so.

I am, sir, very respectfully, your obedient servant,

A. M. EASTMAN.

Colonel RIPLEY, *&c., &c.*

ORDNANCE OFFICE, *Washington, August* 25, 1857.

SIR : By direction of the Secretary of War, you are designated to inspect the field-guns, howitzers, mortars, and altered percussion arms included in the annexed statement, or such of them as may be now at your post. Also, any other field-guns, howitzers, mortars, or small arms on hand, (exclusive of trophy and experimental pieces,) which may be damaged or otherwise unsuitable for the public service.

You will forward to this office an inspection inventory, according to form 11 Army Regulations, with full remarks and recommendations, and duplicate lists according to form 10 same regulations.

Respectfully, &c.,

H. K. CRAIG, *Colonel of Ordnance.*

To COMMANDING OFFICERS *of Arsenals.*

Statement of articles sold at New York arsenal during the third quarter 1861.

4,996 Hall's carbines, (4,996 screwdrivers, 4,996 wipers, 499 spring vises, 499 bullet moulds, 250 boxes packing,) at $3 50 each—$17,486.

Received, this 7th day of August, 1861, of Captain R. H. K. Whiteley, commanding New York arsenal, four thousand nine hundred and ninety-six Hall's carbines, for which I have paid to the said Captain R. H. K. Whiteley the sum of seventeen thousand four hundred and eighty-six dollars, being at the rate of three dollars and fifty cents for each carbine.

ARTHUR M. EASTMAN.

NEW YORK ARSENAL, April 18, 1862.

True copies from original papers in this office.

R. H. K. WHITELEY,
Major of Ordnance.

The entry in the account current of Captain R. H. K. Whiteley, New York arsenal, crediting himself with money received in payment of Hall's carbines, is as follows:

AUGUST 7, 1861.

Amount of draft on assistant treasurer, New York, from J. Pierpont Morgan, esq., in payment for Hall's carbines purchased by A. M. Eastman, $17,486.

UNITED STATES ARSENAL,
St. Louis, Missouri, May 15, 1862.

SIR: Your telegram has been received, and, in the absence of Major Callender, I have the honor to reply. I shall transmit your telegram to Major Callender (with General Halleck) informing him about my action.

Number of Hall's carbines repaired since June, 1861...........542
Number of Hall's carbines now in armory for repair............152

Of which latter 18 have broken stocks—the sides of the boxes in which the receivers work broken out, apparently from the escape of gas through the joints—and two have the barrels broken off about one inch and a half from the muzzle.

The general condition of these arms, as they come from the field for repair, would indicate a great escape of gas through joints, and the residuum of powder left interfering materially with the efficient working of the receiver.

The parts supplied for repair have been principally tumbler and leaf-spring screws and hammers.

In the early period of the war officers complained of these arms, but for many months they are only too willing to use them, as no others have been and apparently cannot be supplied, but the impression is, among those who know and those who do not know, that this arm is very inferior to Sharpe's carbine.

Very respectfully, your obedient servant,

H. R. BUFFINGTON,
First Lieutenant of Ordnance, United States Army, Commanding.

Major P. V. HAGNER,
    Ordnance Department, Washington, D. C.

WASHINGTON, May 13, 1862.

SIR: Referring to your letter to the commission under date of 17th of April, we beg to know whether the particular lot of Hall's carbines sold to Mr. Eastman was ever offered for sale at auction; and if so, we should also be glad to be informed of the date of the last sales of said carbines to which you refer, when, as you state, the prices ranged from one to two dollars, and whether such sales were private or at auction.

Very respectfully, your obedient servant,

J. HOLT, *Commissioner.*

General JAMES W. RIPLEY,
Chief of Ordnance.

ORDNANCE OFFICE,
Washington, May 13, 1862.

SIR : In reply to your inquiry of this date, I have to state that I have no means of ascertaining whether or not the Hall's carbines sold to Mr. Eastman were ever offered at auction. If it be of importance, and you will so inform me, I will make inquiry of the officers who had them in store.

The sales of arms of this kind, referred to in my letter of the 17th ultimo, were made at arsenals in 1859 and 1860; and the sales were advertised in papers far and near, to attract as much attention as possible.

The sales took place at the arsenals and dates as follows :

Watervliet arsenal, September 8, 1859, 69 carbines sold at an average of 90 cents.

Washington arsenal, September 30, 1859, 321 carbines sold at an average of $1 08.

Pittsville arsenal, January 18, 1860, 100 rifled carbines sold at an average of $6.

Pittsville arsenal, January 18, 1860, 1,265 smooth bore carbines sold at an average of $3 50.

Missouri depot, May 14, 1860, 107 carbines sold at an average of $1 15.

Baton Rouge arsenal, May 26, 1860, 7 carbines sold at an average of 25 cents.

Little Rock arsenal, May 28, 1860, 158 carbines sold at $1 each.

St. Louis arsenal, May 30, 1860, 2,579 carbines sold at prices from $1 65 to $1 90.

Allegheny arsenal, June 6, 1860, 28 carbines sold at $1 80.

Leavenworth depot, June 16, 1860, 58 carbines sold at 75 cents.

Mount Vernon arsenal, June 28, 1860, 896 carbines sold at from 49 cents to $1 36.

I am, sir, respectfully, your obedient servant,

JAMES W. RIPLEY,
Brigadier General.

J. WISE, Esq.,
Secretary to the Commission, &c., Washington City.

COMMISSION ON ORDNANCE AND ORDNANCE STORES,
Washington, May 14, 1862.

GENERAL : Referring to your note just received, I have to state that, as a part of the history of the case, the commission does regard it as important to ascertain whether the particular lot of Hall's carbines sold to Eastman was ever offered for sale at auction. If you could conveniently ascertain whether this was done or not and advise us, we should be much obliged.

Very respectfully, your obedient servant,

J. HOLT, *Commissioner.*

General J. W. RIPLEY,
Chief of Ordnance.

The chief of ordnance replied, in answer to the above, that this particular lot of carbines had not been offered at public sale.

P. V. HAGNER,
Major of Ordnance, Assistant to Commission.

NEW YORK ARSENAL,
January 18, 1862.

CAPTAIN: Two days ago I received a note from Simon Stevens, No. 56 Broadway, New York, requesting a copy of my letter to M. A. Eastman of August 20, 1862, which he stated had been sent to you and lost. I declined to give the copy lest it might be used for a very different purpose than originally intended. When I received an order from the chief of the Ordnance department to sell to Mr. M. A. Eastman all the Hall's carbines in store at $3 50 each, I wrote to the Ordnance office for advice, whether or no the appendages and packing boxes were included in the $3 50.

The department being pressed with business, a reply only reached me just before the last delivery, directing me to charge a fair valuation for the appendages and packing boxes. I did so, but the party refused to pay; the understanding Mr. Eastman had with the department was that $3 50 covered all; had bought and had arms delivered at other arsenals without those things being charged extra, and the government never did receive one cent for either appendages or packing boxes. To enforce the charge, I found, would involve a lawsuit, and therefore abandoned it. Mr. Eastman took those carbines east, altered them at an expense of about *one dollar* each, and sold them, I am told, to General Frémont at *five times* their cost. It strikes me Mr. Stevens might use my letter to Mr. Eastman as proof that the latter had paid for the appendages and packing boxes, whereas *he did not*. Three dollars and fifty cents for each carbine was all received by the United States from him.

Yours, respectfully,

R. H. K. WHITELEY,
Major of Ordnance.

Captain F. D. CALLENDER,
Commanding St. Louis Arsenal.

NEW YORK ARSENAL, *August* 20, 1861.

SIR: I have been instructed by General J. W. Ripley, chief of the Ordnance department, to charge you a fair valuation for the appendages accompanying the Hall's carbines, and the boxes in which they were packed, purchased by you from the United States. The cost is as follows, viz:

5,067 screwdrivers, at 25 cents each	$1,266 75
5,005 wipers, at 20 cents each	1,001 00
503 spring vises, at 35 cents each	176 05
503 bullet moulds, at 50 cents each	251 50
250 packing boxes, at $4 each	1,000 00
Amount	3,695 30

These articles are all new and in good order, and will be taken back at these prices should the arms be repurchased by the United States. Your immediate attention to this subject is requested.

Yours, respectfully,

R. H. K. WHITELEY,
Captain of Ordnance.

Mr. A. M. EASTMAN,
Manchester, New Hampshire.

COMMISSION ON ORDNANCE, *April* 14, 1862.

Mr. Simon Stevens, before commission, sworn:

The sale made by me to General Frémont was consummated August 6. The number of arms sold was 5,000. I offered the 5,000 arms to General Frémont on the 5th of August by telegram, as follows:

" NEW YORK, *August* 5, 1861.

" I have 5,000 Hall's rifled cast steel carbines, breech-loading, new, at $22, government standard, .58 bore. Can I hear from you?

" SIMON STEVENS."

And he accepted the whole number, and directed them to be sent to him, also by telegraph in the following words:

" HEADQUARTERS WESTERN DEPARTMENT,

"*St. Louis, August* 6, 1861.

" I will take the whole 5,000 carbines. See agent of Adams' Express and send by express, not fast freight. I will pay all extra charges. Send, also, ammunition. Devote yourself solely to that business to-day.

"J. C. FRÉMONT,

"*Major General Commanding.*"

Question by commission. What day did the guns arrive in St. Louis?

Answer. The first 500 left New York on or about August 23 and arrived in St. Louis two days after. The second lot shipped was 1,500. This left about three days after the first lot. The third lot of 500 left probably two days after the second.

Question. Are you sure that all the 2,500 left New York before September 1?

Answer. I think I am.

Question. What day did the next lot leave?

Answer. The next lot was delayed a few days, may be a week, because the first lot was not paid for as soon as delivered. I telegraphed to General Frémont August 7, asking " when, where, and how the payments were to be made?" Despatch received in reply, " payments will be made upon delivery." After sending 2,500, my engagements required that I should have some money upon them before sending more, consequently the delivery of the second 2,500 was delayed a week or ten days.

Question. The offer to General Frémont made by you was for " rifled cast steel carbines;" in accepting it he ordered them to be sent at once by express; when did you first report to him that the arms were not rifled, and that there would be delay in delivering them?

Answer. August 7, by telegraph, that the first lot would be sent in ten days.

Question. Did General Frémont complain of this delay?

Answer. I do not know that " complain" is the proper word. He telegraphed August 7, urging me to " hurry up guns." I answered immediately, I could send at once the guns as smooth bores at one dollar per gun less, but arrangements were being made for rifling, and that the first lot would go forward in ten days. He answered: " You have done right; go on with the rifling, use despatch, hurry up."

Question. Having forwarded the lot of 2,500, did you get pay for them at once? If so, when and how?

Answer. Mr. Morgan was paid by check on the assistant treasurer at New York, sent by Adams' Express, and dated, I think, September 10, 1861.

Between the day of this check leaving St. Louis and the day of its arrival in

New York, we sent off 1,500 of the second 2,500. All the 5,000 were on the way from New York to St. Louis before the 15th September, and I was informed by Captain Callender were issued to troops before the 24th September.

Question. At what price did you purchase the arms from Mr. Eastman?

Answer. At $12 50 each.

Question. Did you pay Mr. Eastman for implements in addition to the $12 50, and also in addition to the prices stated for boxes?

Answer. I did. I hand in a statement of what I paid Mr. Eastman for implements and boxes—prices as follows:

5,067 screwdrivers, at 25 cents each	$1,266 75
5,005 wipers, at 20 cents each..................	1,001 00
503 spring vises, at 35 cents each..............	176 05
503 bullet moulds, at 50 cents each...........	251 50
250 packing boxes, at $4 each...............	1,000 00
	3,695 30

Question. Has any payment been made by the government upon the second 2,500?

Answer. Mr. Morgan has received none as I am informed, nor has any one for him.

COMMISSION ON ORDNANCE, *May* 13, 1862.

Mr. Edward Savage, of Savage Arms Company, before commission:

Question by Major Hagner. I read a statement by you in reference to Hall's carbines as follows:

"I consider this lot of 5,000 when rifled and with breech enlarged, are now and have always been worth as much as any other carbine in use in the army of the United States;" please state with what arms you have compared it, and whether you would wish this answer to convey the impression that Hall's carbines are correct in the principle of their manufacture, or if not, what defects you know them to have.

I meant to say that I have tried them with the old pattern. Sharpe's without gas-check and with paper cartridges in it, using flask and ball to load the Hall's. In this trial I liked the Hall's best, because the Sharpe's generally reduced too much the cartridge. I never tried Burnside's, Gibbs's, Smith's, or any other, and I do not know how they answer. I do not think the side lever in the way; there is always an escape of gas which I have not found very inconvenient in the gun I use, even not more than in the Sharpe's gun.

Question. How long is it since you commenced making arms for the government?

Answer. Since 1837. I have been making carbines.

Question. Please say what number were generally ordered at one time?

Answer. About 2,000 arms a year. I have had an order for 10,000 at a time.

Question. Did you start the factory?

Answer. No, but I have extended it a great deal.

COMMISSION ON ORDNANCE, *May* 8, 1862.

Mr. J. C. Palmer, president of Sharpe's Rifle Company, before commission, having been sworn:

Question by Mr. Stevens. Are you acquainted with the manufacture of arms?

Answer. I am. I have had eleven years' experience as president or agent of Sharpe's Rifle Company.

Question. Will you state what the government has been paying you for Sharpe's carbines, and what price was offered by the State authorities in July, August, and September, 1861?

Answer. The government paid us $30 for carbines and appendages, never higher or lower. We were offered by Ohio, Illinois, Indiana, and Massachusetts $40 per carbine, by the quartermaster general of these States, during these months. They, or some of them, desired to know if it would be any inducement to us if they should offer $50. I told them that we were under obligations to the general government to turn in the whole product of our establishment, and should do so; and if they desired the arms, they must make applications to the chief of ordnance. We have turned in all our product to the government.

Question. Was there a great demand for carbines about the 1st of August?

Answer. There was, not only for carbines, but for all small arms.

Question. Are you familiar with the construction of Hall's carbines with steel barrels, the last lot was made by North & Savage?

Answer. I know the arm.

Question. What was the value of these arms in August, 1861, if not rifled, with enlarged chamber for fixed ammunition, in good order for service?

Answer. I should say that these arms, if in good condition, might have been sold for $20 to $22 each, with appendages. I would say, in addition, that, to afford a fair profit to the manufacturer, the arm cannot be made and sold for less than $17 to $17 50. By a fair profit I mean from thirty to thirty-three and a third per cent.

Question. Do you suppose that a contract could have been made last August to manufacture Hall's carbines at $17 to $17 50, judging by what was being paid for domestic and foreign arms at the time?

Answer. I cannot say. Such contracts have been made for arms that it is impossible to say what people will not do.

Question. Is your business subject to a commission or agency, or do you sell directly to the government?

Answer. We sell directly to the government. A few arms got into the hands of third parties, and they sold them to the government, both to the War and Navy Departments, at higher prices than ours—at from $5 to $7 above. These were guns contracted for to the third parties prior to the receipt of our orders from the government.

Question. In your transactions with the government was your company subject to the charges for commission incident to ordinary mercantile transactions?

Answer. No, we dealt directly with the government.

Question by commission. Considering the value of Sharpe's carbine to have been $30 in August last to the government, with appendages, what do you think was the value of Hall's carbines?

Answer. I should not exchange one of our carbines for three of the Hall's.

Question. You have stated that you mean by a fair profit thirty to thirty-three and a third per cent.; do you consider that as much as ought to be charged to the government?

Answer. I do.

Question by Mr. Stevens. When you state that the value of Sharpe's carbine was $30 in August last to the government, do you mean to say that that was their value because you had contracted and was bound to deliver them to the government at that price?

Answer. Yes.

Question. Have you not stated that you were offered from $40 to $50 by other parties than the United States government, and could you not have sold them at these prices had you been at liberty to do so?

Answer. I could.

Ex. Doc. 72——31

Question by Mr. Stevens. As Hall's carbines cost the government, when new, $17 50, and Sharpe's $30, what would be the relative difference in the increase of price owing to the demand in August, when you were offered $50 for your carbines?

Answer. My opinion on that subject would be very vague, but I should think that our carbine would sell for more than seventy-five per cent. over Hall's carbine.

JOHN C. PALMER.

COMMISSION ON ORDNANCE,
Washington, June 14, 1862.

Major P. V. Hagner before commission:

Are you acquainted with the Hall-North carbine, which was altered by Marston under the direction of Mr. Stevens?

Answer. I have seen the arms.

Question. After that gun is altered by Mr. Marston, what, in your opinion, is its value?

Answer. Considering the emergency of the times, I should say ten or twelve dollars.

COMMISSION ON ORDNANCE AND ORDNANCE STORES,
Wednesday, June 4, 1862.

Claim of J. Pierpont Morgan—(purchase of Hall's carbines.)

Mr. A. M. Eastman having appeared before the commission, and being duly sworn, was asked by the commission—

1st. Did you or not, in the summer of 1861, sell to Simon Stevens five thousand Hall's carbines? If so, state the date of said sale and the price paid you by him.

Answer. I sold five thousand of Hall's carbines to Simon Stevens the latter part of July or the early part of August—the precise date I cannot now state; but this will appear from the memorandum of agreement signed by myself, which, I believe, has been before the commission; the transaction was to be considered closed upon expiration of the number of days mentioned in that agreement, but the payment was not to be made within that time. The price agreed upon was twelve dollars and fifty cents ($12 50) for each gun, rifled and chambered. Mr. Stevens was to have the work done and paid for; but we made an estimate of the probable expense, and I think it was to be one dollar for each gun. This expense was borne by me to the extent of one dollar per gun, and was deducted from the $12. 50 per gun.

2d question. Were not these carbines the same which you purchased from the United States at $3 50 each?

Answer. They were.

3d question. In the price of $12 50 per carbine paid to you by Stevens, were the appendages and boxes included? And did you or did you not pass them without additional charge to Stevens in the same manner you had received them from the government?

Answer. Nothing was said about the boxes and appendages at the time. Subsequently, there was a negotiation between us in relation to them. The precise amount I do not recollect, but think it was between $3,000 and $4,000 that was to be paid.

4th question. When Mr. Stevens made the agreement with you for these carbines, did he not tell you he was purchasing them for the government?

Answer. He did not; nothing was said on the subject. The boxes and appendages were not specified by Major Whiteley in my bill. After Stevens paid me the $20,000 which he received from his bankers, I went to Governor's island and paid this bill, [through Mr. Morgan.] Subsequently, Major Whiteley wrote to me and also told me that he had received directions to charge for the boxes and appendages. I told him that I had not been charged for them at Frankford arsenal, and supposed they were not to be separately charged for, and as our account was closed and the arms disposed of, it was too late to reopen the matter. He said then that if I had not been called to pay for them at the Frankford arsenal, he supposed it was all right as it was, and no more was said about it. This was after the arms were delivered to me and the bill paid. I made the charge against Stevens, as I found that I was not paid as promptly by him as was agreed, and in consideration of this delay we agreed that I should charge for the boxes and appendages.

5th question. About what time was this agreement?

Answer. I think it was within three or four, not within two weeks of the original sale. I made out the bill for the implements, it was indorsed by him, and the amount was part of the whole amount to be paid to me. Mr. Stevens was aware that Major Whiteley had called upon me to pay separately for the boxes and appendages, and that I had told Major Whiteley that I thought the matter closed, and that I ought not to be called upon then to pay for them, and also that Major Whiteley had told me that should the government repurchase the arms, probably the same amount charged would be paid for the boxes and appendages again. Stevens, being aware of all this, and that I had not paid for these articles separately, agreed to allow me the amount of the bill for them, in consideration of the favor granted him by me, and to take his chance for repayment by the United States. I cannot say as to the exact time when this arrangement was made about the bill for boxes and appendages, but the $20,000 advanced by Mr. Morgan was for me to pay the government, and after the date of that payment Stevens had twenty days to pay me the balance; so that it was after the expiration of the twenty days that the arrangement was made. Mr. Morgan went over to Major Whiteley with Stevens and myself and paid the money to him. The arms were then in Mr. Morgan's possession as security for his advance, and I allowed twenty days for the payment of the balance to me, Mr. Morgan giving me a receipt for the arms. The twenty days were exceeded some considerable time. Had Stevens paid me promptly according to our agreement, I would not have charged him for the boxes and appendages; I might have charged some smaller sum for the boxes.

JUNE 5, 1862.

Mr. A. M. Eastman having appeared before the commission again, was asked as follows:

Question by commission. Look at page 237, report of committee on government contracts, and state whether the answers given by you to the questions— "1. What amount of money did Ketchum pay you?" "Answer. He paid me the balance which was due on the paper—$37,500—for which I indorsed over my paper to him, which held the whole property as security;" and 2. "How much had you previously received from Stevens or other parties?" "Answer. $20,000." State the whole amount received by you for the carbines, including the amount agreed to be paid for boxes and appendages in accordance with the negotiations you have stated were entered into between you.

Answer. The two sums stated did not include what I have received for appendages and boxes, nor what I have received for carbines, additional to the 5,000. I indorsed over my whole account of purchased arms to Mr. Ketchum. This includes about three hundred or four hundred ["still in New York" erased, and "additional" inserted.]

Question by commission. Please look at the paper attached to Mr. Stevens's

evidence, and state whether you recognize it as an original paper in your transactions with him, and whether the sum there given as the amount of value for
appendages and boxes is or is not the amount paid to you for them.

Answer. The paper shown I do not recognize. The amount, I think, is the
correct one paid to me, as I find it corresponds with that given by Major Whiteley as the cost of the boxes and appendages. I wish to say that in stating,
yesterday, "that I made out a bill of implements," it may have been only a
memorandum of account.

ARTHUR M. EASTMAN.

Corrections made by me in Mr. Eastman's presence.

P. V. HAGNER, Major of Ordnance.

Before commission.

Major Hagner stated that upon inquiry at the Ordnance office, no official copy
of the account for the second 2,500 carbines could be found there, and that in
the ordinary course of business it is not probable that such an account would be
there until it was paid.

In the proceedings of the House of Representative's committee, as published,
the following copy of this paper is given, with Captain Callender's answers regarding it. It is, no doubt, correct.

Question. Will you furnish a copy of the bill for the other 2,500 carbines
which have not yet been paid for?

Answer. Yes, sir; it is here.

From No. 13.—The United States to J. Pierpont Morgan, Dr.

1861.   ORDNANCE STORES.

August 7.	2,500 Hall's carbines, at $22	$55,000 00
	5,000 screwdrivers, at 25 cents	1,250 00
	5,000 wipers, at 20 cents	1,000 00
	500 spring vises, at 35 cents	175 00
	500 bullet moulds, at 50 cents	250 00
	125 packing boxes, at $4	500 00
		58,175 00

I certify that the above account is correct and just, amounting to —— dollars
and —— cents, 1861.

The annexed named ordnance stores have been received in good order.

F. D. CALLENDER,
Captain of Ordnance, United States Army.

HEADQUARTERS WESTERN DEPARTMENT,
St. Louis, September 26, 1861.

The above ordnance was purchased by me for the troops under my command.
Captain Callender, ordnance department, will pay the account.

SEPTEMBER 26, 1861.

Not paid for the want of funds.

F. D. CALLENDER,
Captain of Ordnance, United States Army.

This copy I have furnished is as near a copy as I can give the committee.
It was taken merely as a memorandum to assist my recollection.

Question. Who has possession of the original?

Answer. I cannot tell. I suppose, of course, it must have gone to Mr. Morgan, or it may be in the hands of some agent for collection.

Question. To whom did you deliver it?

Answer. I cannot positively say, but most likely to Mr. Howard.

Question. How did it happen that General Frémont's name was not signed to the order of payment?

Answer. The payment had not been made, nor would it be paid until his name was attached to the order.

Question. How does it happen that his name is not attached to the order?

Answer. I can only say that the account was put into this shape to get it into the process of adjustment, according, I suppose, to the wishes of General Frémont and those about him.

WASHINGTON, *June* 12, 1862.

GENERAL: The commission have the honor to report as follows:

CASE No. 97.—J. PIERPONT MORGAN, New York.

Claim for payment of ordnance stores purchased by telegram from St. Louis, dated August 6, 1861, and addressed to Simon Stevens, by Major General Frémont

Referred by special direction of the Secretary of War.

5,000 Hall's rifled breech-loading carbines, cast steel barrels, new, at $22; together with packing boxes and appendages separately charged. Balance claimed $58,175.

The purchase was not made from the claimant, J. Pierpont Morgan, but from Simon Stevens. Morgan having loaned Stevens money, the carbines passed into the possession of Morgan as a security for the advance thus made, and were by him delivered to General Frémont, under the sale made by Stevens to him; and the bills against the government were made out in favor of Morgan. Of these bills—two in number—one, for fifty-five thousand five hundred and fifty dollars, was paid on the 10th of September, 1861, by General Frémont's order; the other, for fifty-eight thousand one hundred and seventy-five dollars, ($58,175,) remains unpaid, and has been referred by the Secretary of War to the commission for its decision.

The commission find the facts in this case to be as follows:

In the year 1857 certain inspecting officers who had been designated to inspect and condemn unserviceable ordnance stores having reported as unserviceable, or of obsolete pattern, all the Hall's carbines then belonging to the United States, the chief of ordnance, in transmitting to the Secretary of War, under date November 5 of that year, an abstract of their report, recommended the sale of certain arms; among others, all the Hall's arms aforesaid.

The recommendation as to these latter was not then acted upon, but various lots of Hall's carbines have been sold by the government from time to time at auction, (letter of chief of ordnance, April 17, 1862,) at prices varying between one and two dollars, except for one lot of rifled carbines, which brought higher prices; the authority for these sales being based on the above recommendation.

In May, 1861, between five and six thousand of these arms still remaining in the possession of the government, of which number more than four thousand had not been in service, Mr. Arthur M. Eastman, of Manchester, New Hampshire, proposed to the chief of ordnance to make certain alterations in them. The offer was declined.

On May 28, 1861, Mr. Eastman, in a letter to the chief of ordnance, proposed to purchase all the Hall's carbines belonging to the government at three dollars, if in good order, and in proportion, if damaged.

This letter was referred, on May 29, by the chief of ordnance to the Secretary of War, with a recommendation that the carbines be sold to Mr. Eastman, "if all of every quality and condition be taken, at the average of three dollars and fifty cents, ($3 50.)" This the Secretary of War approved, under date June 1, 1861. Under date June 2 and June 5, 1861, Mr. Eastman accepted this offer, but stated his wish to take and pay for a thousand carbines at a time, and to have ninety days in which to call for the whole.

In reply, under date June 6, 1861, the chief of ordnance addressed to Mr. Eastman a letter, in which he stated to him that he (Mr. Eastman) must buy and pay for all the carbines before he took any away.

Under date June 11 Mr. Eastman wrote to the chief of ordnance, "I shall be in Washington within a few days and settle the account for the Hall's carbines."

Under date June 18, 1861, Mr. Eastman again wrote to the chief of ordnance, stating that he "was ready to receive and pay for the Hall's carbines," and asking that an order for these arms, to officers in command at the places of deposit, be sent to him, adding that he will take and pay for the arms at once.

Under date June 20, 1861, the chief of ordnance again addressed Mr. Eastman, informing him that instructions had been sent to the commanding officers of the arsenal at Governor's island, New York, and of the Frankford arsenal at Philadelphia, "to sell to him" (Mr. Eastman) all the Hall's carbines on hand, serviceable and unserviceable, and stating that "these arms are to be paid for at once."

This closes the correspondence on the subject of the sale, by the government to Mr. Eastman, of the Hall's carbines.

Throughout the months of June and July no sale was made to Mr. Eastman, and no payment was made by him.

The document next in order, in this case, is an agreement dated Washington, August 1, between Arthur M. Eastman and Simon Stevens, in which, after reciting that said Eastman has purchased of the United States government, and is now the owner of 5,000 carbines known as "Hall's carbines," and that Simon Stevens "agrees to loan to said Eastman the sum of twenty thousand dollars ($20,000) within five days herefrom, and to have a lien upon said property as collateral security for the payment of said loan," it is further agreed that Eastman shall sell to Stevens the said five thousand carbines at twelve dollars and fifty cents ($12 50) each, "deliverable on demand after the loan of the twenty thousand dollars is made."

Four days after the date of the above agreement, namely, on August 5, Mr. Stevens, then in New York, offered, by telegram, the above 5,000 carbines to Major General Frémont, then in command at St. Louis, in these words:

"56 BROADWAY, NEW YORK, *August* 5, 1861.

"I have 5,000 Hall's rifled cast steel carbines, breech-loading, new, at $22. Government standard, fifty-eight. Can I hear from you?

"SIMON STEVENS.

"J. C. FRÉMONT,
    "*Major General Commanding, Cairo, Illinois.*"

General Frémont replied next day, August 6, by telegram, as follows:

"HEADQUARTERS WESTERN DEPARTMENT,
"*St. Louis, August* 6, 1861.

"I will take the whole 5,000 carbines. See agents Adams' Express, and send by express, not fast freight. I will pay all extra charges. Send also ammunition. Devote yourself solely to that business to-day.

"J. C. FRÉMONT, *Major General.*
"SIMON STEVENS."

The day after the date of this last telegram, namely, August 7, 1861, Mr. Eastman bought of the United States government the above 5,000 carbines, payment for the same being made by Mr. J. Pierpont Morgan; the entry in the account current for the quarter ending September 30, 1861, of Captain R. H. K. Whiteley, commanding New York arsenal, being as follows:

"August 7, 1861. Amount of draft on assistant treasurer New York from J. Pierpont Morgan, esq., in payment for Hall's carbines purchased by A. M. Eastman, $17,486."

The above amount of seventeen thousand four hundred and eighty-six dollars ($17,486) was for 4,996 carbines, at three dollars and fifty cents ($3 50) each. These were packed in proper boxes. The appendages usual for such arms, namely, a screwdriver and wiper for each carbine, and a spring vise and bullet mould for each ten carbines, being in the boxes, were delivered along with the carbines, but Mr. Eastman did not pay for them, the sole payment made by or for him being the above seventeen thousand four hundred and eighty-six dollars.

Thus it appears that on June 5, 1861, Mr. Eastman agreed to purchase these carbines at the price fixed by the chief of ordnance, namely, three dollars and fifty cents, ($3 50,) and, on June 11, further agreed to the time of delivery and terms of payment, namely, that the arms should be taken and paid for at once.

That, notwithstanding these agreements, two months elapsed from the date when Mr. Eastman agreed to purchase these carbines without any such purchase being made, or any money being paid by him on account of these arms.

That at the date of the agreement between Eastman and Stevens, (namely, August 1,) in which agreement Eastman avers that he has purchased these arms of the government and is the owner of them, he had, in point of fact, made no such purchase, and the ownership of the arms was in the United States.

That at the time when Stevens offered these arms to General Frémont, (namely, August 5,) and at the time when General Frémont accepted the offer, (namely, August 6,) the arms thus offered and accepted were in store in the New York arsenal, and were still the property of the United States.

Thus the proposal actually was to sell to the government, at twenty-two dollars each, 5,000 of its own arms; the intention being, if the offer was accepted, to obtain these arms by purchase from the government at three dollars and fifty cents each. That intention was carried out (lacking four carbines only) the day after General Frémont accepted the offer. It is evident, also, that the very funds with which this purchase was effected were borrowed on the faith of the previous agreement to sell; so that, if the purchase made by General Frémont is to be regarded as a valid purchase by the United States, the government not only sold, one day, for seventeen thousand four hundred and eighty-six dollars arms which it had agreed, the day before, to repurchase for one hundred and nine thousand nine hundred and twelve dollars—making a loss to the United States on the transaction of ninety-two thousand four hundred and twenty-six dollars ($92,426)—but virtually furnished the money to pay itself the seventeen thousand four hundred and eighty-six dollars which it received.

The question here presents itself whether the purchase thus made by General Frémont was valid and binding on the United States or not.

As to this, the commission find that no law exists authorizing an army officer, of whatever rank, to make purchases of arms for the troops under his command; that no authority so to do was delegated, either by the Secretary of War or by the chief of ordnance, to General Frémont; and, further, that, by a law now in force, it is made the duty of the chief of ordnance, under the direction of the Secretary of War, to make such purchases; for the third section of "An act for the better regulation of the Ordnance department," approved February 8, 1815, (United States Military Laws, 1776 to 1858, pages 231, 232,) provides as follows:

* * * "And it shall also be the duty of the colonel or senior officer of the Ordnance department to furnish estimates, and, under the direction of the Secretary for the Department of War, to make contracts and purchases for procuring the necessary supplies of arms, equipments, ordnance, and ordnance stores."

Had the purchase of these carbines been attempted to be made in accordance with the provisions of the above law, or after consultation with the chief of ordnance, or with his concurrence, or even with his knowledge, the transaction could never have taken place. No public functionary, of sane mind, would have entered into an agreement to purchase, one day, for twenty-two dollars each, the very arms which he was to sell the next day at three dollars and fifty cents each, in order to enable the sellers to carry out their agreement with himself. It would be difficult to find a more striking proof of the wisdom of the provision above quoted from the law of 1815, or of the lamentable consequences which may arise from disregarding it. Nor does the distance of General Frémont's command from the seat of government furnish any excuse for such disregard, seeing that the same time which carried his telegram to New York would have sufficed to carry his requisition over the wires to the Ordnance department at Washington.

Under these circumstances the commission find that General Frémont had no legal authority to make the purchase of the carbines, and, therefore, that the sale made to him by Simon Stevens, as above recited, was without sanction of law, invalid, and null.

It is true, however, and the commission do not overlook the fact, that throughout the summer and autumn of 1861, during the exertions (unprecedented in this and almost in any other country) which were necessary to swell, from what was scarcely the nucleus of an army, our military force to more than half a million of men, organized, armed, and equipped for service—it is true that, under such circumstances, many purchases, both of arms and other military stores, made, from the exigency or necessity of the case, in an informal or illegal manner, have since been ratified and confirmed; some by this commission itself.

The reasons which governed the action of the commission in such confirmations were based on considerations of equity.

In cases, for example, in which an officer in command, pressed by unforeseen emergency, having no delegated authority to purchase army supplies, nor time to ask and receive such authority, was found to have bought only what the necessity of the moment demanded, at fair sale and at prices reasonable under the circumstances; and when the seller, acting in good faith, and either believing that the officer had authority to buy, or that the emergency would be deemed by the government a sufficient justification of an irregular sale, has, in the hour of need, supplied the government wants, the commission, in every such case referred to them, has directed that the account be audited, waiving its informality.

But, in the present case, the essential conditions above set forth are, in a great measure, lacking. The recital already made shows this, in part; the sequel further confirms it, as the following additional particulars abundantly prove.

General Frémont, as his telegram shows, looked to the instant reception of the arms. Mr. Stevens was to devote the day to their shipment and to the obtaining of suitable ammunition, and was to forward both, not by fast freight, but by the more speedy and expensive medium of conveyance, Adams' Express.

But when the purchase was made from the government, and when Mr. Stevens, for the first time, saw the arms, which, two days before, he had telegraphed to General Frémont that he already had in his possession, he discovered that the carbines were not rifled as he had declared them to be. He immediately proceeded to have them rifled and to have the bore of the breech-piece enlarged, so that it corresponded to the diameter of the main barrel to the bottom of the grooves. According to Mr. Stevens's own testimony before the commission, the first lot of 500 carbines was not shipped before August 23, the second lot of 1,500 about three days afterwards, and the third lot of 500 probably two days after that. Mr. Stevens is not sure that the above 2,500 arms were shipped before September 1.

The second lot of 2,500 was delayed until Mr. Stevens was informed that the first lot had been paid for; and was sent off, a portion about September 12, and the remainder about September 15.

Thus the first lot, containing one-tenth only of the whole purchase, was not shipped from New York until sixteen days after that purchase had been made; while the last lot left New York *forty* days after the date of purchase. Mr. Stevens further testifies that he was informed they were issued to troops before the 24th September, that is about *fifty* days after General Frémont's acceptance of them.

It is apparent, beyond all possible doubt, that no exigency of the moment was, in point of fact, supplied by the purchase of these carbines, whatever General Frémont's expectations may have been when he accepted them under the belief that they were ready rifled.

The good faith of the seller in this case is the next matter of inquiry.

Considerable evidence of a circumstantial character, tending to prove that in the transaction of the 6th of August Mr. Stevens was acting as the agent of General Frémont, has appeared before the public. But this is rebutted by a letter of General Frémont to the Hon. C. R. Sedgwick, under date February 22, 1862, which has been referred to this commission, and in which that officer certifies that the carbines in question were purchased by him (General Frémont) " directly from Mr. Stevens, and not through him."

Mr. Stevens, however, when he made the offer to General Frémont, knew that the arms he proposed to sell at twenty-two dollars each were at that moment the property of the United States, and that if his (Stevens) offer was accepted, he would have to furnish the funds to buy them, the next day, from the United States, at three dollars and fifty cents each. It is impossible to regard such a transaction as having been entered upon in good faith, and as having, for such reason, an equitable claim to be confirmed.

In France, during periods of civil commotion, may often be seen inscribed on the bridges, monuments, and other public structures, the words " *committed to the guardianship of the citizens of France.*" In our country it should not be regarded as a romantic stretch of political morality to declare, that all public interests ought to be regarded as under similar guardianship, more especially in times of trial and need like the present. He cannot be looked upon as a good citizen, entitled to favorable consideration of his claim, who seeks to augment the vast burdens, daily increasing, that are to weigh on the future industry of the country, by demands on the treasury for which nothing entitled to the name of an equivalent has been rendered.

Taking the most lenient possible view of this case, Mr. Stevens can be considered only as a broker, bringing to the notice of General Frémont a lot of carbines which another man has to sell at twelve dollars and fifty cents, and whose services are liberally remunerated if he be allowed the usual commission of two and a half per cent.

We now proceed to inquire whether there should be repaid to Mr. Stevens the sums advanced by him in connexion with this transaction to Mr. Eastman; as to the exact amount of which full evidence is before us.

A legal obligation on the part of the government to pay for the guns in question undoubtedly exists; but it does not rest on the contract made between General Frémont and Simon Stevens. It grows out of the fact that the arms did pass into the public service, and were, and still are, held and used as public property. This being so, the government is bound, on the well-known *quantum meruit* principle, to pay to the rightful claimant in this case the fair market value, at the time of sale, of the property so held and used. That value, and that value only, is, in the absence of any binding contract, the measure of the liability of the government arising out of its retention of the carbines.

It remains to be considered what was the fair market value of these arms, and whether the price demanded is a reasonable one.

The carbines in question were of the most recent manufacture of this quality of arm, of better material, and finished with more care, than those of earlier make. But the arm has radical defects which had caused its previous condemnation. Of these, one of the chief is the escape of gas in all directions; inevitable where, as in this case, there is a straight cut through the barrel, leaving an open crack between barrel and breech; a defect always troublesome, sometimes dangerous, increasing the fouling of the gun, and occasionally causing the breaking of the stock. Another defect arises out of the fact that, as the gun can be fired when the breech-chamber is raised, the soldier may shoot off his own thumb. In point of fact, this accident occasionally occurred, and its recurrence operated as an inducement to report the arm as " obsolete."

Add to this, that the arm, in the field during last summer and winter, has exhibited the serious consequences of these defects. By a report made to the commission from the St. Louis arsenal, (under date May 1, 1862,) it appears that the number of these carbines sent to that arsenal alone for repair in the year preceding that date was 792; and of these, eighteen had broken stocks, " apparently," says the officer reporting, " from the escape of gas through the joints."

The best measure of market value is to be found in actual sales between individuals from time to time.

On the 19th of April, 1861, a lot of 300 of these carbines changed hands, at seven dollars and fifty cents ($7 50.) On the 24th of April, another lot of 790 was disposed of, part at six dollars, ($6,) and part at seven dollars and sixty cents, ($7 60,) and these were afterwards resold at ten dollars ($10) each. On the 30th of April, nine dollars ($9) each was paid for 1,000 of this arm, and a few days afterwards ten dollars ($10) was offered and refused for another lot; all in the New York market. This, so far as the commission has been able to ascertain, is (with a single exception hereafter to be noticed) the highest price which these arms reached in changing hands last summer between individuals.

Two depositions, under oath, expressing opinions as to the value of these arms, have been submitted for our consideration.

The first is by Mr. Edward Savage, of Connecticut, an experienced manufacturer of arms. He expresses the opinion that the 5,000 carbines sold to General Frémont, " when rifled and with breech enlarged, are now, and have always been, worth as much as any other carbine in use in the army of the United States." But on personal examination by the commission, Mr. Savage declared that his intention was to compare them only with the Sharpe's carbine, old model, (from which the escape of gas was great,) and that he is not acquainted with the other breech-loaders of the day.

The second is by Mr. Austin Baldwin, whose knowledge of such arms is restricted to his experience as military storekeeper, under President Harrison. This gentleman states that the government paid for the Hall carbine to the manufacturer, at first, twenty dollars, ($20,) afterwards seventeen dollars and fifty cents, ($17 50,) and that as they were made for the government alone, it is, in his opinion, "impossible to fix any price as their market value." He adds, "that in view of their original cost, he thinks the price of twenty-two dollars, ($22,) at the time of purchase, namely, in August, 1861, to have been fair and reasonable."

But the opinion that because these arms were manufactured for the government alone, it was impossible to determine their market value, is evidently a mistake. Mr. Baldwin either was uninformed, or overlooked the fact, that through the months of April, May, June, and July, like arms were in the market, and, as has been shown, changed hands among individuals, at prices varying from six to ten dollars. Thus we are not, as he appears to have concluded, thrown back on the original cost of the weapon, but can refer to actual sales, in order to determine its fair market value.

The opinion of the chief of ordnance, as to the value of the arm in June, 1861, is indicated by the fact that he recommended the sale of all the arms of this description then in possession of the government, (unrifled, however,) at three dollars and fifty cents; but the rifling cost less than one dollar each.

The ordnance officer, who resided in New York during the period of the sale, Major P. V. Hagner, in his testimony before this commission, and in reply to a question as to what, in his judgment, the Hall carbine was worth as altered by Mr. Stevens, expressed the opinion that "considering the exigency of the times," its value was "ten or twelve dollars."

This opinion nearly agrees with that which we may derive from one of the main incidents in this case—the terms, namely, of the contract of August 1, 1861, between two shrewd business men, one agreeing to sell, and the other to buy, 5,000 of these carbines, rifled, at twelve dollars and fifty cents, the expense of the rifling and breech enlarging, estimated at one dollar per carbine, being deducted from the above price, in the payment by Stevens to Eastman.

This would indicate that the market value of the arm had risen from the date of the sales already mentioned to that of the sale by Eastman to Stevens; and that was probably the case. There was no period of the war when the demand for arms was greater than in the early days of August, 1861. Yet, after taking into view every consideration that presents itself in favor of the claimant, the commission is unable to find any evidence which places the market value of the arm, including cost of rifling and enlargement, above the price paid by Stevens to Eastman, especially if to that price is to be added the cost of boxes and of appendages, and the usual percentage of a broker.

Thus, as regards the equitable considerations which present themselves in this case, it appears:

First. That whether an exigency existed or not, no exigency was actually supplied by the immediate delivery of these arms; the expectations of General Frémont in this matter, as indicated in his telegram, having been wholly disappointed.

Second. The circumstances do not indicate good faith on the part of the seller, since his intention was to sell to the government guns which at the time were its own property and in its own possession, and had subsequently to be purchased from it; and that he further intended to do this without the cognizance of the Ordnance department, and on such terms that, were the commission now to confirm the sale, the government would be paying for the gun six times as much as it sold it for, and would be the loser by the transaction to the amount of more than ninety-two thousand dollars.

Third. The price asked, after making every proper allowance for the great demand at the time for cavalry arms, was much above the market value, and was not fair or reasonable, but manifestly exorbitant.

In view of this state of the case, the commission find that the government ought not, either in justice or equity, to confirm the purchase of these carbines at twenty-two dollars.

On the other hand, the commission do not find that the right of the claimant to be paid for these arms at their market value is invalidated by the circumstances, however remarkable, connected with the sale by the government to Eastman, nor by the rate of charge per carbine at which that sale was made; for it is to be conceded that the price of three dollars and fifty cents, though far below the market value of the arm in June, 1861, was recommended by the Ordnance department and approved by the Secretary of War; and while the government was clearly not bound by its offer of sale, at a certain price fixed in June, still to sell at the same price in August, yet it did sell, and thus practically recognized the obligation as still existing.

It further appears that both Mr. Stevens and Mr. Eastman, on examination before the commission, have sworn that the former paid to the latter, for appendages delivered along with the carbines and for packing boxes, the sum of three thousand six hundred and ninety-five dollars and thirty cents, ($3,695 30.) The previous facts in this connexion are as follows:

In the letter to Mr. Eastman of the chief of ordnance, agreeing to sell at three dollars and fifty cents, nothing is said about appendages or packing boxes. Captain (now Major) Whiteley, of the New York arsenal, having received no instructions on this point, wrote to the Ordnance department, asking whether these were included in the three dollars and fifty cents. As no instructions had been given at the time Mr. Morgan appeared ready to make payment, Major Whiteley delivered the carbines boxed and supplied with the usual implements, and rendered to Mr. Eastman the following statement and receipt, which was then signed by the latter:

" *Statement of articles sold at New York arsenal during the third quarter* 1861.

" 4,996 carbines, Hall's,
   4,996 carbine screwdrivers,
   4,996 carbine wipers,
     499 carbine spring vises,   } at $3 50 each, $17,486.
     250 carbine bullet moulds,
     250 boxes, packing,

" Received, this 7th day of August, 1861, of Captain R. H. K. Whiteley, commanding New York arsenal, four thousand nine hundred and ninety-six Hall's carbines, for which I have paid to the said Captain R. H. K. Whiteley the sum of seventeen thousand four hundred and eighty-six dollars, being at the rate of three dollars and fifty cents for each carbine.

                        " ARTHUR M. EASTMAN."

In a reply to his application received some ten or twelve days after the sale, Captain Whiteley was instructed to charge for the appendages and boxes at the usual rates, and, under date August 20, 1861, he addressed a letter to Mr. Eastman informing him of this decision, sending in an account for three thousand six hundred and ninety-five dollars and thirty cents ($3,695 30,) and requesting his immediate attention to the subject. Mr. Eastman (as the commission learn from a letter of Major Whiteley, of date January 18, 1862,) refused to pay for these, alleging that the three dollars and fifty cents covered all.

The government "never did receive a cent," says Major Whiteley, "either for appendages or boxes." He adds, "to enforce the charge I found would involve a lawsuit, and therefore I abandoned it." The claim against Mr. Eastman, however, if originally good in itself, is not invalidated by this delay to press it, but may, at the option of the government, still be maintained against him, yet it would be scarcely just to allow it to be asserted against holders of the property into whose hands, without fraud, it had passed, through the action of a government official. As to such persons, in selling to them the arms at their market value, the sole question is, whether the price fixed upon is such as fairly to include boxes and appendages along with the arms or not.

Under these circumstances, more especially as the government itself actually received nothing for the boxes or appendages, the commission might not unfairly decide against this item, and throw the loss upon Mr. Stevens, on the principle that twelve dollars and fifty cents a gun was a sufficient price to include all. Desirous, however, that the government, in fixing the market value at which it is bound to pay for these guns, should avoid all imputation of having placed that price below a just standard, and willing to give Mr. Stevens the advantage of the inference from his own act, namely, that the guns may, in August, 1861, have been worth twelve dollars and fifty cents each without appendages, the commission decide that the cost of these latter be repaid to Mr. Stevens.

The actual amount paid for the alterations made in these carbines, as appears by detailed accounts submitted to the commission, is three thousand seven hundred and seventy-three dollars ($3,773) for rifling and altering, and two hundred and fifty-nine dollars and seventy-five cents ($259 75) for freight, cartage, and other contingent expenses; together, $4,032 75.

The total amount, then, advanced by Mr. Stevens for these arms is as follows:

5,000 carbines, at $12 50 each	$62,500 00
Deduct amount allowed by Mr. Eastman for altering the same..	5,000 00
	57,500 00
Packingboxes and appendages, paid to Mr. Eastman..........	3,695 30
	61,195 30
Add for rifling, enlarging, and contingencies	4,032 75
Total paid by Mr. Stevens.........................	65,228 05

The amount paid September 10, 1861, (to wit, the sum of fifty-five thousand five hundred and fifty dollars,) the commission decide shall be regarded as a payment on account. Deducting this, there remains unpaid of the sum advanced by Mr. Stevens nine thousand six hundred and seventy-eight dollars and five cents ($9,678 05.)

The commission direct that this amount of $9,678 05, with interest from September 20, 1861, until paid, and the further sum of two and a half per cent. brokerage on sixty-five thousand two hundred and twenty-eight dollars and five cents, ($65,228 05,) namely, the sum of one thousand three hundred and thirty dollars and seventy cents ($1,330 70) be paid to Mr. J. Pierpont Morgan against his receipt for the same in full of all demands against the United States in connexion with this affair.

Under this decision, the price to be paid by the United States for these carbines will be thirteen dollars and thirty-one cents, ($13 31,) being nine dollars and eighty-one cents ($9 81) per carbine, or upwards of forty-nine thousand dollars ($49,000) in all, above the price at which the arms were sold to Mr. Eastman by the United States.

In conclusion, it becomes the duty of the commission to advert to a statement referred to them by the Secretary of War, from one of the most respectable houses in New York, setting forth that they had made large advances in good faith to Mr. Stevens, on the security of his agreement with General Frémont, upon terms which the firm subsequently declined to disclose, and arguing that they ought to be protected against loss in so doing.

The commission will much regret if any loyal and public-spirited business house shall be found to have advanced a sum beyond that above awarded, on the faith of any alleged securities that may have made their appearance in this case. It is to be considered, however, whether the firm in question exercised reasonable caution in the premises.

As to the security upon which they advanced the money, it is to be remarked—

First. That government vouchers, though according to usage transferable, do not, in their circulation, enjoy the immunities which belong to negotiable mercantile paper. The assignee of such a voucher stands in no better position than his assignor, and the former cannot escape the risks to which the latter is exposed. Under any other rule a protection against fraud would be impracticable, since the mere transfer of a government voucher would suffice to render it unimpeachable.

But, secondly, it is in evidence before the commission that, in this case, it was not upon a government voucher that advances were originally made, but merely—according to the testimony of the parties themselves—on a telegram from an army officer of rank, accompanied by a letter introducing Mr. Stevens, but unaccompanied by any proof that the officer in question had been authorized by the Secretary of War, or by the chief of ordnance, to purchase arms for the government. A knowledge of the law of 1815 could not have failed to show the insufficient authority of such a telegram. Nor is it an unfair inference, from the unwillingness evidenced by the house in question, to state the terms on which their advances were made, that, if these terms were disclosed, they might supply evidence that, during the negotiation for funds, doubts as to the sufficiency of the security had actually presented themselves, and that the confidence claimed to have been then felt was largely mingled with distrust.

It is true, that while the house in question (Messrs. Ketchum, Son & Co.) admit that the security on which the advances were made was General Frémont's telegraphic despatch, backed by a private note of introduction, they allude, in the conclusion of their statement above cited, to the large sums advanced by banks and bankers on "certified certificates." But no certified certificate, except for the sum actually paid, namely, fifty-five thousand five hundred and fifty dollars, is to be found in this case. There exists, for the fifty-eight thousand one hundred and seventy-five dollars claimed, only a partially filled up *form* of voucher, bearing an acknowledgment of the receipt of the arms in good order, signed by the ordnance officer at St. Louis, but showing (as the blank spaces disclose) that the required certificate that "the account is correct and just," is filled up by no amount, and remained unsigned by any one; showing, also, that the certificate, apparently prepared for General Frémont's signature, to the effect that "the arms were purchased for the troops under his command," was not signed by that officer. Thus, even if this quasi voucher may have been taken into account by Ketchum, Son & Co., in making some of their later advances, its very appearance was suggestive of the necessity of caution and inquiry regarding it. Nor has it, in point of fact, been shown that it was so taken into account.

Be this, however, as it may, it cannot, with any show of reason, be expected that the government should protect even innocent persons from loss, if these persons have had dealings, however upright, with those who, having acted towards it in bad faith, have lost all claim, equitable as well as legal, to have their accounts allowed, without such reduction in the amount as justice and a reasonable regard for the public interests imperatively require to be made.

We are, sir, very respectfully, your obedient servants,

J. HOLT,
ROBERT DALE OWEN,
Commissioners, &c.

Brigadier General J. W. RIPLEY,
Chief of Ordnance.

CASE No. 98.

T. ROBINSON ROGERS.

T. Robinson Rogers submits copy of an order to furnish 25,000 Springfield muskets, at $20.

NEW YORK, *February* 7, 1862.

SIR: I beg leave to enclose a copy of a contract issued to me on the 24th of December last and accepted on the 2d day of January, 1862, for the manufacture of twenty-five thousand Springfield rifles. To comply with the terms of this contract I have made purchases of large amounts of material sufficient generally to fulfil the whole order, and have made arrangements, and have already purchased part of the machinery to manufacture the same. I shall be fully able to carry out the requirements of the contracts, and expect to commence deliveries of the muskets before the time mentioned.

I have the honor to remain, sir, respectfully, your obedient servant,

T. ROBINSON ROGERS.

Hon. EDWIN M. STANTON,
Secretary of War, Washington, D. C.

ORDNANCE OFFICE,
Washington, December 24, 1861.

SIR: By direction of the Secretary of War, I offer you an order for twenty-five thousand (25,000) muskets of the Springfield pattern, on the following terms and conditions, viz: These arms are to be furnished with the regular appendages, and are to be in all respects identical with the standard rifle musket made at the United States armory at Springfield, Massachusetts, and are to interchange with it and with each other in all their parts. They are to be subject to inspection by United States inspectors in the same manner that the Springfield arms are inspected, and none are to be received or paid for but such as pass inspection, and are approved by the United States inspectors. These twenty-five thousand (25,000) arms and appendages are to be delivered at your armory as follows, viz: not less than five hundred (500) in *each* of the months of July, August and September, 1862; not less than one thousand (1,000) in *each* of the months of October and November, 1862; not less than fifteen hundred (1,500) in December, 1862, and not less than two thousand (2,000) per month thereafter, until the entire twenty-five thousand (25,000) shall have been delivered; and you are to have the right to deliver more rapidly than according to the number of arms before specified, if you can do so. In case of any failure to make deliveries to the extent and within the times before specified, you are to forfeit the right to deliver whatever number may be deficient in the specified number for the month in which the failure occurs. All these arms and appendages are to be delivered by you, and this order, if transferred to another party, is to be thereby forfeited. Payments are to be made in such funds as the Treasury Department may provide, for each delivery, on certificates of inspection and receipt by the United States inspectors, at the rate of twenty dollars for each arm, including appendages. All these arms and appendages are to be packed by you in boxes of the regular pattern, with twenty (20) muskets and appendages in each box, for which a fair price, to be determined by the United States inspectors, will be allowed.

Please signify, in writing, your acceptance or non-acceptance of this order on the terms and conditions herein stated.

Respectfully, your obedient servant,

JAMES W. RIPLEY,
Brigadier General.

Mr. T. ROBINSON ROGERS, *New York, N. Y.*

Before commission, June 18, 1862.

No communication having been received in reply to the letters addressed to T. Robinson Rogers, the commission decide that they will act upon this case without further delay.

The letter signed T. Robinson Rogers, and addressed to the honorable E. M. Stanton, Secretary of War, under date February 7, 1862, having been read, in view of the statements made therein, the commission agree to confirm the order given to him December 24, 1861, to the extent of 20,000 arms, upon the same terms and conditions in like cases.

P. V. HAGNER,
Major of Ordnance, Assistant to Commission.

COMMISSION ON ORDNANCE AND ORDNANCE STORES,
Washington, June 18, 1862.

GENERAL: The commission have the honor to report as follows:

CASE No. 98.—T. ROBINSON ROGERS.

Order by direction of the Secretary of War, dated December 24, 1861. No. 59, page 156. Ex. Doc. No. 67. Referred by direction of the Secretary of War.

To furnish 25,000 muskets, with appendages, of the Springfield pattern, at the price of $20 per gun. Deliveries to be made not less than 500 in each of the months of July, August, and September, 1862; not less than 1,000 in each of the months of October and November, 1862; not less than 1,500 in December, 1862, and not less than 2,000 per month thereafter.—(See Case No. 72.)

The commission find that the above order was not given in accordance with the law and regulations, and that it is not therefore a contract of legal force, inasmuch as it does not contain the express requirements of the law, and was not made "after previous advertisement for proposals repecting the same;" nor can it be regarded as an "open purchase," being for articles which did not require "immediate delivery," but were stipulated to be manufactured and delivered at prescribed distant periods.

They further consider that the number of arms ordered is larger than the wants of the government justify in this case, at the price fixed; and therefore, according to the principles set forth in Mason's case, No. 72, they direct that the order to Mr. Rogers be confirmed, subject to all its terms, to the extent of 20,000 muskets, upon condition that he shall, within fifteen days after notice of this decision, execute bond, with good and sufficient sureties, in the form and with the stipulations prescribed by law and the regulations, for the performance of the contract, as thus modified, resulting from said order and acceptance; and upon his failure or refusal to execute such bond then the said order shall be declared cancelled and of no effect.

The commission further decide that the deliveries under the contract to be executed shall be required at or within the periods stipulated in the original order, but that the number specified may be reduced proportionately to the reduction of the whole number, so that the contract shall be completed within the time allowed in the original order.

We are, sir, very respectfully, your obedient servants,

J. HOLT,
ROBERT DALE OWEN,
Commissioners, &c.

P. V. HAGNER,
Major of Ordnance, Assistant to Commission.

Brigadier General J. W. RIPLEY,
Chief of Ordnance.

CASE No. 99.

ROGERS, SPENCER & CO.

ORDNANCE OFFICE,
Washington, December 26, 1861.

GENTLEMEN: By direction of the Secretary of War I offer you an order for five thousand (5,000) Pettengill pistols, of the army size and calibre, with appendages, on the following terms and conditions, viz: These arms are all to be of the pattern and calibre, and are to be subject to inspection and proof by such inspectors as this department may designate for the purpose. They are to be made according to a pattern to be previously submitted by you for examination and approval at this office, and to serve as a standard in the inspection; and none are to be received or paid for but such as are approved by the United States inspectors as in all respects like and equal in quality to the standard.

These pistols are to be delivered by you at your armory as follows, viz: Not less than one thousand (1,000) in ninety days from this date, and not less than one thousand (1,000) per month thereafter until the whole five thousand (5,000) shall have been delivered. And you are to have the right to deliver more rapidly than according to the number of arms before specified if you can do so. In case of any failure to make deliveries to the extent and within the times before specified, you are to forfeit the right to deliver whatever number may be deficient in the specified number for the month in which the failure occurs.

All these arms and appendages are to be delivered by you; and this order if transferred by you to another party is to be thereby forfeited. Payments are to be made, in such funds as the Treasury Department may provide, for each delivery, on certificates of inspection and receipt by the United States inspectors, at the rate of twenty dollars ($20) for each arm, including appendages. All these arms and appendages are to be packed by you in suitable boxes, with fifty pistols and appendages in each box, for which a fair price, to be determined by the United States inspector, will be allowed.

Please signify in writing your acceptance or non-acceptance of this order on the terms and conditions therein stated.

Respectfully, your obedient servant,

JAMES W. RIPLEY,
Brigadier General.

Messrs. ROGERS, SPENCER & CO.,
New York, N. Y.

Ex. Doc. 72——32

ORDNANCE OFFICE,
Washington, December 26, 1861.

By direction of the Secretary of War I offer you an order for twenty-five thousand (25,000) muskets, of the Springfield pattern, on the following terms and conditions, viz: These arms are to be furnished with the regular append-ages, and are to be in all respects identical with the standard rifle musket made at the United States armory at Springfield, Massachusetts, and are to inter-change with it and with each other in all their parts. They are to be subject to inspection by United States inspectors in the same manner that the Springfield arms are inspected, and none are to be received or paid for but such as pass inspection and are approved by the United States inspector.

These twenty-five thousand (25,000) arms and appendages are to be delivered at your armory as follows, viz: Not less than five hundred (500) in each of the months of July, August, and September, 1862; not less than one thousand (1,000) in each of the months of October and November, 1862; not less than fifteen hundred (1,500) in December, 1862, and not less than two thousand (2,000) per month thereafter until the entire twenty-five thousand (25,000) shall have been delivered. And you have the right to deliver more rapidly than accord-ing to the number of arms before specified if you can do so.

In case of any failure to make deliveries to the extent and within the times before specified, you are to forfeit the right to deliver whatever number may be deficient in the specified number for the month on which the failure occurs.

All these arms and appendages are to be delivered by you, and this order if transferred to another person is to be thereby forfeited. Payments are to be made, in such funds as the Treasury Department may provide, for each delivery, on certificates of inspection and receipt by the United States inspectors, at the rate of twenty dollars for each arm, including appendages. All these arms and appendages are to be packed by you in boxes of the regular pattern, with twenty (20) muskets and appendages in each box, for which a fair price, to be determined by the United States inspector, will be allowed.

Please signify, in writing, your acceptance or non-acceptance of this order on the terms and conditions herein stated.

Respectfully, your obedient servant,

JAMES W. RIPLEY,

ROGERS, SPENCER & CO., *New York.*

NEW YORK CITY, *January* 10, 1862.

We hereby accept and promise to execute the same, on the terms and conditions therein stated, the order from the Ordnance department, under date of December 26, 1861, for 5,000 " Pettengill pistols," of the army size and calibre, with ap-pendages, for the sum of $20 each, to be of the same description and character, and will be delivered as stated in said order. A sample will be furnished with-out delay.

We have the honor to be, very respectfully, your obedient servants,

ROGERS, SPENCER & CO.,

Hon. SECRETARY OF WAR.

NEW YORK CITY, *January* 10, 1862.

We hereby accept and promise to execute the same, on the terms and condi-tions therein stated, the order from the Ordnance department, under date of December 26, 1861, for 25,000 Springfield rifles, with appendages, for the sum of $20 each, to be of the same description and character, and will be delivered as stated in said order.

We have the honor to be, very respectfully, your obedient servants,

ROGERS, SPENCER & CO.

Hon. SECRETARY OF WAR.

WILLOW VALE, *New York*, 1862.

Rogers, Spencer & Co. submit copies of orders to furnish 25,000 Springfield muskets and 5,000 Pettengill pistols.

MANUFACTORY OF ROGERS, SPENCER & CO.
Willow Vale, Oneida county, New York, February 5, 1862.

In the month of December last we presented to your department a sample of the "Pettengill revolver pistol" for examination, which is now in your department; we hold the patent and are the exclusive manufacturers thereof. We think it will be found a safer and better arm than anything heretofore made in the United States. We have been perfecting it for the last two years, until we have arrived at that degree of perfection when we are willing to risk the reputation of our establishment upon its full and final success. The sample presented was .34 calibre, and the largest size previously made. The result of this sample was an order for 5,000 of the army size and calibre, which order we are now filling. And in compliance with an official notice issuing from the department, we send you a statement of what has been done to fill said order.

Immediately upon the receipt of said order we increased our working force from 70 men to 150; employed them in making the tools specially required for this size pistol, such as patterns, gauges, forms, boring tools, mills, &c., since their completion. We have employed our men upon the barrels, cylinders, and lock work, a large amount of which is now made to fill this order; they are so made that every piece shall interchange with each other, upon the principle pursued at the armory at Springfield in the manufacture of the rifle. We are now running one manufactory night and day in order to fill this order, and have so far expended upon it $15,000.

We have also erected a new building, separate and apart from our main factory, expressly for forges and other work connected therewith. At the time we presented this pistol we proposed to make a revolving rifle, (self-cocker,) steel barrel, and four, five, or six shooter, upon the principle of the pistol, to be equal, if not superior, to any arms in use. This proposition was followed by an order for 25,000 Springfield rifles. Two of our firm went immediately thereafter to Springfield to examine the rifle, and more particularly to examine the machinery necessary to make these arms; on their return the order was accepted and the building erected, as spoken of above, for the purpose of doing the work for this order, which we intend to fill; first, however, completing the order for the 5,000 pistols.

We would here suggest, if agreeable to you, that we make a rifle four, five, or six shooter, and present to you for examination, upon the principle of the "Pettengill revolver pistol;" of course it requires time to perfect the tools and machinery even for one gun; yet, if it is not found acceptable to the department, the expense shall be our loss.

A copy of the order for the 5,000 pistols is here enclosed, marked A, and the acceptance of that order, marked A A; also a copy of the order for 25,000 Springfield rifles, marked B, and the acceptance of that order, marked B B.

All of which we respectfully submit.

We have the honor to be, very respecfully, your obedient servants,

ROGERS, SPENCER & CO.,
Willow Vale, Oneida county, New York.

Hon. SECRETARY OF WAR.

N. B.—Since the receipt of these orders we have closed our office in New York city, temporarily used for the sale of the pistols, our manufactory being located at Willow Vale, Oneida county, New York, where we have been located with our factory for the last twenty-five years, and where we should be happy to receive any orders in future. R., S. & Co.

WASHINGTON, *April* 4, 1862.

Rogers, Spencer & Co. ask extension of time in delivery of pistols. State cause of delay.

ORDNANCE OFFICE,
Washington, April 14, 1862.

Respectfully submitted to the Secretary of War. This case seems to be properly referable to the Commission on Ordnance and Ordnance stores.

Inasmuch as the failure to present a sample pistol heretofore appears to have been without fault of the contractors, and as they seem to have gone on in good faith to execute their contract for 5,000 pistols, and now present a well made arm as a sample, I think the extension of time asked for should be granted.

JAMES W. RIPLEY,
Brigadier General.

Referred back to the chief of ordnance with directions to require Rogers, Spencer & Co. to file, *under oath*, a statement of the facts on which they rely to support the within application, specifying in their affidavits the names and residences of the several agents they have employed to represent them before the department, and the duties assigned to or performed by such agents respectively.

By order of the Secretary of War.

P. H. WATSON,
Assistant Secretary of War.

WASHINGTON, *April* 4, 1862.

In the month of December last we proposed to the Ordnance department to manufacture guns and pistols for the use of the government. We received an order from the department, dated December 26, 1861, for the manufacture of 25,000 Springfield muskets and also for 5,000 "Pettengill pistols," of the army size and calibre, the patent for which we exclusively hold.

The order for the pistols required 1,000 to be delivered in ninety days and 1,000 per month thereafter, from the 26th of December, 1861, We found it would take us at least ninety days to make the tools and machinery necessary before we could get out any (even the sample) of this large size pistol, we previously having made none larger than the belt size. We immediately wrote to a gentlemen to call at the department and say that it would be impossible for us to deliver the first 1,000 under four months from the date of said order, and 1,000 per month thereafter. To this application answer was given by the Secretary, that it should make no difference, but to go on and make them. We thereupon accepted the order for the guns and pistols, on the 10th day of January, 1862; and on that day we deposited the same in the post office at Utica, Oneida county, New York, directed to the Secretary of War.

From that day we refused all orders whatever and proceeded at once with all our men and forces to make the tools and machinery necessary for this army size pistol, and we have been at work day and night ever since (and are now so at work) with a large body of men, at great expense, so as to fill the order for said pistols, a large quantity of which we now have in the various process of manufacture.

An order having appeared in public print, signed by the present Secretary of War, requiring within a given time all parties having orders or contracts for fire-arms to file a copy of such order or contract with him, with a statement of what had been done under them. In compliance with this order we did send a copy of the order for the guns and pistols, with a statement of what had been done under them, by mail, directed to the honorable E. M. Stanton, Secretary of War, as required by said order.

By the terms of the order for the pistols we were required to furnish a sample to be approved of as a standard. As before stated, we had to make all the tools and machinery necessary to make this army size and calibre. We could not therefore furnish this sample (worked out by these tools and machinery so that all others would be equal in all respects to the sample) until the completion of said machinery, which was done on the 15th day of March, when we immediately sent, by express, the sample required to a gentleman at Washington, with directions to deliver it to the Ordnance department as the sample required. Not having heard from him (after writing a second time) of the delivery and acceptance of said sample, or the receipt of the same, we came here with a second sample, and now present the same to the department for approval. We now find that the gentleman to whom we sent the first sample was absent on government business, and is now absent, which will account for our not having earlier delivered it.

We have in good faith and in all possible despatch been at work day and night to fill this order for the pistols, and hope we may be permitted to fill it by the delivery of 1,000 per month from the 1st day of April, 1862.

Very respectfully, your obedient servants,
ROGERS, SPENCER & CO.,
Willow Vale, near Utica, Oneida county, New York.

Hon. JAS. W. RIPLEY,
Ordnance Department, Washington.

WASHINGTON, *April* 4, 1862.

In the month of December last we proposed to the Ordnance department to manufacture guns and pistols for the use of the government. We received an order from said department, dated December 26, 1861, for the manufacture of 25,000 Springfield muskets, and als·) for 5,000 Pettengill pistols of the army size and calibre, the manufacture of which under this patent we exclusively hold. The order for the pistols required 1,000 to be delivered in ninety days, and 1,000 per month thereafter from the 26th of December last. We found that it would take us at least ninety days to make the tools and machinery necessary to make this large size pistol, we previously having manufactured none larger than the belt size.

We immediately wrote to a gentleman to call at the department and state that it would be impossible for us to deliver the first 1,000 under four months from said order, and 1,000 per month thereafter. To this application answer was given by the Secretary that it should make no difference, but to go on and make them. We thereupon accepted the order for the guns and pistols on the 10th day of January, 1862, and on that day we deposited the same in the post office at Utica, Oneida county, New York, directed to the Secretary of War. From that day we refused all orders whatever and proceeded at once with all our men and forces to make the tools and machinery necessary to make this army size pistol, and we have been at work day and night ever since, and now are at work with a large body of men, at great expense, to be prepared to complete the order for the pistols, a large quantity of which we now have in the various process of manufacture.

An order having appeared in the public prints, signed by the present Secretary of War, requiring all parties (within a given time) having orders or contracts for fire-arms to file a copy of such order or contract with him, with a statement of what had been done under them; in compliance with this order we did send a copy of the order for the guns and pistols, with a statement of what had been done under them, by mail, directed to honorable E. M. Stanton, Secretary of War.

By the terms of the order for the pistols we were required to furnish a sample to be approved of as a standard. As before stated, we had to make all the tools and machinery to make this army size and calibre. We could not therefore furnish this sample (worked out by these tools and machinery so that all others would be equal in all respects to the sample) until the completion of said machinery, which was done on the 15th day of March, when we sent, by express, the sample required to a gentleman at Washington, with directions to deliver it to the Ordnance department as the sample required. Not having heard from him (after writing a second time) of the acceptance or delivery or receipt of said sample to the department, we came here with a second sample, and present the same to the department for approval. We now find that the gentleman to whom we sent the first sample was absent on government business, and is now absent, which will account for our not having earlier delivered it.

We have in good faith and in all possible despatch been at work night and day to fill this order for the pistols, and hope we may be permitted to fill said order by the delivery of 1,000 per month from the 1st of April, 1862.

ROGERS, SPENCER & CO.,
Willow Vale, Oneida county, New York

Hon. Jas. W. Ripley,
   Ordnance Department, Washington.

Washington City, *District of Columbia, ss:*

On this 7th day of April, 1862, personally appeared before me George C. Tallman, who is personally known to me, and who, being by me duly sworn as the law directs, deposeth and says: That he is a partner in the firm of Rogers, Spencer & Co., doing business at Willow Vale, Oneida county, and in the State of New York, and that he received an order for 5,000 Pettengill pistols from the Ordnance department; and he further deposeth and says that he made a statement and application in reference to said pistols, directed and delivered by him to the honorable James W. Ripley, of the Ordnance department, under date of the 4th of April, 1862, (a copy of which, as near as may be, is hereunto annexed,) and which statement therein contained is in all respects true; and he further deposeth and says that his son, Henry C. Tallman, was the person who called at the office of the Secretary of War to request an extension from ninety days to four months, from which to commence the delivery of said 5,000 Pettengill pistols; and he further deposeth and says Edward D. Tallman, the nephew of said deponent, was the gentleman to whom he sent, by express, the sample of said pistol, so to be by him delivered as therein stated; and he further deposeth and says that no other person or persons whatever have acted as the agent or agents of said Rogers, Spencer & Co., or either of them.

GEORGE C. TALLMAN.

Sworn and subscribed before me this seventh day of April, A. D. 1862.

N. CALLAN, *J. P.* [L. s.]

Before commission, April 12, 1862.

Mr. Tallman, of Rogers, Spencer & Co., came before the commission relative to the contracts of that firm for Pettengill pistols and Springfield muskets, states:

We have given up the hope of making the first three deliveries of Springfield guns in time. We purpose to make the whole arm except the barrel. We have no stocking machines. I think my partner has engaged rough barrels from Mr. Washburne, of Worcester. We have no barrel machinery, and none for locks or mountings. We are first to finish an order for pistols, which cannot be done earlier than the first of August We are allowed upon it four months from March 26, but we have asked for four months from the first of May.

ORDNANCE OFFICE,
Washington, D. C., May 23, 1862.

SIR: In accordance with the request of the commission contained in Major P. V. Hagner's letter of the 14th of April, to have the sample Pettengill pistol examined and reported upon by Captain A. B. Dyer, that officer was directed on the same day to make the inspection and report asked for. I enclose herewith a copy of his report.

Respectfully, your obedient servant,

JAS. W. RIPLEY, *Brigadier General.*

J. WISE, Esq.,
Secretary of Commission on Ordnance Stores.

SPRINGFIELD ARMORY, *May* 20, 1862.

SIR: In compliance with your instructions to me, dated April 14, 1862, directing me to "examine and try the sample Pettengill pistol which will be presented," and to report to the commission on ordnance stores through your office my opinion "of its sufficiency and suitableness in all respects for the purpose for which it is designed," I have the honor to report that Mr. Tallman presented the sample pistol to me for trial about three weeks since; that I carefully examined the workmanship and found it to be good, the parts being as little liable to get out of order as those of any other revolving pistol I have seen.

The firing was accurate, and the penetration good, the balls penetrating three white pine boards one inch thick and embedding themselves in the fourth, at a distance of fifty yards. The calibre of the pistol is .44. The charge twenty-four grains of powder and a conical ball weighing 218 grains. As many as sixty shots were fired. The cylinder which contains the charges is revolved and the pistol is cocked and discharged by pulling the trigger. I regard this as a serious objection, and do not see how it can be corrected. The great distance to be passed over by the trigger in revolving the cylinder and discharging the pistol makes it impossible, even when the pistol is clean, to fire rapidly with ease, and after a few discharges it becomes foul and heated, and the firing is done with great difficulty. I sometimes found it impossible to revolve the cylinder by means of the trigger.

Mr. Tallman was of opinion that the objections could be removed, and asked to be allowed to withdraw the sample pistol in order to have the necessary alteration made. This was allowed. Mr. Tallman returned about two weeks since with the pistol, and it was again tried. When clean it was fired with less difficulty, but after a few discharges it was almost impossible to revolve the cylinder by means of the trigger, and the pistol was again withdrawn.

It was again presented for trial a few days since, and has been fired more than one hundred times. It has worked better than on either of the former occasions, still it has not been free from the objections named above. In my opinion, it is not "suitable in all respects" for the military service.

Respectfully, your obedient servant,

A. B. DYER, *Captain of Ordnance.*

Brigadier General J. W. RIPLEY,
Chief of Ordnance, Washington, D. C.

COMMISSION ON ORDNANCE AND ORDNANCE STORES,
Washington, May 24, 1862.

GENTLEMEN: A report has been received of the trials made at Springfield of the sample pistol submitted by you (as required by your order of December 26) for the "examination and approval of the Ordnance department," and to serve as a standard in the inspection. This report shows that the sample is not satisfactory, and you cannot, therefore, proceed in the manufacture of the arms.

The commission directs me to say that, as their session will soon terminate, and they will have to act previously in this case, they desire to know when your sample, as finally purposed, will be in readiness for trial, and whether you wish to submit anything further for consideration.

Very respectfully, your obedient servant,

P. V. HAGNER,
Major of Ordnance.

Messrs. ROGERS, SPENCER & CO.,
Willow Vale, near Utica, New York.

WASHINGTON, D. C., *June* 4, 1862.

GENTLEMEN: It was on the presentation by us of a pair of the Pettengill pistols, belt size, that the order for 5,000 of the same, army size, was issued to us. We were not making the army size, and could not accept the terms, as to time, of the order. We proposed, however, to accept of it if an extension of the time to the beginning of deliveries of from forty-five to sixty days could be had, to enable us to initiate the making of that size. We were assured that this extension would be granted, and thereupon proceeded with the preparations for and the manufacture of the pistols. We supposed, of course, that the pistols presented had received from government officers such examination and trial as were necessary to a full determination of their qualities, and that we had only to make substantially the same, but of the army size, to satisfy the order We were not suspicious of any irregularities in our negotiations with government.

The making of the pistols had progressed so far that the first 1,000 of them was passing to the assembly room, the fourth 1,000 just entering the works, and all the processes up to the assembling were moving at the rate of 50 pistols per day. As soon as we could, from the first pieces made, we finished and sent forward one as a sample. *Then* we learned that our arm did not stand fully accepted by government, and the order was made for its trial at Springfield. But at this time we had exhausted our working means, and had borrowed largely means to work upon. Borrowed means we could no longer command, *when a doubt had arisen* as to returns, and we were compelled to stop. We had expended upon the pistols and upon the small tools special to that size $23,000 to $25,000.

The report of the trial at Springfield you have. It is favorable to our workmanship, to the action of the pistol as to range and penetration, and to the arrangement and adjustment of its parts, they " being as little liable to get out of order as those of any other revolving pistol" the reporter had seen. The fact that " the cylinder which contains the charges is revolved, and the pistol is worked and discharged by pulling the trigger," is regarded by Captain Dyer " as a serious objection." This objection applies to the most radical distinguishing characteristic of the Pettengill pistol, and the same to those upon presentation of which the order was issued as to these. We could not, therefore, anticipate that objection under our order, and we could not have provided against it in the Pettengill pistol if we had anticipated it, yet we are notified that the arm " is not satisfactory," and that we cannot, therefore, proceed with their manufacture.

We have no disposition to urge upon our government an arm it does not want; but the present shape of the matter is disastrous to us in the extreme, and we therefore request you to consider whether some relief should not be afforded us. Cannot we make for the government some army pistol that we would be at liberty to make, and of which the government is in need, for such prices as are paid to other parties, and on such terms as to time as will enable us to manufacture them advantageously? Our preparations for this work are good. We can do it to the extent of their capacity as cheaply as other parties. Such an arrangement would enable us to work up a large amount of partly-wrought stock which otherwise will be lost. If not in this way, can we not in some other way be restored or relieved from this ruin which must come from the present position of the matter? We are solicitors not only for ourselves, but for our creditors and for our workmen, one hundred and eighty of whom have been suddenly deprived of employment, and we at the same time being deprived of the means of paying them wages already earned, of which they stand sorely in need. We shall be glad to embrace any offer or means of relief which honest men can comply with.

Respectfully,

ROGERS & SPENCER.

The COMMISSION *on Contracts and Claims, &c.*

COMMISSION ON ORDNANCE AND ORDNANCE STORES,
Washington, June 10, 1862.

MAJOR: The commission find that the manufacturers of the Pettengill pistol have involved themselves so deeply on the faith of the order they received, that unless some are received they will be greatly oppressed. Your report is favorable to the workmanship, and you state that the parts are "as little liable to get out of order as those of any other revolving pistol I have seen."

The commission consider, therefore, that as the order was given for *Pettengill's patent pistols*, and as your report shows that the sample cannot be regarded as unserviceable, the manufacturers have an equitable claim to proceed in part with their work upon these arms. The commission therefore request your opinion as to the advantage of requiring the alteration which you state was made in the course of the trial to be applied to all, and also whether any other change should, in your opinion, be required.

Please send by express to my address (Corcoran's building, 15th street) the pistol you tried.

Very respectfully, your obedient servant,

P. V. HAGNER,
Major of Ordnance.

Major A. B. DYER,
U. S. Ordnance Corps, Springfield, Mass.

COMMISSION ON ORDNANCE AND ORDNANCE STORES,
Washington, April 14, 1862.

GENERAL: In the case of Rogers, Spencer & Co.'s order to furnish 5,000 Pettengill pistols, to be inspected in accordance with a sample previously approved, it is represented to the commission that a sample is now ready for inspection and approval, but as yet the inspection has not been made. Your recommendation for an extension of the time for the first delivery is also before the commission.

Before any action can be taken by the commission, they decide that you will direct the sample pistol to be inspected and tried under the direction of Major Dyer, at the Springfield armory, with directions to report to the commission his opinion of the sufficiency and suitableness of the proposed sample.

The commission are averse to considering the other particulars of this case until assured that the requirement of approval of the sample has been complied with.

Very respectfully, your obedient servant,

P. V. HAGNER,
Major of Ordnance.

Brigadier General J. W. RIPLEY,
Chief of Ordnance.

WASHINGTON, D. C., *June* 17, 1862.

GENTLEMEN : Permit us to ask, in view of the circumstances stated in our former letter, that you confirm our order for army pistols to the extent of 2,000 of the number ordered, and so extend to us the time for their delivery as to make it call for the delivery of 400 in the month of August next, and 400 in each succeeding month thereafter until the whole 2,000 are delivered.

If so much is granted to us, we will surrender the order made to us December 26, 1861, for 25,000 Springfield muskets, and make all the pistols to be delivered to correspond in their mechanical action with the sample most approved by Captain Dyer.

We will also, if it is desired, substitute for the thumb screw, which holds the centre-piece in place, one with smaller head and nicked for screwdriver; and with a view of lessening somewhat the disposition to foul around the centre-piece, we will make a *projection on the cylinder* around the pin instead of on the frame.

Respectfully, your obedient servants,

ROGERS, SPENCER & CO.

Hon. JOSEPH HOLT and ROBERT DALE OWEN,
Commissioners, &c.

COMMISSION ON ORDNANCE AND ORDNANCE STORES,
Washington, June 18, 1862.

GENERAL : The commission have the honor to report as follows :

CASE No. 99.—ROGERS, SPENCER & CO.

First order by direction of the Secretary of War, dated Decem'r 26, 1861.—(See page 163, Ex. Doc. No 67.) Second order by direction of the Secretary of War, dated December 26, 1861.—(See page 207, Ex. Doc. No. 67.)—Referred by direction of the Secretary of War.

To furnish 25,000 muskets of the Springfield pattern, with appendages, at the rate of $20 for each gun, including appendages, to be subject to inspection in the same manner the Springfield arms are inspected, and to be delivered not less than 500 in each the months of July, August, and September, 1862; 1,000 in each of the months of October and November, 1862 ; not less than 1,500 in December, 1862, and not less than 2,000 per month thereafter. In case of failure to make deliveries as specified, to forfeit the right to deliver the number deficient for the month.

2d. To furnish 5,000 Pettengill pistols of the army size and calibre, to be made according to a pattern to be previously submitted for examination and approval at the Ordnance office. To be delivered not less than 1,000 on or before March 26, 1862, and at the rate of 1,000 per month thereafter until 5,000 are delivered. Payments to be made at the rate of $20 for each pistol, with appendages, if approved by the United States inspector as in all respects like and equal in quality to the standard. In case of failure to deliver as specified, to forfeit the right to deliver the number deficient for the month.

The commission find that nothing has been done by Messrs. Rogers, Spencer, & Co. in execution of the order for muskets; but that, upon receipt of the order for pistols, they prepared their factory for this work, having been previously engaged in making the pocket size Pettengill pistol, and in machine work.

This required a considerable outlay for machinery and tools, and, as the arms to be made were to be interchangeable with the standard, they postponed all work upon the standard until it could be made by using the completed machines and tools. It was not, therefore, until the 11th of April that they were enabled to present the sample to be used as a standard required in the order for approval by the Ordnance department. At the request of the commission this sample was directed to be tested at the Springfield armory, to determine whether it was in all respects suitable for service. The report made by Captain Dyer, the commanding officer, shows that the arm has certain radical defects due to the principle upon which it is constructed, but that the sample itself was of "good workmanship," the parts not liable to get out of order, the "firing accurate, and the penetration good." As the cocking and revolving is effected by pulling the trigger, it was found to be liable to foul, and difficult of rapid use after a few fires; and as the self-cocking principle has been found to be objectionable for use by soldiers, it is particularly so with this pistol, the hammer being concealed from view. The frame work of the revolver is also of malleable iron. These objections show that the arm is not likely to be of permanent service, and is not a desirable one for the government; and, as the price allowed by the order is very high, it was incumbent upon the commission to require as large a reduction in the number to be furnished as could be made consistent with the terms of the order, and such equitable considerations in favor of the contractors as their expenditures made in good faith might entitle them to. Mr. Rogers, the principal of the firm of Rogers, Spencer & Co., appeared before the commission, and admitted that they could not remove the objections made to the sample furnished as a standard, and could not comply with the terms of the order as to the times of delivery. He also stated that, having no reason to expect the non-success of the army size Pettengill patent, the pocket pistol of this patent being in favor in the trade, the company had expended already so large a sum in special machines and tools, and in work and material partly completed, that they would be subjected to a ruinous loss were the whole order rescinded. The commission requested a proposition from him reducing the number of pistols to be furnished to the smallest number that would protect the company from loss, and conditional upon the surrender of the order held by his company to furnish 25,000 Springfield muskets, in the fulfilment of which he admitted no expense had yet been incurred by them. This proposition having been made in writing by him, the commission agree, in conformity therewith, to direct that the order of the 26th December, 1861, to Rogers, Spencer & Co. for 25,000 Springfield muskets be considered as revoked and annulled, and that no muskets be received thereupon, and that the order to the same company of the same date for 5,000 Pettengill pistols be confirmed to the extent of 2,000 pistols only, at the price stated in the order, and subject to all its terms and conditions except that the monthly deliveries therein stipulated shall be at the rate of 400 pistols per month, commencing in the month of August, 1862, and until the whole 2,000 be delivered, provided that the sample to be used as a standard in the inspection and receipt of the 2,000 pistols, and to which all shall conform, shall be made to correspond in mechanical action with the pistol last tried at Springfield, (to which a label has been attached by the commission,) and that with a view to lessen somewhat the disposition to foul around the centre pin, a projection be made *on the cylinder around the pin*, instead of on the frame. The commission further require that, within fifteen days' notice of this decision, the Messrs. Rogers, Spencer & Co. execute bond, with good and sufficient sureties, in the form and with the stipulations prescribed by law, for the performance of the contract as thus modified resulting from said order and acceptance; and upon the failure or refusal to execute such bond, then the said order shall be declared cancelled and of no effect.

We are, sir, very respectfully, your obedient servants,

J. HOLT,
ROBERT DALE OWEN,
Commissioners, &c.
P. V. HAGNER,
Major of Ordnance, Assistant to Commission.

Brigadier General JAMES W. RIPLEY.
Chief of Ordnance.

NEW YORK, *June* 27, 1862.

GENTLEMEN: I shall protest against any action to cancel the Springfield gun contract issued to Messrs. Rogers, Spencer & Co. I have been for a long while engaged in arranging to manufacture these guns, and the parts are now under manufacture and have been some time. Mr. Rogers, when in Washington, where he had been about one month, was not aware that so much progress had been made, as it has been done principally by one of the other partners, and we expect to deliver guns as soon as any other party. Mr. Stanton informed me and Judge Pierpont that all contracts made in good faith should be carried out by him, and I hope to hold him to his word in this matter if there is any faith in the government. Why should not we be allowed to go on to manufacture as well as others? We will give security if necessary.

I hope if the rumor is true of your intention to annul this contract, you will reconsider it, and give us a fair chance with the rest of the manufacturers.

Yours, very respectfully,

COURTNEY SCHENCK,
Per ROGERS, SPENCER & CO.

Hon. JOSEPH HOLT and R. D. OWEN,
Commissioners.

WILLOW VALE, *(Utica P. O.,) July* 4, 1862.

GENTLEMEN: Yours of the 28th of June, asking for a copy of a letter received by you on that date from us, which you say has been mislaid, has just now come to our hands.

We cannot understand it. We have addressed no letter to you since the date of your report in our case on June 17, and no other party is authorized to subscribe for us.

Very respectfully yours,

ROGERS & SPENCER.

The COMMISSION ON ORDNANCE AND ORDNANCE STORES,

COMMISSION ON ORDNANCE AND ORDNANCE STORES,
Washington, July 1, 1862.

SIR: Your note of the 27th ultimo, addressed to Messrs. Holt and Owen, has been received, and I am directed to reply to it as follows:

Mr. Rogers, the senior of the firm, to which the government gave the order for 25,000 Springfield muskets, has, in writing and in the name of the firm, relinquished that order as part of a plan of adjustment accepted by this commission and by the firm through Mr. Rogers. The order thus relinquished has been declared null and revoked. No one therefore is authorized to deliver arms under the order.

Very respectfully, your obedient servant,

P. V. HAGNER,
Major of Ordnance.

COURTNEY SCHENCK, Esq., *New York.*

WASHINGTON, *July* 7, 1862.

GENTLEMEN: I enclose copies of letters received and written by the commission. Mr. Holt thought he had lost Mr. Schenck's letter and therefore wrote for a duplicate. It was afterwards found.

This will explain the enigma which puzzled you.

Very respectfully, your obedient servant,

P. V. HAGNER,
Major of Ordnance.

Messrs. ROGERS & SPENCER,
Willow Grove, Utica, N. Y.

CASE No. 100.

C. D. SCHUBARTH.

WASHINGTON, *October* 9, 1861.

Caspar D. Schubarth desires a contract with the government for the manufacture of 10,000 breech-loading arms and 20,000 muzzle-loading Springfield rifles.

WASHINGTON, *October* 9, 1861.

Caspar D. Schubarth, doing business at Providence, Rhode Island, desires to contract with the government for the manufacture of ten thousand breech-loading arms, either carbines or rifles, (of his Schubarth patent, 1861,) and twenty thousand muzzle-loading rifles of the description made at Springfield, Massachusetts.

The muzzle-loading rifles at the regular price, twenty dollars each.

The breech-loaders at thirty-five dollars for carbines and thirty-seven dollars and fifty cents each for the larger size, including a bayonet.

I will engage to commence the delivery of arms in March next, and after April will deliver at least two thousand five hundred per month, and two for March and April inclusive.

CASPAR D. SCHUBARTH.

WAR DEPARTMENT, *October* 10, 1861.

Respectfully referred to General Ripley, chief of ordnance, with request to examine the gun and this proposition; then report on both.

THOMAS A. SCOTT,
Acting Secretary.

ORDNANCE OFFICE, *October* 10, 1861.

Respectfully returned. The breech-loading arm was brought to this office yesterday, and the party bringing it was told that it was not considered a suitable arm for the military service and that we did not want to contract for it.

Contracts and orders for muskets on prospective deliveries have already been made to a sufficient extent, and I cannot recommend the acceptance of this proposition.

JAMES W. RIPLEY,
Brigadier General.

ORDNANCE OFFICE, *Washington, October* 11, 1861.

SIR: By direction of the Secretary of War, I offer you an order for twenty thousand muskets, with appendages, on the following terms and conditions, viz: These arms are to be in all respects identical with the standard rifle musket now made at the United States armory at Springfield, Massachusetts, and are to interchange with it and with each other in all their parts. They are to be subject to inspection by United States inspectors in the same manner that the Springfield arms are inspected, and none are to be received and paid for but such as pass inspection and are approved by the United States inspectors. These 20,000 arms and appendages are to be delivered as follows, viz: Not less than 1,000 in each of the months of January, February, and March, 1862, and not less than 2,500 per month thereafter until the whole 20,000 are delivered. In case of failure to make any of these deliveries in or within the times before specified, the government is to have authority to revoke and annul this order immediately. Payments are to be made, in such funds as the Treasury Department may provide, on certificates of insbection and receipt by the United States inspectors, at the rate of twenty dollars ($20) for each arm, including appendages. All these arms and appendages are to be packed by you in boxes of the regular pattern, with twenty muskets and appendages in each box, for which a fair price, to be determined by the United States inspectors, will be allowed.

Please signify your acceptance or non-acceptance of this offer, and the terms and conditions herein specified.

Respectfully, &c.,

JAMES W. RIPLEY,
Brigadier General.

Mr. CASPAR D. SCHUBARTH,
Washington, D. C.

ORDNANCE OFFICE, *Washington, November* 26, 1861.

SIR: By direction of the Secretary of War, I extend the order which was given to you on the 11th of October, 1861, for 20,000 Springfield rifled muskets, by 30,000 rifle muskets and appendages of the same kind; so that the order of the 11th of October, 1861, aforesaid, and this order will comprise together 50,000 Springfield rifled muskets and appendages. These arms and appendages are to be delivered as follows, viz: 1,000 not later than six months from the date of this order; not less than 1,000 per month for the next three months; not less than 2,000 per month thereafter until 25,000 or more shall have been delivered; and the residue to be delivered in four months from the time allowed for the delivery of the first 25,000. All the other terms and conditions of the order of 11th of October, 1861, are to be in full force as regards this order. Your acceptance or non-acceptance of which please signify in writing.

Respectfully, &c.,

JAMES W. RIPLEY,
Brigadier General.

Mr. CASPAR D. SCHUBARTH,
Washington, D. C.

PROVIDENCE, *Rhode Island, February* 24, 1862.

DEAR SIR: I enclose herewith a copy of the first and second order from the War Department for the manufacture of 50,000 Springfield rifle muskets and appendages. These orders were accepted by me in the usual form, but I did not retain a copy of my letters accepting the same. The terms of the last order included the first, and it is under this that I have been acting.

I have been engaged in making fire-arms for over seventeen years, having served my time to the trade, and have an establishment where I have carried on the business, but of course not upon the large scale contemplated in this contract.

The arms contracted for will be put together and finished, ready for inspection at this establishment; but in order to deliver them in the time fixed in the order I have been obliged to contract for the manufacture of such parts of the arms as I could not prepare to make in season for the earliest deliveries, and have so made my contracts as to enable me to deliver the whole number according to the terms of the order.

To do this I have been obliged to engage with other parties for certain parts for the entire number of muskets contracted for, in order to induce them to press forward the numbers I was obliged to obtain in order to fulfil my engagement with the government.

I have 5,000 muskets that in all probability will be ready a month before the specified time of the order. I have 45,000 stocks that are being made for me under contract that will be ahead of my time of delivery.

I have also the same number of barrels contracted for that will be ready in due time. All the parts of the muskets, except the bayonets and guards, which will receive my special attention, are in a satisfactory state of forwardness, and will, without doubt, be ready so I can fulfil my order to the government within the time specified.

Respectfully, your obedient servant,

CASPAR D. SCHUBARTH.

Hon. EDWIN M. STANTON,
    Secretary of War, Washington, D. C.

PROVIDENCE, *April* 19, 1862.

GENTLEMEN : Yours of April 3 was duly received. In reply I would state that I am ready to deliver, according to the order, the first 1,000 muskets, except the barrels, which various causes have delayed from time to time. I am doing the best I can, and shall require a little indulgence in getting them ready. All the parts are now coming along in sufficient numbers to furnish you with the arms according to the order, except the little delay which the barrels may cause. The arms will be assembled at Providence. I can furnish stocks in a few days if any are wanted, and butt plates, tips, cones, and appendages; I have promised no parts to anybody.

Respectfully, your obedient servant,

C. D. SCHUBARTH.

The COMMISSION ON ORDNANCE,
    Washington, D. C.

COMMISSION ON ORDNANCE AND ORDNANCE STORES,
    Washington, May 22, 1862.

SIR : You will please appear before the commission as above, to be examined relative to your contract for Springfield guns.

Very respectfully, your obedient servant,

J. WISE, *Secretary to Commission.*

Mr. C. D. SHUBARTH, *Providence, R. I.*

C. D. Shubarth's testimony is given in the decision of the commission—q. v.

PROVIDENCE, R. I, *June* 2, 1862.

GENTLEMEN : I herein enclose an exact copy of the agreement of copartnership between Ryder, Griffing, and myself, as requested.

Very respectfully, your obedient servant,

C. D. SCHUBARTH.

Hon. Jos. HOLT and R. D. OWEN,
Commissioners on Ordnance and Ordnance Stores,
Washington, D. C.

Agreement made this fifteenth day of February, one thousand eight hundred and sixty-two, between Caspar D. Schubarth, of Providence, Rhode Island, and Frederick Griffing, of Brooklyn, New York, and James M. Ryder, of Pawtucket, Rhode Island, witnesseth :

First. That said Schubarth, Griffing, and Ryder, hereby agree to become copartners together in the furnishing of fifty thousand "Springfield rifle muskets" and appendages to the United States government, in pursuance of an order for twenty thousand of such muskets and appendages, dated October 11, 1861, and a further order for thirty thousand more of such muskets and appendages, dated November 26, 1861, each given on or about the day of its said date to the said Schubarth on the part of the said government, and each heretofore duly accepted in writing by the said Schubarth, and to which said orders reference is had.

Second. Said copartnership shall be considered as commencing from the day of the date hereof, and shall continue until the business necessary to the furnishing of said muskets and appendages shall be completed, but said copartnership shall extend to no other undertaking, business, or transaction whatever.

Third. Said copartnership business shall be carried on under the firm name of " C. D. Schubarth and Company."

Fourth. Said Schubarth hereby contributes to the capital stock of said copartnership the said two orders with said acceptance thereof, and the profits, avails, and benefits thereunto appertaining the same, after the date hereof, to the joint property of said copartners, each of them to own one-third part thereof; and the said Schubarth hereby transfers to said Griffing and said Ryder, each one-third part of all his, said Schubarth's, right, title, and interests in and to said orders, and the profits, avails, and benefits thereof. Said Schubarth also contributes to said copartnership such portion of his time and such services as may be reasonable to be required from him for the proper carrying out on his part of his agreement.

The foregoing shall be all the contribution to said copartnership to be made by said Schubarth, and he shall not be required to furnish any money thereto.

Fifth. Said Griffing and said Ryder agree to furnish to said copartnership all the money necessary for the proper carrying out of said business, and each also agrees to devote so much of his time and such services to said business as may be reasonable to require of him for the proper carrying out on his part of this agreement, and the foregoing shall be the contribution of said Griffing and said Ryder to said copartnership.

Sixth. The net profits arising from said copartnership business shall be equally divided between said copartners.

Seventh. Neither of said parties hereto shall make or use any notes, drafts, or acceptances in the name of said copartnership, or pledge the property or credit thereof in any way.

Witness the hands and seals of the said parties the day and year first above written.

C. D. SCHUBARTH.
FRED. GRIFFING.
J. M. RYDER.

COMMISSION ON ORDNANCE AND ORDNANCE STORES,
Washington, June 9, 1862.

DEAR SIR : I should be much obliged if you could return signed the paper which Mr. Wise left in your hands a few days since. It was carefully prepared immediately after you left, and presents, I think, with entire accuracy your statements before the commission, so far as they bore upon the orders to Schubarth. If, however, you should discover in it any inaccuracies, you will please correct them.

Respectfully, your obedient servant,

J. HOLT.

Hon. J. F. SIMMONS.

COMMISSION ON ORDNANCE AND ORDNANCE STORES,
Washington, May 28, 1862.

SIR : I am instructed by the commission on ordnance and ordnance stores to say that in the progress of their investigations it has become necessary to make further inquiries of yourself in regard to Schubarth's order for 50,000 muskets, now under examination, and they would be gratified if, at some early day, convenient for yourself, you could afford them an interview.

Very respectfully, your obedient servant,

J. WISE, *Secretary to Commission.*

Hon. J. F. SIMMONS.

No answer having been received to the above, a copy of it was sent to Mr. Simmons June 2, 1862. On that day Mr. Simmons called and made a statement before the commission which was written out and transmitted to him for signature.

June 9, Senator Simmons called and presented the paper signed by him, forming part of the decision of the commission, which he requested might be received as his testimony instead of that written out for his signature.

P. V. HAGNER, *Major of Ordnance.*

COMMISSION ON ORDNANCE AND ORDNANCE STORES,
Washington, June 10, 1862.

SIR : I submit for your perusal the enclosed copy of a paper filed with the commission on yesterday by Senator Simmons. You will observe that he states the commissions agreed to be paid him by yourself and partners amount to but $10,000, and that for this sum he holds the notes of the firm. In your deposition before us you said you had promised him five per cent. commissions, amounting to $50,000, and that you felt bound in honor to make this payment, and thought Senator Simmons considered you so bound. There is such a discrepancy between these statements that I have felt it my duty to bring the matter to your notice and ask you to explain it. This I hope you will be able to do by return mail.

In making up our record in the case we should be glad to give you the benefit of any statement you may in reply make to us on the subject.

Respectfully, your obedient servant,

J. HOLT.

Mr. CASPAR D. SCHUBARTH.

PROVIDENCE, *June* 13, 1862.

SIR : Yours of the 10th, covering copy of the papers filed by Mr. Simmons, was received last evening, and I hasten to reply. I do not see as Mr. S.'s statements conflict with my own. He may have concluded, knowing the difficulty I have had to contend with, and the expenses we have incurred in the manufacture of these arms, to have reduced his claim to the amount stated, which would be very satisfactory to me.

With your permission I should wish to remark here, (and as you will perceive from Mr. S.'s statement,) that previous to my going to Washington, in October last, to solicit orders, I had made arrangements to go into the manufacture of arms, and would have been prepared to have given bonds to the government for the fulfilment of the same had it been required of me, which, I understood, is sometimes necessary, and which, in my case, would have proved an advantage to *myself,* inasmuch as the parties then interested with me would have been under more obligation to have carried it through, and have saved me the difficult task of getting parties interested after the public mind had been prejudiced against the government and government contracts by all the newspaper writing and outside talk of the uncertainty of government ever receiving these arms after they were made, &c.

But I have had more faith in the government than *that,* and also those that are now interested with me. We have spent money freely, and have laid ourselves liable for more than we shall be able to pay should the government decline to receive these arms from me.

I mention these things that you can see that I acted in good faith from the very first. It was not my intention or purpose to get a contract merely to speculate on.

Very respectfully, your obedient servant,

CASPAR D. SCHUBARTH.

Hon. J. HOLT,
      Commissioner, Washington, D. C.

CASE No. 100.

C. D. SCHUBARTH, Providence, R. I.

WAR DEPARTMENT,
Washington City, D. C., June 21, 1862.

SIR: In compliance with a resolution of the Senate of this date, directing the Secretary of War to transmit immediately to that body so much of the report of the honorable Joseph Holt and Robert Dale Owen, on the subject of ordnance and gun contracts, as relates to gun contracts of Schubarth, I have the honor to transmit herewith a copy of so much of the report as is called for by the resolution.

Very respectfully, your obedient servant,

EDWIN M. STANTON,
            Secretary of War.

Hon. S. FOOT,
      President of the Senate pro tem.

COMMISSION ON ORDNANCE AND ORDNANCE STORES,
Washington, June 17, 1862.

GENERAL : The commission has the honor to report as follows :

CASE No. 100.—C. D. SCHUBARTH, Providence, R. I.—*Two orders, amounting
to 50,000 arms.*

Order by direction of the Secretary of War, dated October 11, 1862.—(See page 98 Ex. Doc. No. 67)

Order extended by direction of the Secretary of War, under date of November 26, 1862 —(See page 144 Ex. Doc. No. 67.)

To furnish 20,000 muskets, with appendages, identical with the Springfield standard rifle musket, at the rate of $20 for each arm, including appendages. Deliveries to be made of not less than 1,000 in each of the months of January, February, and March, 1862, and not less than 2,500 per month thereafter. In case of failure to make any one delivery as specified, the government is to have authority to revoke and annul this order immediately. The order of October 11, extended " by 30,000 rifle muskets and appendages of the same kind, so that the order of the 11th October, 1861, aforesaid, and this order will comprise together 50,000 Springfield rifle muskets and appendages."

These arms and appendages are to be delivered as follows, viz : 1,000 not less than six months from the date of this order, (November 26 ;) not less than 1,000 per month for the next three months ; and not less than 2,000 per month thereafter, until 25,000 or more shall have been delivered ; and the residue to be delivered within four months from the time allowed for the delivery of the 25,000.

Mr. Schubarth has appeared before the commission and made the following statement under oath :

Barrels.—I propose to have them made in Middletown, by Mr. Ashton. He is to finish the barrels ; they are to be furnished in the rough by Mr. Washburn, and by the Trenton company. Mr. Ashton makes the bargain for them. He superintends the work and supplies the barrels ; we have to provide the machinery. I mean by " we " my partners, James M. Ryder, New Haven, Connecticut, and Frederick Griffin, of Brooklyn, New York. Mr. Ryder resides in Pawtucket, and should be addressed in New York, Lafarge House, or in New Haven. The barrels at first received were not good, but lately are getting better ; the borer found but three in one hundred defective, and they look as if they would finish well. I made an arrangement for 1,000 barrels to be rolled by the Trenton Iron Company, and finished by Field & Horton, of Trenton. I have seen about 600 of these and they promised well. These are for the first delivery. The stocks are to be made in New York, at the Empire Works, at the foot of East Twenty-fourth street.

The *locks*—we are to get 3,000 from Jenks and the rest from Williams, having agreed to accept to the number of 50,000, less what we may be required to buy before he is ready to deliver.

Mountings.—Pecksmith Manufacturing Company, of Suddington, Connecticut, is to make bayonet, butt-plate, and tip. Guard bow and trigger are to be made by Bigelow, of Hartford.

The parts are to be delivered at Providence, to be assembled, and I am to attend to that part.

Implements are to be made in Providence under my supervision.

I came to Washington and got my order through the introduction of the senator from Rhode Island—Senator Simmons. I had a patent breech-loader of my own, and came to Washington to get an order for it, but was told that there was no time for trials, but that Springfield arms were wanting, and I could get an order for them. I proposed making the breech-loaders myself, in Providence; but, upon getting the order for muskets, I found I had not time enough to do all the work under one roof, and determined to branch it out. Nothing was said, either by myself or the Assistant Secretary of War, whom I saw, as to the manner of making them. To raise funds, I took into partnership Mr. Ryder and Mr. Griffin, of Brooklyn; besides this, I promised a commission of five per cent. to the senator I spoke of—Senator Simmons, of Rhode Island—for his services in obtaining the order for me. I gave him no written promise; but when I took Ryder and Griffin into partnership with me I mentioned it to them, and I think the articles of partnership refer to it. I have not concealed the matter, although I have not conversed about it generally; but I recollect mentioning it to some persons. I believe, also, that it was referred to by me in a letter or in a conversation—I am not sure which—with Mr. Norris, of Spring-field. I have since spoken with Senator Simmons many times, as we always talk when we meet about how I am getting along in my business; but no particular reference has been made to this commission.

I offered Mr. Simmons the commission because I heard that it was generally understood that a commission was paid for obtaining contracts. I do not recollect any particular case; but I think that Amos D. Smith, of the firm of Amos D. & J. Y. Smith, of Providence, with whom I first expected to go on in executing the contract, told me that it was customary, before I came to Washington. They afterwards declined to join in, as they thought the terms were too stringent. They advised me to get an increase of number. I then came on here and saw Senator Simmons, who went with me to the Assistant Secretary of War, and the order for increase to 50,000 was given, upon representing to him that the prior number of 20,000 was not sufficient to repay for the investment required to make the arms in the time specified. I consider myself bound to give Senator Simmons five per cent. commission on both orders, and I think he considers me bound to keep my promise. He has said, in several conversations, what produced this impression on me; saying, for example, on one occasion, when talking of rich men in Providence, " I shall be a rich man when I get that commission," or "if I ever get that commission," or words to that effect. I mean to state that my impression that Mr. Senator Simmons expects me to keep the promise I made to him to pay him five per cent. for procuring the orders for me upon the number of arms included in both orders is derived from various conversations with him, the details of which I do not particularly remember. The particular reply of his which I have mentioned may have been spoken jokingly in answer to remarks about rich men in Providence. He said this to me in a room where others were, but I do not know whether they heard it. The paper now shown to me, purporting to be a copy of a letter signed by me, bearing date New York, January 14, 1862, and addressed to Mr. Samuel Norris, I recognize as a true copy of a genuine letter. It was written by Mr. Norris, and signed at his request, and the statements therein are true and correct. I now sign the letter to identify it.

The above testimony (as taken down) has been read to me, and I sign it.

C. D. SCHUBARTH.

Question by the commissioner. Suppose you were not allowed to execute this contract, or suppose the government did not pay you for the arms, would you be bound still to pay Senator Simmons the five per cent. commission promised to him, that is, $50,000?

Answer. Yes, sir, as far as my word of honor is concerned, I should be bound to do so.

Question. Do you think that Senator Simmons considers that you owe him this money should the contract not be confirmed?

Answer. I suppose so. He has performed his part, and I should perform mine.

Question. Were you aware that the offer by you to Senator Simmons, for compensation growing out of a contract between you and the government, was in violation of law; or that the receipt of such compensation by him for such services would be in violation of law?

Answer. No, sir. I understood, on the contrary, that it was customary to make compensation for such services, and I have heard of many cases in which it was said to have been done. In one case, as high as two dollars per pistol is said to have been promised for procuring the order.

I desire to add that I am a Norwegian by birth, and have resided only about twelve years in the United States.

C. D. SCHUBARTH.

The Hon. James F. Simmons, United States senator from Rhode Island' having been interrogated by the commission as to his agency in obtaining these orders to Mr. Schubarth, prepared and submitted for their consideration a paper, which is in the following words:

COMMISSION ON ORDNANCE AND ORDNANCE STORES,
June 2, 1862.

C. D. SCHUBARTH.

Orders, October 11, 1861, for 20,000, and November 26, 1861, for 30,000 Springfield muskets.

Senator Simmons heard the testimony of Mr. Schubarth, given before the commission, under oath, on the 27th May, 1862, read, and said there were some trifling errors therein, and related the actual circumstances, as follows: " While I was in Washington, in October last, on private business, Mr. Schubarth presented a letter of introduction from Messrs. A. D. & J. Y. Smith, a business firm of Providence, Rhode Island, of great wealth and respectability, stating that Mr. Schubarth was the inventor of a breech-loading rifle, and desired to obtain an order from the government to make some of them for the use of the army or navy, and requesting me to assist Mr. Schubarth in obtaining an order, and that if he succeeded they should be concerned in its execution.

" In pursuance of this request, I introduced Mr. Schubarth to the Secretary of War and to General Ripley, and Captain Harwood, of the Navy Department. His arm was tried at the navy yard, and a favorable report made, but the department declined ordering any breech-loaders, but desired Springfield rifled muskets, and gave an order for 20,000.

" Some time during Mr. Schubarth's stay here, while going to or returning from the department, he said he had a letter authorizing him to pay a commission for obtaining an order, and offered it to me to read, but I did not read it, but had no doubt it was so, nor did I doubt the propriety or legality of receiving one for that as for any transaction of business, for men able and willing to pay as the Messrs. Smith were. After my return to Providence, the Messrs. Smith told me the order to Mr. Schubarth was for so small a number, and were to be delivered in so short a time, they must decline the undertaking, as it would not justify the outlay for machinery required. Nothing ever passed between us about commissions to my recollection. In the month of November I was in Washington, on my way south, to Hatteras inlet, and Mr. Schubarth came here and said he could do nothing with the order unless it was made for the same number and as long a time allowed for delivery as other parties had, and requested me to aid him in getting such an alteration, which I did.

" In the month of January following he told me that for some reason or other the Messrs. Smith declined pursuing the business. Soon after I saw him in

New York, and he told me that he had arranged with parties there for means to carry out his contract, and they wanted to have an understanding with me about my commissions. I saw them, and took from them an agreement in writing to pay at certain stipulated times (I think in about a year from this time) the amount agreed upon. The agreement was without qualification or condition, and had no connexion with what the government might subsequently do, only binding themselves to a due execution of the order on their part. Under and in pursuance of this agreement, they subsequently gave me one note payable in August and one in September next, both amounting to ten thousand dollars, which I expect will be paid, as I have no doubt of their responsibility.

"J. F. SIMMONS."

The apparent discrepancy between the statements of Mr. Schubarth and Senator Simmons, as to the compensation due to the latter, may be thus explained. It would seem that the partners of Mr. Schubarth are responsible to the senator for but $10,000, and for this sum they executed to him their notes; but Mr. Schubarth, as he has sworn, considers himself bound to keep his original promise to pay five per cent., or $50,000, as the commission agreed on, and he thinks Senator Simmons also regards him as so bound, and he gives his reasons for this opinion. On this point—the personal liability of Mr. Schubarth himself, under his original undertaking—Senator Simmons is entirely silent. Upon bringing to Mr. Schubarth's notice this seeming conflict of statement, he replied in terms which leave the impression that he was not cognizant of the arrangement between his partners and Senator Simmons; and he says, " He [the senator] may have concluded, knowing the difficulty I would have to contend with, and the expenses we have incurred in the manufacture of these arms, to have reduced his claim to the amount stated, which would be very satisfactory to me."

The first inquiry which arises out of the facts thus presented is, as to how far, if at all, the contract with Mr. Schubarth is affected by Mr. Simmons's connexion with it. There are but two acts of Congress which can be regarded as bearing on this question. The first is that approved April 8, 1808, which provides, under a severe penalty, that "no member of Congress shall, directly or indirectly, himself or by any other person in trust for him, or for his use or benefit, or on his account, undertake, execute, hold, or enjoy, in the whole or in part, any contract or agreement hereafter to be made or entered into with any officer of the United States in their behalf, or with any person authorized to make contracts on the part of the United States;" and a violation of this provision is declared to be a high misdemeanor, rendering null and void the contract, and subjecting the party to a fine of three thousand dollars.

The second is that of February 26, 1853, the third section of which declares that "any senator or representative in Congress who, after the passage of this act, shall, for compensation paid or to be paid, certain or contingent, act as agent or attorney for prosecuting any claim or claims against the United States, or shall in any manner, or by any means, for such compensation, aid or assist in the prosecution or support of any such claim or claims, or shall receive any gratuity, or any share of or interest in any claim from any claimant against the United States, with intent to aid or assist, or in consideration of having aided or assisted, in the prosecution of such claim, shall be liable to indictment, as for a misdemeanor, in any court of the United States having jurisdiction thereof, and on conviction shall pay a fine not exceeding five thousand dollars, or suffer imprisonment in the penitentiary not exceeding one year, or both, as the court, in its discretion, shall adjudge."

It seems to us quite clear that the services rendered by Mr. Simmons were not of the character referred to in the act of 1853. The term "claim," as there employed, imports an unsettled and probably contested money demand against the government. The proposal of Mr. Schubarth, in aid of which Mr. Simmons acted, was not at all of this nature, but simply an offer to manufacture guns, out of which a claim against the government might or might not thereafter arise.

To bring the case within the operation of the act of 1808, it would be necessary that the contract should be either in Mr. Simmons's name, or be held, executed, and enjoyed, in whole or in part, in trust for him, or for his use or benefit. None of these conditions exist. The contract is in the name of Schubarth, and is held and to be executed solely for the use and benefit of himself and partners. Mr. Simmons has no interest in it whatever. If the $10,000 due him for his services was to be paid out of funds to be received from the government under the contract, or if such payment was to be dependent upon the execution of the contract by either of the parties thereto, he would, to that extent, have an interest in it, and it would in consequence be declared null and void. It is fully proved, however, both by Mr. Schubarth and himself, that the obligation to pay him his fee, as agreed upon, is absolute and unconditional, and that whether the contract is executed or not, his rights are precisely the same. As, therefore, the case is not within the language or meaning of the act, we do not feel justified in assuming it to be within the evil its provisions were intended to remedy.

We are satisfied that Mr. Schubarth is personally innocent of any illegal or immoral purpose, and of all consciousness of violating the policy of the government. He is a foreigner, not very intimate, it may be assumed, with our institutions; and in offering compensation to Senator Simmons, he only did what he was assured by intelligent business men (Americans by birth) was customary. His conduct is chargeable to a vicious system of administration, which, in abandoning the law, forces the citizen to seek the patronage of his government by purchase through mercenary agencies, instead of obtaining it by open and honorable competition.

Senator Simmons, also, we doubt not, regards his action in accepting this compensation as strictly legal, and we cannot, in the present condition of the legislation of Congress upon this subject, contest his opinion. That, however, the receipt of a large moneyed reward by a member of the United States Senate for such services rendered for one of his constituents is in harmony with the spirit of our institutions we cannot but deny. It was certainly not the slight labor of accompanying Mr. Schubarth to the War Department, and urging his proposals upon the Secretary, for which the above charge of $10,000 was made. It was Mr. Simmons's supposed influence over the executive department of the government, resulting from his official position, that was thus bought and sold. If we understand the theory of our government aright, the influence which a member of Congress, as such, exercises over the administration of the departments is as much public property as is his vote in the Capitol. While the latter is so carefully protected from being brought into conflict with his personal interests, why is not the former entitled to the same guardianship? Congress, however, comprehensive as has been its legislation upon the subject, has not thought proper to embrace in its prohibitions the class of cases to which that under consideration belongs; and, however deplorable, we must treat as legal such charges made by members of Congress until the body to which they belong shall otherwise declare.

The order to Mr. Schubarth, as extended, was not given in accordance with law and the regulations, and does not constitute a contract of legal force, since it does not embody the express requirements of the law, and was not made "after previous advertisement for proposals respecting the same;" nor can it be regarded as an "open purchase," being for articles which did not require "immediate delivery," but were stipulated to be manufactured and delivered at prescribed distant periods. The outlays of Mr. Schubarth, however, made in good faith, in preparation for the manufacture of these guns, entitle him to the equities recognized in Mason's case, No. 72. For the reasons set forth in the decision rendered in that case, it is determined that the order, as extended to fifty thousand, be confirmed for thirty thousand muskets only, from which number must be deducted the thousand already forfeited for non-delivery within six months from November 26, 1861; and from this number must also be deducted any other muskets which may become due according to the stipulations of the order, but which shall not be delivered before the execution of the bond hereinafter required; which confirmation is made subject to the terms of the order, and upon condition that Mr. Schubarth shall, within fifteen days after notice of this decision, execute bond with good and sufficient sureties in the form and with the stipulations prescribed by law and the regulations for the performance of the contract as thus modified, resulting from said order and acceptance; and upon his failure or refusal to execute such bond, then the said order shall be declared cancelled and of no effect.

We are, sir, very respectfully, your obedient servants,

J. HOLT,
ROBERT DALE OWEN,

Brig. Gen. J. W. RIPLEY,   *Commissioners, &c.*
Chief of Ordnance.

CASE No. 101.

J. B. BUTTERFIELD.

Proposal of Joseph B. Butterfield to make 50,000 Butterfield rifles or 50,000 Springfield rifled muskets.

PHILADELPHIA, *December* 12, 1861.

I respectfully propose to manufacture and supply to the United States government 50,000 rifles similar to sample now in the War Department, (calibre .58, with angular bayonets, and all implements usual with army guns, subject to full and usual inspection,) recommended by Colonel Kingsbury, and approved with recommendation, to the honorable Secretary, by Major General George B. McClellan; or, if preferred by the department, will manufacture the same number of improved Springfield rifled muskets on same terms, viz: $20 each, and deliverable after date of contract as follows: 3,000 in six months, 3,000 in seven months, 5,000 in eight months, 5,000 in nine months, 5,000 in ten months, 5,000 in eleven months, 5,000 in twelve months, 5,000 in thirteen months, 5,000 in fourteen months, 5,000 in fifteen months, and 4,000 in sixteen months, making a total of 50,000.

Very respectfully,

JOSEPH B. BUTTERFIELD.

Hon. SIMON CAMERON,
Secretary of War.

HEADQUARTERS ARMY OF THE POTOMAC,
Washington, December 4, 1861.

SIR: In compliance with the instructions of the commanding general, I have examined the arms presented by Mr. Butterfield. The rifle musket appears to be an efficient and desirable arm; it is of the .58 inch calibre, and modelled after the Enfield rifle. With a substitution of the triangular for the sword bayonet, it is an arm of which more than 50,000 are wanted for immediate issue to the army of the Potomac. The revolver is of the calibre of Colt's navy pistol; brass mounted, and can be furnished at $16. The rifle and pistol can each be delivered at the rate of 400 per week, and after thirty days at the rate of 1,000 per week.

Very respectfully, your obedient servant,

C. P. KINGSBURY,
Colonel, Chief of Ordnance Army of Potomac.

Colonel A. V. COLLUM,
Assistant Adjutant General, Secretary, &c.

Respectfully referred to the honorable Secretary of War. The rifle musket alluded to seems to be a very good weapon, far better than those I have thus far seen from Europe.

GEORGE B. McCLELLAN,
Major General Commanding.

ORDNANCE OFFICE,
Washington, December 24, 1861.

GENTLEMEN: By direction of the Secretary of War, I offer you an order for fifty thousand (50,000) muskets, with appendages, of the Springfield pattern, on the following terms and conditions, viz: These arms are to be furnished with the regular appendages, and are to be in all respects identical with the standard rifle musket made at the United States armory at Springfield, Massachusetts, and are to interchange with it and with each other in all their parts. They are to be subject to inspection by United States inspectors in the same manner that the Springfield arms are inspected, and none are to be received or paid for but such as pass inspection, and are approved by the United States inspectors. These fifty thousand (50,000) arms and appendages are to be delivered at your armory as follows, viz: not less than one thousand (1,000) in *each* of the months of July, August, and September, 1862; not less than two thousand (2,000) in *each* of the months of October and November, 1862; not less than three thousand (3,000) in December, 1862, and not less than four thousand (4,000) per month thereafter, until the entire fifty thousand shall have been delivered; and you are to have the right to deliver more rapidly than according to the number of arms before specified, if you can do so. In the case of any failure to make deliveries to the extent and within the times before specified, you are to forfeit the right to deliver whatever number may be deficient in the specified number for the month in which the failure occurs. All these arms and appendages are to be delivered by you, and this order, if transferred to another party, is to be thereby forfeited. Payments are to be made in such funds as the Treasury Department may provide for each delivery, or certificate of inspection and receipt by the United States inspectors, at the rate of twenty dollars ($20) for each arm, including appendages. All these arms and appendages are to be packed by you in boxes of the regular pattern, with twenty (20) muskets and appendages in each box, for which a fair price, to be determined by the United States inspector, will be allowed.

Please signify, in writing, your acceptance or non-acceptance of this order, on the terms and conditions before stated herein.

Respectfully, your obedient servant,

JAMES W. RIPLEY,
Brigadier General.

JOSEPH B. BUTTERFIELD & Co.,
Philadelphia, Pa.

PHILADELPHIA, *February* 4, 1862.

Joseph B. Butterfield & Co. have a contract for 50,000 Springfield rifle muskets; have commenced the making of some parts of the weapon, and expect to fulfil their contract with government in good faith.

PHILADELPHIA, *February* 4, 1862.

SIR: In accordance with your published instructions of the 28th ultimo, we beg leave to submit the following:

We have a contract for fifty thousand (50,000) Springfield rifle muskets, at twenty dollars each, with appendages, from the Ordnance bureau, dated December 24, 1861, signed by James W. Ripley, brigadier general.

Said contract was obtained through written request of Major General George B. McClellan upon the War Department, after his inspection and approval of sample gun made by us, (now in the office of the Assistant Secretary, T. A. Scott, esq.;) and the letter of Colonel Kingsbury to that effect, indorsed by the major general, is on file in the War Department.

In pursuance of this, we have commenced, at our manufactory, the making of some parts of the weapon, and have entered into contracts for further machinery for the purpose of making locks, stocks, bayonets, &c., to the amount of sixty thousand dollars, ($60,000,) under a penalty for the faithful performance on our part, which machinery will be delivered to us in the months of April and May next, enabling us to fulfil our contract with the government in good faith.

We have at present one factory, with ample machinery, in active operation, and another one prepared to receive the other for our heavier work, and will then employ in all about 400 men.

The parties connected are practical men, and have abundant means to fulfil their obligations entered into with the government.

Very respectfully,

JOS. B. BUTTERFIELD & CO.

Post office address: *Box* 1,045, *Post Office, Philadelphia.*

Hon. EDWIN M. STANTON,
        Secretary of War.

PHILADELPHIA, *April* 16, 1862.

GENTLEMEN: Your letter of 4th April did not reach us till we saw it advertised, your secretary having neglected to put on the post office address, (furnished him by the writer when in Washington,) *Box* 1,045, *Philadelphia post office;* and as our manufactory is out of town, it did not reach us by delivery.

We shall be prepared to comply with our contract delivery of 1,000, commencing in July. Of this we feel well assured, although we have been retarded by a difficulty as to barrels, which we think has been overcome.

We shall be prepared in a short time to furnish you with a detailed list of machinery, &c., and also advise you as to whether we can finish any parts to others, which thus far we have not undertaken to do.

Very respectfully,

JOS. B. BUTTERFIELD & CO.,
        Box 1,045, *Post Office.*

Messrs. JOSEPH HOLT, R. D. OWEN, and Major HAGNER.

N. B.—Will the secretary be good enough to notice our post office address.

PHILADELPHIA, *June* 7, 1862.

GENTLEMEN : You will doubtless remember that we appeared before you in the first week of your session, and stated at the time we had already ordered additional machinery to the amount of some $60,000, on account of our order from the government for 50,000 guns.

On the 9th day of March we received a letter from the Assistant Secretary of War, Mr. P. H. Watson, dated March 8, authorizing us to proceed to Springfield and get samples and forgings, and such information as might be necessary to carry out our order, an extract from which is here given.

" By direction of the Secretary, I have to inform you that the chief of ordnance, to whom the matter was referred, reports as follows : Messrs. Butterfield & Co. can obtain all proper facilities to enable them to execute this order for 50,000 Springfield rifle muskets by applying at the United States armory at that place, exhibiting this order."

Acting on this authority, as a reaffirmation of our order, (Mr. Watson having, in a personal interview, previously refused to give it, giving as his reason that it would *amount to a confirmation of the same,*) we have steadfastly proceeded in the work ; and having fully completed all our arrangements for machinery and materials for the whole 50,000 guns, are able to report that we shall faithfully execute the order.

Very respectfully,

JOSEPH B. BUTTERFIELD & CO.

Hon. JOSEPH HOLT and R. DALE OWEN,
Commissioners.

Before the commission, June 18, 1862.

Mr. Stephens, of the firm of J. B. Butterfield & Co., appeared and states that his proposal to the government was to make a special arm ; that, instead of these, he received an order for 50,000 Springfield muskets ; upon receipt of this order he made arrangements with a moneyed man to advance capital, but that in consequence of the publication of Mr. Stanton calling for copies of contracts, these arrangements fell through ; that having had an interview with Mr. Stanton, in which he assured him that if arms were made and delivered as stipulated in the order they would certainly be received, he returned to Philadelphia and got a second moneyed man to promise capital, and asked for and obtained the promise of a sample arm from Springfield ; that in consequence of the appointment of the commission, and the rumors about annulling contracts, these arrangements fell through ; that when called upon by the commission for his statement in writing of what had been done, he was awaiting their action, as he could make no definite arrangements, and therefore made no report to the commission ; that at present he purposes to get all the guns made for him, and to deliver such as he can under the terms of his order. He considers that his case differs from others, and asks the confirmation of the original order by the commission.

He further states that he can deliver 500 guns in July, and has made his arrangements in anticipation. The arms are to be assembled at Springfield, under Mr. Norris's superintendence. All detailed arrangements have been made through him, and he is responsible to the company (B. & Co.) for the execution of the order. Mr. Camman, of New York, is interested, and he has made the arrangements with Mr. Norris. This has been done within the last two or three weeks ; he cannot say definitely.

COMMISSION ON ORDNANCE AND ORDNANCE STORES,
Washington, June 18, 1862.

GENERAL : The commission have the honor to report as follows:

CASE No. 101.—J. B. BUTTERFIELD, New York.

Order by direction of the Secretary of War, dated December 24, 1861.—(No. 63, page 161, Ex. Doc. No. 67)
Referred by direction of the Secretary of War.

To furnish 50,000 muskets, with appendages, of the Springfield pattern, at the price of $20 per gun. Deliveries to be made of not less than 1,000 in each of the months of July, August, and September; not less than 2,000 in each of the months of October and November; not less than 3,000 in December; and not less than 4,000 per month thereafter.—(See Case No. 72.)

The commission find that the above order was not given in accordance with the law and regulations, and that it is not therefore a contract of legal force, inasmuch as it does not contain the express requirements of the law, and was not made " after previous advertisement for proposals respecting the same;" nor can it be regarded as an " open purchase," being for articles which did not require " immediate delivery," but were stipulated to be manufactured and delivered at prescribed distant periods.

They further consider that the number of arms ordered is larger than the wants of the government justify in this case, at the price fixed, and therefore, according to the principles set forth in Mason's case, (No. 72,) they decide that the order of Mr. Butterfield be confirmed, subject to all its terms, to the extent of 25,000 muskets, upon condition that he shall, within fifteen days after notice of this decision, execute bond, with good and sufficient sureties, in the form and with the stipulations prescribed by law and the regulations for the performance of the contract, as thus modified, resulting from said order and acceptance; and upon his failure or refusal to execute such bond, then the said order shall be declared cancelled and of no effect.

The commission further decide that the deliveries under the contract to be executed shall be required at or within the period stipulated in the original order, but that the numbers specified may be reduced proportionately to the reduction of the whole number, so that the contract shall be completed within the time allowed in the original order.

We are, sir, very respectfully, your obedient servants,
J. HOLT,
ROBERT DALE OWEN,
Commissioners, &c.
P. V. HAGNER,
Major of Ordnance.

Brigadier General J. W. RIPLEY,
Chief of Ordnance.

CASE No. 102.

G. H. PENFIELD.

ORDNANCE OFFICE, *March* 21, 1862.

The within claim of G. H. Penfield for ordnance, &c., furnished under his order of October 11, 1861, with a copy of that order, and of all papers relating thereto, is respectfully submitted to the Secretray of War for reference to the commission appointed by order of the 13th instant.

JAMES W. RIPLEY,
Brigadier General.

ORDNANCE OFFICE,
Washington, October 11, 1861.

SIR: By direction of the Secretary of War, I offer you an order for fourteen field batteries complete, each to consist of six 6-pounder bronze rifle guns, with carriages, caissons, implements, and equipments, as prescribed at page 305, Ordnance Manual; one forge and one battery wagon, with contents, as prescribed at pages 307 to 316, Ordnance Manual; harness complete for six horses, two wheel and four leading, for each gun-carriage, caisson, forge, and battery wagon, and one hundred rounds of ammunition (one-sixth shot, one-sixth canister, and two-thirds shell) for each gun; the whole to be delivered complete and ready for service in the field. All the articles are to be subject to regular inspection and proof by such officer as this department may designate for the purpose, and are to be of the patterns and quality of similar articles in the United States service. They are to be delivered as follows, viz: two batteries complete on or before the first day of November next, and from and after that date two batteries per week until the whole fourteen batteries complete, hereby ordered, are delivered. In case of any failure to deliver in or within the times before stated, the government is to be under no obligation to take any of the articles then remaining undelivered under this order, but may or may not do so, at its option. Payments will be made in such funds as the Treasury Department may provide, on certificates of inspection and receipt by the United States inspector, at said prices per battery complete, as may be determined to be fair and just by Major P. V. Hagner and Lieutenant G. T. Balch, according to the average of the prices they have paid or may be paying for similar articles as contracts or purchases, or by valuation for any of the articles not so obtained. In case of failure to fill this order in accordance with its conditions as to time and all other respects, the government may immediately revoke and annul it. Please signify, in writing, your acceptance or non-acceptance of this order, on the terms and conditions herein specified.

Respectfully, your obedient servant,

JAMES W. RIPLEY,
Brigadier General.

Mr. G. H. PENFIELD, *Washington, D. C.*

P. S.—It is understood that an additional quantity of ammunition for the batteries will be supplied hereafter, on requisitions from the governor of Illinois, when wanted.

J. W. R.

ORDNANCE OFFICE,
Washington, October 29, 1861.

SIR: As desired by Governor Richard Yates, in his letter to you of the 24th instant, the order of October 11, 1861, for fourteen batteries of artillery is so modified as to allow the twelve batteries, remaining after the first delivery, to be delivered at the rate of two batteries per week from and after November 10, 1861, instead of the 1st of November, as in the original order.

Respectfully, your obedient servant,

JAMES W. RIPLEY,
Brigadier General.

Mr. G. H. PENFIELD, *Washington, D. C.*

To the commissioners on contracts and claims for ordnance and ordnance stores

I respectfully beg leave to submit the following statement:

On October 8, 1861, I wrote to Governor Yates, of the State of Illinois, and General James W. Ripley, of the Ordnance office, a proposal in writing, of which the following is a copy:

"WASHINGTON, *October* 8, 1861.

"SIR: I propose to furnish the United States, for service with Illinois troops, fourteen field batteries, each six 6-pounder bronze rifle guns, for using 'James's patent projectiles,' with carriages, caissons, harness, saddles, and all fixtures complete and ready for the field. Also 500 rounds of ammunition for each gun, with James's patent shot and shell—one-third shot and two-thirds shells—the shells to be charged and ready for use; the delivery as follows, (at the manufactory:)

"Two batteries, with carriages, caissons, harness, saddles, &c., with 500 rounds of ammunition each, by or before the first day of November next; from and after that time, I will deliver two batteries, with all fixtures and ammunition therefor, each week, until this contract is filled, and I have delivered the full number of fourteen batteries, &c., &c.

"The price of the above-named property to be the same as has been usual for similar property to General James or Mr. Ames.

"Respectfully, your obedient servant,

"G. H. PENFIELD, *Agent.*

"Hon. SIMON CAMERON,
  "*Secretary of War, Washington, D. C.*"

General Ripley notified Governor Yates that this proposal was satisfactory, and that a written order, in accordance with the terms of the proposal, would be ready for my acceptance by 12 o'clock of that day. On calling at the Ordnance office to receive and accept the order as agreed on, General Ripley refused to give it to me, but offered for my acceptance a new order, of which the following is a copy:

"ORDNANCE OFFICE,
  "*Washington, October* 11, 1861.

"SIR: By direction of the Secretary of War, I offer you an order for fourteen field batteries complete, each to consist of six 6-pounder bronze rifle guns, with carriages, caissons, implements, and equipments, as prescribed at pages 306 and 316, Ordnance Manual, harness complete for six horses (two wheel and four leading) for each gun-carriage, caisson, forge, and battery wagon, and one hundred rounds of ammunition (one-sixth shot, one-sixth canister, and two-thirds shells) for each gun; the whole to be delivered complete and ready for service in the field. All the articles to be subject to regular inspection and proof by such officer as the department may designate for the purpose, and are to be of the pattern and quality of similar articles in the United States service. They are to be delivered as follows, viz: two batteries complete on or before the first day of November next, and from and after that date two batteries per week, until the whole fourteen field batteries complete, hereby ordered, are delivered. In case of any failure to deliver in or within the times before stated, the government is to be under no obligation to take any of the articles then remaining undelivered under this order, but may or may not do so, at its option. Payments will be made in such funds as the Treasury Department may provide, on certificates of inspection and receipt by the United States inspector, at such prices per battery complete as may be determined to be fair and just by Major P. V. Hagner and Lieutenant G. T. Balch, according to the average of the prices they have paid or may be paying for similar articles on contract or purchases, or by valuation for any of the articles not so obtained. In case of failure to fill this order in accordance with its conditions as to time and all other respects, the government may immediately revoke and annul it. Please signify, in writing, your acceptance or non-acceptance of this order, on the terms and conditions herein specified.

"Respectfully, your obedient servant,

"JAMES W. RIPLEY,
"*Brigadier General.*

"Mr. G. H. PENFIELD,
"*Washington, D. C.*"

This order varied very materially from the original, as agreed on by General Ripley, Governor Yates, and myself.

Among other variations, it reduced the amount of ammunition to be furnished from five hundred to one hundred rounds for each gun, making a total variation of thirty-three thousand six hundred rounds, (33,600.) I therefore refused to accept it. The agent left by Governor Yates to take care of the interest of the State of Illinois afterward presented me the order, with the following addition made by General Ripley:

"P. S.—It is understood that an additional quantity of ammunition for the batteries will be supplied hereafter, on requisitions from the governor of Illinois, when wanted.

"J. W. R."

Understanding that the "*additional quantity of ammunition*" referred to in this postscript was intended to cover the remaining 400 rounds of ammunition for each gun, and believing that requisitions therefor would soon be made by the governor of Illinois, and that an order to fill the requisitions so made would be given to me, I accepted the order as amended.

The batteries, harness, guns, and a part of the ammunition, have been delivered, inspected, and received by the government.

By referring to the order, it will be seen that the prices to be paid for the batteries were to be determined by Major P. V. Hagner and Lieutenant G. T. Balch, "according to the average of the prices *they* have been or may be paying for similar articles on contract or purchases, or by valuation of the articles not so obtained." Major Hagner, as I am informed, was not consulted, and had nothing whatever to do in determining the prices proposed to be paid me. Nor were the prices that *he* had been "paying for similar articles on contract or purchases" taken into account in making the "*average*" of prices for the articles to be delivered on this order; nor was he a party to the "*valuation*" of the articles not so obtained. The whole matter was placed in the hands of Lieutenant Balch, who performed the duties in a manner calculated to do me great injustice. In determining the prices he failed to give any consideration to the facts that the demand at that time for all the articles necessary for these batteries was so great that the prices were very considerably enhanced, and that from the shortness of the time allowed to fill this order I was compelled to purchase the required articles wherever I could find them, without regard to cost. He seems to have been governed by his own estimate of the value of the articles, and not by the market value, nor by the "average price" that he and Major Hagner had been or might be paying for similar articles.

I claim that under the order as given to and accepted by me General Ripley had no right to allow this duty to be performed by Lieutenant Balch alone; and in view of that fact, and of the manner in which the duty was performed, I ask that the action of Lieutenant Balch be disregarded, and that I may be paid for all the articles furnished on this order the same prices that have been paid for similar articles by various States as well as by the government of the United States.

I also claim that under the amendment to the order I am now entitled to an order from the government for such a number of shot and shells as will fill the requisition from Governor Yates now on file in the War Department.

G. H. PENFIELD, Agent.

United States to G. H. Penfield, D<small>R.</small>

1861.

Nov. 18. For 14 field batteries, each six 6-pd'r rifle guns :
925, 924, 917, 920, 918, 917, 918, 918, 914, 921, 921, 914, 908, 880, 865, 874, 871, 882, 882.

19 guns, 17,169 lbs., at 46 cts.........	$7, 897 74	
Rifling 19 guns, at $50...............	950 00	
Sighting 19 guns, at $20..............	380 00	
Boxing.....................	47 50	
		$9, 275 24

Dec. 13. 919, 915, 919, 918, 917, 917, 923, 923, 910, 926, 917, 914, 920, 925, 907, 913, 917.

17 guns, 15,600 lbs., at 46 cts.........	7, 176 00	
Rifling 17 guns, at $50...............	850 00	
Sighting 17 guns, at $20..............	340 00	
Boxing.....................	42 50	
		8, 408 50

Dec. 21. 3,200 6-pd'r shell, 800 6-pd'r shot, 800 6-pd'r canister; total, 4,800 projectiles,

at $2 25.........................	10, 800 00	
Boxing.....................	240 00	
		11, 040 00

1862.

Jan'y 7. 907, 906, 909, 914, 905, 906, 916, 915, 913, 902, 919, 916, 915.

13 guns, 11,853 lbs., at 46 cts.........	5, 452 38	
Rifling 13 guns, at $50...............	650 00	
Sighting 13 guns, at $20..............	260 00	
Boxing.....................	32 50	
		6, 394 88

March 6. 918, 916, 911, 915, 916, 918, 917, 922, 920, 917, 920, 914, 924, 917, 920, 921, 910, 920, 921, 918, 923, 914, 912, 915, 899, 922, 914, 908.

28 guns, 25,667 lbs., at 46 cts.........	11, 806 82	
Rifling 28 guns, at $50...............	1, 400 00	
Sighting 28 guns, at $20..............	560 00	
Boxing.....................	70 00	
		13, 836 82

March 12. 500 6-pd'r shot, 2,000 shell, 500 canister;

total, 3,000 projectiles, at $2 25.....	6, 750 00	
Boxing.....................	150 00	
		6, 900 00

March 18. 100 6-pd'r shot, 400 shell, 100 canister;

total, 600 projectiles, at $2 25.......	1, 350 00	
Boxing.....................	30 00	
		1, 380 00

Carried forward..................   57, 235 44

1862.	Brought forward.............			$57,235 44
March 18.	914, 919, 914, 923, 917, 909, 919.			
	7 guns, 6,415 lbs., at 46 cents.........	$2,950	00	
	Rifling 7 guns, at $50.................	350	00	
	Sighting 7 guns, at $20..............	140	00	
	Boxing......	17	50	
				3,458 40
March 1.	For 196 sets harness, at $270..........	52,920	00	
	Boxing, at $3 50....................	686	00	
				53,606 00
March 1.	84 gun-carriages and limbers, with implements complete....................	34,700	00	
	Boxing......	63	00	
				34,763 00
March 1.	84 caissons and limbers, with implements complete, at $425 each.............	34,700	00	
	Boxing......	210	00	
				34,910 00
March 1.	14 battery wagons, with implements complete, at $1,050....................	14,700	00	
	Boxing......	252	00	
				14,952 00
March 1.	14 travelling forges, with tools and stores complete, at $550......	7,700	00	
	Boxing......	196	00	
				7,896 00
				206,820 84

Cr.

By cash received from Mr. Ames—			
For bill November 18.........................	$9,275	24	
For bill December 13.........................	8,408	50	
			17,683 74
By stores purchased by harness-makers of Captain Balch, (the inspector,) see details in his certificate of inspection...............................	15,243	73	
			32,927 47
Balance due................................ .			173,893 37

SPRINGFIELD, MASSACHUSETTS,
March 7, 1862.

SIR: I have the honor to acknowledge the receipt of your telegram of the 6th, asking for a reply to your letter of February 27, in relation to the Penfield contract. Your letter was received on the 28th, but I was unable to collect and put in shape the data required until the 4th instant, when I replied to it. I desire to correct my statement of deliveries therein enclosed, by adding 10 N. M. 6-pounder rifled guns, delivered January 7, making forty-nine guns delivered on the contract up to March 1. I yesterday inspected twenty-eight more, making seventy-seven already delivered; the remaining seven, with the last of the projectiles, will be shipped next week, thus closing the whole order.

Ex. Doc. 72——34

I observe that Mr. Ames charges in his bills for these guns fifty dollars for rifling and twenty dollars for sighting. These prices I consider *exorbitant*. In my opinion the charge for rifling should not be one cent over ten dollars, and that for sighting not over eight. The price charged for the projectiles, two dollars and twenty-five cents each, is beyond all reason. At seven cents per pound, the average cost is, say seventy-seven cents; one and a quarter pound of powder, say twenty-five cents; cartridge-box, twelve cents; labor to complete, five cents; or total, one dollar and seventeen cents. Certainly one dollar and twenty-five cents is all they are worth, even at the high price of seven cents for the patent and shot.

By the terms of the contract I am to fix prices on articles according to what I have paid for similar ones. As I have never made any purchases of guns or projectiles I have left the prices of these stores to be fixed by the department, but I have thought it proper to give my views of the prices charged by Mr. Ames.

The prices for harness, carriages, caissons, equipments, tools, and stores have been fixed by me after much careful deliberation, and are, as I believe, just.

I have given Mr. Penfield, by the hand of Mr. Ames, certificates for the harness and for the carriages, equipments, and stores. I enclose herewith my price list, on which these certificates are based, for your information in settling with the contractor.

Very respectfully, your obedient servant,

GEO. T. BALCH,
Captain of Ordnance.

General J. W. RIPLEY,
Chief of Ordnance, Washington, D. C.

COMMISSION ON ORDNANCE AND ORDNANCE STORES,
Washington, May 9, 1862.

GENERAL: The papers in the Penfield case, sent to the commission, do not include any complete account against the United States agreeing with his claims.

We have four inspection certificates, with accounts attached, dated two on the 6th and two on the 12th of March, but these only embrace, 1st, 28 6-pounder guns, rifled and sighted; 2d, 13 6-pounder guns, rifled and sighted; 3d, 4,800 projectiles; 4th, 3,000 projectiles.

Captain Balch's letter, of March 7, mentions 84 guns actually inspected, additional ammunition, and harness, carriages, caissons, equipments, tools, and stores.

Please send the other accounts if they have been rendered.

Very respectfully, your obedient servant,

P. V. HAGNER, *Major of Ordnance.*

Brigadier General J. W. RIPLEY,
Chief of Ordnance.

ORDNANCE OFFICE,
Washington, D. C., May 10, 1862.

SIR: I have to acknowledge the receipt of Major P. V. Hagner's letter of the 9th instant, requesting information in regard to the Penfield contract, &c.

On the 18th of November, 1861, Captain Balch inspected and received nineteen rifled guns under this contract, and on the 29th of November the bill for them was presented to, and reported for payment by, this office.

On the 13th of December, 1861, Captain Balch inspected and received 17 rifled guns under the contract, and on the 19th of December the bill for them was presented to, and reported for payment by, this office.

Copies of these bills are herewith enclosed.

No other accounts, that I am aware of, have ever been presented to me for payment. I have requested Captain Balch, to whom was assigned the inspection and receipt of all stores furnished under this contract, to make a statement of the stores received under this contract, and also one of the certificates he has furnished the contractor. As soon as these papers are received they will be transmitted to the commission.

Respectfully, your obedient servant,

JAS. W. RIPLEY, *Brigadier General.*

J. WISE, Esq.,
Secretary to Commission on Ordnance Stores.

Before commission, May 19, 1862.

Mr. Penfield states: I have made out my bill, item for item, at the rates paid me for two batteries, consisting of six 6-pounders and one 12-pounder each, (the 12-pounder excepted, which I furnished for the State of Illinois, by order of the President, through Colonel Fouke, member of Congress from Illinois.) This bill had been examined at the Ordnance department, audited and paid long since, and I supposed there would be no question regarding the present bill.

The articles have been made and ready for inspection ever since the periods specified in the contract, and I offered in batteries, as stipulated, and they should have been inspected and paid for in batteries. To the present time thirty-six of the guns have been paid for (without my knowledge at the time) to Mr. Ames, and the charges for rifling and sighting, now objected to, are there allowed. The bills were rendered in connexion with other work done by Mr. Ames, and the guns included as if furnished as usual, through mistake of the clerk. I only know of the bill having been rendered some time afterwards from Mr. Ames. These payments are credited in my bill. There is another credit for "stores purchased from Captain Balch, the inspector." This is for harness, irons, &c., &c., which were obtained by the manufacturer of the harness from Captain Balch. The inspection certificates, with bills attached, have been handed in by Captain Balch, having been made without my knowledge or concurrence in any way. They are only of value to my accounts, (as far as my consent is required,) as certificates of inspection and receipts for the articles, not for the prices of the articles, as these should have been determined as required by my order.

The payments already made have required of me to procure funds. All the wood work bill, and I believe about $25,000 on harness, and Cooper & Pond's bill (who furnished battery wagons and stores and forges and stores) have been settled. Governor Yates came to me about those batteries because he knew I had furnished batteries previously to the State, and my first order was given by Colonel Fouke because he wanted carbines with his two batteries, which the President authorized him to procure, and I, being agent of Sharpe's factory, agreed to furnish the carbines, and he asked me to make a contract including batteries and all.

Mr. Penfield wishes to add that as the government has not given him the benefit of Major Frazer's inspection at the time at which he was entitled to it under the order, he submits that as the articles have been placed in service, and many of them used up, there remains no other rule for adjusting the correct price than comparison with the bills actually paid to him and to others by the government for articles of the same kind and quality and pattern.

As to the additional order for projectiles, a large portion of the 400 rounds per gun has already been made up, in anticipation of an immediate order for that number upon the receipt of Governor Yates's requisition as stipulated in the postscript of the order would be done upon the governor's requisition.

I stated publicly, upon the receipt of the order as originally written, limiting the number of rounds to 100 per gun, that I would not accept it, and I handed the letter to Judge Kellogg, who brought it back to me the next day with the postscript, and he told me that if the guns and projectiles proved satisfactory to Governor Yates, upon the trial ordered, the governor would certainly make the requisition; so that the only risk seemed to be whether they would succeed, and I felt confident of this and accepted.

Before commission, May 19, 1862.

Hon. Wm. Kellogg, House of Representatives, states: I was in Washington with Governor Yates, and went with him to the War Department, to endeavor to procure batteries of James's guns for use by our (Illinois) State troops. We saw Mr. Scott, and also General Ripley, and it was agreed that if they could be had they should be ordered. I knew of Mr. Penfield's connexion with this matter, and seeing him, asked that he would make a proposition. He did so, and we took it to the Ordnance department. His proposition was to furnish with each gun 500 rounds of ammunition. Governor Yates was to leave town immediately, and we left the Ordnance office under the impression that the proposition as made would be accepted. Afterwards it was found that General Ripley made the number of rounds only 100 per gun; I objected to this on the grounds that we ought to have a larger supply for guns to be used so far from the point of supply of the ammunition, and also that we should require a large supply in practice, the troops being inexperienced. Mr. Penfield objected for some reason he did not explain to me. General Ripley contended that it was the usual and sufficient amount for a first supply. Mr. Scott, Assistant Secretary of War, agreed to modify by increasing the number to 200 rounds per gun; but as I still objected to less than 500, it was at last stated that a postscript would be added to the order promising an additional supply in case Governor Yates made requisition for it. This I preferred to an order for 200 loads, and it was acceptable to Mr. Penfield. We have received the guns and other articles; they have been issued to our troops, and the governor has made a requisition for 400 rounds additional. The payment by the government it was agreed was to depend on the success of these guns and batteries. This was to be judged of by Governor Yates. The test was to be made in Illinois. Mr. James went to Illinois and tried them; they were also tried by our troops in action. Governor Yates became convinced from the reports of the officers that the guns and projectiles were entirely satisfactory, and he wrote to me asking me to procure two 12-pounder guns to replace two of the 6-pounders in each battery, and also to procure the additional number of rounds of ammunition. I took the requisition to Secretary Stanton, but he declined to order the additional supply. I then went to the President, and he wrote requesting the Secretary to fill the whole requisition of Governor Yates, if consistent with the public interests. Mr. Stanton still declined, and I returned to the President, who wrote asking why the ammunition could not be supplied. I have since had no connexion with the matter.

COMMISSION ON ORDNANCE AND ORDNANCE STORES,
Washington, May 20, 1862.

SIR: The commission direct me to inform you that it will be necessary for them to have the original bills for articles purchased by you and supplied to the government, under your order for fourteen batteries for the State of Illinois, in order that they can form an opinion in your case as submitted to them. Will you please produce them at your earliest convenience. They will be returned to you in a short time.

Very respectfully, your obedient servant,

P. V. HAGNER,
Major of Ordnance.

Mr. G. H. PENFIELD, *National Hotel.*

Receipts of ordnance and ordnance stores by Capt. G. T. Balch, Springfield, Mass., under the Penfield contract of October 11, 1861.

Date	Principal agent	Sub agent, who is the manufacturer	Place received	6-pounder N. M. brass guns, rifled, 3.80 caliber	6-pounder carriages, complete	6-pounder caissons	Travelling forges A	Battery wagons C	Sets of implem'ts and equipments	James's 6-pounder shot	James's 6-pounder shell	James's 6-pounder canister	Sets of harness, complete, wheel and lead	Sets of tools and stores for forges A	Sets of tools for battery wagons C	Batteries complete
1861.																
Nov. 9	James T. Ames	F. W. Parmenter	Chicopee. Mass		6	6										
14	Cooper & Pond	....do....	Troy, N. Y			12	4	4						4	4	
14	James T. Ames	James T. Ames	....do....				1							1	1	
18	....do....	....do....	Chicopee, Mass	19												
20	Cooper & Pond	F. W. Parmenter	Troy, N. Y			4				300	1,200	300				
30	....do....	Augt. Viele	....do....		8											
30	James T. Ames	Cooper & Pond	West Troy, N. Y					1								
30	....do....	James T. Ames	Troy, N. Y													
Dec. 9	Cooper & Pond	....do....	Springfield, Mass			4			1							
13	....do....	Augt. Viele	Chicopee, Mass	17	12	8										
26	....do....	F. W. Parmenter	West Troy, N. Y				6							6	6	
28	....do....	Cooper & Pond	Troy, N. Y					6								
31	James T. Ames	E. Gaylord	....do....			26										
9 & 20	....do....	James T. Ames	Chicopee, Mass						4	300	1,200	300				
31	....do....	E. Gaylord	....do....										336			
1862.																
Jan. 3	....do....	James T. Ames	....do....	10									168			
10	....do....	....do....	....do....		28	26										
7	Cooper & Pond	J. M. Quimby & Co.	Newark, N. J													
11	....do....	S. B. Althouse & Co.	New York, N. Y	3												
11	James T. Ames	El Gaylord	Chicopee, Mass													
14	....do....	J. T. Ames	....do....			18							168			
21	....do....	E. Gaylord	....do....													
22	....do....	....do....	....do....													
29	Cooper & Pond	Augt. Viele	West Troy, N. Y													
31	....do....	F. W. Parmenter	Troy, N. Y				3	3						3	3	
Feb. 22	Cooper & Pond	Cooper & Pond	....do....		12	6				200	800	200	168			
24	....do....	....do....	New York, N. Y										168			
24	....do....	James T. Ames	Chicopee, Mass		18								168			
28	....do....	....do....	....do....						9							
Mar. 6	James T. Ames	James T. Ames	....do....	28									168			
12	....do....	....do....	....do....							500	2,000	500				
18	....do....	....do....	....do....	7						100	400	100				
18	....do....	....do....	....do....													
			Total deliveries...	84	84	94	14	14	14	1,400	5,600	1,400	1,176	14	14	

(All Invoiced to Gov. R. Yates, Springfield, Ill.)

GEO. T. BALCH, *Captain Ordnance Corps.*

WASHINGTON, D. C., *May 16, 1862.*

List of certificates given for ordnance and ordnance stores received under the Penfield contract of October 11, 1861.

No.	Date.	Certificates.	Amount.
	1861.		
7	Nov. 18	For 13 N. M. and 6 O. M. rifled 6-pounder guns, (19) ...	$9,285 24
11	Dec. 13	For 17 N. M. 6-pounder guns, rifled and sighted.........	8,418 50
	1862.		
13	March 6	For 4,800 James's rifled projectiles.....................	11,040 00
14	....do....	For 13 6-pounder guns, rifled and sighted...............	6,394 88
16	....do....	For 28 6-pounder guns, N. M., rifled...................	13,836 82
18	12	For 3,000 James's rifled projectiles	6,900 00
19	18	For 600 James's rifled projectiles	1,380 00
21	....do....	For 7 6-pounder guns, rifled and sighted	3,458 40
		All of the above certificates were to order of J. T. Ames.	
1	1	For 14 batteries complete, consisting of the carriages, caissons, forges, and battery wagons, with implements, equipments, tools, and stores complete	70,020 01
2	1	For 392 sets artillery harness, wheel, and 784 sets lead ..	37,284 27
		To order of G. Penfield.	
			168,018 12

GEO. T. BALCH,
Captain Ordnance Corps.

WASHINGTON, D. C., *May 16, 1862.*

ORDNANCE OFFICE, *Washington, D. C., May 16, 1862.*

SIR : Referring to my letter of the 10th May, in relation to the papers in the case of the Penfield contract, I now enclose herewith a list of certificates given by Captain G. T. Balch, for ordnance and ordnance stores received by him under G. H. Penfield's contract of October 11, 1861.

A statement of the different parties from whom the above stores were received, and the dates when received. Statement of the prices allowed by Captain Balch for each article furnished under the head of artillery carriages, implements, equipments, and stores, showing how the amount stated in certificates Nos. 1 and 2 to G. H. Penfield was made up. Be pleased to return the last paper to this office when no longer required.

Respectfully, your obedient servant,

JAS. W. RIPLEY, *Brigadier General.*

J. WISE, Esq., *Secretary to Commission on Ordnance Stores,*
Washington, D. C.

Before commission, May 19, 1862.

General James states :

No price less than $50 for rifling and $20 dollars for sighting has been ever paid for my guns, and no price less than $2 25 has been paid for a round of 6-pounder ammunition of my patent to my knowledge. There are ten grooves in a 6-pounder, about five-eighths inch wide. They are one-sixteenth of an inch deep in the centre, and reduced to one-twentieth at the sides, and they are of a progressive depth from barrel to muzzle, .05 deeper at the breech. The twist varies also, starting straight. The machine regulates the twist and progressive depth, and cuts only one groove at a time. The charge for making projectiles, according to Ames's charges, made it necessary to charge $2 25 for so small a number as 8,400 projectiles. This cost would be reduced. I think, if I went elsewhere instead of to Ames's, and if 10,000 were ordered, but I wrote to Mr. Penfield that I would not take the order at all, when I heard that only 8,400 rounds were ordered, as the profit was so small at that number, even at $2 25.

I know, of my own knowledge, that the bills handed in by Mr. Penfield for carriages, caissons, implements, and harness are the same in amount, precisely, as charged to him by Mr. Ames and myself. And I would say further, that Mr. Ames and myself have charged for the above articles the exact amount of bills paid by us a long time since. Mr. Ames and myself receive our profit from the guns and projectiles, and the prices for the guns and projectiles, as charged by Mr. Penfield, are the same, precisely, as charged by Mr. Ames to the government and to several of the States, when dealing directly with him.

COMMISSION ON ORDNANCE AND ORDNANCE STORES,
Washington, May 19, 1862.

GENERAL : The commission request that you will please state the price paid to Miles Greenwood, of Cincinnati, for rifling and sighting brass guns. Also the like price paid to Alger & Co., and to any others. Also the price of 6-pounder projectiles of different makers for rifled guns, fixed and unfixed, with or without charge of gun. Also the prices paid for Wiard's batteries, with such details as may admit of a comparison with James's or others.

Very respectfully, your obedient servant,

P. V. HAGNER,
Major of Ordnance.

Brigadier General J. W. RIPLEY,
    Chief of Ordnance.

COMMISSION ON ORDNANCE AND ORDNANCE STORES,
Washington, May 24, 1862.

GENERAL : The commission has directed that the appraisement of the articles furnished by Mr. G. H. Penfield, under your order of October 11, required to be made by Major P. V. Hagner and Lieutenant (now Captain) Balch, not having been so made, should, if possible, be now made by those officers, and they request that this duty may be performed as soon as can be consistent with the other duties of these officers, and that a report be made to the commission by them.

Should you be able to spare Captain Balch for the time necessary, on Monday or Tuesday next, they request that the necessary orders be given for the meeting of these officers in one of those days.

Very respectfully, your obedient servant,

P. V. HAGNER,
Major of Ordnance.

General J. W. Ripley, Chief of Ordnance.

COMMISSION ON ORDNANCE AND ORDNANCE STORES,
Washington, May 24, 1862.

SIR : The commission direct me to inform you that, as it appears from your order to "furnish fourteen batteries," &c., the price to be paid by the United States was to be determined by Major P. V. Hagner and Lieutenant G. T. Balch, in accordance with certain rules therein set forth, they direct that such scale of prices be now fixed by them, it appearing that this stipulation has not been heretofore carried out. As Major Hagner and Lieutenant (now Captain) Balch are both at present in the city, the commission will require that they perform this duty at the earliest convenient time, and notice is hereby given to you in order that you may furnish for their use any information you desire.

The papers in your case, now on file with the commission, will be placed at the service of these officers.

Very respectfully, your obedient servant,

P. V. HAGNER, *Major of Ordnance.*

Mr. G. H. PENFIELD, *Washington.*

COMMISSION ON ORDNANCE,
Washington, May 31, 1862.

SIR : The officers appointed by the terms of your order, dated October 11, to fix the prices to be paid for the articles furnished by you under that order have prepared their report, and have submitted it to the commission. If you have any suggestions to make, or corrections to propose for the consideration of the commission in reference to that report, they will be heard on Monday next.

Very respectfully, your obedient servant,

J. WISE, *Secretary, &c.*

Mr. G. H. PENFIELD, *National Hotel.*

Before commission.

Major Hagner states that he finds at the Ordnance office that Mr. James's shot, shell, and canister have been charged at the same price heretofore, although other makers usually make a difference.

ORDNANCE OFFICE, *Washington, May* 24, 1862.

SIR: In compliance with the request of the commissioners of the 19th instant, I report that the price paid to Miles Greenwood for rifling 6-pounder bronze guns was $50 each. His bills, when presented at this office, charged for rifled guns at 55 cents per pound, which, at the established price for smooth-bore guns, would allow $78 each for rifling them; but the bills were reduced, before payment, to the usual prices of 46 cents per pound for the guns, and $50 each for rifling them.

The price paid to C. Alger & Co. for rifling and *sighting* such guns is $50 each.

The price paid to J. T. Ames for rifling similar guns is $50 each, and for sighting them $20 each, amounting together to $70 each.

R. P. Parrott's charge for *sighting* guns with graduated sights, fixed complete, is $7 50 each.

The prices paid for 6-pounder projectiles, for rifled cannon without cartridges, are as follows, viz:

	Price.	Weight.	Cost.
Shells—James's	$1 95	each, 11½ lbs. each,	17 cents per lb.
Hotchkiss's	1 50	" 13½ "	11$\frac{1}{9}$ "
Parrott's	1 45	" 14½ "	10 "
Schenkl's	1 37½	" 9½ "	14½ "
Schenkl's fuze, extra	62½	"	
Solid shot—James's	1 95	" 13$\frac{8}{10}$ "	14$\frac{1}{8}$ "
Hotchkiss's	1 25	" 13½ "	9¼ "

The price of all the shells, except Schenkl's, includes a fuze. His fuze is of a peculiar kind, more expensive, and preferred by the artillery, and is often required for use in projectiles of other kinds. The bills for rifle projectiles charge by number at a stated price; but as they differ considerably in weight, the cost per pound is the proper standard for comparison. Ten cents per pound appears to be a fair price for 6-pounder rifle shot and shells, including a common fuze, except the Schenkl, which includes a pressed paper sabot, and is, therefore, more expensive.

The price paid for Wiard's batteries, which consists each of two 12-pounder and four 6-pounder steel guns, is $11,500 each. These differ from all other models, and give no just basis for a comparison with other batteries. For five batteries of bronze guns, (four 6-pounders and two howitzers,) manufactured in St. Louis—

The price paid for the six guns was	$2,448 00
For the carriages, without implements	3,958 00
Cost of each battery	6,406 00

Three batteries of Parrott's 10-pounder rifled guns, procured by the State of New York for a regiment of United States volunteer artillery, were purchased by the United States.

The price paid for the guns	$1,182 00
For the carriages, with implements	4,137 67
Cost of each battery	5,319 67

Two batteries of bronze 6-pounder rifled guns were furnished by G. H. Penfield, for the use of General McClernand's brigade of Illinois troops, for which the United States paid—

For the six guns	$2,988 46
And for the carriages and implements	6,736 50
Cost of each battery	9,724 96

The prices of the several parts of the batteries, including ammunition, are stated in detail in the two latter bills, and, as they may be useful to the commissioners, they are here stated:

	Parrott's.	Penfield's.
For six guns	$1,137 00	$2,553 46
For rifling the same (Parrott's is included in the price of guns)	..	300 00
For sighting same	45 00	120 00
6 gun-carriages and implements	1,690 67	2,550 00
6 caissons and implements	1,710 00	2,550 00
1 travelling forge	275 00	550 00
1 battery wagon	275 00	1,050 00
Tools and stores for forge and wagon, not separately charged in Penfield's	187 00	..
Boxing, not separately charged in Parrott's	..	51 50
Cost of guns, carriages, and implements, complete for one battery	5,319 67	9,724 96
42 sets of harness, for two horses each, including boxes	3,360 00	3,919 00
3,600 projectiles, with powder and cartridges	5,580 00	8,100 00
Cost of each battery, including harness and 600 rounds of ammunition, for each gun	14,529 67	21,743 96
	4,650 00	
	9,879 67	....

In all of the batteries mentioned, except Wiard's, the carriages and implements were similar, and of the established United States models; but the guns differed, Parrott's being made of iron, and the others of bronze.

The prices charged for the St. Louis and Parrott batteries are about the same as have usually been paid, and are considered just and reasonable. The batteries delivered by G. H. Penfield were furnished under a contract made with him in August last by P. B. Fouke, in which the prices were stated in detail. This department had no agency in making that contract, nor any knowledge of it, until after the batteries had been sent to Cairo. The prices specified in that contract are, therefore, not regarded as precedents in adjusting other accounts for similar articles. The largest part of all the artillery carriages which have been procured by this department were purchased without implements, at prices varying from $275 to $285 each, averaging about $280 each, which amounts to $3,920 for the fourteen carriages composing a battery. Many of these were manufactured by the same persons who made the carriages delivered by G. H. Penfield under the order to him of October 11, 1861.

Respectfully, I am your obedient servant,

JAS. W. RIPLEY,
Brigadier General.

Mr. J. WISE,
Secretary of Commission on Ordnance Stores.

In the matter of G. H. Penfield.

To the commissioners on contracts and claims for ordnance and ordnance stores:

In the report of Major Hagner and Captain Balch, affixing prices to the articles furnished the United States under an order from General Ripley, October 11, 1861, they have affixed prices to James's patent shot and shell. I claim that they had no right to do this.

By the terms of the contract the *batteries complete* were to be paid for at such prices as Major Hagner and Captain Balch might determine to be fair and just, according to the average of prices they had paid or might be paying for similar articles, but this did not give them any right to determine the prices of the projectiles. They are not a part of the batteries, and therefore were not subject to appraisal; and even if they had been a part of the batteries, being, as they are, a patented article, they are not "similar" to any other article, and the only *fair* and *just* rule by which their prices could be determined is the price at which "James's" projectiles of this size have already been sold, have always been sold by the patentee.

I also object to the prices named in said report, because they are not such prices as the government has paid for "similar" articles, as will be shown in the following cases:

The government is paying Miles Greenwood, of Cincinnati, for bronze guns and rifling, as follows: for bronze guns, 46 cents per pound; for rifling bronze guns, $5\frac{7}{10}$ cents per pound.

The 84 guns which I have furnished weigh 76,704 pounds, which,

at $5\frac{7}{10}$ per pound for rifling, would amount to	$4,372 12
84 guns, at $50 each, is	4,200 00
Balance in my favor of	172 12

Mr. Alger, who rifles "bronze" guns for the government, in his account of February 19, 1862, I find the following as having been paid: "For rifling and sighting one 26-pounder bronze gun, with two wrenches, $100."

The contract requires the "batteries complete" to be made according to pages

306 to 316, Ordnance Manual. After having been thus made, an alteration was required by the inspector, for which I am charged in Cooper & Pond's account (on file with the commission) $15 each on 196 wagons, &c., &c., while Major Hagner and Captain Balch allow me $10 each on 90 wagons, making a difference of $2,040 for work not contemplated in the contract. The harness-maker, E. Gaylord, charges me $270 per set, while Major Hagner and Captain Balch allow me $265 per set. The reasons are set forth in Mr. Gaylord's letter, on file.

By the delay on the part of the Ordnance bureau in inspecting the property and fixing the prices to be paid me I shall be subjected to great loss. Had the Ordnance bureau inspected the first two "batteries complete" and fixed the prices to be paid, agreeable to the terms of the contract, I should have known what was "the average of the prices they (Major Hagner and Captain Balch) have paid or may be paying for similar articles on contracts or purchases," and should have taken care to purchase at such prices.

The commissioners will bear in mind that I did not seek this contract, but only consented to undertake it at the urgent request of Governor Yates. The short time was objected to, among other things. My proposition made to the Secretary of War was what Governor Yates and myself understood at the time to have been accepted by General Ripley.

I should have received the money on the delivery of each two "batteries complete," and thus been saved a large amount in interest money, had the property been inspected as contemplated in the contract.

In conclusion, I respectfully ask the commission to save me from the great loss I shall suffer if the prices reported by Major Hagner and Captain Balch be confirmed, and also that a perfect record be made of the proceedings had before the commissioners, so that I may be able to further prosecute my just demands, if necessary.

Respectfully, &c., G. H. PENFIELD.

COMMISSION ON ORDNANCE AND ORDNANCE STORES,
Washington, June 20, 1862.

GENERAL : The commission have the honor to report as follows :

CASE No. 102.—G. H. PENFIELD, Washington, D. C.

Order by direction of the Secretary of War, dated October 11, 1861. Account rendered by G. H. Penfield, or by his authority, November 29, 1861, for 19 guns, December 13, 1861, for 17 guns, to the Ordnance department.

March 21, final account rendered and referred (with certificates of inspection and appraised value of articles by Lieutenant Balch and statement by Mr. Penfield) to the commission, by special order of the Secretary of War.

Letters indorsed by the President and Secretary of War, March 8 and April 1, 1862, subsequently referred.

To furnish 14 field batteries complete, each to consist of six 6-pounder bronze rifle guns, with carriages, caissons, implements, and equipments, as prescribed in Ordnance Manual, harness (two wheel and four lead sets) for each carriage, caisson, forge, and battery wagon, and one hundred rounds of ammunition (one-sixth shot, one-sixth canister, and two-thirds shell) for each gun. The whole to be complete and ready for service in the field. All the articles to be subject to regular inspection and proof, to be of prescribed quality and pattern. To be delivered, two batteries prior to November 1, 1861, and two batteries weekly thereafter until all are delivered. In case of failure to deliver as stipulated, the government is to be under no obligation to take the deficient articles. Payments to be made at such prices per battery as may be determined to be fair and just by Major P. V. Hagner and Lieutenant G. T. Balch, according to the average of the prices they have paid or may be paying for similar articles on contract or purchases, or by valuation for any of the articles not so obtained.

The commission found, upon commencing their examination, that the appraisement directed in the order to be made by Major P. V. Hagner and Lieutenant (now Captain) Balch had not been made, and therefore (as both these officers were then in Washington) we called upon the chief of ordnance to require them to make the appraisement of the articles delivered, as contemplated by the order. This they have done, and have prepared and submitted to us a paper fully setting forth their action, a copy of which was furnished Mr. Penfield, that he might offer any objections he desired. He has opposed the adoption of the appraisement, as thus reported, on the following grounds, which have been duly considered:

1st. "The appraisers have fixed prices to James's patent shell and shot. They have no right to do this, as they are not part of the batteries, and also as James's patented shell and shot are not *similar* to any other."

It is considered that all the articles called for by the order given to Mr. Penfield were directed to be appraised by these officers; and as the cost of the three kinds of projectiles is not the same, and as a particular proportion of each was furnished, it was necessary to establish a value for each kind. The appraised value of the shells agrees very nearly with that charged, but that of the solid shot and canister is less, as shown by comparing the weight and component parts with other patented shot and canister nearly similar.

As it has been proven by the evidence before the commission of the patentee and manufacturer that the price charged by Mr. Penfield for the projectiles in the proportion furnished is the same as charged heretofore to all buyers, the government included, and as Mr. Penfield was obliged to furnish *James's patent* projectiles, made only by one manufacturer, and could not have been expected to buy them at less than the usual rates, the commission consider that the "valuation" required of the appraisers should have rested upon the sales actually made to the government and others, and that the liability of the government in settling with Mr. Penfield must be measured by such price, and therefore direct an extra allowance for the 5,600 projectiles equal to the difference between the amount allowed by the appraisers for projectiles and that charged by Mr. Penfield, viz: two thousand three hundred and eighty dollars, ($2,380.)

2d. "That the price allowed for rifling and sighting is not as high as paid to other parties."

The commission find that the sum allowed is greater than paid to some others, although less than was paid to one party—Miles Greenwood. In this case the manufacturer, but recently established as a founder of cannon, charged for *rifled* bronze guns per pound much higher than the usual price for smooth-bore bronze guns. This charge was not allowed, but as a maximum allowance, in consideration, no doubt, of the fact that he was a beginner in the business, and at a time when the government needed such guns, and that the definite contract required by law had not been made prior to his commencing the work, the price of 46 cents per pound was allowed for the guns, and $50 per gun for rifling. In several other cases, however, these operations have been paid for to beginners in the business, also, at much lower rates, and as these guns were furnished by Mr. Ames, one of the largest and most experienced *makers* of bronze guns in the country, the commission consider the price allowed abundantly ample. The Phœnix Iron Company report, through Major Laidley, that the cost of rifling their three-inch wrought iron cannon is only $1 25, and the allowance by the appraisers of $36 per gun can only be justified, therefore, because approaching the "average" paid, though largely exceeding a "just" price for the work done. The charge for *sighting* is also in excess of that paid to others, $7 50 per gun having been paid, while $14 per gun is allowed.

3d. The charge for alterations upon 196 wagons, at $15 each, "has been reduced to 90 wagons, at $10 each."

The commission find that, in point of fact, only 90 carriages were altered, the others having been made by the same manufacturers who were making correctly for the department, and that the allowance of $10 for the alteration is in excess of the cost by at least two dollars.

4th. "The allowance per set for harness is less than charged to Mr. Penfield." The price allowed is in excess of that paid to many manufacturers, and a separate charge has been granted for *whips and nose-bags*, although these articles were furnished with the harness without charge by all the manufacturers employed by Major Hagner, except in a single case.

The commission consider that much of the delay and trouble complained of by Mr. Penfield must be ascribed to the fact that, although he undertook to procure the numerous articles composing these batteries, he did not (as he himself testified before the commission) see personally to his engagements, but merely intrusted the supply to other parties, without special contracts or agreements as to prices.

The explicit terms of the order given to him could leave no doubt that he should not in any case *exceed* the prices paid by Major Hagner and Lieutenant Balch, whose future appraisement might have been made to bind others as it bound him, particularly as these same parties were generally employed by them to manufacture. As these officers could have been applied to at any time for information which would have shielded him from all risk of loss, the commission consider that it cannot be admitted, in face of the terms of the order and the ready means of complying safely with those terms, always open to Mr. Penfield, that the government can be held responsible for any lavish expenditure or excessive allowance that may have been thus carelessly made.

The extra allowance beyond the valuation of Major Hagner and Captain Balch, heretofore directed, is upon the ground, as already intimated, that, as these projectiles were patented, and had never been sold at lower prices than those now charged for them, the government in ordering them must have expected to pay for them, as they did for the batteries, at customary prices. In reference, however, to the batteries, of which purchases had been previously made, and were then from time to time being made, by these officers, the "average" price which they paid for them is made by the terms of the order conclusive as to the rates at which they are to be accepted from Mr. Penfield by the government. The appraisement as to the batteries becomes thus, in effect, part and parcel of the contract, and we have not felt authorized to disturb it, either by reduction or increase.

The improvidence of using the services of a "middle man" to fill so extensive an order, instead of employing directly the manufacturers, was apparent to all, and therefore the chief of ordnance in his order very properly attempted to guard the public interests by the requirement that the prices allowed should not exceed what the government would itself have to pay or was paying; and this strict requirement should have either prevented Mr. Penfield from accepting the order given him, or have made it obligatory on him not to advance the market price by paying higher than was proper for articles of which the government was the only purchaser. His own safety, as well as his duty to the government, demanded this, and any excess thus paid by him was an injury to the public interest, probably affecting future supplies to even a greater extent than the amount so charged to and by him.

Mr. Penfield has argued before the commission that the delay in the inspection and appraisement of the first two batteries operates now to his disadvantage, in not having given him earlier warning of the prices to be allowed, so that he could have stopped at once his larger payments to others. This complaint cannot be regarded as well founded, inasmuch as he failed to use the equally decisive means within his reach, by inquiring of the officers named in his contract, who were purchasing at the time. The government could not have anticipated that with such carefully limited powers he would have exceeded fair market prices, yet the bills rendered show a large excess over prices paid to the same parties for the same articles by these officers. The moment for making the inspection was not stipulated in the order, and of course had to be dependent upon the exigencies of the service. No payment was promised for partial deliveries, although it appears that two payments were made for guns, and the final inspection, it is stated, was made without delay as soon as all the batteries were complete.

It is therefore directed that the account of Mr. Penfield be examined and audited as usual, allowing for each battery, with one hundred rounds of ammunition, in accordance with the report hereto attached, by Major Hagner and Captain Balch, the sum of twelve thousand nine hundred and ten dollars and eighty-five cents, ($12,910 85,) with the addition of two thousand three hundred and eighty dollars ($2,380) for extra allowance upon 5,600 projectiles, and deducting the amounts already paid on this account.

The position which Mr. Penfield claims to occupy in this transaction is altogether anomalous. He voluntarily engaged to furnish these batteries at "the average price" at which they had been and were being bought by two accomplished ordnance officers, who, it may be assumed, made their purchases on the best possible terms for the government. As he was not a manufacturer of any of the articles, and had, so far as it appears, no connexion with any such manufacturing establishment, his undertaking was in effect to buy the batteries, and supply them to the government at their market value, and to make from his own funds all advances required for the purpose, an undertaking which, if fairly executed, would necessarily leave him without profit or compensation, either for his services or expenditures, and this is the attitude he has taken before the commission, and with which he professes to be content. At the same time he presents these excessive bills. This is a mystery which we do not pretend to explain, but which leaves upon our minds the impression that if the terms of the contract with the government are insisted on, in view of the relations subsisting between the manufacturers and sellers of the batteries and Mr. Penfield, the latter will not be permitted to suffer, but will be held to pay for the batteries only at the same rates at which the same parties had sold and were then selling them to the government. We have no doubt but that this will be the result. In, however, holding Mr. Penfield to his engagement which, as a "middle-man," he made with the government, and which, as stated, leaves him without profit, we feel it but just to allow him, although he does not demand it, a fair commission for the service he has rendered.

It is therefore directed that, in addition to the amount adjudged to be due upon the purchases, there be paid to Mr. Penfield, in full of all claim whatever upon the government growing out of the order of the 11th October, a commission of two and a half per cent. upon one hundred and eighty-three thousand one hundred and thirty-one dollars and ninety cents, ($183,131 90,) the total amount of the bill as sanctioned by the commission. The rate of commission thus granted must be regarded as liberally compensating Mr. Penfield for the slight services he professes to have rendered.

His claim to be permitted to continue in the unusual position of serving the government without compensation, in obtaining 400 more rounds of ammunition for each of these guns, rests upon a postscript to the order of the chief of ordnance, wherein it is stated that "an additional quantity of ammunition for the batteries will be supplied hereafter on requisitions from the Governor of Illinois when wanted;" and a letter from Governor Yates to the Secretary of War, dated March 1, 1862, requesting, among other things, "500 projectiles for each gun of the fourteen batteries named above." Mr. Penfield shows that he sought an order for 500 rounds per gun in his original proposal; but admits that it was denied him, and that no promise would be given more satisfactory than the one stated in the postscript above quoted; but he insists that the circumstances under which this was given to him induced him to look upon it as equivalent to a promise. We cannot so regard it. Supplies of ammunition must depend upon the wants of the service in the kind and price, as well as the quantity. The interests of the government must be the guide at the time it may be needed.

No stipulation was given as to quantity or kind by the words of the postscript; and as Mr. Penfield was not the recognized agent of James's projectiles only, and of none others, no assurance can be inferred that the additional ammunition to be furnished "when wanted" (upon requisition of the governor of Illinois) was to be of that kind, or, admitting that the kind might be designated by the governor, it cannot be claimed that the price charged and allowed in this account (evidently unreasonable and extravagant) can now be admitted.

By the indorsement of the Secretary of War upon the letter of Governor Yates it is shown that, in his opinion, the request could not be complied with "without detriment to the service," and the commission consider that this should be regarded as a conclusive judgment upon the claim as urged by Mr. Penfield, and that no additional order should be given through or by him.

We are, sir, very respectfully, &c.,

J. HOLT,
ROBERT DALE OWEN,
Commissioners.
P. V. HAGNER,
Major of Ordnance, Assistant to Commission.

Brigadier General J. W. RIPLEY,
Chief of Ordnance.

WASHINGTON, *May* 31, 1862.

The undersigned, in compliance with instructions, beg leave to submit the following report of prices per battery, complete, determined by them to be fair and just, according to the average of the prices they have paid on contracts or purchases, or by valuation for any of the articles not so obtained, viz:

1. 6-pounder bronze guns, (78 new model, 6 old model:)
   Freight, 76,700 pounds, at 46 cents $35,283 84
   Rifling 84 guns, at $36 .... 3,024 00
   Sighting 78 guns, at $14 .... 1,092 00
   Boxing 84 guns, at $2 50 .... 210 00

2. 84 6-pounder carriages, at $280.......................... 23,520 00
   84 6-pounder caissons, at $285 .... 23,940 00
   14 battery wagons, at $290............................... 4,060 00
   14 forges, at $290....................................... 4,060 00
   14 sets of implements, tools, and stores, at $1,081 82........ 15,145 48
   Additional allowed on the battery fitted by Ames with harness, after deducting for deficiencies, as per statement of Captain Balch 20 00
   Altering pole straps of 44 caissons and 46 carriages, (90,) at $10 .... 900 00
   Allowance for boxes, (in addition to 74 boxes, at 75 cents,) 37 boxes, at $1..................................... 37 00

3. 1,176 sets of harness, (392 at $47 50; 784 at $42) 51,940 00
   196 boxes, at $3... 588 00

4. 8,400 projectiles:
   5,600 shells, at $2 20.................................... 12,312 00
   1,400 shot, at $1 50 .... 2,100 00

1,400 canister, at $1 50.................................. $2,100 00
840 boxes, at 50 cents 420 00

                                                           199,752 51
Deduct amount of bill for harness, irons, &c................ 15,243 73

                                                           165,508 78
Payments made on account to James T. Ames, (November 18,
$9,275 24; December 13, $8,480 50)........ .... 17,683 74

Balance now due G. H. Penfield 147 825 04

Price per battery of Mr. Penfield, (price of guns 46 cents per pound,) with
100 rounds per gun, 6-pounders, 180,752 ÷ 14 = $12,910 85.

Price paid for Wiard's battery, (price of guns 64 cents per pound) of four
6-pounders and two 12-pounders, with tools and stores, complete, and 100
rounds per gun, $11,500.

Price paid R. P. Parrott for battery (price of guns 25 cents per pound) of six
guns, complete, with tools and stores, and 100 rounds of ammunition per gun,
$9,879 67.

Respectfully submitted.

> P. V. HAGNER,
> *Major of Ordnance.*
> GEO. T. BALCH,
> *Captain Ordnance Corps.*

The CHIEF OF ORDNANCE.

WASHINGTON, *July* 15, 1862.

GENTLEMEN: Understanding that you are about to make a report of the
cases that have been examined before you, I respectfully request that the
papers herewith sent, and numbered from 1 to 13 inclusive, be published in connexion with your report in my case.

Respectfully, your obedient servant,

> G. H. PENFIELD.

Hon. J. HOLT and ROBERT DALE OWEN,
Commissioners, &c., &c., &c.

The papers enclosed in the above letter had been submitted to the commission
by Mr. Penfield, and considered by them, and were subsequently withdrawn by
Mr. Penfield. Those not published in the case are now appended, as requested
by Mr. Penfield.

No. 1 same as No. 3 ante.

No. 2. Original order to Mr. Penfield—same as No. 1 ante, without the
indorsement by the chief of ordnance, but having indorsements, first signed A.
Lincoln, dated March 26, 1862, and second signed Edwin M. Stanton, Secretary
of War, dated April 1, 1862, which follow.

No. 3. Letter from Governor Yates to the Secretary of War, dated March 1,
1862, with two indorsements—*first* signed A. Lincoln, March 8, 1862, and *second*
signed Edwin M. Stanton, Secretary of War.

No. 4. Letter from G. H. Penfield to General J. W. Ripley, dated October 28,
1861.

No. 5. Letter and bill from E. Gaylord, dated May 22, 1862.

No. 6. Bill of sundries bought of Cooper & Pond.

No. 7. Copy of letter from Cooper & Pond, dated May 22, 1862.

No. 8. Letter from James T. Ames, dated March 27, 1862.

No. 9. Copy of agreement, signed G. H. Penfield, dated ———.
No. 10. Letter to G. H. Penfield from Governor Yates, dated June 7, 1862.
No. 11. Same as No. 13 ante.
No. 12. Same as No. 14 ante.
No. 13. Same as No. 17 ante.

P. V. HAGNER,
Major of Ordnance.

ORDNANCE OFFICE,
Washington, October 11, 1862.

SIR : By direction of the Secretary of War, I offer you an order for fourteen field batteries complete, each to consist of six 6-pounder bronze rifle guns, with carriages, caissons, implements, and equipments, as prescribed at pages 307 to 316 Ordnance Manual; harness complete for six horses (two wheel and four leading) for each gun-carriage, caisson, forge, and battery wagon; and one hundred rounds of ammunition (one-sixth shot, one-sixth canister, and two-thirds shell,) for each gun—the whole to be delivered complete and ready for service in the field. All the articles are to be subject to regular inspection and proof by such officer as this department may designate for the purpose, and are to be of the pattern and quality of similar articles in the United States service. They are to be delivered as follows, viz : Two batteries complete on or before the first day of November next, and from and after that date two batteries per week, until the whole fourteen field batteries complete hereby ordered are delivered. In case of any failure to deliver in or within the times before stated, the government is to be under no obligation to take any of the articles then remaining undelivered under this order, but may or may not do so, at its option. Payments will be made, in such funds as the Treasury Department may provide, on certificates of inspection and receipt by the United States inspector, at such prices per battery complete as may be determined to be fair and just by Major P. V. Hagner and Lieutenant G. T. Balch, according to the average of the prices they have paid or may be paying for similar articles on contracts or purchases, or by valuation for any of the articles not so obtained.

In case of failure to fill this order in accordance with its conditions as to time and all other respects, the government may immediately revoke and annul it.

Please signify, in writing, your acceptance or non-acceptance of this order, on the terms and conditions herein specified.

Respectfully, your obedient servant,

JAS. W. RIPLEY,
Brigadier General.

Mr. G. H. PENFIELD,
    Washington, D. C.

P. S.—It is understood that an additional quantity of ammunition for the batteries will be supplied hereafter, on requisitions from the governor of Illinois, when wanted.

J. W. R.

[Indorsements upon letter from chief of ordnance to G. H. Penfield dated October 11, 1862.—(See ante No. 1.)]

I understand a requisition has been made by Governor Yates, according to the memorandum at the bottom of this contract, and that the requisition is refused. Will the Secretary of War please tell me why is this ?

A. LINCOLN.

MARCH 26, 1862.

The Secretary of War has the honor to report that the above-mentioned requisition is not complied with—

1st. Because, if necessary for the army, the commanding general of the army is the proper person to make the requisition, in the regular manner, through the Ordnance department.

2d. It involves large expenditures of public money, when the treasury is in straitened circumstances, which can only be justified through requisitions in the proper official channels.

EDWIN M. STANTON,
Secretary of War.

APRIL 1, 1862.

STATE OF ILLINOIS,
Executive Department, Springfield, March 1, 1862.

SIR: The government, at my special request, a few months since contracted for fourteen batteries of the James rifled gun, six-pounder calibre, and a limited quantity of the James projectiles, weighing about fourteen pounds each.

The reports showing the superiority of this gun and projectile, both as regards range, accuracy, and execution for field service over that of all others at the battle of Fort Donelson, leads me to request that there be furnished to the State of Illinois in the shortest time practicable, seven batteries of 12-pounder calibre James rifled guns, with carriages, harness, implements, &c., &c., complete and ready for field service, together with the following fixed ammunition to each gun, viz: two hundred and twenty-five (225) shells; two hundred and twenty-five (225) canister, and fifty (50) solid projectiles, weighing about twenty-four pounds each; and also 200 shell, 200 canister, and 100 solid projectiles for each of the guns of the fourteen batteries named above, weighing about fourteen pounds each, all to be of the James model.

Very respectfully,

RICHARD YATES,
Governor of Illinois

Hon. EDWIN M. STANTON,
Secretary of War, Washington, D. C.

MARCH 8, 1862.

The within is from the governor of Illinois. I understand the seven additional batteries now sought are to be six-gun batteries; and the object is to mix them with the fourteen batteries they already have, so as to make each battery consist of four 6-pounders and two 12-pounders. I shall be very glad to have the requisition filled if it can be without detriment to the service.

A. LINCOLN.

The within application has been considered by the War Department, and cannot be complied with at present without detriment to the service.

EDWIN M. STANTON,
Secretary of War.

WASHINGTON, *October* 28, 1861.

SIR: The two batteries provided to be delivered during the month of October, in my contract with you of the 11th instant, are now ready for inspection at the manufactory of James T. Ames, esq., Chicopee, Massachusetts.

I have to request that you order them inspected as soon as possible, and that you will also direct how they are to be shipped, and have also to request that you direct the inspection of the balance of the batteries provided for in said contract to be inspected, agreeable to the terms of the contract.

I enclose a letter from Governor Yates, of Illinois, and have to ask that the modifications of the said contract of the 11th instant be made which is contemplated in said enclosed letter.

I have the honor to be, very respectfully, your obedient servant,

G. H. PENFIELD.

Brigadier General J. W. RIPLEY,
Ordnance Department.

CHICOPEE, *Massachusetts, March* 10, 1862.

G. H. Penfield to Emeseer Gaylord, DR.

To 196 sets of artillery harness, 6 to a set, $270	$52, 920
Boxing	686
	53, 606

CR.

October 15, 1861, by cash advanced	25, 000
	28, 606

CHICOPEE, *Massachusetts, May* 22, 1862.

DEAR SIR: In answer to your request of the 21st instant, I have to say that I have charged you for the harness $5 (five dollars) per set more than I am in the habit of charging for harness for similar use, and I do it because they have cost much more, as I was requested by Captain Balch to furnish better goods in this order than I had furnished in other government orders. I have not charged you as much extra as the real cost to me amounts to, as per statement on some of the items   I am sure I do not vary much from facts when I say that the harnesses are really worth ten dollars per set more than harness commonly furnished on government orders for the same purpose. Below I give you the extra cost on some of the parts:

Extra on 6 collars per set, each 50 cents	$3 00
Extra on 3 whips per set, each 40 cents	1 20
Extra on 6 halters per set, each 15 cents	90
Extra on 2 breechings per set, each 10 cents	20
	5 30

Very truly yours,

EMESEER GAYLORD.

G. H. PENFIELD, *Washington, D. C.*

177 BROADWAY, *(opposite Howard Hotel.)*

Mr. George H. Penfield, (guarantied by Mr. James T. Ames,) bought of Cooper & Pond, importers and manufacturers of guns, rifles, pistols, and gun materials:

84 gun-carriages, 6-pounders	$325 00	
Altering 84 poles and addition of 84 pole straps	15 00	
Leather buckets, instead of gutta-percha as agreed, difference on same, each	6 00	
Implements, as per agreement	64 50	
	410 50	$34, 440

Boxing, &c.		$83
84 caissons for above	$325 00	
Altering poles and pole straps	15 00	
Leather buckets, instead of gutta-percha as agreed	6 00	
Implements, as per agreement	60 50	
	406 50	34, 146
Boxing, &c.		190
14 battery wagons	375 00	
Altering poles and straps	15 00	
Leather buckets, &c.	6 00	
Implements furnished by us, not including the leather work	475 00	
Sets of boxes, &c., for inside of carriages	25 00	
	896 00	12, 544
Boxing, &c.		112
14 forges	375 00	
Altering poles and straps	15 00	
Buckets	6 00	
Implements, as per agreement	127 00	
	523 00	7, 322
Boxing		90
		88, 927

NEW YORK, *May* 22, 1862.

DEAR SIR : Enclosed we hand you bill of the gun-carriages, &c., as requested. We are sorry to see this matter so delayed. When we took the order to make carriages it was understood that we were to deliver two batteries per week, commencing November 7. We were ready, but you did not take them or commence taking them until January, which subjected us to considerable loss, as we were constantly paying out cash for the work and material. Had you given us longer time we could have made them for less money, but the short space of time obliged us to pay more for everything; parties knowing our wants took advantage of the circumstances. Again, the alteration of the poles and substituting of pole straps was contrary to what we had agreed upon—although it made them so much better—still we were not aware we should have to make an alteration until they were inspected, when we had to go to the expense of new iron work and pole straps, which made quite an item of difference. They were made exactly as Major Hagner had been having them made during the whole season. There were many other reasons and alterations made by us, which we have mentioned before, which we have made no memorandum of. In relation to implements would say, we have seen some implements, &c., made for the western country, and if we could have furnished such we could have named less prices; as, for instance, we saw some tarpaulins sent from here to Ohio which were not worth one-sixth of what ours were, ours being made of the best of cotton duck, when that was at its highest price, while they were made of the commonest stuff imaginable. We spared no pains to give you the very best of materials. Our expenses of transportation were very large, also travelling expenses, and our young man who gave it his whole attention for three or four months, and to whom we pay large wages, and we do not think this to be unreasonable.

This bill does not include leather work which you got some other party to make.

Respectfully,

COOPER & POND.

Mr. G. H. PENFIELD, *Washington,*

WASHINGTON, *March* 27, 1862.

DEAR SIR : I have examined your amount of the fourteen batteries, and the prices are the same as we have charged the government and several of the States who have purchased similar articles.

Respectfully, yours,

JAMES T. AMES,
Chicopee, Massachusetts.

GEORGE H. PENFIELD, Esq.

WASHINGTON, D. C., *October* 10, 1861.

Whereas the undersigned have, with the consent of Governor Yates, agreed to furnish to the general government, for the use of the troops of the State of Illinois, fourteen batteries of James's rifled cannon, with projectiles and equipments, as per specifications to-day agreed upon between the undersigned and the United States Ordnance department, the undersigned agree to submit to fair test, (under such inspection as the governor of Illinois may prescribe,) at Springfield, the first two cannon, to be delivered at Springfield during the present month, and that the government of the United States shall not be bound to receive or pay for any of said cannon or equipments unless the same shall, upon said test, prove satisfactory.

G. H. PENFIELD.

STATE OF ILLINOIS,
Executive Department, Springfield, June 7, 1862.

DEAR SIR : My recollection of the facts relative to your contract with General Ripley to deliver to me fourteen batteries of James's rifled cannon is as follows :

You presented your proposition to General Ripley and he, after reading, said he would have the contract ready by 12 or 1 o'clock of that day. I then left the city, with the understanding that General Ripley had accepted your proposition, and that he would make the contract in conformity with that proposition. If I remember the proposition correctly, I was to be furnished by the government 500 rounds to each gun.

The guns have done splendid execution on our various battle-fields, and I do not understand why there should be unwillingness to carry out the contract.

Respectfully, yours,

RICHARD YATES.

G. H. PENFIELD.

CASE No. 103.

CAPTAIN T. J. RODMAN AND CHARLES KNAPP.

WAR DEPARTMENT,
Washington City, D. C., April 2, 1862.

GENERAL : Application has been made to this department to repay, or make allowance, for patent fees on cannon manufactured under orders issued by you upon a plan patented to Captain Thomas J. Rodman, and as the Secretary of

War has no knowledge of any such orders he directs me to ask you to report to him:

1. Whether contracts or orders have been given by you for the manufacture of cast-iron cannon upon a plan or plans patented to any person or persons; and if so, to whom?

2. Whether any, and if any, what, sums have been paid, directly or indirectly, by the government for patent fees on such cannon, and on account of what patent or patents have such sums been paid?

3. What price per pound has been paid for such cannon made under patented plans, and what price per pound for cannon of the same calibre made upon unpatented?

4. Whether any instruction or direction has been given by any officer connected with the Ordnance bureau to any contractor or applicant for a contract, as to the price on the pound weight of the cannon made by him, that he would be expected to pay as patent fees?

Very respectfully, your obedient servant,

P. H. WATSON,
Assistant Secretary of War.

Brigadier General J. W. RIPLEY,
Chief of Ordnance.

ORDNANCE OFFICE, *April* 14, 1862.

SIR: In compliance with your instructions of the 2d instant, I have the honor to report, that orders have been given for the manufacture of cast-iron cannon upon the plan patented by Thomas J. Rodman. The first order for the manufacture of such cannon, on which a payment of patent fees was allowed, was given by the Secretary of War on the 16th of November, 1859. A copy of the order and of the letter on which it was indorsed is herewith communicated.—(No. 1.)

A copy of this order was immediately transmitted by this department to all the founders then engaged in manufacturing cannon for the United States, who were at the same time required to conform to it in all cannon to be thereafter cast.

Messrs. Knapp, Rudd & Co. cast at Fort Pitt foundery, in 1860, thirty-nine eight-inch columbiads in conformity with the order. The manufacturers were paid the usual price of 6½ cents per pound, established many years before for cannon of that calibre. And in conformity with the order the United States paid to Charles Knapp, the proprietor of the patent, $3,037 68, being 20 per cent. on the cost of 26 of those cannon. No other founders cast any cannon on the Rodman plan, and no other payment on account of patent fees has been made.

The account for the patent fee on the remaining 13 of the guns cast by Knapp, Rudd & Co. was disallowed, because of the revocation of the order of November 15, 1859, by another order, of which the following is a copy:

"WAR DEPARTMENT, *January* 21, 1861.

"The order of the 16th November, 1859, being regarded as incompatible with the third section of the act of June 23, 1860, is revoked.

"J. HOLT,
"*Secretary of War, ad interim.*"

The third section of the act referred to in this last order was repealed February 21, 1861.

Knapp, Rudd & Co. were, on the 21st of February, 1861, notified by this department of the revocation of the order of November 16, 1859, and were informed that in future no payments on account of patent fees would be made by the United States. Mr. Knapp protested against this revocation, in a letter dated March 5, a copy of which is enclosed.—(No. 2.) The attention of the department was again called to the subject in a letter from Major A. B. Dyer, who has for several years past been extensively engaged in experimental firing and proof of cannon, in which he urges the importance of *requiring that all heavy guns* hereafter made for the government shall be cast on a core, and cooled from the inside.

The subject was referred to a board of officers, who were required to fix a suitable price for such cannon. Copies of Major Dyer's letter, and of the report of the board of officers, dated December 19, 1861, are herewith submitted.— (Nos. 3 and 4.)

In accordance with these recommendations, orders were given to the founders to cast the heavy cannon in the manner recommended. Copies of these orders, dated December 22, are herewith submitted.—(No. 5.) The price fixed in these orders is $7\frac{8}{10}$ cents per pound, being an advance of 20 per cent. on $6\frac{1}{2}$ cents, the price usually paid for guns cast solid. This price is paid by the United States to the manufacturer, the latter compensating the proprietor of the patent for the privilege of using it. The sum required by the latter for this privilege is one cent per pound, as will be seen by his letter of December 23, 1861, a copy of which is herewith submitted.—(No. 6.) Copies of the same were communicated to the several founders who had received orders for cannon. Since that date, Knapp, Rudd & Co. have manufactured and delivered forty-four thirteen-inch mortars, and four ten-inch columbiads cast on the Rodman plan, for which they have been allowed $7\frac{8}{10}$ cents per pound. Parties applying for orders for the manufacture of cannon are informed of the price allowed, and of the sum required as patent fees by the proprietor of the patent, as above stated.

There appears to be no doubt that the endurance and safety of heavy cannon which are cast on a core and cooled from the interior are much greater than those cast solid. A condensed statement of the relative merits of all the guns cast for the purpose of trial by both methods is given on page 133 of the published reports of Captain Rodman, and more extended comparisons are given on pages 134, 135, 277, and 278, of the same volume.

The opinions of General Totten, and of several other experienced officers of the army, are given in letters accompanying the letters of Charles Knapp, dated May 17, 1861, which are herewith submitted.—(No. 7.)

I submit also a copy of a letter just received from Captain Rodman, dated 11th instant, which gives a brief history of proceedings in relation to his plan of casting cannon on a core, and cooling from the interior.—(No. 8.)

Respectfully, I am, sir, your obedient servant,

JAMES W. RIPLEY,
Brigadier General.

Hon. EDWIN M. STANTON,
Secretary of War.

MAY 13, 1862.

Referred to honorable J. Holt and honorable Robert Dale Owen, special commissioners on ordnance contracts, &c. By order of the Secretary of War.

P. H. WATSON,
Assistant Secretary of War.

WASHINGTON, D. C., *November 14, 1859*

SIR: In reply to your inquiry what would be a fair equivalent for the right to cast heavy ordnance in the manner proposed by Captain Rodman, I have to say that, judging from the relative endurance of the six different pairs of guns which have been fired to extremity to test the value of this mode of casting guns, I am of the opinion that for guns of large calibre an advance of 20 per cent. on the cost of the gun would not be more than a fair percentage for the use of the patent right.

In every case in which guns cast in this way have been compared with those made of the same metal, but cast in the ordinary manner, the hollow cast gun has endured at least three times as many discharges as the solid cast gun, and in some cases very many more; thus proving that, in these six instances, the hollow guns were worth more than 300 per cent. more than the solid cast guns, and I know of nothing to make the trials thus far made exceptional cases.

Very respectfully, I am, sir, your obedient servant,

T. T. S. LAIDLEY,
Brevet Major, Captain of Ordnance.

Hon. John B. Floyd, *Secretary of War.*

[Copy of indorsement on above letter.]

War Department, *November* 16, 1859.

The Ordnance bureau will make arrangements with all the founders who are to make heavy ordnance for it, to have all such cannon cast hollow, after the plan called "Rodman's plan." The free use of the right to cast cannon for the land service after this plan will be secured by the Ordnance bureau to each founder, by the payment for such use of twenty per cent. on the cost of each from the appropriation for the armament of fortifications, to Mr. Charles Knapp, the proprietor of the patent. The price for the finished cannon at the founderies will remain the same as now paid.

J. B. FLOYD, *Secretary of War.*

Washington City, *March* 5, 1861.

Colonel: I have received a copy of your letter to Knapp, Rudd & Co., dated February 21, in which you state that the order of the Secretary of War dated November 16, 1859, requiring all heavy ordnance to be cast hollow, has been revoked.

I respectfully state, in reply, that I have instructed the Fort Pitt foundery to continue to cast columbiads on the Rodman plan, and I hereby enter my protest against the revocation of the order of November 16, 1859, for the reason that said order vested in me certain valuable rights of which I may not legally or justly be summarily divested. I claim that said order, duly accepted and partially fulfilled on my part, and confirmed by the department by several payments thereon, is in fact and in law a contract which cannot be cancelled without the consent of both parties.

As a citizen, possessed of information which warrants it, I protest against the revocation of said order, for the reason that it is due to our country and its defenders that the best and most durable guns should be procured, and the records of your office afford incontrovertible evidence that guns cast from the same iron, on the Rodman plan, are greatly superior to those cast in the usual manner.

The law of June, 1860, under which I suppose you revoked the order of November, 1859, having been repealed on the ———, 1861, leaves it quite competent for you to now revive the order of 1859, which you are respectfully requested to do.

With great respect, your obedient servant,

CHARLES KNAPP.

Colonel H. K. Craig, *Chief of Ordnance.*

WASHINGTON, D. C., *December* 19, 1861.

SIR: The importance of improving the quality of our heavy guns has for several years engaged my particular attention, and the interest I take in the subject induces me to address this communication to you.

That the columbiads now on hand cannot be relied on for service has been established beyond question by the bursting of a large number of them in experimental and other firing. To correct this evil several modifications have been made within the last two or three years in the mode of casting and in the models of those guns, and as experiment has shown, with marked improvement in the quality of the guns. Indeed, the proper model and method of casting have been so well demonstrated, that they may now be safely established by regulation, and no time can be so favorable for it as the present. We have no columbiads of the established models on hand, and but few of the various models authorized within the last two or three years have been made. Our system may therefore be regarded as about to be commenced. The professional interest which I feel in securing for the department *the very best guns* which can be made impels me to urge upon you the importance of *requiring* that *all heavy guns* hereafter made for the department shall be cast on a core and cooled from the inside. Theory indicates this mode of casting as superior to that heretofore followed, and it is fully sustained by numerous trials made in this country and in England.

Seven pairs of guns have been made in this country and proved to extremity by firing, and in *every* instance the hollow cast gun has exhibited the greatest endurance, the ratio being quite as much as three to one in its favor.

I have recently been informed by Colonel Wilmot, of the royal artillery, that two pairs of 13-inch mortars (one hollow and the other solid cast) were made in England and tested by firing with equal charges under like circumstances. Neither solid cast mortars endured as much as (800) eight hundred fires. Both of those cast hollow endured (2,000) two thousand rounds without bursting. With this accumulation of evidence of the superiority of the hollow method of casting heavy guns before us, we ought not to hesitate to require all heavy guns made for the department to be cast hollow and cooled from the inside.

Very respectfully, your obedient servant,

A. B. DYER,
Captain of Ordnance, Brevet Major U. S. Army.

Brigadier General J. W. RIPLEY,
Chief of Ordnance, Washington.

ORDNANCE OFFICE,
Washington, December 19, 1861.

SIR: The officers to whom you referred the subject of fixing a suitable price for 8 and 10-inch columbiads, after due consideration have the honor to make the following report, viz:

1st. They consider it important that all pieces of these calibres should be cooled from the interior in casting.

2d. In view of the fact that the Navy Department pays 7.73 and 8.23 cents per pound for its 9 and 11-inch guns, respectively, the undersigned consider that 7.8 cents per pound is fair and reasonable for 8 and 10-inch columbiads cast hollow, more especially as they consider the latter named cannon more durable than the former.

The undersigned are prepared to extend the foregoing recommendation to all cast-iron cannon made by direction of the Ordnance department.

Respectfully, your obedient servants,

A. B. DYER,
Captain of Ordnance and Brevet Major U. S. Army.
T. J. RODMAN,
Captain of Ordnance.
J. G. BENTON,
Captain of Ordnance.

General J. W. RIPLEY,
Chief of Ordnance, Washington City, D. C.

ORDNANCE OFFICE.
Washington, December 22, 1861.

SIR : I am directed by the Secretary of War to submit to you the following proposition, viz:

That you furnish to the United States government all the eight and ten-inch columbiads that you can make at your establishment in the next twelve months; these pieces to be cast hollow and cooled from the interior. The price allowed to be 7.8 cents per pound; to be paid after the pieces have passed the proof and inspection by an officer of the Ordnance department. The proportion of the two calibres will be determined as soon as practicable.

The department reserves to itself the right to change the mode of casting and cooling, and to modify the price correspondingly, should it be deemed necessary to do so at any time.

Please signify your acceptance or non-acceptance of the foregoing proposition.

Respectfully,

JAMES W. RIPLEY,
Brigadier General.

Captain R. P. PARROTT,
West Point Foundery, Cold Spring, New York.

A similar letter was on the same day addressed to Cyrus Alger & Co., Boston, Massachusetts, and Mr. Charles Knapp, Washington, D. C.

WASHINGTON CITY, *December 23, 1861.*

GENERAL : You are hereby authorized to inform Messrs. Parrott & Alger that my charge to them for the use of the Rodman patent, for cooling guns, will be one cent per pound of the finished weight of all guns received for service by the United States.

Very respectfully, your obedient servant,

CHARLES KNAPP.

General J. W. RIPLEY, *Chief of Ordnance.*

WASHINGTON CITY, *May 17, 1861.*

COLONEL: I ask your attention to my letter to Colonel Craig, under date of March 5, 1861, protesting against his revocation of the order of the Secretary of War, dated November 14, 1859.

The superiority of guns cast on the "Rodman plan" is already established by the records of your office. I however have the honor to add to these by transmitting herewith commendatory letters from General Totten, Major Barnard, and Captain Wright, of the engineers; also from Majors Symington, Maynadier and Laidley, Captain McNutt and Lieutenants Crispin and Baylor, all of whom have, in performance of official duty, had occasion to form an opinion, and whose views, as to the superiority of the plan, are singularly harmonious.

The superiority of these guns being established, it would seem to be a duty to procure them, and only them. It may, however, be thought that increased cost of these guns is an element to be considered; that inferior guns at low prices are as judicious a purchase as superior guns at higher prices. On this subject I state that the cost of eight and ten-inch columbiads per pound, including the royalty paid to me under the order referred to, is less than that of Dahlgren's nine and eleven-inch navy guns, cast in the usual way.

I ask that Colonel Craig's letter of February 21, 1861, revoking the order of the Secretary of War, dated November 16, 1859, be recalled.

With great respect, your servant,

CHARLES KNAPP.

Lieutenant Colonel J. W. RIPLEY, *Chief of Ordnance.*

WASHINGTON, *April* 12, 1861.

DEAR SIR: I have time to reply only briefly to your inquiry as to my opinion of the value of "the Rodman plan of casting heavy ordnance."

From the experiments that I witnessed with the fifteen-inch gun, the examination of its condition after long continued firing, similar examinations of a ten-inch gun that had been fired some thousand times, and from the explanation of the process given by Captain Rodman, I incline to think very favorably of it.

Very respectfully, your obedient servant,

JOS. G. TOTTEN.

CHARLES KNAPP, Esq.

NEW YORK, *April* 15, 1861.

MY DEAR SIR: I give my most unqualified approbation of the principle of hollow casting for heavy ordnance, invented by Captain Rodman. I believe it to be founded on sound scientific principles, and, moreover, I believe it the *only proper* way to cast large guns.

The results of experience, so far as they have come under my observation, confirm the superiority which theoretical considerations attribute to the hollow casting principle.

I should be much interested in seeing a 20-inch gun, and believe that in going up to that calibre we should secure all that we desire for sea and defence.

I am yours, respectfully,

JAMES BARNARD, *Major of Engineers.*

Mr. KNAPP.

WASHINGTON ARSENAL, *April* 2, 1861.

SIR: In reply to your letter of March 29, requesting the expression of my opinion in regard to the value of the "Rodman method of casting and cooling heavy ordnance," I have respectfully to state, without touching upon the theory of the method, which is fully and clearly set forth in Captain Rodman's report on the subject, including the results of his preliminary experiments and tests, that I witnessed the process of the casting of heavy guns by this method, and examined some of them after they had been subjected to a series of firing with heavy charges, and in two instances, where comparative trials had been made with guns of similar pattern, cast hollow and solid, in all of which one very important result was determined, that is, the very slight enlargement of the bore of the hollow cast guns compared with those of the solid cast, a result due to the greater hardness and density which the hollow casting and cooling gives to the metal around the surface of the bore.

With regard to the endurance of guns cast hollow and solid at the Fort Pitt foundery in Pittsburg, the reports of comparative trials, made at different times, exhibit results greatly in favor of the hollow cast. From these facts, then, I am clearly of opinion that the Rodman method of casting and cooling heavy ordnance is more certain of giving a good enduring gun than the method of casting them solid.

I am, very respectfully,

JOHN SYMINGTON, *Major of Ordnance.*

CHARLES KNAPP, Esq.

FRANKFORD ARSENAL, *April* 8, 1861.

SIR: In compliance with your request that I would give you my opinion in regard to the mode of casting iron cannon of which you are the patentee, known as the Rodman plan, I have to state:

The theory of Captain Rodman so plainly demonstrated the advantages of that plan as to leave little or no doubt about the results that would attend its practical trials. These trials, in repeated instances, particularly in those last made, have proved the superior wear and greater endurance of the hollow cast guns so fully and decidedly as to leave no doubt in my mind of the great advantages to be derived from adopting that mode of casting; advantages which, in my opinion, far outweigh the original cost.

I am, very respectfully, your obedient servant,

WILLIAM MAYNADIER,
Captain of Ordnance.

CHARLES KNAPP, Esq., *Washington.*

WASHINGTON, *April* 12, 1861.

DEAR SIR: Your note of the 10th instant, asking my opinion as to the value of the Rodman plan of casting heavy ordnance, is received.

I gave considerable attention to this mode of casting ordnance many years ago, when it was first suggested by Captain Rodman; I satisfied myself that it was based upon sound and scientific principles.

Subsequent consideration of the subject, and the careful examination I had the opportunity of making, as a member of the board which was convened at Fort Monroe to witness and report upon the firing of the 15-inch gun cast upon this plan, confirmed the conclusion to which I had at first arrived of the great superiority of this mode over the method of solid casting.

I should not hesitate therefore to recommend this method, in all cases of heavy calibres particularly, nor do I see any reason to doubt its successful application to a greater calibre even than the 15-inch, should such ordnance be considered desirable.

Very respectfully, your obedient servant,

H. G. WRIGHT.

CHARLES KNAPP, Esq., *Washington, D. C.*

FORT MONROE ARSENAL,
Virginia, April 17, 1861.

MY DEAR SIR: My opinion of the great superiority of hollow cast guns over those cast solid is already to be found on record in the War Department, given in answer to a call from the Secretary of War, but I have no objection to repeating it, and the grounds on which that opinion is based. The theory of what takes place in the two modes of casting seemed to me to be perfectly reasonable, and as convincing as any mere theory could be.

When to this theory was added the proof of actual experiments, repeated some five times, in every case the hollow gun showing its superiority, and under circumstances not calculated to develop the advantages of the hollow casting to the greatest degree, all place for cavil or doubt as to which mode made the best guns was at an end, and the superiority of the hollow gun established with a degree of certainty that it would seem to me no unbiased mind could resist.

I would state that I was charged with the firing of one pair of 10-inch columbiads, cast, one solid, the other hollow, and observed the progressive changes in the two with great care and attention.

The superiority of the hollow gun was very apparent, though neither was broken.

Very respectfully and truly yours,

T. T. S. LAIDLEY,
Brevet Major, Captain of Ordnance.

CHARLES KNAPP, *Washington, D. C.*

ALLEGHENY ARSENAL, *April* 3, 1861.

DEAR SIR : Your letter of the 29th ultimo, requesting my opinion of the merits of Captain Rodman's method of casting cannon, has been received, and, in reply, I beg leave to state that it is my opinion that his method has decided advantages over any other that has heretofore been pursued.

The method heretofore followed of casting heavy cannon solid has been found defective to a degree such that guns thus cast have, in many instances, burst after a few rounds. This is owing undoubtedly to the fact of the cooling of the metal taking place from the exterior, causing contractions from the centre, and thus weakening the gun where strength is most needed to resist the effects of the explosion of the charge of powder.

In case of casting hollow and cooling from the centre the contractions are towards the centre, and the metal as it cools becomes more and more solidified and strengthened, and the result ought to be a more enduring gun than when the cooling takes place from the exterior. The trials so far show that this is the case, and leave no doubt in my mind as to the superiority of the method of casting hollow over that of casting solid.

As to the economy of the two methods, I do not consider that it should be taken into the account, as the one that will give the most enduring guns should always be preferred.

Very respectfully, your obedient servant,

J. McNUTT, *Captain of Ordnance.*

CHARLES KNAPP, Esq.

ALLEGHENY ARSENAL, *April* 4, 1861.

DEAR SIR : In reply to your request for an expression of my views relative to the merits of the plan of casting cannon on hollow cores and cooling from the interior, as originated and applied by Captain Rodman, of the ordnance corps, I have to state that, in my judgment, this mode of fabrication will enable us to produce guns of a decidedly superior quality, in point of strength and endurance, to those cast solid. I am led to this conclusion not only by a belief in the soundness of the principles upon which the plan is based, but also by the important fact that in the comparative trials which have been made of the two methods of casting—some of which have come under my immediate personal observation—the superiority of the hollow mode has been established. In the casting of large masses of iron solid, which are necessarily cooled from the exterior, there is no doubt, from our knowledge of the manner in which solidification takes place under these circumstances, but that the result is the production at the centre of the mass of iron comparatively to that on the exterior, more or less soft, porous, and otherwise defective, and that the resulting strains of compression at the exterior and tension at the interior, induced by this mode of cooling, directly favor the action of powder in its tendency to burst our guns. It is, therefore, apparent, besides the defects of injurious strains, that the softer and weaker iron of the casting will be found surrounding and constituting the bores of our solid cast guns, the very position where, for endurance, the stronger and more elastic metal should only, if possible, have place.

These inherent defects of solid cast guns, which evidently must tend to diminish their endurance, is, I believe, in a great measure remedied by the hollow mode, the interior and more rapid cooling utilizing the strains developed in solidification, rendering them antagonistic to the bursting effort of the charge. and securing the denser and more superior metal at the interior, where it is evidently needed.

The trials which have been made, comparing the two methods, exhibiting a greater endurance on the part of the hollow cast guns, in many instances marked, offered ample proof that this is the case. In no instance, I conceive, was this superiority more strikingly displayed than in the last pair of trial guns experimented with at Pittsburg, and subsequently at Fortress Monroe; for although they have both equally endured several thousand rounds without breaking, yet an examination of the bores shows the solid one to be worn to such an extent as to be rendered, in my opinion, unfit for service, whilst the hollow one remains comparatively uninjured. With this mode of casting, and with the application of the mechanical tests which experiments and a better appreciation of the requisites of good gun metal, here shown to be important in determining the qualities of iron, I believe we shall not only improve the strength of our ordnance but also arrive at some degree of *uniformity* as regards the ultimate endurance of cannon, a desideratum of the highest importance, and which, it cannot be said, we have heretofore attained. No experimental research or effort should be spared to attain this important end—a really reliable gun evidently being worth any cost which its efficient manufacture may demand.

Yours, truly,

S. CRISPIN, *Lieutenant of Ordnance.*

CHARLES KNAPP, Esq.,
  Washington, D. C.

FORT MONROE ARSENAL, *April* 3, 1861.

DEAR SIR: Your letter of March 30, requesting my opinion of the value of Captain Rodman's method of casting and cooling guns, was duly received. In reply, I would state that I not only think but know that it produces a gun in every way superior to the common method of casting guns solid and cooling them from the exterior. I have seen the two methods fairly and thoroughly tested together and under the same circumstances, and there can be but one opinion as to which is the best method from those experiments. One important fact I will state resulting from trials I have seen and made with the guns from the two methods, and which will show plainly the superior value of the hollow cast gun. A gun of a large calibre, (and it may be true with small calibres,) solid cast, becomes unserviceable from the action of the gas on the bore eating it into deep furrows and grooves over the seat of the shot in about 1,000 or 1,200 rounds, whereas a gun of the same calibre, hollow cast, (Captain Rodman's method,) will be serviceable after a considerably greater number of rounds. I could state some more facts in regard to the two methods, but as you merely ask for my opinion, I think I have said enough to show my opinion of the value of Captain Rodman's method of casting and cooling guns.

Yours, truly,

T. G. BAYLOR, *Lieutenant of Ordnance.*

Mr. CHARLES KNAPP.

WATERTOWN ARSENAL, *April* 11, 1862.

SIR : In reply to your letter of the 2d instant, calling for a concise history of all the circumstances attending the change in the mode of casting iron cannon, from the solid to the hollow, with interior cooling, &c., I have to state as follows :

My attention was first directed to the improvement of the quality of iron ordnance by the history of the large gun on board the steamer Princeton, in 1844. My investigations soon satisfied me that a gun, free from all strain at the moment of ignition of a bursting charge within it, would begin to break at the surface of the bore, and, consequently, that in order to avail ourselves of the entire strength of all the material in a gun, the metal should be thrown upon a strain, the exterior portions being under a strain of extension, and the interior under one of compression.

My first proposition for accomplishing this object was to make a cast-iron core, of which to form the bore of the gun, that should have sufficient thickness to give it the requisite longitudinal strength, and then wind it with consecutive layers of iron wire, of proper form, in cross section, and tightly drawn on with a constant tension.

This plan was referred to (then) Major R. L. Baker, of the Ordnance department, who did not encourage the project.

I was about this time, (1845, I think,) at my own request, placed on foundery duty, to superintend the casting of 8-inch columbiads, at the Fort Pitt foundery, in addition to my duties as second in command at the Allegheny arsenal.

Observation on the contractions of iron in passing from the fluid to the cold, solid state, made on guns, car wheels, and other castings, soon satisfied me that the solid cast gun, which is necessarily cooled from the exterior, was left upon a strain just the reverse of what my previous investigations satisfied me ought to exist. It then occurred to me that if cooling from the exterior left the gun upon a strain the reverse of what it should be, cooling from the interior would leave it in just the condition required to develop its greatest strength.

Reflection soon satisfied me of the practicability of cooling guns from the interior.

About this time being ordered on temporary duty at Richmond, Virginia, I stopped on my way at the Ordnance office and conveised with the acting chief of ordnance, Lieutenant Colonel G. Talcott, on this subject, urging him to authorize experiments to test the practicability of casting guns hollow and cooling them from the interior.

In this conversation I stated my full conviction both of the practicability of cooling guns in this way and of the superiority in quality of the guns so cooled over those cast and cooled in the ordinary way.

Colonel Talcott expressed himself as being in doubt as to the practicability and the utility of the proposed method, giving it as his opinion that if I should succeed in casting a gun in this way it would have a hard cylinder around the bore, and another around the exterior, with an open or spongy space between. He further stated that the want of funds precluded the possibility of making the experiments at that time. Nothing was said of patenting the process, for I had no idea at that time of doing so. No further action was had in the matter till in, I think, 1846, when being again ordered, on temporary duty, to Richmond, Virginia, I stopped, en route, at the Ordnance office, where I met Colonel Bomford, who was then preparing to cast his 12-inch gun.

The subject of hollow casting was again discussed, by Colonel Bomford, Colonel Talcott, and myself, and I again urged the trial of the hollow mode of casting, which now, as I thought, appeared to be viewed with more favor, especially by Colonel Bomford, who encouraged me in the hope that he would cast his 12-inch gun in that way. Still, nothing was said about patenting the process, for I did not yet think of doing so, if I could get government to make the trial. I returned to my station, and not long after learned that Colonel Bomford had cast his 12-inch gun solid.

I felt disappointed, and was then urged by my friends to patent the process, and Messrs. Knapp & Totten, then proprietors of the Fort Pitt foundery, offered to incur all expenses necessary to test the practicability of casting and cooling guns in that way, provided I would patent the process and assign to them one-half interest in said patent. But being still uncertain what might be the views of the department on the subject, no steps were taken till after I had had another interview with Colonel Talcott.

In this interview I asked him if there were any likelihood that the department would authorize the experiments which I had requested, to which he replied that he did not think there was. I then asked him if there would be any impropriety in my patenting the process, and getting it tested by private parties, and whether or not he would have any objection to my doing so, to which he replied, certainly not, and appeared entirely satisfied to dispose of the subject in that way. On my return to Pittsburg, after this interview, I accepted the offer of Messrs. Knapp & Totten, and took steps for obtaining the patent, which was issued in August, 1847, and the first gun was cast hollow and cooled from the interior in that year, the cooling being effected by circulating air through the core barrel; and all the expenses being borne by Messrs. Knapp & Totten. Other guns were made in this way, except that water was used for cooling, and several were lost before the method was fully perfected, the loss being sustained wholly by Messrs. Knapp & Totten.

Having fully established the practicability of casting and cooling guns in that way, the Ordnance department was asked to adopt it, and Colonel Talcott went with me to Mr. Marcy, then Secretary of War, to whom I exhibited the patent and explained the principles involved and the benefit in increased endurance and greater safety of guns, especially those of large calibre, expected to result from this mode of casting and cooling, and my recollection is that Colonel Talcott recommended to Mr. Marcy the trial of a pair of "8-inch guns," with the view of adopting this mode if the result of the trial should establish the superiority of the guns cast in that way. I *know*, however, that I left the War office and the Ordnance office with the full understanding that a trial would be made to test the relative endurance of guns made of the same iron; one cast solid and cooled in the ordinary way, and the other cast and cooled on the new mode. Before any trial was made, however, I was ordered to Camargo, Mexico, from which place my first written communication to the Ordnance department on this subject was sent in June, 1848.

This communication is on file in the Ordnance office. In January, 1849, I went to Washington specially on this business, being authorized by Messrs. Knapp & Totten to make the proposal for them to furnish the trial guns at their actual cost, and my recollection is that I fixed the price to be paid for them at four and one-half cents per pound. Before I left the city Mr. Totten arrived and went with me to the Ordnance department, where the subject of making the trial guns was again alluded to, and Mr. Totten remarked that the price I had named would not pay the actual expenses of making the guns, but that he would adhere to it, remarking, at the same time, that he supposed there would be objection to his gathering up the pieces of the broken guns. Colonel Talcott no said no, that he might have all the pieces he could find after the guns were broken.

On these terms the first pair of trial guns (8-inch columbiads) was cast and proved in 1849. And although the hollow cast gun endured about three times as many rounds as the solid, the result was not deemed satisfactory by the government, for the reason that neither gun endured as much as it was thought a good gun should; the solid gun having burst at the 85th fire, and the hollow one at the 251st.

Another pair of 8-inch and a pair of 10-inch were now ordered to be made, of a different variety of iron, and tested. These guns were made and tested in 1851; the solid 8-inch gun burst at the 73d fire, while the hollow one endured without bursting 1,500 rounds. The solid 10-inch gun burst at the 20th fire, and the hollow one at the 249th. These results were not regarded by the department as satisfactory, the endurance of the 8-inch hollow gun being regarded as accidentally great, and that of the 10-inch as not great enough.

The department then ordered a pair of 32-pounders to be tested, which was done in 1852. The result was, that the guns endured 1,000 service rounds each; the solid one burst at the sixth fire of the first increase, while the hollow one endured twenty rounds of this increase, and burst at the first fire of the second increase, the charge being sixteen pounds powder and two shot.

The department was not yet satisfied either to adopt or wholly reject the new mode, and in 1856 another pair of 10-inch guns were ordered, made, and tested, the result being that the solid gun burst at the 26th fire, and the hollow one at the 315th.

The department could not yet decide to adopt or reject the new mode, while it was now, as it had been previously, urged by Mr. Knapp and myself that the experiments were conclusive as to the superiority of the new mode. It was also about this time suggested that the treatment of the iron of which the trial guns were made might have been such as to impair its quality, and that reliable guns were being made of some variety of iron at the West Point foundery; therefore, in compliance with instructions of Colonel Craig, then chief of ordnance, dated February 10, 1857, a board of officers, composed of Colonel B. Huger, Captain A. B. Dyer, and myself, submitted, on the 16th of same month, a programme of experiments, for the purpose, among other things, of testing the relative endurance of guns made of the same variety of iron, but melted in furnaces of different construction, and to further test the relative endurance of solid and hollow cast guns. In accordance with this programme, iron enough for six ten-inch guns was selected at the West Point foundery, and in August, 1857, a set of triplicate guns were cast from it—a solid gun at the West Point foundery, and a solid and a hollow gun at the Fort Pitt foundery. The result of the trial of these guns was, that the West Point gun burst at the 169th fire; the Fort Pitt solid gun at the 399th fire; the hollow gun having endured without rupture 1,600 rounds.

My recollection is, that it was after the trial of these guns that Mr. Knapp proposed to me to buy out my interest in the patent, and I accordingly sold it to him.

It was intended to duplicate the trial last referred to, but when, the following year, it was about to be repeated, it was ascertained that a portion of the selected iron left at the West Point foundery had been used, and consequently that a duplicate set of triplicate guns could not be made. It was ordered, however, to cast and prove another pair of ten-inch guns from the remainder of the selected iron that had been sent to the Fort Pitt foundery. This pair of guns had an increased thickness of metal in the breech, and the bores were terminated by hemispheres. They have been fired 4,082 service and two proof charges each, and neither gun burst, the solid gun being greatly more deteriorated than the hollow one. This includes all the trials that have been made for testing the relative endurance of solid and hollow cast guns. The expenses of these trials have been borne mainly by the United States. The price paid for trial guns not having, as I have been told by Mr. Knapp, been equal to their actual cost. The expenses and the risk incurred in establishing the practicability of casting and cooling guns on the new mode were borne exclusively by Messrs. Knapp & Totten.

In selling my interest in the patent to Mr. Knapp, I obligated myself to procure an extension of said patent, if practicable. This I did, and an extension of seven years was issued in August last.

I am, very respectfully, sir, your obedient servant,

T. J. RODMAN,
Captain of Ordnance.

General J. W. RIPLEY,
Ordnance Office, Washington, D. C.

COMMISSION ON ORDNANCE AND ORDNANCE STORES,
Washington, May 23, 1862.

CAPTAIN: In the course of the investigation now making by this commission, under the authority of the Secretary of War, in reference to "charges made and sums paid for patent fees," it is found necessary to inquire of you as to the terms of sale of your patent right to Mr. Knapp, or to the company of which he is a partner. The commission, therefore, request that you will furnish to them copies of such terms of sale as may have been agreed upon between you and the company, or between you and Mr. Knapp.

Should you prefer, and your duties at Watertown permit, the commission authorize me to say that they would be glad to have you appear before them, and will sanction your journey, should you be able to do so.

Very respectfully, your obedient servant,

P. V. HAGNER,
Major of Ordnance.

Captain T. J. RODMAN,
U. S. Ordnance Department, Watertown Arsenal.

WATERTOWN ARSENAL, *May 30, 1862.*

MAJOR: Yours of the 23d instant, conveying the request of the commission on ordnance and ordnance stores that I would send them a copy of the terms of sale of patent from me to Mr. Knapp, or appear in person before them, has been received. I had hoped to be able to appear before them, but finding that my duties here will not admit of my doing so at this time, I have the honor to enclose herewith a copy of the terms of sale agreed upon between Mr. Knapp and myself, as requested.

I am, very respectfully, your obedient servant,

T. J. RODMAN,
Captain of Ordnance.

Major P. V. HAGNER.

Terms of sale.

This agreement, made and entered into by and between Thomas J. Rodman, of the United States army, and Charles Knapp, of the city of Pittsburg, Pennsylvania, witnesseth:

That whereas the said Rodman has by an instrument in writing, bearing even date herewith, assigned and transferred to the said Knapp, his administrators, executors, and assigns, all his remaining interest in certain letters patent under the seal of the Patent Office of the United States, bearing date the 14th day of August, A. D. 1847, for a new and useful improvement in casting ordnance, &c., whereby the entire interest in said letters patent becomes vested in said Knapp:

Now, the said Knapp, for and in consideration of the transfer above cited, does hereby covenant and agree for himself, his heirs, executors, and assigns, to pay to the said Rodman, his heirs, executors, administrators, or assigns, the full sum of one-half of one cent per pound of the finished weight of all cannon and other castings, on which the said Knapp may receive a royalty for the use of said patent, payable from time to time as he, the said Knapp, may collect said royalty. And the said Knapp hereby binds himself, his heirs, executors, administrators, and assigns, to reserve and require payment of royalty in all cases of sale, transfer, assignment, (except in the case of the sale to the United States hereinafter referred to,) of any interest in or right to use said patent, and to use all due diligence in the collection of said royalty whenever it becomes due and payable, and to treat the portion belonging to said Rodman strictly as a "trust fund," to be paid over without any delay.

And it is hereby further agreed by said Knapp, that, in the event of his selling the said patent to the United States government, he will, in the article of transfer, limit the conveyance to the boundaries of the said United States and Territories, and, upon the consummation of the sale, he will pay to the said Rodman or his legal representatives the sum of fifty thousand dollars.

The said Knapp further agrees to make all proper exertion and effort to procure an extension of said patent on or before its expiration. In case he has not previously effected a sale thereof to the United States, and in the event of his procuring such extension, it is hereby mutually agreed, that for and during the term of such extension or extensions the contract shall remain in full force. It is further agreed, that in the event of it being thought to be for the interest of the said Rodman and Knapp to endeavor to introduce the use of said patent in any foreign country, the said Knapp shall, at his own proper expense, make the effort, and any money received from any foreign government or individual for the use thereof shall be divided equally between the parties hereto—that is to say, the said Rodman shall receive one-half and the said Knapp shall receive the one-half thereof.

The said Knapp further covenants and agrees that the Fort Pitt foundery, nor any other in which he is or may become interested, shall use the patent aforesaid in making any castings without paying the said Rodman the amount per pound hereinbefore stated.

It is hereby agreed that in the event of the said Knapp, or his legal representatives, failing fully and promptly to comply with the conditions and covenants contained in the foregoing, then it shall be the right and privilege of the said Rodman to resume possession of the interest in said patent which he has transferred to the said Knapp by an instrument having even date herewith, and to assume control of the entire patent, or any extension or extensions that may be had thereon; in which event the said Rodman shall pay to the said Knapp one-half the amount received for the use or sale of said patent, from time to time as he may receive it, after deducting all his expenses in conducting the business.

In testimony whereof, the said Rodman and Knapp have hereunto set their hands and seals, as of the twentieth day of October, A. D. 1858.

T. J. RODMAN. [L. S.]
CHARLES KNAPP. [L. S.]

In presence of—
    NICHOLAS K. WADE.

A true copy.

T. J. RODMAN,
Captain of Ordnance.

Before commission.

Major Hagner states:

That he learns from Captain Benton, at the Ordnance office, that our new model eight-inch and ten-inch columbiads cast solid—the cost price of which is $6\frac{1}{2}$ cents per pound—have answered thus far very well, no guns having failed.

The ten-inch columbiads were used at the siege of Fort Pulaski. No doubt they were fired a good deal, although the number of rounds has not been reported. The charge used was 20 pounds of powder and a solid shot weighing 128 pounds. 26 ten-inch columbiads and 75 eight-inch columbiads have been delivered up to this time.

It is believed that the model of these guns is very good, much superior in strength to the old model, although the new guns are lighter than the old.

The trial commenced at Pittsburg and completed at Old Point Comfort—in which two ten-inch of the new model, one cast hollow by Rodman's plan, and one solid, as usual, each endured, without bursting, 4,082 fires—show remarkable strength due to the model, as guns of the old model of the same metal cast solid had burst very early in the proof.

It is reported that the English have recently tried some heavy mortars cast solid and *hollow*, (according to Rodman's plan,) and that the solid ones burst after 700 or 800 fires, while the hollow cast endured 2,000.

I roughly calculate the expenses as follows:

Powder, 232,970 pounds	$42,000
Shot, total weight of rounds fired, 1,619,334 pounds—charge $\frac{1}{15}$	4,000
Guns, 114,000 pounds, at $4\frac{1}{2}$ cents per pound	5,130
" 75,250 pounds, at $5\frac{1}{2}$ cents per pound	4,138
Other expenses	4,732
	60,000

The actual price paid for guns, and the number of shot used, may be very different, probably greater than estimated.

COMMISSION ON ORDNANCE AND ORDNANCE STORES,
Washington, June 27, 1862.

GENERAL: The commission request to be informed of the number of heavy cannon "cast hollow and cooled from the interior," received from all sources since your orders of 22d December, 1861.

Very respectfully, your obedient servant,

J. WISE, *Secretary.*

Brigadier General J. W. RIPLEY,
Chief of Ordnance.

ORDNANCE OFFICE,
Washington, July 14, 1862.

SIR: The number and weight of heavy guns cast hollow and cooled from the interior since December 22, 1861, are as follows:

22 columbiads, weight	330,996 lbs.
69 13-inch sea-coast mortars	1,185,489 lbs.
Total weight	1,516,485 lbs.

Respectfully, I am your obedient servant,

JAMES W. RIPLEY,
Brigadier General.

J. WISE, Esq.,
Secretary to Commission on Ordnance, &c.

COMMISSION ON ORDNANCE AND ORDNANCE STORES,
Washington, July 2, 1862.

GENERAL : The commission have the honor to report as follows :

CASE NO. 103.—Captain T. J. RODMAN, United States Ordnance department, and CHARLES KNAPP, Pittsburg, Pennsylvania.

Report by chief of ordnance upon letter of April 2, 1862, written by order of the Secretary of War. Specially referred by direction of the Secretary of War, dated May 13, 1862.

April 2, 1862, Secretary of War requires " to know whether contracts or orders have been given by the Ordnance department for the manufacture of cast-iron cannon upon a plan patented to any individual ; whether any sum has been paid directly or indirectly by the government for patent fees ; what price per pound has been paid for the cannon made under the patented plans, and what for cannon of the same calibre made under the unpatented plans ; and whether any instruction or direction had been given by any officer connected with the Ordnance bureau to any contractor, or applicant for a contract, to the effect that he would be expected to pay any sum as patent fee."

The papers submitted to the commission show that the inquiries made by the Secretary of War refer to certain orders given by the chief of ordnance December 22, 1861, and later to several founders to furnish all the 8-inch and 10-inch columbiads they could make in the next twelve months at a price of $7\frac{8}{10}$ cents per pound. The guns are required to be " cast hollow and cooled from the interior," and notice was given to the parties receiving orders that a " payment of one cent per pound as a patent fee is required by the holder of the patent-right."

The history of the case is very fully given by the chief of ordnance, as well as by Captain Rodman, of the Ordnance department, the officer to whom the patent-right was granted for the process of " casting cannon hollow and cooling from the interior," and the papers show that the claim of Captain Rodman as inventor, and the fact of a patent having been granted to him, have been made known at different times to different Secretaries of War, and that the payments made for patent fees, either directly or indirectly, have been either ordered by the Secretary or, as at present, concurred in by the chief of ordnance.

It appears from Captain Rodman's statement to the commission that as early as 1845, when on duty at the Pittsburg arsenal and superintending the casting of cannon in the foundery adjacent, reflection upon the subject of casting cannon led him to study the theory of the effects of cooling on large masses of iron, and to write out a demonstration to prove the advantages that would be obtained by casting large guns hollow and cooling from the interior, and also the injury to the strength of the gun by the plan in use of casting solid and cooling from the exterior. As an improvement, he suggested that cast-iron guns should be cast with a core for the bore smaller than the finished bore, and that the casting should be cooled by conducting a stream of air or water through this bore, so as to commence the cooling from the interior.

In passing through Washington about this time, Lieutenant Rodman conversed with the chief of ordnance upon the subject, and requested to have the matter tested by actual trial. In reply, it was stated that no money was then available ; and although an interest was manifested both by Cols. Bomford and Talcott, doubts were expressed as to the correctness of the theory—General Talcott supposing that the effect of this mode of cooling would be to produce a dense layer of metal around the bore, and another of like quality on the outside of the gun, with porous metal between these layers.

The proprietors of Fort Pitt foundery, where Captain Rodman was engaged superintending the casting of cannon for the government about this time, advised him to patent the process, and offered to be at the expense of testing the practicability of casting and cooling guns, according to his plan, if he would take out letters patent, and assign one-half the interest to them.

Before accepting this offer he made it known to the then chief of ordnance, who considered that there could be no impropriety in the course proposed. Thereupon he sought and obtained a patent in August, 1847, and assigned one-half interest to Messrs. Knapp & Totten, proprietors of the Fort Pitt foundery, who soon thereafter cast a hollow gun, which was cooled by passing a stream of air through the interior.

" Messrs. Knapp & Totten," Captain Rodman reports, " bore the entire expense of this trial, and also of others, in which water was used to cool the iron— several guns being lost before the mode was perfected, and the loss wholly sustained by Messrs. Knapp & Totten." The result of the experiments made was considered by the founders as fully establishing the practicability of casting and cooling guns in this way ; and upon stating this to Colonel Talcott, the acting chief of ordnance, he accompanied Captain Rodman to the then Secretary of War, Mr. Marcy, and after full explanations, and the exhibition of his patent, Captain Rodman understood that orders would be given immediately to cast two 8-inch cannon, one by his method, and one by the ordinary method, for comparative trial, to test the value of the invention in improving the endurance of heavy guns.

Before this trial was made Captain Rodman was ordered to Mexico, and he sent from Camargo, in June, 1848, his first official written report upon the subject, now on file in the Ordnance office.

In January, 1849, having been authorized by Messrs. Knapp & Totten to propose in their names to furnish a pair of trial guns, at their actual cost, Captain Rodman visited the department and obtained authority to have cast two eight-inch columbiads by the Messrs. Knapp & Totten, for which they were to be paid at the rate of $4\frac{1}{2}$ cents per pound, and to have the broken guns " after proof." This appears to have been the first trial made with large guns ; and the first the cost of which was borne by the government. " The result of it was not deemed satisfactory," says Captain Rodman, " as neither gun endured as much as a good gun should ;" the " solid " cast gun having burst at the 85th fire, and the " hollow one " at the 251st. Another pair of eight-inch and a pair of ten-inch guns were made and tested in 1851, the " solid " eight-inch bursting at the 73d fire, while the " hollow " one endured 1,500 rounds without bursting ; the " solid " ten-inch burst at the 20th fire, and the " hollow " one at the 249th. These results were still deemed unsatisfactory, as *three* of the *four* guns showed very insufficient endurance. In 1852 a pair of 32-pounders were cast and tested, and both endured over 1,000 service rounds, and several *increased charges;* the " hollow" one more than the " solid" one ; but not so much more as to prove an important superiority. Again, in 1856, another pair of 10-inch guns was ordered and again the result was unsatisfactory, from the early failure of both guns ; the " solid" one at the 26th fire, and the "hollow" one at the 315th. As it seemed probable from the small endurance of the " solid" guns made at the Fort Pitt foundery, (thus repeatedly shown in these comparative trials,) that the treatment of the iron there might have impaired its quality—" reliable" guns being made at the time of the same character of iron as the West Point foundery— the ordnance board to which was referred the subject of a " proper programme of experiments to test the effect of the kind of furnace used in melting the iron, upon the endurance of the gun, and also the relative endurance of guns cast solid and hollow," recommended, in February, 1857, the casting of six ten-inch guns, of iron selected at the West Point foundery, in sets of three, one to be cast solid at West Point, and one hollow and one solid at Fort Pitt. The first three tried in August, 1857, still failed to settle previous doubts, as both the solid guns cast at Fort Pitt and West Point proved to be inferior to the usual endurance ; the superiority of the " hollow" one to both was, however, evident, as it endured without rupture 1,000 service rounds. It was intended to duplicate this last trial the next year, but as a portion of the selected iron had been inadvertently used for other purposes, this could not be done. The ordnance board at this time recommended a change of pattern in our columbiads, considering that the existing model, although good guns had been made according to it, was not the most suitable for endurance, and that this defect might account, in part, for recent failures in those guns. This recommendation was approved, and two ten-inch guns were cast from the West Point iron remaining at Fort Pitt foundery, upon this new model; with a view to test the new form as well as the mode of cooling. The result of this trial, showing the unparalleled endurance of both these 10-inch guns, (which have withstood 4,082 service and two proof charges without breaking,) while proving that the new model must be regarded as an essential improvement, leaves the question of the comparative superiority of Rodman's plan for guns of this model still unsettled. Subsequent service with solid cast guns made after this model has thus far shown that guns so made may probably be amply strong for service, as no gun of this model has yet failed, although many are in use. The officers who superintended the trial above noted report that, though both guns remained whole, the gun cast hollow is in much better condition, and did not commence to show traces of wear as soon as the others. Up to this stage, therefore, although some advantages had been shown in every comparative trial in favor of the guns cast by Captain Rodman's plan, there is no decisive proof that cast-iron guns thus made will be uniformly reliable, or that guns of the new model, cast solid, will not be sufficiently so. Both modes of casting by the old model failed in some cases and endured in others, and all the guns cast upon the new model have endured well, whether cast by the one plan or the other. The mechanical arrangements for cooling from the interior, so far as to show the proper course to be pursued, had been satisfactorily established at the expense of the founders prior to any expense being incurred by the government; but for all the castings the government had paid, at rates covering the cost of manufacture, and had also borne the expense for powder, shot, labor, &c., necessary in making the experiments, and Captain Rodman's services as an ordnance officer, superintending this work, had been continued at the foundery. The actual amount of extra expense incurred by Messrs. Knapp & Totten in making these guns, rather than solid ones, has not been stated; but on the part of the government, besides the services of Captain Rodman in part only devoted to this matter, the cost price of guns, ammunition, and labor, consumed in the various experiments may be roughly estimated at about $60,000. As the invention is one only of use to the government, and the proof of its merit the essential feature of its value, it may be justly claimed that the expenditures testing the merit had given the government a large interest in it—an interest that should not have been overlooked in any transfer of it as a marketable commodity. The untried suggestion was valueless; proof of its merit required government aid; it was granted to a liberal extent, and whatever advantage may accrue, it was the alchemy of government aid that converted the suggestion into gold to the extent of value it had been shown to have. In the case of an improvement, patented by an officer of ordnance, recommended for trial to the ordnance board of 1858, it was advised that the trials should be made, it being understood that "the trials are to be made for the public benefit and not for the interests of the individual officer." This decision, it would seem, is based upon the view taken above.

It appears, however, that prior to the completion of the last trial above recorded, (October 20, 1858,) while the government was still experimenting, unable to adopt yet unwilling to reject a plan that had given promise of improving our cast-iron cannon, Captain Rodman assigned and transferred to Mr. Knapp all his remaining interest in the letters-patent granted to him August

14, 1847, and entered into an agreement in consideration of the transfer. A copy of this agreement has been furnished to the commission by Captain Rodman. By the terms of this instrument, it appears that one-half of one cent per pound of the finished weight of all castings on which the said Knapp may receive a royalty for the use of said patent is to be paid to Captain Rodman, from time to time, as the said Knapp may collect said royalty. And it is further agreed by the said Knapp that in the event of his selling the said patent to the United States government he will in the article of transfer limit the conveyance to the boundaries of said States and Territories, and upon confirmation of the sale he will pay to the said Rodman or his legal representatives the sum of fifty thousand dollars. The said Knapp also agrees to make all proper exertion and effort to procure an extension of said patent, and that in the event of his procuring such extension it is mutually agreed that for and during the time of such extension or extensions this contract shall maintain its full force. In case it shall be to the interest of the said Rodman, for reasons stated, to resume possession of the interest in the said patent which he has transferred to the said Knapp by an instrument bearing date herewith, (no copy of which has been furnished to the commission,) in that event the said Rodman shall pay to the said Knapp one-half of the amount received for the use or sale of said patent, from time to time, as he may receive it, after deducting all his expense in conducting the business.

November 16, 1859, without the recommendation of the ordnance board, (required by article 1377 General Regulations of the Army, edition 1861,) the then Secretary of War, Mr. J. B. Floyd, directed the adoption of this mode of casting heavy guns, ordering that arrangements should be made to cast all heavy cannon after the "Rodman plan," and that "the free use of the right to cast cannon for the land service after this plan should be secured by the Ordnance bureau to each founder, by the payment from the appropriation for armament of fortifications, for such use, of twenty per cent. upon the cost of each gun to Mr. Charles Knapp, the proprietor of the patent. The price for finished cannon at the founderies will remain the same as now paid." A copy of this order was transmitted to all the founders then engaged in manufacturing cannon for the United States; and in 1860 thirty-nine 8-inch columbiads were cast after this plan at the Fort Pitt foundery, and were paid for at the rate of 6½ cents per pound—the usual price established some years previously; and Mr. Charles Knapp, the proprietor of the patent, was paid, in addition, $3,037 68, being twenty per cent. upon the cost of twenty-six of these cannon. The account for the patent fee upon the remaining thirteen of these guns, rendered later by Mr. Knapp, was disallowed by decision of the Secretary of War ad interim, Mr. J. Holt, January 21, 1861, "being regarded as incompatible with the —— section of the act of June 23, 1860." Messrs. Knapp, Rudd & Co. were accordingly notified that the "order of November 16, 1859, was revoked, and that no payment on account of patent fees would be made by the United States." No other founders than the proprietors of the Fort Pitt foundery have ever cast guns under the "Rodman plan," and no other payment has been made expressly as patent fees than the one above stated.

Mr. Knapp protested against the revocation of the order of November 16, 1859, and as the third section of the act of June 23, 1860, was repealed on the 21st of February, 1861, the basis upon which this payment was denied no longer exists. To complete the history of the case, as shown before the commission, it should be here stated that in August, 1861, Captain Rodman applied for and obtained an extension for seven years of his original patent grant, which would have expired in that month.

In December, 1861, the chief of ordnance finding it necessary to give immediate orders for casting, and having recommendations from officers of the department the most practiced in experimental firing with heavy cannon favorable to Rodman's plan, submitted the subject to a board of officers composed of Brevet

Major Dyer, Captain Rodman, and Captain Benton, directing them to "fix a suitable price to be paid for 8-inch and 10-inch columbiads." December 19, 1861, the board reported that: First. They consider it important that all pieces of these calibres should be cooled from the interior in casting. Second. In view of the fact that the Navy Department pays $7\frac{73}{100}$ and $8\frac{23}{100}$ cents per pound for its 9 and 11-inch guns, respectively, the undersigned consider that $7\frac{8}{10}$ cents per pound is fair and reasonable for 8-inch and 10-inch columbiads cast hollow, more especially as they consider the latter named cannon more durable than the former. The undersigned are prepared to extend the foregoing recommendation to all cast-iron cannon made by direction of the Ordnance department.

It has been explained to the commission that the prices above quoted as those paid for navy guns were established after calculations, based upon the price of army guns, of the greater labor and expense of finishing guns, according to the method adopted over army guns of like size, the rough casting of the navy guns as compared with its finished size, and the loss of metal and amount of workmanship being greater. As an increase of expense attends the fabrication of the army gun in consequence of being cooled from the interior, no part of the increase over $6\frac{1}{2}$ cents per pound, the price paid for guns cast solid, is absorbed in the cost of fabrication.

In accordance with the recommendations above quoted, propositions were made to the founders then employed by the government, Mr. Parrott, Mr. Alger, and Mr. Knapp, asking them "to furnish to the government all the 8-inch and 10-inch columbiads that they could make in the next twelve months, the pieces to be cast hollow and cooled from the interior; the price allowed to be $7\frac{8}{10}$ cents per pound." The founder was, of course, to make all the necessary arrangements for the privilege of casting and cooling the guns as required.

By letter dated December 23, 1861, the chief of ordnance was authorized by Mr. Charles Knapp to inform Mr. Parrott and Mr. Alger that "my charge to them for the use of the Rodman patent for cooling guns will be one cent per pound of the finished weight of all guns received for service by the United States." This price it will be seen leaves an increase of a cent per pound to these founders over and above that heretofore paid for like guns cast solid; but the proprietor of the patent may claim one cent and three-tenths per pound from others without reducing the usual profits to the founder casting heavy guns. Mr. Alger declined the proposal of the department, and although Mr. Parrott accepted it, he has as yet done nothing to carry it out, being fully occupied with other work. Mr. Knapp, however, accepted the proposal, and in his acceptance stated that he expected to be able to deliver from 1,000 to 1,200 guns within the time specified. Prior to June 1, 1862, sixty-nine mortars and twenty-two columbiads, weighing 1,516,485 pounds, have been delivered by Mr. Knapp, upon which he has received, or claims payment at the rate of $7\frac{8}{10}$ cents per pound. As the calculated weight of cast-iron guns required to complete the armament of the forts is 71,411,364 pounds, should all of these be cast hollow, the total royalty to Mr. Knapp will amount to $928,347, of which Captain Rodman's share may be $357,000.

The commission having thus stated all the details of this case serving to show the extent of the interests involved affecting the government and the present holder of the patent right, find it to be their duty to consider the propriety of the sale of the patent by Captain Rodman and of his continuing interest in it while an officer of the army. It appears that in all the steps taken by Captain Rodman prior to the sale of the patent, he acted after consultation with his superior officers, but it does not appear that the terms of that sale were known to them at the time payments were made for its use.

Intelligent and zealous officers, especially those in the scientific corps of the army, charged with conducting experiments in new fields, or supervising operations under novel circumstances, are frequently called upon to make the scientific theories, mechanical principles, or economical arrangements for the progress of work more or less familiar in practice elsewhere, subservient to new purposes. Valuable suggestions thus made, if found to be of importance to the government, entitle the officer to suitable reward and distinction, and it should be the policy of the government to give encouragement to talent of this kind by special executive or legislative action.   As officers in charge of government establishments enjoy great advantages in maturing designs suggested by their current duties, they do not stand in fair competition as sellers of patent rights with those not having such advantages.

If these valuable inventions thus made and matured are sold to citizens, who may claim a degree of remuneration according to the government need of the invention, in the end the government pays more for such inventions than if made by others, and may be thus injured rather than benefited by the possession of such a class of ingenious officers.

Payment for such patent rights must also, generally, be based upon the extent of use that may be made of them, and the officer in his duties would thus find himself hampered by appeals to his personal feelings or interests to extend their use or over estimate their value.   Should he receive a patent for an invention of immediate advantage to the government, the law and regulations allow of but one mode by which he can secure pecuniary benefit to himself while he is in the military service.   He must apply to Congress so that the recompense for its use "may be authorized by law and explicitly set out in the appropriation."— (See Article 1003 General Regulations of the Army.)

Article 1002 (of the same regulations) forbids "any officer or agent in the military service to purchase from any other person in the military service, or make any contract with any such person to furnish supplies or services, or make any purchase or contract in which such person shall be admitted to any share or to any benefit therefrom.

As is evident by the articlesof agreement between Mr. Knapp and Captain Rodman, each officer or military agent paying for or making a contract for the casting of heavy cannon under the orders given out by the Ordnance department in December last, or under like orders, commits an infraction of this article.

It having been shown that large expenditures have been made by the United States in testing the merits of Captain Rodman's suggestion, and that probably the suggestion itself was the fruit of his official position and labors, we think the government has a fair claim to insist that these facts shall be considered in estimating what it shall pay for the use of the invention thus originating and matured, and this claim may be justly asserted not only against Captain Rodman himself, but against his assignees, having notice of the circumstances on which it rests.   With all these circumstances Mr. Knapp, the assignee now before us, was, without doubt, well acquainted.

This view, however much it may influence the government hereafter in determining the amount of compensation it will make for the use of the invention, is unimportant in reference to our present decision.   The order to Mr. Knapp for the casting of cannon at a price of which a continuing royalty to be paid to Captain Rodman was an acknowledged part, being in violation of law and against public policy, was *null* and *void* in its entirety, and under it, as a contract, nothing is due.   Our decision that the cannon shall be paid for at current rates, and in exclusion altogether of the illegal element of compensation for the invention, does not rest upon the order, but upon the reception and retention of the guns by the United States.

The commission therefore consider that—

1. Captain Rodman, being an officer of the army, could not legally sell to the government the right to an invention of which he was the claimant.

2. That the use of it cannot now be paid for by the government to the

personal emolument of Captain Rodman while he holds his commission in the army; and

3. That the rates of charge which have been imposed for its use by the government are unreasonable and extravagant.

The commission therefore direct, that while Captain Rodman remains an officer or agent in the military service, no higher rate than $6\frac{1}{2}$ cents per pound be paid for the guns ordered to be "cast hollow and cooled from the interior," and that payments heretofore made to Mr. Knapp at $7\frac{8}{10}$ cents per pound for such guns be considered as on account, and in future settlements with him $1\frac{3}{10}$ cents per pound be deducted from such sums as have been thus paid, that being the amount claimed for royalty.

Should it be deemed essential to give further orders to use this plan of casting and cooling, so long as Captain Rodman continues in the army the government should use the invention as private property taken for public use, leaving the compensation to be fixed by Congress on such terms as may be deemed proper.

The commission recommend that application should be made at once by the War Department to Congress to establish a fair measure of compensation for the free use of the patent granted to Captain Rodman, now having about six years to run, as in the event of his withdrawal from the army it may become competent for an officer to contract with Mr. Knapp for the use of this invention, the compensation for which should be limited by law.

We are, sir, very respectfully, your obedient servants,

J. HOLT,
ROBERT DALE OWEN,
Commissioners.
P. V. HAGNER,
Major of Ordnance, Assistant to Commission.

Brigadier General J. W. RIPLEY,
Chief of Ordnance.

CASE No. 104.

INDIANAPOLIS ARSENAL.

Captain Sturm wants powder, fuzes, and money.

UNITED STATES MILITARY TELEGRAPH,
Received March 8, 1861, from Indianapolis, Indiana, March 8.

Captain H. Sturm, ordnance officer at the arsenal, needs cannon powder, Borman fuzes, &c., badly, to fill urgent and large requisitions from different points. He has telegraphed twice to General Ripley, but no answer; will you please urge the general to answer and allow Captain Sturm to purchase such materials as he may need. Assistant Secretary Scott intimated when here that this would be done. Captain Sturm is a faithful officer and works day and night. This accounts for the delay in his reports; they will be sent on Monday next. He also needs seven thousand (7,000) dollars to pay hands, &c.

O. P. MORTON, *Governor of Indiana.*

Hon. E. M. STANTON, *Secretary of War.*

MARCH 8, 1862.

Referred to chief of ordnance for immediate report. By order of Secretary of War.
P. H. WATSON,
Assistant Secretary of War.

Governor O. P. MORTON.

Brigadier General Jas. W. Ripley's report on telegram of Governor Morton.

ORDNANCE OFFICE, *Washington, March* 8, 1862.

SIR: The telegram of Governor Morton, of this date, is herewith returned. I also enclose two telegrams from Captain Sturm, the officer in charge of the arsenal at Indianapolis, which have been received at this office.

As this department has large supplies of field ammunition on hand to meet requisitions, and as this telegram of Captain Sturm is obscure in one particular, it was thought proper to defer action on it until his explanatory letter was received. This letter has not yet been received, hence the delay.

With regard to this arsenal at Indianapolis, I would state for the information of the War Department that it is a State establishment, and not under the control of this department further than this department has been frequently called upon to supply money and materials to carry on its operations.

On the 31st of December last I addressed a letter to the Hon. Robert Dale Owen, the agent of the State of Indiana, in which occurs the following sentence: "I do not deem it advisable to continue the preparation of ammunition for small arms, or for artillery, further than may be necessary to consume the materials which have already been provided at the arsenal at Indianapolis for that purpose.

"Such additional supplies, if any, as it may be necessary to have there, can be provided by timely requisitions on this office from the Allegheny or some other United States arsenal."

In view of the fact that the supplies called for by Captain Sturm are large in amount, and as there is an ample supply of field ammunition on hand, I would respectfully recommend that the issue be delayed until Captain Sturm's report is received.

Advances of money are only made to the regular disbursing officers of this department.

Respectfully, &c.,

JAS. W. RIPLEY,
Brigadier General.

Hon. E. M. STANTON, *Secretary of War.*

Indorsed on envelope, in the handwriting of the Secretary of War:

"Referred to the ordnance commission.   STANTON."

P. V. HAGNER,
Major of Ordnance.

WASHINGTON, *March* 19, 1862.

Captain H. Sturm presents accounts in triplicate for material purchased for Indiana arsenal by order of Colonel Thomas A. Scott, Assistant Secretary of War.

ORDNANCE OFFICE, *March* 21, 1862.

Respectfully returned. These accounts, amounting to $40,495 59, have been examined. They are all of the same character, and not one of them has any evidence of the authority required by law (3d section of the act approved February 8, 1815) for the purchase of ordnance, arms, equipments, or ordnance stores, or that the articles purchased have been delivered to any United States officer, or applied to the United States service. This office has therefore no authority to approve any of them, and cannot recommend their payment.

JAMES W. RIPLEY, *Brigadier General.*

WASHINGTON, *April* 6, 1862.

Robert Dale Owen submits statement and makes suggestions concerning the arsenal at Indianapolis, Indiana.

WASHINGTON, *April* 6, 1862.

SIR: Pressed by urgent letters from the State of Indiana in regard to the accounts of the Indianapolis arsenal, I beg leave to make to you the following statement:

When Governor Morton, of Indiana, was last in this city, after conference with the Secretary of War, it was, as he informed me, agreed as to the said arsenal as follows:

1. That it should not be adopted as a government arsenal, there being no legal authority for so doing; but

2. That it should be allowed to proceed, as heretofore, in the manufacture of ammunition, and to present its accounts, monthly, to the Ordnance department.

3. That these accounts, when duly authenticated, and the prices approved by the Ordnance department, should be passed as those of any individual furnishing to the government similar ordnance stores.

In pursuance of this agreement such monthly accounts have been forwarded to the Ordnance department; but they have not been acted on.

I called upon the chief of ordnance in regard to this matter, and he informed me that he believed he had no authority in the matter, having only verbal information that such an arrangement had been made by the Secretary.

In this way the accounts remain unaudited. This will produce serious embarrassment, and may even arrest operations at the arsenal. As it is daily supplying ammunition to our western armies, the consequences of any disappointment in the supply might be serious.

I submit the facts, praying that you will be so kind as to take them into consideration, and to act in the premises as you deem best.

I am, sir, your obedient servant,

ROBERT DALE OWEN,

Hon. P. H. WATSON,
Assistant Secretary of War.

Referred to Brigadier General J. W. Ripley for report, by order of the Secretary of War.

P. H. WATSON,
Assistant Secretary of War.

ORDNANCE OFFICE, *Washington, May* 2, 1862.

James W. Ripley, brigadier general, submits two accounts for articles fabricated at and materials purchased at the Indiana State arsenal; and, also, abstract of the correspondence in relation thereto.

ORDNANCE OFFICE, *Washington, May* 2, 1862.

SIR: I submit herewith an account, amounting to $71,044 40, for ammunition fabricated by the State of Indiana at its arsenal, Indianapolis, on account of the United States; which account has been presented by Colonel D. G. Rose, who is delegated by Governor Morton to collect the amount.

I also again submit the account presented by Captain H. Sturm on the 19th ultimo, which amount, in the aggregate, to $40,495 59, and which are stated to be for materials purchased for Indiana arsenal by order of Colonel Thomas A. Scott, Assistant Secretary of War.

With these papers I submit an abstract of the correspondence which has taken place in relation to this arsenal and the fabrication thereat of ammunition on account of the United States.

In view of this correspondence, and of the complicated nature of the accounts—for although the United States have furnished much material, such as powder and lead, and accounts are presented for large quantities of materials said to have been purchased for the United States, no credit seems to be given for the same, and the account heretofore paid, and the one now presented, are both for finished cartridges at a given price per thousand, and the price of some of these, charged at $11 50 and $13 50, is greatly in excess of the price reported by Hon. R. D. Owen, who, in a letter of 27th December, 1861, states it to be, for the same kind of cartridge, $8 88 and $10 75, and in a letter of 19th March, 1862, $9 97 as the cost to the State—I therefore respectfully recommend that the whole subject be placed in the hands of an officer, with instructions to proceed to Indianapolis to examine into the matter on the spot; to see that proper credit be given for the materials furnished by and purchased on account of the United States, that the articles be charged at a fair price, and to give proper certificates for such amount as he shall find to be due for ammunition and supplies which may have been procured and fabricated for and applied to or held for the use of the United States. That as soon as this shall have been done all connexion of government with this arsenal to cease, and all such ammunition and material as shall then belong to the United States to be removed to St. Louis arsenal, or to such other place of deposit as may be deemed advisable.

Very respectfully, your obedient servant,

JAS. W. RIPLEY, *Brigadier General.*

Hon. E. M. STANTON,
      Secretary of War.

Approved.

The chief of ordnance will detail a competent officer to investigate the accounts and make report, subject to the approval of the Ordnance bureau and of this department.

EDWIN M. STANTON,
Secretary of War.

INDIANA ARSENAL, *May* 8, 1862.

GOVERNOR: Enclosed please find a statement of ammunition on hand at this arsenal and now waiting the order of the chief of ordnance at Washington. On the 7th of April I forwarded to General Ripley a statement of all the ammunition then on hand and ready for delivery to any place he might direct, but up to this time I have received no answer from him. About the same time that I forwarded this to General Ripley, a bill for the ammunition manufactured during the first quarter, ending March 31, 1862, and amounting to $71,044 40, was also forwarded to Washington for payment. This bill, as per agreement between yourself and the Secretary of War, was duly certified to by Laz. Noble, adjutant general of Indiana. Since then I have made more ammunition, amounting in all to some $18,000. I have also purchased a large quantity of materials for ammunition, at cash figures, and the parties from whom I purchased are very anxious to receive their pay. There are now employed at this arsenal 325 persons, mostly females, who have either husbands, brothers, or some other relatives in the army; these mostly depend upon the money they earn in the arsenal for their daily bread, and it is extremely necessary that some means should be devised by which they can be paid regularly once a month.

Governor, can you not possibly make some arrangements by which the money necessary to pay the hands, and other claims, can be procured? You can form no idea how much it is needed by them. The total indebtedness of the arsenal at this date, including amount due in pay-roll, amounts to nearly $100,000.

The amount of ammunition sold to the United States in April 1, 1862, amounts to $71,044 40; ammunition made during the month of April amounts to about $18,000—making a total of $89,044 40.

I am, sir, very respectfully, your obedient servant,

H. STURM, *Captain Commanding.*

His Excellency Governor O. P. MORTON,
Indianapolis, Indiana.

EXECUTIVE DEPARTMENT,
Indianapolis, May 10, 1862.

SIR: General Ripley persistently declines carrying out the agreement in regard to the Indiana arsenal. The accounts duly certified were forwarded over a month ago, but they are not passed. I learn from the Hon. Mr. Owen that General Ripley puts the delay on the ground that he has no "written authority to act;" and Colonel Rose, who was recently at Washington on this business, informs me that the general based his refusal to make the settlement on the fact that a large lot of lead, and perhaps some other material, has been supplied to the State by the United States, for which credit had not been given in the accounts. (Upon this latter point I refer you to Captain Sturm's statement, herewith enclosed, marked A.) He also stated to Colonel Rose that he would send some one here to inspect the arsenal and examine the accounts, and that he would recommend the removal of all the public property to St. Louis, and suspend the operation of the concern.

We have contracted debts on account of the arsenal, for labor and materials, to the amount of nearly $10,000, most of it since the arrangement respecting the arsenal was concluded, which indebtedness I expected to pay out of money to be received from the United States; but the delay in passing the accounts, if continued much longer, will make it necessary to borrow money and pay the same to save the credit of the State.

The continuance of the arsenal is a matter of no pecuniary interest to the State, but only to those who are employed in it and who are dependent on it for the means of subsistence. It was started as a matter of necessity in the beginning, and rendered most excellent service in furnishing large supplies of ammunition of the best quality to the army—east, west, and south—and has continued to do so up to the present time. And feeling a pride in its success, it would be a source of gratification to our people if it could proceed prosperously in what seems to us to be a *good work.*

The plain truth is, that General Ripley is hostile to the continuance of the arsenal here, and has been from the time it was first brought to his attention, although I am credibly informed that he procures large quantities of fixed ammunition to be prepared, under contract, by private parties in Philadelphia and elsewhere, at rates exceeding those charged by this State, and certainly procuring no better article. I know of no reason why ammunition prepared by private individuals should be preferred to that manufactured here, unless it is furnished at cheaper rates or of better quality, and can only attribute General Ripley's course to his early and continued hostility.

If it were not for the pride I have in the matter, the outstanding debts that must be paid, and the sudden ejection of several hundred persons from employment, most of whom are very poor and have no other means of livelihood, operations would be suspended at once, and I should not say another word about it.

It is unpleasant to present the State in the attitude of a suppliant asking for the examination of her accounts and the continuance of the patronage of the government in a matter in which she has no interest beyond the public good and the honorable employment of her citizens. The struggle with General Ripley has been going on quite *six months*, and must end, as I am thoroughly tired of it. We obtained a settlement last winter for ammunition issued to the army before that time, after great trouble and after sending two agents to Washington, and finally going myself, and then only by positive order of Mr. Secretary Cameron. I enclose herewith a copy of a letter addressed to me by Captain Sturm, superintendent of the arsenal, (marked B;) also sundry statements, which I submit for your consideration in connexion with the foregoing.

I have the honor to be, sir, very respectfully, your obedient servant,

O. P. MORTON,
Governor of Indiana.

Hon. EDWIN M. STANTON,
Secretary of War, Washington.

Indorsed on envelope, in the handwriting of the Secretary of War: "Referred to the ordnance commission."

P. V. HAGNER,
Major of Ordnance.

STATE OF INDIANA, EXECUTIVE DEPARTMENT,
Indianapolis, May 10, 1862.

SIR: The Hon. David C. Branham, one of our most eminent citizens, being on a visit to our regiments in Virginia, will call on you, at my request, for the purpose of procuring, if possible, an adjustment of the accounts of the State for ammunition furnished to the United States. He will deliver to you a letter from myself, and a number of other papers, relating to that matter.

I bespeak for Mr. Branham an early interview and your kind attention, and have the honor to be, very respectfully, your obedient servant,

O. P. MORTON.

Hon. EDWIN M. STANTON,
Secretary of War, Washington.

INDIANA ARSENAL, *May* 12, 1862.

GOVERNOR: In answer to your inquiry in regard to material furnished to me by the United States government, permit me to state that, on the 5th day of February, Colonel T. A. Scott, Assistant Secretary of War, while here examining our arsenal, requested me to continue the manufacturing of ammunition, authorizing me at the same time, in presence of your military secretary and the assistant adjutant general, to purchase such materials as I might require, and to forward the bills for the same, certified by me, to Washington, for payment; stating, at the same time, that in future supplies should be sent to me by the chief of ordnance, upon my requisition for the same. Being in want of certain materials at the time, and the demand for ammunition in the department of the Ohio being very pressing, I, in compliance with these instructions, telegraphed to General Ripley for buckshot, lead, and powder. A telegram from him, dated February 7, on file at this office, authorized me to purchase such buckshot as I might require. In a subsequent telegram, dated at Washington, February 15, he says: "I have ordered 300 barrels of musket powder and 100 tons of lead to be sent to you from the New York arsenal. In the meantime purchase such lead as you may require, at 7¼ cents per pound, if it cannot be obtained for less." I then purchased 100 tons of lead from Messrs. Fugate & Hildebrand, of this city, at from 6½ to 7 cents per pound. While this was being worked up, and having no hope of receiving the lead from the New York arsenal in time, I purchased 100 tons from N. Corwith & Co., Galena, Illinois, at 6¼ cents per pound. And as the powder mentioned in General Ripley's despatch did not arrive, I also purchased 150 barrels of government proof powder from J. W. Donohue, Mr. Dupont's agent at Cincinnati. This powder lasted me until the beginning of

April; and although the powder sent by General Ripley arrived here March 8, I could not, in justice to the State, credit the United States with it in the bill for ammunition manufactured during the first quarter, ending March 31, 1862, as I had not used a single pound of it for any ammunition mentioned in that bill. The lead mentioned in General Ripley's despatch was not sent from the New York arsenal until April 2, and did not arrive here until April 8, and of course came several days after the bill against the United States had been made out. During the month of April I made ammunition to the amount of $25,000, and in that bill the United States will of course be credited with the amount of powder and lead received. I must state, however, that, owing to the delay in shipping the lead from New York, (it being near two (2) months after it was ordered by General Ripley to be shipped,) I was under the necessity, as stated before, of purchasing lead, which has lasted me until the beginning of May, at which time all the lead received from the United States was yet untouched.

I am, sir, very respectfully, your obedient servant,

H. STURM,
Captain Commanding.

His Excellency Governor O. P. MORTON,
Indianapolis.

Abstract of correspondence in relation to arsenal at Indianapolis, and of the expenses incurred on account of the United States.

October 9, 1861.—Governor Morton encloses a statement of ammunition made at the arsenal and supplied to troops for service of the United States to date; asks if government will furnish funds to meet actual expenses thereof, &c.

October 18, 1861.—Governor informed by Ordnance office that money can only be refunded by the regular disbursing officers of the department, and that if an account of the expenditure is forwarded, with a certificate that the ammunition charged for is held for the United States, the amount thereof will be remitted.

November 6, 1861.—Governor Morton telegraphs that ordnance officer has not yet arrived to inspect arsenal. (Application to this effect must have been verbal, as none such appears of record.)

November 7, 1861.—Lieutenant Crispin is directed to proceed to Indianapolis to examine the arsenal there, and to give his views as to the advisability, &c., of making ammunition there, instead of at the United States arsenal.

November 19, 1861.—Governor Morton telegraphs that he has requisition from Kentucky for 100,000 cartridges and a large quantity of field ammunition; that arsenal is suspended for want of funds, and that he will start it at once.

November 20, 1861.—The governor is informed that before accepting his offer to make ammunition, inquiries will be made of General Buel to ascertain if his want cannot be supplied in the usual manner.

December 11, 1861.—Lieutenant Crispin reports the result of his visit to Indianapolis arsenal; describes it and its facilities, but thinks that all the wants of the army in that region of the country can be supplied by timely requisitions from United States arsenals, without having resource to State establishments. This report is communicated to Hon. Mr. Owen, State agent, December 30, and he is informed that it is not deemed advisable to continue the preparation of ammunition at that place further than may be necessary to consume the materials which have been purchased for the purpose, and that if supplies are needed by the State they can be supplied from United States arsenal.

January 8, 1862.—Hon. Mr. Owen, State agent, presents an account for ammunition, amounting to $68,701 60. The purchase of this ammunition from the State is authorized by the Secretary of War on the same day. He approves the voucher, and it is paid by the treasury.

Ex. Doc. 72——37

February 6, 1862.—Captain Sturm, the superintendent of the arsenal, reports that, by advice of Colonel T. A. Scott, Assistant Secretary of War, he was changing some 3-inch ammunition, and, by same advice, had purchased lead and other materials.

February 14, 1862.—Captain Sturm telegraphs for powder and lead, stating he had to fill a large order immediately.

February 15, 1862.—Captain Sturm is authorized to purchase lead and buck-shot, and informed that 300 barrels of powder and 100 tons of lead would be sent to him.

March 5, 1862.—Governor Morton telegraphs Secretary of War, saying that supplies asked for be sent.

March 5, 1862.—Secretary of War is told that the arsenal is a State estab-lishment; that Captain Sturm had been asked to explain his telegram, which explanation had not been received; that the departmeut had been called on to supply money and materials; that the supply of field ammunition at arsenals was ample; quoted extract from letter to Mr. Owen of December 30, 1861, and recommendation made that issue of articles called for be delayed till Captain Sturm's report be received.

March 19, 1862.—Hon. Mr. Owen urges that funds be remitted to carry on the operations of the arsenal, stating that four hundred hands were employed; that price of cartridges was very low; that funds were wanted, and also authority to purchase materials. A report was made upon this the same day, and refer-ence made to reports of the 5th and 13th of March on the same subject.

March 19, 1862.—Captain Sturm presents account, amounting to $40,495 59, for materials purchased by order of Colonel Thomas A. Scott, Assistant Secre-tary of War, for Indiana arsenal.

March 21, 1862.—Report made to Secretary of War, referring to law on the subject, and declining to recommend payment of the same.

April 30, 1862.—Colonel D. G. Rose presents account ($71,044 40) for ammunition furnished during first quarter of 1862.

ORDNANCE OFFICE,
Washington, May 20, 1862.

James W. Ripley, brigadier general, transmits, by authority of the Secretary of War, the accompanying accounts for ammunition furnished the United States from the Indiana arsenal.

ORDNANCE OFFICE,
Washington, May 20, 1862

SIR: Understanding that several papers were before the commission in rela-tion to the account for ammunition, &c., furnished to the United States from Indiana arsenal, I have been authorized by the Secretary to transmit to you the accompanying papers on the same subject.

They embrace several accounts, presented by Captain H. Sturm, for materials purchased for use at the arsenal on behalf of the United States, and one account, presented by Colonel Rose, for a large quantity of ammunition furnished during the first quarter of 1862. Also some correspondence on the subject.

I respectfully submit these papers as authorized, and request that they may be adjudicated in connexion with other accounts, &c., which may be before you in connexion with the Indiana State arsenal.

Very respectfully, your obedient servant,

JAS. W. RIPLEY,
Brigadier General.

Hon. J. HOLT,
Of the Commission on Contracts, &c.,
for Ordnance and Ordnance Stores, Washington City.

INDIANA ARSENAL, *May* 27, 1862.

SIR: Enclosed please find returns of ordnance and ordnance stores fabricated, issued, and remaining on hand at Indiana arsenal March 31, 1862, which I was requested by Governor O. P. Morton to send to you.

In the bill of the State of Indiana against the United States now before your commission you will find charged some ammunition—viz: 100,000 blank musket, 77,000 Mississippi rifle, (calibre .54,) 100,000 Colt's rifle, 61,000 Colt's navy revolver, 102,400 army percussion caps, 145,000 revolver percussion caps, 225 signal rockets, 480 portfires, 11,000 blank pistol cartridges—which does not appear in the return of ordnance stores manufactured during the first quarter in this year, for the reason that it was manufactured and issued during the last quarter of 1861, and accounted for to the chief of ordnance in the return for said quarter. But this ammunition never has been charged to nor paid for by the United States. The most of the ammunition appearing as on hand, as per return, also that manufactured since, has, however, been issued during the last six days, by order of Brigadier General Ripley and Major General Halleck; and at the end of this month I shall forward to you the proper returns and vouchers, together with a bill for ammunition manufactured during the last two months.

I am, sir, very respectfully, your obedient servant,

H. STURM,
Captain Commanding.

Mr. WISE,
Secretary of Commission on Ordnance and Ordnance Stores,
War Department.

ORDNANCE OFFICE, WAR DEPARTMENT,
Washington, June 10, 1862.

SIR: By request of the quartermaster general of the State of Indiana, I submit herewith a statement of the circumstances under which a supply of small-arm ammunition was asked for and forwarded from the Indianapolis arsenal, Indiana, on the 18th of May. On the 17th of May I received a telegram from Lieutenant Buffington, at St. Louis arsenal, Missouri, a copy of which is enclosed, requesting that a supply of ammunition be sent to General Halleck's army at Corinth. As this army was then on the eve of a battle, on which much depended, I took immediate measures to forward an abundant supply. Telegraphic requisitions were made on the officers in charge of the Louisville depot, Allegheny arsenal, Pennsylvania, Indianapolis State arsenal, and the State depot at Columbus, Ohio; and on the 18th there was forwarded from these places ammunition as follows:

From Louisville depot..................	5,500,000,	assorted.
From Allegheny arsenal	720,000,	"
From Indianapolis arsenal..............	3,033,000,	"
From Columbus arsenal	1,893,000,	"
Total...........................	11,146,000,	"

A copy of the invoice forwarded from Indianapolis is enclosed.

Respectfully, your obedient servant,

JAMES W. RIPLEY,
Brigadier General.

J. WISE, Esq.
Secretary to Commission on Ordnance Stores.

[United States Military Telegraph, War Department, Washington, D. C.]

ST. LOUIS ARSENAL, *May* 17, 1862.

I supply the whole west with ammunition; have sent millions; but General Halleck wants more elongated rifle, calibre fifty-four, (54,) fifty-eight, (58,) and sixty-nine, (69.) If any available, send it to Captain Brench, steamer Rocket, Pittsburg Landing, Tennessee, and advise me.

A. R. BUFFINGTON,
United States Army, Com'g Arsenal.

General J. W. RIPLEY,
  Chief of Ordnance.

Invoice of ordnance and ordnance stores turned over by Captain H. Sturm, commanding Indiana State arsenal, to Captain James A. Ekin, assistant quartermaster United States army, Indianapolis, for transportation to Pittsburg Landing, Tennessee, in obedience to order for supplies, No. —.

No. of boxes or packages.	Marks	Total contents.	Weight.
921	[B]	921,000 rifle elongated ball, with caps, cal. .69 ---	
908		908,000 rifle elongated ball, with caps, cal. .577 --	
221		221,000 rifle elongated ball, with caps, cal. .54 . --	
21		21,000 buck and ball, with caps, cal. .69 ---------	
63		63,000 buck and ball, no caps, cal. .69 ----------	
52		52,000 Colt's rifle, with caps, cal. .54 ----------	320,000
159		159,000 Mississippi rifle, no caps, cal. .54 -------	
57		57,000 Colt's rifle, no caps, cal. .54 ------------	
30		30,000 Sharpe's carbine --------------------	
601		601,000 musket round ball, cal. .69 -----------	
3,033		3,033 packing boxes ------ ----------------	

I certify that the above is a correct invoice of ordnance and ordnance stores turned over by me, this 18th day of May, 1862, to Captain James A. Ekin, assistant quartermaster United States army, for transportation to Captain Bronce, Pittsburg Landing, Tennessee, per steamer Rocket.

H. STURM, *Captain Commanding.*

Copies of telegraphic despatches to Captain H. Sturm, superintendent of Indiana State arsenal, for ammunition and ordnance stores.

EVANSVILLE, *October* 2, 1861.

Send to-morrow a large supply, except round shot, for these (6) 6-pounders. The demand is pressing.

JAMES E. BLYTHE.

H. STURM.

LOUISVILLE, *October* 28, 1861.

Send me 600,000 Colt's rifle cartridges.

GENERAL SHERMAN.

H. STURM.

LOUISVILLE, *November* 17, 1861.

Send here by first train 3,000 friction primers, 100,000 percussion caps, 40,000 Mississippi rifle cartridges.

GENERAL SHERMAN.

H. STURM.

CAMP HENRI, KENTUCKY,
November 23, 1861.

Send me 100,000 Enfield cartridges, calibre .577.

GENERAL WOOD.

H. STURM.

JEFFERSONVILLE, *December* 24, 1861

Send immediately 100,000 blank cartridges.

M. IGOE, *Quartermaster.*

General J. H. VAGIN.

LOUISVILLE, *Kentucky, January* 16, 1862.

Please send me four hundred thousand elongated ball cartridges, calibre .69, immediately.

T. EDSON, *Lieutenant of Ordnance.*

Captain STURM.

LOUISVILLE, *February* 3, 1862.

Can you not send immediately to Lieutenant Edson two hundred canister 3-inch guns, and four hundred case shot for same?

J. H. GILLMAN, *Captain U. S. Army.*

Captain STURM.

LOUISVILLE, *February* 9, 1862.

If you have any Burnside cartridges, please send 40,000. Answer.

T. EDSON, *Lieutenant of Ordnance.*

H. STURM.

LOUISVILLE, *February* 8, 1862.

How many Burnside cartridges can our regiment be furnished with immediately?

T. R. DUDLEY.

Governor O. P. MORTON.

LOUISVILLE, *February* 11, 1862.

When can you send me some of the 3-inch ammunition? It is very necessary for immediate use.

T. EDSON, *Lieutenant of Ordnance.*

Captain H. STURM.

LOUISVILLE, *February* 13, 1862.

Send me some Parrott ammunition per express, if you can.

T. EDSON, *Lieutenant of Ordnance.*

Captain STURM.

LOUISVILLE, *February* 18, 1862.

Please send me 100,000 elongated ball cartridges, calibre .715, as soon as possible.

T. EDSON, *Lieutenant of Ordnance.*

Captain H. STURM.

LOUISVILLE, *March* 6, 1862.

Please send me 500,000 elongated ball cartridges, calibre .69.

T. EDSON, *Lieutenant of Ordnance.*

Captain H. STURM.

LOUISVILLE, *March* 7, 1862.

In addition to the 500,000 cartridges ordered yesterday, send me 500,000 Enfield cartridges, calibre .577.

T. EDSON, *Lieutenant of Ordnance.*

H. STURM.

LOUISVILLE, *April* 5, 1862.

Send me 100,000 Enfield and 100,000 elongated, calibre .69, cartridges, to-day, if you can.

T. EDSON, *Lieutenant of Ordnance.*

Captain STURM.

CAMP PEA RIDGE, *Arkansas, April* 3, 1862.

Send to me

    125 projectiles, James's rifled.
    175 percussion shells, rifled.
    100 canister.
    325 blank cartridges,
    500 friction primers.

CAPTAIN KLAUSS, *1st Battery Ind. Vols.*

Captain STURM.

MONTEREY, *Tennessee, May* 9, 1862.

Send to me 80 fixed 3-inch canister shot.

CAPTAIN KIDD, *14th Battery Ind. Vols.*

Captain STURM.

ST. LOUIS, *Missouri, September* 23, 1861.

Send to me 500 projectile James's rifled guns.

MAJOR GENERAL FRÉMONT.

Governor O. P. MORTON.

CAMP LARAMIE, *Missouri, February* 4, 1862.

Send to me

    50 percussion shells, James's rifled.
    80 solid shot, James's rifled.
    100 blank cartridges, 1¼.
    50 blank cartridges, 1.

CAPTAIN COCKIFAIR, *3d Battery Ind. Vols.*

Captain STURM.

FORT LEAVENWORTH, *February* 14, 1862.

Send to me

    400 percussion shells, James's rifled.
    100 projectile shells, James's rifled.
    200 canister, James's rifled.

CAPTAIN RABB, *2d Battery Ind. Vols.*

Captain STURM.

JEFFERSON CITY, MO., *March* —, 1862.

Send to me

    103 percussion shells, James's rifled.
     60 canister shot.
     80 round shot.
     78 case.
    100 blank cartridges, ½.
  1,571 friction primers.

CAPTAIN COCKIFAIR, *3d Battery Ind. Vols.*

Captain STURM.

COMMISSION ON ORDNANCE, *June* 16, 1862.

GENERAL: The commission desire to allow a settlement of the Indianapolis arsenal claim so far as to pay at current rates (or below if the charge made is less) for such ammunition as may have been issued by your orders, or to duly commissioned officers under exigencies, detailing the arsenal, with payment already made, and the value of stores delivered to the arsenal by the United States. For this purpose they have called upon Captain Sturm to produce all the receipts he may have for issues made. He has done this for the 1st quarter, 1862, stating that the prior receipts have been forwarded to your office.

The commission request that you will allow the clerk who has examined Captain Sturm's accounts in your office to report here with the accounts, so that a statement may embrace all issues and receipts to date.

I will endeavor to dispense with his service as soon as possible.

Very respectfully, your obedient servant,

P. V. HAGNER,
Major of Ordnance.

General J. W. RIPLEY,
Chief of Ordnance.

STATE OF INDIANA,
Executive Department, Indianapolis, June 13, 1862.

DEAR SIR: Captain Sturm leaves to-night for Washington on business connected with our arsenal. Will you have the kindness to afford him all the assistance in your power in effecting a settlement of our accounts with the government?

We are sadly in want of funds to pay debts contracted for labor and materials, and will be compelled to suspend operations very soon unless some relief is afforded. The delay in passing our claims is unaccountable. The arsenal is now in better condition for work than ever before. The ammunition turned out is first class, and is needed and issued as fast as manufactured. Captain Sturm is a skilful and energetic man, and his management is very satisfactory. If anything is to be done for us, pray urge that it be done speedily.

By order of Governor Morton.

Very respectfully, &c.,

W. H. H. TERRELL,
Military Governor.

Hon. ROBERT DALE OWEN, *Washington.*

COMMISSION ON ORDNANCE AND ORDNANCE STORES,
Washington, June 28, 1862.

GENERAL: The commission have the honor to report as follows:

CASE No. 104.—INDIANA STATE ARSENAL.

Claim for payment for ammunition fabricated and issued to various persons. Letters from the governor and agent of the State of Indiana, of various dates, and from the chief of ordnance, relative to this arsenal and the work in progress there. Bills rendered April 8 and June 1, 1862, amounting to $118,705 40.

Referred by special order of the Secretary of War.

Arsenal established at Indianapolis by direction of Governor Morton, of Indiana, April 27, to make ammunition for use of regiments of the State under marching orders for actual service, there being no ammunition on hand or obtainable at the time. Bill rendered by agent of State, Robert Dale Owen, January 7, 1862, and payment made by order of Secretary of War, amounting to $68,701 60.

Payment of bills of April 8 and June 1 suspended by chief of ordnance for orders of the Secretary of War.

The commission find that in order to supply necessary ammunition to regiments under orders for Virginia in April, 1861, the governor of Indiana ordered Captain Sturm, then an officer of State artillery, to start a laboratory at Indianapolis, using enlisted labor for the purpose; that in a day or two it was found advisable to send back the soldiers to their companies and employ suitable hired labor. Captain Sturm being an experienced laboratorian, was detached from his company, and as he had not been fully mustered into the United States service, was continued in charge as a State officer. He commenced at once to erect buildings and purchase materials from State funds to manufacture in large quantities all the various kinds of ammunition for field pieces and small arms.

Being also ordnance officer of the State, such ordnance stores as were sent to the governor for issue to Indiana regiments mustered into the service of the United States were under his charge, and by degrees a considerable quantity of military munitions belonging to the United States was accumulated at this State arsenal. Issues and receipts of such, as well as of ammunition fabricated there, have been made by order of the governor, as the necessities of the public service, in his opinion, required. Thus an arsenal has grown up under Captain Sturm's care which has been of great service at times in providing ordnance supplies for the several large armies operating in Western Virginia, Kentucky, Tennessee, Missouri, and Kansas. Issues have been made upon requisitions by generals commanding departments or divisions by ordnance officers at the depots in Kentucky and Tennessee, and sometimes by commanding officers of regiments and posts or companies. Requisitions by the chief of ordnance and United States ordnance and general officers have been in every case promptly complied with by Captain Sturm, without special reference to the governor, but in all other cases the governor approved the requisitions before issues were made. In October, 1861, the Secretary of War visited the arsenal, and having fully informed himself of the operations going on, verbally requested the governor (as stated to the commission by Captain Sturm) to continue fabricating ammunition, and by his order an account, amounting to $68,701 60, was paid January 7, 1862, to the agent of the State of Indiana, for certain stated quantities, of various kinds, at prices considered reasonable by the chief of ordnance, the quantities paid for having been in part issued (as above stated) and in part remaining still in the arsenal. Captain Sturm submitted to the chief of ordnance soon afterwards a return of all property and stores on hand at the arsenal belonging to the United States up to December 31, 1861, as is required from United States arsenals, but no direct charge of the arsenal in the details of its operations has been assumed by the Ordnance department. As the law does not permit the establishment of a United States arsenal in this manner, nor the purchase or issue of ordnance stores and supplies without the authority of the chief of ordnance, the case was reported to the Secretary of War in November, 1861, and an officer sent to examine the arsenal and to report his views as to the advisability of making ammunition there instead of at the United States arsenals. December 11 Lieutenant Crispin, the inspecting officer, reported the results of his visit, "and that, in his opinion, all the wants of the army in that region of the country can be supplied, by timely requisitions from United States arsenals, without having recourse to State establishments." This report was communicated to the Hon. Robert Dale Owen, agent of the State of Indiana, December 30, and he was informed "that it was not deemed advisable to continue the preparation of ammunition at Indianapolis further than may be necessary to consume the materials which have been obtained at cost prices of the various kinds of ammunition as charged in the account.

The commission decide, therefore, that, in adjusting the accounts of the arsenal against the United States, the payment already made should be considered as " on account," and that all such stores as have been duly issued and receipted for, by troops in the service of the United States, be charged against the government as purchased from the State of Indiana, leaving the balance to be paid for when actually received by a United States officer. In order to show the condition of this account for ammunition, so that a settlement may be made for it at once, the commission has had prepared, by Captain Sturm, a return of all the ammunition issued since the commencement of the work, from which the quantity paid for has been deducted, and from the remainder is also deducted the quantity turned over for transportation to agents, and not yet receipted for by the officers to whom it was directed to be issued. The receipt of the balance has actually been acknowledged by officers duly commissioned in the United States service, who are accountable for its proper use.—(See return, marked A, and vouchers.)

The whole expense of fabrication has been borne by the State of Indiana, and if the issues had been made by proper authority the account for this balance would have been regular and in form. The prices charged in the bills rendered, (see vouchers January 7, 1862, and bills of April 8 and June 1, 1862,) are deemed by the commission to be reasonable and just, as the prices include payment for all expenses by the State for the care and preservation of all the United States stores at the arsenal (except small arms) up to June 1, 1862. Considering the condition of the country at the time, the commission approve of the issues to the several officers, as made without objection on account of insufficient authority, and direct the payment to the State of Indiana at the prices charged in bills of April 8 and June 1, 1862, for all issues, as soon as sufficient evidence is afforded that the stores were used in the government service, or are now in the hands of its officers, deducting on the account the amount due for lead and powder furnished by the government to the arsenal. The portion of the ammunition turned over to transportation agents cannot be paid for until evidence is furnished that these agents have duly acquitted themselves of their responsibility. Such "purchased for the purpose, and that if supplies are needed by the State, they can be furnished from United States arsenals." Subsequently, however, to fill the requisitions for the supply of the army in the field (reported to be urgently necessary for immediate use) additional materials were purchased; and on the 15th February, in answer to the request of Captain Sturm, the chief of ordnance promised an immediate supply of powder and lead, and authorized the purchase of buckshot and lead. March 5, 1862, the chief of ordnance having been called upon by the Secretary of War, again reported : "That the arsenal is a State establishment," and quoted from his letter to Hon. Robert Dale Owen of December 30. "No action, however, was taken, and operations at the arsenal have since been continued without restriction as to the amount of materials actually on hand, the governor proposing, with the concurrence of the Secretary of War, to render monthly accounts for such quantities of ammunition as may be used by the United States."

The two accounts now before the commission have been forwarded in accordance with this arrangement.

It is stated that these include the whole amount fabricated, (and not yet paid for,) prior to June 1, 1862, crediting the United States with the value of the powder and lead received from the government and used in preparing the ammunition. All thus fabricated, however, had not been issued when the accounts were rendered; the balance remaining under the charge of Captain Sturm. A large portion of this balance has been recently issued upon direct orders of the chief of ordnance.

Captain Sturm has appeared before the commission and presents returns of property on hand at the close of the first quarter, 1862, and also abstracts of issues and receipts, and of articles purchased and fabricated, supported by vouchers. These papers have been examined, and show that, in addition to the ammunition supplied, many repairs have been made to ordnance stores in actual service, and articles purchased for artillery and cavalry, and issued (as in the case of ammunition) sometimes without due authority. Captain Sturm has not been paid by the United States for his services at the arsenal, but from the first by the State, and this expense, as well as all other expenses for labor and material, in preparing ammunition, and in repairs and issues and care of ordnance stores, (except small arms,) have been included in computing the evidence, Captain Sturm states can be obtained and will be forwarded. As the guardianship of ordnance stores belongs by law to the Ordnance department, the commission consider that arrangements should at once be made to place the stores now belonging to the government at the Indianapolis arsenal under the exclusive authority of the chief of ordnance, so that all disbursements of public money, and all issues of stores be made by his orders. If a temporary ordnance depot be necessary at Indianapolis, it should be administered as in the case of other ordnance depots, and be broken up as soon as the exigency requiring it may cease. Should a depot be established there, the ammunition remaining on hand would then be in charge of a United States officer, and should then be paid for at the rates above directed. An abstract (marked B) has been rendered by Captain Sturm, showing the articles purchased to complete the equipments of different batteries organizing for the field. These articles should be taken up upon the returns and duly accounted for, and the commission direct that they likewise be purchased from the State of Indiana, and paid for at such prices as the government is accustomed to pay for like articles; the issues made of these articles being sanctioned, in consideration of the circumstances, although not made by due authority. In conclusion, the commission consider it due to Captain Sturm to say that the papers submitted to them, as well as the satisfactory explanation he has given of every transaction connected with the case, prove that he has managed the establishment with great probity and intelligence, and greatly to the advantage of the government service, and that if now duly commissioned as a captain in the military service, they consider it advisable that he should be detailed for ordnance duty, and be ordered to report to the chief of ordnance.

We are, sir. respectfully, your obedient servants,

J. HOLT.
ROBERT DALE OWEN.

Brig. Gen. J. W. RIPLEY,
    Chief of Ordnance.

CASE No. 105.

DANIEL TREADWELL AND SEYFERT, McMANUS & CO.

WASHINGTON, *May* 15, 1862.

SIR: The improvement of ordnance by increasing it in strength and size has been the principal subject of my labors and thought for more than twenty years. I have done this with great pecuniary loss and against great discouragements. All this is well known to most of the officers of the ordnance of both services of the United States.

It seems to me now, however, that if your department will accord to me a contract or order for a number of guns, such as are now constantly ordered from others who are pursuing their business under the light which they have borrowed from my inventions, I may be put in the way of obtaining my long-sought end, and that the government may, without any extra expense or risk, be put in possession of better guns than are attainable by any other means. I therefore solicit from your department an order for the three following kinds of guns:

1st. For 50, of $7\frac{3}{8}$ inches calibre, to weigh, say 9,000 pounds, and carry a rifled shot of 100 pounds; the guns to be covered from the breech to the trunnions with wrought-iron hoops or bands, "put on under great strain," in the manner invented by me and since followed in England by Captain Blakely, and in this country by Captain Parrott. The price of these guns to be 18 cents a pound.

2d. For 30, of 9 inch calibre, to weigh, say 16,500 pounds, to carry a rifled shot of 184 pounds; to be hooped from the breech to 1 foot in front of the trunnions in two *layers*; the hoops to be put on as the above, and also to be secured to the gun and to each other by screw-threads, as described in my patent and represented in drawing No. 2, herewith presented; the trunnions to be formed upon one of the hoops. The price of these guns to be 25 cents a pound.

3d. For 20, of 10½ inches calibre, to weigh, say 27,000 pounds, and carry a rifled projectile of 300 pounds; to be hooped like the preceding, and the hoops (if desired) to be carried over the whole length of the gun. The price for these also to be 25 cents a pound.

The government not to be bound to take any of the 100-pounders which are not delivered within 18 months, nor of the 184-pounders that are not delivered in 27 months, nor of the 300-pounders that are not delivered within three years. But I should confidently expect to complete the order much within the above specified time, and should make every effort to that end.

My works and workmanship and materials to be at all times open to the inspection of a government officer. The guns to be subjected to such tests as may be agreed upon, and every question of the intent and understanding of the parties that may arise to be settled by reference.

My desire to obtain an order in the above form is not founded in mere pecuniary interest, but to obtain a mechanical success, and at the same time to put the government in possession of the strongest and best possible guns in the shortest possible time. Drawings of the two proposed modifications of my gun are herewith presented. These may be changed in any of their details to suit the wishes of the department, if they do not interfere with the essential principle on which the improvement is founded.

I am, sir, with great respect, your obedient servant,

DANIEL TREADWELL.

Hon. EDWIN M. STANTON,
Secretary of War.

Permit me to subjoin to the foregoing communication a computation of the respective forces of the 9 and 10½-inch guns, as proposed to be made by me, in terms of "work done" or destructive effect of their shot under velocities of 1,500 feet a second, as compared with a 15-inch gun carrying a shot of 430 pounds with a velocity of 1,000 feet a second.

9-inch gun; shot, 184 *lbs.; velocity*, 1,500 *feet.*—$1,500^2 = 2,250,000 \times 184 =$ 414,000,000 *destructive power.*

10½-inch gun; shot, 300 *lbs.; velocity*, 1,500 *feet.*—$1.500^2 = 2,250,000 \times 300 =$ 675,000,000 *destructive power.*

15-inch gun; shot, 430 *lbs.; velocity*, 1,000 *feet.*—$1,000^2 = 1,000,000 \times 430 =$ 430,000,000 *destructive power.*

Very respectfully,

DANIEL TREADWELL.

ORDNANCE OFFICE,
Washington, May 21, 1862.

SIR: I have examined the propositions submitted by Mr. Treadwell, which you referred to this office, and now report that the methods invented by Mr. Treadwell for the manufacture of cannon of large calibre were published by him several years since. His methods, as now proposed, may be briefly stated to consist in making the initial tube, which forms the bore and breech of the-gun, in one piece of cast-iron; and then to strengthen the tube by covering it with successive hoops of wrought-iron screwed on under suitable tension; the hoops to cover a part or the whole length of the tube, and to consist of one or more layers over each other, as the size and strength of the gun may require.

This method of construction appears to promise a maximum strength with any given weight of material in as high a degree as any other method now known or practiced. The most successful trials of projectiles, recently made in England, to penetrate iron targets were, according to newspaper reports, made with cannon constructed on similar principles, which tends to confirm Mr. Treadwell's theory.

At the present time it is an object of great importance to artillerists to give the highest possible velocity to projectiles of great weight, in order to penetrate and destroy heavy iron-clad defences ; and whatever means may be devised for giving greater strength and safety to large cannon will promote that object.

Among all the numerous methods which have recently been suggested for improving large cannon, I have not seen any which appears better adapted to that purpose than those proposed by Mr. Treadwell. I am, therefore, of opinion that his invention is worthy of a trial.

His processes of manufacture are, however, very expensive, and cannon made as he proposes will cost much more than is now paid for any other large cannon of equal weight. His proposition to make one hundred guns of different sizes at the prices named will, if accepted, require an expenditure of about $340,000. I think it would be inexpedient to make a contract involving so large an amount for any untried weapon, however confident may be the expectations of its ultimate success. Before making any contract for a large quantity of new weapons, an actual trial of one or more of them should be made, in connexion with such others now in use as are designed for similar service. The trials to be so arranged as would demonstrate conclusively the relative merits or de- merits of the new invention compared with models already in service. What- ever practical value the new invention might be found to possess, either in capacity for powerful work or for prolonged endurance, would thus be satis- factorily ascertained.

If it shall be decided to make a trial of Mr. Treadwell's cannon, I would. suggest that one or two of large size, say 8 or 10-inch bore, and rifled, be ordered upon the condition that, if on trial they proved to be satisfactory, they should be paid for at a stipulated price. And, also, that the department may then, at its option, order an additional number for service at prices not exceeding those stated in Mr. Treadwell's proposition.

Respectfully, I am your obedient servant,

JAMES W. RIPLEY,
Brigadier General.

Hon. E. M. STANTON,
Secretary of War.

READING, PENNSYLVANIA,
February 22, 1862.

SIR: We propose to cast and manufacture, according to specifications fur- nished by your bureau, two hundred and fifty, or any less quantity you may designate, of 8-inch or 10-inch guns, commencing with nine, to be completed during the month of March, twenty during the month of April, and thirty dur- ing each subsequent month till contract is completed, at the rate of seven and eight-tenth cents ($7\frac{8}{10}$ cents) per pound.

Respectfully,

SEYFERT, McMANUS & CO.

General J. W. RIPLEY,
Chief of Ordnance.

Our iron has been tested by the Navy Department and pronounced of a superior quality for ordnance. A copy of the report of the ordnance officer who tested the guns has been furnished you.

ORDNANCE OFFICE, *February* 27, 1862.

Respectfully submitted to the Secretary of War. If Messrs. Seyfert, McManus & Co. will prove their ability to fabricate suitable and reliable cast-iron heavy cannon by first preparing a trial 10-inch columbiad, to be made and tested in conformity with the specifications in the proposed form of ordnance herewith enclosed, then I recommend that they shall have an order for fifty 10-inch and fifty 8-inch guns, to be delivered in not more than six months from the time of trial of the test-gun, and on the terms and conditions stated in the enclosed form. I further recommend that the same conditions be required of all founders proposing to make guns who have not heretofore proved satisfactorily the quality of their metal and their ability to make good cannon.

JAMES W. RIPLEY,
Brigadier General.

Report received July 3, 1862.

Referred to the commission on ordnance and ordnance stores for examination and report. By order of the Secretary of War.

P. H. WATSON,
Assistant Secretary of War.

COMMISSION ON ORDNANCE,
Washington, July 3, 1862.

SIR: By direction of the commissioner I respectfully return the papers relating to Mr. Treadwell's proposition to make a number of cannon of different calibres according to his method, at 25 cents per pound, and also the papers accompanying Seyfert, McManus & Co.'s proposal to cast 8-inch and 10-inch columbiads at $7\frac{8}{10}$ cents per pound.

The manufacture of guns, according to the plan of Mr. Treadwell, will involve the construction of peculiar machinery, requiring a large outlay, and therefore, even at the high price per pound named by him, he could not undertake to make a single *trial* gun unless the ultimate necessity of using such guns promised repayment. At present that necessity is not apparent, as neither the *solid cast* nor the *hollow cast* of the present model have been shown to be deficient in any of the requirements for service. *None have yet burst,* and the trial 10-inch guns of this model, one cast solid and one hollow, have endured better than any guns on record (4,082 rounds each.)

There seems to be no *necessity,* therefore, at present, to use a more costly material than cast-iron at $6\frac{1}{2}$ cents per pound.

In the decision of the Rodman case, No. 103, the commission has given its recommendation in case his method, now costing $7\frac{8}{10}$ cents per pound, should be deemed of necessary use to the government, but, at present, experience does not justify us in proscribing the cheaper method of casting solid, proven to be safe and durable for guns made after our latest model.

Should future trials prove that cast-iron alone, cast solid or hollow, is not sufficiently reliable, the next most economical substitute is to *band* the cast-iron with wrought-iron.

Many plans for doing this have been suggested. As Mr. Treadwell's seems the most difficult and expensive to execute, it would not be advisable to adopt it on a large scale until the failure of others shall have shown the necessity, and a trial of it its sufficiency.

Very respectfully, your obedient servant,

P. V. HAGNER,
Major of Ordnance.

Hon. E. M. STANTON,
  Secretary of War.

Proposed form of order for heavy cannon.

SIR: You are hereby authorized to make for the United States one 10-inch gun, in conformity with drawings to be furnished by the department, and with the following specifications, viz:

The gun is to be made of cold, blast, charcoal iron, cast hollow and cooled from the interior, and to have a tenacity of metal of not less than thirty thousand pounds per square inch, this to be determined by testing specimens taken from the sinking head of the gun, and from a cylinder cast from the same heat and from metal of the same quality as that from which the gun may be cast. This cylinder to be cast on end, in dry sand moulds, to be seventy-two inches high, with an elliptical base whose major axis is twenty-four inches and its minor sixteen inches; you to cut the specimens from the gun-head, and a slab four and a half inches thick from the cylinder, by planes parallel to and equidistant from the axis of the cylinder and the minor axis of the base. This gun to be ready for trial in not more than three months from this date, and as much sooner as you can get it ready.

This department will test the specimens and furnish the ammunition and prove the gun. Should your trial gun fail to endure one thousand rounds, with service charges of powder, as heretofore used for trial guns, viz: 200 rounds with solid shot, and 800 rounds with shells, it will not be paid for at all. Should it endure this test, this will be your authority for making 10-inch and 8-inch guns, to be delivered in — months from the date of the trial, under the following conditions: The guns to be made of the same quality of iron as that of the trial gun, this department to have the right to test the iron during the process of fabrication, you to furnish at least one specimen from the head of each gun, and slabs from cylinders, as above described, at the option of the department, not to exceed one for every ten guns. The guns all to endure the proof established by this department for guns of these calibres. For all guns received from you, under this authority, including the satisfactory trial gun, you will be paid at the rate of seven and eight-tenth cents per pound, net weight. Failure to comply with these stipulations is to forfeit this authority.

Respectfully, your obedient servant.

———— ————,
Brigadier General.

———

CASE No. 106.

COLONEL O. DE FORREST.

Colonel O. De Forrest submits copies of orders to procure 2,280 sets of horse equipments, 2,280 army revolvers, and 2,280 sabres.

CAMP HARRIS, ANNAPOLIS, MARYLAND,
February 10, 1862.

SIR: In response to the circular of the War Department of 29th ultimo I have the honor to submit the following: Copy of order to Colonel O. De Forest, commanding "Ira Harris Guards," from Brigadier General James W.

Ripley, dated September 16, 1861, authorizing the purchase of six hundred and seventy-five (675) sets of horse equipments, six hundred and seventy-five (675) revolver pistols, six hundred and seventy-five (675) sabres; also copy of additional order, dated October 30, 1861, for purchase of one thousand (1,000) sets of horse equipments, one thousand (1,000) revolver pistols, one thousand (1,000) sabres; also copy of additional order, dated November 22, 1861, for purchase of six hundred and five (605) sets of horse equipments, six hundred and five (605) revolver pistols, six hundred and five (605) sabres.

That under the several orders above enumerated I have contracted with J. B. Butterfield & Co. for the delivery of twenty-two hundred and eighty pistols; with H. G. Leisenring for the delivery of the same number of sabres; with D. D. Conover, of the city of New York, for the same number of horse blankets; and with Lacy & Phillips, of Philadelphia, for six hundred and five sets of horse equipments, the balance of the horse equipments having been furnished by Major Hagner, being the only ones that could be obtained, notwithstanding strenuous exertions were made to obtain them.

In addition thereto I also annex a copy of order to same, from Acting Quartermaster General Sibley, for the "purchase of horses for his men as fast as they were mustered into service;" and that the whole number, twenty-two hundred and eighty horses, have been purchased, of which some twelve hundred (1,200) have been delivered and are in the service, and only one thousand (1,000) paid for up to this date, the balance being ready for delivery, and only awaiting the remittance of funds to the proper disbursing officer in New York or at any other point which the department may, in its judgment, determine.

Inasmuch as the efficiency of the regiments known as the Ira Harris Guards cavalry has been much impeded by the difficulties attendant upon the non-procurement of horses and arms, the department will indulge me, I trust, in expressing the hope that early action may be taken to secure the horses now purchased and awaiting delivery. The arms and equipments referred to above, it is proper to mention, will, it is presumed, all be ready for delivery within the next thirty days.

Very respectfully, your obedient servant,

O. DE FORREST,
Colonel Commanding.

Hon. EDWIN M. STANTON,
Secretary of War.

This letter and claim having been repudiated by Colonel De Forrest, (as stated by Colonel Maynadier,) the commission directs the papers to be returned to Ordnance office.

P. V. HAGNER,
Major of Ordnance.

ORDNANCE OFFICE.
Washington, September 16, 1861.

SIR: You are authorized to procure for your regiment six hundred and seventy-five (675) sets of horse equipments, six hundred and seventy-five revolver pistols, and six hundred and seventy-five sabres, which articles are to be inspected by Major Hagner, in New York, and will be paid for on certificate of inspection by him, at such prices (not exceeding those paid for similar articles) as he may certify to be fair and just.

Respectfully, your obedient servant,

JAMES W. RIPLEY,
Brigadier General.

Colonel O. DE FORREST,
Commanding Ira Harris Guards.

ORDNANCE OFFICE,
Washington, October 30, 1861.

SIR : You are authorized to procure for your regiment one thousand sets of horse equipments, one thousand revolver pistols, and one thousand sabres, which articles are to be inspected by Major Hagner, in New York, and will be paid on certificates of inspection by him, and evidence of delivery to a United States officer, at such prices (not exceeding those paid contractors for similar articles) as he may certify to be fair and just. This is in addition to the cavalry equipments and arms which you were authorized to procure by letter from this office of September 16, 1861.

Respectfully, your obedient servant,

JAMES W. RIPLEY,
Brigadier General.

Colonel O. DE FORREST,
Commanding Ira Harris Guards, No. 4 Pine street, New York.

ORDNANCE OFFICE,
Washington, November 22, 1861.

SIR : You are authorized to purchase for your regiment six hundred and five sets of horse equipments, and the same number, each, of revolver pistols and sabres, which articles are to be inspected by Major Hagner, in New York, and will be paid for on certificates of inspection from him, and evidence of delivery to a United States officer, at such prices (not exceeding those paid contractors for similar articles) as he may certify to be fair and just. This is in addition to the cavalry equipments and arms which you were authorized to procure by letters from this office of September 16 and October 30, 1861.

Respectfully, your obedient servant,

JAMES W. RIPLEY,
Brigadier General.

Colonel O. DE FORREST,
No. 4 Pine street, New York.

ORDNANCE OFFICE,
War Department, Washington, June 11, 1862.

GENTLEMEN : Your letter of the 10th instant is received. I have to request that you will enclose to this office a copy of Colonel O. De Forrest's order to you to make the pistols you report ready for inspection.

Respectfully, your obedient servant,

JAMES W. RIPLEY,
Brigadier General.

Messrs. J. B. BUTTERFIELD & Co.,
Philadelphia, Pennsylvania.

No answer has been received at the Ordnance office up to this date, June 23, 1862.

PHILADELPHIA, *June* 10, 1862.

SIR : Under your orders to Colonel O. De Forrest, Ira Harris cavalry, of the dates of September 16, October 30, and November 22, to purchase twenty-two hundred and eighty pistols, which orders were subsequently given us by him to make and deliver, and in pursuance of which we have thus far expended over ten thousand dollars for alteration of tools and new machinery and materials, (some delay having necessarily been caused by the alteration of tools, having previously made a smaller arm,) the entire parts being nearly all made, we are now ready to commence putting the same together in the course of the next week, when they will be ready for inspection.

Will you oblige us by stating, by return mail, where we shall present them for inspection, whether at our factory or at the arsenal?

Very respectfully,

J. B. BUTTERFIELD & CO.,
Box 1045 Post Office, Philadelphia, Pennsylvania.

Brigadier General J. W. RIPLEY,
Chief of Ordnance Bureau, Washington, D. C.

ORDNANCE OFFICE,
War Department, Washington, June 23, 1862.

SIR: I enclose herewith the following papers relating to the order of Colonel O. De Forest to Messrs. J. B. Butterfield & Co.

Colonel O. De Forest's letter to the Secretary of War, February 10, 1862, ($\frac{547}{32}$ H.) Messrs. J. B. Butterfield's letter of June 10 to this office (791) and a copy of my reply thereto.

Respectfully, your obedient servant,

JAMES W. RIPLEY,
Brigadier General.

J. WISE, Esq.,
Secretary Commission on Ordnance Stores.

WILLARD'S HOTEL, *June 18, 1862.*

Colonel O. De Forest was authorized to purchase horse equipments, pistols and sabres. Purchased nothing but horse equipments.

Dr. C. L. Rowand made contract with Butterfield & Co., for 2,280 pistols, thinking himself authorized by me; asks the favor to have them inspected and paid for.

Received June 24, 1862.

ORDNANCE OFFICE, *June 24, 1862.*

Respectfully referred to the commission on ordnance and ordnance stores, to be read in connexion with the De Forest case.

JAMES W. RIPLEY,
Brigadier General.

WILLARD'S HOTEL,
Washington, D. C., June 18, 1862.

GENERAL: I was authorized, by orders from your department of September 16, October 30, and November 22, 1861, to procure for my command horse equipments, pistols and sabres. Finding that your department could furnish as good an article as I could purchase myself, and much more speedily, I purchased nothing except 605 setts of horse equipments from Messrs. Phillips & Co., of Philadelphia, but have since learned that Dr. Charles L. Rowand, whose assistance I desired, and who co-operated with me in raising my brigade, thinking himself authorized by me, made a contract with Messrs. Butterfield & Co. for 2,280 pistols, an article of superior value, and which should be adopted by our government. He informs me that they have never been received by you, but that they are ready for delivery.

Will you do me the favor to have them inspected and paid for? It will relieve from great pecuniary difficulties the contractors who have expended a large sum of money to manufacture them, and from great uneasiness and trouble.

Very respectfully, your obedient servant,

O. DE FOREST,
Colonel Ira Harris Guard and 5th N. Y. Cavalry.

General JAMES W. RIPLEY,
Chief of Ordnance.

Before commission, June 24, 1862.

Major Hagner states that he has just received a letter addressed by Colonel De Forest, of the Ira Harris Guard, 5th New York cavalry, to General Ripley, and indorsed by the general, "Respectfully referred to the commission on ordnance and ordnance stores, to be read in connexion with the De Forest case," dated Ordnance office, June 24, 1862."

This case was before the commission in May last, having been referred, with others, by the Secretary of War. Colonel De Forest was notified by letter dated April 1, 1862, that the commission desired his attendance, but he has not answered the letter nor appeared before the commission.

About the 31st of May, Colonel Maynadier sent a message to the commission from the ordnance office, stating that Colonel De Forest was then at his office and requested that the papers in his case might be sent there. They were delivered to the messenger and soon after returned to me with a note in pencil from Colonel Maynadier, the original of which I attached to the papers. It is as follows:

"MY DEAR MAJOR: I have shown the letter to Colonel De Forest who repudiates it, and says he never wrote it.

"Yours truly,

"W. M."

The letter referred to is that addressed to the Secretary of War, dated February 10, 1862, enclosing copies of General Ripley's orders of September 16, October 30, and November 22, 1861, now with the papers.

Upon receipt of this note the commission decided that no action was necessary on their part, and directed the papers to be returned to the Ordnance office, which was done. The following indorsement was placed upon the letter;

" ORDNANCE OFFICE,
" *Washington, May* 31, 1862.

" This letter and claim having been repudiated by Colonel De Forest, (as stated by Colonel Maynadier,) the commission directs the papers to be returned to the Ordnance office."

Colonel De Forest now writes to the chief of ordnance, under date of June 18, 1862, referring to the orders given to him in September, October, and November, to purchase supplies for his command and states : " finding that your department could furnish as good an article as I could purchase myself, and much more speedily, I purchased nothing except 605 sets of horse equipments from Messrs. Phillips & Co., of Philadelphia, but I have since learned that Dr. Charles L. Rowand, whose assistance I desired, and who co-operated with me in raising my brigade, thinking himself authorized by me, made a contract with Messrs. Butterfield & Co. for 2,280 pistols, an article of superior value and which should be adopted by our government. He informs me that they have never been received by you, but that they are ready for delivery. Will you do me the favor to have them inspected and paid for." No copy of contract has been presented, and no statement made as to the price or the time agreed upon. Messrs. Butterfield & Co. have also notified the chief of ordnance by letter dated June 10, 1862, that they were ready to commence putting together the work prepared by them under an order from Colonel De Forest for 2,280 pistols, and asking where they are to be inspected. Upon receipt of this letter the Messrs. Butterfield were requested by letter, from the chief of ordnance, dated June 11, " to enclose a copy of Colonel De Forest's letter to you to make the pistols you report ready for inspection."

No answer had been received to this letter up to July 15, 1862.

In the absence of the copy of the contracts, and not informed of the price, the commission cannot decide upon the most advantageous course to be pursued in this case. No obligation rests upon the government, however, to carry out an agreement not made by its orders, but under an error by an unauthorized agent. The commission therefore direct that nothing be received under such contract or agreement; but that, should it be deemed advisable to purchase the pistols stated to have been made, it shall be done, after proper trial and in open market, at such price, compared with the present prices of revolvers, as may be fair and just.

J. HOLT, *Commissioner.*
P. V. HAGNER,
Major of Ordnance, Assistant to Commission.

CASE No. 107.

E. TOWNSEND.

Before commission, July 2, 1862.

Account of E. Townsend for shot, &c., purchased by General Lockwood, $504.

It appearing to the commissioner that these stores, &c., were necessary for the public service, the price reasonable, and the purchase made by order of the general commanding, the account was indorsed as follows:

" The enclosed account, received from the War Department, is approved by the commission, and the payment recommended."

J. HOLT, *Commissioner.*

JULY 2, 1862.

ALPHABETICAL INDEX OF THE ARMS MAKERS